AMAZING ACHIEVEMENTS

AMAZING ACHIEVEMENTS

A CELEBRATION OF HUMAN INGENUITY

Nigel Hawkes

THUNDER BAY

P·R·E·S·S

A Marshall Edition
Amazing Achievements
was conceived, edited, and designed by
Marshall Editions
170 Piccadilly
London
W1V 9DD

Copyright © 1990, 1991, 1993, 1996 Marshall Editions
Developments Ltd

Thunder Bay Press
5880 Oberlin Drive
Suite 400
San Diego
CA 92121-9653

Library of Congress Cataloging-in-Publication Data in Progress

ISBN 1-57145-038-6

Printed and bound in Italy

Contents

Introduction

To build and to explore are among the most basic of human instincts. In every successful culture there have been people driven by the urge to create something big and memorable, or to extend their range by striking out into the unknown. A million years ago, *Homo erectus* left Africa on the first great journey of exploration, spreading slowly through Asia and Europe to populate the world. No monuments record that great diaspora, for man's earliest ancestor lived in simple structures that have long since disappeared. Only with the development of agriculture and the birth of cities ten thousand years ago did the techniques arise to perpetuate a culture through its buildings, from the enigmatic stone circles of the Celts to the splendour of the pyramids and the immensity of the Great Wall of China.

This selection of structures and journeys cannot hope to be comprehensive, but it can try to be representative. The unifying theme is one of superlatives; vernacular buildings, for all their charms, are excluded. What links the Panama Canal to the Vatican Palace, to Mount Rushmore and to the Great Wall of China, is the streak of megalomania that drives the world's great builders. The urge to create something big and memorable — to leave a deep footprint in history — seems to unite all peoples and every culture. Behind every great structure, there is usually a great man (or, less often, a woman): an engineer, an architect, a priest, a war-lord, or a president.

The same considerations lay behind the choice of journeys. The more successful cultures have had a curiosity about the world around them and a belief that over the horizon is a place where life is easier, the Sun warmer and the Earth more fruitful. The great journeys that first established the shape of the oceans and continents were made not in pursuit of abstract knowledge, but of wealth and power. Great builders and great explorers are united by the desire to dominate, by conquering space and distance.

The oldest structures in the book are those erected by the Egyptians, while the newest are the huge scientific instruments of Chile and Switzerland designed to study the infinities of space or the infinitesimal structure of the atom. Between the two lies the whole history of building and civil engineering: a collection of palaces, churches, monumental sculptures, bridges, dams, canals, railways and tunnels which qualify for inclusion by their boldness, scale, or sheer eccentricity.

The journeys, too, range from the epoch-making to the frankly bizarre. Columbus and Magellan may seem to have little in common with Thomas Stevens, the pioneer cyclist who blundered his way around the world on his penny-farthing in 1884, but they are united by the spirit of adventure and by the fact that they were the first to achieve what they did. Those who succeeded in making pioneer journeys, or in establishing new records for speed and endurance, were those who had provided themselves with the best machines, so it is their vehicles as well as their journeys that must be celebrated. Each was designed to improve on what had gone before, with a specific purpose in mind: to explore the Earth; to test the toughness of a machine and its design; to carry ever greater loads; to provide the most opulent surroundings in which to travel; to reach the Moon.

The structures, vehicles, and journeys described here are chosen because they are the first, the biggest, the fastest, the toughest, or the most singular, but the principle has not been followed slavishly. Some are included because they tell an interesting story or represent a landmark in technique, others because their curious qualities commend them.

Some equally worthy subjects have been omitted, on grounds of familiarity: many books have been written about the pyramids of Egypt, but the much larger pyramid of Cholula in Mexico remains obscure, largely unvisited and poorly understood. No book of manageable size can pretend to be comprehensive, so interesting and important buildings denied a full description are listed at the end, together with a timetable of the vital steps in transportation.

Section I: *Structures*

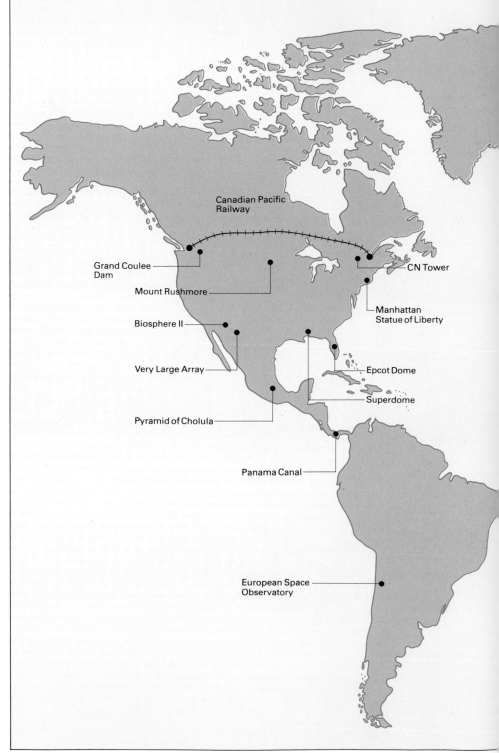

Canadian Pacific Railway

Grand Coulee Dam

CN Tower

Mount Rushmore

Manhattan Statue of Liberty

Biosphere II

Very Large Array

Epcot Dome

Superdome

Pyramid of Cholula

Panama Canal

European Space Observatory

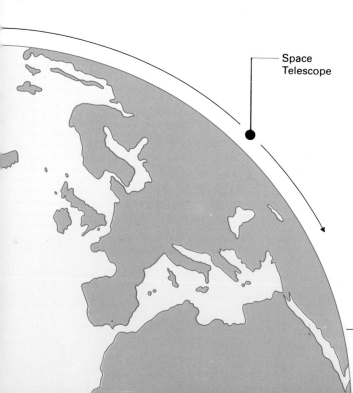

Space Telescope

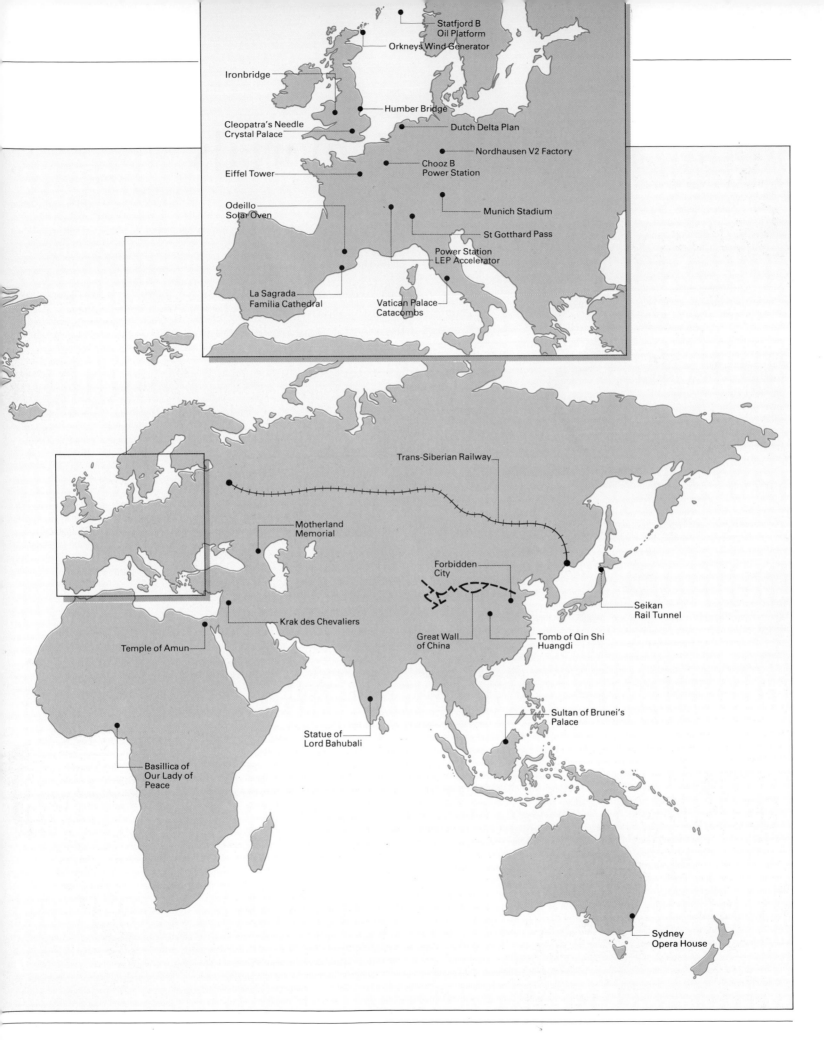

Statfjord B
Oil Platform

Orkneys Wind Generator

Ironbridge

Humber Bridge

Cleopatra's Needle
Crystal Palace

Dutch Delta Plan

Nordhausen V2 Factory

Chooz B
Power Station

Eiffel Tower

Munich Stadium

Odeillo
Solar Oven

St Gotthard Pass

Power Station
LEP Accelerator

La Sagrada
Familia Cathedral

Vatican Palace
Catacombs

Trans-Siberian Railway

Motherland
Memorial

Forbidden
City

Seikan
Rail Tunnel

Krak des Chevaliers

Temple of Amun

Great Wall
of China

Tomb of Qin Shi
Huangdi

Statue of
Lord Bahubali

Sultan of Brunei's
Palace

Basillica of
Our Lady of
Peace

Sydney
Opera House

CHAPTER ONE

Monolithic Memorials

Sculptors know that to achieve an impact, ostensibly life-size statues gain by being rather larger than life. Praxiteles made his statue of Hermes carrying the infant Dionysus 7 feet tall, while Churchill's statue in Parliament Square, London, overtops the living Churchill by quite a margin. Michelangelo went even further: his David was more than 14 feet tall because it was originally intended to occupy a space high on the Cathedral of Florence. But few sculptors have had the daring, the equipment, the time — or the money — to take this process to its logical conclusion.

Huge, monumental sculptures many times life size have the ability to strike directly at the emotions — or so the sculptor of Mount Rushmore, Gutzon Borglum, believed. In an age when everything was big, sculpture, he asserted, needed to be gigantic. It was not a new idea. The Egyptians, with the Sphinx and their obelisks carved from a single block of stone, had already proved that sheer size can take the breath away. In the tenth century AD, Jaina sculptors in southern India produced from the solid rock a holy image of Lord Bahubali so vast that tourists still come to marvel at it today. And Borglum himself had been involved in an unsuccessful attempt to improve the best-known monumental sculpture of all, the Statue of Liberty in New York Harbour.

The first Chinese emperor, Qin Shi Huangdi, opted for numbers rather than size, surrounding his mausoleum with no less than 8,000 warriors made of fired clay. The effect was the same: the terracotta army was meant to impress by its sheer bulk, and it does. So does the gigantic Motherland statue in Volgograd, even though as a work of art it is not a great success.

Huge sculptures have no purpose but to add glory to an image. They celebrate a victory, an idea, or a human life. They speak powerfully across the centuries and the cultures in a language that all can understand, enduring when smaller works of art are lost, transported, or destroyed. Of all structures, these are the ones most likely to survive into eternity.

Monolithic Memorials
Cleopatra's Needles
Tomb of Qin Shi Huangdi
Statue of Lord Bahubali
Statue of Liberty
Mount Rushmore
Motherland Memorial

London's Egyptian Obelisk

Fact file

Obelisks 3,500 years old that are a tribute to the craftsmen of ancient Egypt

Creator: Tuthmosis III

Built: c1504–1450 BC

Material: Granite

Height: London 68ft 6in; New York 69ft 6in

Weight: London 186 tons; New York 200 tons

Among the most remarkable memorials of the ancient civilization of Egypt are obelisks, slender pillars with four flat sides tapering to a point, cut from a single piece of granite. Highly polished and decorated with inscriptions and drawings, the obelisks were created almost 4,000 years ago with the most basic of tools.

The largest, weighing 455 tons and more than 105 feet high, was commissioned by the Pharaoh Tuthmosis III and now stands in the Piazza San Giovanni in Laterano, Rome, but an even larger one still lies unfinished in the quarry near Aswan from which the obelisks came. Two of the most interesting, also commissioned by Tuthmosis III, were erected like sentinels at the entrance to the Temple of the Sun at Heliopolis, just north of modern Cairo. Later these two acquired the name of Cleopatra's Needles, and were moved to new sites in London and New York. How were these huge blocks of stone quarried and cut without the use of metals? How were they moved without the use of wheels, and raised upright without cranes, scaffolding or even pulleys?

The purpose of the obelisks appears to have been part religious, part ceremonial. They were erected in honour of the sun god, and the first of them went up at Heliopolis, the main centre of worship. But the inscriptions on the obelisks glorified the achievements of earthly rulers: territories conquered, rivals defeated, and the anniversaries of a king's reign. Cleopatra's Needles carry inscriptions down the centre of each side extolling the virtues of Tuthmosis III, and further hieroglyphics, added 200 years later, record the victories of another great Pharaoh, Rameses II.

Cleopatra's Needles are made from red granite and may have come from the very same quarry in Aswan where the even larger unfinished obelisk still lies. If the quarry workers had not come across an unexpected crack in the granite, forcing them to abandon work, it would have been the biggest obelisk of all, standing more than 135 feet high and weighing 1,168 tons. For archeologists it is among the most precious of finds, for it shows how all the other obelisks were made.

First, the quarry engineers had to locate an area of perfect stone from which an obelisk could be cut in a single piece. This was done by sinking test shafts down into the rock. Once a site had been chosen, the first stage was to smooth the upper surface of the rock by removing uneven areas. Bricks were heated and placed on the surface, then doused with cold water. The effect was to fracture the rock surface, making it easier to remove.

The next stage was to cut down on either side of the obelisk, creating trenches. The clue as to how this was done comes from the discovery of balls of the mineral dolerite lying around the quarry. Such balls, between 4 and 12 inches in diameter, and weighing 10 lb or more, occur naturally in the Eastern Desert, from which they had been brought. Mounted on rammers, the stones were lifted and then brought down with great force on the rock, so crushing it. At any time, several thousand men would have been at work, in groups of three, two standing and raising the ramrod, the other squatting down to direct the blow. To maintain the rhythm, a chanter would intone.

Progress must have been very slow, and it probably took six months to a year for the teams to cut down to the full depth needed. The next step was to detach the bottom of the obelisk from the rock, and according to the English archeologist Reginald Engelbach this was also done by pounding. First an area beneath the obelisk would have to be prepared, to form a gallery in which to work. Then wooden beams would be used to support the obelisk as it was progressively cut away by pounding horizontally. Some believe that wooden wedges were used, either by progressively driving them in to force it to crack, or by inserting the wedges and wetting them, allowing the expansion of the wood to exert the force. Others believe the whole job was done with the dolerite balls.

Decoration of the obelisks may have begun while they were still at the quarry, although the chances are that final decoration, including covering the upper surfaces and the point—the pyramidon—with gold, was left until the obelisk was upright in its final position.

The next problem was getting the obelisk out of its pit in the quarry, on to barges and down the Nile to its final resting place. Hundreds of men would have used great balks of timber as levers, lifting first one side of the obelisk and then the other, packing fresh material under it at every lift. In this way it might have been raised by stages to a height almost equal to that of the surrounding rock, and a passage cut to enable it to be pulled away.

Some doubt exists over whether rollers were used to ease the movement of the obelisks. None has ever been found, but without them up to

London's obelisk is situated on the Embankment beside the River Thames. Before decoration the surfaces of the stone were rubbed smooth and flat, using emery powder or dolerite balls. The smoothness was checked by pressing against it a flat surface covered with red ochre to mark the high spots. These would be ground down, and the surface checked again. Inscriptions were cut into the surface with emery, perhaps using copper blades to apply the abrasive. Copper was the only hard metal available to the Egyptians, but on its own was not hard enough to cut stone.

6,000 men, pulling 40 ropes, would have been needed to overcome friction. At the edge of the Nile, it is assumed that barges were drawn up and virtually buried in sand, perhaps at a time when the river was low and the barges could rest on the bottom. Then the huge obelisk would be dragged on top of the sand embankments and the sand removed from around and beneath it, allowing it gradually to settle on to the barge. When the river rose at the annual flood, the journey to the obelisk's final destination began.

Tuthmosis III created at least seven obelisks,

five in Thebes and two in Heliopolis. Four survive, but not one remains in its original position. The two Cleopatra's Needles have had an extraordinary history. For 1,500 years they stood at Heliopolis, while Egypt fell successively under the rule of the Ethiopians, the Persians, and the Greeks under Alexander the Great. He founded Alexandria, where later Queen Cleopatra ruled as the last of the Ptolemaic dynasty and built a palace on the edge of the Mediterranean dedicated to Julius Caesar.

When Cleopatra died in 30 BC, Egypt fell once

London's Egyptian Obelisk

more under foreign domination, this time the Roman Empire, and the two obelisks from Heliopolis were moved to a new site at the water gate to Cleopatra's palace. Centuries later they had acquired the name Cleopatra's Needles, although in reality they dated from a period 15 centuries before she was even born.

There they stood for a further 1,500 years as Cleopatra's palace fell into ruin and disappeared. At some point—it is not clear when—one of the two obelisks fell to the ground, where it was seen half-covered in sand by the traveller George Sandys in 1610. When Napoleon Bonaparte landed in Egypt in 1798, with the intention of taking the Middle East from the Turks, it was the Royal Navy and a British army that defeated him. In gratitude, the Turks, restored to power, were glad to accept the suggestion that the British should take home with them the obelisk that had already toppled. Napoleon had had it in mind to take them both, and wires had already been attached to the upright obelisk ready to pull it down.

It was, however, another 65 years before anything was done about this offer, years in which the obelisk lay on the ground and was abused by passing tourists, who were inclined to chip pieces off it as souvenirs. By 1867, the obelisk was in dire peril, for a Greek merchant named Giovanni Demetrio had bought the land on which it lay and was proposing to develop it. Unable to move the obelisk intact, he was ready to break it up and use it as building material. The man who came to the rescue was General Sir James Alexander, who heard of the threat, roused public opinion and helped to devise a scheme for bringing the obelisk to London.

A special tube-shaped craft was designed to carry the obelisk, estimated to weigh 185 tons, on its ocean voyage to England. *Cleopatra*, as the floating cigar-tube was called, was put in tow of a tug, the *Olga*. So long as the weather was calm, all went well, although communication between the two vessels was difficult and the *Cleopatra* pitched like a see-saw. Worse things were to come, however. In the Bay of Biscay, a storm struck, and the tow-rope had to be cut. When the weather eased and *Olga* went in search of the *Cleopatra*, she had completely disappeared.

But *Cleopatra* had not sunk. Lying low in the water, with the seas pouring over her, this curious vessel was spotted by another British ship, the *Fitzmaurice*, which with enormous difficulty towed her into Ferrol harbour upside-

CLEOPATRA'S NEEDLE—PROPOSED SCHEME FOR TRANSPORTING THE MONUMENT TO ENGLAND

LONGITUDINAL SECTION OF THE CYLINDER

EXTERIOR OF THE CYLINDER CONTAINING THE NEEDLE

down. From here she was, in due course, recovered, after the salvage claim with the owners of *Fitzmaurice* had seen settled. She was brought into the Thames and her precious cargo raised into its present position on the Embankment. Her twin was transported to the US in 1880 aboard a rather more seaworthy vessel, and erected in Central Park, New York.

The two obelisks—and others, now in Paris, Istanbul and Rome—were taken from Egypt before the modern world had developed a conscience about stripping a nation of its cultural treasures. Rome acquired its collection of 13 obelisks in ancient times, as did Istanbul, while London, Paris and New York obtained theirs in the nineteenth century. The irony is that they all now stand virtually ignored, dwarfed by modern buildings and surrounded by traffic. People who would pay large sums of money to travel to Egypt to see them in their original surroundings never give them a second thought where they stand today.

The tube in which Cleopatra's Needle was brought to London was built in Alexandria and holed by a sharp stone as soon as it was launched. Once patched and refloated, the cylinder was fitted with 2 keels, a cabin and deck. Higher rates of pay had to be paid by the English captain to the 6 crew, such was the fear about the vessel's safety.

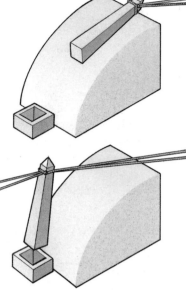

The method the Egyptians used *for raising obelisks (above) entailed, according to the French archeologist Henri Chevrier, the construction of huge embankments leading to a curve descending to the plinth. Sand to stop the obelisk falling too fast would be removed, allowing it to settle in a notch in the plinth at an angle of about 34 degrees. Ropes would be used to pull it upright.*

Raising of the needle *on the Adelphi Steps beside the Thames in September 1878. It was unloaded and hauled up the steps using hydraulic jacks and screw traversers. Once on its plinth, a huge wooden framework was built over the obelisk to raise it sufficiently high to swing it into the vertical plane with steel cables. The needle was so finely balanced about its centre of gravity that the beam holding it could be swung by one man.*

The Terracotta Army

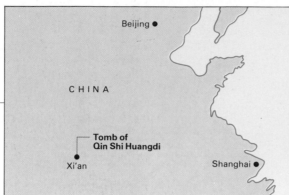

Fact file

One of the world's most spectacular burial sites

Creator: Qin Shi Huangdi

Built: 246–209 BC

Material: Terracotta

Number of figures: Approximately 8,000

The soldiers and horses (opposite) have been left in the pits where they were discovered, although extensive restoration has been necessary on the most badly broken figures. It is estimated that about 600 horses, 7,000 warriors and 100 chariots will be unearthed. The Qin horses were bred with powerful lungs to gallop for long distances at high speed.

In March 1974 workers at the Yanzhai Commune, 18 miles from the ancient Chinese capital of Xi'an, were worried that their harvest would be lost as a result of drought. Searching for water, they dug a well and stumbled instead across one of the most spectacular archeological discoveries of the twentieth century. They found a few fragments of terracotta, sculpted and fired into the shape of warriors and horses.

Since then, archeologists have unearthed an entire army of terracotta warriors and believe that ultimately there may be as many as 8,000 of them, figures a little larger than life-size, carved with enormous skill and buried for more than 2,000 years. They provide a glimpse into the world of the first emperor to unite China, Qin Shi Huangdi, a remarkable man who created the first totalitarian society on earth and ruled it with a combination of efficiency and utter ruthlessness.

The warriors were created as an entourage to guard the emperor and to guide him into the next world. He was born in 259 BC, and came to the throne of the state of Qin as a 13-year-old boy in 246 BC. Almost immediately, despite his youth, work began on a splendid tomb which was to be his home after death. It was another 36 years before he occupied it, years in which he annexed the six other independent kingdoms of China and became the first emperor. As a warrior and administrator, Qin Shi Huangdi has had few equals in history. He unified the Great Wall of China, linking together separate walls built by earlier northern states. His army was equipped with swords and arrowheads made of bronze, and crossbows powerful enough to penetrate armour, yet light enough to be carried by mounted archers. The triggers were far more sophisticated than any that were to appear in Europe for many centuries.

Qin Shi Huangdi created a centralized, auto-cratic state, with a uniform code of law, a single currency and set of weights and measures and a written language. He built a network of tree-lined roads, 50 paces wide, radiating outward from the Qin capital, Xianyang. He ruled by force, and fear: the law provided for whole families to be executed for the crimes of one member, and millions of men were drafted into the army and civilian labour force. He permitted no independent thought, burning books and burying scholars alive. He set the pattern of authoritarian rule which has survived in China to this day.

During his life Qin Shi Huangdi created several palaces, plus a huge mausoleum, which has yet to be excavated. The history books tell us that beneath this mound of earth some 250 feet high is a tomb chamber whose ceiling is decorated with pearls, representing the stars, while the stone floor is a map of the Qin empire, the rivers glittering with mercury to represent water. The tomb was filled with treasures and fitted with booby traps in the form of crossbows primed to fire at any intruder. Here the emperor was buried in 209 BC, the year after his death. Buried alive with him were his wives—none of whom had borne him any children—and the craftsmen who knew the secrets of the tomb.

Whether these stories are true must await the excavation of the tomb. The terracotta army, clearly designed as a guard, was found about a mile east of the mausoleum, and all of its number face eastward, perhaps because the emperor expected any revengeful attack from the six conquered kingdoms to come from that direction. Scholars have speculated that this was merely a storage place—but why the warriors did not join the emperor after his death is not clear. As guards, they proved ineffective. Within three years of his death, the emperor's tomb had been plundered by a rebel general, Hsiang Yu, who also discovered the terracotta army in its underground vaults. He ordered the roof to be set alight and it collapsed on the figures, breaking many of them and covering them in mud.

The warriors have been found in three separate pits. The largest contains up to 6,000 soldiers and more than 100 horses. It is more than 250 yards long, 70 yards wide, and 17 feet deep. The floors are paved with brick and the pit consists of a series of trenches or corridors, divided by earthen walls, and roofed originally with beams, woven mats, and alternate layers of plaster and earth up to ground level. So far, about 1,000

The Terracotta Army

warriors and 24 horses have been excavated, a small fraction of the total the pit is believed to contain. The horses, in teams of four, pull wooden chariots of which little has survived the centuries. The other two pits are similar, but smaller, with about 1,000 warriors in the second and 68 in the third. From the arrangement of the third pit, it appears to have represented the command headquarters where officers controlling the other two pits were stationed.

The warriors themselves range in height between 5 feet 8 inches and 6 feet 5 inches, somewhat larger than the average height in Qin times. They were made by a combination of moulding and hand-modelling. Several dozen different moulds were used to make the heads, producing rough castings which were then finished off by hand to create individuality.

For each warrior, ears and moustaches were made in separate moulds and attached later, and headgear, lips and eyes also show signs of having been made separately. The material of which they were made is clay, which when fired shrinks by about 18 percent, so the unfired figures must have been considerably larger. Heads and bodies were made separately, then joined together. To ensure that they stood upright, thicker layers of clay were used in the lower parts of the body.

The faces of the warriors have been classified by some scholars into 30 different types, but fall into ten broad categories, described by the Chinese written characters they most nearly resemble. The face like the character which is pronounced "you", for example, belongs to the mightiest of the warriors, and is broader in the cheekbone than in the forehead. The opposite face, with forehead broader than cheekbones, represents the Chinese character "jia" and is found most commonly among the vanguard, since its appearance is alert and resourceful. Many of the faces have tightly closed lips and staring eyes, to create the feeling of bravery and steadiness. Others show vigour, confidence, thoughtfulness, or experience.

The skill of the carvers has created an army of recognizable types, no two of whom are exactly the same. They are neither mechanical copies of real warriors, nor mere imaginative figures; rather, they represent a gallery of ideal types such as one might find in a well-run army, ranging from the young and enthusiastic subaltern to the wise and experienced sergeant.

The armour worn by the warriors is also skilfully executed, showing that the sculptors

were familiar with Qin armour. The pieces of battledress were individually made, and fit their wearers perfectly. The horses are carved with similar vigour, and meet the requirements for fine horses laid down by Qin writers several hundred years earlier: pillarlike forelegs, bowlike hind legs, high hoofs, slim ankles, flared nostrils and a broad mouth. The horses' saddles are decorated with tassels, and were originally painted red, white, brown and blue and made to represent leather. There are no stirrups, suggesting that the horsemen in the emperor's army had no need of them.

In December 1980 a remarkable find was made 20 yards to the west of the emperor's tomb mound: a pair of bronze chariots, complete with horses and charioteers. Unlike the terracotta warriors, these are two-thirds life-size, but are modelled with even greater delicacy and skill.

The hangar protecting the pits covers an area of 19,000 square yards. The burial of the army replaced the earlier practice of human and animal sacrifice. The army was deployed with archers at the front, chariots on the right flank and the cavalry on the left, surrounding lines of infantry interspersed with chariots.

The brick-paved floors can be seen beneath these warriors (left), who all face east. It is thought the direction may have reflected Qin Shi Huangdi's fear that a revengeful attack would be most likely to come from the 6 kingdoms he conquered. The depth of the figures indicates why the army was found only when farmers were drilling for water.

The armour of the warriors (above right) has provided invaluable information on the state of military technology; this is an infantryman. It is now known how armour was designed for generals, cavalrymen and charioteers. Even the hair of warriors (right) was individually finished, as well as all their facial features.

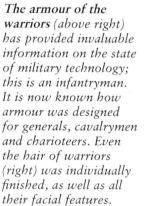

The bronze chariots have survived far better than the wooden ones pulled by the terracotta horses, and provide a reliable model of what a Qin chariot was actually like. Horses and charioteers were originally painted, but have now faded to a greyish white. The horses' bridles are decorated with gold and bronze decorations. Few doubt that other remarkable finds will be made as excavation of the tomb proceeds.

The entire army, evidence of the supreme power and megalomania of Qin Shi Huangdi, must have taken hundreds of craftsmen many years to complete. If it was supposed to preserve the emperor in death, it failed; but it has brought down to us an extraordinary insight into the world of China's first emperor, a world in which supreme craftsmanship coexisted with cruelty and violence. No more spectacular memorial exists than Qin Shi Huangdi's terracotta army.

How the warriors may have looked

The Museum near the excavated pits contains a display of figures painted as it is thought they once looked. Firing the fine-textured clay figures gave them a smooth finish which was then painted with pigments mixed with gelatine to give them an even more life-like appearance. Only traces of this paint remain.

The Granite Icon

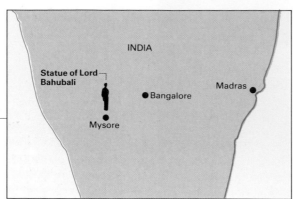

INDIA

Statue of Lord Bahubali

Bangalore

Madras

Mysore

INDIA

SRI LANKA

Fact file

Believed to be the tallest monolithic statue carved out of a single piece of rock

Builder: King Chamundaraya

Built: 981

Material: Granite

Height: 57 feet

Every dozen years or so, followers of the Jaina religion make a pilgrimage to a small town, Shravana Belgola, in Karnataka in southern India. There, on top of a hill, stands a monolithic statue of a naked man, some 57 feet high and carved out of solid granite a thousand years ago. From a platform erected around the head of the statue, the pilgrims pour water, milk, ghee, curds and sandalwood paste in various colours over the holy image in a ceremony as ancient as the statue itself. The great statue gleams in the sun as the priests chant mantras and sound gongs. The ceremony was last performed in 1981, the thousandth anniversary of the statue's creation.

The story of how this remarkable statue was carved is lost in the mists of time, and buried by the accretion of myths and legends which surround it. The statue depicts Lord Bahubali, one of the sons of Rishabha, the founder of the Jaina religion and a king who decided to renounce worldly power in the search for righteous living and salvation. Realizing the ephemeral nature of success in this world, Rishabha abandoned his two wives and more than 100 children to seek enlightenment in the forest. Before leaving he appointed one son, Bharata, to run his kingdom of Ayodhya, and awarded another, Bahubali, the principality of Pondnapura. Bharata became a powerful ruler, but of his brothers only Bahubali refused to accept his overlordship.

The two brothers fought, according to legend, first by staring one another down, then by fighting in water, and finally by wrestling. Bahubali won all three contests, and at the end of the wrestling bout held his brother high and prepared to dash him to the ground. Suddenly he was overcome by remorse and disillusionment, and put Bharata gently down. Without a moment's hesitation, he then left for the forests, pulled out his hair and stood still, his arms at his sides and his feet straight ahead, as he sought enlightenment. He stood like this for a whole year, while ants built nests around his feet and the creepers of the forest began to wind around

The climb to the statue up 614 steps carved out of the rock begins near a "tank" in Shravana Belgola (left). Since the statue is concealed by cloisters built around it during the 12th century, ascending pilgrims see it in its totality only at the last moment. The dramatic impact of losing sight of the statue and then suddenly seeing it again at close quarters (right) is awe-inspiring. The statue, here with scaffolding ready for the annointing ceremony, is visible from 15 miles away.

The Granite Icon

his legs. Finally Bharata and two of Bahubali's sisters came to the forest to offer homage, and his resentment and pride finally disappeared. Bahubali then achieved the highest states of enlightenment known to the Jaina religion.

Bahubali's statue, on top of a hill 3,350 feet high, is believed to have been created in AD 981 under the command of a powerful general named Chamundaraya, a king of the Ganga dynasty. Contemporary descriptions of how the work was done do not exist—a long inscription on an elaborately decorated column erected at the same time by Chamundaraya, which might have held the secret, was obliterated when a later record was inscribed on it in 1200.

At the site of the statue itself, inscriptions in three languages—Kannada, Tamil and Marathi—make it clear that it was Chamundaraya who had the image made, but do not say how it was done. Since the statue is enormous and carved from a single piece of granite, it must have taken many workmen years to create it.

The statue is carved in the round from the head to the lower half of the thighs, with the rest in bold relief. The shoulders are broad, the waist narrow, and from the knees downward the legs are somewhat out of proportion. The arms hang straight down the sides with the thumbs turned outward. The whole figure exudes serenity. At Lord Bahubali's feet are carved anthills with serpents, and creepers wind their way up his legs. The granite of which the statue is carved is smooth, homogenous and hard—the ideal material for such a huge work of art. Ever since its creation the image has been one of the wonders of India.

The statue has many names and several curious features. It is often called the Gommata or Gommateshwara, either because Gommata was another name for Chamundaraya, because the word means beautiful, or because it means a hill or hillock. Its only visible flaw is a shortened forefinger on the left hand, and a variety of explanations has been put forward to explain this. One is that Chamundaraya ordered the finger to be mutilated because the image, when the carvers had finished their work, was simply too perfect. By deliberately damaging it, he sought to avert the evil eye.

Another theory is that the statue was damaged as an act of revenge in the reign of King Vishnuvardhana in the twelfth century. The king, who had lost a finger, was angered when a Jaina guru refused to accept food from his

The head-annointing ceremony, or Mahamastakabhisheka, *is known to have taken place in 1398 and has since been held regularly. Women are responsible for pouring offerings over the head of the statue. The influx of a million pilgrims (right) for the ceremony in 1981 necessitated construction of 7 satellite towns.*

The naked Indras, priests of the Jaina temples, direct the ceremony of Mahamastakabhisheka. In 1780 it was recorded that they worshipped the 1,008 shining metal pots that were used to carry sacred water up the hill to be poured over the head of Bahubali.

mutilated hand. In revenge, he abandoned the Jaina religion and ordered the statue damaged as an act of revenge. After such colourful legends, it is almost a disappointment to record that the most likely reason for the flaw is that the carvers came across a fault in the rock, which caused the end of the finger to fall off. To make the best if it, they carved a fingernail on to the end of the shortened finger.

The conservation of the statue of Lord Bahubali is the responsibility of the Archaeological Survey of India. Since it has stood unprotected for more than a millenium, time has begun to weather its smooth grey surface. In addition, the fact that huge quantities of milk, ghee and curds have been poured over the statue at irregular

Tall, ornate scaffolding is required to enable the offerings to be poured over the head of Lord Bahubali. Once the statue was finished, King Chamundaraya arranged to have it annointed with milk. But however much he poured over its head, the milk would not descend below the naval. Then an old woman named Gullakayajji arrived with a few drops of milk in the skin of an eggplant, and poured it over the statue. It not only covered the statue but flowed down to the valley, forming a pond. This miraculous event is commemorated with a statue to Gullakayajji, within the cloister that surrounds the statue.

Offerings at the feet of the statue indicate the the variety of substances with which its head is annointed: coconut milk, yoghurt, ghee, bananas, jaggery, dates, almonds, poppy seeds, milk, gold coins, saffron, yellow and red sandalwood pastes, sugar and, at the ceremony in 1887, precious gems of 9 kinds.

intervals has resulted in an accretion of grease, and the growth of moss and lichen. More alarming were the appearance of small cracks all over, and particularly on the face, and the development of pitted areas where the stone had begun to flake off. Beginning in the early 1950s, a series of experiments was carried out to determine the best way of removing the grease, cleaning and repairing the statue.

Before the ceremony of *Mahamastakabhisheka*, the statue now receives a preliminary coat of paraffin wax in solvent oil, which allows the greasy materials in the milk and other offerings to flow soothly over the stone, without getting into its pores. Such treatment also makes it much easier to clean the statue afterwards.

Although it is the largest, the statue of Lord Bahubali at Shravana Belagola is not the only iconographic image of him. There are four copies of it, the biggest at Karkal, which was carved in 1432 and stands around 40 feet tall. A second version at Enur, carved in 1604, is 33 feet tall. A magnificent bronze Bahubali, dating from the ninth century, is in the Prince of Wales Museum of Western India in Bombay. But none can compete with the original, its grandeur enhanced by the mystery of its creation. It stands, as one writer put it, "like a giant over the rampart of an enchanted castle, uninjured, though darkened by the monsoons of centuries, its calm gaze directed eastward toward a nearby mountain range mantled with forests."

Monument to Freedom

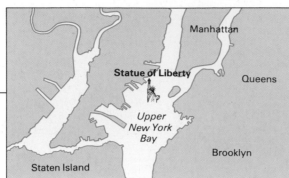

Fact file

The tallest monument in the world when given by France to the United States of America to mark the centenary of its independence from Great Britain

Designer: Frédéric-Auguste Bartholdi

Built: 1875–86

Materials: Copper, iron

Height: 306 feet 8 inches

Bedloe's Island, a 12-acre island in Upper New York Bay, provided the perfect site for the statue. Named after its owner, Isaac Bedloe, the island is visible to all shipping using the harbour and entering the Hudson River, making the statue a prominent landmark.

No statue expresses a more powerful symbolism than the colossal sculpture of a woman holding aloft the torch of freedom which dominates the harbour of New York. For 17 million immigrants from Europe, for whom she was the first sight as they reached American shores, the Statue of Liberty meant a new life in a new land. One of those immigrants remembers: "She was a beautiful sight after a miserable crossing that September. She held such promise for us all with her arm flung high, the torch lighting the way."

This was exactly how the statue's sculptor, Frédéric-Auguste Bartholdi, had envisaged his great lady: "Grand as the idea which it embodies, radiant upon the two worlds". The suggestion of such a statue was first made at a dinner party held near Versailles in 1865 by the historian and politician Edouard de Laboulaye. It was intended to symbolize the friendship between France and the United States at the time of the American Revolution, and mark the hundredth anniversary of the US as a nation. Bartholdi, a young sculptor with an established reputation, was a guest at the dinner and supported the idea. When he visited the US in 1871 he quickly identified the right site, on a small island in Upper New York Bay, south west of Manhattan, and back in France he began work on the first small models of a woman holding a torch.

Raising the money for the Statue of Liberty did not prove easy. Lotteries and dinner parties held by the Franco-American Union in France eventually financed the statue, while the huge pedestal upon which it was to stand was built from American contributions, raised with the powerful support of Joseph Pulitzer and his newspaper, *The World*. Bartholdi settled upon a statue built of beaten sheets of copper, mounted on a framework of iron: bronze or stone would have been too expensive and too heavy to transport. He knew the method would work, for he had seen the seventeenth-century statue of St

Carlo Borromeo, by G.B. Crespi, at Lake Maggiore in Italy, which stands 76 feet high. Bartholdi decided to create a statue twice as high, the largest in the world.

To design the supporting structure he first consulted Eugène-Emmanuel Viollet-le-Duc, the high priest of the Gothic revival in France. But he died in 1879 with the task incomplete, and Bartholdi turned to Gustave Eiffel, a daring engineer and specialist in structures of iron. Eiffel proposed supporting the statue on a central iron tower anchored firmly in the pedestal. The tower would consist of an iron truss, with diagonal bracing. From this strong framework, a secondary structure would be hung, approximating to the shape of the statue, and from this secondary framing a series of flat, springy iron bars would connect directly to the statue's skin.

The skin of the statue consists of 300 copper plates, beaten into shape by the technique known as *repoussé*. First Bartholdi made a series of clay models, of increasing size, in which he refined and perfected the form of the statue. From Bartholdi's one-third scale models, craftsmen at the workshops of Gaget, Gauthier et Cie in Paris made full-scale plaster copies, which were then used to form moulds by surrounding them with a wooden framework. The copper sheets were then created by beating them into shape on the inside of the wooden moulds. Thin copper sheets only $\frac{3}{32}$ of an inch thick were used, each overlapping with the next, and rivet holes were drilled to fix neighbouring sheets together. To ensure that the method really worked, the statue was temporarily assembled in the courtyard of Gaget, Gauthier. By 1885—nine years late for the bicentennial it was supposed to celebrate—the statue was finally on its way to New York.

There, work on the huge pedestal had also been delayed. It had been designed by the American architect Richard Morris Hunt, a specialist in the *beaux-arts* style. The pedestal is no mean construction in itself, standing 89 feet high on a 65-foot foundation. The style eventually selected by Hunt is vaguely Egyptian in style, strong and simple, and enhances the statue placed on top of it. Building of the pedestal began in 1883 and was completed in 1886, by which time the sculpture had been waiting for 15 months in its crates. It was removed and reassembled, working upward from the ground without exterior scaffolding. As the framework

Monument to Freedom

Full-size plaster copies of the statue's components were made in Paris, around which was built a "negative" wooden form, reversing the model's contours. Traditional wood lath-and-plaster techniques were used to make the life-size copies.

The incongruous sight of Liberty towering over the Paris factory of Gaget, Gauthier. Attaching the copper sheets from the bottom up, this temporary assembly used only 1 rivet in 10 so that it could be easily taken apart and packed into 210 crates for shipment to New York.

rose, the workers attached the skin, leaning over the side to install the rivets. In October 1886 the statue was finally dedicated.

The methods of construction worked well, but had one important flaw. The iron armature rods reacted electrolytically with the copper skin, causing corrosion which, by 1980, had destroyed much of the strength of the structure. The rods had swollen, causing rivets to shear or fall off and allowing rainwater to seep in, which exacerbated the problem. The inner surface of the copper had been painted many times, in an attempt to preserve it, but that had trapped water and in some places it was only the paint that was keeping together pieces of broken armature bar. The torch, and the structure supporting the raised right arm, were in particularly bad shape.

A major restoration project was launched to ensure that the statue would survive a second century. Every armature rod in the structure was replaced with new rods of stainless steel, working slowly through the statue and replacing a few at a time so that it would retain its integrity. The old bars were removed, and exact copies made in the new material and replaced, using the original rivet holes. It took a year to replace 10,000 feet of armature bars.

The most important repair of all was the replacement of the torch. Bartholdi had wanted to make the torch glow by projecting a strong light from the torch platform on to the flame itself, which was gilded, but the plan was dropped at the last minute for fear that the strong light would dazzle ships' pilots in the harbour. Instead, portholes were cut and lights installed within, producing a feeble result which Bartholdi compared with the light of a glow-worm. In 1916, the American sculptor Gutzon Borglum, creator of Mount Rushmore, converted the flame into a lantern by cutting holes in it, installing amber-coloured glass, and mounting a light inside. The flame was now nothing like the one Bartholdi had designed, and it also began to leak, creating further corrosion which weakened it.

By the time of the 1980s restoration, the flame was in such poor condition that it required complete replacement. The decision was taken to restore the lamp to as near Bartholdi's original as possible, and to remove the Borglum lantern and display it in the statue's museum. Appropriately a French firm, Les Métalliers Champenois from Rheims, won the contract for the job, and produced a gilded flame as close to the original as could be contrived. Modern lights—far more intense than any available for use in Bartholdi's day—were installed, so that today the flame glows at night just as he originally hoped it would.

The torch and flame
were the first parts of
the statue to reach the
United States, being sent
to the Philadelphia
Centennial Exposition
in 1876. After being
displayed in Madison
Square Park, New
York, they were
returned in 1883 to
Paris where the design
of the flame was
altered.

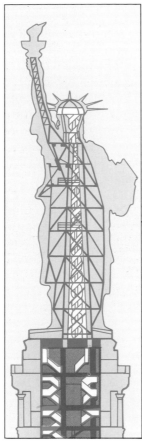

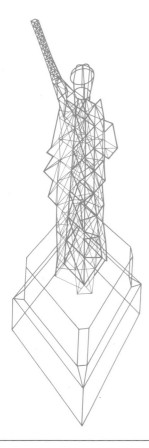

A computer diagram
(left) of the statue's iron
skeleton, made during
the statue's restoration
between 1982 and 1986.
The network of
armatures attached to
the central tower was
the only part based on
Viollet-le-Duc's ideas.
The two spiral
stairways (above)
connect the base with
the crown, which has a
25-window observation
platform for 30 visitors.

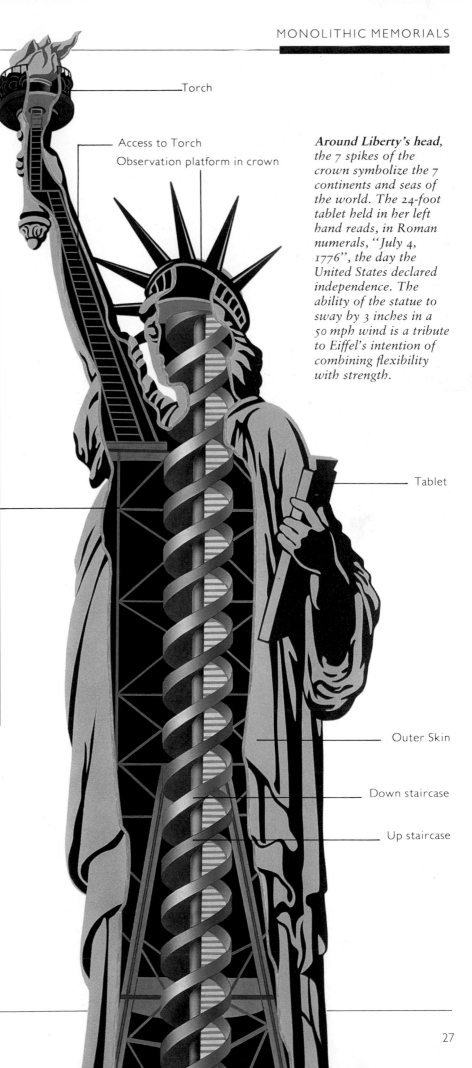

Torch

Access to Torch
Observation platform in crown

Around Liberty's head,
the 7 spikes of the
crown symbolize the 7
continents and seas of
the world. The 24-foot
tablet held in her left
hand reads, in Roman
numerals, "July 4,
1776", the day the
United States declared
independence. The
ability of the statue to
sway by 3 inches in a
50 mph wind is a tribute
to Eiffel's intention of
combining flexibility
with strength.

Tablet

Outer Skin

Down staircase

Up staircase

Builders of a Nation

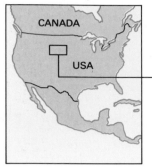

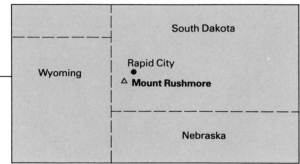

Fact file

The world's largest sculpture, carved out of a granite cliff face

Sculptor: Gutzon Borglum

Built: 1927–41

Material: Granite

Height: 60 feet

Rock excavated: 450,000 tons

In the Black Hills of South Dakota, USA, the sculptor Gutzon Borglum created the world's most gigantic piece of sculpture by carving the faces of four American presidents into a granite cliff. Each face is about 60 feet high, and some 450,000 tons of rock had to be removed by explosives, pneumatic drills and chisels to create the group. They have noses 20 feet long, mouths 18 feet wide and eyes 11 feet across. Given bodies on the same scale, the four presidents depicted—George Washington, Thomas Jefferson, Abraham Lincoln and Theodore Roosevelt—would stand about 460 feet tall.

The creation of Mount Rushmore took more than 15 years, though most of that time was spent not on the rock but on the stump, trying to raise the money needed. The idea came from Doane Robinson, a lawyer and writer who in the early 1920s held the post of official historian in South Dakota. In 1923 it occurred to him to

encourage more tourists to come to the state by commissioning a massive sculpture in the Black Hills. After failing to interest the sculptor Lorado Taft, Robinson put the idea to Gutzon Borglum. He had found the right man, perhaps the only man, with the confidence and skill needed to turn his dream into a reality.

Borglum was a successful sculptor with a taste for publicity and very little tact. The son of a Danish immigrant, he studied art in San Francisco and Paris, and worked for three years in London before establishing himself in New York. He created 100 statues for the Cathedral of St John the Divine in New York, and developed a taste for huge sculpture with a head of Abraham Lincoln carved from a 6-ton block of marble, now in the Capital Rotunda in Washington.

By then he was convinced that huge sculptures were needed to match the spirit of what he called the Colossal Age. "Volume, great mass, has a greater emotional effect upon the observer than quality of form", he wrote. "Quality of form affects the mind; volume shocks the nerve or soul centres and is emotional in its effect." Grumbling that there was not a monument in America as big as a snuff box, Borglum set out to remedy the deficiency. He found his canvas at Mount Rushmore, a great cliff of granite 400 feet high and 500 feet long, towering like a battlement of stone above pine trees and fresh vegetation.

Although Borglum asserted more than once that raising the money for the job would be simple, this was far from the truth. Eventually, however, Borglum, Robinson and the two senators from South Dakota persuaded Congress to set aside $250,000, half the expected cost, with the rest to be raised by public donation. The bill passed Congress and was signed into law by Calvin Coolidge just in time; within months the Stock Market crash of 1929 had wiped out whole fortunes and no money would have been available for such an apparently frivolous enterprise as carving faces on a mountain.

Outwardly, Borglum was certain that now he had sufficient money to make a start he could do the job. But he knew very little about the rock and was ignorant as to whether it would prove to be workable. Nor did he set out with any preconceived ideas of what the finished sculpture would look like. The head of Washington, he decided, must be dominant, so he set out to sculpt it without finally deciding where the other heads would ultimately be. The only successful

Foreman William Tallman hanging from the lower rim of Jefferson's eyelid, when the eye was still at a rough stage. To prevent the eyes having a dead look, Borglum carved a ring, or pupil, several feet across and deep enough to ensure that it was always in shadow; in the centre a peg of rock was left to reflect light within the pupil.

way to proceed, he asserted, was to shape the forms to the existing stone: "Sculptured work on a mountain must *belong* to the mountain as a natural part of it; otherwise it becomes a hideous mechanical application." Once the head of Washington was complete, he would determine how best to blend the next head with it.

He had chosen Mount Rushmore partly because the close-grained rock appeared to be carvable. It was immensely tough, but even so had a weathered surface which had to be cut away to expose smooth undamaged stone suitable for sculpture. For the first head, that of the first President, George Washington, Borglum cut away about 30 feet of rock. The most recessed head of the group, Theodore Roosevelt, required the removal of 120 feet of rock.

The problem of creating convincing faces for the four presidents was solved by a simple method invented by Borglum. First he prepared models, one-twelfth the size of the final sculpture, so that one inch on the models represented one foot on the mountain. At the centre of the head of each model he mounted a swivelled pointer, with a protractor plate to measure the exact angle, to right or left, to which it was pointing. From the pointer hung a plumb line, which could be moved in and out along the pointer and raised or lowered. Every point on the face of the model could then be defined by the angle of the pointer, the position of the suspension point, and the vertical fall of the plumb line. A similar pointer, but much bigger, with an arm 30 feet long, was then mounted at the centre of what was to be the head on the mountain. Measurements taken from any point on the model could be transferred to the same point on the rock, and marks made to show how much rock had to be removed. Men were trained to use the system, which proved simple and effective. It was the only measuring system needed to complete the entire sculpture.

The men Borglum hired to do the work were miners and quarrymen, familiar with pneumatic

Mount Rushmore *(5,725 feet) dominates the surrounding terrain and provided Borglum with smooth-grained granite that faced east, the best direction for the fall of light on the carvings. The final order of George Washington, Thomas Jefferson, Theodore Roosevelt and Abraham Lincoln was achieved pragmatically, beginning with Washington.*

Builders of a Nation

drills and explosives, but hardly used to working hanging like spiders on the face of a mountain almost 6,000 feet high. To reach their place of work, they strapped themselves into devices rather like a child's swing, and walked backwards over the cliff as a winchman wound out the cable supporting them. To gain any purchase when drilling into the rock, they would first attach two bolts and a chain, which they put around their backs so that they were able to press against it. The rock was so hard that drill bits quickly became blunt, and a full-time blacksmith was employed to sharpen them.

To begin shaping each face, the drillers first created egg-shaped volumes of clean rock, with the surface 3 to 6 feet proud of the final profile. Then the pointers got to work, transferring to the rock the instructions for shaping it. By honeycomb drilling and chiselling, the rough outlines of the face were created, and finishing touches added at the instructions of Borglum, who had a genius for recognizing what was needed to make the faces come to life. Inspired touches were the way in which he suggested Lincoln's beard by vertical lines in the rock, and Roosevelt's spectacles by the bridge over the nose and just a hint of the outline of the frame around the eyes.

Work on the monument went on throughout the 1930s, with frequent pauses when money ran out or the weather proved too unpleasant. By the time Borglum died, on 6 March 1941, Mount Rushmore was all but finished. The final touches were carried out by his son Lincoln Borglum, who had started work as a pointer on the project at the age of 15. The final cost was just under £1 million. In only one place—on Jefferson's upper lip, where an area of uncarvable feldspar was found—did the sculpture need patching. A small piece of granite 2 feet long by 10 inches wide was pinned into place and cemented with molten sulphur. Today some 2 million people a year come to the Black Hills to see the Mount Rushmore National Memorial, justifying all of Doane Robinson's original hopes.

To celebrate the monument's fiftieth birthday in 1991, a renewal scheme costing $40 million is being undertaken. This will include the first structural analysis of the sculptures, to ensure that cracks in the rock are not growing. If repairs are needed they will be carried out, and the survey will provide other knowledge needed to manage what the Mount Rushmore superintendent Dan Wenk calls "this great resource".

The greatest alteration made by Borglum was to relocate the head of Jefferson after work had begun. As seen from the road, it was to have been to Washington's left (below) but the rock was unsound and Borglum disliked the perspective. However, a crack in the rock through Jefferson's nose in the new location forced him to tilt the head back.

Jefferson's rough-hewn face shows the technique of "honeycombing" in which a series of close-set holes was drilled and the honeycombed rock between removed with a chisel. The granite proved so hard that Borglum had to abandon his intention not to use dynamite, since the use of pneumatic hammers would have taken decades. After honeycombing, lighter pneumatic hammers, known as "bumpers", were used to chatter against the rock, smoothing the outlines and creating details.

Jefferson's complete head, with Washington beyond, before work began on Roosevelt or Lincoln. Jefferson is the only one of the four to be portrayed as he looked before becoming president. The number of men working on the monument varied according to the weather and the availability of funds; it was sometimes as few as one, sometimes as many as 70 but an average was about 30. Work began at 7.30am after the climb up 760 steps to the mountain top. Supplies were brought in by the cableway anchored beside Jefferson's head.

Borglum's models were used to transfer his design on to the mountain using his "pointing machine" that related to a swivelled pointer in the centre of the head of each model (above).

The pointer (right) had a protractor plate to measure angles, while a plumb line which could be moved along the pointer, raised or lowered, enabled measurements to be transferred.

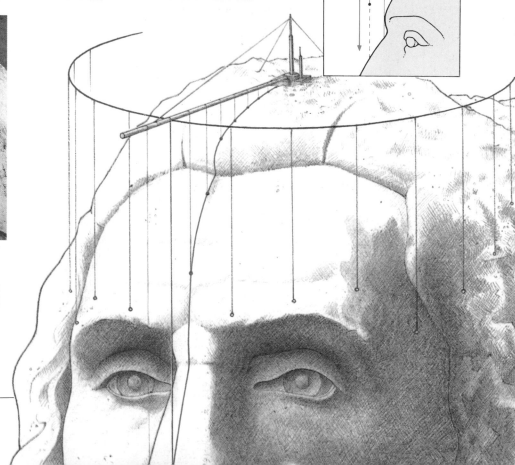

Monument to Victory

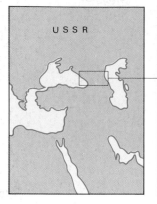

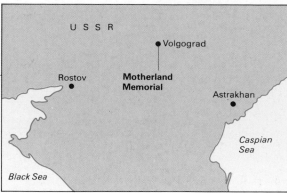

Fact file

The world's largest full-figure statue

Sculptor: Yevgeni Vuchetich

Built: 1959–67

Material: Reinforced concrete

Height: 270 feet

In the winter of 1942–43, one of the decisive battles of World War II was fought on the banks of the Volga at Stalingrad. German forces had broken through in August 1942 along a 5-mile front north of Stalingrad, and the Soviet 62nd Army faced encirclement and destruction by the German 6th Army, commanded by General Friedrich Paulus, and the 4th Panzer Army.

What followed was one of the most remarkable defences ever mounted, a battle in which every person available was mobilized to defeat the enemy. Both attackers and defenders endured appalling hardship, and terrible casualties: between February 1943, when the battle was won, and April 147,200 German dead and 47,700 Russians were buried. Of the 48,190 houses standing at the start of the battle, 41,685 were destroyed by bombing, fire, or artillery bombardment.

Some of the toughest fighting of all took place on a small hill to the north of the central part of the city. Mamayev Hill, named after the Tartar Khan Mamai who once made his camp on it, was listed on the combat maps as "Height 102"—its elevation in metres. The fight for possession of this crucial vantage point lasted for more than four months at the end of 1942, and it was here, on 26 January 1943, that units of the Soviet 21st Army advancing from the west joined up with the 62nd Army which had borne the brunt of the defence of the city. The German troops were cut in two, and defeated.

So intense was the fighting that the hill itself was altered in shape, and despite the severity of the winter it remained black, for the snow was melted by the heat of gunfire. When spring came, no grass grew. Every handful of earth from Mamayev Hill contained seven or eight pieces of shrapnel.

This hill still dominates the city, whose name was changed to Volgograd after Stalin's death

and posthumous disgrace. Now it is the site of the grandest war memorial in the Soviet Union, with its centrepiece a huge sculpture in reinforced concrete representing Mother Russia, somewhat sparsely clad, calling upon her sons to rise in her defence. The Motherland statue, created by the sculptor Yevgeni Vuchetich, is the largest full-figure statue in the world. From the base of her pedestal to the tip of the sword she holds aloft, Motherland stands 270 feet tall. The sword alone, made from stainless steel, is more than 90 feet long and weighs 14 tons.

The statue is certainly impressive, a landmark from every point in the city, but it is only one element in a majestic war memorial that is meant to be experienced as an unfolding drama. The whole concept was created by Vuchetich after he emerged in 1959 as the winner of a competition to design a fitting memorial for the dead of Stalingrad. It took 8 years to complete and was not finally opened until 15 October 1967.

Vuchetich, who died in 1974, was a prolific creator of sculptures glorifying the Soviet people and their triumph in the Great Patriotic War. He carried out more than 40 busts of generals, officers and soldiers, and at least ten Soviet cities have monuments by him. He was also responsible for a magnificent memorial to the Soviet Army in Treptow Park in East Berlin. Born in 1908 in Dniepropetrovsk, Vuchetich was educated at the Rostov School of Arts and at the Academy of Arts in Leningrad. He fought in the war, and suffered shell-shock. Afterwards he worked in the Grekov Studio of Painters of Battle Pieces.

The memorial he designed for Volgograd is didactic and uncompromising, a Politburo speech in stone. It begins at the foot of the hill, on Lenin Avenue. A stone mural depicts a procession making its way up the hill, the faces of men and women etched with grief but full of Socialist determination as they carry flowers, wreaths and banners to honour the memory of the dead. At the head of the procession are a man, his hand stretching out in the direction of the hill, and a girl carrying a modest bunch of flowers. They point the way to a flight of stairs that leads to a gently rising avenue of poplar trees. As soon as you set foot on the pathway, the huge Motherland figure is visible on the summit of the hill. She is standing against the wind, her scarf blown to one side. She seems to be shouting something, and pointing toward the Volga. The message needs no interpretation; she is calling on

Monument to Victory

her children to defend their country.

But before the huge figure is reached, you pass a smaller one, of a soldier emerging from a pool of water. Stripped to the waist and holding a grenade in his right hand and a sub-machine-gun in his left, this idealized member of the Red Army is no stripling, for he stands a full 40 feet high. Vuchetich called this sculpture "Fight to the Death" and said that it represented the whole Soviet people preparing to deliver a devastating blow to the enemy. "His figure, hewn from the beetling rock, becomes, as it were, a mighty bastion against Fascism" said Vuchetich, whose prose had something in common with his sculptures.

Behind this symbolic chunk of Socialist Realism, Vuchetich had the interesting idea of building two huge walls, converging in perspective and intended to convey the idea of a massive ruin. Like the rest of the memorial, they are carried out on a gigantic scale, more than 160 feet long and nearly 60 feet high. The walls, blackened by fire, are covered with inscriptions and scenes of the fighting. "Forward, only forward!" reads a typical one. At the end of the right-hand wall a real incident in the battle is depicted. A young member of the Komsomol (the Communist Youth Organization), Mikhail Panikakha, with no grenades left, is said to have destroyed a German tank by flinging himself on it with a flaming Molotov cocktail in his hand. Both he and the tank were consumed in the ensuing inferno.

The next stage in the ascent is Heroes' Square, a large open space with surrounding walls containing more depictions of heroism. Yet further and you reach the Hall of Military Glory, grey concrete walls outside but an enormous glittering hall within. The walls shine with gilt and copper inlay, and in the centre of the hall a huge hand faced with marble chips holds up a torch which carries the eternal flame. The torch is inscribed with the words "Glory, Glory, Glory", and the flame is surrounded by a guard of honour from the Volgograd garrison.

Perhaps uncertain that the many reliefs, inscriptions and sculptures would, unaided, make their effect on the Soviet public, Vuchetich and his colleagues also use sound to establish the appropriate mood. At the Ruined Walls can be heard the music of Bach, and the sound of wartime songs, the crash of gunfire, the shouts of the soldiers and the crackling voice of a radio announcer. In the Hall of Military Glory, it is

The Memorial Complex took over 8 years to build, entailing the excavation of over 1.3 million cubic yards of earth and the laying of over 26,000 cubic yards of concrete. To the left of Motherland is "The Grief of a Mother", which helps to balance the mass of the Hall of Military Glory on the opposite side of the square. The mother bending over the body of her lifeless son echoes the image of Pieta, expressing the human relationship between Christ and the Virgin.

Schumann's "Traumen", solemn and sad.

Around the Hall of Military Glory (also called the Pantheon) is yet another square, this time called the Square of Sorrow. Here there is another statue, "The Grief of a Mother", showing a woman bending over the body of her dead son. Finally there is another short climb to the base of the pedestal of Motherland herself. Along the concrete pathway that meanders its way up the grassy slopes are graves of Heroes of the Soviet Union who fell in the battle. "To Senior Lieutenant of the Guards Khazov Vladimir Petrovich, Hero of the Soviet Union, Eternal Glory!" "To Master Sergeant Smirnov Pavel Mikhailovich, Hero of the Soviet Union, Eternal Glory!"

As the path wanders to and fro, the statue is seen from different vantage points. Finally you are right beneath her feet and as you look up you notice, in the words of one Soviet writer, that the

The statue of **Motherland** (left) is not fixed to its pedestal, its own great weight providing the only support. The scarf blowing away behind the neck alone is said to weigh 250 tons. The statue is imposing from all angles.

colossal statue with her widely outstretched and highly raised arms has encompassed half the sky. Glinka's hymn "Glory" plays gently in the background. On winter evenings the statue is illuminated by searchlights.

The whole ensemble is typically Soviet, representing one of the principal justifications claimed by the Soviet Communist Party for ruling the country—victory in the Great Patriotic War. For sincere Communists, and for veterans of the war, visiting Motherland is an emotional experience. For younger more cynical Russians, it tends to be seen as a grandiose production of the years when Leonid Brezhnev led the country into stagnation. Motherland's local nickname is "Brezhnev's Auntie". But nobody should complain: in an earlier era it would not have been a statue of Mother Russia brooding over Volgograd, but of Stalin himself. And that would have been a lot harder to swallow.

"Fight to the Death" (above) is on the central axis of the complex and is made of a solid block of waterproof reinforced concrete faced with granite slabs. Birches, the typical tree of Russian forests, surround the pool from which the statue arises.

The Hall of Military Glory (left) is decorated with 34 mosaic banners with black ribbon fringes that bear the names of 7,200 Soviet soldiers who fell at Stalingrad. The floor is inlaid with black, grey and red marble.

CHAPTER TWO

Architectural Achievements

G reat buildings are designed to make a statement. Some glorify God, or symbolize the power of a ruler—temples, cathedrals and palaces have been built ever since man first laid one stone on another. Some are monuments to wealth, or instruments of war; others are shrines to culture or to sport. Several reflect a desire evident through the centuries to build ever higher, creating structures which have tested contemporary building technology to the limit—and sometimes beyond it. Many towers have collapsed when ambition has outstripped knowledge of the laws governing stresses; one of the most remarkable towers to have fallen was the Gothic spire at Fonthill, which is featured in the Gazetteer.

Although the purpose of these buildings may vary, without a function they could hardly have been created, for architects, unlike other artists, cannot work without a client ready and willing to pay the bill.

All the buildings described here have some claim to be unique. They are either the first, the biggest, the tallest, the most original or the most fantastic of their kind. Some can claim, like the Crystal Palace, the Eiffel Tower or the New Orleans Superdome, to have carried the art of building into new territory. Others have been chosen because they reflect the obsessions of a single man, like Antonio Gaudí or Felix Houphouet-Boigny, determined to leave a statement in stone or concrete behind them. There are mysteries like the great pyramid of Cholula, science fiction fantasies like Biosphere II, and near-follies such as the Sydney Opera House in which a beautiful idea demanded to be translated into reality, however difficult that turned out to be.

Every important culture has produced great buildings; sometimes it is the only thing they have left behind. Here are a selection of the most remarkable among them, the work of architects and builders over the past four thousand years. If architecture is frozen music—as a German philosopher once claimed—here are some of the loudest and the sweetest sounds man has ever contrived to make.

Architectural Achievements
Temple of Amun
Pyramid of Cholula
Pyramids: shrines of the ancients
Krak des Chevaliers
Vatican Palace
Forbidden City
Crystal Palace
Paxton's Influence
Sagrada Familia Cathedral
Gaudi's creative genius
Eiffel Tower
Eiffel's other works
Manhattan
Epcot Dome
Munich Olympic Stadium
Sydney Opera House
Superdome
CN Tower
The tallest towers
Sultan of Brunei's Palace
Basilica of Our Lady of Peace
Biosphere II

Shrine to the God of the Wind

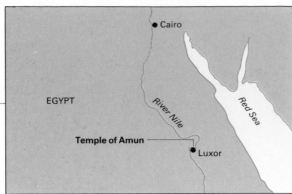

Fact file

The largest religious building ever constructed

Builders (major constructions):
Tuthmosis I—Ramesses II

Built: c1524–1212 BC

Material: Granite, sandstone and limestone

Area (Great Court):
10,668 square yards

On the banks of the Nile, at a place the Egyptians called the birthplace of all the world, lies the largest religious building ever constructed. The Temple of Amun at Karnak (once ancient Thebes) is more than a building, for its history stretches over 1,300 years. It is a record of Egyptian civilization, laid layer on layer in a vast and confusing muddle that impresses more by its bulk than its beauty. At its height, when Thebes ruled over Egypt, Amun's temple was served by 81,000 slaves, and was paid tribute in gold, silver, copper and precious stones from 65 other cities and towns. The many buildings on the site have one thing only in common: they were built to glorify the great god Amun, and to ensure their builders long life and great power.

The ancient Egyptians had many gods, and built shrines to propitiate them. Some gods had a purely local significance, but others were elevated to the status of "great gods"—like Re, the sun god, recognized as the source of life beyond his origins in Heliopolis, and Amun, the god of wind and of fertility, who was originally worshipped only in Thebes. With his wife Mut and son Khonsu, Amun formed a royal trinity,

becoming "King of the Gods". But even the greatest of gods were not in conflict with one another, and could incorporate each other's qualities. In this way, under the patronage of powerful rulers, Amun acquired the character of the sun god, Re, becoming Amun-Re and gaining greater eminence, at least in Thebes. Increasingly, other gods came to be seen as facets of Amun, who, by absorbing many gods into one, came close to being a single, all-sufficient god such as those in the Judaeo-Christian tradition.

The creation of the Temple of Amun coincided with the rise and fall of Thebes. Today all that is left is the temple itself, because the great city of Thebes was built, like all Egyptian domestic buildings, of mud bricks and has not survived. Even the houses where the Pharaohs lived were of brick, their furniture designed to last only a lifetime. The temple, however, was different. It was meant to last into eternity and was made of granite, sandstone and limestone, quarried and shaped with the most primitive of tools and techniques.

The granite came from quarries at Aswan, limestone from Tura near Cairo, and sandstone from many places along the Nile Valley. The softer stones appear to have been quarried with an implement like a pick, but no such surviving tool has ever been found. Stone slabs for building appear to have been dressed with a saw, probably made of copper and using an abrasive mineral such as quartz to increase its cutting power. Holes could be drilled with hollow circular drills, also made of copper; the cylindrical drill cores produced by the use of such an instrument have been found, although neither saw nor drill has survived.

The building methods used by the Egyptians were fairly primitive. The Temple of Amun, for example, has virtually no foundations. So long as the pillars could be laid on the underlying rock, that was considered sufficient. At Karnak, flooding carried away the flimsy foundations of the huge Hypostyle Hall, causing 11 columns to fall in 1899. This provided a chance to examine the foundations, which turned out to be little more than a trench packed with sand to provide a level surface, and a yard or so of small stones loosely laid on top.

The largest and most splendid building at Karnak is the Hypostyle Hall (from the Greek word meaning "below pillars") and consists of a forest of columns—originally there were 134 of them. This was the greatest building produced in

The Sacred Lake (left), bordering the south-east part of the temple complex, symbolizes Nun, the eternal ocean in which the priests of Amun purify themselves. The 134 columns of the Hypostyle Hall (right) are arranged in 16 rows, and those in the central double row are 69 feet high. Every surface is decorated with reliefs and inscriptions.

Shrine to the God of the Wind

ancient times, and covered an area 339 feet long by 169 feet broad. Down the centre runs a double row of columns 33 feet in circumference and 69 feet high.

To either side are seven further rows of columns, each 48 feet high. Originally the whole area, big enough to accommodate the Notre-Dame in Paris, was roofed with stone blocks, rising higher in the centre and with windows along the clerestory of the nave providing light for the interior.

Creating this huge building was an astonishing achievement, given the simplicity of the tools available. The pulley was not known to the Egyptians, and the blocks making up the pillars and the roof were pulled into place up ramps made of mud bricks. Scaffolding was used, but only on a small scale for the decoration and finishing of the stone. The men who built the temple worked in gangs with fixed shifts. A diary of the work done by each group was kept, together with records of the weight of copper tools issued to each man, and notes of excuses given for absence. The workmen were paid with food, wood, oil and clothing, and sometimes received a bonus of wine, salt or meat.

The Hypostyle Hall was planned and started by Ramesses I, who ruled for just two years before being succeeded by his son Seti I in 1318 BC. The hall was completed by Ramesses II, who succeeded his father in 1290 BC and ruled for 67 years. Ramesses II was a great builder, creating more temples and monuments than all the other Pharaohs, including the temples at Abu Simbel.

The decoration on the outside of the hall includes the depiction of Ramesses II's war against the Hittites, and includes the actual text of the final peace treaty, the first non-aggression treaty ever negotiated. It also includes a prayer to Amun for help when Ramesses II had been abandoned by most of his army and was faced by the might of the Hittites. "I call to thee, my father Amun. I am in the midst of strangers whom I know not. All the nations have banded together against me. I am alone and no one is with me . . . But I call and see that Amun is better for me than millions of footsoldiers and hundreds of thousands of charioteers." The northern wall depicts the battles of Seti I in Lebanon, southern Palestine and Syria.

The hall as we see it today is the result of major reconstruction, mostly by French archeologists. When it was rediscovered by Napoleon and his army at the end of the eighteenth century,

The use of calyx capitals to columns (left) provides a support 12 feet in diameter, enough to hold 100 men.

The decoration in the Hypostyle Hall has provided archeologists with valuable information. The Egyptians used little vaulting and no arches, their temples consisting of many pillars roofed over with flat blocks of stone. The limited span of limestone and sandstone necessitated numerous columns.

Ram-headed sphinxes (right) line the western approach to the Temple of Amun, from the River Nile. With sun discs on their heads and a statue of the Pharaoh under their chins, they symbolize the sun god's strength (the lion) and his docility (the ram).

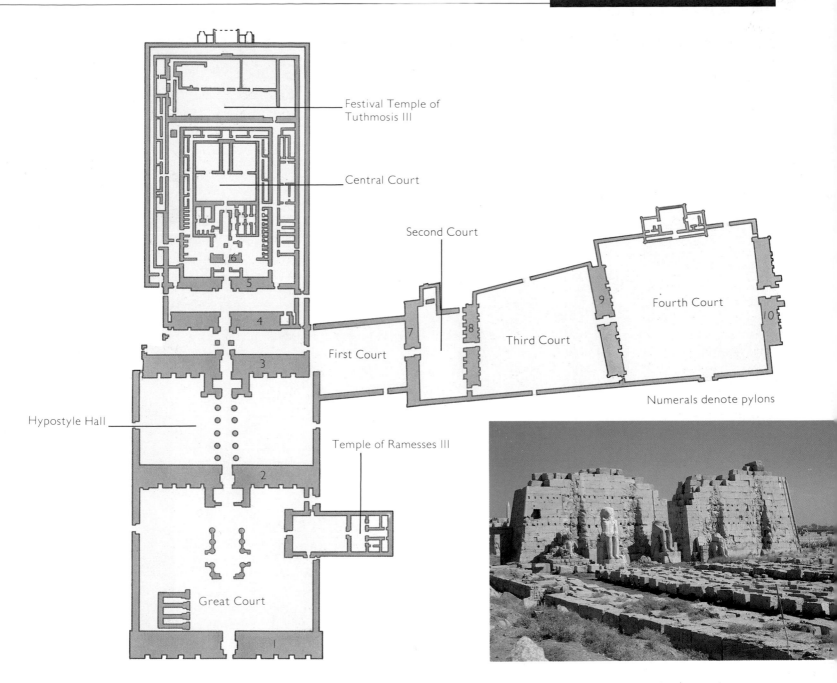

Festival Temple of
Tuthmosis III

Central Court

Second Court

First Court

Fourth Court

Third Court

Numerals denote pylons

Hypostyle Hall

Temple of Ramesses III

Great Court

the hall was ruined. Pillars had either fallen or were leaning, the sand had encroached and almost buried it. Long years of reconstruction followed, to produce the complete building—less roof—that we can see today.

The Hypostyle Hall is just one of 20 temples, shrines and ceremonial halls at Karnak. The last structure to be built there, the giant pylon, or gates, was erected by the last native rulers of ancient Egypt, the Ptolemaic Pharaohs. This huge gateway is 49 feet thick, 143 feet high, and 370 feet wide. One wall, incomplete, still shows the rough finish of the stonework before it was finally dressed, and still in place are the remains of the brick ramps up which the blocks were hauled to make the wall.

Through the gates lies an open court built by the Libyan Pharaohs of the XXII Dynasty (945–715 BC) and on the southern wall of this court is one of the finest examples of an Egyptian temple, the temple of Ramesses III, consisting of a forecourt, pillared hall, and sanctuary.

The whole area of the site is sufficient to accommodate 10 European cathedrals. It is an imperial statement on behalf of a god whose temple, at its peak in the time of Ramesses III, controlled at least 7 percent of the population of Egypt and 9 percent of the land, 81,000 slaves, 421,000 head of cattle, 433 gardens and orchards, 46 building yards and 83 ships. Discoveries are still being made by archeologists here; as recently as 1979–80, a complete shrine came to light, which is one of the most important discoveries in recent years.

The 8th pylon was built by Queen Hatshepsut. Pylons were introduced at Karnak by Amenhotep III (1417–1379 BC) and guard each side of the entrance to a temple. The walls slope inward, and the façades were usually decorated with scenes of conquest by whichever ruler built the pylon. Grooves were incorporated for ornamental flag poles.

Legendary Mexican Tomb

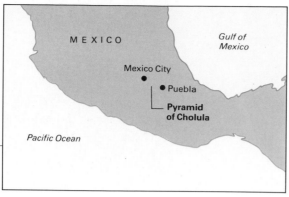

Fact file

The world's largest pyramid

Built: 2nd–8th centuries

Material: Adobe

Height: 200 feet

Base: 1,400 feet square

Near the quiet, sleepy town of Cholula in Mexico a pretty colonial church, its dome tiled in green and gold, sits on top of an odd-looking hill that rises from the plain. The church was built by the Spanish conquerors of Mexico, and is known as Nuestra Señora de los Remedios. It is one of many Christian churches in the town, but its builders may have been unaware that it crowns a much more remarkable religious structure. The hill on which it stands is not a natural feature at all, but the world's largest pyramid and the biggest ancient structure in the New World. It is, in fact, not one pyramid but at least four, each built on top of a previous construction.

The great pyramid, 1,400 feet along each side and some 200 feet high, was already in ruins and covered in dense green brush when the Spaniards first arrived. Building probably began on the site in the first or second centuries AD, and the successive increases in the size of the pyramid continued until the end of the eighth century, although modifications were made up until the twelfth century. Many thousands of people must have been involved in building such a huge structure, under the command of a priestly caste which exercised complete power. The earlier, buried pyramids at Cholula are contemporary with two other great pyramids at Teotihuacán, a bigger city 100 miles to the north and at its height the capital of a considerable empire.

The great pyramid at Cholula is built of adobe—unbaked brick—faced with small stones and then coated with either plaster or clay. Inside the pyramid there is a network of tunnels, in which many of the walls bear paintings, and a staircase of cut stone that leads through the inside of the pyramid to the flat summit. Outside the pyramid is a plaza more than an acre in area, which originally gave access to the staircase which led up the pyramid face.

Around the plaza are buildings, some with murals similar in style to those found at Teotihuacán, but at least one in a different style, namely a mural more than 150 feet long showing a ceremonial drinking scene that might have taken place at the time of the harvest. The figures, depicted life-size in a free-flowing style, are all men, with the exception of two wrinkled old women. The scene is one of abandonment, with the drinkers, mostly nude, showing distended stomachs which suggest that imbibing had been under way for some time. The mural is believed to have been painted between the second and third centuries.

Like the people of Teotihuacán, the god worshipped at Cholula was Quetzalcoatl, a creature with the feathers of a quetzal bird and the body of a snake. The feathers of this bird, which lives in a small area on the border between Mexico and Guatemala, were greatly prized in ancient Mexico for their rarity and beauty, so that the word "quetzal" eventually came to mean anything precious.

But who were the people who built the world's greatest pyramid? Nobody knows. They predated the Toltecs, who took over the region after their decline, and the Aztecs. But little is known about their language, customs, or the extent of their political control in the centuries during which the pyramid was being built. The huge size of the structure, and the organization that went into creating it, suggest that the society was controlled by an élite who commanded loyalty over a considerable area.

The better preserved ruins at Teotihuacán provide some clues about Cholula, for it is clear that the two places were linked. The city there was laid out on a grid plan, covering 8 square miles. Its main thoroughfare, the Avenue of the Dead, started at a huge pyramid, the Pyramid of the Moon, and passed in front of an even larger one, the Pyramid of the Sun. Along the length of

Legendary Mexican Tomb

this avenue were further pyramid-shaped platforms with flat tops, with a temple on each.

The huge Pyramid of the Sun, which rises to a height of 216 feet from a base about 750 feet square, is reckoned to have taken 30 years to build, using a work force of 3,000 men. About a million cubic yards of material was used to create it. The pyramid at Cholula, though not quite as tall, has a base almost four times as large, and is reckoned to have involved the shifting of 4.3 million cubic yards. Thus we may perhaps guess that it would have taken as many as 10,000 workmen a total of 40 years to build.

In practice, however, the building took place in stages, with the smaller pyramids providing a base for the later ones, so it is probable that the structure was created over a period of hundreds of years, with pauses as each successive pyramid was completed. For comparison, the Great Pyramid of Cheops, one of the original seven wonders of the world, was originally 481 feet high (now 449 feet, since the loss of the point at the top) and its base was 756 feet in each direction. It contains a total of 3.36 million cubic yards of material.

The people who built the pyramids at Cholula and Teotihuacán had only simple stone-age tools but were able to use them to create not only the monumental architecture of the pyramids, but also pottery and sculpture. On the east side of the great plaza at Cholula, archeologists found a huge stone slab, weighing 10 tons, carved along its vertical edge with a motif of serpents entwined with one another. On the west side of the pyramid, a stylized serpent's head was found, carved in a rectilinear style.

The makers of these artefacts do not appear to have been warriors. Neither Teotihuacán nor Cholula have any fortifications, which may explain how the priestly civilizations that created both disappeared so rapidly when nomadic warrior tribes arrived from the north. Teotihuacán at its peak was a city of at least 125,000 people, perhaps even as many as 200,000, which makes it larger than Athens at the height of its power. Yet it disappeared abruptly and completely in about AD 750 (some say earlier). Cholula was never as large, and may have survived a little longer, but it too was eventually overrun and its culture obliterated.

By the time Cortés arrived in Mexico, the city of Cholula had passed through the hands of at least three waves of conquerors. The best known of these were the Toltecs, who are said to have

taken control of the city in 1292, to be displaced in 1359 by the kingdom of Huexotzingo. Though neither of these peoples shared the religious convictions of those who built the pyramid, they continued to regard it as one of the wonders of the nation. Cortés himself reported that Cholula, a city whose exterior was "as fine as any in Spain", had 20,000 houses, and 400 pyramids.

At the beginning of the nineteenth century, the first tentative attempts to understand the ancient civilizations of Mexico were made by the German explorer and scholar Alexander von Humboldt. He was the first in modern times to measure the size of the pyramid, which he described as "a mountain of unbaked bricks",

The material used in much of the construction of the pyramid is adobe, which was faced with small stones and given a thick coating of plaster or clay. This render was then painted. The Spanish are said to have built 364 churches in Cholula.

Several stone monuments (left) have been found by excavation, though they were broken and have had to be repaired and re-erected where they once stood. This monument on the east side of the plaza is about 12 feet high with a missing top. Around the perimeter is an interlocking scroll design.

Tunnelling through the pyramid has helped to determine that there were at least 4 major superimpositions as the structure was steadily enlarged (above). The earliest measured 373 feet by 353 feet by 59 feet high, and the last phase increased it to 1,400 feet square and a height of about 200 feet, covering approximately 46 acres.

and he was struck by its similarity to the pyramids of ancient Egypt and to the Ziggurat of Belus in Babylon. He speculated about a link between the builders of these monuments.

Curiously, there is also a link between the pre-Conquest legends about the pyramid and those of the Biblical flood and the Tower of Babel. According to Humboldt, the pyramid was built after a great flood had devastated the land. Seven giants had saved themselves from the waters, and one of them built the pyramid in order to reach heaven. But the gods, angered by this plan, hurled fire at the pyramid in order to destroy it. Cortés was said to have been shown a meteorite, bearing a resemblance to the shape of a toad,

which had fallen on top of the pyramid.

A structure as large and as mysterious as the pyramid of Cholula is bound to attract myths, which can be dispelled only slowly by scientific efforts to understand the culture that created it. Excavations began at Cholula in 1931, and have continued since, with more than 4 miles of passages dug through the structure to expose its secrets. It is these excavations that have revealed the successive layers of pyramid-building, and cleared the platforms and squares of centuries of earth and dense greenery. But precise details about the people who built Cholula, how they did it, and why they disappeared so rapidly and so completely, remain to be discovered.

Excavations on the perimeter of the pyramid base have revealed a number of large plazas and courtyards surrounded by platforms. Protected by 30–35 feet of earth, they were in good condition, but the buildings had disintegrated. Only a small part of the site has been excavated.

Pyramids: Shrines of the Ancients

The earliest pyramids were constructed by the ancient Egyptians, and the first was the tomb built for the Third Dynasty king, Djoser (*c*2668–2649 BC). Its shape was almost an accident of its location; it required height to establish a dominant image so a square was enlarged, both at the base and with additional steps of brick. For the next millennium every king of note was buried beneath a pyramid. The largest was the pyramid of Cheops which held the record as the world's tallest structure for longer than any other—from *c*2580 BC until AD 1307 when it was overtaken by Lincoln Cathedral, England. The pyramids of central America were built much later, and were temples rather than tombs.

The Temple of the Giant Jaguar, Tikal, Guatemala
Situated in the largest of the Mayan cities, the pyramid is thought to date from about AD 800. The temple takes its name from the motif on a carved lintel. One side has been partially restored to reveal the succession of 9 terraces, surmounted by a 3-roomed temple. Within the temple a tomb was found; it contained a vaulted chamber with the remains of a skeleton adorned with 180 items of jade and buried with pearls, alabaster, pottery and shells. There are 7 other substantial pyramids in Tikal, which once covered 46 square miles.

The ziggurat at Ur
The ziggurat or temple tower is the principal ruin in the ancient city of Ur, in modern Iraq, which was inhabited c3500 BC. Ziggurats, like pyramids in central America, are thought to have been surmounted by temples, or to have encased burial chambers, as in Egypt.

The Pyramid of the Moon, Teotihuacán, Mexico
The pyramid covers 160,000 square feet at its base and provided the focus of the city, begun about AD 30. The other great pyramid in the city was consecrated to the Sun; Sun and Moon were represented by huge stone idols covered in gold.

The Pyramids at Giza, Egypt

Situated south west of Cairo is the world's largest pyramid, today measuring 449 feet in height—decay has reduced it from an original 481 feet. In its full form it contained $10\frac{1}{2}$ million cubic feet of material, and it is estimated that the pyramid contains 2.3 million blocks of limestone, each weighing $2\frac{1}{2}$ tons. The largest of 3 pyramids at Giza, it was built by Khufu (known to the Greeks as Cheops) who reigned in ancient Egypt from c2589–2566 BC. It was during the reign of his father, Sneferu, that the smooth-sided pyramid replaced the stepped kind.

The Soothsayer Pyramid, Uxmal, Mexico

The Mayan city of Uxmal is in northern Yucatan. The pyramid's total height is about 114 feet, made up of 4 distinct sections in an unusual elliptical form, surmounted by the base of a temple which is reached by 2 staircases. Restoration work has revealed that the pyramid has at least 5 building periods, reflecting the Mayan custom of superimposing new work on old. The name is derived from a legend about a dwarf whose soothsaying skill helped him to become king, whereupon he built himself this imposing pyramid.

Stronghold of the Crusaders

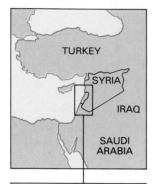

Fact file

The principal stronghold of the Crusaders which never fell to force of arms

Built: Successively strengthened between 11th and 13th centuries

Maximum wall thickness: 80 feet

Maximum garrison: 2,000

Headquarters of the Hospitallers: 1142–1271

Considered by many to be the finest medieval castle surviving today, Krak des Chevaliers is a reminder of the Crusades—religious passions that for two centuries drove thousands of men to war in a foreign land. The greatest fortress built by the Crusaders in the Holy Land, it was held by the Knights of the Hospital of St John for 130 years between 1142 and 1271. Standing on a spur dominating a fertile plain in what is now Syria, Krak was as nearly impregnable as any fortress ever built, falling finally as a result of a trick. T.E. Lawrence called it "perhaps the best preserved and most wholly admirable castle in the world".

Like other Crusader castles, Krak was built to defend the conquests made by Christian armies that had travelled to Palestine at the end of the eleventh century to liberate the holy places from Moslem occupation. The Crusades were inspired by Pope Urban II at the Council of Clermont in 1095, when he promised that Crusaders would be absolved from sin, would gain great wealth if they lived, or go straight to heaven if they died. Christ would be their leader in a Holy War. The effect was electrifying. "Never, perhaps, did the single speech of a man work such extraordinary and lasting results" one historian has written. The warlike sentiments of an increasingly confident and adventurous European nobility were sanctioned by the religious purposes of the Crusades.

After the First Crusade had succeeded in recapturing Jerusalem in 1099, many of the Crusaders left for home, their vows fulfilled. But some stayed, creating Crusader states along a narrow strip around the eastern shores of the Mediterranean. To protect these states from Moslem attack they built castles; the greatest of them was Krak des Chevaliers. Its name is a mixture of Arabic and French: Kerak, the Arabic for fortress, was corrupted into Krak, and the Chevaliers were the Knights of St John, who took over an earlier castle on the same site in 1140 and greatly improved it.

Krak was one of a network of Crusader castles standing on mountain peaks from the borders of Syria in the north to the deserts south of the Dead Sea. They were usually no more than a day's ride apart, and they were able to signal to one another at night by fires set on the battlements. They had their own water supplies, either in reservoirs cut from the rock or from natural springs, and they could withstand a siege for months, even years. They provided a system of defence which enabled the Franks and their successors to hold off a far greater number of Moslems for two centuries.

Krak was situated in the Crusader state known as the County of Tripoli, first established by Raymond of St-Gilles, Count of Toulouse. He died in 1105 and his successors first took possession of a small castle on the site, called the Castle of the Kurds, in 1110. They quickly improved it, but by 1142 the ruling Count of Tripoli, perhaps finding the responsibility for such an important castle too much for him, gave it to a religious military order, the Knights of St John, or Hospitallers. This order had run a hospital for pilgrims in Jerusalem and had earned the gratitude of Crusaders. Rewarded by the warriors whose wounds they had treated, the Knights of St John became a powerful and wealthy organization. It was during their occupation that Krak became the foremost castle in the Holy Land. Most of the work was done after an earthquake in 1202, which destroyed some of the existing fortifications.

Krak's plan is concentric, with two circles of walls interspersed with a series of towers. The masonry is massively solid, and the design epitomized the concept of defence in depth which reached its finest expression in this building. The succession of walls is designed to prevent surprise attacks, and to keep the siege instruments of attacking forces far enough away to prevent them from reaching the heart of the castle. The walls are made of masonry blocks 15 inches high by as much as a yard long, with a core of rubble and mortar, as was the usual medieval practice.

Below the three towers of the keep is a massive sloping wall, the talus, which drops more than 80 feet into a moat which also served as a reservoir. The angle of the wall, which Arabs called "the mountain", is puzzling, because its slope appears to make it easier for besieging forces to climb it. When T.E. Lawrence visited Krak in 1909 he was able, barefoot, to climb more than half way up this wall. He argued that its purpose could not be to prevent attackers undermining the walls, since the castle stands on rock, or as protection against battering rams, since its thickness—80 feet—would have been excessive. The reason must have been to prevent attacking troops getting so close to the wall that they were protected from the defenders' fire.

The same purpose is served by the placement of machicoulis around many of the castle's walls.

These are small boxes projecting from the walls close to the top. The object is to provide a secure point overlooking besieging troops from which fire could be directed at them, or stones or hot materials dropped on their heads. The machicoulis at Krak are small, meaning barely 16 inches across, and would have been big enough only for a single soldier.

To prevent attacking forces from attempting to rush the gateway and burst through, the entrance passage twists and turns through three "elbows"—abrupt changes of direction which make a blind charge impossible. The entrance is also defended by a drawbridge, a moat, four gates, a machicoulis, and by at least one portcullis.

In the days before the use of gunpowder, Krak was impregnable. During the occupation of the Knights of St John, a garrison of about 2,000 people was quartered here. A windmill stood on the north wall, grinding corn. Meetings and banquets were held in the hall, built in the thirteenth century, while the Latin Mass was chanted daily in the Chapel. The Wardens of the

Krak stands on a steep hillside *at a height of 2,300 feet with a commanding view. Most of the towers are round rather than square, to minimize damage from siege catapults. The arched entrance and square tower beyond are of post-Crusader construction.*

Stronghold of the Crusaders

South strongwork

Inner Castle

Outer Castle

Outer moat

Box-machilcoulis

Loopholes

The three tallest towers comprise the keep, built at the only point exposed to direct assault—the south. Previously keeps had been sited at the strongest point of defence, which was recognized as a tactical error. Beneath them is the sloping talus, thought to have been designed to keep attackers away from the wall and so make them an easier target.

An aerial reconstruction from the north east (right). In the foreground is the main gate; the chapel tower is that immediately beyond the main gate, with two lancet windows. The windmill was for grinding corn. Towers could not be roofed over to protect defenders, due to lack of wood or slate.

castle occupied rooms in the south-west tower, the same rooms in which T.E. Lawrence found the governor of the province living, with his harem, when he visited Krak in 1909.

There were assaults, but they failed. In 1163 the Emir Nur ed-Din besieged Krak, but made the mistake of taking a siesta one day outside the walls. The Knights poured out, surprised him, and put his army to rout. A generation later the great military leader Saladin marched his army up to the walls, took a good look, and retreated without even attempting a siege.

As time passed, however, the power of the Crusaders in the Holy Land began to fade. One after another the fortresses fell: Jerusalem in 1244, and Antioch in 1268. Krak found itself increasingly surrounded by hostile forces, growing every day more confident. In 1268, the Grand Master of the Knights of St John wrote to Europe for help, declaring that the bastions of Krak and Markab between them had only 300 men left to defend them against the Saracens. No help came, and in 1271 Sultan Beibars surrounded the castle with his army, and managed to penetrate the first defensive walls. But the talus, and the huge towers, defeated him. Within their walls the Knights could have held out for months.

Finally, Beibars devised a ruse. A letter, cleverly faked so as to appear genuine, was delivered to the defenders of the castle. It purported to come from the Count of Tripoli, and it instructed the garrison to surrender. The Knights emerged from their stronghold, and Krak fell. They were given a safe passage to the coast and rode away, leaving their castle behind them. All that is left, as one writer put it, are "the shadows of the kestrels cruising above, and the sun-scorched stones".

Warden's tower

Wall-walk

Refectory

Chapel

The vaulting of the Cloister reflects the quality of Krak's stonework. The chamber of the Grand Master of the Hospitallers in the Warden's Tower has particularly fine work— delicate pilasters, Gothic vaulting and a decorative frieze.

The outer wall was overlooked by the concentrically placed inner wall, built on higher ground to provide support to the first line of defence. Both dominated the surrounding plain.

Main gate

Main gate to inner ward

Escarpments

The Sacred City

The Vatican, one of the smallest states in the world, contains the second largest and most magnificent church. It also boasts the world's most famous ceiling—in the Sistine Chapel—and the world's largest collection of antique art, in the Vatican Museum. It has, in addition, a huge and famous library. Nowhere else are so many treasures of the Renaissance collected within so small a space.

It was here that St Peter, Christ's apostle and the first of the popes, was martyred, probably in the year AD 67. He was buried by his fellow Christians in a simple tomb on the sloping side of the Vatican Hill. Above this tomb was later built a great basilica by Constantine the Great which, despite the depradations of Goths, Huns, Vandals and Saracens, stood for more than a thousand years.

By the time of Pope Nicholas V (1447–55) the old building was tottering, its walls bulging 6 feet out of true and apparently ready to fall at any moment. Nicholas decided to replace it with a new building, but little was actually done until the papacy of Julius II (1503–13). Julius resolved to build a new St Peter's that would "embody the greatness of the present and the future . . . and surpass all other churches in the universe". He chose as the architect Donato Bramante.

Bramante devised a building in the shape of a Greek cross, with four arms of equal length, crowned by a magnificent central dome. The foundation stones were in place by 1507, and by 1510, 2,500 labourers under Bramante's direction had completed the four colossal piers that determine the size of the central crossing point. Bramante died in 1513, and in 1514 Pope Leo X appointed the young Raphael as chief architect. Raphael had already completed the decoration of the Vatican's State Apartments—the Stanze—with a series of paintings. He did not, however, contribute very much to the design of St Peter's before he died in 1520 at the age of 37.

Raphael was an agreeable man who obviously tried to make life pleasant for others, sometimes with alarming results. He allowed the masons working on St Peter's to leave holes in the foundations, to provide storage space for their lunches, tools and firewood. A few years later the hollow sections began to crumble and had to be replaced with solid masonry to make them strong enough to hold up the weight above.

Progress was slow after Raphael's death and stopped altogether during 1527, when Rome was sacked by invading Spanish forces. By the time

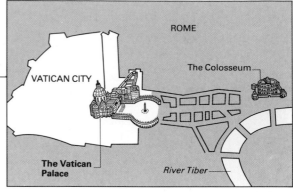

work resumed in the 1530s, the piers finished so long before by Bramante were sprouting a lush growth of grass and weeds. The plans were changed by Antonio de Sangallo in the 1540s, but after a series of rows and the death of Sangallo and his successor in 1546, the elderly Michelangelo, then 71, was summoned by Pope Paul III to take charge.

Reluctantly Michelangelo assumed full responsibility, then worked on the building without pay for the rest of his life. He demanded *carte blanche*, and got it. He could make any changes he wished, even demolishing parts of the basilica which were already finished, and could draw on

Fact file

The greatest concentration of Renaissance art in the world

Architect, St Peter's Basilica: Bramante, Michelangelo

Built: 1507–1612

Materials: Stone and brick

Length: 694 feet

Area: 54,402 square feet

The Vatican City State (left) covers an area of 108 acres and contains 30 streets and squares, 50 palaces, 2 churches beside St Peter's, a radio station, a railway station and a printing works. In the right foreground is Castel Sant' Angelo, built by Hadrian in AD 130.

The Papal Altar seen from the principal entrance to St Peter's. Above the altar is Bernini's baldacchino, 95 feet high and supported by 4 gilded spiral columns, and above that Michelangelo's dome with an internal height of 452 feet and a diameter of 157 feet.

The Sacred City

money without having to keep formal records. The St Peter's of today is largely the achievement of Michelangelo, who shrugged off a torrent of criticism and several attempts to discredit him by jealous rivals. By the time he died in 1564 he had devoted 17 years to the building, under five popes. And by then the huge drum which carries the dome was complete.

It took another 26 years to complete the dome, after endless further delays. It was not until 1590 that the final stone was in place and Pope Sixtus V was able to offer a solemn Mass of Thanksgiving in the basilica. The dome as completed is not quite what Michelangelo intended, being taller and more pointed than his design.

Models show that the structure was also changed. Michelangelo's design consisted of three brick shells, one inside the other, but the finished dome has only two. Its structure consists of 16 stone ribs, with the gaps between them filled with bricks, laid in herring-bone patterns. Three rows of windows admit light into the

St Peter's Square (above) is an image known throughout Christendom for the Pope's weekly Angelus blessing and seasonal messages. Bernini's colonnade of 284 columns and 88 pillars in 4 rows carries an Ionic entablature and balustrade on which stand 140 statues of saints.

The dome of St Peter's is surmounted by a lantern, a copper ball 8 feet in diameter, and a cross. A complex of staircases runs through the dome and lantern into the ball itself.

The Pinacoteca (left) is the Vatican's picture gallery, comprising 15 rooms in the Lombardi Renaissance style and opened in 1932. Napoleon compelled Pius VI, who formed the collection of Old Masters, to surrender the best works to France in 1797, although 77 were recovered in 1815.

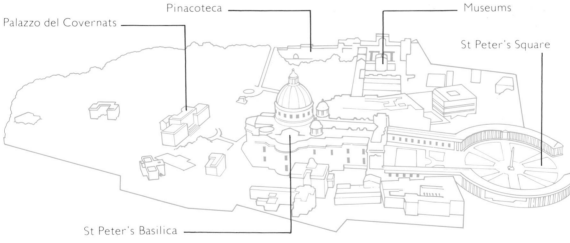

Palazzo del Covernats

Pinacoteca

Museums

St Peter's Square

St Peter's Basilica

The Vatican Museums (above) contain the largest collection of art and antiquities in the world, with several thousand items of sculpture and 460 Old Masters. The main part of the collection dates from the time of Pope Clement XIV (1769–74) and is made up of Etruscan, Egyptian and Greek antiquities, many of which were found in Rome. Besides the 15 rooms of the Picture Gallery is the Museum of Modern Religious Art, housed in 55 rooms under the Sistine Chapel. The Vatican Library holds some 800,000 books, 80,000 manuscripts and over 100,000 engravings and woodcuts.

The view from the dome of St Peter's (right) across Bernini's piazza and down Via della Conciliazione, a creation of Mussolini which entailed the demolition of 2 streets lined with old houses. At the end of the street is the Ponte Sant' Angelo, which also carries statues by Bernini—10 huge angels set up on the balustrade in 1668.

The Sacred City

A spiral staircase with barely perceptible risers links the entrance to the Vatican Museum, flanked by Statues of Raphael and Michelangelo, with the galleries above. From the main entrance of the museum to the Sistine Chapel—the highlight of any visit to the Vatican—is a walk of about ½ mile down marble corridors.

space between the two shells, and a narrow staircase runs upwards to the massive lantern on the top. Three chains were built into the dome during construction to prevent it spreading under the weight of the lantern, but 150 years later it became clear that this was not enough. Cracks began appearing as the ribs bulged outwards. Five more chains were inserted in 1743 and 1744, and a sixth in 1748. Since then there has been no further sign of movement.

In 1598, Clement VIII engaged Guiseppe Caesari to design the mosaics that decorate the inside of the dome, depictions of Christ, the Virgin Mary, apostles, saints and popes. Through the *oculus* at the very centre can be seen God bestowing blessings on mankind. Around the lower rim is an inscription in dark blue letters 5 feet high: *Tu es Petrus et super hanc petram aedificabo ecclesiam meam et tibi dabo claves regni caelorum* (Thou art Peter, and upon this rock I will build my church, and I will give unto thee the keys to the Kingdom of Heaven).

Even now the basilica was incomplete. The problem was that as designed by Michelangelo it did not include the whole area covered by Constantine's church, large parts of which had yet to be demolished. Should land hallowed by so many centuries of worship be allowed to fall outside the perimeter of the new building? Pope Paul V decided to extend the nave, turning

The splendour of the Vatican is reflected in the elaborate decoration of even a waiting room in the Secretariat of State. These walls were painted by Raphael, who was appointed Superintendent of Roman Antiquities by the Medici Pope Leo X (1513–21).

Bramante and Michelangelo's Greek cross into a Latin cross. Carlo Maderna designed the new nave, and an army of 1,000 men working night and day finished it by 1612.

One final detail remained, and it is the one that makes St Peter's instantly recognizable—the semi-circular colonnades that surround the huge Piazza di San Pietro, designed by Bernini and completed by about 1667. There are 284 columns, in the Doric/Tuscan order, and 88 pillars.

St Peter's was the work of many hands, over more than a century and a half. The ceiling of the Sistine Chapel, by contrast, was the work of one. Goethe said that nobody who had not seen the Sistine Chapel could have a complete conception of what a single man can accomplish. That man, of course, was Michelangelo, commissioned in March 1508 by Pope Julius II to paint the 12 apostles on the ceiling of the chapel. He agreed, reluctantly, and decided to do much more than that; to cover the whole ceiling, 10,000 square feet, with a huge fresco, a medium with which he was not even especially familiar. He called for assistants: seven applied, but after a short trial

all were sent on their way. Michelangelo locked the door and started the task alone.

He worked lying on his back on a scaffolding, paint dripping in his eyes and hair, and insistently nagged by Julius who kept demanding when he would finish. "When I can" Michelangelo replied. Working conditions were so uncomfortable that Michelangelo found he could not read a letter unless he held it above his head and tilted his head back. The job took him four years to finish, and then he signed it not with his own name, but with an inscription giving the honour of its completion to God—the alpha and omega, through whose assistance it had been begun and ended. The result was one of the great triumphs of the Renaissance, a joyous and glorious fresco that has been admired unstintingly ever since.

While Michelangelo was at work in the Sistine Chapel, Raphael was decorating the state rooms in the Vatican Palace. The four *Stanze*, as they are called, were the apartments used by Pope Julius II. The frescoes Raphael executed here are among his greatest works.

The Sistine Chapel takes its name from Sixtus IV (1471–84) who rebuilt it as the private chapel of the popes. Its chief glory is the barrel-vaulted ceiling frescoes by Michelangelo who, between 1508 and 1541, painted what has been described as a poem on the subject of creation, based on figures from the Old and New Testaments. Restoration of the frescoes began in 1980 and work on the main part was completed 10 years later amidst fierce controversy over its merits: opinion ranged from "an artistic Chernobyl" to high praise.

The Imperial Labyrinth

Fact file

For centuries the most mysterious and awe-inspiring palace in the world

Builder: Yung Lo

Built: 1406–20; mostly rebuilt

Materials: Wood and tiles

Number of rooms: 9,000

At the heart of Beijing (Peking) is the place "where earth and sky meet, where the four seasons merge, where wind and rain are gathered in, and where yin and yang are in harmony"— the Imperial Palace, or Forbidden City. In this huge complex of buildings the Ming emperors and their successors, the Manchus, ruled China for 500 years, attended by concubines and eunuchs and a few trembling bureaucrats who had to turn the orders of the "Sons of Heaven" into action. No ordinary citizen was allowed to step within its walls.

The Forbidden City that can be seen today lies on a site originally chosen by the Mongol rulers of the Yuan Dynasty (1279–1368) but was laid out by the third Ming emperor, Yung Lo, who ruled between 1403 and 1423. He came to power after a revolt against the grandson of the first Ming, Hung Wu, who has been described as "the harshest and most unreasonable tyrant in all of Chinese history". Hung Wu's violent temper and unreasonable cruelty so terrified his officials that if called to an audience with the emperor they would say their last goodbyes to their families.

When Hung Wu died he was succeeded briefly by his 16-year-old grandson, who was soon overthrown by his own uncle. Despite his name, which means Everlasting Happiness, Yung Lo was as tough, cruel and capricious as Hung Wu. He decided to shift the capital of China from Nanjing, closer to his own power base in northern China. In 1404 he began the reconstruction of Beijing, and the bulk of the Forbidden City was created between 1406 and 1420, using up to 100,000 craftsmen and as many as a million labourers. Its construction was one of the greatest building feats in history.

The plan to which Yung Lo built was said to have been given to him in a sealed envelope by a famous astrologer. It is based on geomantic principles, with each important building repre-

senting a part of the body. It lies along a single straight line, the axis of the Universe, in which the emperor's role was "to stand at the centre of the Earth and stabilize the people within the four seas", according to the Confucian sage Mencius. The main axis runs north and south, with a series of courtyards and pavilions succeeding one another in rigid sequence. The whole area covers about 250 acres, and is surrounded by a moat and also by a wall 35 feet high, with four doors.

The city is divided into two sections, with the buildings of state (including six main palaces) in the first and the residential buildings behind. The whole includes 75 halls, palaces, temples, pavilions, libraries and studios, linked by courtyards, paths, gardens, gates and walls. Altogether, there are reputedly a total of 9,000 rooms.

The Forbidden City was built not in stone, but wood. As a result, its buildings deteriorated or were destroyed far more quickly by fire, rot and insect attack than if they had been of more permanent materials. Of the buildings that stand today in the Forbidden City few are very old by the standards of Europe. Many were destroyed when the city was sacked and looted by the Manchu armies at the overthrow of the Ming Dynasty in 1644, and were rebuilt by the Qing emperor Qian Long (1736–96). Further additions were made by the Empress Dowager Cixi during the nineteenth century. Why the Chinese emperors did not choose to build more permanently is not clear, for their own mausoleums were built in stone. The most persuasive explanation is that the emperors were more concerned with the life eternal than life on Earth, and therefore devoted greater energy and resources to creating enduring structures that they would occupy after death.

Architecturally, two things are particularly striking about the Forbidden City: the exotic curves of the roofs, and the brilliant colour of the

buildings. Although their method of constructing roofs could have been adapted to build in planes rather than curves, it seems that the Chinese preferred curves for aesthetic reasons. They enjoyed the contrast between the straight lines of the pillars and the base of the buildings and the languorous curves of the roof.

Entering the Forbidden City through the Wumen, the Meridian Gate—originally reserved for the use of the emperor—there is a huge courtyard. From the heights of the gate the emperor would review his armies, survey prisoners to determine who should live and who should die, and announce the new year's calendar to the court. His power was so absolute that

it was for him to designate the days and months of the year. When inspecting his troops, he would be flanked by elephants provided by his Burmese subjects.

Beyond this courtyard and through the smaller Taihamen (Gate of Supreme Harmony) lies a second, larger court in which the major imperial audiences would be held. The whole court of perhaps 100,000 could be accommodated here, and they would enter through the side gates—civilians to the east, soldiers to the west—before standing in silence before the emperor and prostrating themselves nine times.

Facing them as they gave obeisance was the first of three main ceremonial halls, set one

The courtyard between the Meridian Gate, the southerly entrance to the Imperial City, and the Gate of Supreme Harmony (on the left) is the first of several large open spaces between the principal halls. Between the parallel balustrade runs a stream crossed by 5 bridges, intended to symbolize the 5 virtues.

The Imperial Labyrinth

The view from Prospect Hill, looking south towards Meridian Gate and Tiananmen Square, shows the uniform sweep of the roofs and the scale of the city. In the foreground is the principal northern gate, the Gate of Divine Military Genius.

behind the other on a raised marble terrace called the Dragon Pavement. The Taihedian (Hall of Supreme Harmony), originally built in 1420 and restored in 1697, is the largest building in the Forbidden City, covering more than half an acre and standing 115 feet high. No building in the whole of Beijing was permitted to be higher. It was used for special state occasions such as the emperor's birthday. Here was his throne, with two elephants of peace at its feet and a screen behind symbolizing in dragon motifs both longevity and the unity of earth and heaven. Twenty columns support the roof, the six in the centre being decorated with the imperial dragon.

In the second, smaller hall, the Zhonghedian (Hall of Perfect Harmony), the emperor prepared himself and put on the imperial regalia for these ceremonies, while the third, the Baohedian (Hall of Protecting Harmony), was used for Palace Examinations, the system by which candidates for positions in the administration were chosen. The principle was to pick candidates by merit: the origin of all modern meritocracies. In practice, there was much corruption,

and the examinations became increasingly formalized, demanding only the learning by heart of the tenets of Confucius. In this hall, the Emperor also received rulers bringing tribute. The anterooms to the hall have now been converted into galleries to display imperial relics and the gifts given by foreign rulers—many still in their original wrappings, conveying the Chinese contempt for the tribute of barbarians.

Beyond the three great halls, in the Inner Court, are the buildings where the emperors lived. The first, the Qianqinggong (Palace of Heavenly Purity) was the residence of the last four Ming emperors. The last, the Kunninggong (Palace of Earthly Tranquillity) was where their empresses lived, and where the emperor and empress traditionally spent their wedding night. The actual wedding chamber, a small room painted entirely in red with decorative emblems symbolic of fertility, was last used in 1922 for the child wedding of Puyi, the last Manchu emperor. Between these two halls was the Jiaotaidan (Hall of Union, or Vigorous Fertility) which was used for birthday celebrations, and for storing the seals of previous emperors. On display here

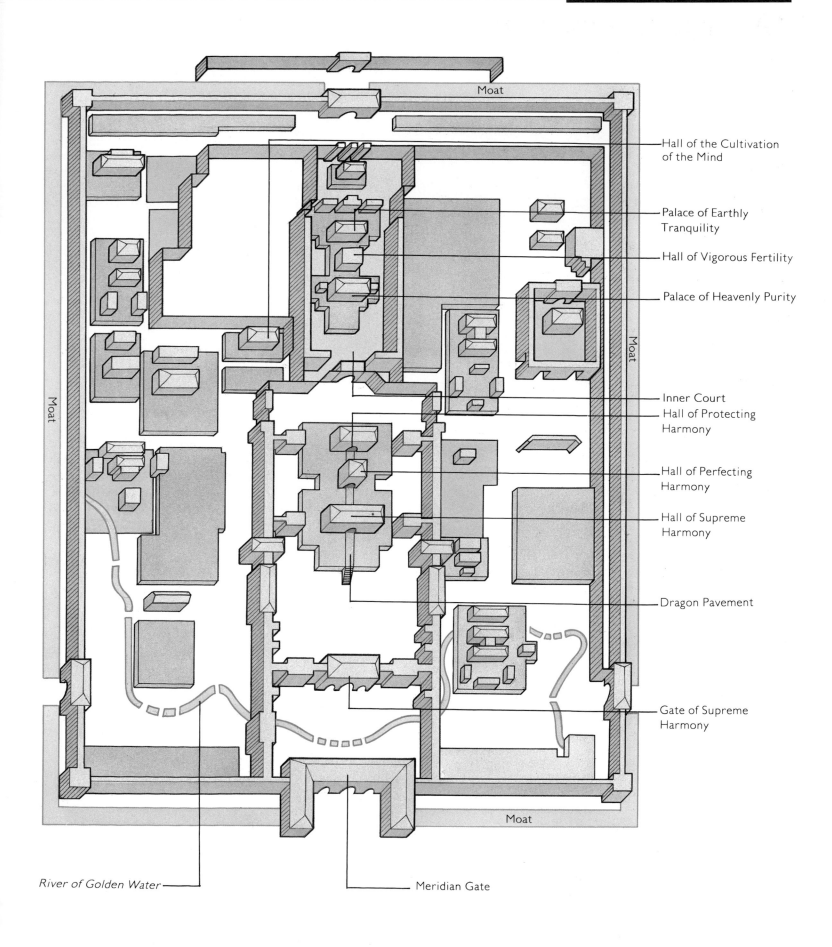

Hall of the Cultivation of the Mind

Palace of Earthly Tranquility

Hall of Vigorous Fertility

Palace of Heavenly Purity

Inner Court

Hall of Protecting Harmony

Hall of Perfecting Harmony

Hall of Supreme Harmony

Dragon Pavement

Gate of Supreme Harmony

Moat

Moat

Moat

Moat

River of Golden Water — Meridian Gate

The Imperial Labyrinth

The Dragon Pavement *leads through the 3 main halls between the Gate of Supreme Harmony and the Gate of Heavenly Purity. Steps flank a bas-relief of dragons which was reserved exclusively for the imperial palanquin. The last imperial occupant of the palace was Puyi, subject of Bertolucci's film* The Last Emperor.

today is one of China's inventions, the clepsydra (water clock), 2,500 years old.

The Hall of Heavenly Purity, which is surrounded by a complex of houses, medical consulting rooms, libraries and living quarters for palace servants, was the place where the emperors left the instructions concerning the succession. Each emperor would write the name of his chosen successor on two slips of paper, keeping one and concealing the other behind a plaque on the wall inscribed with the words "Upright and Bright". On the emperor's death his advisers would recover the two slips and compare them. If the same name was found on both, the chosen successor would be named.

These six halls form the main north–south axis of the Forbidden City. Their purpose was principally ceremonial, and the emperors actually spent most of their time in another building to the west, the Yangxindiang, or Hall of the Cultivation of the Mind. Within the entire complex they lived their whole lives, seldom setting foot outside among their people. Few ruling families have been more remote, autocratic, or self-indulgent. Their meals were gargantuan, their sexual appetites satisfied by hundreds of concubines, and the daily routines of the palace carried out by eunuchs, the only male attendants allowed to live within the Forbidden City.

The role played by the eunuchs during the Ming dynasty became increasingly dominant. They were employed because it was thought they would be loyal and reliable, having no families of their own, and no prospect of illicit relations with the palace women. Most of them were recruited from the ranks of criminals who had been castrated as a form of punishment; pathetically, since the Chinese belief was that no person who was not whole could aspire to heavenly happiness, they would carry their scrotums around with them, or at least ensure that they were buried with them when they died. Hung Wu had tried to limit their number to 100, but by the end of the Ming era in 1644, there were 70,000 eunuchs in the Forbidden City, and another 30,000 on administrative duties outside.

As the Ming emperors declined in vigour, the power of the eunuchs increased. By the 1620s, the power of the government fell first into the hands of a concubine, and then into those of a 52-year-old eunuch, Wei Chung-hsien. Wei became so influential with the emperor, a 15-year-old boy whose principal interest was carpentry, that he became the virtual ruler. Temples were erected in his honour, while opponents were executed in numbers "beyond calculations", according to the official history of the Ming. Wei lost his power only when the emperor suddenly died, and he was forced to commit suicide to avoid arrest. The Ming dynasty soon fell to the Manchus, who burned part of the Forbidden City and melted down the silver.

In the nineteenth century, the Forbidden City did fall under the power of a concubine, the autocratic Empress Dowager Cixi. Her power derived from the fact that of all the emperor Hsien Feng's concubines, she was the only one to provide him with a son and heir. He died when the child was only five, and Cixi assumed power, fighting off other courtiers. When her son died at 19 she struck again, insisting on the appointment of another young emperor so that her regency could continue. When this emperor took the throne and began to introduce reforms, Cixi struck for a third time, returning from semi-retirement to take power once more.

Narrow-minded, brutal and xenophobic, Cixi made common cause with the members of a group called the Society of the Righteous and Harmonious Fists, who blamed foreign imperialists for China's ills. When the society—known to Westerners as the Boxers—attacked missionaries, Cixi refused to accede to Western

The use of colour throughout the Forbidden City is determined by the different elements of the buildings: the raised podiums upon which they are built are white; the pillars and walls are dull red (far left); and the roofs are brilliant golden yellow (left). This colour was reserved exclusively for imperial use.

demands for their suppression. In June 1900 they attacked foreign-owned buildings and legations in Beijing, and swung Cixi behind them. In August, Western forces arrived to rescue the besieged diplomats, invading the Forbidden City and putting Cixi to flight. But disagreements among the Western forces enabled her to return, and she arrived once more in Beijing in January 1902. Finally she attempted to introduce the reforms that 30 years earlier might have preserved the dynasty as a constitutional monarchy, but it was too late. In 1908 she died, and in 1911 the revolution led by Sun Yat Sen triumphed.

Attempts to restore imperial rule during the 1920s failed, and in the 1930s many valuable

objects were looted from the Forbidden City under the Japanese occupation. The retreating forces of Chiang Kai-shek took away still more in 1949, as they abandoned mainland China for exile in Taiwan before the Communist forces of Mao Zedong. On 1 October 1949 Mao stood on the terrace of the Gate of Heavenly Peace and proclaimed the birth of the People's Republic of China: the latest dynasty to rule China.

Today the Forbidden City provides the backdrop to the mass rallies held in Tiananmen Square, which were particularly associated with the Cultural Revolution and the cult of Mao whose portrait has been incongruously hung on the Gate of Heavenly Peace.

The intricate carpentry under the eaves (above left) was purely ornamental. On some buildings it became so elaborate that an extra colonnade had to be placed under the outer edge to support the weight. Ferocious bronze lions flank the Dragon Pavement (above right).

Paxton's Inspiration from Nature

Fact file

The world's first exhibition building constructed of glass and iron

Designer: Joseph Paxton

Built: 1850–51

Materials: Wrought and cast iron, glass

Length: 1,848 feet

Width: 408 feet

Few buildings have been designed so swiftly, or erected at such breakneck pace, as the Crystal Palace. It took less than a year from the moment Joseph Paxton conceived the building to the day in 1851 when it was opened by Queen Victoria to house the Great Exhibition. More than twice the size of St Paul's Cathedral, it covered 19 acres of Hyde Park, and in its central transept a full-grown elm tree 108 feet high was comfortably accommodated. The design called for 4,500 tons of cast and wrought iron, 6 million cubic feet of timber and 300,000 panes of glass, and was itself revolutionary, paving the way for modern steel-framed buildings. The actual construction of the building took just seven months.

Paxton formulated his brilliant idea at exactly the right moment. The Great Exhibition was intended to demonstrate Britain's pre-eminence in engineering, and its principal patron was Prince Albert. A distinguished Royal Commission had been established to plan and organize the Exhibition, and had delegated the decision on the building to a committee of engineers and architects which included Charles Barry, architect of the Houses of Parliament, Isambard Kingdom Brunel, and Robert Stephenson. After wading through 245 sets of plans submitted to them, they were at their wits' end. In desperation they produced a design of their own—largely the work of Brunel—and, equally desperately, the commissioners accepted it. It was awful, envisaging a huge, squat, brick warehouse with a vast iron dome on the top. It would have required at least 16 million bricks, and even if enough could have been found, it is doubtful if there would have been time to lay them all. The plans were greeted with horror by *The Times* and many shared its views.

Into this frenzied atmosphere stepped Joseph Paxton, the Duke of Devonshire's head gardener. Paxton, born in 1803, was a farmer's son, with little formal education. The duke had spotted his talents and hired him at the age of 23 to run the gardens at Chatsworth. There Paxton had worked wonders, digging lakes, diverting streams and shifting hills to beautify the duke's estates. There he built a lily house, using the principle behind the leaf structure of the giant water lily *Victoria regia* for the framework. It had not been finished long when Paxton decided to apply the same methods to the design of a building for the Great Exhibition. Although it was at the eleventh hour, the committee was prepared to consider his design, providing they had it in their hands within two weeks. "I will go home and in nine days time I will bring you my plans all complete," Paxton told them.

He went straight to Hyde Park to look at the site, and was confirmed in his decision to build a greatly enlarged version of his lily house. Such a design had many advantages: it would be quick to erect and, having no mortar or plaster, would be dry and ready for occupation; it could be taken down just as easily, and put up somewhere else, answering the critics who said the Exhibition was going to destroy Hyde Park; and if no permanent site could be found, at least the materials would be worth a lot as scrap.

During a railway board meeting three days later, an inattentive Paxton made his first drawings; although mere jottings, they contained the essence of the design, a rectilinear building rising in tiers. The pillars were to be of iron, the walls of glass. In a week, the plans were complete. It took another week for the building contractor, Fox & Henderson, and the glass manufacturer to produce precise costings. They determined that Paxton's building, with its 205 miles of sash bars, 3,300 iron columns, 2,150 girders and 900,000 square feet of glass, could be built for £150,000, or for £79,800 if they could keep the materials after the building had been taken down. The committee had no choice but to accept—even the higher figure was lower than the estimate for their own design.

Once construction began, the genius of Paxton's design became apparent. The iron columns, hollow to take the rainwater flowing off the roof, could be erected with remarkable speed and girders laid across the top. Once the workmen got into the swing of it, they could raise three columns and two girders in 16 minutes, as Paxton himself reported. As the first storey progressed, other teams came along behind to build the second. Special machinery on site made the miles of "Paxton guttering"—

The revolutionary techniques employed in the construction of the Crystal Palace perfectly complemented the idea of the Great Exhibition—to illustrate Britain's industrial pre-eminence. It was opened by Queen Victoria and Prince Albert (below).

Paxton's Inspiration from Nature

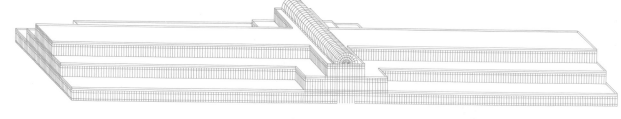

Paxton's design was derived from the lily house he built for the Duke of Devonshire, itself based on the principle of radiating ribs and cross-ribs which Paxton observed in a lily at Chatsworth.

wooden rafters hollowed out on top to act as gutters, with channels inserted on the underside to carry away water which condensed on the inside of the glass.

The arches of the transept, which transformed a huge glass box into an elegant building, were made of wood and were lifted into place from above. Once they were in position, glazing began. In one week, 80 men fixed 18,000 panes of glass. For their productivity the glaziers sought a rise from 4 shillings to 5 shillings a day and went on strike. Fox & Henderson reacted in typically Victorian fashion, dismissing the strike leaders and giving the rest a chance to go back to work—at the old rate. They did.

Everybody was astonished as the building rose so fast above Hyde Park. It was *Punch* that gave it its name—the Crystal Palace—and William Thackeray wrote a verse or two in celebration:

As though 'twere by a wizard's rod
A blazing arch of lucid glass
Leaps like a fountain from the grass
To meet the sun!

By now critics were fewer, although some proclaimed that a strong wind or a shower of hail would cause the building to collapse. *The Times* suggested that the official salute, due to be fired on the opening day when Queen Victoria arrived, would "shiver the roof of the Palace, and thousands of ladies will be cut into mincemeat". No such disaster occurred, and opening day, 1 May 1851, was an unparalleled triumph. "The sight as we came to the middle was magical," wrote Queen Victoria in her journal, "so vast, so glorious, so touching." By then the huge building had been filled with millions of objects, many of them attesting to the vigorous lack of taste of mid-Victorian Britain.

The exhibition proved a huge success, its profits being used to finance more permanent London buildings which grew into today's complex of museums between the Brompton Road and Hyde Park—the Victoria and Albert, the Science and the Natural History museums.

The speed of construction was a tribute to Paxton's genius: the use of shear-legs, pulleys and horses obviated the need for scaffolding; the girders bolted simply to the columns (below left).

More than six million visitors went through the turnstiles before the Exhibition eventually closed on 11 October.

Paxton was anxious that his masterpiece should survive and led a campaign to leave it where it stood in Hyde Park. But opposition was too strong, and Parliament rejected the proposal. But by then Paxton had raised £500,000 to buy the building and a new site for it, on 200 acres of wooded parkland on the summit of Sydenham Hill, on London's southern outskirts. Here it was rebuilt, even bigger and more splendid than before. The Sydenham Crystal Palace was half as large again as the one in Hyde Park, with a vaulted roof from end to end and a transept doubled in width. When built, it was filled with extraordinary objects: courts representing the different periods in the history of art, hundreds of sculptures—some of them colossal—trees,

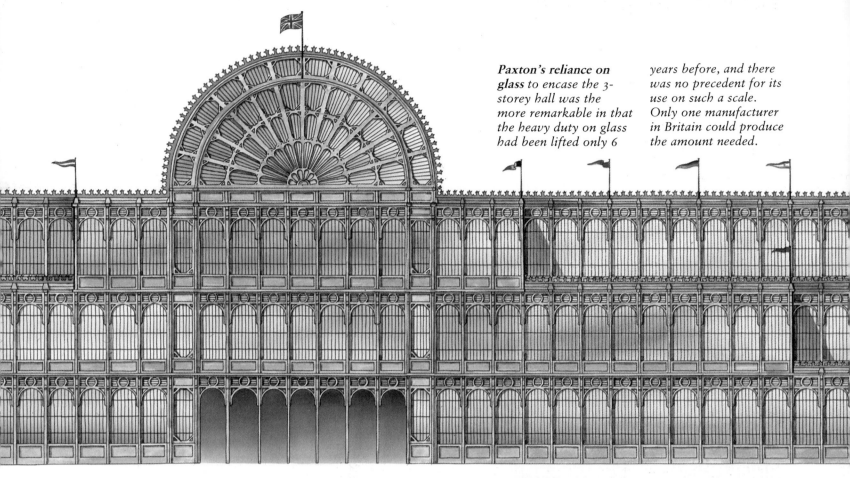

Paxton's reliance on glass to encase the 3-storey hall was the more remarkable in that the heavy duty on glass had been lifted only 6 years before, and there was no precedent for its use on such a scale. Only one manufacturer in Britain could produce the amount needed.

The transept running at right angles to the building was the brilliant idea of the exhibition committee. It was prompted by the strong opposition to felling trees on the site; a 108-foot high transept would enable a group of elms to be kept (left).

It took 900,000 square feet of glass to cover the Crystal Palace. The glass was $\frac{1}{16}$ inch thick and supplied by Chance Brothers of Birmingham. The glaziers worked from small trolleys with wheels that fitted into the gulleys on Paxton's gutters, propelling themselves along. Rainwater flowed down the gentle ridge-and-

furrow roof into gutters and down the 8-inch hollow columns. The Times warned that the "concussion [of guns firing the opening day salute] will shiver the glass roof of the Palace, and thousands of ladies will be cut into mincemeat".

Paxton's Inspiration from Nature

Paxton's Influence

The Sydenham Crystal Palace was not Paxton's preferred solution to the problem of what to do with the building when the Great Exhibition closed on 11 October 1851. He had hoped that it could remain in Hyde Park and be converted into a Winter Park and Garden with an abundance of trees and plants. Parliament rejected the idea, but Paxton had already raised £½ million to buy a site and re-erect the building.

Besides creating at Sydenham Hill the intended botanical collection, Paxton had copied statuary, urns and vases from early civilizations, and built stupendous fountains that rivalled Versailles. The 2 towers at each end (above) were built by Isambard Kingdom Brunel to supply the necessary head of water. When completed 12,000 jets used 7 million gallons an hour.

art galleries, a hall of fame, a theatre, a concert hall with 4,000 seats and room in the centre for a Grand Orchestra of 4,000 musicians and a Great Organ with 4,500 pipes.

The Crystal Palace at Sydenham was not a museum, or a concert hall, or a huge park; it was all three at once, perhaps the first example of what are today called Theme Parks. A family could spend the whole day there, enjoying the setting and spectacle, and finishing in the evening with a huge firework display for which the place became famous. It was here, too, that a large audience first watched moving pictures. There were balloon ascents, high-wire acts, shows, exhibitions, conferences, pantomimes and spectacular events such as the staging of an invasion in which an entire village was destroyed in front of 25,000 spectators. The Crystal Palace provided for the first time a leisure centre where people from any background could enjoy their free time.

All this came to an end on 30 November 1936. A small fire broke out in a staff lavatory and, despite efforts to put it out, spread with alarming speed. The wood of the floorboards, the walls and the sashes burned fiercely, defeating the efforts of 89 fire engines and 381 firemen to put it out. It was the biggest and most spectacular event ever staged at the Crystal Palace, visible from all over London. People flocked to watch as the great building was destroyed. By morning it had gone. In the gloom of the 1930s there was never a serious chance it would be rebuilt.

Joseph Paxton was born in 1803 at Milton Bryant, near Woburn in Bedfordshire, into a family in poor circumstances. Through hard work and intelligence, he came to the notice of the Duke of Devonshire; at 23 Paxton was put in charge of the Duke's gardens at Chatsworth.

The principles behind the construction of the lily-house at Chatsworth and the Crystal Palace were to have a profound effect. The train sheds at King's Cross, St Pancras and Paddington were derived from his work. Even more important was the establishment of the ideas of system building, and of the option to rely on an interior framework rather than an exterior wall for a building's strength.

The train shed for the Midland Railway's London terminus was designed by R.M. Ordish and W.H. Barlow, who had helped Paxton with the Crystal Palace. The lattice cast-iron ribs supporting the roof are tied together by girders under the platforms.

The Bond Centre, Hong Kong

Built by the Australian entrepreneur Alan Bond, this skyscraper office block is typical of the thousands of office buildings worldwide that employ glass as a curtain wall and are based on a system of prefabrication that reduces costs—and limits the freedom of the architect.

Willis Faber Dumas offices, Ipswich, England

Designed by Foster Associates and completed in 1975, this building exemplifies the reduction of the outer wall to a weathershield, having no structural function. Internal steel or concrete frames and replacement of window frames by silicone or neoprene joints enables the curtain wall to be made entirely of glass.

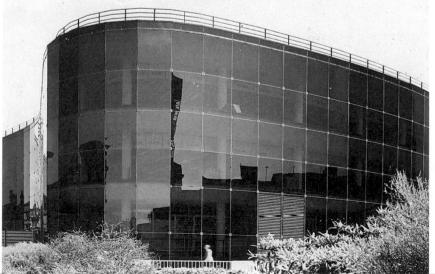

Gaudi's Gothic Masterpiece

Fact file

The world's most unorthodox cathedral

Architect: Antonio Gaudí y Cornet

Built: 1882–

Material: Stone, brick, steel and concrete

Height: 557 feet

Seating: over 13,000

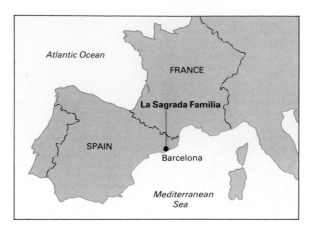

For more than a hundred years, a church has been under construction in Barcelona. It is huge, fantastic, and unfinishable, the dream of an architect whose imagination ran away with him. The cathedral of La Sagrada Familia—the Sacred Family—is a building unlike any other, where pillars lean and branch like trees, and huge pierced towers stand silent before an empty nave. It has been described as a work of genius, and as the product of a diseased imagination: few building sites have excited such strong and contrary emotions.

La Sagrada Familia began as a perfectly respectable neo-Gothic church, to be built in the "New City" area of Barcelona, and financed by the Spiritual Association of the Devotees of St Joseph. Its purpose was to exalt St Joseph and the Holy Family, symbols of family life and thus the basis of the social order. A site was bought, the local diocesan architect, Francisco de Paula del Villar, produced a design, and the foundation stone was laid in 1882.

Quite soon the architect fell out with the association and was replaced by a young man of only 31, Antonio Gaudí. What began for Gaudí as an architectural commission became a lifelong obsession, a devotion blending religious observance and art into a consuming passion. He never completed the building; it remains unfinished. But it is the greatest sight in Barcelona and one of the most extraordinary conceptions in the whole of Western architecture.

The style adopted by Gaudí for La Sagrada Familia is difficult to describe, for it has no exact counterpart elsewhere. It borrows from Gothic, but the curling, almost liquid shapes of the stonework owe a lot to Art Nouveau. It is as if the drawings of Aubrey Beardsley, or the silverwork of the English Arts and Crafts Movement, had been turned into stone. Gaudí's main

The site of the High Altar (left), *placed beneath the central cupola. Gaudí's concept for the High Table envisaged Christ on the cross as the only ornament, with a vine winding around the foot of the cross. The 7 apsidal chapels would be dedicated to the joys and sufferings of St Joseph.*

The Facade of the Nativity (right) *on which work began in 1891. It took until 1930 to complete. The 4 bell towers are dedicated, from left to right, to the Holy Apostles Barnabas, Simon, Thaddeus and Matthias. Facing east the façade is lit by the rising sun.*

Gaudí's Gothic Masterpiece

influences appear to have been John Ruskin and William Morris, and the French neo-Gothic architect Viollet-le-Duc. He worked on the church for so many years between the acceptance of the commission in 1883 and his death in 1926 that it also reflects his own changing views about architecture and religion.

Gaudí's first step was to make the church bigger. He would have liked to alter its position, too, but the foundations were already laid. For the first ten years or so he continued building the crypt, in more-or-less Gothic style, his main innovation being to introduce naturalistic ornamentation. But from the 1890s, his ideas blossomed. He abandoned Villar's plain ideas, substituting a profusion of decoration, with floral, human and animal motifs.

By 1895 he was designing the east façade, a controversial decision since the people of Barcelona were already becoming impatient, and the west façade, which faced the city, appeared a more urgent priority. Gaudí justified his decision by pointing out that the theme of the east façade was the birth of Christ, and thus it must be built before that of the west, whose theme was the Passion. Gaudí already saw the church not as a building to be finished as quickly as possible, but as a religious expression in its own right, a catechism in stone.

His plans grew ever more ambitious and complex. Around the church were to be 18 pointed towers with, at the centre, a great tower 557 feet high—as high as Cologne Cathedral and far higher than either St Paul's in London or St Peter's in Rome. Gaudí intended the towers to symbolize the 12 apostles, the 4 evangelists, the Virgin Mary and, the tallest of all, Christ himself. The three façades of the church Gaudí saw as representing the birth, death and resurrection of Christ.

This rich use of symbolism is also seen in the details of the design. Gaudí appears to have abhorred plain surfaces. What strikes the visitor is the sheer dynamism of the decoration, with animals, plants, figures, trees and sculpture occupying every square foot. Many of the sculptures would have been framed in colour if Gaudí had lived to see them completed. Around the whole building he planned a cloisterlike structure which would have shielded the inner sanctum from the noise of the street.

The four towers of the east façade, each 328 feet high, were the last parts of the church constructed under Gaudí's direction, and he

lived to see only the southernmost tower finished, which is dedicated to St Barnabas. Since his death and a long interruption from 1936—when the Spanish Civil War stopped work—to 1952, building has continued. But it is far from complete even today. However, an attempt is being made to complete the church in time for the Olympic Games at Barcelona in 1992.

The glory of Gaudí's conception can only be appreciated in a fragmentary way, as when the interior is illuminated at night, and the light floods out through the pierced stonework. Then La Sagrada Familia represents, as Gaudí hoped it would, the expression in masonry of Christ's words: "I am the light of the world."

La Sagrada Familia was in a part of Barcelona not built up until this century. The contrast between the hue of the stone on the Façade of the Nativity (above) and the newer towers behind, illustrates the effect of decades of urban pollution. The Coronation of the Virgin is above the central main door.

The interior of the Façade of the Nativity. The position of statues was determined by Gaudí pragmatically: full-size plaster models were put in place in the early morning light while he watched from a distance. They were then moved about according to his wishes. Gaudí was so concerned with day-to-day details that he often slept on site.

A detail of the Façade of the Nativity (below) illustrates the riot of decoration and symbolism that covers every surface of the exterior. Showing the section above the central doorway, which represents Charity, under the windows is the nativity scene. The musician-angel on the right replaces one destroyed in 1936 during the Spanish Civil War.

The pinnacles of the towers above the Façade of the Nativity are encrusted with mosaics and pearl shapes, and they represent the episcopal attributes of the cross, mitre, crook and ring. The words "Hosanna" and "Excelsis" are alternately rendered in vertical letters.

Gaudi's Creative Genius

Antonio Gaudí y Cornet, born on 25 June 1852 at Reus, Tarragona, was a fervent Catalan and a devout Catholic whose buildings are the artistic expression of the Catalan political revival. Despite a humble background, Gaudí's strong character and intelligence took him in 1873 to the Provincial School of Architecture in Barcelona.

Although staunchly Catalan—he refused to speak Castilian—he was conservative both in his private and his spiritual life. Gaudí neither married nor travelled, nor did he establish a school of architecture. His was a vision that died with him, at a moment when the geometric and functional International Style of modern architecture was in the ascendant.

Park Güell (right) was intended by Gaudí to be comparable to an English garden suburb, but only the park was built. He worked there until 1914 and it is now the city's public area, containing a church, arbours, sculpture and Greek Theatre. This is the Hall of 100 columns.

Casa Batlló in Barcelona (above) was a remodelling of an existing building. Between 1905 and 1907, Gaudí covered the plain building with a mosaic portraying sky, clouds and water, gave it a dragonlike roof of glazed scales, and inserted slender columns in the windows, prompting the building's nickname, "House of Bones".

The terrace of the open-air theatre in Park Güell (right) has a serpentine curlicue of benches made from shards of ceramic, glass and porcelain, and even the bottoms of plates and bottles from local potteries. Besides being cheap, the materials encouraged spontaneous composition. In his pragmatism, Gaudí was more like a medieval craftsman than an architect.

Gaudí's use of natural forms was influenced by the writings of the art critic John Ruskin. Rather than take elements from nature, Gaudí used them as whole as possible: besides this lizard in Park Güell (above), he incorporated in his work flowers, seeds, trees, snails, dogs, fish scales, bone and muscle.

Mosaics are used on the house in Park Güell to emphasize the building's form. The use of brightly coloured ceramic tiles was introduced to Iberia by the Arabs. Gaudí's love of ornament, colour and unusual forms testifies to a sense of humour as well as form. Gaudí is revered in Barcelona for the vigorous and sometimes playful buildings he bequeathed the city.

Stairway to the Sky

Fact file

The world's most distinctive tower, built to commemorate the centenary of the French Revolution

Designer: Gustave Eiffel

Built: 1887–89

Material: Wrought iron

Height: 990 feet

Eiffel's tower dominates the Paris skyline with an elegance that even its early critics finally admitted.

France's most instantly recognizable landmark, the Eiffel Tower, was denounced as an eyesore when first proposed. "A dishonour to Paris and a ridiculous dizzy tower like some gigantic and sombre factory chimney" declared a group that included the writers Alexandre Dumas and Guy de Maupassant and the composer Charles Gounod. Today it is impossible to imagine Paris without its "tragic lamppost", "inverted torch-holder" or even "Grand Suppositaire"—all descriptions applied to it at various times.

The tower was built for the 100th anniversary of the French Revolution, which was marked by a huge exhibition, the *Exposition Universelle*, in Paris. The organizers considered a number of schemes for a centrepiece for the exhibition, including the bizarre idea of a model guillotine 1,000 feet high. The best idea came from Gustave Eiffel, an engineer who was already well known as an expert in wrought iron. He had built bridges, domes and roofs using this reliable material, at that time cheaper than steel. The tower had been suggested to him by two juniors in his engineering company, Maurice Koechlin and Emile Nougier, who did the preliminary calculations. Eiffel took the idea to the organizers of the *Exposition* and convinced them to back the project.

The aim was to construct the world's tallest building, 984 feet high. At the time, the record was held by the Washington Monument in Washington, DC, a stone obelisk that was 554 feet high. The tallest ancient building was the Great Pyramid of Cheops, at 482 feet. Eiffel's target was to build a structure almost twice as high as anything that had gone before.

His design was a structure of wrought-iron ribs, held together by rivets and resting on a solid masonry foundation. Unlike a bridge, where a large number of the struts are identical, the tower required many different components, which were individually designed by a team of 50 engineers under Eiffel's direction. Each component had a maximum weight of 3 tons to ease construction.

The actual building of the tower began in January 1887. Steel caissons 50 feet long, 22 feet wide and 7 feet deep were filled with concrete and sunk into the subsoil to form the foundations. Upon these the wrought-iron structure began to rise at the end of June. The components were lifted by cranes, and so accurate was their manufacture that even when the tower rose 164 feet above ground the holes in the prefabricated parts matched exactly. This was important, because wrought iron cannot be welded; it must be fastened together with rivets. Once the first platform had been completed (by 1 April 1888), the cranes were hoisted on to it.

Work continued steadily throughout 1888, and by the end of March the following year the tower had reached its full height. One of the more remarkable statistics is that nobody was killed during the construction, although an Italian workman died while installing the elevators, after the tower had been inaugurated. The tower weighed 9,547 tons and was built of 18,000 components, held together with 2.5 million rivets. The workforce consisted of only 230 men, 100 of them to make the parts and 130 on site to put them together. The final height of the tower was 990 feet, or a fraction more in hot weather when it expands by a further 7 inches.

On 31 March a small party climbed the 1,792 steps to the top of the tower to hoist the French *tricolore*, a vast flag more than 23 feet long by 15 feet wide. Toasts were drunk in champagne, to cries of "Vive la France! Vive Paris! Vive la République!". The descent from the platform, *The Times* reported, "was found to be as trying as the ascent had been, and lasted 40 minutes". On the ground, tables were laid for a celebration attended by 200 workmen, the engineers who designed the tower, and the prime minister, M. Tirard, who admitted that he had not at first been enthusiastic about the tower, but was now prepared to make an *amende honorable* and concede that he had been wrong.

Stairway to the Sky

Now that the tower was up, many of its critics found it much more elegant than they had expected. It was lighter and more graceful than it had appeared in the drawings. Gounod retracted his criticisms and *Le Figaro* celebrated the tower's opening with a tribute in verse to its creator: "Gloire au Titan industriel / Qui fit cet escalier au ciel" (Glory to the industrial Titan who built this stairway to the sky).

Nor did the gloomy predictions of financial disaster come true. The tower cost 7,799,401 francs and 31 centimes to build—about 1 million francs more than Eiffel had predicted—but it attracted a huge number of visitors. In the last five months of 1889 alone it was visited by 1.9 million people, who paid 2 francs to get to the first platform, a further franc to get to the second, and another two to reach the top. By the end of the year, 75 percent of the total cost had been recovered. It went on to become a highly profitable enterprise, although the 1889 attendance was not exceeded until the advent of mass tourism in the 1960s. In 1988, a total of 4.5 million people visited it.

Originally designed to last for only 20 years, the tower is still going strong after 100. During the 1980s it underwent a major facelift, costing $28 million. One job was to remove excess weight which had gradually been added to the structure over the years. Some 1,000 tons, including a revolving staircase 590 feet high, were removed.

The Eiffel Tower has always been operated as a commercial enterprise. M. Citroën, the motor car manufacturer, temporarily owned the publicity rights and rigged up an imposing system of lights by which flames appeared to creep up from the base of the tower to the top. More usefully, the tower formed an excellent platform for radio and, later, television transmitters.

The tower is painted a muddy brown colour, which the French call *marron*. The paint's full name is *brun Tour Eiffel*, and 45 tons of it are applied to the structure every seven years. Inevitably, it has been the scene of many suicides; some 400 people have thrown themselves off it. The first parachute jump was made in 1984 when a British couple, Mike McCarthy and Amanda Tucker, slipped past security guards and jumped from the top, landing safely. An elephant once walked to the first platform, and two motorcyclists managed in 1983 to ride trail bikes up the 746 steps to the second platform, turn round and come down again without mishap.

Two elevators serving the first floor were to a French double-deck design to carry 50 people. During World War II a mysterious fault prevented Hitler from using them, compelling him to climb the tower on foot. When the city was freed in 1944, the turn of a screw released them.

Hydraulic jacks were incorporated into the base of the tower's 16 columns (4 for each pier). They enabled the piers to be adjusted so that they were perfectly horizontal for the band of girders situated at first-floor level.

A

The Stages of Construction
Prefabrication of sections was a revolutionary innovation, forced on Eiffel by the close deadline for completion. He decided that the 7 million holes in the girders would be drilled off site, leaving only riveting to be done in situ *using portable forges*. 5,300 drawings specified the location of holes.

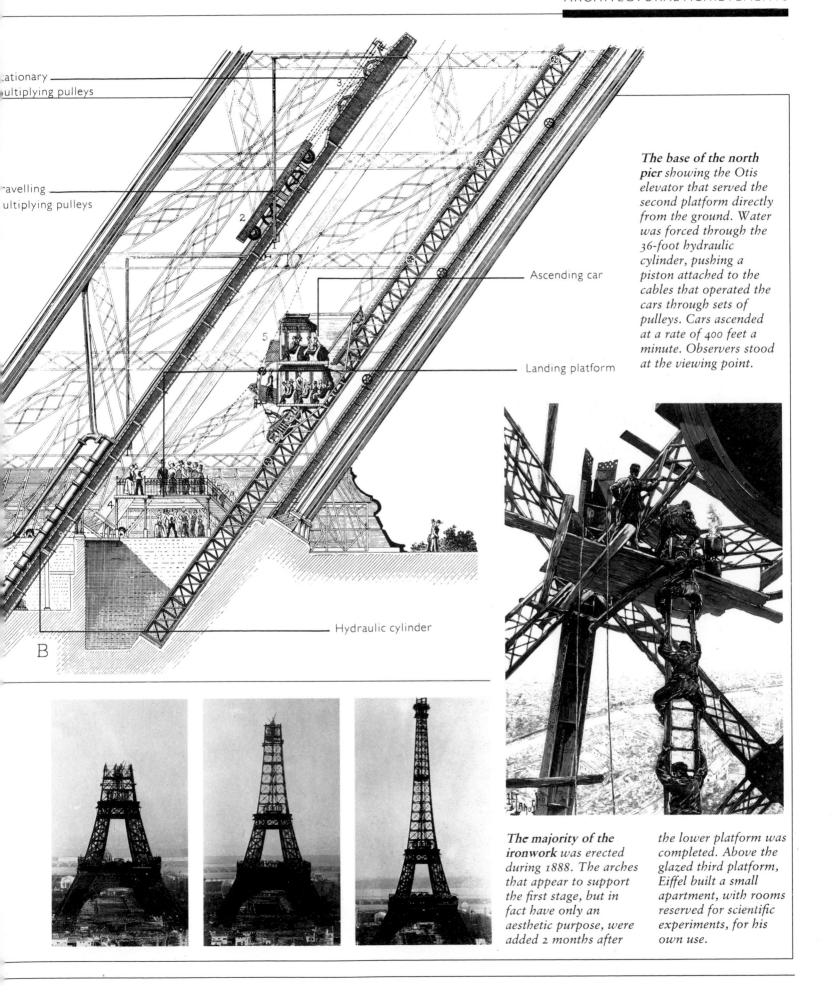

ationary
ultiplying pulleys

ravelling
ultiplying pulleys

Ascending car

Landing platform

Hydraulic cylinder

B

The base of the north pier showing the Otis elevator that served the second platform directly from the ground. Water was forced through the 36-foot hydraulic cylinder, pushing a piston attached to the cables that operated the cars through sets of pulleys. Cars ascended at a rate of 400 feet a minute. Observers stood at the viewing point.

The majority of the ironwork was erected during 1888. The arches that appear to support the first stage, but in fact have only an aesthetic purpose, were added 2 months after the lower platform was completed. Above the glazed third platform, Eiffel built a small apartment, with rooms reserved for scientific experiments, for his own use.

Eiffel's Other Works

Alexandre Gustave Eiffel was born in Dijon on 15 December 1832. After graduating in chemistry in Paris, he joined a company manufacturing railway equipment, which encouraged him to give up chemistry for civil engineering. At the early age of 25 he was put in charge of the construction of a bridge over the Garonne River at Bordeaux. He adopted a new method of pile driving, and his success in completing, on schedule, one of the largest iron structures of its day, helped to establish his name.

During a recession, Eiffel opted to become a freelance consulting engineer and soon set up a metalworks in Paris. His growing reputation led to contracts for bridges as far afield as Peru, Algeria and Cochin China as well as countless viaducts and bridges for railways in Europe. But his skill extended to all forms of engineering: a harbour for Chile; churches in Peru and the Philippines; gasworks, a steelworks and dam in France; and lock gates for Russia and the Panama Canal. The tower for the Paris Exposition was but the climax of a remarkable career.

Eiffel died at the age of 91 on 27 December 1923 at his mansion on Rue Rabelais, Paris.

Bon Marché Department Store, Paris, France
Eiffel's designs for ironwork were grounded in rigorously worked-out calculations which enabled him to build with the minimum of ironwork without sacrificing strength or rigidity. He even published a formula applicable to all wrought-iron structures which eliminated much of the guesswork from calculating stresses and strains. The lightness of his designs is evident in the Bon Marché department store in Paris (above and left) which Eiffel built with L.-C. Boileau in 1869–79.

The Nice Observatory, France

Situated in the Alpes-Maritimes, the Nice Observatory (left) was the largest such dome in the world when completed by Eiffel in 1885. Eiffel produced the ironwork of the dome, 74 feet in diameter, which rotated on a frictionless ring that enables the 110-ton dome to be moved by hand.

The Garabit Bridge, France

This viaduct in the Massif Central (below) was second only to the Eiffel Tower in Eiffel's pantheon of engineering achievements. When opened in 1884, it was the highest arched bridge in the world, at 400 feet above the Truyere River. The arch of 541 feet supported a railway deck 1,850 feet in length.

The Steel and Concrete Forest

Fact file

The world's greatest concentration of skyscrapers

Length: $12\frac{1}{2}$ miles

Width (maximum): $2\frac{1}{2}$ miles

Length of electric cable under Manhattan: 17,000 miles

The island of Manhattan, $12\frac{1}{2}$ miles long by $2\frac{1}{2}$ miles wide, has the world's most sensational skyline. Here, in the heart of New York, huge buildings soaring almost out of sight are constantly being constructed, often to be demolished within years and replaced by ever-taller structures. Manhattan is never finished, for no sooner is a new building erected than the architects, engineers and builders move on to another site and start again.

Space is so limited that there is no alternative but to build upward, and as techniques have improved so the height of Manhattan's tallest buildings has increased. From the Flatiron Building of 1903 to the Empire State Building of 1931 and the World Trade Center of 1971, Manhattan has usually been able to boast the world's tallest habitable building. Even when that title has been wrested from it by an exceptional building elsewhere, Manhattan can claim to have the greatest concentration of skyscrapers in a single place.

Much ingenuity has gone into making it possible. Until Elisha Otis developed his "safety hoister", buildings were limited to the height people were prepared to climb on foot, and that was generally no more than about six storeys. Otis invented a safety device that locked his elevator in place even when the cable supporting it was cut, and showed it off at the New York World's Fair in 1854. Using cast-iron frames, it was already possible to build higher, and by 1875 the Western Union Building on Lower Broadway reached ten storeys. By the end of the century the Pulitzer Building on Park Row had exceeded it. Topped by a huge cupola, this building was a mixture of old and new; it had a core supported by wrought-iron columns, but its outer walls rested on masonry up to 9 feet thick.

Traditional buildings require thick walls to support their bulk; the taller they are, the thicker their walls must be at ground level. Given the limitations of space in Manhattan, that would have set an upper limit to the builders' ambitions had it not been for the evolution of the steel-framed building, in which all the internal and external loads are carried by the frame and transmitted by it to the foundations.

The first of these was William Jenney's ten-storey Home Insurance Building in Chicago, built in 1884. The first in New York was probably the Tower Building at 50 Broadway, designed in 1888 by Bradford Lee Gilbert, on a site only 21 feet wide. If he had followed traditional methods, all but 10 feet of Gilbert's building at ground level would have had to be solid masonry. Instead, he built what he described as "an iron bridge truss, stood on end"— a building 13 storeys high in which the iron framework went all the way up. To calm the fears of the owner, Gilbert himself promised to take the top two floors, so demonstrating his confidence that the building would stand. Like many of New York's pioneering skyscrapers, Gilbert's building has given way to something else, but his method opened the way to even taller structures.

One of the most striking is the Flatiron Building, situated on a narrow triangular site the shape of a flat-iron at the junction between Broadway and 5th Avenue at 23rd Street. Its 20

Lower Manhattan looking north. The World Trade Center is the tall building on the left. The Empire State Building is the tallest building in the middle distance. On the extreme right is the Brooklyn Bridge spanning the East River.

The Steel and Concrete Forest

The World Trade Center, built between 1966 and 1973, is an unusual development for the USA in that it was financed by two states, the Port Authority of New York and New Jersey. The intention was to bring together over 1,000 businesses and government agencies involved in international trade; over 60 countries are represented. Half the 16-acre site was reclaimed from the Hudson River, and the underground foundation work was 6 storeys deep. The tallest tower, of 110 storeys, is 1,350 feet high.

storeys were built on a steel frame clad with decorative stonework and served by six Otis hydraulic elevators. It was built by the George A. Fuller construction company, which boasted that it was the strongest building ever erected. Unlike many pioneering buildings it survives today, and is New York's oldest skyscraper.

But it was soon dwarfed by much bigger buildings of which the most striking was the 792-foot Woolworth Building, a Gothic tower on Broadway built in 1913 for F.W. Woolworth, founder of the chainstore that still bears his name. This has 60 floors from sub-basement to top, each floor with generous 12-foot ceilings—a use of space that could not be justified economically today. The inner structure of this building is steel, but its outer decoration is of terracotta, elaborately modelled into complex shapes and traceries. So profitable were the Woolworth stores that the building cost of $13.5 million was paid out of cash flow as construction proceeded.

The steel structure of the Woolworth Building, like all skyscrapers of the period, was riveted together. The rivets were inserted red-hot into prepared holes in the steel columns, and shrank as they cooled, tightening their grip and holding the steel pieces firmly together.

This was how New York's most famous skyscraper, the Empire State Building, was put together in 1930–31. When you stand on the observation tower 1,250 feet above 5th Avenue, it is disconcerting to think of the riveters who stood here on narrow steel beams, tossing red-hot rivets around with nothing but air beneath them. The building's graceful design, with higher levels set back by increasing amounts from the ground line, was the result of New York's building code of the time, which specified that a tower could not simply go straight up. The architect, William Lamb, produced 15 different designs before selecting the one that was finally built.

Work began at the height of the Depression and went on at a hectic pace; there were days when it rose by more than a storey. The building contains 60,000 tons of steel beams, produced in

The Empire State Building was the world's tallest building when built, in 1930–31, its 102 storeys reaching 1,250 feet. Designed by Shreve Lamb & Harman, its construction was so well planned and executed that it was built within 18 months and some occupants moved in 4 months ahead of schedule. The reason for the gradually recessed walls of the tower lies with New York's building code, which prohibited a straight rise from the street for more than 125 feet. A further reduction in plan was required at the 30th floor.

The Woolworth Building held the record for the world's tallest office building for almost 20 years after its completion, in 1913, at 761 feet. Designed by Cass Gilbert it remains one of the most highly regarded skyscrapers, and was given protected landmark status by New York City in 1983. So successful were F.W. Woolworth's 5c and 10c stores that the $13¼ million bill for construction was paid out of income. The building's ceiling heights—over 12 feet— are much more generous than today's developers would allow. The tower is covered in terracotta and all details reflect its Gothic intentions.

Pittsburgh and delivered on a relentless schedule which had many beams in place only three days after they had been made. The entire weight of the building is 365,000 tons.

The planning of the construction has gone into legend. Every day a progress chart and a printed timetable were issued. They listed every truck that would be arriving, what it would be carrying, who was responsible for it, and where it should go. Space in Manhattan is so tight that buildings can seldom afford the luxury of a builder's yard for storing materials during construction. Each steel piece was numbered to make sure it went into the correct place, and on each floor as the building rose a small gauge railway was built to carry materials to the right spot. Unloaded at ground level on to small carts, materials were lifted by derricks to the upper floor, placed on the track, and then wheeled to the precise spot they were needed.

A trip up the Empire State Building is one of the unmissable treats of a visit to New York, and two million people every year ride its express elevators which reach the 80th floor in less than a minute. Further elevators continue to the glass-enclosed upper observatory at the 102nd floor level. Above that rises a TV mast which itself is as tall as a 22-storey building.

Initially, the public doubted the strength of the structure, but all uncertainties on that score were removed in July 1945 when a US Air Force bomber approaching Newark airport in fog and rain smashed into the building at the 78th and 79th floors. The crew of 3 and 11 people inside were killed in the impact, but the building itself stood firm. The riveters had done their work well.

Today's techniques are rather different. Steel structures are held together by bolts, or by welding, rather than rivets. The men who dangle high above the streets putting them together are called ironworkers, or steel erectors. They are armed with spud wrenches, a tapered point on one end to jam in the holes to force a beam into position, a spanner on the other to tighten a nut on to a bolt to hold the two pieces together.

Other skyscrapers use no steel at all, but are made of concrete, poured on site into wooden moulds known as forms. The vertical pillars that separate the floors and hold them up are cast around a sprouting mass of steel reinforcing bars, while the floors themselves are made by pumping concrete on to a temporary wooden floor covered with a mesh of reinforcing bars.

The Steel and Concrete Forest

Between 4 and 8 inches of concrete are poured, a shallow edge around the outside of the building preventing its escape, and levelled.

Within a day or so the concrete is strong enough to walk on, and the wooden floor is removed and raised to the next level to create another storey. Temporary wooden beams may be inserted to hold the concrete floor in place while it develops its full strength, which takes several weeks. As each floor goes up, surveyors check the building is not getting out of true. The concrete floors in steel-framed buildings are created in much the same way.

The final stage in creating a skyscraper is to put into place the outer panels, which will form the walls. Because they bear no structural loads, they can be made of a wide variety of materials, including stone, brick, aluminium, stainless steel, tile, glass or concrete. The panels are made in factories and delivered to the site on trucks, hoisted into place and attached with bolts or other fasteners to the building's frame.

Old buildings can be given a "face-lift" by removing all the original panels and replacing them with something more fashionable, at a fraction of the cost of rebuilding the entire structure. Glass panels, which may be tinted or have a mirror-like surface, require special handling. The huge pieces of glass, up to an inch thick, are lifted with special suction cups to avoid damaging the edges as they are put into place.

The older buildings of Manhattan, like the Chrysler and Empire State buildings, are built of immensely strong steel and are very rigid, able to resist the force of the wind. Tests show that even in a high wind the Empire State Building bends only very slightly, less than $\frac{1}{4}$ inch at the 85th floor.

More modern buildings have less substantial steelwork, in order to reduce costs, so may need sophisticated arrangements to avoid sway. One example is at the Citicorp Building on Lexington Avenue, where a special damper in the form of a 400-ton block of concrete has been built into the 59th floor. The block is connected to the frame of the building by shock-absorber arms, and can be "floated" on a thin film of oil. When the wind blows strongly, oil is pumped under the block to lift it and allow movement. But because of the block's huge inertia, it moves only slowly and, through its links with the frame, stops that from moving also.

Beneath the ground lie the hidden but vital foundations upon which the stability of the

A head for heights was the obvious requirement for men working around a skeleton of girders hundreds of feet above the ground. A worker relaxes (below) while working on the Chrysler Building in 1928.

Erectors and Riveters

Until welding of steel girders became the glue of skyscrapers, the racket of riveting reverberated around Manhattan. Steel erectors would guide the girders into position, where they were secured by a riveting gang of 5 men. A "punk" supplied the "heater" with rivets to be heated on a forge. Glowing rivets were hurled to the "catcher" who collected them in a bucket, tapped each to remove cinders and rammed it into a hole for the "bucker-up" to hold while the "driver" flattened the end with a compressed-air hammer.

A steel erector uses the quickest way to reach his work on the Empire State Building in 1930. The Chrysler Building is in the background. A gang might put in 800 rivets during a 7½-hour shift. Up to 38 gangs worked on the Empire State Building, at a time when no ear protection was available.

Erection of the Empire State Building steelwork (right), of 102 storeys, took just 6 months. As the Waldorf-Astoria Hotel was being demolished to make way for the Empire State Building, the stock market crashed, indirectly reducing the developer's costs: of the construction estimate of $44 million, about $20 million was saved.

An Iroquois steel erector (right) in front of the Chrysler Building in 1962. The Iroquois, who once inhabited New York State, are not the only workers of Indian ancestry to show a particular aptitude for work amongst the high girders; the Mohawk Indians from a reservation near Montreal have been at work pushing up the Manhattan skyline since the 1920s.

The Steel and Concrete Forest

building depends. The World Trade Center, built between 1966 and 1971 and briefly the tallest building in the world, has some of the most remarkable foundations ever built. An area equal to 16 football fields was dug out to a depth of six storeys, all below the level of the Hudson River.

To make this possible, a trench had to be excavated around the outside down to the depth of the bedrock, and filled with concrete to create a huge coffer dam. Then 1.2 million cubic yards of soil were removed to create the foundations for two towers 110 storeys high, rising to 1,350 feet. The soil removed was used to create 23 acres of new land on the banks of the Hudson River at Battery Park City next to the Trade Center. The twin towers at the Trade Center were briefly the tallest structures in the world, before being overtaken by the Sears Tower in Chicago, which is 1,454 feet high.

If New York property millionaire Donald Trump has his way, the title of the world's tallest building will return to New York. He has plans for a massive complex called Television City, on a 75-acre site on Manhattan's West Side. Trump bought the site, an abandoned rail yard, for $95 million in 1984, one of the best bargains since Dutch settlers bought Manhattan from the Indians who originally lived there for $24 worth of trinkets. On this site Trump intends to build six 70-storey towers (and one of 65 storeys) surrounding a central spire 150 storeys high, 216 feet taller than the Sears Tower. The project includes huge TV studios, apartment buildings, shopping malls and parks. It is the biggest project in Manhattan since the Rockefeller Center went up in the 1930s. "The world's greatest city deserves the world's greatest building", says Trump. "This is to be a great monument, majestic."

Trump has already built one 68-storey Trump Tower in Manhattan, on 5th Avenue next door to Tiffany's. It has a huge atrium, soaring upward for six floors, down which pours a constant stream of water in the world's highest indoor waterfall. The lobby gleams with acres of rose-red marble, there are smart boutiques selling expensive clothes and jewellry, and those who live in the apartments above enjoy magnificent views of Central Park. It is a flashy and highly fashionable building, and there seem no technical reasons to suppose that Trump cannot also carry off his even more ambitious vision in Television City.

"Donjons of a New Feudalism"

Central Park Lake in 1909 (below) and almost the same view in 1934 (bottom). In the centre of the later view is the Chrysler Building. The tall building with the gabled roof, centre left, is New India House.

So the *Illustrated London News* described the forest of skyscrapers that had grown up in Manhattan by 1934, when it presented an extraordinary comparison between the New York skyline of that year and just 25 years earlier. In 1909 the first buses were replacing horse-drawn carriages, and the fire service was still not mechanized; by 1934 the Empire State Building was dominating the Manhattan skyline and Lindbergh's solo flight across the Atlantic was already a memory 7 years old.

The Flatiron Building (left) was built with 6 Otis hydraulic elevators. It was Elisha Otis's steam-powered "safety hoist" that enabled architects to disregard the previous constraint of a reliance on stairs. Otis's breakthrough was the invention of a good braking system. Elevators in the Rockefeller Center travel nearly 2 million miles a year.

Continuous rebuilding in Manhattan (above) is not a new phenomenon: when the Flatiron Building was being erected in 1901, the nearby Hotel Pabst had been demolished after only 4 years. This view looking south east down 42nd Street shows the Pan-Am Building beyond the construction site and the Chrysler Building to the right of centre.

The Geodesic Golfball

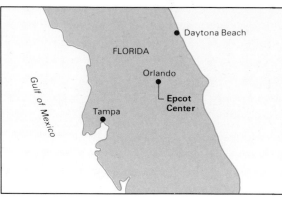

USA

FLORIDA

Daytona Beach

Orlando

Epcot Center

Gulf of Mexico

Tampa

Fact file

The largest privately financed construction project ever undertaken

Builder: Walt Disney World

Built: 1966–82

Area: 260 acres

Walt Disney, the creator of Mickey Mouse and Donald Duck, had a dream. It was to create a futuristic city somewhere in America, complete with homes, schools, parks and jobs for all, where harmony would reign amid an environment planned by the best designers and engineers. That, at least, was what he sketched out on his table napkin some time in 1959. He even had a name for the people who would make this dream come true: he called them "imagineers".

What he got—or more accurately, what the corporate imagineers created 16 years after his death—was a theme park, set in 260 acres of land south west of Orlando in Florida. Epcot, originally supposed to stand for Experimental Prototype Community of Tomorrow, is not a community at all. Nobody lives there permanently, and at night it dies. By day, it is a thriving entertainment centre that attempts to educate while it is providing fun.

The building of Epcot was an extraordinary achievement, the largest privately financed construction project ever undertaken. Ground-breaking on the site took place in October 1979; it was opened on time on 1 October 1982. It cost $1 billion, double the estimate, and employed 600 Disney designers and engineers, 1,200 consultants, and 5,000 construction workers. To help pay for it, Disney executives went out into the world of commerce and persuaded a number of blue-chip companies to provide sponsorship. They ended up with seven, who put up $300 million over ten years. In exchange, they had their names attached to a pavilion apiece.

To an ordinary eye, the site Disney chose was not an appealing one; much of it was swamp, filled with muck, a peatlike organic material with a 95 percent water content. Drilling showed that in places this muck was 160 feet deep. Before the land could even take buildings and roads, it had to be either removed or consolidated. A total

of 2.5 million cubic yards was removed, and replaced by 5 million cubic yards of clean material, while in the swampier areas the cushion of muck was simply compressed by 15 feet, covered with a blanket of sand, and turned into lagoons and lakes, with water up to 10 feet deep on top of it.

On this reconstituted ground, the Disney engineers erected buildings that house exhibitions, movies, restaurants, rides and instant townships representing the cultures of nine nations, including Britain, France, Italy and China. The theme is set by the most striking building of all, Spaceship Earth, a huge golfball that is the first completely spherical geodesic dome ever built. It is also the biggest, standing 180 feet, or 18 storeys, tall. It is made of steel framing clad with faceted aluminium panels, and stands on three pairs of steel legs.

Inside the huge sphere there is a spiralling ride that takes place in darkness, so that in fact one might as well be inside a boring square building. Its theme is communication, and it is sponsored by AT&T. The ¼-mile spiral ride passes various key events in human history—Cro Magnon Man painting the walls of his cave, Greek dramatists declaiming, Michelangelo labouring on the ceiling of the Sistine Chapel, Gutenberg manipulating type, and so on. The Disney publicity states that the hieroglyphics are authentic, the ancient dialects correct, and the costumes for the 65 animated figures have been exhaustively researched.

At the very top of the ride, there is a realistic simulation of floating in outer space before the descent. Forty thousand years of human history are condensed into 15 minutes, and the ride is so loaded with technological wizardry that, to begin with at least, it frequently went wrong. "We're sorry for the delay. Our journey in time has stopped for the time being", disembodied

The Geodesic Golfball

Spaceship Earth (above) has been built to withstand wind speeds of up to 200 mph—Florida is prone to hurricanes. The perfectly spherical geodesic dome rests on 6 steel legs 30 feet wide that raise it 15 feet above the ground. The interior of one of the 17 major pavilions, "Journey Into Imagination" (left), explores the latest ways of producing images, and creates dramatic effects for visitors.

voices declared as the vehicles ground to a halt. "I have seen the future and it kept breaking down", one visitor concluded.

The hidden services of Epcot are to many people its most interesting feature. It has, for example, a fibre-optic telecommunication system (one of the first installed anywhere in the world), a pneumatic rubbish disposal system, PeopleMovers that are driven by linear induction motors, and an all-electric monorail that takes people to and from the neighbouring Disney World complex. (Monorails have been appearing in cities of the future for at least the past 25 years, though they seem no nearer to becoming part of the real world.) The waste at Epcot is used as fuel, to provide air conditioning and cook the food the visitors eat. There is a central security system that monitors 4,000 critical points for fire or distress and, as in all Disney theme parks, the cleanliness is extraordinary. Litter is scarcely allowed to hit the ground before it is whisked away and consigned to the pneumatic disposal systems, a possible model for the city of the future.

Epcot is divided into two sections, Future World (which includes the Spaceship Earth geodesic dome) and World Showcase. Future World consists of eight separate pavilions, including the Universe of Energy (courtesy of Exxon), where visitors are transported around in vehicles each accommodating 96 people. The electricity is supplied by 80,000 solar cells, providing 70 kilowatts, and the vehicles are directed by wires embedded in the floors of each room. There are two theatres, where the vehicles are rotated into position by turntables that are suspended on air, so that the occupants can experience multiscreen entertainments, or models of Mesozoic creatures lumbering around with the aid of silicon chips and solenoids.

A second pavilion in this section, The Land, is sponsored by Kraft. This time the tour is made by boat, and is accompanied by sounds, smells and hot winds: the chickens not only look like chickens, they smell like them too. It includes advanced agricultural techniques, such as a conveyor belt with lettuces growing in mid-air, their roots sprayed with water, subterranean irrigation systems, and fish farming.

The World Showcase is quite different, rather less like a vision of the future and more like a traditional Disney theme park. The pavilions here attempt the familiar idea of many a World's Fair, a "condensation" of the culture of many

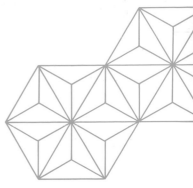

The framework of the geodesic dome consists of 1,450 steel beams covered with waterproof neoprene sheeting. The external cladding of nearly 1,000 triangular aluminium panels (left and above) is bolted on to the steel framework. The sphere has a diameter of 165 feet and a volume of 2.2 million cubic feet, but the darkness prevents visitors gaining any sense of size.

The monorail (below) has become a feature of most World Fairs and futuristic representations, but of few cities. The existing monorail system to transport guests around Walt Disney World was extended by 7 miles to take in Epcot, much of it on an elevated beamway designed for speeds up to 45 mph. The beamway is of precast, prestressed, post-tensioned concrete with spans of 120 feet.

nations complete with the olde English pub, a Chinese garden, a souk from Morocco. Here the illusionists' art perfected by generations of successful cartooning is seen at its best. None of the buildings is made of the proper materials—glassfibre predominates—but it is all put together with enormous skill. Even the flaws that a real building might have, such as a chip in the stucco, have been faithfully recreated.

"Of course it is hokey" admitted one architectural critic, impressed despite himself. "But it has been so carefully considered and so expertly executed by real artisans (Disney raised the mastery of glassfibre to craft, and an art director accompanied each construction crew) that it bears the signature of the skilled human hand in design and execution."

The Glass Tent

Fact file

One of the world's most extraordinary roof structures covering Europe's largest hall

Architect: Guenther Behnisch and Partners

Built: 1966–72

Materials: Concrete and glass

Roof area: 89,700 square yards

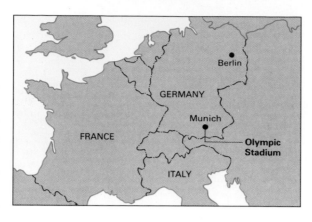

The stadium's roof at sunset resembles a Bedouin tent. The 58 masts that hold up the roof are so positioned that the pressure on the glass and on the frame in which the panes sit is equalized.

Creating the right environment for the Olympic Games has become a major challenge and a huge expense for the city that wins the right to stage them. Few have met this challenge more successfully than Munich, the Bavarian city that was the site for the games of 1972. The eye-catching stadium designed for those games by the Stuttgart architects Guenther Behnisch and Partners has never been equalled. Even today, almost 20 years since it was built, it remains one of the most remarkable structures in Europe.

The feature that distinguished the Munich stadium was its extraordinary roof, which consists of 89,700 square yards of acrylic glass plates, supported in a tentlike structure by huge masts and cables. It looks like a cobweb, too delicate to survive the first storm, but that is an illusion. The stadium is still in full use today, having staged more than 3,500 sporting, cultural and commercial events attended by more than 30 million visitors since the Olympic Games ended.

The Olympic Park, as it is called, is in fact a lot more than just a graceful roof. In addition to the stadium, it includes two halls, an indoor swimming pool, an ice-rink, a cycling stadium, a lake, and a tower 941 feet high which is one of the highest buildings in Europe. The roof flows across a large part of the park, providing cover for both of the stadiums, the Olympic Hall, the swimming pool and the pedestrian areas.

Planning began in 1966 when the International Olympics Committee awarded the games of the XXth Olympiad to Munich. The site was on the former army training grounds of the kings of Bavaria, and the adjoining Oberwiesenfeld airfield, a total of 225 acres.

The first element to be finished was the Olympic Tower, which had been planned before the city won the games. Built of reinforced concrete with two viewing platforms and a restaurant at the top, the tower was completed in 1968. It is used for TV broadcasting, as well as proving a considerable tourist attraction. There are two elevators, operating at 22 feet per second, to carry the two million visitors a year up to the viewing platforms or the 230-seater restaurant, which revolves through 360 degrees in 36, 53 or 70 minutes, depending on the speed setting. The entire tower weighs 52,000 tons.

The view from the tower includes the whole Olympic Park, the city of Munich and in the distance, the Alps. It provides a spectacular perspective on the roof which billows like canvas below. The structure is supported by 58 masts, which in turn are fastened to anchors in the ground by steel guy ropes. The masts are all placed on the periphery of the roof, so that inside the stadium there are no obstacles to a perfect view. From the masts further cables support the roof itself, which rises to a series of points where the cables are attached.

The roof consists of a series of acrylic glass plates, up to 9 feet 9 inches square and just $\frac{1}{6}$ inch thick. The glass is intended to be self-cleaning, since crawling about on the roof is not an easy task. It depends on the rain, snow and frost to remove dust and dirt that settles on it; fortunately, Munich is not heavily industrialized.

Each of the plates is surrounded by light metal rails, into which they are sealed by neoprene rubber buffers to make the system waterproof, and to allow for movements that can occur as a result of changes in temperature or during storms. The light metal framework does not, however, actually support the weight of the roof. That is done by a second network of cables that run across the roof in both directions at a spacing of 30 inches and are attached directly to the glass plates, not to the framework.

The connection between the supporting network and the glass is made by a series of steel bolts about 4 inches long attached to the plates.

The Glass Tent

The joint is once again buffered with a neoprene washer, to equalize pressure and to take up any shocks. In total, there are 137,000 such joints over the entire roof. Effectively the roof thus consists of a network of cables running in two directions at a 30-inch spacing to produce a grid, supported from above by the masts and anchored to the ground at various points. From this web hang the glass plates. The arrangement is designed so that pressure is equalized over the surface of the glass, and no pressure is exerted on the frames in which the glass sits. This is intended to eliminate the possibility of one of the frames distorting and allowing a plate to fall.

The roof covers just over half of the Olympic Stadium, with the other half unprotected. The stadium is built of reinforced concrete and at its highest point the west stand rises to a height of 110 feet. The capacity of the stadium is 78,000, of whom 48,000 are seated. The football pitch, on which West Germany won the 1974 World Cup final, is heated by about 12 miles of plastic piping under the turf, which ensures that the pitch is playable even in the worst conditions. The stadium has also been used for concerts by pop groups, and it was here that the Pope blessed the Catholics of Germany. The World Congress of Jehovah's Witnesses has also been held here.

The Olympic Hall, used for handball and gymnastics in the 1972 games, is a completely covered arena with seating for 14,000 people, a capacity unmatched anywhere else in Europe. The hall is 585 feet long, 390 feet wide and 136 feet high. The tent roof covers it, while the walls consist of a glass façade up to 60 feet high. The Olympic Hall has staged six-day cycle races, Davis Cup tennis matches, the World Ice Hockey championships, performances of *Aïda* and concerts by Tina Turner and Luciano Pavarotti. It is one of the largest and most flexible spaces anywhere, able to host a schools sports gala one day, a pedigree dog show the next, and moto-cross races the day after.

The Olympic Park also boasts one of the finest swimming-pool complexes in Europe, with five separate pools—designed for competition, diving, training, practice and a special pool for children. Like the Olympic Hall, the pools are covered by the roof, with a glass façade rising to more than 80 feet in places providing the walls. This creates the effect of an outdoor pool, even though it is protected from the weather and can seat 2,000 people. During the games, temporary seating was provided to more than quadruple the

The adaptability of the roof structure is evident in this view from the Olympic Tower. The system enables large and small halls and stadia to be linked by a continuous ceiling of glass, which gives the site a cohesion and unity that separate units could not achieve.

capacity, bringing it up to 9,360.

Providing a site for the Olympics has proved a good investment for Munich. The total cost of landscaping the site, and building the many sports facilities, cost DM 1,350 million, two thirds of which was covered by revenue raised by the organizing committee, the sale of Olympic coins, a TV lottery and a public lottery. Half the rest was financed by the Federal Republic government, the other half jointly by the Bavarian State and by the city of Munich. Given a repayment term of six years, the city was able to finance its share out of the current budget each year—and finished with a sports complex any city would envy. It is a tragedy that the games for which the complex was built will be remembered principally for a terrorist attack on Israeli athletes which overshadowed the performances on track and field; but the Olympic Park has proved a great success in the years since then.

The Olympic Tower
*dominates the Munich
skyline and affords the
best view of the
Olympic Park. Erected
in 1962, before most of
the buildings that form
the Park, the Tower is
941 feet high and
weighs 51,200 tons.
Elevators ascend the
tower until 11.30 pm,
giving visitors ½ hour to
enjoy the lights before
the last ride down.*

**Deterioration of the
neoprene joints** *(above)
will eventually
necessitate their
complete replacement.*

The Stadium *(left)
accommodates 52,448
seated spectators and
20,608 standing, and
there are 240 seats for
press, television and
radio reporters with 20
commentators' cabins.
The West Stand is built
over the athletes' and
technical facilities. The
2 indicator boards are
so large that 48,000
light bulbs are used.*

Australia's Architectural Symbol

AUSTRALIA

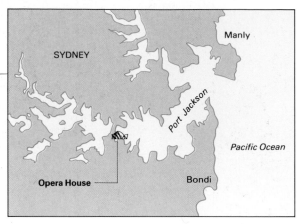

SYDNEY

Manly

Port Jackson

Pacific Ocean

Opera House

Bondi

Fact file

One of the most distinctive buildings in the world, that required novel construction ideas

Designer: Jorn Utzon

Built: 1959–73

Materials: Pre-stressed concrete and glass

Weight of roof: 26,800 tons

Area of glass: 1½ acres

Sydney Opera House has become an Australian symbol as instantly recognizable as the kangaroo or the koala. Its gleaming white roofs cluster like overlapping shells on a promontory that juts into Sydney Cove, creating a building that looks beautiful from any angle.

Beneath the shells are five separate halls—for symphony concerts, operas, chamber music and plays—as well as an exhibition hall, 3 restaurants, 6 bars, a library and 60 dressing rooms. The Opera House has a thousand rooms and 11 acres of usable floor space. A million ceramic tiles cover the roof, and 67,000 square feet of specially made glass fill the open ends of the shells. Behind the creation of this extraordinary building lies the inspiration of one architect and the work of many, combined with the skills of the structural engineers who made it possible. There is no other building like it, anywhere. It is unlikely there ever will be.

The design was the prize-winning entry in a competition launched in 1955 by the Premier of New South Wales, Joseph Cahill, to create a

national opera house on a magnificent site in Sydney Harbour. Bennelong Point is named after an Aborigine befriended by the commander of the First Fleet, Captain Arthur Phillip RN, who landed with Australia's first convict settlers in Sydney Cove in 1788. From 1902 it was occupied by a huge red-brick tram depot, which was demolished to make way for the Opera House.

To the astonishment of the world, the contest was won by a little-known Danish architect, 38-year-old Jorn Utzon, who had few completed commissions to his credit. Almost all he had built were 63 houses near Elsinore in 1956, and a smaller housing project near Fredensborg. For the Opera House, Utzon had produced a design so graceful and daring that it simply swept the others aside. He provided few details. "The drawings submitted are simple to the point of being diagrammatic" the judges concluded. "Nevertheless, as we have returned again and again to the study of these drawings, we are convinced that they present a concept of an opera house which is capable of being one of the great buildings of the world."

Faced with this wonderful but difficult design, the New South Wales Government might have lost its courage; it was under no obligation to build the first prize winner. It could have saved itself a lot of money, and years of argument, if it had chosen a simpler but more ordinary structure. But it did not. It accepted Utzon's design and at his suggestion appointed Ove Arup and Partners, the British-based firm founded by a Danish engineer, as structural consultants.

The first stage was to clear the site and build the podium, the deep, flat platform upon which the building stands. Work on that began in 1959, before it was clear that Utzon's shells could even be built. The assumption at this stage was that the roofs would be made of a vault of concrete poured in one operation into curved wooden or steel moulds. That would, however, have been prohibitively expensive, so Utzon came up with another idea.

He suggested instead that the shells should be made of prefabricated concrete ribs, standing next to one another, and that they should all have the same spherical curvature. He showed that all the shells could be made from sections taken from the surface of a sphere 246 feet in radius, like pieces cut from the skin of an orange. But instead of casting the shells as one piece, they would be made up of ribs, cast in separate sections on site from a relatively small number of

The two principal halls (left)—for opera on the left and orchestral concerts on the right— appear joined from most angles; in fact, like the small set of shells covering the restaurant (right), they are divided by a passageway. The buildings cover 4¼ acres of the site area of 5½ acres, and the 5 auditoria provide seats for 5,467.

Australia's Architectural Symbol

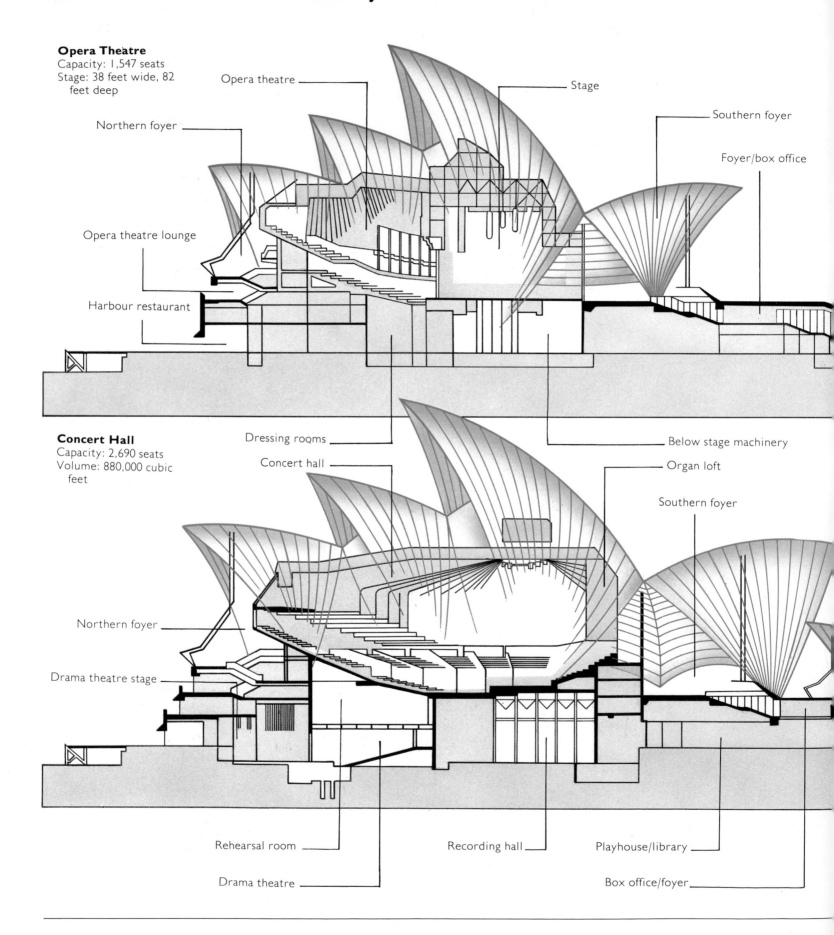

Opera Theatre
Capacity: 1,547 seats
Stage: 38 feet wide, 82 feet deep

Opera theatre

Northern foyer

Opera theatre lounge

Harbour restaurant

Stage

Southern foyer

Foyer/box office

Concert Hall
Capacity: 2,690 seats
Volume: 880,000 cubic feet

Dressing rooms

Concert hall

Below stage machinery

Organ loft

Southern foyer

Northern foyer

Drama theatre stage

Rehearsal room

Recording hall

Playhouse/library

Drama theatre

Box office/foyer

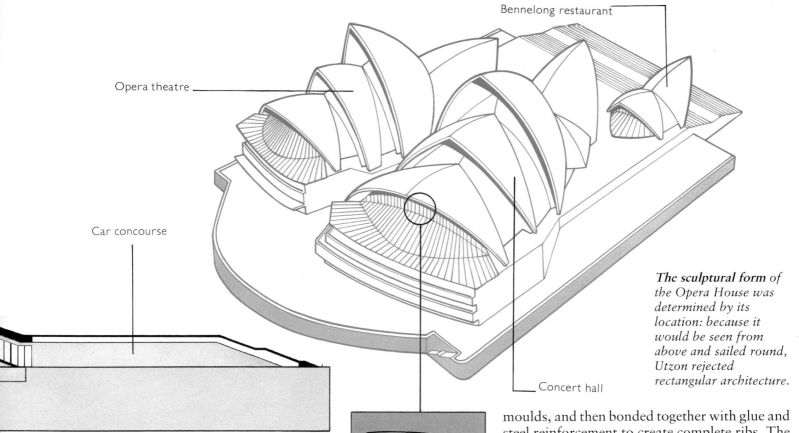

Bennelong restaurant

Opera theatre

Car concourse

Concert hall

The sculptural form of the Opera House was determined by its location: because it would be seen from above and sailed round, Utzon rejected rectangular architecture.

Bennelong restaurant

Car concourse

Staircase to foyer

The choice of glass to fill the mouths of the shells was made by Utzon at an early stage, but the technical problems of supporting such a vast area, and of keeping out the noise of shipping sirens, were daunting. Utzon was determined to avoid a vertical wall since it would "kill the unsupported shell effect"; consequently he opted for a broken line.

moulds, and then bonded together with glue and steel reinforcement to create complete ribs. The ribs stand so close together they almost touch, and are linked to one another by a concrete joint. The outside of the shells is then covered by a layer of ceramic tiles.

Selecting and placing the tiles was a huge problem. Utzon regarded the choice of roof covering as vital: "The wrong material would ruin the appearance", he wrote. It would have to gleam in the sun, survive large temperature variations, keep itself clean, and retain its character for many years. To find such a material, Utzon looked to the ancient world, and decided that ceramic tiles were the only answer. The use of the spherical curves for the ribs meant that the surface could be covered successfully with tiles of a single size, $4\frac{3}{4}$ inches square.

Two different surface finishes were used, one glossy and white, the other matt and buff in colour, to give the roof its distinctive pattern. The tiles, made by Hoganas in Sweden, were laid on the roof in prefabricated trays, or "lids". These were assembled by laying the tiles face downward on a form and pouring concrete over their backs to bond them together. The complete lid, which could be as much as 33 feet long by 7 feet 6 inches broad, was then removed from the form and bolted to the roof by phosphor-bronze bolts. The entire roof contains 4,253 lids, made up of 1,056,000 individual tiles.

One of the mysteries of the building is how the

Bennelong Point is one of the finest situations chosen for a public building, backed by the green acres of the Royal Botanic Gardens and Government House grounds. In April 1964, when the P&O liner Canberra passed the site, work was beginning on the halls.

shells are supported, apparently on only two points, without the use of pillars. This is achieved by linking the large shells to smaller ones facing in the opposite direction, so that the two form a unit. Since each shell touches the ground at two points, this means that the unit is squarely set on four legs. The smaller "louvre shells", as they are called, are barely noticeable, but without them the roof could not stand up.

Another tricky problem was devising a system for glazing the open ends of the shells. Utzon always intended to use glass for most of the shells, but finding a way to support it was difficult. The glass walls were eventually supported on vertical steel mullions which extend all the way up the mouths of the shells. From these mullions run bronze glazing bars into which the panes are embedded in silicone putty. There are 2,000 panes of glass, ranging in size from 4 feet square to 14 feet by 8 feet 6 inches, in more than 700 different sizes, worked out by Ove Arup and Partners using a computer. The glass itself is $\frac{3}{4}$ inch thick and consists of two layers, one plain and one amber, joined together by an interlayer of plastic. This structure increases the strength of the windows, reducing the danger from falling glass inside the building, and also produces better sound insulation.

By 1966, work on the main structure was well advanced, but little had been done inside the building. Utzon had fallen out with government officials over methods of construction and the awarding of subcontracts. A new state government, elected to office in May 1965, was becom-

ing anxious about the costs of the building, already certain to exceed the original estimates by a wide margin. Suddenly, in February 1966, Utzon resigned as architect to the Opera House. Despite appeals from the government to return to the project as a member of the architectural team, not its supervisor, he stuck to his decision. His letter of resignation contained the gnomic sentence: "It is not I but the Sydney Opera House that created all the enormous difficulties." Soon after he left Australia, never to return.

His task was finished by a team of Australian architects, so that while the exterior of the building bears Utzon's stamp, the interior does not. Decisions were also taken which changed

The partly completed shells in June 1965 illustrate the prefabrication of the roofs, which are made of 2 rows of concrete ribs that curve inwards to meet at the centreline. The roofs required 2,194 precast segments, which were made in a casting yard on the site.

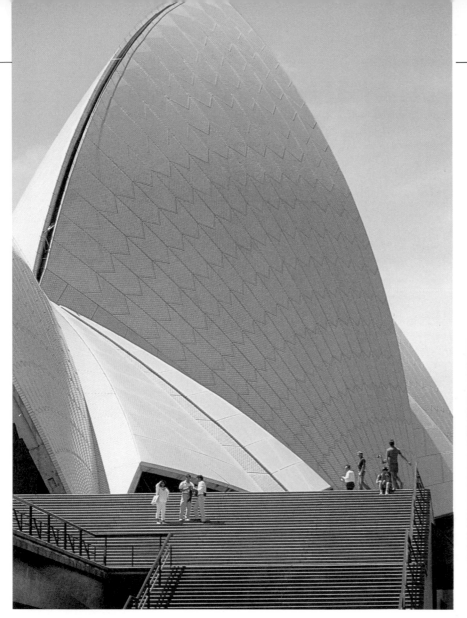

The tiling of the roof posed huge difficulties and required surveying techniques using computers to resolve them. The impossibility of using regularly shaped tiles on Utzon's original shells, whose contours altered continuously, forced a change in shell design.

the nature of the building, committing the largest hall (which seats 2,690) not to opera but to orchestral music. Utzon had believed that it could serve both purposes, but a panel set up to advise the government after his departure recommended otherwise. As a result, the Sydney Opera House is unable to stage the grandest of operas, which require complex stage machinery and a large orchestra pit. The hall used for opera, which seats 1,547, was originally intended for plays, and does not have a pit large enough. As a result, says conductor Sir Charles Mackerras, "it's very nearly impossible to do anything adequately". When the Australian Opera puts on Wagner's Ring, they have to use a reduced version. Though large-scale operas are put on in the bigger hall, it lacks proper stage machinery.

Because of these shortcomings, opera lovers have always regarded the house as something of a fraud: an opera house containing a large concert hall not suitable for opera and a smaller hall satisfactory only for small-scale works. Defenders of the decisions taken after Utzon's departure argue that the term Opera House has always been a misnomer anyway, because the competition rules made it clear that opera was not the building's primary function.

Despite the arguments, the building was eventually completed, and opened by Queen Elizabeth II in October 1973. The original estimate given by Joseph Cahill had been A $7 million (£3.5 million); the final cost came to A $102 million (£50 million), the vast majority raised by lotteries. The state government breathed a sigh of relief and began to enjoy the international praise for its stunning new building.

However, by March 1989, Parliament was warned that urgent repairs were needed, at a cost of A $86 million (£42 million), if the building were not to be irretrievably damaged. Tiles had begun falling off the roof, which was leaking, as were some windows and walls. Sealants used on the concrete ribs, expected to last for 20 years, had deteriorated after only ten. Whatever the cost, the building would be maintained at the highest standard, the New South Wales Arts Minister told Parliament, but the Opera House is clearly going to remain demanding for years to come.

The ceiling of the Concert Hall is designed to create a space with acoustic properties suitable for music and speech. A hollow raft composed of layers of concrete, plasterboard and plywood is suspended from the ceiling. The cavity conceals and allows access to wiring and air-conditioning ducts. The floor is of laminated brush box.

The Ultimate Stadium

The world's largest indoor stadium, in the centre of New Orleans, is a colossal multi-purpose building with the biggest dome ever constructed. The roof alone covers almost 10 acres, rising in the centre to the height of a 26-storey building. Halfway through building it, the subcontractor entrusted with the job walked out, claiming that the design simply would not work. The architects who designed it kept calm, found a new subcontractor and finished the job. More than 15 years later the building is a huge success which has vindicated the design and the decision of the Louisiana Stadium and Exposition District to build it.

The Louisiana Superdome is not the only enclosed stadium suitable for sports events, rock concerts and political conventions in the US, but it is the biggest. Its dome is 680 feet across and 273 feet high in the centre, and its seating can accommodate up to 75,000 people for sports events, or more for special events such as concerts.

Planning began in 1967 when LSED announced its intention of creating such a building in a derelict part of downtown New Orleans, then occupied by rusting railway tracks and abandoned warehouses. The contract was won by the New York firm of Curtis and Davis Architects and Planners, who formed a joint venture with the St Louis engineering consultants Sverdrup & Parcel and Associates. The contract was awarded early in 1971, and the first concrete pile was driven into the soft Louisiana mud in August 1972.

The key to the economic success of the building was flexibility, so that it could be used for a range of sports—American football, baseball, basketball, and even tennis—as well as conventions, trade shows, theatrical productions, and large-scale closed circuit TV events. The architects sought to produce a building "large enough to house the most spectacular extravaganza and small enough to accommodate a poetry reading", in the words of the leader of the design team, Nathaniel C. Curtis Jnr. For this reason, a number of meeting rooms and convention facilities were placed immediately behind the main stadium seating.

Satisfying the needs of a variety of sports is more difficult, for baseball needs the biggest field, while football attracts the most spectators, and basketball and tennis are usually played in smaller arenas where the atmosphere is more intimate. To meet these different requirements,

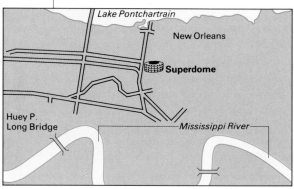

Fact file

The world's largest indoor stadium covered by the world's biggest dome

Designers: Curtis and Davis

Built: 1971–75

Materials: Steel and concrete

Width of dome: 680 feet

15,000 seats along the lower concourse can be moved to and fro. In their rear expanded position, they provide the maximum area for playing baseball, but for football they can be moved forward 50 feet to give spectators the ideal view close to the touchline. For tennis, an entire section of the east stand, with 2,500 seats, can be moved right across the field to form a compact arena on the west side of the stadium.

The building is supported on 2,100 prestressed concrete piles driven 160 feet down to bedrock. At the lowest level are three tiers of parking for 5,000 cars. Above that is a floor of offices, and above that again the convention floor. At a height of 160 feet above the ground, a circular ring of welded steel supports the domed roof. This tension ring, 680 feet in diameter, is in the form of a truss 9 feet deep and 18 inches across. Designed to withstand the immense forces exerted by the dome, the tension ring is made from 1¼-inch steel, prefabricated in 24 sections that were welded together in place. To ensure the reliability of the welds, they were carried out in the controlled atmosphere of a tent-house that was moved around the circumference of the ring from joint to joint.

The dome itself consists of a framework of structural steel radiating outward from a central "crown block". During construction, the dome was supported by 37 temporary towers, each

The Superdome's design was consciously intended to facilitate the range of activities that were held in the amphitheatres of ancient Greece, from sport to poetry readings. Determining the optimun seating arrangements around the different-shaped fields for football and baseball (right) required the computer analysis of 200 schemes.

with a hydraulic jack on top so that the entire dome, when complete, could be lowered on to the tension ring which was to support it. The dome's structure is formed by 12 curved radial ribs running outward from the centre, linked by six sets of circumferential ribs and braced by a series of other struts to create a diamond pattern. The weatherproof surface on top consists of 18-gauge sheet steel panels, followed by a 1-inch layer of polyurethane foam and finally a sprayed-on layer of hypalon plastic. The idea was to create a homogeneous skin with no joints, and with enough flexibility to allow the structure to expand and contract by several inches in response to temperature changes.

For the same reason, the tension ring on which the dome rests is supported by pinned connections that can hinge to allow movement. Up to 8

The Ultimate Stadium

The Superdome's location in downtown New Orleans was chosen to take advantage of existing public transport and highway systems, and 20,000 commercial parking spaces nearby (left). The white plastic covering to the roof, designed to avoid joints, was sprayed on inside a cocoon for protection from the weather.

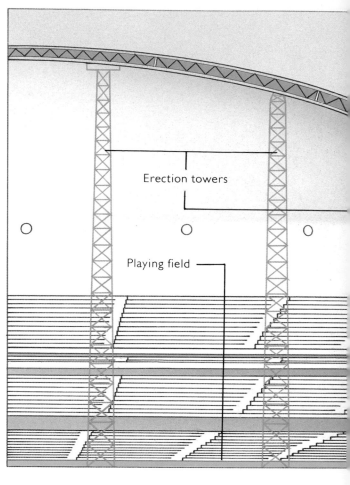

Erection towers

Playing field

The frequency of hurricane winds in New Orleans necessitated wind tunnel tests on a 1:288 scale model which proved that the Superdome could withstand sustained winds of over 150 mph and gusts up to 200 mph. The steel framework of the walls and roof required 20,000 tons of steel from Pittsburgh, delivered by barge up the Mississippi River.

inches of movement occurs in normal conditions. Between the dome and the outer wall is a trench 4 feet deep by 8 feet wide which forms a gutter to collect the rain falling on the roof. This trench, or gutter tub, can hold the equivalent of 1 inch of rain falling on the roof; to avoid overtaxing the sewers of New Orleans, the flow of water away from the gutter is controlled by drain pipes that do not allow it all to escape at once.

When the structure of the dome was complete, the hydraulic jacks on the top of each tower supporting it were removed, one by one, until it rested completely on the tension ring. The fabricators of all the steelwork in the Superdome, American Bridge, had estimated that when support was removed from the centre of the dome, it would settle by 4 inches under its own weight. They were delighted when the

actual settlement turned out to be $3\frac{1}{2}$ inches.

The circular shape of the domed roof creates an immense amount of lift as winds blow across it, acting rather like an aircraft wing. This is counteracted by the weight of the roof itself, assisted by a 75-ton TV gondola suspended inside the stadium from the centre of the dome. The gondola contains six giant TV screens, each 22 by 26 feet, sound systems, and lighting. A control room projects the TV pictures on to the screens from six projectors in the upper tier seats, and can provide instant replays, TV pictures from other stadia or events, or messages. The height of the gondola can be adjusted. For football it is placed about 100 feet above the field, but is raised to 200 feet for baseball to prevent stray balls hitting the screens. For theatrical events the gondola can be lowered to whatever height the director prefers, or the six screens replaced by two larger ones for showing sports events, motor racing or theatre productions from outside.

Given the very soft soil under the foundations, there was a theoretical danger that one or other

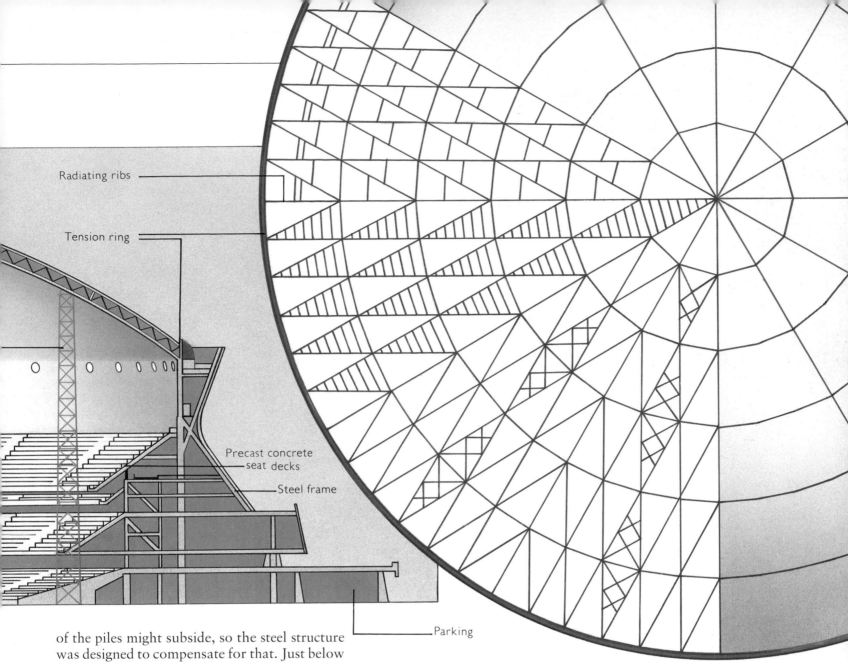

Radiating ribs

Tension ring

Precast concrete
seat decks

Steel frame

Parking

of the piles might subside, so the steel structure was designed to compensate for that. Just below the tension ring very heavy steel cross-bracing was added to the structure, so that if a column were to sink, load would be redistributed to the two neighbouring columns. In theory, the bracing is strong enough to suspend completely a settling dome column, although in practice this will not happen. Settlement only happens under load, and as the bracing redistributes that load, settlement stops.

The Superdome first opened its doors on 3 August 1975. Since then it has been home several times to America's biggest football game, the Superbowl, housed the Republican National Convention in 1988, and an address by Pope John Paul II to 88,000 schoolchildren in 1987. It holds the record for the biggest indoor concert crowd in history (87,500 to hear the Rolling Stones in 1981) and has become a major tourist attraction in its own right, with some 75,000 people a year attending its daily tours. The grass on which football and baseball are played is artificial, AstroTurf 8—or Mardi Grass as the

Superdome operators call it. At first, the Superdome was managed by the State of Louisiana, but it lost money and was handed over to a private firm, Facility Management of Louisiana, which has achieved much better results.

The total cost of the building was $173 million, and in its first ten years of operation it cost an additional $99.2 million, for interest and repayment on the bonds sold to finance it, operating subsidies, and capital improvements. But a study by the University of New Orleans shows that the benefits to the area far exceed the costs. It estimates that new money brought to the area by the Superdome is almost $1 billion over that period, while the benefit to the rundown section of the city where it was built could not have been achieved in any other way. In 1970 the area was one of urban decay; today it is one of the showcases of the business district.

The 6-ring lamella roof-framing system was constructed on a patented configuration in which a diamond pattern is created by imposing parallel ribs on the 12 radial ribs and 6 rings. Each ring is made up of numerous small lattice trusses.

Symbol of a City

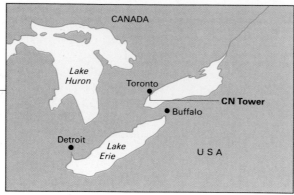

Fact file

The world's tallest unsupported structure

Builder: Canadian National Railways

Built: 1973–76

Material: Concrete

Height: 1,815 feet 5 inches

Weight: 130,000 tons

Cost: $57 million

The skyline of downtown Toronto is dominated by a pencil-slim tower that soars above the office blocks around it. The CN Tower, a structure of the television age, was built by Canadian National Railways for the practical purpose of eliminating "ghosting" that ruined the picture on many local screens. It has achieved much more than that. Today it is the symbol of Toronto's newfound confidence, the tallest unsupported structure in the world, visited by nearly 2 million tourists every year.

The tower rises 1,815 feet 5 inches from its base to the tip of its lightning rod. It weighs 130,000 tons, and its concrete and steel foundations rest on a bed of specially smoothed shale 50 feet below ground. Construction began on 6 February 1973 and took just 40 months, at a cost of $57 million. In cross-section the tower forms the configuration of a Y, which tapers gently as it rises. More than 1,100 feet up, a doughnut-shaped bulge is wrapped around the tower: it is a

seven-storey building, the Skypod, containing the equipment needed for TV broadcasting, a revolving restaurant, two observation decks, a night-club and two small picture theatres. Higher still, at 1,500 feet, is another even more vertiginous observation platform, the two-storey Space Deck, whose windows curve in toward the floor to enable the brave to look vertically downward, a spine-tingling experience; on a clear day one can see for 100 miles.

The tower was built by pouring high-quality concrete into a huge mould, called a slipform, supported by jacks which gradually inched it upward. As it climbed, the slipform was reduced in size to produce the taper of the tower. Because of the speed of construction—up to 20 feet a day—normal testing of the strength of the concrete (which involves waiting seven days for it to harden) could not be used, and special accelerated tests had to be adopted.

Extraordinary efforts were made to ensure the tower did not lean or develop a twist. In addition to a plumb bob (a 250-lb steel cylinder suspended on a wire down the centre of the tower's hexagonal core) optical instruments were used to take measurements every two hours. The result was a tower 1,815 feet and 5 inches high which deviates only $1\frac{1}{10}$ inches from a perfect vertical.

The top 335 feet of the tower consist of a steel transmission mast, assembled from 39 sections by lifting them into place one by one suspended from a huge Sikorsky S64E helicopter. This flying skyhook lifted and placed the sections in

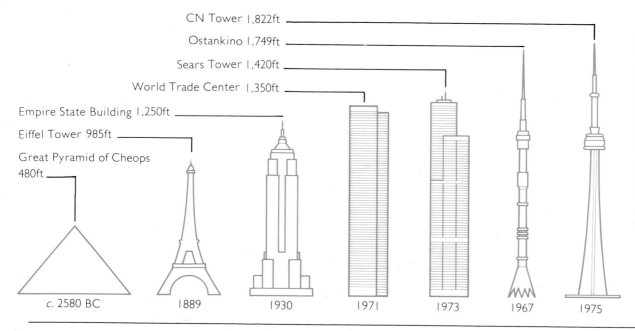

CN Tower 1,822ft
Ostankino 1,749ft
Sears Tower 1,420ft
World Trade Center 1,350ft
Empire State Building 1,250ft
Eiffel Tower 985ft
Great Pyramid of Cheops 480ft

c. 2580 BC   1889   1930   1971   1973   1967   1975

The height of the world's tallest unsupported building has almost doubled (left) in less than 100 years between the completion of the Eiffel and CN towers. The lighting of the CN Tower (right) has to be reduced during the spring and autumn bird migrations to avoid attracting them, thus risking fatal collisions.

Symbol of a City

three and a half weeks, instead of the six months it would have taken by more conventional methods.

The tower was designed to resist the worst weather imaginable, and then some. A wind of 130 mph is expected to occur once every thousand years; the tower was built to withstand one twice as strong. If you were bold enough to go up to the Skypod in a 130 mph wind, you would find yourself wobbling in an elliptical path through a distance of about 10 inches. But the movement would be so slow that it would be barely perceptible. The steel television mast would bend far more, oscillating through an 8-foot path, so special lead counterweights have been added to damp out the effect. The tower is a wonderful place to watch a thunderstorm, since it acts as a lightning conductor for all the surrounding buildings. Each year it is struck by lightning at least 60 times, the charge being harmlessly grounded to earth.

A greater danger with structures that rise as high as the CN Tower is the formation of ice high above the ground. Melting slabs of ice are reported to have fallen from the Ostankino Tower in Moscow, the second highest in the world, threatening the life of anyone below. In Toronto, the danger has been eliminated by ice-proofing areas where ice might form, such as the roof edges of the Skypod. In some places heating cables have been inserted, while in others a sheath of shiny plastic has been attached, on which ice cannot cling.

Visitors are carried up the tower in lifts which zoom upward at 1,200 feet a minute, as rapid a rate of climb as a jet taking off. The speed and acceleration of the lift were carefully calculated so that it is fast enough to be enjoyable, but not so fast as to cause alarm, nausea, or fainting fits. There is a glass wall to see the view, but the lifts have also been designed to provide a cocoonlike sense of security. The lifts have independent power supplies and can empty the tower quickly in an emergency, but to reassure visitors, there is also a staircase of 2,570 steps.

The tower has been the scene of many stunts. The first man to parachute off it was a member of the construction crew, Bill Eustace, also known as "Sweet William", on 9 November 1975. He was sacked. In 1979, the record for dropping an egg was smashed when Patrick Baillie, 17, threw a Grade A egg undamaged from 1,120 feet into a specially designed net. All this and better TV pictures too.

A Sikorsky S64E helicopter was used to locate the crane that was mounted on top of the Space Deck during construction. It was then used to position the 39 sections of the antenna that sits on top of the Space Deck; the heaviest section of the antenna weighs 8 tons.

Painting parts of the transmission mast (below) took 4 men 11 days, working 1,815 feet above the railroad tracks. The mast is protected from ice build-up by a glass-reinforced plastic covering 2 inches thick.

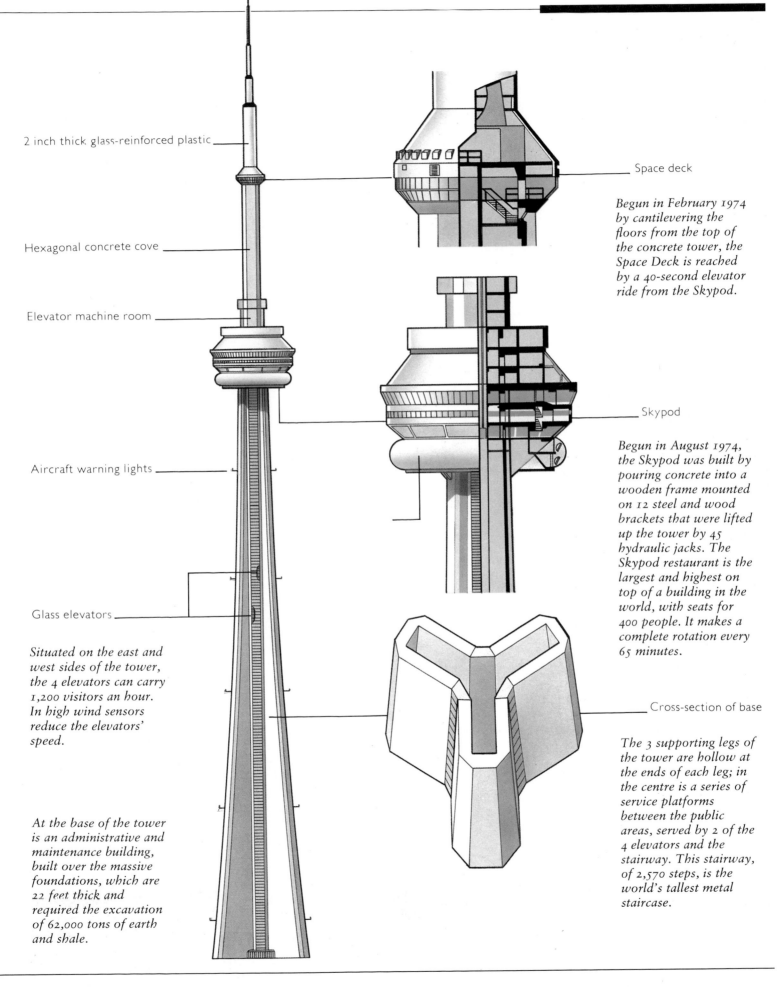

2 inch thick glass-reinforced plastic

Hexagonal concrete cove

Elevator machine room

Aircraft warning lights

Glass elevators

Space deck

Begun in February 1974 by cantilevering the floors from the top of the concrete tower, the Space Deck is reached by a 40-second elevator ride from the Skypod.

Skypod

Begun in August 1974, the Skypod was built by pouring concrete into a wooden frame mounted on 12 steel and wood brackets that were lifted up the tower by 45 hydraulic jacks. The Skypod restaurant is the largest and highest on top of a building in the world, with seats for 400 people. It makes a complete rotation every 65 minutes.

Cross-section of base

Situated on the east and west sides of the tower, the 4 elevators can carry 1,200 visitors an hour. In high wind sensors reduce the elevators' speed.

At the base of the tower is an administrative and maintenance building, built over the massive foundations, which are 22 feet thick and required the excavation of 62,000 tons of earth and shale.

The 3 supporting legs of the tower are hollow at the ends of each leg; in the centre is a series of service platforms between the public areas, served by 2 of the 4 elevators and the stairway. This stairway, of 2,570 steps, is the world's tallest metal staircase.

The Tallest Towers

One of the 7 wonders of the world was the Pharos of Alexandria, a tower built to help navigation off the Mediterranean port during the reign of Ptolemy II, who died in 247 BC. It is estimated to have been about 350 feet high, with a lantern section on top. It collapsed in 1326.

Successive ecclesiastical buildings have held the record for the tallest structure in the world until the Washington Memorial took the record for just 5 years in 1884. Since World War II, radio and television masts have held the record, the current holder being the Warszawa Radio mast near Plock in Poland which is 2,120 feet 8 inches high, or over $\frac{2}{5}$ mile. Plans for ever taller towers are continually made.

Bishop Rock Lighthouse, England

Standing between the Scilly Isles and the Lizard, Cornwall, this lighthouse was the first indication for many mariners that the transatlantic crossing was almost over, besides warning of submerged rocks. It is the tallest lighthouse in Britain, with a height of 156 feet 10 inches to the helipad, which is a recent addition.

Washington Monument, USA

It took 36 years to build the obelisk that stands between the Capitol and the Lincoln Memorial in Washington, DC. Completed in 1884, it forms the keynote of a plan proposed in 1791 by a French officer, Pierre L'Enfant. It was not until 1901 that Congress agreed to implement his scheme. The monument, 555 feet high, can be ascended by elevator.

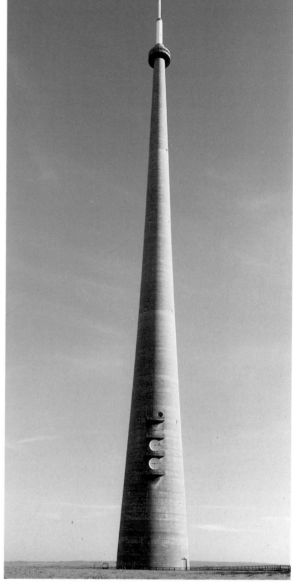

Marine Tower, Yokahama, Japan
The tallest lighthouse in the world stands in Yamashita Park, Yokohama, and measures 348 feet in height. Built of steel, it has a luminous intensity of 600,000 candles and a visibility of 20 miles.

Emley Moor, Yorkshire, England
Built by the Independent Broadcasting Authority, this transmitter is the tallest self-supporting structure in Great Britain, at 1,080 feet. Completed in 1971, it replaced a taller, stayed mast of 1,265 feet which was brought down by icing in March 1969. The mast encases a room at 865 feet and weighs, with the foundations, 14,760 tons.

A Private Xanadu

South China Sea

Sabah

Sultan's Palace

Bandar Seri Begawan

BRUNEI

Sarawak

BORNEO

Kalimantan

BORNEO

INDONESIA

Fact file

The world's largest
occupied palace

Architect: Leandro V.
Locsin

Built: 1982–86

Materials: Concrete,
steel and marble

Floor area: 50 acres

*Sultan Hassanal Bolkiak
was born on 15 July
1946. He was not
expected to become the
29th Sultan, since
Hassanal's father
inherited the title from
his brother in 1953. The
throne room (opposite)
seats thousands.*

The richest man in the world also possesses the longest name. His Majesty Paduka Seri Baginda Sultan and Yang Di-Pertuan, Sultan Hassanal Bolkiah Mu'izzaddin Waddaulah Ibni Al-Markhum Sultan Haji Oamr Ali Saifuddien Sa'adul Khairi Waddien is quite a handle, even if another four lines of honours and titles are omitted . . . Collar of the Supreme Order of the Chrysanthemum, Grand Order of the Mugunghwa, and similar decorations.

The Sultan of Brunei shuns the press, and as a result the details of his magnificent palace, the biggest occupied residence in the world, have largely been obscured in a flurry of lawyers' letters. The least awestruck account of the Sultan and his extraordinary lifestyle comes from the writer James Bartholomew, in his book *The Richest Man in the World*, from which most of the present account is derived.

The Sultan's wealth is based on oil. His small nation of 230,000 people virtually floats on it. It provides free education, health care and subsidized housing for the people, and tops up the Sultan's already bulging bank accounts. According to most estimates, his wealth now amounts to at least $25,000 million, which makes him worth more than General Motors, or ICI, Jaguar and the National Westminster Bank combined. He earns at least $2,000 million a year, or $4.5 million a day—$4,000 dollars a minute. He never has to worry where the next billion is coming from. The estimated $350 million that the palace cost came, in any case, from state funds, not the Sultan's personal fortune.

The Sultan possesses houses all around the world. When in Britain, he often stays at the Dorchester Hotel, which he owns, although he also has a house in Kensington Palace Gardens, another in Hampstead, and a huge property in the suburb of Southall. Once he bought a house near Guildford in Surrey, sight unseen, and

drove off to visit it, following another car driven by somebody who knew the way. The two cars became separated, so the Sultan no longer had any idea which way to go. He persevered, however, and in due course reached Guildford. But despite driving around for two and a half hours in search of the house, he failed to find it. He concluded that a house that was so difficult to find was not worth having, so he sold it.

All these houses pale into insignificance compared with his palace in Brunei, the Istana Nurul Iman. The Sultan only decided to build it in the early 1980s, and resolved that it be finished in time for Brunei's independence from Britain early in 1984. Its design and construction were therefore something of a race against time. The architect, Leandro V. Locsin, a distinguished Filipino with uncompromisingly modern tastes, was given just two weeks to come up with a design. The contractors were allowed two years to complete the building, which contains 1,778 rooms. Hardly surprisingly, many things went wrong.

The man who won the contract to build the palace was Enrique Zobel, a Filipino businessman who had met the Sultan playing polo. Zobel persuaded the Sultan that there was no time to put the palace out to tender, and it would be better if he handled the entire job himself. Zobel appointed Locsin, who produced two alternative designs in a hurry. He had never seen the site, or talked to the Sultan, which made his task harder. One design was ultra-modern, the other contained some Islamic motifs and was far less radical. Locsin preferred the first, but the Sultan chose the second. As the design progressed, however, Locsin reverted more and more to his own taste, and away from that of the Sultan.

To help with construction the American project engineers Bechtel were signed up. They recommended that the roof of the throne room, originally to be made of prestressed concrete, should instead be of steel. The demands on this roof are considerable, since as well as spanning a very large area it supports 12 huge chandeliers each of which weighs a ton. There are four thrones, the extra two designed to accommodate a visiting royal couple. Behind the four thrones is a 60-foot Islamic arch, with two further arches inside it, all covered in 22-carat gold tiles.

The banqueting hall, by far the largest in the world, can seat 4,000 people. It, too, has chandeliers and arches tiled in gold. There are 18 lifts, 44 staircases, a total floor area of just over

A Private Xanadu

The palace (above) is situated in a huge compound, seen here beyond the gold-topped Omar Ali Saifuddin Mosque and city of Bandar Seri Begawan. Many of the inhabitants live in kampongs, *water villages in which the houses are built on stilts, like those beyond the mosque.*

Locsin's roof design (above) echoes the roofs of the longhouses that are common in parts of south-east Asia. Much of the effect is lost by not being able to look down on the roofs, since the palace is on a hill. Locsin was not to know this, having never visited the site.

50 acres, and an underground car park big enough for 800 cars. The Sultan likes cars, owns at least 110 himself and tends to buy them in threes, so as to be able to vary the colour. He owns several dozen Rolls-Royces, some of which do not have number plates and have never been used. A full-time Rolls-Royce engineer is employed to look after them.

Royal suites inside the palace are provided for members of the royal family, each the equivalent in accommodation to a large house. In all, the suites occupy 900 rooms. Originally, the whole of the interior of the palace was to be covered in marble, but as costs rose that idea was modified. The estimate for the marble alone, ordered by Bechtel, came to $17 million. Alarmed at the size of the bill, Zobel took over the task of buying the marble, altered the specification slightly, and got the bill down to a mere $10 million.

Because the whole building was erected in

The side of the palace overlooking the river (above) has been likened to a multi-storey car park. The palace has 257 toilets and a sewage-treatment plant capable of handling 300,000 gallons a day, adequate for a village of 1,500 people.

such haste, neither architect, contractor nor interior designer ever really discovered what the Sultan's tastes were. Both Locsin and the interior designer, Dale Keller, favoured austere modern designs, but the Sultan's taste runs more to antique or reproduction furniture and decoration of the fancier kind—what designers call "Louis Farouk" style (Louis-Quatorze out of King Farouk). The two styles clashed, and the Sultan has had several rooms completely gutted and rebuilt closer to his own taste.

The entrance to the palace is up a long drive that circles around the entire building before reaching the front, beside which water cascades over huge granite steps. Inside the carved wooden doors, 16 feet high, permanently guarded by two soldiers, is a promenade that runs alongside water. In the middle of the water is an island on which a small orchestra performs. Access is provided by an underground passage

Independence celebrations in 1984 (left) provided the deadline for the palace's completion; in fact, work was still continuing in 1986. The Islamic arches in the principal rooms are covered in gold. The palace is lit by 51,490 light bulbs and 564 chandeliers.

leading to stairs that emerge in the centre of the island. At the end of the promenade, stairs and escalators lead to the main public rooms, the throne room and the banqueting hall.

Architectural critics who were invited to see the palace on its opening were not altogether impressed. *Le Monde* suggested that its pomp was not always in the best of taste. The American magazine *House and Garden* re- marked that the rooms did indeed possess astounding glamour and exoticism, but that it was impossible not to be reminded of *The Wizard of Oz* when one looked at the door to the throne room, or of *The King and I* "as one slowly advances toward the gilded, wing-eaved canopy beneath which the Sultan and his Queen sit on state occasions". The most favourable account, inspired by the architect, appeared in the Ameri- can magazine *Connoisseur*, which accounted the building "a grand success". Yet this irritated the

Sultan, who issued a writ claiming that Locsin was in breach of his contract in talking about the palace to anybody.

It was perhaps as a result of these setbacks that the Sultan decided to build another palace in Brunei, for the use of his second wife, Queen Mariam, a former air hostess. This palace, the Istana Nurulizza, is a smaller, more intimate building, but it still cost $60 million to build and another $60 million to decorate. It includes a high-tech study for the Sultan, with a filing cabinet that descends from the ceiling at the touch of a button, automatically displaying the precise file the ruler has demanded. The couple's son, Prince Azim, had his own personal suite despite being only five years old at the time. It was as pretty as a fairytale, full of knights, castles, and little cottages lost in the forest. But in due course all this elaborate decoration was torn out to be replaced with something more adult.

The reception hall has a marble floor with bold geometric patterns in black. Italian marble of 38 different kinds covers a total of 14 acres inside the palace, while the outside is clad in travertine marble. The Privy Council Chamber is lined with Moroccan onyx, said to be from the very last block of this marble in the world.

The Biggest Church in the World

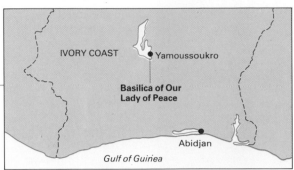

Fact file

The world's largest church, modelled on St Peter's, Rome

Creator: President Felix Houphouet-Boigny

Built: 1987–89

Materials: Marble, steel, concrete and glass

Height: 520 feet

Length: 632 feet

Seats: 7,000

The great cathedrals of Europe took whole lifetimes to build, generation after generation of medieval craftsmen working on buildings which they would never see completed. We live in a more impatient age. The biggest church in the world has recently been finished in just three years. What is more, it is not in Europe, close to the sources of marble, steel, concrete and stained glass from which it was built, but in the empty savannah of the Ivory Coast, miles from any-where. The Basilica of Our Lady of Peace is the grandest architectural gesture of the century, a declaration of faith that cost at least £100 million and that will stand as a beacon to the Christians of Africa—or, as others see it, as the ultimate folly of an old man with intimations of mortality.

The creator of Our Lady of Peace is President Felix Houphouet-Boigny, who as a child of ten had to travel miles to his baptism from his home village of Yamoussoukro, which had no Cath-olic church. Eighty years later, the basilica in Yamoussoukro is his response, a church modelled on the pattern of St Peter's in Rome. Tactfully, the basilica's dome is a fraction lower than St Peter's, but the crown and golden cross on top soar to 520 feet, which make it 70 feet higher than the original. It is 632 feet long (20 feet more than St Peter's) while its dome is three times as wide as the dome of St Paul's in London, and the whole of Notre-Dame in Paris would fit inside it several times over. The bronze canopy over the altar is as high as a nine-storey building.

Inside, the basilica has seating for 7,000 and standing room for another 11,000. Outside, the 7-acre marble slab on which it stands provides room for 320,000 more people to participate in services, although the day when that happens is likely to be a distant one. Yamoussoukro, a small town developed by Houphouet-Boigny as the Brasilia of the Ivory Coast, has no more than 30,000 inhabitants, and only about 4,000 of them are Roman Catholics. Abidjan, the capital around which most of the Ivory Coast's popula-tion lives, lies 160 miles away to the south—and it already has a modern Catholic cathedral. Even on important feast days, there seems to be little prospect of overcrowding at Our Lady of Peace.

The idea of the basilica occurred to Houph-ouet-Boigny in 1987. According to the senior engineer responsible for much of the work in Yamoussoukro, Pierre Cabrelli, the President decided that what he wanted to build next was a magnificent church. "I was amazed," Cabrelli told *The Times*. "Who today builds a basilica? Then I asked what was the deadline. The President said that the Pope comes to Africa every four years, that he had been here the year before, and so 'how much time do you have? You work it out'."

The basilica could not have been completed in the time available without modern methods of construction, or without the labour of up to 2,000 men who worked two 10-hour shifts a day. The engineers responsible came from abroad, but the workmen were locally recruited and developed an intense pride in what they had achieved. To criticisms that the basilica was a folly that a poor country such as the Ivory Coast could ill afford, one craftsman retorted: "When they built St Peter's, were there no hungry people in Rome? When England after the Great Fire built itself St Paul's, were there no poor and homeless in London?"

One of the great glories of the building is the dome; the lining of light blue stucco tiles is pierced with 29 million holes that act as a baffle for sound. At its very top are brilliant rings of light blue and dark blue stained glass, leading the eye to the very centre of the cupola, where it finds

Yamoussoukro's local inhabitants are the only people ever to have witnessed construction of so huge a basilica in so short a time; it was erected in just 3 years whereas St Paul's in London took 35 years and St Peter's in Rome 109. Only about 15 percent of the Ivory Coast's population is Roman Catholic; most cling to traditional animist cults.

a representation of a white dove of peace.

The basilica is not the only big building in Yamoussoukro. Houphouet-Boigny, or "Houph" as he is widely known, has transformed his sleepy home town with a vast presidential palace, a marble-fronted conference hall (which has so far housed a single conference), a five-star hotel with its own golf course, three universities and a hospital. The dusty road that leads from Abidjan has been converted into a six-lane highway as it approaches these splendours, most of which stand half-empty amid the encroaching African jungle. While the national university in Abidjan is seriously overcrowded, those in Yamoussoukro, designed in *grande-école* French style, are magnificently empty.

*The **completed basilica** awaiting consecration by Pope John Paul II on 10 September, 1990, when 150,000 attended the service. Over 7,000 dignatories were seated inside (above). The area of stained glass (left)— 80,000 square feet— eclipses any other ecclesiastical building. Over 4,000 shades of glass produce dramatic effects in the 10-storey high windows.*

The Biggest Church in the World

The 272 columns, using Corinthian, Doric and Ionic orders, reach up to 100 feet and were built of concrete to save time and money. Other elements of the building also use modern methods—the dome is of light grey anodized aluminium over polyurethane insulation. Modern techniques are employed to create a Renaissance structure.

Equipped with everything the student could desire, they teach only engineering and agriculture.

In many other countries, such fantastic spending would condemn Houphouet-Boigny as a megalomaniac intent on destroying his country in order to create a memorial to himself. But many of those who come to Yamoussoukro to mock find the criticisms dying in their throats. It is true that, according to figures from UNICEF, the money spent on the basilica might have been used to vaccinate the Ivory Coast's 10 million people against six diseases—diphtheria, measles, whooping cough, polio, tetanus and tuberculosis—which claim thousands of victims every year. Furthermore, the Ivory Coast faces economic catastrophe, with a debt of $8 billion on which payments have had to be suspended. But for some Houphouet-Boigny's own sincerity and the splendour of what has been achieved make such criticisms seem irrelevant.

Until 1980, Houphouet-Boigny had achieved remarkable things for his country, once a colony of France. While many newly independent nations in Africa had degenerated into tribal conflict and poverty, the Ivory Coast was a huge success. An economy based on cocoa, coffee and cotton had created wealth and stability. The regime, though dominated by a single man, was benign and liberal. Then the prices of raw materials began to decline, as the world turned away from chocolate. To pay the guaranteed prices to the cocoa growers, the Ivory Coast ran up the highest per capita debt in Africa. Instead of being able to present Yamoussoukro as the crowning glory of his success, Houphouet-Boigny was forced to defend it against harsh criticism, both internal and external.

He claimed that all the money it had cost had come from his own purse, a suggestion that provokes some chuckles but is not wholly impossible. He was already a rich man when he became president, and is said to have invested the family wealth skilfully. Taxed with the suspension of debt repayments in 1988, when the cost of the basilica was put at £80 million, he asked "How could my little £80 million help?" When criticisms came from France, he was exasperated: "How can a people who are proud of Versailles, of Notre-Dame, of Chartres, not understand?" he pleaded. The Ivorian Minister of Information, M. Laurent Dona Fologo, was less subtle. He called the criticism "racist" because, he said, critics obviously "cannot stand

to see Africans with something big, beautiful, and lasting".

In part to deflect criticism, in part to ensure it will survive him, Houphouet-Boigny offered the completed basilica to the Vatican, a gift which threw the civil servants of St Peter's into something of a tizzy. How could they turn down such a magnificent expression of the Catholic faith in a continent full of unbelievers? After three months' thought, and some negotiation, they accepted the gift but only on condition that the upkeep will be borne by the Ivory Coast. A special fund has been established by Houphouet-Boigny in the Vatican Bank from which will be drawn the £1.7 million a year the upkeep of the basilica is expected to cost. The Vatican is also believed to have extracted a promise from the President that he will increase spending on his people's health and education. In return,

Precast concrete was the main material used to build the basilica, the sections being erected by 6 cranes running on rails (left). Granite was imported from Spain, steel from Belgium, marble for the peristyle from Italy and glass from France.

The basilica's rotunda with the cupola ready to be placed on top of the dome. Although the dome itself is slightly lower than St Peter's, the cupola and golden cross make the overall height greater. At night the dome is lit by 1,810 1,000-watt lights.

Houphouet-Boigny persuaded the Pope to visit Yamoussoukro in January 1990 to inaugurate the basilica.

Whether the building is seen as a gigantic caprice or as a beacon for Africans depends on the eye of faith, and on what becomes of it after Houphouet-Boigny dies. When the cathedral was finished at the end of 1989 he was at least 84 (some say over 90) and had been president for 35 years. He was unwilling to discuss the question of his successor until the basilica was completed for fear that he might not survive to see it finished were he to reveal his intentions. Once his influence is gone, can the unkind climate of Africa be kept at bay? Will the faithless poor be prepared to sustain a dream in which they have no share? The history of Our Lady of Peace is likely to be just as interesting and unpredictable as the story of its construction.

A window frame about to be lifted into position above the portico. The air-conditioned basilica requires a maintenance staff of 25, of whom 8 do nothing but wash and polish the marble of the square and peristyle on which an open-air congregation would stand. Others spend all day polishing the 7,000 reddish-brown iroko hardwood pews.

World within a World

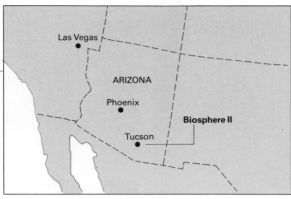

God created the Earth in six days, according to the Book of Genesis. In the desert 40 miles north of Tucson, Arizona, a team of scientists and visionaries is attempting to reproduce that feat. They are taking a little longer and may not get quite such a satisfactory result; but the project is testing techniques of building to the limit and if it works will provide a mass of information that may be useful in managing life on Earth, and in planning new settlements in space.

The project is called Biosphere II, and the object is to produce a completely sealed environment which will simulate the behaviour of the Earth. Within two huge glasshouses, an entire ecosystem will be created, providing all the food, water and air needed to keep alive eight people who will spend up to two years inside. Air, water and wastes will all be recycled, and natural weather patterns mimicked. Nothing will be allowed to enter or leave the sealed container, which consists of two linked space-frame structures covered in glass.

Inside one will be a five-storey building in which the experimenters will live, a tropical rainforest, a region of desert, an ocean complete with a coral reef and tides, a savannah region, and a selection of birds, reptiles, insects and small mammals. The other structure will be used for intensive agriculture. In all, some 3,800 plant and animal species will inhabit Biosphere II, whose name reflects the fact that it is not the first experiment of this kind. Biosphere I is the Earth, that abused but still functioning planet the Arizona pioneers are seeking to mimic.

Building such a revolutionary structure has created considerable problems. One of the most difficult is ensuring that the inside is completely isolated from the outside. A normal well-sealed building exchanges its air completely one to three times every day. Biosphere II is designed to exchange all the air within it only once in its entire lifetime, which is set at 100 years. "No matter how you define airtight, that is still an awesome specification," says Peter Pearce, president of Pearce Structures Inc, a California firm that won the contract to design and build the space frame. It is the first time that any builder has ever attempted to achieve such a result. Pearce says that it is more like building a space shuttle than a building.

On top of the concrete foundations a thin stainless-steel liner has been inserted, rising at the edges to form a seal to the glass walls of the building. The basic structure consists of ribs of steel, linked together in a novel way and with the panes of glass sealed directly to the steel with a silicone material. The design was produced by Pearce in four months, after scientists had realized that no existing glazing system was capable of doing the job.

The structural principle that lies behind it is the space frame, a very strong and flexible building system based on attaching steel tubes together in triangular shapes. Space frames are inherently stronger than traditional structures, use less material, and can be built in many different shapes. One of the two structures in Biosphere II—the agricultural space—consists of a series of circular vaults, while the other is pyramidal in form.

The organization behind the project is called Space Biosphere Ventures, whose Chief Executive Officer is Margaret Augustine; and it has been funded by Edward Bass, a Texan who has invested $30 million to get Biosphere II built. When finished, Biosphere II will cover an area of 3.1 acres, rise to 85 feet at its highest point, and enclose a volume of 7 million cubic feet of air. In addition to the apartments for the eight researchers, it will incorporate laboratories, computer and communications facilities, workshops, libraries and recreation

facilities. The "biospherians", as they call themselves, will not be cut off totally from the outside world; they will be able to watch TV, listen to the radio, or talk to colleagues outside by telephone.

The eight biospherians are hoping to enter the sealed environment in September 1990, if the builders have finished it by then. Once inside, they will breathe oxygen created by the plants around them. Water will evaporate and form "clouds" inside the glass, rising to the highest point in the building where cooling coils will condense it back into water. Then it will flow down the 50-foot high mountain an through a miniature rainforest into an artificial ocean, which is 35 feet deep, and from which evaporation will occur. The only thing that will come from outside is energy, and information.

The Sun will supply much of the energy, but electricity will also be fed in to run various mechanical systems, including the artificial wave-maker which is necessary if coral is to grow in the ocean. The heat of the Sun will be controlled by louvres that can open and close. Botanists are hoping that the steel parts of the space frame, which cut out some light, will not prevent plants from growing normally.

Most of the food eaten by the inhabitants of Biosphere II will come from intensive farming techniques developed at the University of Arizona. A total of 140 different crops will be grown, with waste products recycled to provide nutrients. Vegetables, including cucumbers, tomatoes, lettuce and broccoli, fruits such as

The unique outlines and space frames of Biosphere II were influenced by Buckminster Fuller, whose work is admired by the designer of the frame, Peter Pearce. The various "biomes" will replicate rainforest, tropical savannah, salt- and fresh-water marsh, desert, ocean and a thorn-scrub forest, as well as intensive agriculture.

World within a World

The aquaculture bay (below) provides the surroundings for lunch. The "biospherians" will eat some of the fruit and fish that the biosphere will provide. Milk will be produced by African pygmy goats and chickens will supply eggs and meat.

Hydroponic tomatoes: the root systems are kept in darkness and draw their nourishment from water impregnated with nutrients. About 20,000 square feet will be devoted to intensive agriculture. Produce from the greenhouse is sold to cover costs.

papaya, bananas and strawberries, and cereal crops such as wheat, barley and rice can all be grown in this way. Fertilizer will be provided from the waste products of the fish grown in the fish farm. The builders have been obliged to avoid using any curing agents in the concrete foundations, for fear that it would migrate into the soil and poison the occupants, or at least interfere with their experiments.

Biosphere II is not the first attempt at survival in a totally enclosed system. Inhabitants of spacecraft face similar problems, and experiments have been carried out on the ground in the Soviet Union since the 1960s. Large bottles containing sealed gardens are a simple example of the principle, and one of those, at the University of Hawaii, has been functioning

successfully without human intervention for 20 years. SBV have done their own experiments, in a much smaller test module designed to test the principles.

In March 1989 a marine biologist, Abigail Alling, emerged unharmed after five days inside the module, which SBV claims is the longest time any human being has ever occupied a completely sealed ecological system. The object of the experiment was to test the systems for controlling the accumulation of toxic gases. Some of the Soviet experiments had to be terminated when toxic gases such as sulphur dioxide, nitrogen dioxide, ammonia, carbon monoxide, ozone and hydrogen sulphide increased to a dangerous level. In Biosphere II, such gases will be controlled by forcing the air through soil con-

The aquaculture bay will generate some food for the biospherians, but it will also provide nutrients for crops in soil beds irrigated by fish water. These nutrients result from the excretion of ammonia in fish wastes; the naturally present bacteria in the biofilter tank convert this to nitrates which are used to fertilize crops.

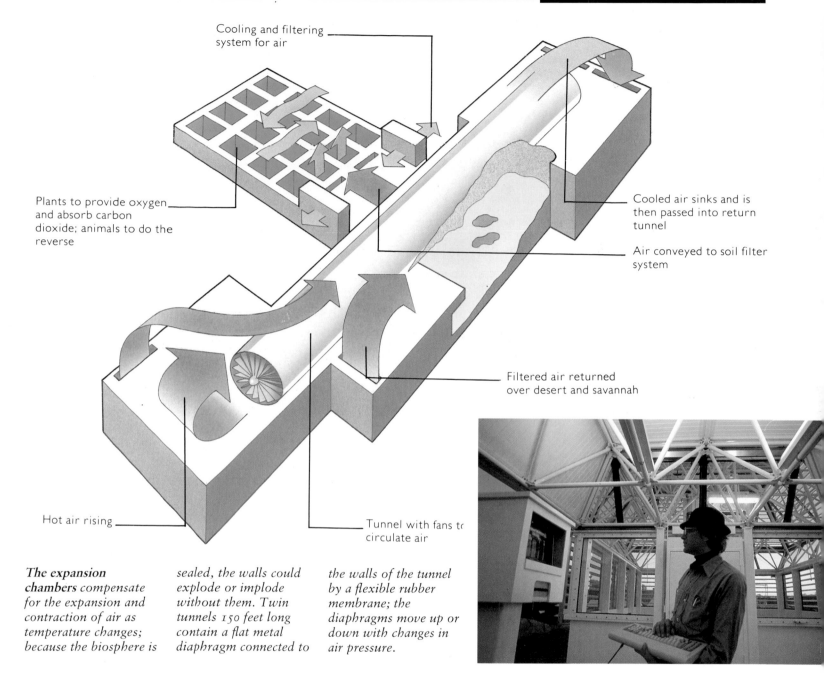

Cooling and filtering system for air

Plants to provide oxygen and absorb carbon dioxide; animals to do the reverse

Cooled air sinks and is then passed into return tunnel

Air conveyed to soil filter system

Filtered air returned over desert and savannah

Hot air rising

Tunnel with fans to circulate air

The expansion chambers compensate for the expansion and contraction of air as temperature changes; because the biosphere is sealed, *the walls could explode or implode without them. Twin tunnels 150 feet long contain a flat metal diaphragm connected to* *the walls of the tunnel by a flexible rubber membrane; the diaphragms move up or down with changes in air pressure.*

A test module for the biosphere, of 17,000 cubic feet, was built to test materials, techniques and the computer monitoring systems. By using it to test the closed-system dynamics of ecosystems that will be replicated in the biosphere, many potential problems were overcome. Each series of experiments was for a 3-month period.

taining microbes which should convert the toxic gases into harmless chemicals.

The air inside the enclosure will be circulated mechanically, since it is impossible to simulate the movements of the atmosphere on such a small scale. A set of 3,500 sensors have been installed to measure the conditions and to control the rate of air circulation. Monitors have also been installed to ensure that the building really is as leak tight as it is supposed to be.

The experiment has at least two purposes. One is to try to understand better how the Earth itself functions, what are the critical parameters, and how it might be better managed. A second is to lay the ground rules for constructing habitable colonies in space. If such colonies are to function successfully, they will need to be self-supporting,

since transporting food and fuel from Earth will be far too expensive. That would be like expecting the colonists who settled in the New World in the seventeenth century to be supplied for ever by convoys of vessels crossing the Atlantic from Europe.

The whole concept of Biosphere II is futuristic. And since it is not the kind of thing many official research organizations would dare to finance it needed the patronage of a philanthropist to get it started. But many respectable scientists have been consulted, and take the idea seriously. One of them, Carl Hodges, Director of the Environmental Research Laboratory at the University of Arizona, admits it may not work. "We could get the balance wrong," he says. "It's a big step, but big steps are the most fun."

CHAPTER THREE

Feats of Civil Engineering

Human mastery over nature is measured by the achievements of civil engineers, the men (and increasingly women as well) who bridge rivers, dam lakes, build roads and railways, dig canals and erect coastal defences to defeat the power of the sea. Once finished their works are easily taken for granted, unless they should fail, when the air is loud with lamentation. For unlike other forms of engineering the work of civil engineers is expected to last for ever, a permanent modification of the natural world. They must work for posterity as well as for their clients.

Some civil engineering works are so huge and permanent that they even outlast the purposes that gave rise to them. The Great Wall of China, perhaps the most remarkable construction in the history of civilization, still leaps from crag to crag across the immensity of that country, although the threat it was meant to counter has long disappeared. The Panama Canal altered geography permanently, even if ships should one day cease to use it. A desert in the state of Washington, arid and uncultivable since man first discovered it, was turned into productive farmland by the Grand Coulee Dam. And the coastline of the Netherlands has been remodelled radically—and, the Dutch hope, permanently—by the Delta Plan, one of the greatest but least heralded feats of civil engineering this century.

Civil engineering can also change perceptions. The nation of Canada might not have survived at all but for the long ribbon of steel, in the form of the Canadian Pacific Railway, that stitched it together. The dream of capitalizing on the riches of Siberia would have remained even more remote without the Trans-Siberian and BAM railways. And the concept of a united Europe would seem less realistic but for the railways and roads that tunnel beneath the barrier of the Alps, linking Germany and Switzerland to Italy.

As the world's reserves of fossil fuels diminish, the search for alternative sources of energy is bound to accelerate, with schemes like the Orkney turbine to exploit wind power, and the solar oven in France to harness the power of the Sun.

The tasks of civil engineering, for all their permanence, are never complete. As one great project ends, another, even more ambitious, swims into view, made possible by improving techniques. Since the very first roads and bridges were built, humans have pursued a desire to adapt and utilize nature, and there is no sign we will ever desist.

Feats of Civil Engineering
Great Wall of China
Panama Canal
Canals across the world
Canadian Pacific Railway
Trans-Siberian Railway
Grand Coulee Dam
Dams: harnessing the power of water
Dutch Delta Plan
St Gotthard Pass
The world's greatest highways
Ironbridge
Humber Bridge
Bridges of distinction
Statfjord B Oil Platform
Orkney Wind Generator
CHOOZ-B Power Station
Odeillo Solar Oven

The Longest Bastion

Fact file

Described as the greatest construction enterprise ever undertaken, the Great Wall took 20 centuries to complete and refine

Original builder: Qin Shi Huangdi

Built: 3rd century BC–17th century AD

Materials: Earth, stone, timber and bricks

Length: 2,150 miles

Qin Shi Huangdi (221–210 BC), the first emperor of China, who began the Great Wall. Though his reign was brief, Qin established the political form by which China was to be ruled until 1911. He is best known for the army of terracotta horses and warriors found near his tomb in Xi'an.

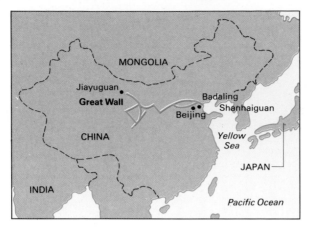

The greatest construction project ever carried out by man stretches 2,150 miles across China along a twisting, curving course that has been compared to the body of a dragon. Created over a period of more than 1,800 years by millions of soldiers and workmen, the Great Wall of China runs from the Yellow Sea near Beijing to the Jade Gate at Jiayuguan, which marked the outer limits of Chinese influence and the beginning of the Central Asian wilderness. The wall formed the boundary between Chinese civilization and the barbarians lying to the north, the point at which the spread of Chinese culture finally petered out in the mountains and deserts where nomads eked out a precarious existence. The Great Wall thus represents "the most colossal tide-mark of the human race" in the words of the American scholar Owen Lattimore.

The wall was begun in the reign of the First Emperor, Qin Shi Huangdi, who waged a war of conquest and finally united China in 221 BC. Before that, as early as the fifth century BC, there had been smaller walls built by local rulers, many of which were destroyed by Qin. He established a ruthless and efficient empire, with a system of criminal justice, a network of new roads, and a bureaucracy that controlled where people lived and how far they could move. Criminals were treated harshly, while those unwilling to work were drafted into the army and despatched to the farther corners of the empire. It was these people who were the first builders of what we now call the Great Wall.

According to contemporary history books, Qin sent his top general, Meng Tian, at the head of an army of 300,000 men to put down the barbarians in the north and to build a wall following the terrain, using natural obstacles and passes to form an impenetrable barrier.

The wall we see today is, however, mostly of much later construction, dating from the Ming dynasty (1368–1644). Its purpose was the same as that of Qin's—to prevent invasions from the north and mark in an unambiguous way the borders of the empire. The best-preserved section of the Ming dynasty wall lies between Beijing and the sea, a 400-mile stretch of masonry running eastward along the high ridges of the Yanshan mountains to Shanhaiguan.

In between these two periods, other rulers of China also set their stamp on the wall, putting millions of unwilling labourers to work on different sections. Qin Shi Huangdi used his army, plus half a million peasants, to create his wall. More than 600 years later, in AD 446, Taiping Zhenjun called up 300,000 labourers to build another section, while in AD 555 Tian Bao press-ganged 1.8 million peasants for work.

There were periods when interest in the wall declined; the Tang dynasty, which began in AD 618, considered attack the best line of defence, and created a strong army rather than reinforce the wall. But when the Mings took over, the wall regained its priority in the scheme of things. The wall we see today is thus the product of millions of men, but a single idea.

The materials used include earth, stone, timber, tiles and, during the Ming dynasty, bricks. Because transportation was difficult, local ones were employed: stones in the high mountains; earth on the plains; sand, pebbles and tamarisk twigs in the Gobi Desert; oak, pine and fir from forests around Liaodong in the north east. Many of these materials made an impermanent wall; thus it is the stone and later brick-and-tile sections that have survived. During the Ming dynasty, kilns were built on the spot to create the bricks and tiles, as well as the lime used to bind them together.

The building materials were carried by human effort, on a man's back or on carrying poles. Sometimes the labourers formed a human chain, passing the stones or bricks from hand to hand up the mountain side. Handcarts were also used, and large rocks were hauled with windlasses or moved with levers. Donkeys carried baskets loaded with bricks and mortar, while goats are also said to have been pressed into service, the bricks tied to their horns.

The earthen walls of the Qin dynasty were made by erecting shuttering in the forms of posts and boards along the line of construction, and then filling the space between with soil. Layers of earth 3–4 inches thick were laid and then

The Longest Bastion

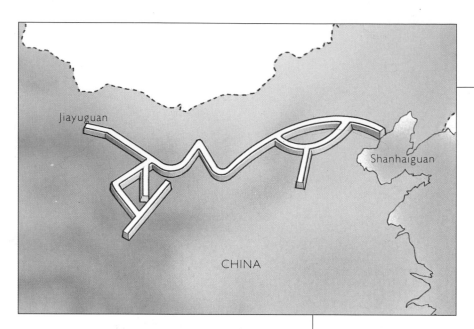

Jiayuguan

Shanhaiguan

CHINA

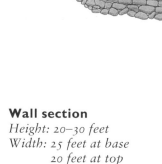

Watchtower

hammered solid with mallets before laying subsequent layers. Similar methods were used in the Ming period, except that each successive layer was deeper—by 8 inches or so. This technique was well developed in China, since it was often used for building the walls of houses.

Masonry sections were built by first levelling the ground and laying a series of courses of stone slabs to form the foundation. The faces of the wall were then constructed from stone, and the gap between them filled with small stones, rubble, lime and earth. Once the wall was tall enough, the top was made in the form of layers of brick, either laid on a slant for gentle inclines or in the form of a staircase if the slope was more than 45 degrees.

One of the most astonishing features of the Great Wall is the way it makes use of the defensive qualities of the ground, often striking out along a ridge, only to curve back on itself to follow the natural features and dominate the high ground. At key points forts and towers were built from which to survey the land commanded by the wall. These points naturally tended to be the places where the enemy would seek to attack—mountain passes, road junctions, or bends in a river on flat land. As an encyclopedia written during the Tang dynasty puts it: "Beacon towers must be built at crucial points of high mountains or at turning points on flat land."

Although the function of the wall was defensive and utilitarian, many of its details were designed with a real sense of style. Towers, gates and forts were often beautifully detailed, in a wide variety of architectural styles. There were

The route of the wall is not a single line, since it incorporates a series of walls built by successive rulers. The early walls were rudimentary and had to be rebuilt.

The wall clings to the ridges as it snakes over the mountains. Wherever the gradient was less than 45 degrees, bricks lining the walkway followed the contour of the wall; where it exceeded that angle, steps were created.

Wall section
Height: 20–30 feet
Width: 25 feet at base
20 feet at top

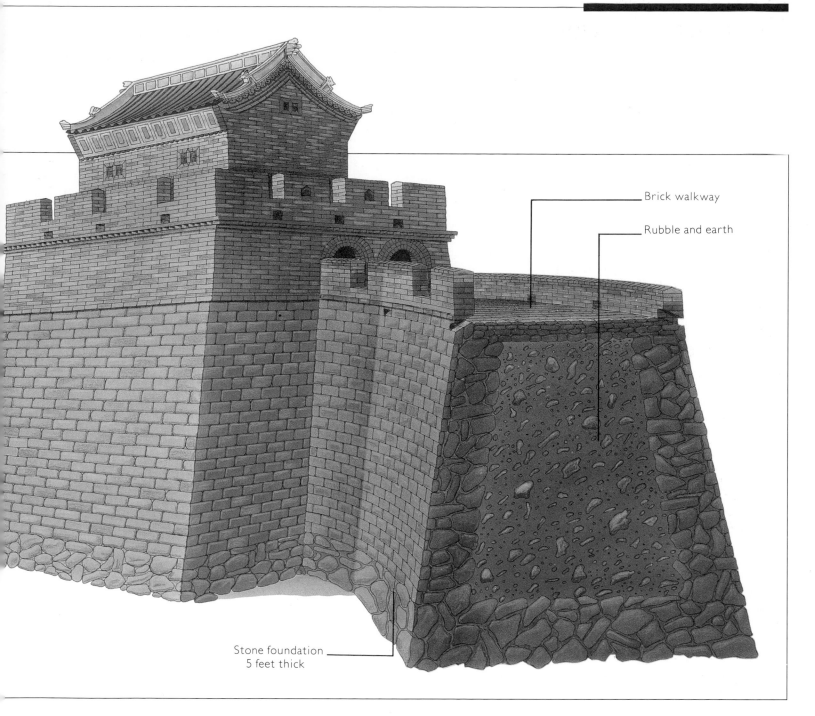

Brick walkway

Rubble and earth

Stone foundation
5 feet thick

Watchtowers

Generally 40 feet square in plan and up to 40 feet high, watchtowers are estimated to number about 25,000. Beacon towers, placed at a maximum distance of 11 miles, used wolves' dung, sulphur and nitrate to produce a column of smoke to indicate to adjacent towers the strength of an attack. At night dry timber was used.

also temple buildings and shrines along the wall, as well as tea-houses and clock towers.

The wall itself stood about 22–26 feet high, and equally broad at its base, narrowing to about 16 feet at the top. (These measurements apply to the best-preserved section of the wall, near Beijing, which dates from the Ming period.) Every 200 yards or so, an archway on the Chinese side of the wall gave access to a staircase leading to the top of the wall; the top served as a pathway as well as a line of defence, enabling troops to move swiftly, ten abreast, along its length to reinforce a garrison under attack.

On the inner edge was a 3-foot parapet to reduce the risk of falling off, and battlements up

to 6 feet high provided protection on the outer edge. Every 100–200 yards was a projecting platform, forming a buttress to strengthen the wall, and a place from which soldiers could bring fire to bear on enemies trying to climb the sides of the wall.

At similar distances were placed ramparts, two- to three-storey buildings in which the soldiers lived. About 30–40 feet high and 120–180 feet square, the ramparts were topped by an area from which cannons could be fired. Each rampart was garrisoned by between 30 and 50 soldiers under the command of a petty officer.

When an attack came, the soldiers used a well-established system of signals for indicating its

The Longest Bastion

general in command. When an attack came, all nine were brought under the command of the Minister of War. Each military zone had its headquarters in a city along the wall, or in an important fort, in close communication with the capital. At its peak, the system worked well.

To the Ming dynasty, the wall was all that stood between them and the Mongol hordes, who had begun the creation of their empire under Genghis Khan at the beginning of the thirteenth century. Despite the Mongols' small numbers and modest army of only 250,000 men, their ferocity enabled them to breach the Great Wall and conquer China. By the end of the thirteenth century their empire stretched in a great swathe across Asia and Europe, from Korea to Poland and Hungary in the north, and from south China to Turkey in the south.

The great emperor Kublai Khan, grandson of Genghis, emerged as emperor in 1260, ruling China with considerable skill. After his death, however, Mongol dominance began to crumble, until the Mongols were finally thrown back behind what remained of the wall and Zhu Yuanzhang established the Ming dynasty.

Given this background, it is hardly surprising that particular attention was paid to reinforcing the wall as the only way of preventing another successful assault from the Mongols. Zhu sent his nine sons north to head the nine garrisons defending the wall, and more and more fortifications were built. Building continued throughout the entire Ming dynasty, and the bulk of the wall as we know it today was created during that period, between 1368 and 1644.

A wall so prodigious as that built by the Chinese could not fail to charm Europeans, once they became aware of it. Dr Johnson was especially enthusiastic, and would have liked to have visited the wall himself. One day James Boswell, his biographer, remarked to Johnson that he too would like to visit the wall if he did not have his children to look after. In a famous retort, Johnson remarked: "Sir, by doing so, you would do what would be of importance in raising your children to eminence. There would be a lustre reflected on them from your spirit and curiosity. They would at all times be regarded as the children of a man who had gone to view the Great Wall of China. I am serious, Sir."

In 1909 the American writer William Edgar Geil became one of the first westerners to follow the entire course of the wall, and became immensely enthusiastic. He claimed that the

importance. One beacon fire and one salvo meant between 2 and 100 enemy; two beacon fires and two salvos meant up to 500, and so on, up to five fires and five salvos, which meant an attack by more than 10,000 enemy troops.

In times of peace, the soldiers grew their own food on land close to the wall, so as to remain self-supporting. They kept guard, and monitored the movement of merchants crossing the wall with goods for sale. The upkeep of the wall was their responsibility, and they were given strict instructions about how to maintain it. Their weapons included gunpowder, invented during the Ming dynasty, which was used for various types of grenade. Real artillery was not then available, or it would have proved much more difficult to defend the wall, but the siege crossbow and a version of the Roman catapult were used for firing large projectiles over considerable distances. Swords, spears and cudgels were effective in close combat, and mounted cavalry were also employed.

The length of the wall, claimed during the Ming period as 10,000 li (4,000 miles), was divided up into nine military zones, each with a

The Great Wall was seen by the Chinese as a dragon with its head drinking from the Bo Hai Sea at Shanhaiguan (above). The head is a section 76 feet long which protrudes into the sea, and was damaged by a British force invading in 1900 to quell the Boxer uprising. The gate at the first fort is known as "The First Pass Under Heaven".

The wall at Gubeikou in Hebei Province, where a military unit was set up under the Ming dynasty to guard a dozen passes, of which the most important was Gubeikou itself. It was here that the first British Ambassador to China first saw the wall, in 1793.

The unrestored sections of the wall vary in dilapidation from ridges of earth to stone sections that require little restoration. This example of unrestored wall is adjacent to the restored section visited by tourists at Badaling, east of Beijing.

builders of the wall had been ahead of the senseless militarism of Europe. In the 1980s, more than four million people every year have followed Geil's footsteps, though few have ventured further than the well-preserved section of wall within an easy coach trip from Beijing. One who did was William Lindsay, a university research worker from Merseyside, England, who was hailed by the New China News Agency in 1987 as the first foreigner to run unescorted and alone along 1,500 miles of the Great Wall. The journey, a combination of running, walking and limping, took 78 days, with a four-month break in the middle.

During the twentieth century, the Chinese have lacked the resources to maintain the wall in the manner it merits. Some short stretches are magnificent, but other parts, out of reach of tourists, have been allowed to decay. The wall today no longer has any defensive role, though Chinese troops used it as a highway in the war against the Japanese. But it remains one of the wonders of the world, a work of man on the scale of nature, an astonishing example of human strength, ingenuity and endurance.

Joining the Oceans

Fact file

The world's largest and most costly engineering project when built

Engineers: de Lesseps, John Stevens, George W. Goethals

Built: 1881–89, 1904–14

Length: 51 miles 352 yards

The building of a canal to link the Atlantic and the Pacific was the largest and most expensive engineering project ever undertaken. It took more than 40 years from its conception to the first transit by an ocean-going ship. It employed tens of thousands of men and broke new ground in engineering, planning, medicine and labour relations. It was the final fling of nineteenth-century European optimism—and the first evidence that the United States had become a great power. It changed geography, dividing a continent to unite the oceans and even helped to create a new nation, Panama.

The story began in 1870, when two ships of the US Navy were despatched to the Isthmus of Darien, the narrow neck of land joining the Americas, to establish where a canal might be dug. The objective was clear: from New York to San Francisco around Cape Horn was a journey of 13,000 miles, taking a month to complete. Through a canal it would be only 5,000 miles. Yet the difficulties of cutting a canal through this narrow strip of land—only 30 miles across at its narrowest point—could hardly be overestimated. Driving a railway across it in the 1850s had taken five years and cost six times the estimate. Thousands had died of cholera, dysentery, yellow fever and smallpox.

However, before further action was taken by the US, a group of French financiers obtained a concession to construct a canal from Colon to Panama. Their choice of engineer was Ferdinand de Lesseps, a French diplomat and politician who had made his name building the Suez Canal. He arrived in Panama City in 1880 and after a cursory survey decided to build a canal along the Chagres River and the Rio Grande, linking the Atlantic and Pacific at sea level and following closely the line of the railway. No sooner had work begun than people began to die. Panama was a hell-hole, one of the unhealthiest places on earth: mosquitoes bred in millions in swamps and pools of water; proper drainage did not exist; and the medical knowledge of the French

pioneers was simply inadequate. One of those who laboured on the canal was the French painter Paul Gauguin, who arrived in 1887 full of dreams of buying land and living for nothing on fruit and fish. He hated the place, and the people. As soon as he had made enough money, Gauguin left for Martinique.

In 1889 de Lesseps' company crashed, his dream of a canal at sea level having proved impracticable. Failure was followed by scandal: Ferdinand de Lesseps was accused of corruption, and the collapse of the company became a French *affaire* in which governments fell and reputations were ruined. A total of $287 million had been spent—far more, at the time, than had ever been spent on any peacetime operation—at least 20,000 had died, and just 19 miles of canal had been dug. It was a deep and humiliating failure for France.

By the turn of the century, however, the United States had regained enthusiasm for the canal, and opened negotiations with the Government of Colombia, of which Panama was then a department. The Colombians rejected a proposed treaty but, with tacit encouragement from President Theodore Roosevelt, a group of Panamanians declared themselves independent. Within two days, their government was recognized by Washington. For the sum of $10 million, plus $250,000 a year from 1913 onwards, Roosevelt won agreement from the new government to dig the canal.

The first task, without which all else would fail, was to control disease in Panama. An Army doctor, Colonel William Gorgas, was appointed to take charge of the hospitals and sanitary arrangements. It was an inspired appointment, for Gorgas had already been largely responsible for eliminating yellow fever in Cuba, by controlling the mosquito *Stegomyia fasciata*. By eliminating both this and the *Anopheles* mosquito, responsible for malaria, Gorgas transformed the prospects for success in Panama.

But there was still a canal to be dug. Unlike de

Gatún Lake, bisected by the canal channel, was created by a dam and sets of locks at each end and forms the central part of the canal. The most formidable challenge to the builders was Culebra Cut (right), now called the Gaillard Cut. Every day 60 steam shovels filled trains with spoil; often they were engulfed by the collapse of the channel walls, which became a more frequent occurrence from 1911 as the cut grew deeper.

Lesseps, the American engineers made no attempt to build a canal at sea level. Instead, they designed a series of locks to carry the ships up and down, a far more practical scheme. But the amount of digging to be done was still prodigious. The toughest section of all was the Culebra (now Gaillard) Cut, an 8-mile stretch between Bas Obispo and Pedro Miguel. Here a man-made canyon was created through a mountain, driven by steam shovels, explosives and a workforce of 6,000 men. It took seven years and 61 million pounds of dynamite, more explosive energy than had been expended in all the wars the US had ever fought. The noise was tremendous, the dangers enormous, the loss of life barely calculable.

The trouble was the instability of the rock. As it was removed from the sides of the cut, the

Joining the Oceans

Ships pass from the Caribbean Sea to the Pacific Ocean in an easterly direction.

Larger vessels have reduced clearance within the locks. There are 3 pairs of locks at Gatún, and at the other end of the lake, 1 at Pedro Miguel and 2 at Miraflores.

Electric locomotives at each lock act as land tugs, hauling ships through, using a powered windlass and 800 feet of steel cable, with the smoothness of a piston through a cylinder.

A cross-section through the canal illustrates the rise of the canal to Lake Gatún, whose surface level ranges from 82 to 87 feet above sea level. The surface of Miraflores Lake is at 54 feet above sea level.

Gatun Locks

Caribbean Sea

Colon

Gatun Locks

Gatun Dam

Gatun Lake

PANAMA CANAL

Gatun Lake

Panama Railroad

Can

Gaill

Pan American Highway

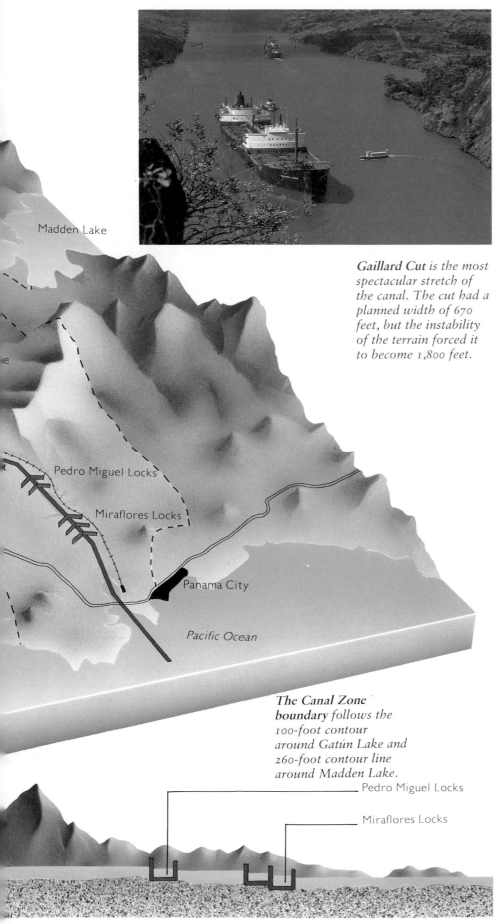

Gaillard Cut *is the most spectacular stretch of the canal. The cut had a planned width of 670 feet, but the instability of the terrain forced it to become 1,800 feet.*

Madden Lake

Pedro Miguel Locks

Miraflores Locks

Panama City

Pacific Ocean

The Canal Zone boundary *follows the 100-foot contour around Gatún Lake and 260-foot contour line around Madden Lake.*

Pedro Miguel Locks

Miraflores Locks

walls literally began to bulge as pressure drove them outward. The same effect even caused the floor of the cut to rise, sometimes astonishingly fast, by 15 to 20 feet. It was disheartening indeed. Everything was tried to stop the falls, including plastering the walls with concrete, but all failed. The concrete crumbled and fell, together with the rock. The only way was to reduce the slope of the walls until stability was achieved, and that meant the intended narrow defile becoming a saucer-shaped depression.

The great chain of locks at each end of the canal, the biggest such structures ever built, were another source of wonder. Stood on end, these locks would tower above most buildings in Manhattan today, except for the Empire State, the World Trade Center and a few others. Yet they are not simply buildings, but machines which work as smoothly as a sewing-machine. It took four years to build them, beginning in August 1909. They were built in pairs, to take two lines of traffic at once.

The locks are made of concrete, poured into huge wooden forms. The floor of each chamber was 13 to 20 feet thick, while the walls were as much as 50 feet thick at floor level, narrowing in a series of steps on the outside to only 8 feet at the top. The total quantity of concrete poured to make all 12 chambers was 4.4 million cubic yards. The concrete remains in perfect condition.

The walls of each chamber are not solid, but threaded with huge passageways through which water runs to fill and empty the chambers. The water comes from Gatún Lake and Miraflores Lake and is fed into the bottom of each set of chambers, where it flows through 70 holes to lift the ships smoothly and gently. A similar set of holes is used to drain the chambers, lowering ships if they are moving in the other direction. The flow of water is controlled by sliding steel gates, running on roller bearings, which can be raised and lowered across the culverts.

At the end of each chamber are huge gates, each weighing hundreds of tons. Made of steel plate riveted to a backbone of steel girders, they swing together to form a flattened "V". They were designed to float, so that in use they would exert the least possible force on their hinges. Each leaf is 65 feet wide and 7 feet thick, but their height varies with their position. The largest, at Miraflores, are 82 feet high and weigh 745 tons.

The life-blood of any canal with locks is water. Because Panama is a country with ample rainfall, until recently there seemed no danger

Joining the Oceans

that the canal would run dry. However, the lakes rely on the surrounding rain forest for replenishment of the water lost to the sea each time a ship passes through the canal. Extensive felling of the forest has reduced the flow of water into the lakes by destroying the rain forest's ability to act as a giant sponge; there is now serious concern that a shortage of water will jeopardize the canal's future operation.

The flow of water over the spillway at Gatún is used to generate electricity, which in turn powers everything else on the canal—the valves, the lock gates, and the small, specially designed locomotives which travel along tracks laid at the top of the lock chambers, towing the ships through. No ship was to travel through the locks under its own power, for fear that it would get out of control and smash through the safety chains and into the lock gates.

Everything, except the operation of the locomotives, was designed to be under the control of one man and a single control panel. On this panel are depicted all the functions of the locks—the gates, the valves, the water levels, and next to each is a simple control switch. Switches can only be moved in the correct order, so that it is impossible, for instance, to try to open the lock gates against a head of water.

The control panels have ensured that the canal has worked like clockwork since the day the first ship went through it. That took place on 7 January 1914, with little ceremony, when an old French crane boat, the *Alexandre la Valley*, made the first complete transit through the canal. On 3 August the *Christobal*, a cement boat, became the first ocean-going ship to travel from ocean to ocean, and the *Ancon* was the first passenger ship to cross, on 15 August. But the Culebra Cut still had problems to present, and in October a huge collapse blocked the entire canal. There were further falls in 1915, and dredging has continued to this day.

Ten years after it opened, more than 5,000 ships a year were passing through the canal, and by 1939 the number reached 7,000. After World War II it doubled, and hit a peak of about 15,000 ships a year in the early 1970s. The greatest toll ever paid by a ship was $42,077.88 by the *Queen Elizabeth II* in March 1975; the smallest, 36 cents, by Richard Halliburton, who swam through the canal one day at a time in the 1920s. He even persuaded the authorities to let him swim through the locks, and, like any other vessel, paid a toll based on his weight.

Creators of the Panama Canal

An enterprise on the scale of the Panama Canal requires men of rare calibre to see it through to success. Four such men became involved with its construction.

President Theodore Roosevelt

If a single person were to be credited with the creation of the Panama Canal, it would be Roosevelt. His ambition was to make the United States a global force, the "dominant power on the shores of the Pacific Ocean". As Secretary to the Navy, Governor of New York, and later President, Roosevelt campaigned vigorously for the canal, though for many years he believed that it should go through Nicaragua, not Panama. As President he connived in the creation of Panama, then overrode the wishes of Congress by giving supreme powers over the construction of the canal to one man, George Goethals.

Although three presidents were involved in the creation of the canal—Roosevelt, Taft and Wilson—it was Roosevelt who made the idea of it inspiring and inevitable. "The real builder of the Panama Canal was Theodore Roosevelt" according to Goethals. It could not have been more his own creation "if he had personally lifted every shovelful".

The gates at Gatún Locks during construction.

John Frank Stevens

Stevens was an engineer with an extraordinary record of success in constructing railways when Roosevelt appointed him to build the canal in 1905. In 1886 he had built a railway line 400 miles long through swamp and pine in upper Michigan, surviving disease, attacks by Indians and wolves, and the bitter cold of the North American winter.

When appointed to build the canal, Stevens inherited a mess; a year had passed, $128 million had been spent, but little achieved. There was still no plan, and no organization. Materials delivered to Panama were piled in heaps, and engineers were leaving as quickly as they could find passage on ships. Food was in short supply, disease rampant, and morale low.

Stevens stopped the work, and started to plan: he gave full support to proper sanitation, and reorganized the railways, essential to take away the spoil; he built a cold storage plant to provide decent food; he provided houses for his engineers and told them to send for their wives and families; and he built baseball fields and clubhouses, arranged concerts and created a healthy community.

Stevens lobbied hard for a canal with locks, and finally got his way. In 1906, he welcomed Roosevelt to the canal—a visit that swayed American opinion. Then, in February 1907, he wrote a long letter to Roosevelt complaining of exhaustion, of being constantly criticized, and describing the canal as "only a big ditch" whose utility had never been apparent to him. He asked Roosevelt for a rest, but the President took the letter as a resignation, and accepted it at once.

George Washington Goethals

Stevens' successor was George Goethals, a Lieutenant-Colonel in the Corps of Engineers. Roosevelt appointed him to chair the commission of seven which Congress had insisted be appointed, but made it clear that he was the boss.

When Goethals had examined the works in the company of Stevens, he paid tribute to Stevens's work: "there is nothing left for us to do but just . . . continue in the good work".

Goethals was a stiff, hard-working man who had few relaxations. He was tough, energetic, and not greatly loved, but he was a good picker of men and a good delegator. Every Sunday morning, between 7.30 and noon, any employee with a grievance or a complaint could come and see him. Goethals' Sunday morning sessions, in which he played a combination of father confessor and judge, were a totally new innovation in labour relations. They won him the support of the workforce, without which the canal could not have been built.

Goethals was indomitable. When the walls of the Culebra Cut collapsed yet again, destroying months of work, Goethals hurried to the spot. "What do we do now?" he was asked. "Hell, dig it out again", replied Goethals. So they did, and went on doing until the canal was finally completed.

Dr William C. Gorgas

All the work of the engineers would have been to no avail without the work of Dr Gorgas, the man who brought the endemic diseases of Panama under control.

With the enthusiastic support of Stevens and Roosevelt, Gorgas eliminated mosquitoes, which he believed to be the carriers of the diseases. It might not have worked; knowledge was scanty, and Gorgas's opponents said that money was being wasted. But he was right. Within 18 months of his arrival, yellow fever was eradicated, and malaria was also coming under control.

Gorgas also had proper pavements and drains laid, hospitals built and sanitation provided. The country that had been the graveyard of De Lesseps' hopes was rendered tolerably healthy, in one of the most remarkable feats of public health ever accomplished.

Canals across the World

Credit for the first canal appears to rest with the Chinese, though there is evidence of a form of canal dating from about 4000 BC in Iraq; certainly the oldest recorded and still working waterway made by human hand is the Grand Canal linking Tianjin and Hangzhou, which was built between 485 BC and AD 283. It was also in China that the first pound lock was built, using two sets of gates to raise or lower boats between two levels.

The earliest canals in the West were short sections made to avoid obstacles impeding the navigation of rivers. Subsequently canals have been built to bypass whole rivers, to extend navigation from a river to a town, and to link rivers, lakes and seas. The longest canal joins the Volga River at Astrakhan with the Baltic Sea at Leningrad, a distance of 1,850 miles.

The Grand Canal
Like China's Great Wall, the Grand Canal was built in sections over many centuries. It uses parts of rivers, has been rebuilt, enlarged or rerouted, making it impossible to give a definitive length, but remodelling in the 13th century gave a route of 1,100 miles. Its main function was to help the collection of taxes paid in the form of rice grains. Today the canal carries 2,000-ton ships, but its usual traffic is smaller barges, like these in Suzhou.

The Suez Canal
A link between the Red and Mediterranean seas dates back to Herodotus (died 424 BC) who wrote of a canal from Suez to the Nile. Though Napoleon had a survey made for a canal, the idea lay dormant until 1833 when the eventual builder, Ferdinand de Lesseps, became involved. Doubts about the scheme delayed the start of work until 1860. Mechanical diggers removed about 100 million cubic feet of spoil, and the 100-mile-long canal was opened in 1869. This panorama shows Suez in the foreground and Port Said at the far end.

The Corinth Canal

A canal to link the Aegean and Ionian seas was begun under Emperor Nero in AD 67, but work ceased with his death. It was not until 1882 that it was resumed under a Hungarian engineer. The two ends, in the gulfs of Corinth and Aegina, were protected by breakwaters and the approaches dredged. The canal is a 4-mile cutting with an average depth of 190 feet.

The Ronquières Inclined Plane

Perhaps the greatest canal structure in the world is situated on the canal between Brussels and Charleroi. The mile-long incline was opened in 1968 and rises 223 feet to cut out 28 locks and a 1,149-yard tunnel. Barges are transported up and down in water-filled tanks that can accommodate 1,350-ton barges; each tank weighs 5,–5,700 tons.

Lines across a Nation

Fact file

One of the greatest railway construction feats

General Manager: Cornelius Van Horne

Built: 1881–85

Length (Montreal–Vancouver): 2,920 miles

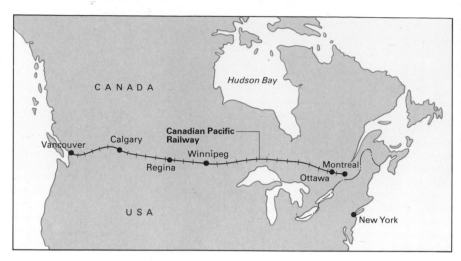

A tunnel near Rogers Pass which provided continual problems for the early operators of the CP. The death of 58 people due to a snowslide on the railway in 1910 prompted construction of the Connaught Tunnel, at 5 miles the longest double-track tunnel on the continent. From one vantage point in the Pass, Rogers could see 42 glaciers.

In 1871 the Conservative Prime Minister of Canada, John A. Macdonald, promised the colonists of British Columbia a railroad linking them to the east—within ten years. It was, said his Liberal opponent, Alexander Mackenzie, "an act of insane recklessness". Imprudent it may have been, but Macdonald had a dream: a British North America stretching from coast to coast, held together by a single line of steel. Without the railway, he feared, the nation could not be created, nor could British Columbia be persuaded to join the new confederation formed by Ontario, Quebec, New Brunswick, Nova Scotia and Manitoba.

The enterprise was epic in scale. Not only was the country enormous and thinly populated, but a transcontinental railway would have to run through some of the most inhospitable geography imaginable. At the time of Macdonald's pledge, large areas of the North West were hardly explored. Great mountain ranges and bottomless areas of muskeg swamp would somehow need to be surveyed and conquered if the promise were to come true. And how was a small nation of 3½ million people to find $100 million, the estimated cost of the railroad?

Things began badly, with a financial scandal and the fall of Macdonald's government. During the 1870s little was done except for the construction of branch lines and a tentative beginning on the main line at Fort William, Ontario. But by 1880 Macdonald was back in power and work began in earnest. By spring 1881 the financial problems had been ironed out and construction began at Portage la Prairie, west of Winnipeg. In November that year, a remarkable man, Cornelius Van Horne, was appointed General Manager of the Canadian Pacific Railway and

charged with the task of building the railway. It was an inspired appointment, for Van Horne was a man of enormous energy, unquenchable optimism and considerable railway experience.

Van Horne swore that he would build 500 miles of track during 1882, and the whole railway in five years, half the time allowed by the government. He recruited 3,000 men and 4,000 horses and set to work across the prairie from Flat Creek to Fort Calgary. In April there were floods, in May snowstorms. By the end of June, hardly an inch of line had been laid.

People began to express doubts about the whole enterprise, but then began a construction blitz without parallel in railway history. From Winnipeg the line began to stretch across the country; every day, 65 flat trucks or box cars of supplies were dumped wherever the track ended, providing the raw materials for driving it onward. Ahead of them across the plains were the grading crews, flattening the ground with scrapers pulled by teams of horses. Accompanying them were bridging crews, throwing wooden bridges across rivers and streams, desperately trying to keep ahead of the track-layers.

By the arrival of winter, Van Horne had missed his target, but not by much. He had built 417 miles of track, 28 miles of sidings, and graded another 18 miles ready for the track-layers the following year. But where exactly was the track heading? That was an embarrassing question to ask in the winter of 1882. Van Horne and his men were moving as fast as they could across the prairie towards a double row of mountains—the Rocky Mountains and the Selkirks—without knowing a route over them.

The task of finding a route had been given to Major A.B. Rogers, a surveyor whose habit of

cursing at his workmen had given him the nickname of "Hell's Bells Rogers". He was honest, tough and ambitious. He was promised that if he could find a pass that would save the railway a 150-mile detour, he would be given a $5,000 bonus and have the pass named after him.

But first Rogers chose a route through the Rockies, selecting Kicking Horse Pass which was surveyed with extraordinary difficulty. Even the Indians avoided the Pass, regarding the treacherous gorge as too difficult for horses. An eastern pass was no good without a western exit from the mountains, but a route through the Selkirks was even harder to find. After several expeditions that courted death when supplies ran out, Rogers finally stumbled through spruce woods on to upland meadows from which a stream

flowed in opposite directions. A route that Rogers' detractors said was impossible had been found. The pass was given his name and the railway honoured their promise of a $5,000 cheque, though Rogers refused to cash it, preferring to hang it on the wall.

Kicking Horse was passable, but only just. As the railway inched across the map, money began to run low and economies were demanded. The contract with the government stipulated that the maximum gradient anywhere on the line was to be 2.2 per cent, or 116 feet in a mile. To achieve that through Kicking Horse would have involved building a tunnel 1,400 feet long, which would have delayed matters by a further year. Instead, a "temporary" line was built from the summit down into the valley at a gradient double

Lines across a Nation

A CP local train in 1900. Riding on the buffer beam at the front of a locomotive was considered one of the best ways to enjoy the spectacular scenery through which the CP passes in the west; in 1901 the party of the future King George V and Queen Mary rode in such style, well covered with travelling rugs, for a section near Glacier, British Columbia.

that permitted in the contract, and four times the maximum desirable. This was the notorious "Big Hill", 8 miles long, which for 25 years would terrify drivers and passengers alike.

The very first train that tried to descend the Big Hill ran away and fell into the river, killing three men. Safety diversions were installed and manned night and day. Every train had to stop at each one, and reset the points to the main line before going on. At the top of the hill, every passenger train stopped and had its brakes checked. A maximum speed of 6 mph was allowed, and guards jumped off from time to time to make sure the wheels were not locking. Going up was just as hard, needing four big engines for a 710-ton train of 11 passenger coaches. Not until 1909 was this notorious danger spot bypassed, by the expedient of driving two spiral tunnels into the mountain, by which the trains descended at gentler grades while curving round in a complete circle.

Construction of the line around the north edge of Lake Superior was another back-breaking assignment. The rock—granite striped with quartz—was hard, the winters tough, the summers made intolerable by flies. So much dynamite was needed to blast the line through that Van Horne established three factories, each

capable of turning out a ton a day. In the summer of 1884, 15,000 men were working on this stretch of line, costing $1.1 million a month in wages alone. In winter 300 dog teams, working non-stop, were needed to keep the men supplied.

By the beginning of 1885, the line was nearly finished, but so was the money to pay for it. Until the trains began to operate, there was no cash flow to offset the tremendous expenditure. The government refused to step in, and financial catastrophe threatened. At the end of March, just when all seemed lost, a rising in the North West by disaffected white settlers, backed by Indians, saved the situation. A force of 3,300 militiamen had to be sent west to quell the

The last spike is driven home at Eagle Pass by the eldest of the 4 CP directors present, Donald A. Smith, on 7 November 1885. The portly gentleman to his left is Van Horne, General Manager of the CPR, whose secret, he said, was "I eat all I can; I drink all I can; and I don't give a damn for anybody". The tall white-bearded man between them is Sir Sandford Fleming, who in 1862 first put before the government a considered plan to build a railway to the Pacific. Smith bent the first spike.

Stoney Creek Bridge on the long climb up to Rogers Pass being crossed by a transcontinental train with dome cars. Built in 1893, and reinforced in 1929, this steel arch of 336 feet replaced an earlier trestle viaduct dating from the opening of the line. Government cutbacks in 1990 abolished what has been described as the world's most spectacular rail journey.

The wheat plains of Manitoba proved easy country across which to build a railway. The gangs created an embankment 4 feet above the prairie, with ditches 20 yards wide on either side to prevent the line being blocked by snow.

Laying continuous welded rail near Lake Louise, Alberta, is a far cry from the basic and harsh conditions under which the line was built, though on good days 5 miles of track might be laid by the workmen. Their pay was between $1 and $1.50 for a 10-hour day. Their diet was salt pork, corned beef, molasses, beans, oatmeal, potatoes and tea. Lack of fruit gave them scurvy.

rebellion, and the unfinished railway was the only means of doing so swiftly enough to be effective. Van Horne promised to get them all to the North West within ten days, reasoning that no government could refuse aid to a railway that had helped it to crush a rebellion.

The journey was a nightmare, with the men travelling on flatcars or on horse-drawn sleighs along the unfinished sections, in bitter cold and snow. But they arrived and successfully quelled the revolt. Even so, the government would not help the railway until it came within a hair's breadth of collapse. On 10 July 1885, when Parliament was meeting to discuss aid, one of Canadian Pacific's creditors pressed for payment of a $400,000 debt. It was due for payment at 3 pm. At 2 pm, the House of Commons voted to provide more money. The railway was saved.

The final spike was driven at Eagle Pass on a dull November morning. All the leading figures in the railway, men who had come close to ruin to make it a reality, were on the spot to see it finished. There were cheers and the shrill whistle of a locomotive. Van Horne, called upon for a speech, made a short one: "All I can say is that the work has been done well in every way." Then the whistle sounded again, and a voice cried, "All aboard for the Pacific!"

Tracks through the Taiga

Fact file

The world's longest railway

Built: 1891–1904

Length: 5,900 miles

Duration of journey: 170 hours 5 minutes

Time zones traversed: 7

Few railways have been built under greater difficulties, or with more confusion, than the great line that runs 5,900 miles from Moscow to Vladivostock across the Siberian wastes. After constant false starts, and despite the urging of Tsar Alexander III, who declared in 1886, "It is time, it is high time!", actual building did not start until May 1891 at the eastern end, and a year later in the west. That it started at all was largely thanks to Sergius Witte, a railway enthusiast who was appointed Finance Minister and who, through brilliant financial stratagems, was able to repair Russia's crippled economy and provide the necessary money for the railway.

The building of the line was divided into sections, under the control of different engineers. The westernmost section, starting at Chelyabinsk, ran in a virtually straight line for 900 miles across level plains. But there were no trees to make sleepers, and all-out work was only possible for four months of the year.

Excavation was by pick and shovel, and to save money sleepers were more widely spaced than in Europe or North America, while the actual rails were made of much lighter steel. Ballast beneath the track was virtually nonexistent; in many places the sleepers were laid on the earth. Progress, despite the problems, was rapid, with track being laid at the rate of $2\frac{1}{2}$ miles a day in summer conditions, and the first 500 miles of the western section was opened in September 1894. By August 1895 the Ob, one of Siberia's longest rivers, had been reached.

The crews built bridges as they went along, wooden structures over small rivers and streams, more substantial crossings of stone and steel for rivers like the Ob and the Yenisei. They built well, for many of these steel bridges survive today, despite the impact of thousands of tons of melting ice on the stone piers every spring. The cold claimed countless lives, for the gangs perched a hundred or so feet above the frozen rivers had little protection, and often allowed their bodies to become so chilled that they could no longer grasp the supports and fell on to the ice below. Most of the masons were Italians, who earned 100 roubles a month ($50).

Cast steel for the bridges came from the Urals, cement from St Petersburg, steel bearings from Warsaw, all brought along the newly built line at agonizingly slow speeds. Before bridges were built, the lines were sometimes laid bodily across the ice, frozen in place by constant douches of water. The few passengers alighted and walked across, while the driver gingerly tested the ice by driving on to it.

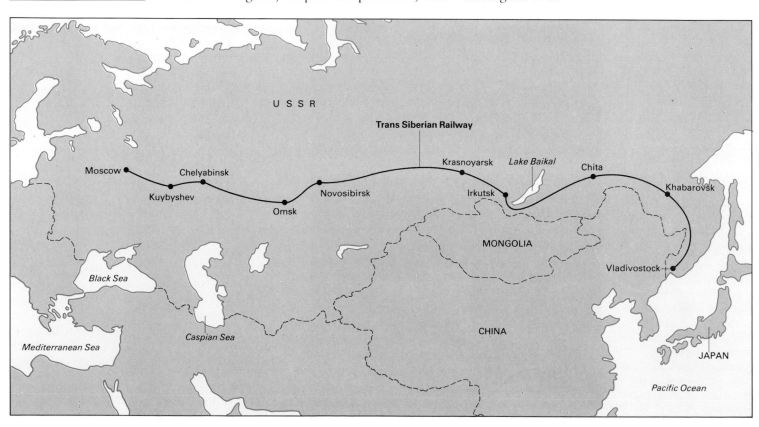

The seemingly endless forest through which much of the railway passes is seen here east of Krasnoyarsk, where it crosses the River Yenisei on a 1,010-yard viaduct of 6 spans. Beneath the emblem of Soviet railways (right) a plate bears the legend "Moscow to Vladivostock", which has only recently been opened to Western travellers.

Meanwhile another construction party had leap-frogged ahead to the mid-Siberian sector, where driving a railway through the virgin forest of the Siberian taiga was even more difficult. A passage 250 feet wide (to reduce the risk of fire from sparks) had to be cut through the forest, and rails laid on ground that was frozen until July, then turned into a boggy swamp. With 66,000 men at work by 1895 the mid-Siberian line was finished by mid-1898, that is in five years rather than the seven allowed.

The most difficult section of all still lay ahead, a 162-mile segment around the southern edge of Lake Baikal. Since construction would take some years, it was decided to take trains across the lake, the world's largest body of fresh water; ice-breaking train ferries were built on the River Tyne in England, taken apart, transported to Siberia and reassembled. Construction began in 1899, and was finished in feverish haste in 1904, after the war between Russia and Japan had broken out. So hasty was the work that the first train over the line derailed ten times. But on 25 September 1904 the line was opened, and it was possible for the first time to travel from the

Tracks through the Taiga

Atlantic shores of Europe to the eastern shores of Asia on uninterrupted rails. It had taken 13 years and 4 months, and it had cost $250 million.

Today the journey from one end of the railway to the other takes more than eight days, with 97 stops. Despite the achievement of building the line, and its economic and strategic importance, travel on the Trans-Siberian has never been as luxurious as on European trains such as the Orient Express, or especially exciting. The landscape unrolls day after day, unchanging and monotonous. The food is notorious; one writer remembers a week with nothing to eat but semolina and a kind of omelette. Nor are accidents unheard of. In June 1989 the world's worst-ever rail accident happened on the line 750 miles east of Moscow, when liquid gas from a leaking pipeline exploded as two packed trains were passing. More than 800 people died.

In the past 15 years the Soviet Union has built a second line across Siberia, the Baikal–Amur Mainline, or BAM. It runs for 2,000 miles across Siberia, passing north rather than south of Lake Baikal, and well to the north of the old line.

Construction workers were recruited from Turkey, Persia and Italy, and even convicts from a prison near Irkutsk were requisitioned. They received a promise that 8 months' labouring was equal to a year off their sentence.

This cutting near Lake Baikal indicates the reason for the section of line around the lake being the last to be completed. It passes through 40 tunnels and numerous rock-hewn cuttings.

The Russian Imperial arms of Nicholas II emblazoned over the entrance to the viaduct across the Volga between Syzran and Kuybyshev.

Ob' station, to the west of Novosibirsk, a small, ornate station with decorative bargeboards. The poor standard of engineering work on the railway meant that early speeds were slow: the Siberian Express averaged only 20 mph.

Passenger accommodation in the early years of the railway ranged from a sub-European standard train de luxe to converted goods vans (left), although use of the latter was usually for convicts, immigrant trains of compulsory exiles to Siberia, and even troops.

A Concrete Triumph

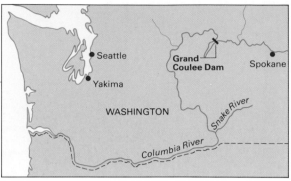

Fact file

When planned, the largest hydro-electric scheme in the world

Constructors: Mason-Walsh-Atkinson-Kier Co

Built: 1933–

Material: Concrete

Height: 550 feet

Length: 4,173 feet

The world's largest concrete dam—and the largest concrete structure in the world—lies on the Columbia River in the State of Washington, in the north-west United States. It is also one of the largest hydro-electric power plants in the world, and its huge irrigation pumps are big enough to pump dry most of the rivers in the USA. Its construction in an isolated and thinly populated area of the US during the Depression years was one of the great achievements of the Work Projects Administration, President Franklin Roosevelt's bid to restore prosperity and jobs to a nation in trouble.

The dam had two purposes, three if the provision of jobs is included. The principal one was to supply irrigation water to more than a million acres of desert land—known as the coulee country—in central Washington, good soil that needed only water to make it fertile. It used to be said that a jackrabbit had to carry his lunch and a canteen of water just to cross the coulee country, and the area was littered with empty farmsteads, broken windmills, and abandoned equipment. The second purpose was to generate electricity, some of which would be used to drive the irrigation pumps.

Geology had created the setting for the dam. Millions of years ago a glacier advancing southwards from Canada had cut off the flow of the Columbia River and forced it into a new channel. This channel was eventually eroded by the river to a depth of 900 feet, 5 miles wide, and 50 miles long, before the glacier retreated and allowed the river to return to its original course. The channel that was left was the Grand Coulee, dry along its entire length.

The Grand Coulee project envisaged a huge concrete dam across the new course of the river, creating a lake 151 miles long stretching back towards Canada, and two smaller earth dams across the Grand Coulee itself, to turn it into a storage reservoir for irrigation. Because the glacier had raised the level of the river, the storage reservoir in the Grand Coulee lies about 300 feet above the high-water mark in the lake below, so pumps are needed to carry the water up to it. From here, the water is distributed through canals to the high and arid lands on the plateau of the coulee country.

The main dam is of prodigious size, 4,173 feet long and at 550 feet as tall as a 46-storey building. It contains 10,979,641 cubic yards of concrete, and raised the level of the river by 350 feet. It depends entirely on its mass to resist the pressure of water, the river being too wide for an arched dam. Preliminary engineering work began in 1933, and the first contract was let at the end of that year.

In order to build the dam on sound foundations, temporary cofferdams made of steel piling and timber were constructed to narrow the width of the river and expose the bedrock below. Two U-shaped cofferdams were built, one on either side of the river, leaving a gap just 500 feet wide for the river to flow through. Water was pumped from the areas inside the cofferdams, and the rock exposed. Once the areas were dry, the concrete dam was constructed outward from each bank toward the middle, leaving some low areas as spillways. Then two more cofferdams were built above and below the dam, diverting the river over the spillways so that the central part of the river could be pumped dry and the last 500 feet of the concrete laid.

The concrete was poured as a series of columns 50 feet by 50 feet which extended from the bedrock to the full height of the dam. The columns grew 5 feet at a time, with 72 hours between each successive pour to give the concrete time to begin curing.

When curing, concrete generates heat in a chemical reaction. If this heat is not removed, a huge concrete structure will increase in temperature over a period of months, and expand. When

curing is complete, and the temperature falls, it will shrink, creating cracks. To prevent this happening, special cooling pipes made of thin wall steel tubing an inch thick were set into the concrete as it was poured, and cooling water pumped through.

When the columns of concrete were finally cool and set, the small gaps between them caused by shrinkage were filled by pumping in a cement and water grout through a network of pipes embedded into the concrete as it was poured. The shrinkage between each block was tiny—only $\frac{3}{32}$ of an inch—but over the length of the dam that added up to about 8 inches. The grout sealed the blocks, making a watertight dam.

A novel problem emerged during the building of the dam, and was solved in an unusual way. At the east end of the dam, the bedrock was no sooner exposed than it was covered by a huge volume of plastic clay, which kept creeping forward and defeated all attempts to stop it. Timber and concrete obstacles were set up, but to no avail. The volume of clay involved was 200,000 cubic yards, so removing it would have been time-consuming and expensive. Finally the engineers had the idea of freezing the leading

The Grand Coulee Dam is the main dam; the more recent Forebay Dam, which is still to be fully completed, is the shorter, angled dam on the left. Behind the dam the lake extends for 151 miles toward British Columbia, with an average width of 4,000 feet and a depth of 375 feet. The lake is a new haven for wildlife.

A Concrete Triumph

Excavated spoil from the east side was carried 4,000 feet across the river by conveyor belt (top) to Rattlesnake Canyon where 13 million cubic yards of spoil were deposited. Cement was brought from 5 plants in Washington state and stored in steel silos before being combined with sand and gravel in mixers 100 feet high (above).

edge of the clay to form a dam that would hold the rest back. A 3-mile length of pipe was placed in an arc in the toe of the sloping mass of clay, and brine at a temperature of zero degrees Fahrenheit circulated through it. This froze the front edge of the clay into the shape of an arch 20 feet thick, 45 feet deep and 110 feet long.

Between August 1936 and April 1937 an ice plant kept the clay frozen while the bedrock was prepared and the dam constructed until it was above the level of the clay. After that, the ice plant was switched off, and the clay once more allowed to move. It had cost $35,000, but saved many times that much.

The lake created by the dam holds water amounting to 20,000 gallons for every citizen of the US, but such is the flow of the Columbia River that it could fill the lake in two months, or in one month in the flood season. At each side of the river, hydro-electric plants were built, initially with a total output of 1,920 megawatts. Power from these is used to drive 12 pumps located on the west side of the river behind the dam. The capacity of each of these pumps, 1,600 cubic feet per second, is enough to irrigate 120,000 acres of land.

The pumps send water through conduits 13 feet in diameter to the higher reservoir, built in the upper Grand Coulee. This was created by building two earth dams about 100 feet high, one

The first phase of the Forebay Dam under construction in 1971 at the west end of the Grand Coulee Dam (right). A close-up shows the construction of the 6 penstocks (below)—tubes that feed water into the turbines. Their 40-foot diameter is over twice the size of those in the original power plant. Each penstock is made up of cylindrical sections, or "cans", which are lowered down rails and welded in place.

Two trestles, each 3,000 feet long (above), were built to enable concrete to be placed in the columns. Cranes with a reach of over 115 feet could travel along the trestle, picking up bottom-emptying buckets that were brought on to the trestle by railway from the concrete mixers. Concrete could be placed at 1 cubic yard every $5\frac{1}{2}$ seconds.

about 2 miles from the Grand Coulee Dam and another near Coulee City. Between these two dams a reservoir 27 miles long was created, and filled with water pumped 300 feet up from the big reservoir below. From here the water flows 10 miles to the heads of two canals, the 150-mile east-side canal and the 100-mile west-side canal, from which it is distributed to farms through shorter lateral channels.

Since 1970, a new scheme to increase the output of the hydro-electric plants has been under way. This has involved removing some 250 feet of the existing dam at the east end, and building a new dam, joined to it and angled away downstream. The new turbines are built into this

dam, a simpler task than taking apart the old dam to replace the turbines installed in the 1930s. To remove the end of the original dam, a cofferdam was first built to isolate it, then it was carefully demolished block by block by toppling the blocks over downstream using dynamite.

Simultaneously, penstocks—huge tubes to carry the water to the turbines—were being constructed downstream of where the new section of dam was to go. The ultimate output of the plant, when all phases of the contract are complete, will be 10,080 megawatts. Only one other plant in the world, the Itaipu power station on the Parana River on the borders between Brazil and Paraguay, exceeds this.

Harnessing the Power of Water

The earliest known dam was a series of stone-faced earth dams at Jawa in Jordan, dated to *c*3200 BC. Earthen irrigation dams in the Tigris and Euphrates valleys were followed by the first known rock-filled dam, near Homs in Syria, built *c*1300 BC. The skills of dam building spread to India, Sri Lanka and Japan. The first known arch dam, achieving strength through the same principle as an arch bridge, was built on the Turkish/Syrian border during the reign of Justinian I (AD 527–65).

In the twentieth century, the generation of hydroelectric power has become the principal justification for many dams, a development pioneered by Sir William Armstrong whose Northumberland home was the first in the world to be lit by this method.

Kielder Dam, England
The largest dam in Britain, Kielder's embankment measures 3,740 feet in length and contains almost 7 million cubic yards of earth. Loss of countryside through flooding is often the cause of opposition to dams, but Kielder has won praise for the way it has been landscaped. The reservoir of 2,684 acres supplies water to a large part of northeast England.

Tucurui Dam, Brazil
The capacity for dams to alter beyond recognition substantial areas of land is illustrated by this $4 billion dam on the Tocantins River. The dam, of 84 million cubic yards, turned the river into a chain of lakes 1,180 miles long. Hydroelectricity has been so widely adopted that about 20 percent of the world's electricity is derived from water-driven turbines. Much of the work on turbines was done by the British engineer Charles Parsons, who invented the steam turbine in 1884.

Itaipu Dam, Brazil
Built at a cost of $11 billion on the Parana River on the Paraguay/ Brazil border, Itaipu power station began generating power in October 1984 and will produce 13,320 megawatts from the 18 turbines in the dam. It is the world's most powerful dam, although a much more powerful project is planned for the Tunguska River in the USSR. It is hydroelectric schemes in Brazil that have aroused the greatest opposition to the international bank loans that finance such projects, seen by many as ecological disasters. One of the biggest schemes in Brazil, Plan 2010, envisaged constructing 136 dams to supply Brazil's energy needs for the next 2 decades. It would have entailed the flooding of an area the size of the United Kingdom and displaced 250,000 Indians from their traditional rainforest.

Taming the Seas

Fact file

The world's largest sea barrier

Built: 1958–86

Materials: Prestressed concrete and steel

Length: Eastern Scheldt, 2,743 yards

The Netherlands are not known as the Low Countries for nothing. The Dutch people have struggled against flooding for nine centuries, pioneering the building of dykes, dams and canals to tame the sea and to recover new land for agriculture. At the same time, they have used their easy access to the sea to become a major shipping and trading nation, with the port of Rotterdam holding its position as Europe's busiest. In October 1986 Queen Beatrix inaugurated the biggest and most advanced sea barrier anywhere in the world, the culmination of a plan that had been in progress for almost 30 years.

The Dutch Delta Plan, unlike the damming of the Zuider Zee, was not designed to create new land from the sea. Its object has always been to reduce the danger of catastrophic flooding, which in the past has periodically swept aside the dykes and engulfed large areas of the country. The last great disaster was on the night of 31 January–1 February 1953, when huge areas were inundated by the combination of a spring tide and a severe north-westerly gale. Hundreds of dykes were swept away, 395,000 acres of land flooded, and 1,835 people lost their lives in the worst flood ever to hit the Netherlands.

Plans had already been started for a system of dams, but the disaster created much more urgency. In 1958 Parliament passed the Delta Act, a bold attempt to remodel the whole coast of south-west Netherlands, preventing any future danger of floods, while keeping open the waterways giving access to the ports of Rotterdam and Antwerp.

The plan envisaged a series of dams and surge barriers, some with locks and discharge sluices, to force the saltwater back toward the sea, prevent flooding, and improve fresh-water management in the country. The plan was put into action step by step, starting with the smaller projects and gradually moving to more difficult ones as experience was gained. It involved five primary dams, five secondary dams, the strengthening of dykes along the New Waterway which leads to Rotterdam and the Western Scheldt which leads to Antwerp, and the building of two major bridges. The first primary dam to be built, the Veerse Gat, sealed off an estuary with a tidal volume of 6,200 million cubic feet; the last, the Eastern Scheldt, had a tidal volume of 77,500 million cubic feet.

The height of the dams was set at a level approximately 3 feet higher than the level reached in the 1953 flood. The chances that such a level will be exceeded were calculated at less than one in 10,000 for the most important economic areas—giving a 1 percent chance of a flood topping the barriers in any 100 years—and one in 4,000 for the rest. Among the greatest problems faced in building the dams were scouring by the sea, which tends to wash away the foundations, and devising ways for closing the final gap in the dam when it was virtually complete. At the Haringvliet Barrage, for example, huge underwater "aprons" had to be built on either side of the dam, consisting of a nylon mattress with layers of graded gravel and rocks on top of it. The barrage had to have gates strong enough to resist the force of the sea, spanning sluiceways big enough to pass ice in winter.

Two methods were used for closing the final gaps in the dams. One was to build a series of prefabricated concrete caissons, which could be placed in position at slack water, gradually narrowing the gap until the final caisson was placed. Once the water had been dammed in this way, the rest of the dam could be built around the caissons. This was the method used at the Veerse Gat Dam. The alternative was to build the dam outward from either shore, and then run a cableway across between the two ends. The cableway carried cars loaded with stone which

Schaar construction dock (above), in which the prefabricated piers of the Eastern Scheldt barrier were built. The dock is divided into 4 by dykes; as soon as all the piers in a compartment were complete, it was flooded to enable a vessel to lift them, one by one, and drop them in position. The Delta Plan was devised to prevent inundation of low-lying land (right).

were hauled out to the middle and their load dumped into the gap, gradually filling the breach until the stone emerged from the water. This method was used at Grevelingen Dam.

The last and biggest task in the Delta Plan was the damming of the Eastern Scheldt, a huge body of tidal water, with a barrier more than 5 miles long. Final closure was planned for 1978. But a strong campaign was launched in favour of keeping the Eastern Scheldt open, in order to preserve the natural environment. Sealed off, it would have lost its role as a nursery for North Sea fish, and its attraction to the seabirds that flock to the sandbanks at low tide. The growing of shellfish would also have been eliminated if the Eastern Scheldt became an inland lake cut off

Taming the Seas

from the sea. Against that, those anxious for the greatest possible safety from flooding, and the improvement of agriculture, wanted the dam.

After years of argument the Dutch government ordered a study to see if it were possible to modify the dam, providing instead a barrage that would stay open all the time, except when a storm surge was expected, when gates would be closed to prevent flooding. The danger was that such a plan would retain as a permanent feature of the barrage the most dangerous stage in the closure operation, which many engineers regarded as foolhardy. Despite that, the Dutch government decided to bow to the pressure from the environmentalists, and turn the dam into a barrage, despite the engineering difficulties.

The design of the barrage consists of 65 prefabricated concrete piers between which 62 sliding steel gates have been installed. The gates are more than 17 feet thick and 130 feet wide. With the gates in the raised position, the tidal range behind the barrier would remain three-quarters of what it was originally, thus preserving the natural environment.

The barrage is built across the three main tidal channels of the Eastern Scheldt, with the rest of the crossing consisting of a dam. When the gates are closed, the forces exerted on the gates and the piers are enormous. The foundations must be designed so that these forces do not shift the piers, which would cause jamming of the gates.

The piers are placed on the sea bed on top of foundation mattresses, the purpose of which is to absorb changing water pressure in the subsoil so that the fine sand under the mattress is not washed away, thus weakening the foundations. Slight variations in the level of the mattresses were compensated for by additional concrete mattresses of varying thickness, before the piers were placed on top and sunk into place. They are not attached to the sea bed by any piling, but remain in place simply by virtue of their weight.

Around the base of each pier a sill was constructed of graded layers of stone, each layer becoming larger the closer it is to the surface. The bigger stones in the upper layers prevent the smaller ones below being swept away. The top layer consists of basalt rocks weighing between 6 and 10 tons, designed to ensure that if a gate should fail to close the current rushing through it will not carry away the stone and endanger the barrier.

The piers are linked by two sets of sills, made

Foundation mattresses (above) for the piers were made in a special plant and consisted of successive layers of sand, fine gravel and coarse gravel on a plastic base. Each more than 650 feet long, 140 feet broad and 1 foot thick, they were laid by a special rig aboard 2 ships, followed by a second smaller mattress laid on top.

of concrete. The lower sills each weigh 2,500 tons and link the piers underwater. The smaller upper sills weigh 1,100 tons and form the upper edge of the opening through which the tide passes when the gates are open.

The operation of the gates is tested at least once a month, and it takes about an hour to close or open them all. If they are closed too quickly, it can affect the wave movements inside the barrier. While emergency closure to prevent flooding is a rare occurrence, the gates are used to fine tune the amount of water flowing in and out of the Eastern Scheldt.

The barrier was finally completed in 1986, the largest Dutch public works project since the Second World War, costing $2.4 billion. In the spring of 1990 it successfully staved off a flood of potentially disastrous proportions.

The 65 prefabricated piers (left) *were built in the Schaar construction dock. Each pier is the height of a 12-storey building, weighs 18,000 tons and took 1½ years to complete. Work began on a new pier every 2 weeks so that their installation would be an uninterrupted process. In 4 years, 589,000 cubic yards of concrete were used to make the piers.*

Placing the 18,000-ton piers in water up to 100 feet in depth demanded accuracy to a few inches. A U-shaped vessel, the Ostrea (right), *lifted a pier, transported it to the site and manoeuvred it into position with the help of its 4 rudder propellers, 2 in the bow, 2 in the stern. Another vessel held the Ostrea steady while the pier was lowered into place.*

The steel gates (right) *are more than 17 feet thick and 130 feet wide, the precise dimensions being determined only after the piers were in place. The height of the gates varies from 77 feet to 155 feet, depending on their position in the channel. Their weight ranges from 300 to 500 tons.*

The completed storm surge barrier showing the vertical hydraulic cylinders protruding above the capping units. Each gate is opened and closed by 2 cylinders operated from the central control building.

Conquest of the Alps

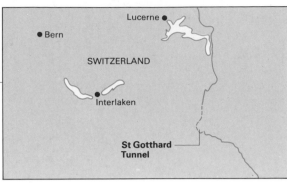

From Göschenen in the Swiss canton of Uri to Airolo, in Italy, is just 10 miles through the road tunnel under the Alps which was opened in 1980. But providing a route between the two places by road or rail had taxed the ingenuity of engineers for hundreds of years. Today it is possible to drive all the way from Hamburg in West Germany to Reggio di Calabria in the toe of Italy without ever leaving a motorway, thanks to the tunnel—the longest road tunnel in the world.

The St Gotthard Pass has always been important because of its position on a direct line joining Milan with the Rhine valley. By Alpine standards it is not particularly high—6,936 feet above sea level, but it was never easy going, due to an awkward obstacle on the Swiss side, the narrow and precipitous Schöllenen gorge above Göschenen. At the beginning of the thirteenth century, unknown engineers managed to span this gorge with a narrow wooden bridge some 100 feet above the Reuss River. The approach to the bridge, along vertical cliffs of stone, was formed by a wooden walkway 80 yards long, fastened to the rock with chains. It was a major achievement of medieval technology, known locally as the "Devil's Bridge" because only the Devil would have had the ingenuity to create it.

In 1595 the wooden bridge was replaced with a stone arch, and in 1707 the first Alpine tunnel, the Urnerloch, was driven through the mountainside to replace the walkway. It was 80 yards long, and excavated by Petro Morettini of Ticino. It was just 12 feet by 10 feet, too narrow for carriages, although in 1775 an English mineralogist named Greville drove a light chaise through it, becoming the first person to cross the St Gotthard by vehicle. In 1830 the gallery was widened to take full-size carriages.

By then it had been the setting for an extraordinary clash in 1799 between a force of 21,000 Russian troops led by General Suvarov and the armies of Revolutionary France. In a 12-hour battle fought on the Italian side of the St Gotthard Pass, Suvarov defeated the French, but in retreating they destroyed the Devil's Bridge and left the Urnerloch defended by a rearguard. In a bitter battle, many Russians died as they tried to dislodge the French, succeeding finally by finding a ford across the river. The bridge was repaired and Suvarov led his men across.

Between 1818 and 1830, the road across St Gotthard was greatly improved by the Uri canton, which was almost ruined by the expense of the operation. In those days the passes did not close in winter, but were kept open by hardy *cantonniers* who went out after snowfalls with ploughs, pulled by oxen, to cut a narrow passage through the drifts. Passengers were transferred from carriages to horse-drawn sleighs, enveloped in fur coats and blankets, and taken over the top through the paths the oxen had carved out. Special passing places were provided, in which the horse going up had the right of way. At the summit of the pass was a hospice, where travellers could be thawed out and fed.

By 1850, the railways could bring travellers to either side of the great Alpine passes, but it still required carriages, horses, and sleighs to get them over. During the 1860s the first Alpine tunnel, under Mont Cenis, was successfully dug, and in 1871 Germany, Italy and Switzerland signed an agreement to subsidize the digging of a tunnel through the St Gotthard massif. The man who won the contract was Louis Favre of Genoa, and it destroyed him. Tough penalty clauses for late completion of the tunnel threw his company into bankruptcy, and Favre himself died a broken man before the tunnel was finally opened in May 1882 after ten years of work.

A principal trouble was water, which poured into the workings with the force of a fire hose, and forced workers to excavate the tunnel up to their knees in water. Dynamite was no sooner placed in holes to blast the rock than it was

The approaches to the Gotthard railway tunnel from both directions required engineering as impressive as the tunnel itself. From the north, on grades as steep as 2.6% or 1 in 37½, the line describes a complete circle within the Pfaffensprung Tunnel, followed by 2 other tunnels, besides crossing numerous viaducts. The southern approach (above) was equally dramatic, with 2 spiral tunnels above this crossing of the Ticino River in the Piottino Ravine.

washed away as a yellow sludge. The temperature in the tunnel was tropical and disease flourished, with men and horses dying or being forced to give up work. Air was pumped to the working face by compressors, and used to drive the drills and provide air to breath; but the compressors were not up to the job, and miners found themselves gasping for air.

The greatest problem of all was the collapse of the roof in a section of tunnel 1½ miles from the Swiss end. The tunnel had been driven at this point through unstable gypsum and feldspar, which in contact with the moist air began to liquefy, exerting such huge force on the tunnel linings that it crushed them. It took two years to solve the problem, which was achieved by building a massive granite wall more than 8 feet thick, carrying an arch 4 feet 8 inches deep, which proved strong enough finally to hold back

Conquest of the Alps

The safety tunnel
(above) runs parallel
with the main tunnel.
Of horseshoe shape and
8 feet high by 9 feet
wide, it is lit but
unlined and connected
to the main tunnel every
300 yards where there
are lay-bys for vehicles.

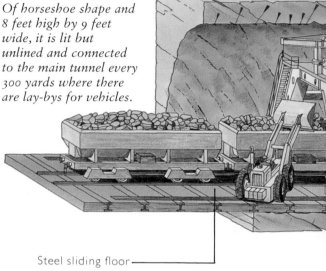

Steel sliding floor

Full-face excavation
was carried out by
drilling jumbos which
each weighed 36½ tons
and had 5 hammer
drills, powered by
compressed air. Smaller
drills (above) were used
to make holes for bolts
to secure the protective
wire netting above the
working area until steel
supports could be
installed.

the sticky mass. It was an expensive delay.

The final cost of the tunnel was 57.6 million francs (£2.3 million) which was 14.7 million francs (£590,000) more than Favre had bid. In today's circumstances, and given the huge difficulties overcome, that may seem a modest overspend but the railway company insisted his firm bear the loss—a judgement upheld by the courts—and that he also pay forfeit money of £230,000 for late completion. Favre was already dead, but these harsh conditions ensured that his company disappeared also. He was not the only victim: the St Gotthard Tunnel cost the lives of 310 workmen, and incapacitated another 877.

Today the same mountain has been pierced by a second tunnel, which carries the road. That, too, proved a tough undertaking. Work began in 1969, and the tunnel was finally opened 11 years later, in September 1980. Under pressure from Swiss motoring organizations, a safety tunnel was built parallel to the main tunnel and 100 feet away to provide an escape route in the event of fire. The two tunnels follow a curving path through the mountain, partly to provide shorter ventilation tunnels accessible from the existing pass, and partly to avoid tricky rock. In addition, it was felt that driving around a gentle curve for 10 miles, together with some changes of gradient, would be less tiring and potentially hazar-

dous than holding a perfectly straight course.

Drilling of the tunnel began from both ends on 5 May 1970, using a conventional tunnelling method in which rock was broken up by explosive charges and then removed by road or rail vehicles from the working face. The safety tunnel and the four ventilation tunnels were excavated at the same time, the safety tunnel running slightly ahead to provide warning of poor ground conditions. The main tunnel is 25 feet wide, allowing for a single carriageway in each direction, and 14 feet 6 inches high.

One innovation in the drilling of the tunnel was the use of a "sliding floor", made of steel, and more than 250 yards long. As excavation proceeded, the floor was moved forward, providing a sound surface for trucks coming to take away the rock, and a platform from which to build the lining to support the tunnel roof. To ensure that the tunnel ran in the right direction, a system of nine laser beams was used, mounted at

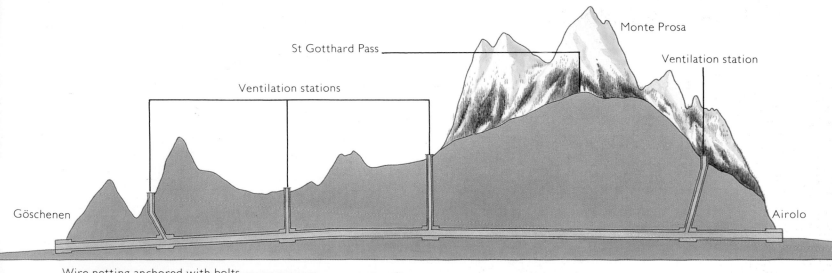

Monte Prosa

St Gotthard Pass

Ventilation station

Ventilation stations

Göschenen

Airolo

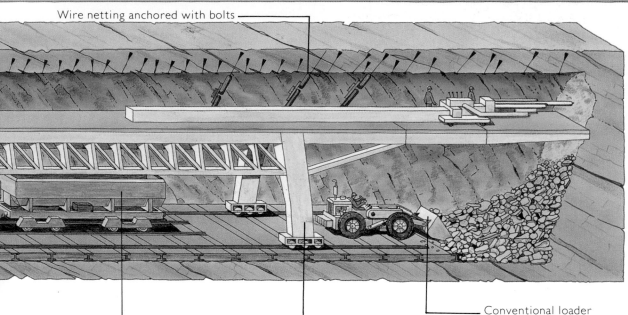

Wire netting anchored with bolts

Six ventilation plants (above), together consuming up to 24 megawatts, work to remove potentially lethal exhaust fumes. At full power they are capable of changing the air in the tunnel within 6 minutes, but when traffic is light, a computer controls fans to avoid wasting power.

Conventional loader

Railway truck for spoil removal

Supporting platform and cantilever arm

the opening of the tunnel and pointing forward to mark out the profile for the excavation. After every advance of 350 yards, they were moved nearer the face and aimed in the right direction for tunnelling to proceed. At one point, about $\frac{1}{2}$ mile from the northern portal, the tunnel passes directly underneath the rail tunnel, with a gap of only 16 feet of rock, so care was needed with blasting to avoid damage to the older tunnel.

About 730 workers were employed, half at each end, and they joined up in March 1976. In spite of the safety precautions taken, 19 died in accidents during the excavation. The tunnel they built is filled with special systems to ensure the safety of its users. Lighting is continuous, with every tenth light connected to a separate, independent power supply.

Within the tunnel, and on the approaches to it, there are signalling systems to control the flow of traffic, which has to filter down from the two-lane carriageways on the approach roads to the

A protective platform (above), 32 yards long and 5½ yards high with a cantilever arm of 15 yards, enabled simultaneous work on the excavated arch and removal of blasted rock.

single carriageways in the tunnel. Along the full length of the tunnel there are shelters on the east side which lead directly to the safety tunnel, and on the west side are niches, with fire extinguishers and emergency telephones, within which people can take cover in the event of fire or accident. The tunnel is also fitted with fire alarm systems and TV monitors, while radio systems enable drivers to listen to their radios as they go through, and hear any emergency warnings.

Like Favre, the tunnellers met difficult rock and an unexpected amount of water under the St Gotthard massif, delaying the opening of the tunnel for three years. Its final cost was 690 million Swiss francs (£175 million) which was more than twice the original budget. Inflation accounted for half the increase, and the difficult rock for a quarter. Some extra money was also spent on preparing the way for a future second tunnel, when the capacity of the present one (1,800 vehicles per hour) is reached.

The World's Greatest Highways

The first roads were little more than tracks that developed into trade routes, of which the most famous were the silk routes between Persia and China. The first surfaced roads were made by the Egyptians, who built polished stone causeways to facilitate the carriage of stone blocks for the pyramids. However, it is the Romans who are renowned for their skills in creating straight roads across their empire.

The development of wheeled vehicles called for better roads, leading from the work of British engineers on turnpike roads, through the auto-bahns and autostradas of the 1930s, to today's multi-lane highways. Concern over their environmental impact is now forcing a reappraisal of road schemes and traffic growth.

The Appian Way
Completed between the Porta San Sebastiano in Rome and Capua in 312 BC by the censor Appius Claudius, the Via Appia (below) was the most important of the consular roads. Later extended to Benevento and Brindisi, it was surfaced with huge polygonal blocks of basaltic lava, and lined for the first part with family tombs and temples.

Los Angeles Interchange
Of the world's cities, Los Angeles is probably the most wedded to the automobile: a million cars a day carry 3.3 million commuters along 725 miles of generally clogged freeway, producing so much poisonous smog that radical solutions are being considered to try to stop the city choking to death.

The Pan-American Highway
The world's longest road begins in Texas (several places contend for the honour) and runs for over 15,500 miles through Panama City to Valparaiso in Chile; from there it turns east to cross the Andes, seen here near Arequipa in Peru, to Buenos Aires. Short gaps exist in Central America, and there is an extension to Brasilia.

Darby's Metal Masterpiece

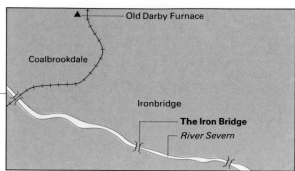

Fact file

The world's first iron bridge, built over the River Severn

Designer: Thomas Farnolls Pritchard

Built: 1777–79

Materials: Cast iron and stone

Length: Span of 100 feet 6 inches

Weight of iron: 378 tons 15 cwt

"From Coalport to the Ironbridge, two miles, the river passes through the most extraordinary district in the world", wrote a Shrewsbury man, Charles Hulbert, at the end of the eighteenth century. Everywhere, he said, were iron works, brick works, boat-building establishments, retail stores, inns and houses.

Hulbert was describing the first district in England, and the world, to feel the impact of the Industrial Revolution. It was a change so radical and complete that it has dominated human lives ever since. And the most eloquent symbol of that revolution is the bridge Hulbert mentions, a bridge made of iron across the River Severn. From the beginning the bridge was a source of wonder: the dramatist and song-writer Charles Dibdin wrote that "though it seems like network wrought in iron, it will apparently be uninjured for ages". Uninjured, it stands today.

The idea for the bridge came from a Shrewsbury architect, Thomas Farnolls Pritchard. The bridge would replace a ferry across the gorge of the Severn between Madeley and Broseley, reducing the delays and inconveniences, particularly in the winter, caused by the poor boat services. Why Pritchard opted for cast iron is less clear, although in the parliamentary bill giving assent to the bridge, passed in the spring of 1776, the options were widened to include structures of "cast iron, stone, brick or timber". The petition to Parliament merely claimed that it would be "of public utility" if the bridge were to be constructed of cast iron—presumably on grounds of longevity and strength, and in order to demonstrate the possibilities of the material.

By the summer of 1776, indeed, the trustees were split between the radicals, led by the ironmaster Abraham Darby III, who favoured the cast-iron structure, and the conservatives who preferred a more conventional solution. Fortunately Darby, though outnumbered, held the majority of the shares and was able to get his way. Pritchard and Darby estimated, between

them, that the bridge would be built for £3,200, of which £2,100 was to go on more than 300 tons of cast iron and £500 on dressed stone. These figures turned out to be a considerable underestimate, and during the building of the bridge financial catastrophe was never far away.

Darby, chosen by Pritchard to be the builder of the bridge, was the third member of his family to carry the same name. His grandfather, Abraham Darby I, devised in 1709 a method of making iron in a blast furnace using coke rather than charcoal as the source of carbon. The discovery, although of enormous long-term importance, was taken up only slowly by other iron makers. The reason was that for the time being there was no great shortage of charcoal, and coke worked well only if the ore and the coal were carefully chosen. But by 1755 his son Abraham Darby II, also working in Coalbrookdale, had built a blast furnace using coke that was fully competitive with charcoal and produced cast iron of high quality. It was his son, the third in the Darby dynasty, who was to apply this material to the building of the bridge.

The first designs by Pritchard were for a single-span bridge of 120 feet, with four sets of curved iron ribs, each 9 inches by 6 inches in section. But by July 1777 the span had been reduced to 90 feet, and the design changed slightly. It was subsequently increased once more, to 100 feet 6 inches, to accommodate a towpath along the banks of the Severn, and this is the bridge that was eventually built. On 21 December 1777, when work had hardly begun, Pritchard died, leaving the task to Darby.

The biggest castings in the bridge are the main ribs, each of which weighs $5\frac{3}{4}$ tons. At the time, the blast furnaces of Coalbrookdale produced little more than 2 tons of iron at a time, so the ribs could not have been poured into moulds directly from the blast furnace. The chances are that a special remelting furnace was set up on the banks of the river, and used to melt iron that had been made earlier in the blast furnace, before it was poured into sand moulds.

The advantage would have been that the heavy and fragile castings would not then have had to be manhandled for just over a mile from the Coalbrookdale foundry to the river bank. Though strong in compression, cast iron is a brittle material that required careful handling until it was safely in place. Once erected, the design was such that the forces exerted on the ribs were predominantly compressive.

Considering the contemporary interest in the structure, accounts of its construction are scanty. It appears that most of the work of raising the ribs was carried out in about six weeks in the summer of 1779, beginning with the raising and securing of the first pair of ribs on 1 and 2 July. Some 25 to 30 men were employed on the job. Darby's accounts record the purchase of large amounts of timber, which were used to build a scaffold from which the ribs were suspended on ropes and lowered until they joined in the middle.

In mid-August, the account books record the spending of £6 on ale, which we may guess was to celebrate the completion of the fitting of the ribs. By late November, the same books show the removal of the scaffolding, so it is safe to assume that by then the bridge was complete.

How much the bridge cost is another uncertainty, but contemporary accounts put it at not less than £5,250. Darby appears to have found the additional £2,000 over his original estimate out of his own pocket, and it came close to ruining him. For the rest of his life his property was heavily mortgaged, suggesting that he bought immortality at some sacrifice.

The design of the iron bridge was very conservative and provided a generous margin of safety, for the load-bearing properties of cast iron were not then fully understood. But Darby,

The importance of the Iron Bridge and the surrounding area in the history of industrial development is reflected by UNESCO's decision to declare them a World Heritage Site.

Darby's Metal Masterpiece

or Pritchard, made a small error by failing to allow for the fact that a bridge of iron would be much lighter than one of stone. In a stone bridge, the weight is such that the arch presses outward with great force, requiring embankments to resist movement. In the iron bridge the outward pressure was less, so the embankments moved slowly inward, raising the crown of the arch.

In the early years of the nineteenth century, two additional side arches were added to the bridge, but earth movements continued and cracks were identified. At the beginning of the twentieth century, various additional straps and braces were added to strengthen the structure, which was closed to road traffic in 1934. By the end of the 1960s, continuing movement of the abutments had created some anxiety about the future of the bridge.

Consulting engineers advised that to prevent further movement of the abutments, the foundations of the north abutment should be strengthened and a strut inserted under the water to keep the abutments at a fixed distance apart. The strut took the form of a reinforced concrete slab laid in a trench in the bed of the river, together with walls at each end running up the inside walls of the abutment. Despite flooding and many difficulties, the work was completed during low water in the summers of 1973 and 1974, ensuring the iron bridge will survive for another 200 years.

The successful completion of the bridge in 1779 began a period of bridge-building in cast and wrought iron which lasted a century. By the early 1790s, a huge bridge was built over the Wear at Sunderland, a single arch of 236 feet, yet containing less iron than the bridge at Coalbrookdale. In 1795 floods on the Severn swept away many bridges, but the iron bridge held fast, further increasing its fame and advertising the advantages of cast iron.

The iron bridge itself survived largely because Coalbrookdale, after leading the way into the Industrial Revolution, became something of a backwater. The centres of industry moved to Manchester, Glasgow, Newcastle and other great towns. If traffic over the Severn had continued to grow during the nineteenth century, there is little doubt that the iron bridge would have been replaced by something bigger and more modern; but it did not. As a result, it remains a unique survivor of a bygone age, and the centre of a flourishing museum which has taken over the historic sites of Coalbrookdale.

A bridge "of very curious construction" was how the subscribers described Pritchard's design, based on the principles of carpentry and employing dovetail and mortice-and-tenon joints. No screws or rivets were used.

Coalbrookdale and the Iron Bridge were the first industrial sites to become a tourist attraction, visited by many eminent travellers and commemorated in paintings, coins, jugs, tankards, glasses and even fire-grates. Besides the Darby ironworks, the banks of the river and its environs were lined with brick, tile and china works, warehouses and loading wharfs. The bridge was of great value to the district's trade.

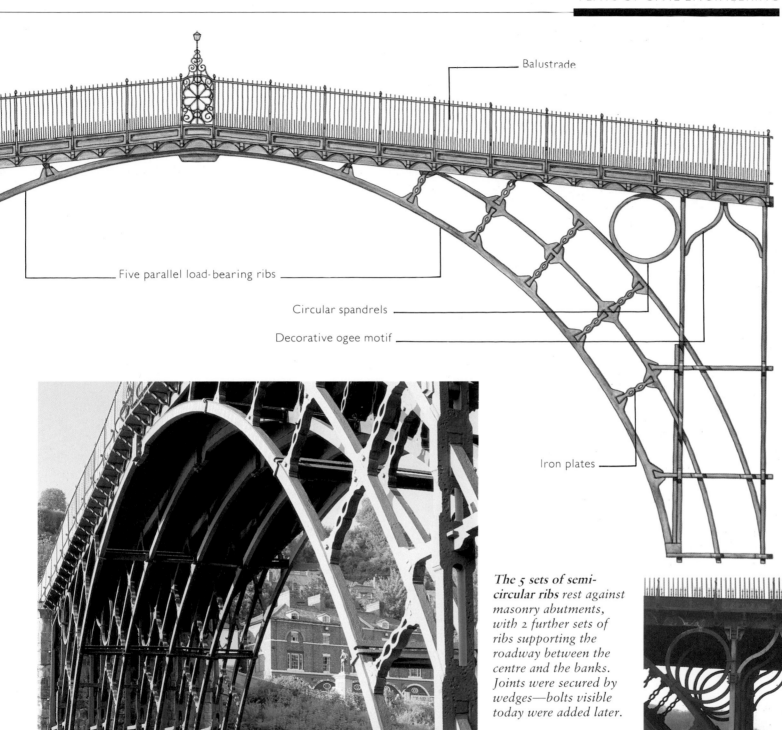

Balustrade

Five parallel load-bearing ribs

Circular spandrels

Decorative ogee motif

Iron plates

The 5 sets of semi-circular ribs *rest against masonry abutments, with 2 further sets of ribs supporting the roadway between the centre and the banks. Joints were secured by wedges—bolts visible today were added later.*

Circles strengthen and decorate the spandrels, *while ornate ogee-headed braces join the 2 vertical members beside the abutments. The design demanded castings of great accuracy.*

The Longest Span

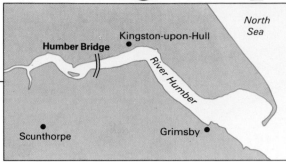

Fact file

The world's longest single-span suspension bridge

Designer: Freeman Fox

Built: 1972–81

Material: Reinforced concrete and steel

Length: 4,625 feet

The world's longest single-span suspension bridge crosses the Humber Estuary, linking together the two halves of the English county of Humberside. It combines the world's longest single span—1,410 metres, or 4,625 feet—with one of the world's fastest accumulating debts. Since the day it opened in 1981, tolls collected from vehicles crossing it have never equalled the interest charges on the money borrowed to build it, so the debt has steadily risen. Critics have called it "the bridge from nowhere to nowhere", and traffic has never come close to meeting the estimates made before it was constructed. It is, none the less, a fine structure, beautiful to look at and a daring piece of engineering.

The bridge was designed by the British company Freeman Fox & Partners, consulting engineers. The main deck is supported by two massive steel cables solidly anchored at each side of the estuary, and carried over the top of concrete towers so that they hang in a graceful catenary curve above the river. The cables are attached by high-tensile steel ropes to a series of shallow boxes which form the roadway. This type of construction is well proven, and is used for bridges requiring very long single spans, such as the Verrazano-Narrows Bridge in New York,

the Bosphorus Bridge in Istanbul, Turkey, and the Severn Bridge linking England and Wales (the last two also the work of Freeman Fox).

The first stage in the construction was to build the anchorages and the towers. On the north bank, both could be built on a solid bed of chalk which comes close to the surface at Hessle. The southern bank was more difficult, with no chalk but a bed of Kimmeridge Clay, 100 feet below the surface, which formed a sufficiently solid base. The southern tower was actually constructed some 510 yards out into the river, with the anchorage at the water's edge. To provide a sound foundation for the tower, concrete caissons were used—huge open circular constructions designed to sink gradually under their own weight as they were built, finishing with their lower edges some 8 yards into the clay. The caissons gradually sank as material was removed from inside them by a grab, but struck underground water which quickly washed away the bentonite, a mineral material used to lubricate the surface of the concrete and ease penetration into the ground. This caused huge difficulties and long delays; ultimately the height of the caissons had to be increased, and 6,000 tons of steel billets temporarily piled on top to create

The Humber Bridge differs from its near rivals in several ways. Topography and geology prevented the usual near symmetry of the side span measurements, though the bridge's length masks the asymmetry. The use of reinforced concrete rather than steel for the towers had been confined to bridges with spans less than half the size.

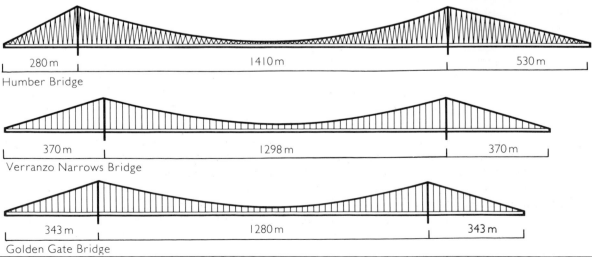

| 280 m | 1410 m | 530 m |

Humber Bridge

| 370 m | 1298 m | 370 m |

Verranzo Narrows Bridge

| 343 m | 1280 m | 343 m |

Golden Gate Bridge

sufficient weight to make the caissons sink to their final positions.

The towers themselves were built of reinforced concrete, poured into forms carried by a platform that could be raised on jacks as the towers went up. Each tower is 158 yards tall, and they rose at a rate of up to $6\frac{1}{2}$ feet a day. The Barton tower, at the southern side of the bridge, was completed in just ten weeks.

The first step in creating the bridge was to throw a footbridge across the river, using six wire ropes carried across in a boat and then pulled into position. The footbridge, a temporary arrangement, was to enable workmen to get into position across the river for the erection of the main support cables which involved some 11,000 tons of wire. During the "spinning" of the cables (as the operation is called, although no actual spinning is involved) the individual strands of wire were carried across in the form of a loop around a wheel carried to and fro by a tramway. Men were stationed at 100-yard intervals along the walkway to handle the wire as it was spooled out. Slowly the cable was built up to its ultimate diameter of 27 inches. At intervals bands were attached around the cables, from which to attach the hangers which would support the decking. The cables were finally coated with red lead paste and wrapped with $\frac{1}{7}$-inch (3.5mm) wire, using special wrapping

The length of the span compelled the designers to allow for the curvature of the Earth: the towers are built exactly 36mm out of parallel. Extensive wind tunnel tests were carried out on models of the deck and towers, and provision was made for a total movement and deflection of just under 9 feet between the ends of the spans.

The Longest Span

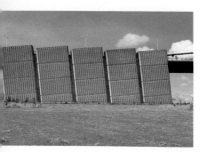

The anchorages for the cables were constructed of reinforced concrete sections covered by glass-reinforced panels to form a decorative ribbed finish.

Trolley for lifting box sections

Main cable

Each main cable is made up of 14,948 parallel wires, each of $\frac{1}{5}$ inch diameter, totalling 41,000 miles in length. To simplify erection, the cables were grouped into 37 strands, each of 404 wires.

machines, before being given five coats of paint to protect them against the weather.

After erection of the bridge's decking, the last stage was to apply the final road surface to the boxes, a $1\frac{1}{2}$-inch (38mm) layer of mastic asphalt, chosen because it is dense enough to stop water penetrating to the steel beneath, and flexible enough to bend to a limited extent without cracking. A total of 3,500 tons of asphalt was needed to complete the roadway.

There is no doubt that the bridge is an engineering and aesthetic success. Although no concessions were made in the design in an attempt to make it beautiful, its austere mathematical simplicity never fails to impress.

The financial statements of the Humber Bridge Board, responsible for running it, are rather less exquisite, consisting as they do largely of red ink. Partly as a result of delays in the foundations for the Barton tower, the bridge was late in opening. Work began on site in April 1973, and the bridge was not opened to traffic until the summer of 1981. The cost also increased enormously, principally as a result of inflation. Instead of the £28 million estimated in 1972, the final cost was £90 million. That, combined with interest during construction, left the bridge with a debt of £151 million on the day it opened. Since then, as interest charges exceed income from tolls, the debt has done nothing but rise. By 1987 the debt was £300 million, by 1989 it totalled £350 million. The Freight Transport Association estimated that if nothing was done, the debt would amount to £576 million by 1993, more than £21,500 million by 2023 and a stupendous £248,247 million by the year 2043. Although tolls bring in around £9 million a year, this is not sufficient, and increasing the tolls would not help as many fewer people would use the bridge. The toll for a car, at £1.60, is already the highest in Britain. However, there is a glimmer of hope that the British government, which lent the money to build the bridge, may agree to write off a proportion of the debt, and give the bridge a chance of breaking even.

The hollow trapezoidal boxes that form the bridge's deck are a distinguishing feature. The steel boxes are lighter than the usual stiffened truss, allowing savings to be made in cables, towers, anchorages and foundations, and the "streamlined" shape reduces wind loading on the bridge. Maintenance is also easier.

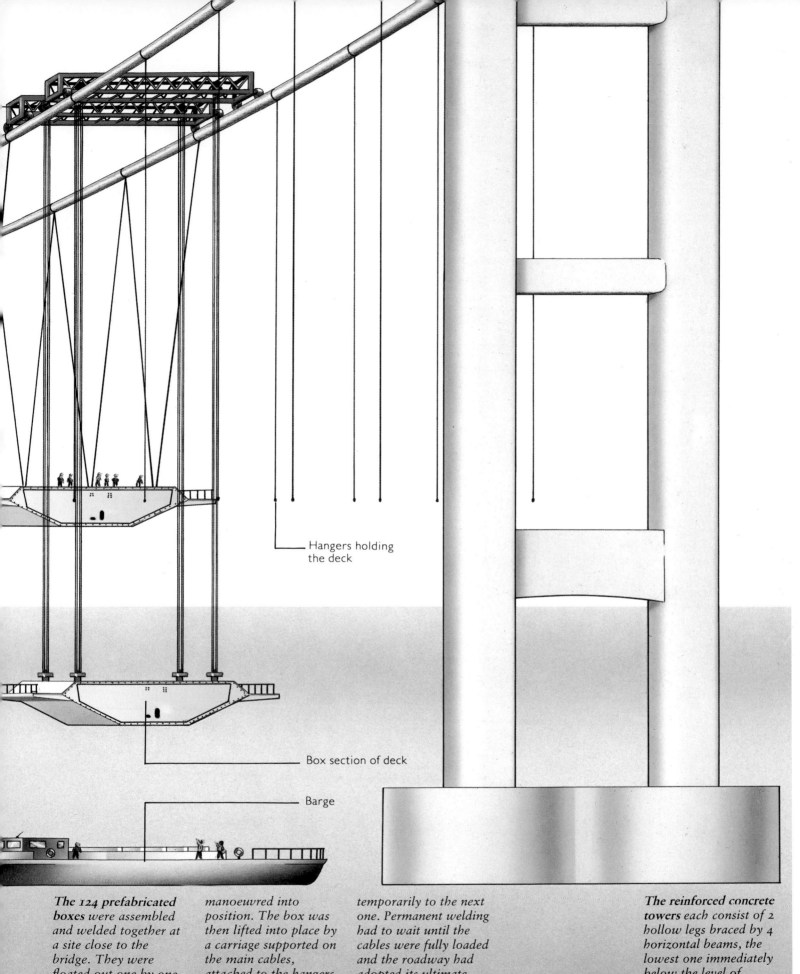

Hangers holding
the deck

Box section of deck

Barge

The 124 prefabricated boxes *were assembled and welded together at a site close to the bridge. They were floated out one by one on barges and* manoeuvred into *position. The box was then lifted into place by a carriage supported on the main cables, attached to the hangers and connected* temporarily to the next *one. Permanent welding had to wait until the cables were fully loaded and the roadway had adopted its ultimate position.*

The reinforced concrete towers *each consist of 2 hollow legs braced by 4 horizontal beams, the lowest one immediately below the level of support for the deck.*

Bridges of Distinction

Bridges have been built since primitive peoples threw a tree trunk across a stream to produce the first beam, or girder, bridge. The principal distinction between the three main types of bridge—girder, arch or suspension—is the way the forces exerted by the bridge's weight are displaced. In the case of a girder or cantilever bridge (a series of girders balanced on supporting piers), the weight simply rests on the ground. An arch bridge exerts an outward thrust on its abutments and a suspension bridge pulls its cables into tension from the anchorage points sited at each end.

Sometimes the principles are combined, but all bridges are permutations of these basic types. The earliest were built of wood, followed by the use of stone, brick, iron, steel and concrete.

The Sydney Harbour bridge

Built by Dorman, Long of Middlesbrough, England, between 1924 and 1932, the steel arch, supported by granite pylons, was half as long again and required twice as much steel as the largest previously built. The span is 1,650 feet and was built to carry 4 railway lines and a 57-foot wide road. It was tested by 72 locomotives weighing 7,600 tons.

The Great Seto bridge

Opened in 1988 it provides a rail and road link between the largest of Japan's 4 main islands, Honshu, and the smallest, Shikoku. The 6 spans and viaducts total almost 8 miles and it is the world's longest double-decker bridge carrying cars as well as trains. Of the 6 spans, 3 are suspended, 2 are cable-stayed and 1 is a conventional truss. It cost about $8,180 million.

Clapper bridge, Devon

Crossing the East Dart River at Postbridge on Dartmoor, Devon, the bridge was built to carry the Plymouth to Moretonhampstead pack-horse route. It is thought to date from the thirteenth century when the traffic in tin and agricultural produce developed. Built of outcropping moorland stone, huge slabs of unchiselled granite rest on piers and buttresses of the same material. Similar examples are found in Spain, and the oldest surviving datable bridge is of slab construction—the bridge over the River Meles in Izmir, Turkey, which was built about 850 BC.

Luiz I bridge, Oporto

Spanning the River Douro at Oporto in Portugal, the bridge was completed in 1885 to the design of T. Seyrig. He had worked with Gustave Eiffel to produce the very similar Pia Maria bridge close by, opened in 1877. The latter carries a railway line over the single deck whereas the Luiz I bridge bears one roadway on the top of the arch and another provides the tie at the foot of the arch. The Luiz I bridge has a 566-foot arch, and both were built by cantilevering from the river banks. A similar design was used by Eiffel for his railway viaduct at Garabit in France which, at 400 feet above a gorge, was the highest arched railway bridge in the world.

Massive Seabed Structure

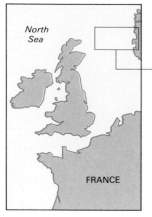

Fact file

When completed, the largest object ever built

Builder: Norwegian Contractors

Built: 1978–81

Material: Concrete and steel

Height: 890 feet

Weight: 824,000 tons

Submerged to the same depth as Statfjord B, the Manhattan skyline would scarcely break above the waves.

In August 1981, the heaviest man-made object ever moved was towed slowly through the western Norwegian fjords toward the North Sea. It was the Statfjord B oil platform, 824,000 tons of concrete and steel, more than 630 feet tall from the oil storage tanks at the bottom to the helicopter deck at the top, and built at a cost of $1,840 million.

Five tugs pulled the huge platform, while three more restrained it from behind to retain control as it wound its way safely through some very narrow fjords. Once in the open sea, the three at the back cast off and the five at the front pulled the platform along at speeds of up to 3 mph. In five days, after a tow of 245 nautical miles, it reached its station, 112 miles due west of Songefjord and 115 miles north east of the

Shetland Islands. Water was pumped into the tanks and the platform settled on the bottom within 50 feet of its planned position.

Statfjord B was then the biggest object produced in an heroic era of offshore engineering. Because the platforms that produce oil from the North Sea are so remote, and so much of them lies below the surface, few people have any conception just how vast they are. From ocean floor to the top of its oil derrick, Statfjord B stands 890 feet, nearly twice as tall as the Great Pyramid at Cheops and not far short of the 1,052 feet of the Eiffel Tower. It is almost 115 times heavier than the latter, nine times heavier than the world's biggest warships (the American Nimitz class aircraft carriers) and three times heavier than each tower in the world's biggest office building, the World Trade Center in New York. Such a structure on land would be an object of huge interest—in the middle of the North Sea, it is almost forgotten.

Statfjord B is a gravity platform, one that rests on the seabed under its own immense weight. The base consists of 24 cells made of reinforced concrete, built in a dry dock in Stavanger. From them rise four hollow legs, also of concrete. Mounted on top is a separate steel structure, the deck, weighing 40,000 tons. This includes all the equipment for drilling the wells and producing 150,000 barrels of oil a day, together with a 200-bed hotel where the workers live, and a helicopter landing pad on the roof. Platforms such as these are production well, refinery, hotel and airport all in one.

The base and the deck were built separately, then mated at sea in an operation which called for supreme precision. The deck, supported by barges, and the base were floated out to Yrkjefjorden, a sheltered deep-water fjord. The top of the four legs in the base matched four short tubes which projected from the bottom of the deck. The trick was to manoeuvre the deck exactly into the right position over the base, then add ballast to the barges to lower the deck while at the same time raising the base by pumping out water from its storage cells. Shifting such huge masses about in the ocean so precisely is a nerve-wracking task. The forces of inertia are so great that the slightest error can chip off huge chunks of concrete as the two huge masses meet. But in 37 hours the entire weight of the deck had been successfully transferred to the base, and the two fastened together by more than 100 4-inch bolts.

Placing the complete platform was another

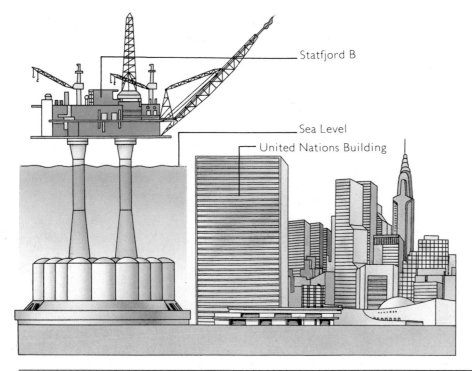

Statfjord B

Sea Level

United Nations Building

Massive Seabed Structure

Statfjord B was the first 4-leg concrete offshore platform to be built. Once the cells of a platform base are completed, 1, 3 or 4 shafts, or legs, are built by the same slipforming techniques employed to build the cells, continuing until the *final height is reached. The shafts have an inner diameter of 75 feet at the base. Two shafts are used for drilling, 1 is the Riser shaft for the oil and the 4th is the Utility shaft, housing loading pumps and ballast water controls.*

The cell structure at the base contains 24 individual concrete cylinders, or cells, in a concentric formation. Four are extended to form the platform's shafts; the other 20 are storage cells 75 feet wide by 210 feet high for crude oil, which not only assist in smoothing off-loading operations but help to stabilize the platform.

tricky operation. Once manoeuvred into position after its tow, water was pumped into the ballast cells to sink the platform on to the seabed. Around the bottom of the concrete base, a skirt made of steel cut approximately 13 feet into the seabed as the platform settled. Six tugs pulling outward in the form of a star positioned the platform and held it steady while ballast was added, monitored by more than 100 sensors and measuring devices.

Once the skirt began penetrating the seabed, water was pumped from beneath it, and finally the small gaps between the bottom of the base and the seabed were filled by pumping in concrete. The result was a platform placed in the right position and vertical to within a fraction of a degree. It will withstand the worst the North Sea can throw at it, waves 100 feet high and winds of more than 100 mph, without shifting so much as half an inch.

Platforms such as Statfjord B are a world of their own, a universe of noise and power and ceaseless activity. Gas turbines generate enough electricity to run a small town, while inside the huge concrete legs runs a network of pipes and cables of nightmarish complexity. Two legs on Statfjord B are used for drilling the 32 wells, which do not go straight down but curve outwards in a sweeping parabola to reach the farthest corners of the field. Another leg, used for pumps and piping, has 13 separate floors served by lifts.

From the dark oily water of the bilges at the bottom, hundreds of feet below the surface of the sea, you can look upwards, the poet Al Alvarez has written, "as if from the bottom of one of Piranesi's imaginary prisons—a vast enclosed shadowy place, with gangways and galleries and ominous, purposeful machinery, all of it disproportionate to the human scale".

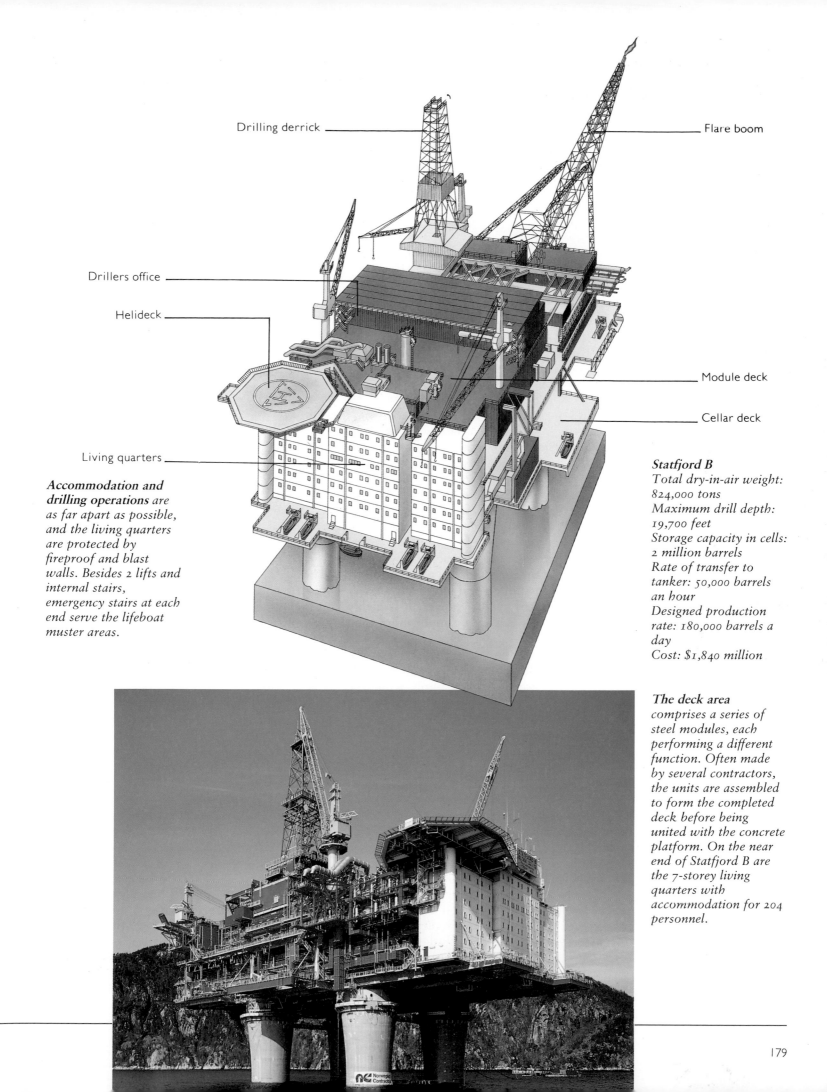

Drilling derrick

Flare boom

Drillers office

Helideck

Module deck

Cellar deck

Living quarters

Accommodation and drilling operations are as far apart as possible, and the living quarters are protected by fireproof and blast walls. Besides 2 lifts and internal stairs, emergency stairs at each end serve the lifeboat muster areas.

Statfjord B
Total dry-in-air weight: 824,000 tons
Maximum drill depth: 19,700 feet
Storage capacity in cells: 2 million barrels
Rate of transfer to tanker: 50,000 barrels an hour
Designed production rate: 180,000 barrels a day
Cost: $1,840 million

The deck area comprises a series of steel modules, each performing a different function. Often made by several contractors, the units are assembled to form the completed deck before being united with the concrete platform. On the near end of Statfjord B are the 7-storey living quarters with accommodation for 204 personnel.

Generators of the Future

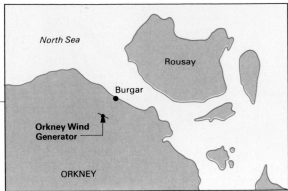

Fact file

The world's most powerful wind generator

Builder: Wind Energy Group

Built: 1985–87

Material: Concrete

Height: 145 feet

Length of rotor: 195 feet

The wind has been used as a source of energy since the seventh century AD, when the first windmills appeared in Persia. From medieval times until the invention of steam power, wind- and watermills represented the summit of technology, machines that could grind corn and pump water, producing far more power than man or animals could. By 1840 there are reckoned to have been about 10,000 windmills at work in England and Wales.

But these beautiful machines have little in common with the new design of wind generators, designed to produce electricity, which have been built since the early 1970s in response to the rising price of fossil fuels and increasing anxiety about the safety of nuclear power. It is highly unlikely that they can ever supply more than about 5–10 percent of the generating needs of developed countries, but even that is a substantial market. At current construction costs, 5 percent of the British power supply would be worth £6,000 million in construction contracts, which explains why a number of big companies have taken an interest.

To make a useful contribution to national electricity generation, as opposed to supplying isolated homes and communities with an intermittent supply, wind generators need to be big. The first attempt to produce such a machine was made by an American engineer, Palmer Putnam, in the 1940s. On the top of a mountain called Grandpa's Knob 2,000 feet up in the Green mountains of central Vermont, Putnam built a tower 110 feet high with a two-bladed, propeller-shaped rotor mounted at the top. It was designed to generate 1.25 megawatts, a substantial output, and went into service on an experimental basis in October 1941.

The generator was not a huge success, suffering many breakdowns and finally failing in March 1945 when one of the blades flew off. The experience at Grandpa's Knob has been repeated many times since, because the fluctuating forces at the root of the blades produce metal fatigue which causes fracture and destruction of the machine. Recent experience suggests that this problem has yet to be entirely overcome.

Where Palmer Putnam went, many other engineers have followed. The world's biggest wind generator was inaugurated in November 1987 on top of Burgar Hill, on the island of Orkney off the coast of Scotland. The generator, LS-1, has a two-bladed rotor mounted at the top of a concrete tower 145 feet high. The machine was designed to generate a peak output of 3 megawatts, and sufficient electricity year-round to supply 2,000 homes connected to the Orkney grid. It cost £12.2 million to build.

LS-1 was constructed by the Wind Energy Group, a joint venture involving Taylor Woodrow, GEC, and British Aerospace. The huge rotor was built by British Aerospace at its Hatfield plant. The tower had meanwhile been constructed using conventional slipforming techniques. On top of it was placed a steel top, or frustum, 20 feet high and weighing 33 tons, which houses the electrical generator. This was made by Seaforth Maritime in Scotland. To it was attached a 66-ton nacelle, built by British Aerospace, which carries the rotor, primary gearbox, bearings, and brake.

The Orkney machine, like all large wind generators, is designed to produce a steady output under a range of wind speeds. In breezes of less than 15 mph, or Force 3 on the Beaufort Scale, it produces nothing. When the wind rises above that speed the rotor cuts in, and reaches maximum power of 3 MW at winds of 37 mph.

At high wind speeds of more than 60 mph, or Force 10, the machine cuts out to avoid damage. The entire construction is designed to survive hurricane force winds of 155 mph. At an average mean wind speed of 24 mph at the hub height of the machine, it will generate 9,000 MW hours per year—equivalent to a continuous 1 MW output 24 hours a day, every day of the year.

Power from the rotor is first transmitted to the primary gearbox inside the nacelle. The output from this gearbox runs downward into the frustum, through a secondary gearbox and into the generator. The rotor turns at a speed of 34 rpm—about as fast as a long-playing record on a turntable—and the two gearboxes multiply the speed up to the generator's 1,500 rpm. The generator speed is fixed by the need to synchron-

Generators of the Future

ize the output with the 50 cycle per second mains supply. The machine, which is intended to be experimental, is extensively equipped with sensors to measure power output, rotor blade loads, wind speeds and other variables. The signals are fed by fibre optic cable to a computer-based data acquisition system located some 100 yards from the machine.

Although LS-1 is the largest wind generator to date, other machines almost its equal have been built in Sweden, Germany, and the US. So far, experience with the big machines has been mixed. The fatigue problem has defeated several of them, and there have also been difficulties synchronizing their output to the grid, which is vital if they are to become reliable suppliers of power. The grid supplies an alternating current which reverses direction 50 times a second, and new power stations have to get into step with all the others when they come on line, so that the peaks and troughs of the supply coincide.

There have been difficulties achieving this with wind-power machines because their speed is not absolutely constant. The force of gravity on the blades makes them slow down slightly when they are moving between 6 o'clock and midnight, and accelerate between midnight and 6 o'clock. This can produce fluctuations in output which make synchronization difficult. In LS-1, a hydraulic coupling between the rotor and the gearbox damps down the oscillations.

Experience with smaller machines has so far been rather better. The greatest concentration of them is in the state of California, where "wind farms" already supply enough energy for 20,000 homes, saving 2.2 million barrels of oil a year. One prime site is the Altamont Pass, near San Francisco, where winds blow almost continuously, and thousands of wind-power machines dot the landscape. By 1988, California had 16,000 wind turbines supplying electricity, most of them in the 150–300 kilowatt range, much smaller than LS-1. Tax incentives have helped the developments in the US, as they have in Denmark and the Netherlands.

In the long run, the future of wind energy will depend on reliability, cost, and environmental acceptability. Most cost estimates at present suggest that wind-generated electricity is roughly competitive with coal and nuclear generation, but certainly not dramatically cheaper. Operating experience suggests that big machines will also need a lot of servicing, spending perhaps a third of their lives out of

commission. Costs of small- to medium-sized machines are, however, falling as more are built, which could improve the economic prospects.

The environmental acceptability of wind power is another key issue. While enthusiasts for alternative energy sources tend to favour wind power over oil, coal or nuclear energy, it is not yet clear that the general public would be happy to see every windy site, and many seashores, occupied by huge wind turbines. To make inroads into total energy consumption, hundreds or even thousands of machines like LS-1 would have to be built, each requiring a substantial area. Such machines cannot be built right next to each other because that reduces the wind and increases buffeting. Wind farms may be green, but is their effect on the environment entirely benign? That is an intriguing and difficult question to which environmentalists may yet have to find an answer.

LS-1 under construction on Burgar Hill (above). Orkney is known for its bitter weather and regular gales, making the site ideal. Though not the first wind generator on Burgar Hill, it is much the largest. The forerunner of LS-1 can be seen beyond the construction site; the MS-1 has an output of 250kW compared with LS-1's 3MW.

The rotor is built in 5 sections, of steel and glass fibre-reinforced plastic and weighs 63 tons. Measuring 195 feet from tip to tip, it is just longer than the wing span of a Boeing 747 jumbo jet. The enormous forces on the rotor make it the most vulnerable component to metal fatigue.

Assembly of the rotor took place in a large hangar where it was tested both statically and dynamically before being taken apart and shipped to Orkney. The angle or pitch of the rotor can be adjusted by hydraulic power (below), the mechanism fitting into the hub. The outer 30 percent of the blades can be feathered to adjust their speed for a constant output.

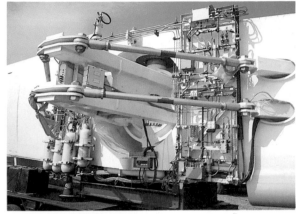

An internal hoist enabled the rotor to be lifted up to be united with the primary gearbox in the nacelle. The 65-ton nacelle and 32-ton frustum, containing the generator, had to be put in place by crane. A 4-person elevator provides access to the nacelle for operations and maintenance personnel.

Nuclear Goliath

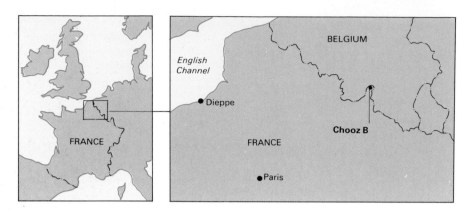

BELGIUM

English Channel

Dieppe

Chooz B

FRANCE

FRANCE

Paris

Fact file

Europe's largest nuclear power station

Builder: Electricité de France

Built: 1982–

Output: 2,800 megawatts

Area of site: 331 acres

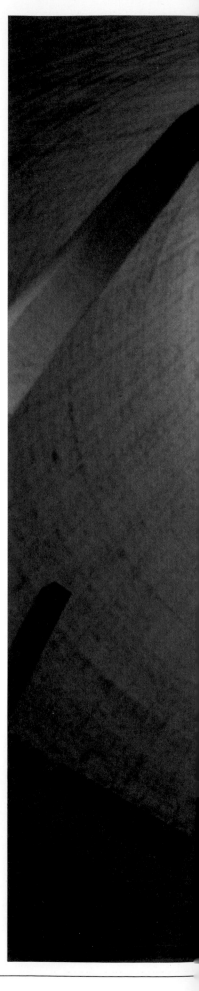

No other form of engineering combines power and precision in quite the same way as do nuclear power stations. They are vast machines, costing hundreds of millions of pounds, and powerful enough to supply all the electricity for a huge city. Yet they are put together with a clockmaker's precision, and in conditions of cleanliness that would do credit to an operating theatre. The biggest in Europe, and among the very biggest in the world, is Chooz B, which, when finished in 1993, will generate 2,800 megawatts from two pressurized water reactors set in a curve of the River Meuse in France close to the border with Belgium.

The years since 1979 have not been happy ones for nuclear power. The accidents at Three Mile Island in 1979 and Chernobyl in 1986 have brought home the consequences of error in a technology that offers much, but at a price. Many nations have stopped building nuclear plants altogether. Not so France, which possesses uranium but lacks indigenous sources of coal or oil and embarked in the early 1970s on an ambitious plan of nuclear investment.

In 1973 France produced less than a quarter of its energy from its own resources. By 1986, it produced 46 percent, and it expects to exceed 50 percent during the 1990s. This has been achieved by building nuclear plants on all the main rivers of France and along the coastline. Today France has more than 50 reactors in operation. The three biggest, still under construction, are at Chooz on the Meuse and at Civaux on the Vienne. At Chooz, where there is already a much smaller reactor, Chooz A, there will be two 1,400 MW reactors; at Civaux, one.

Part of the French success in this huge and costly programme has come from building a single type of reactor, increasing in size only gradually, and gaining enormous expertise in putting the reactors together. The pressurized water reactor was originally developed by Westinghouse in the United States, based on a scaled-up version of the reactor used to power nuclear submarines. But the French had little hesitation in abandoning their own home-grown designs in favour of a reactor made in America. The design has since been considerably developed.

All nuclear power stations have certain things in common: uranium fuel, usually in the form of pellets of uranium dioxide; a coolant to remove the heat produced by the nuclear reaction, and generate steam; and a moderator, the purpose of which is to slow down the neutrons produced by nuclear fission and improve the functioning of the reactor. In a PWR, ordinary water is used as both coolant and moderator. The heat generated by the fuel is transferred to the water inside a steel vessel at a pressure of about 2,000 lb per square inch, or 130 times normal atmospheric pressure. The water temperature rises to more than 570°F (300°C), but the water does not boil because it is under such great pressure. Instead it flows in tubes through a steam generator, where it gives up its heat to a second set of tubes, also carrying water. This water, which is not pressurized, does boil, producing steam which is then fed to turbo-generators to produce electricity.

The most critical component in a PWR reactor is the pressure vessel, for if it should fail catastrophically there would be a massive leak of radioactive material into the reactor building, and perhaps also to the outside world. The pressure vessels at the Chooz B plant are typical. They are cylinders 44 feet high and with an inner diameter of 14 feet 6 inches, made from steel almost 9 inches thick, and weigh 462 tons. On top is a dome-shaped lid which is bolted firmly down during normal operation, but which can be removed when fuel needs replacing—once every year at Chooz B. The standards of manufacture of the pressure vessel and pipework

Nuclear Goliath

which carries the cooling water in and out need to be of the very highest. So far, the care has paid off: there have been no catastrophic failures of pressure vessels in commercial nuclear reactors.

Inside the pressure vessel is a network of fuel rods, each about 14 feet long and less than ½ inch in diameter. Inside each rod are pellets of uranium oxide in which the proportion of fissile uranium-235 has been artificially increased to about 3 percent. The rods are arranged into fuel assemblies, which each contain 264 rods, held together on a grid with spacers. The Chooz B reactor has 205 such assemblies—a total of 54,120 fuel rods. The fuel assemblies occupy the lower half of the pressure vessel and are surrounded by a cylindrical sheath. Water flowing through pipes at the top is directed down to the bottom of the pressure vessel between the sheath and the walls, and then flows upward through the gaps between the fuel rods in the centre. As it does so it removes heat from the fuel rods and increases in temperature before flowing out through a separate set of pipes to the steam generator.

The PWR is a very compact design, with all the heat generated in a comparatively small volume. It is therefore vital to maintain a flow of water at all times, because if it were to fail the reactor could overheat and melt down. Coolant flow is necessary even after the reactor has been shut down, for it still continues to generate intense heat through radioactive decay. This is why PWRs are always fitted with emergency core-cooling systems, independent of the regular circuits, to ensure adequate cooling at all times.

The much bigger structures that tower over the reactor buildings at Chooz B are cooling towers. Due to the laws of thermodynamics, not all the heat generated by the nuclear fuel can be turned into electricity – more than half of it must be discarded.

The purpose of cooling towers is to remove the heat from the water and disperse it into the air. Air flows in at the bottom and rises naturally to the top as a result of the chimney effect of the structure. Meanwhile, warm water is sprayed over a network of vanes between which the rising air flows. The result is to heat the air— which leaves from the top of the tower as a plume loaded with water vapour—and to cool the water. The cooled water is then released into the River Meuse; but even now it is not quite cold, and will raise the temperature of the river by 1.8°F (1°C). This, claims Electricité de France,

is too little to have any measurable effect on the life of the river.

The final key element in the plant is the turbo-generator which turns the steam into electricity. At Chooz B, the turbo-generators are among the biggest ever built, capable of generating 1,400 MW and weighing 3,150 tons. At one end is a steam turbine, in which steam is allowed to expand through series of fans arranged along a common shaft, forcing it to turn at 1,500 rpm. Attached to the same shaft at the other end of the machine is an electrical generator which produces the electricity.

Chooz B will take ten years to complete, and is expected to cost 15,000 million francs ($2,640 million) at 1985 prices. Building it will employ 1,600 people; operating it will need between 500 and 550. Work began on site in July 1982 and the first reactor is expected to come on stream in 1991, with the second following in 1993.

Cooling towers are a feature common to coal-fired and inland nuclear power stations. Nuclear plants by the sea generally dispose of waste heat by allowing it to flow away in the form of hot water into the ocean, where its effect is minimal. River-based plants cannot do this, because the river water would soon be lukewarm and cause enormous ecological damage.

The foundation ring of a cooling tower (below), showing the anti-turbulence, finned pillars, which look too insubstantial to support the concrete tower. Heat exchanging machinery covers the floor of the tower.

The reactors are surrounded by a concrete vault housed in a double-walled structure (above), the containment building. This provides successive layers of protection to isolate radiation from the outside world in the event of a leak.

Part of a steam generator (right) which utilizes heat generated by the PWR to produce steam in a secondary system, which in turn powers the turbo-generator. Each generator contains 5,600 U-shaped tubes.

The dome over the PWR has an inner and outer casing, strengthened by anti-fracture steel reinforcement (above). Almost 261,500 cubic yards of concrete are required for each reactor and fuel building and its associated cooling tower.

Harness of the Sun

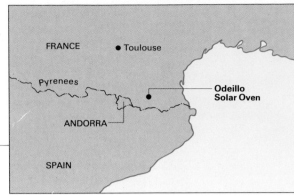

Fact file

The largest solar-powered generating plant in Europe

Builder: National Centre for Scientific Research

Commissioned: 1969

Material: Glass

Area of mirror: 20,000 square feet

The tower in front of the fixed mirror houses the furnace which receives the concentrated solar rays from the mirror.

The energy that reaches the Earth from its star, the Sun, is many times greater than that actually used by the humans on our planet. The amount that falls just on the roads and freeways of the United States is more than double the world's total consumption of coal and oil. But solar energy is widely spread: at best, the amount falling on an area of 1 square yard on a sunny day is around 1,000 watts. If the weather is cloudy, it might be only a fifth of that.

To make effective use of the Sun's energy, it has to be concentrated. This principle has been understood since ancient times. Archimedes is supposed to have attacked the Roman fleet at Syracuse in 214 BC by reflecting solar rays on to their ships with a system of mirrors arranged on the shore. The Athenians and the Aztecs lit their sacred flames with the help of concave mirrors, and countless campers have done the same for their bonfires with convex lenses. In the eighteenth century a Swiss physicist, Horace-Benedict

de Saussure, cooked a little soup—we do not know what sort—by using a series of lenses to focus the Sun's rays on to an oven, and the famous chemist Antoine Lavoisier constructed a solar furnace in 1772, using two lenses mounted on a wooden chariot. With this device he was able to create temperatures that exceeded 2,700°F (1,500°C).

The use of solar energy in this way seems to have been particularly fascinating to the French. In 1945 the chemist Felix Trombe, who specialized in the study of high-melting refractory materials, was asked by the French National Centre for Scientific Research (CNRS) to study the subject in depth. He used an old radar dish 6 feet in diameter, silvered on the inside to reflect light, to achieve temperatures of more than 5,400°F (3,000°C). It was as a result of his experiments that a laboratory was set up in the western Pyrenees, at the fort of Montlouis, to continue the work. Close by, at Odeillo, was built one of the most impressive and successful of solar furnaces. It came into service in 1969.

The Odeillo furnace uses a series of flat mirrors, arranged on terraces on a hillside, to reflect the Sun's rays on to a parabolic mirror 138 feet wide. There are 63 flat mirrors, known as heliostats, arranged on eight terraces. The heliostats can turn both horizontally and vertically to track the Sun and ensure that its rays are always reflected exactly on to the central parabolic mirror. The movement is carried out automatically, under hydraulic power. A computer controls the hydraulic system.

The parabolic mirror is fixed, and focuses the light falling on to it. It is a characteristic of parabolic mirrors that parallel rays of light reflected from them all pass through the same point, called the focal distance; at Odeillo this point is 58 feet in front of the parabolic mirror. The mirror itself consists of 9,500 small mirrors, each just under 18 inches square, creating a total surface area of some 20,000 square feet. The light from this mirror is focused on to the furnace, which is mounted in a tower fixed at the focal point of the mirror. All the heat is not concentrated at a single point, but into an area just 16 inches across. This produces immensely high temperatures, up to 6,870°F (3,800°C).

Because the air in the Pyrenees is clean, little dirt is deposited on the mirrors and any that is tends to be removed by frost and snow. The heliostats need cleaning only every two years or so, while the parabolic mirror was cleaned only

Harness of the Sun

twice in its first 16 years of operation. The furnace operates for around 1,200 hours every year and requires little servicing of its hydraulic and electronic control gear.

The advantage of the solar furnace is the intensity of the heat source and its great purity. Unlike other methods of reaching such high temperatures, there is no danger of contamination, which has made it useful for the production of materials such as a vanadium oxide semiconductor used by Kodak in certain photographic films. It can also be used to investigate the resistance of materials to sudden changes of temperature. By using specially cooled shutters, the heat can be turned on and off in a period as short as $\frac{1}{10}$ of a second, creating very rapid cycles of heating and cooling which would cause most materials to shatter. The thermal tiles used to protect the American space shuttle when it re-enters the atmosphere, and the protective material on missiles have been tested in this way.

There is, of course, another way in which the concentrated heat of the Sun can be used. By raising steam, it can generate electricity and replace coal, oil or nuclear generating plants. Near Odeillo there is a 2.5 megawatt plant based on this principle, using 200 mirrors arranged in a semicircle to reflect sunlight towards a tower 328 feet high. This is the largest solar-powered generating plant in Europe, but there is a much bigger establishment at Barstow in California, named Solar 1.

This plant uses 1,818 mirrors to focus the sunlight on to a boiler at the top of a tower 255 feet high. First tested in 1982, Solar 1 is capable of generating 10 megawatts, and cost $141 million to build. It is situated in the Mohave Desert, which enjoys more than 300 cloudless days a year. But it occupies about 100 acres of land, which is an indication of just how much space is needed for a solar power station, even in ideal circumstances. To generate the whole of the United States' power supply in this way would mean occupying much of the desert lands with power stations. Nations less favoured with solar energy, like Britain, could simply not find the space to justify such plants.

Unlike Odeillo, the Barstow plant does not have a complex parabolic mirror. Instead, its sun-tracking mirrors focus the light on to a single receiver mounted on top of the tower. The receiver consists of a series of pipes, painted black to absorb energy better, through which flows a fluid. In the simplest plants the fluid may

be water, which is converted to steam by the heat, and the steam used to generate electricity in conventional turbines. An alternative is to use molten salts, which are an excellent medium for storing heat, and divert the problem of handling high-pressure steam up at the top of the tower. The salt is heated by the concentrated solar rays, and flows through pipes to the ground, where it gives up its heat in heat exchangers to water, generating steam to produce electricity.

The Barstow plant has proved very successful, and has been followed by a series of schemes in the US to replace the conventional boilers of power stations with "power towers" using solar energy. One survey in the 16 south-western states suggested that up to 13,000 megawatts of solar energy could be used in so-called repowering schemes, replacing about 11 percent of the oil and gas being consumed at present by the electricity utilities.

The size of the mirrors necessary to generate a commercially worthwhile amount of power (above), and their obtrusiveness in the landscape, militate against their adoption on a large scale. However, as the costs of fossil fuels rise, harnessing the Sun's energy will become an increasingly attractive prospect.

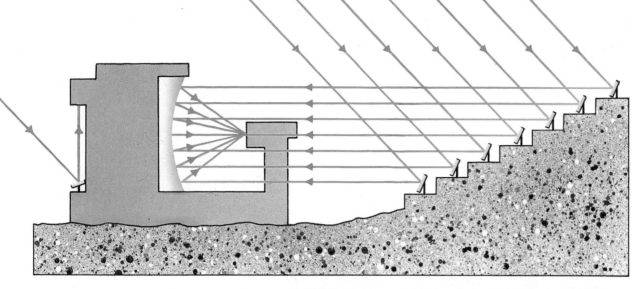

The intensity of the solar radiation at the focal point of the mirror's rays is 12,000 times more powerful than normal solar rays when the furnace is operating at maximum capacity; in average conditions it is 2,000 times more powerful.

Banks of heliostats (right)—flat mirrors that reflect the Sun's rays on to the main, parabolic mirror—require a large amount of space, and need to be in a stepped pattern to maximize their effectiveness. At Odeillo, the heliostats are each 24 feet by 20 feet, giving a total area of collection of 30,000 square feet.

The number of overcast days in temperate climates (left) is the principal drawback to the exploitation of solar energy in such climates. Yet the Sun's energy is so great that its potential compels extensive research: in 2 weeks, the solar energy falling on Earth is the equivalent of the world's entire initial reserves of coal, oil and gas.

CHAPTER FOUR

Underground Engineering Achievements

We know more about the surface of the Moon than we do about the ground 10 miles beneath our feet. Despite every achievement of engineering, the Earth's crust remains unknown territory into which we have scarcely ventured. The mantle and the core that lie below the crust are even more remote. The deepest wells drilled go down no more than 10 miles, and then only with huge difficulty. Attempts to reach the Mohorovicic Discontinuity—the point at which crust gives way to mantle—were abandoned in the 1960s when the costs of the venture soared out of control.

It was an experience familiar indeed to tunnel engineers. As the barrier that has divided Britain from the rest of Europe for so long is finally undermined by the Channel Tunnel, the costs and complexities of boring tunnels are constantly rehearsed. There is hardly a tunnel that has ever been dug, anywhere, without exceeding its budget. Even in Japan, where the world's longest rail tunnel was completed during the 1980s at huge and uncovenanted expense, construction had taken so long that the airlines had taken most of the traffic. Moreover, the cost overrun meant that there was no money left to build the railway for "bullet" trains that might have won the passengers back. No one, it seems, can produce a formula that is entirely right.

The sinister nature of the subterranean world, and the sense of fear it provokes, are nowhere stronger than in the catacombs, where early Christians were laid to rest like lost souls each to its own filing cabinet. A similar unease pervades the long tunnels of the world's greatest underground factory, in the Harz Mountains of Germany, where slave labourers from the conquered nations were put to work building a new and terrible weapon, the ballistic missile, during World War II. Compared with these, the light and cheerful tunnel that houses the world's biggest atom-smasher at CERN, the European particle physics laboratory, seems wholly beneficent. Here a vast machine buried in the stable rock is used to probe the fundamental nature of the universe. Tiny particles too small to imagine whirl round at fantastic speeds before smashing into one another, a concept as peculiar in its way as the ancient myths that once gave the nether world such notoriety.

Underground Engineering Achievements
Catacombs
Nordhausen V2 Factory
LEP Accelerator
Seikan Rail Tunnel
Great tunnels

Subterranean Mausoleum

On the outskirts of Rome lies a honeycomb of subterranean passages where the bodies of the early Christians were buried. The catacombs, as they are called, date from a period when being a Christian was a dangerous activity. Here were laid the bodies of some of the early popes, and of Christians martyred by Roman emperors determined to stamp out the Church. Alongside them are ordinary Christians, men and women who shared the conviction that burial of the dead was a supreme duty if they were to participate in the resurrection in which all Christians believe.

The digging of the catacombs, a process which went on for several hundred years, was the task of a group of men called *fossores*, or diggers. The marks of the picks they used to carve out the passages in the soft rock can still be seen today. By the middle of the third century, when the Church was under very strong pressure, many men must have been employed as *fossores* in order to have created such a labyrinth of tunnels. About 40 different sets of catacombs are known, most of them close to the main roads that run into the city. The total length of tunnel is difficult to calculate, since the catacombs run to and fro like a maze, usually occupying several levels, but they amount to many miles.

The *fossores* who created them lived a cold and gloomy life, hacking away in narrow tunnels with only the dead for company; it was no task for the faint-hearted. Sometimes they would be required to carve out underground rooms, 10 feet or more square, which served as crypts for an entire family. There seems little doubt that some of them supplemented their incomes by stealing anything of value from older graves.

Later, as waves of invaders swept through Rome, the very existence of the catacombs was forgotten, and they remained unvisited for hundreds of years. They were then rediscovered at the beginning of the seventeenth century by an enthusiast named Antonio Bosio, who appears to have spent most of his life after the age of 20 searching for them. He would set out on foot from the centre of Rome and spend whole days looking for entrances to the catacombs. He rediscovered about 30 of them, and published his results in his book *Roma Sotterranea*, Subterranean Rome. Proper archeological study followed in the nineteenth century. In 1854, when Pope Pius IX was told by the archeologist G.B. de Rossi that the graves of the early popes had been rediscovered, he initially refused to believe it. Inscriptions, however, left no doubt that these were, indeed, the last resting places of five popes from the third century.

Why did the early Christians go to such enormous trouble to bury their dead? Catacombs are not, in fact, an exclusively Christian custom, and they are found all over the Mediterranean, particularly in Malta, Sicily, Egypt, Tunisia and Lebanon. But the fact that after his crucifixion Christ's body was laid in a sepulchre, with a stone to cover the entrance, must have helped make the idea popular to his followers.

Another reason was undoubtedly the danger of persecution. Under the Emperor Valerian, for example, Christians were forbidden to visit cemeteries, and all burials within the walls of Rome were forbidden by law. To protect the mortal remains of the Christian martyrs, they were taken from ordinary graves and concealed in catacombs where they were less likely to be disturbed. These burial places then became centres of pilgrimage, and ordinary Christians began to express the wish that when they died they should be laid as close as possible to the bodies of the martyrs.

A further consideration may have been limitation of space, encouraging a system of burial where successive tombs are buried ever deeper in the ground. A final factor was the wish of living Christians to visit the dead on the anniversary of burial, there to celebrate the Eucharist. For a persecuted Church it was clearly much easier to do this privately underground than in a more conventional cemetery. There is, however, no reason to suppose that the catacombs were used as secret places for worship. The largest rooms in any of the catacombs can accommodate no more than 40 people, and by the third century there were at least 50,000 practising Christians in Rome, so an underground service would not have been very convenient.

The ground around Rome was ideal for tunnelling, consisting of a soft *tufa* that was

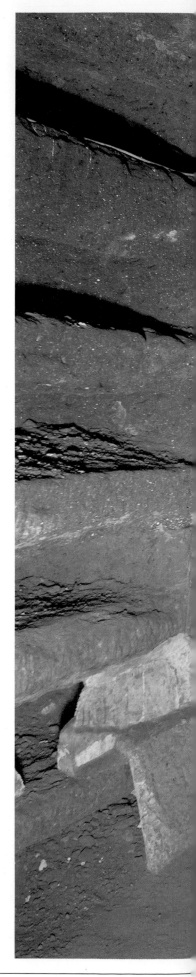

Subterranean Mausoleum

The Catacombs of St Calixtus (right) were the official burial place of the bishops of Rome, and named after Callistus who was put in charge of the cemetery by Pope Zephyrinus. Callistus was himself elected pope after 18 years administering the cemetery. The catacombs are on five levels and contain many frescoes. The papal crypt still has Greek inscriptions of the early martyred popes from the 3rd to 4th centuries.

The Columbarium in the privately owned Vigna Codini (above) has space in its largest room for 500 urns containing cremated remains. The term "Columbarium" was applied to such rooms on account of their resemblance to the holes in the walls of a dovecote, which is the principal meaning of the word, "columba" being the Latin for dove.

quarried to form the basis of a strong mortar used by the Romans for building. Often a catacomb began at an entrance into a hillside originally dug by quarrymen to extract *tufa*. A passage was dug into the ground, and new passages cut at right angles to it, perhaps leading to further passages parallel to the first one. Sometimes the passages, 7–10 feet high and 3–4 feet wide, went down for as many as five distinct levels, with light wells drilled to the surface to let some sunshine penetrate the gloom. Neighbouring catacombs often joined up, creating a veritable warren of passages, in which it is easy to get lost.

The simplest grave was a kind of shelf, dug into the walls of the passage, in which the body was laid, wrapped in two layers of linen. The space was then closed by sealing it with tiles. Such graves are known as *loculi*. Alternatively, there were tomb chambers, or *cubicula*, in which

a whole family might be buried, the equivalent underground of the family vaults in an ordinary cemetery. Along the passages oil lamps were cemented into the walls, together with vases for perfume to sweeten the air. Sometimes a child's toy, or a coin, was also cemented into the wall close to a tomb. Most of the tiles have been torn off by grave robbers.

What little we know about the *fossore* who dug these catacombs comes from the drawings that are found on the walls. They wore a short tunic, and carried a lamp with a chain and spike attached, so that it could be driven into the wall and hung to supply light. They also carried a basket for removing the material they hacked from the walls with their picks. *Fossore* clearly regarded themselves as more than mere grave-diggers, with a status approaching that of the clergy. They were also artists, decorating the catacombs with simple carvings and paintings of

A catacomb near Via Latina (left) was discovered as recently as 1955 during building work. It is thought to date from between AD 320 and 360 and to have been the preserve of a few wealthy families. Some frescoes depict subjects never before encountered in the catacombs, such as Greek mythology. This picture in a cubiculum depicts Alcestis after being rescued from Hades by Hercules who returns her to her husband Admetus.

no great merit, but fascinating for the light they cast on the early Church.

In the period when Rome was attacked by successive waves of invaders, the bodies of many of the Christian martyrs were removed from the catacombs and taken into the churches and basilicas. In AD 609, for example, 28 wagon loads of relics are said to have been taken to the church of S. Maria ad martyres, and the Lombard invasion of 756 did enormous damage to the cemeteries outside Rome, encouraging more relics to be brought into churches in the city by Pope Paul I (757–67).

Paschal I (817–24) had the bodies of 2,300 martyrs transferred to the church of S. Prassede. By this time, the catacombs were almost empty, and began to be forgotten. From the ninth century, until the time of Bosio in the seventeenth, they slumbered quietly, visited by very few. Bosio's work encouraged others to venture down, but few were willing to believe that these were really Christian burial places. Many relics and paintings were destroyed by enthusiastic but amateurish exploration.

The paintings that do survive in the catacombs are important because they are almost the only remaining forms of Christian art from the era when the Church was persecuted. Early church buildings have all perished, but the simple decoration of the catacombs survived. Many of the paintings depict scenes from the Old Testament—the Fall, Noah's Ark, and Abraham's sacrifice of Isaac are particularly common.

There are also many New Testament scenes, such as the baptism of Jesus, and many of his miracles. By far the most common of these is the raising of Lazarus, of which more than 50 examples have been found in the catacombs—an understandable theme to find in a place devoted to the dead.

The Catacombs of Saints Pietro and Marcellino (above) are the most pictorially decorated in Rome. Representations of the Fall are common, not only in paintings but on sarcophagi and on glass cups. A version in the Via Latina catacombs shows Adam and Eve being expelled from Eden by God, *who was portrayed without inhibitions in early Christian art.*

Factory beneath a Mountain

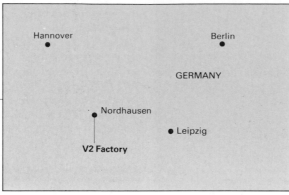

Fact file

The world's largest underground factory

Builder: Third Reich

Built: 1936–42

Length of tunnels: 7 miles

Area: 1.27 million square feet

On the evening of 8 September 1944, without a hint of warning, a huge explosion blew a hole 20 feet deep in the middle of Staveley Road in the London borough of Brentford and Chiswick. Three people were killed, one a young soldier walking down the road, another a three-year-old baby. They were the first-ever victims of a ballistic missile, the V-2. It had been launched from a mobile platform parked on a suburban street in The Hague, then under German occupation. Sixteen seconds after the first explosion, a second V-2 landed in Epping, without killing or injuring anybody.

The V-2 was the secret weapon that Hitler hoped would bring him victory in the war. Together with the flying-bomb, the V-1, it was assembled in an extraordinary underground factory in the Harz Mountains, in Lower Saxony. Protected by 200 feet of rock, and with their entrances carefully concealed from the air, the underground tunnels at Nordhausen remained intact and invulnerable until the end of the war, when they were overrun by troops of the US 1st Army. By then they had produced the vast majority of the 1,403 V-2 missiles fired at London, together with many more used against targets in Belgium. The Nordhausen plant is the largest underground factory ever created.

Work began in 1936 when, as part of the German preparations for war, the state-controlled oil storage firm Wirtschaftliche Forschungs GmbH drew up plans for an underground storage depot under Kohnstein Hill near Nordhausen. The rock was anhydrite (calcium sulphate), ideal for the purpose since it is dry, soft, and easy to tunnel, yet strong enough for long, continuous galleries without extra support. The material excavated was used as a raw material for the production of cement, sulphur, and sulphuric acid.

By the time the complex was complete in 1942, there were two service tunnels, more or less parallel to each other and about 180 yards apart, running into the hill. Each tunnel was just over 1 mile long, 35 feet wide and 25 feet high. At intervals of about 40 yards the tunnels were linked by 43 cross-galleries, arranged like the rungs of a ladder, each about 30 feet wide and 22 feet high. The 7 miles of tunnel gave a floor area of 1.27 million square feet. Huge cylindrical tanks were installed in the cross-galleries for storing fuel, but in 1943 these were removed on the orders of the German Ministry of War Production, and the whole complex requisitioned for the production of weapons.

After successful Allied air raids on Hamburg, the ball-bearing factories at Schweinfurt and the research centre at Peenemünde where the V-weapons were developed, a bomb-proof factory was needed, and Nordhausen was the ideal candidate. The southern half of the complex was handed over to Mittelwerk GmbH for the manufacture and assembly of V-1 flying bombs (less wings) and V-2 rockets (without warheads). The northern part was given to the Junkers company for the assembly of Jumo 004 jet engines for Messerschmitt 262 fighters, and Jumo 213 piston engines for the older Focke Wulf 190 fighters.

Few changes were needed. An electricity supply was laid on from a nearby power station, and a cavern 75 feet high was hollowed out so that completed V-2 rockets could be stood vertically for testing the electrical components. During August and September 1943, prisoners were moved from other concentration camps to provide the work force.

Toward the end of October, the whole camp was moved underground and the prisoners—mostly French, Russian and Polish, but with some German political prisoners, too—were billeted in three chambers which were dark,

damp and full of dust. They slept in bunks four tiers high, working 12-hour shifts. When one shift went off to work, the other tried to sleep in the same dirty bunks, covering themselves with the same blankets. There were no latrines—empty carbide barrels, cut in half, had to serve—and it was a walk of over ½ mile to a water tap.

Albert Speer, the German armaments minister, visited the plant in December and recorded his impressions in his autobiography, published after the war. "The conditions for these prisoners were in fact barbarous, and a sense of profound involvement and personal guilt seizes me whenever I think of them. As I learned from overseers after the inspection was over, the sanitary conditions were inadequate, disease rampant; the prisoners were quartered right there in the damp caves, and as a result the mortality . . . was extraordinarily high."

As a result of Speer's orders, a concentration camp was built above ground to house the prisoners, and conditions improved. More and more prisoners were sent to the camp, until the pool of slave labour reached about 20,000. The SS issued strict orders forbidding private contact between the convicts and the German staff. On

A partially completed V-2 being examined by a US soldier after the capture of Nordhausen by General Omar Bradley's army on 11 April 1945. Hitler had ordered destruction of the entire plant before capture, but it was left almost untouched after the evacuation of the specialists and workers.

Factory beneath a Mountain

no account was news of what was happening at Nordhausen to reach the outside world.

The first three V-2 missiles were delivered from Nordhausen on New Year's Day 1944, and by the end of January another 17 had been completed. From then on production built up rapidly, with 250 missiles being delivered in June. The production of the V-1 began later, in July 1944, and 300 were delivered that month. While the V-2 was a highly complex and sophisticated weapon, the V-1 was cheap and crude. Both were effective, and in London there was a good deal of Blitz humour over which was more terrifying—the V-1, whose engine could be heard until it cut out, leaving an agonizing wait for the bang, or the V-2, which arrived without any warning at all. One London woman, from Streatham, was philosophical about the V-2, regarding it as one might a thunderbolt: "By the time it had arrived, you were either dead or it had missed", she said. But the writer James Lees-Milne, who was living in Chelsea, was in no doubt that the V-2 was far more alarming than the V-1, because it gave no warning: "One finds oneself waiting for it and jumps out of one's skin at the slightest bang or unexpected noise, like a car backfire or even a door slam."

The entrances and ventilation shafts of the factory had all been well camouflaged. The missiles were loaded on to rail wagons or lorries in the tunnels, and canvas covers tied in place. The trains then ran out of the tunnels and on to the German railway network, on their way to the launching pads close to the Channel. These precautions successfully concealed the plant from reconnaissance aircraft, and the only hint of its importance came from interrogation of a German prisoner of war in the late summer of 1944. An American plan to attack the plant by dropping huge amounts of napalm on the tunnels and ventilation shafts, to create a fire that would suffocate those inside, was rejected, fortunately for Nordhausen's slave workers.

During December 1944, a total of 1,500 V-1s and 850 V-2s were produced at the underground plant, and its success and invulnerability led to proposals to increase its floor area sixfold. New tunnels were begun to house a plant to manufacture liquid oxygen (one of the fuels used by the V-2), a second factory for aero engines, and a refinery to produce synthetic oil. But all came to an end on 11 April 1945, when US forces reached the area. They stayed for about six weeks, carrying out a minute examination of the factory

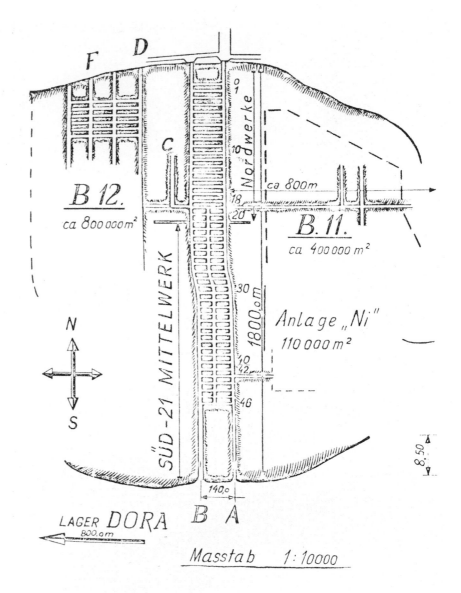

The Mittelwerk factory was engaged in machining components for, and assembly of, flying bombs and rockets. Situated at Niedersachswerfen, near Nordhausen, the factory had 2 equidistant tunnels that passed right through the hill, each taking a standard gauge railway line for the supply of materials and loading of rockets.

and its products, before handing it over to the Red Army. Nordhausen had been allocated to the Soviet zone of Germany, which subsequently became the German Democratic Republic.

Had the V-2 come sooner, its effect on the outcome of the war might indeed have been decisive. As it was, some 1,403 were launched at London, killing 2,754 people and injuring another 6,532. Many more were launched at targets in Belgium in the last months of the war—1,214 at Antwerp alone. Its designers, including Werner von Braun, went to the US after the war and designed rockets for the Western Allies. Combined with a nuclear warhead, the ballistic missile became the ultimate weapon in whose precarious balance of terror the world has existed ever since.

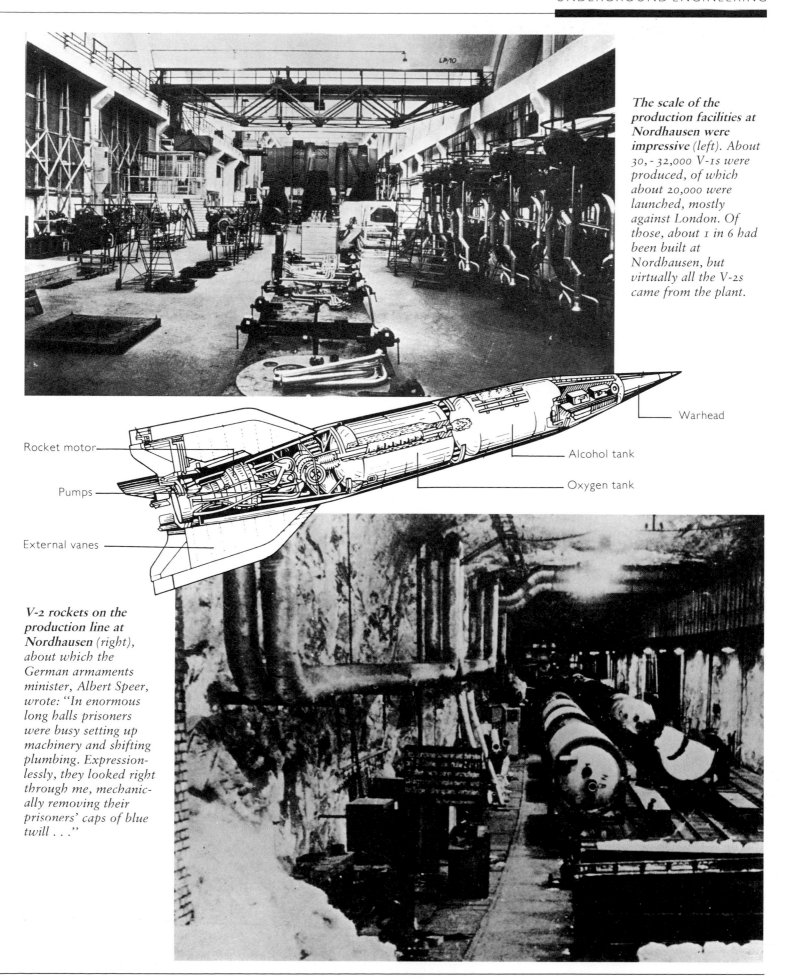

The scale of the production facilities at Nordhausen were impressive (left). *About 30,-32,000 V-1s were produced, of which about 20,000 were launched, mostly against London. Of those, about 1 in 6 had been built at Nordhausen, but virtually all the V-2s came from the plant.*

Warhead

Rocket motor

Alcohol tank

Pumps

Oxygen tank

External vanes

V-2 rockets on the production line at Nordhausen (right), *about which the German armaments minister, Albert Speer, wrote: "In enormous long halls prisoners were busy setting up machinery and shifting plumbing. Expressionlessly, they looked right through me, mechanically removing their prisoners' caps of blue twill . . ."*

Giant Collision Tunnel

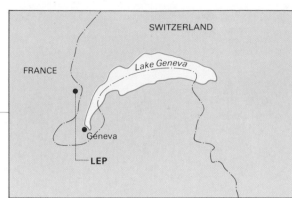

Fact file

The world's largest scientific instrument

Builder: European Council for Nuclear Research (CERN)

Built: 1983–89

Length of tunnel: 17 miles

Cost: £500 million

The scale of machinery (opposite) within LEP can be gauged from the detectors in the experiment halls at the points of collision: the apparatus in L3 is mostly encased in a magnet that contains 6,500 tons of steel; Delphi is equipped with the world's largest super-conducting magnet. The annual budget, shared by 450 physicists from 39 institutions, is close to £200 million.

The world's largest scientific instrument lies in a tunnel 17 miles long on the border between France and Switzerland. The large electron-positron collider, or LEP, is a machine for accelerating sub-microscopic particles to speeds close to the speed of light, before smashing them together and watching the results. The ring is as large in circumference as the Circle Line on the London Underground. Arranged along a tunnel 12 feet in diameter are 4,600 huge magnets to guide the beams of particles through an evacuated tube. More than 60,000 tons of technical equipment have been installed to create a machine that consumes 70 megawatts of electrical energy—enough for a large city. From the surface this huge construction is scarcely visible.

Particle physicists use the biggest machine in the world to study the smallest particles, the fragments of matter from which the entire universe is made. Once it was believed that the atom was the smallest particle that could be created, but scientists have long since shown that atoms themselves consist of yet smaller particles—electrons, protons, neutrons and others. One cannot take atoms apart with a scalpel, or look at them through a microscope; only brute force will break the bonds that hold them together. So the process of discovery has consisted of dissecting atoms by force, and then hurling the constituent parts at one another as hard as possible and watching the bits that fly off.

The greater the relative speed of particles, the more complete the rupture when they collide. Since the first particle accelerators were built in the 1930s, they have become bigger and bigger as the energy—and hence the speed—of the particles has increased. At LEP, two different sorts of particles are accelerated, in different directions, then collided together like two vehicles in a head-on crash.

Electrons, discovered by J.J. Thomson at the University of Manchester during the 1890s, are very light particles carrying a negative charge. Positrons were first found by Carl Anderson at the California Institute of Technology in 1932, and as their name suggests are positively charged. They are in fact identical to electrons except for their charge. The fact that both these particles have electrical charges makes it possible to guide them using magnets, and increase their speed using radio-frequency fields.

What happens at LEP is that the electrons and positrons travel around the evacuated tube of the accelerator in bunches. Because they have opposite charges, the magnetic and electrical fields make them travel in opposite directions until, at the will of the experimenters, they collide. When they do, they annihilate each other, creating for a fraction of a second a burst of high energy that mimics the state of the universe at the moment of its creation. Instantly the energy rematerializes as particles again, but in that fraction of a second the scientists have created the conditions they wish to study.

Accelerators must be big because if particles are made to go round a very tight circle, they lose energy much too fast and slow down. So bigger energies require bigger accelerators, and that means more expensive ones. The point has long been passed when individual universities, or even individual European nations, could afford to build competitive accelerators on their own. So in 1954 twelve European nations got together to form CERN (Conseil européen pour la recherche nucléaire), a collaborative venture in which all shared the costs. Two more nations have since joined and the organization, based in Geneva, has changed its name to the more accurate European Laboratory for Particle Physics. CERN, however, remains the acronym by which it is known around the world.

Planning for LEP began in the late 1970s when it was realized that in order to keep up with the American laboratories CERN would need a new and bigger machine. Approval was given in December 1981, and actual work began in September 1983. The machine produced its first electron-positron collisions in August 1989, less than six years later.

LEP was built underground for a variety of reasons. Doing so provides a stable and secure foundation for a machine that, despite its size, must be positioned and maintained with extraordinary precision. There are, in any case, few areas of land flat enough to create a circle more

Giant Collision Tunnel

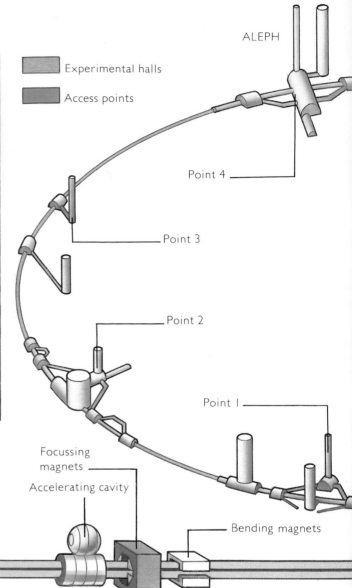

ALEPH

Experimental halls

Access points

Point 4

Point 3

Point 2

Point 1

Focussing magnets

Accelerating cavity

Bending magnets

Vacuum chamber

Collision

An aerial view of the LEP site *(above), showing the route of the tunnel. The border between France and Switzerland is marked by the dotted line, with Switzerland in the* *foreground. The small circle within LEP on the left marks the circuit of the Super Proton Synchrotron, one of 3 accelerators built between 1954 and the construction of LEP.*

Each collision of electrons and positrons *produces enough information to fill a telephone directory, but so sophisticated are the monitoring equipment and high-speed computers that only unusual or interesting data is recorded for analysis. Within the vacuum chamber, the circulating electrons are accelerated, bent and focused.*

than 5 miles in diameter without considerable tunnelling or the building of embankments, particularly close to Geneva. And by burying the machine out of sight, CERN made sure of obtaining permission from the local authorities for the project.

The actual site of LEP is a small stretch of land between Lake Geneva and the Jura mountains. The tunnel is almost but not quite circular, consisting of eight straight sections 550 yards long, linked by eight arcs each 3,000 yards long. Most of the tunnel was drilled through a soft rock called molasse, using full-face boring machines. They were lowered to the level of the tunnel through 18 shafts running from the surface to a level between 160 feet and 480 feet below the surface.

The boring machines, guided by a laser beam to ensure they were precisely on course, cut their way through the molasse, and the tunnel behind

was lined with precast concrete rings. The largest excavations in the tunnel are the experimental halls, huge underground caverns where the beams of electrons and positrons collide and instruments are set up to detect the results. A total of 1.83 million cubic yards of spoil was removed and dumped on land of low agricultural value close to the tunnel. Finally topsoil was replaced, and the land returned to farming.

Once the tunnel was complete it was fitted out with the tube around which the particles travel, and the bending and focusing magnets that guide them. Because the particles must not collide with any other matter as they move, the tube containing them must be completely evacuated. The electrons and positrons each travel more than 100 times the distance between the Earth and the Sun as they whirl around, so removing the last traces of air from the vacuum tube is critical. The beam runs through the centre

Point 5

High-frequency cavities (right) to accelerate the electron beams are situated on the straight sections of the tunnel.

Radio-frequency power for the 128 cavities is produced by 16 klystrons, which bunch electrons crossing a gap.

OPAL

The underground structures punctuating the tunnel are reached by shafts at equidistant points (1–8). The tunnel passes through the width of the 4 halls in which experiments on the collisions are conducted, each specializing in different areas of research.

LEP tunnel

Point 6

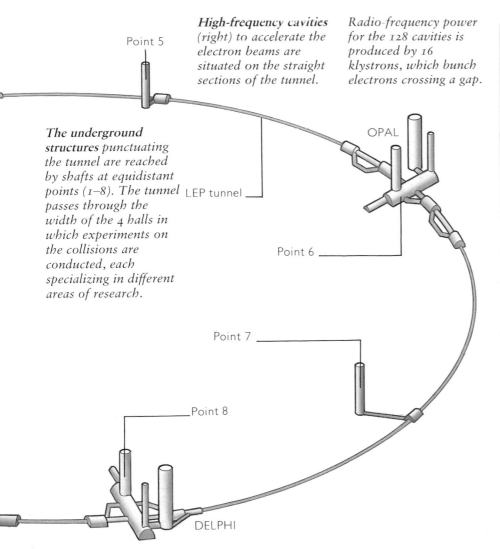

Point 7

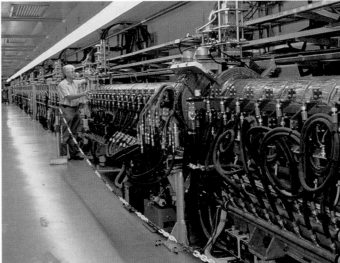

Point 8

DELPHI

---

of an oval tube with pumps along it to maintain the vacuum.

Arranged along the course of the tube are 3,368 dipole magnets which bend the beam and keep it on course, and 816 quadrupole magnets which focus the beam, keeping it sharp and narrow. In addition, 128 accelerating cavities boost the speed of the particles. In all, this hardware amounted to 14,000 tons of steel and 1,200 tons of aluminium, and it was carried to the appropriate position around the ring using a monorail system. Measuring instruments of extreme precision were used to position the magnets to within four-thousandths of an inch.

The actual detectors used to measure the results of the collisions are themselves spectacular objects, more than 30 feet long and the same in diameter, straddling the pipe where the beam runs. There are four such detectors, designed by huge teams of scientists. The detector for the experiment called L3, for example, is as big as a five-storey building and is literally crammed with electronic instruments.

LEP was finished on time, and cost 1.3 billion Swiss francs (£500 million), just 5 percent more than the initial budget. Within weeks of starting up, it had demonstrated its worth by confirming that all matter is made from just three families of subatomic particles. This proof of what theoretical physicists call the Standard Model was a triumphant vindication of the effort and money put into the world's biggest and most sophisticated machine. It represented another step on the way to the physicists' holy grail, the so-called TOE, or Theory of Everything, which would explain the entire workings of the universe from the smallest particle to the largest heavenly body. When that is achieved, the physicists will have worked themselves out of a job, but none is worrying about that just yet.

The linac injector (above) supplies the electrons and positrons which are then stored until they are fed into the Proton Synchrotron (PS) followed by the Super PS; these are interconnected accelerators which give the particles their first big boost in energy before they are fed into LEP where they are taken to even higher speeds.

Railroad under the Sea

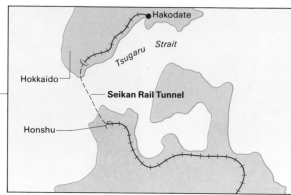

Fact file

The world's longest and most costly tunnel

Builder: Japan Railways

Built: 1971–88

Length: 34 miles

Minimum depth below sea: 275 feet

The world's longest and most expensive tunnel lies clean, dry and hardly used beneath the Tsugaru Strait between the islands of Honshu and Hokkaido in Japan. Only 15 trains a day each way pass through this extraordinary tunnel, 34 miles long and dug through some of the most difficult rock ever encountered. It took twice as long as expected, and cost almost ten times as much. Completing it was "a technological achievement without parallel in the world" according to the Japanese Minister of Transport who opened it in March 1988. But while the tunnellers laboured underground, the Japanese passengers took to the skies. By the time the first train rolled through, air services were already so well established between the two islands that few wanted to travel by train.

The tunnel represents the partial fulfilment of a dream that has inspired Japanese engineers since 1936—to link all the islands of Japan together by train. Originally the line was to go even farther north to the island of Sakhalin, then on to Korea, which was a Japanese colony. But Sakhalin fell to the Soviet Union in World War II, and Korea became independent. So a modi-

The Tsugaru Strait is prone to extreme weather and violent currents that close it for at least 80 days a year. It was the loss of 5 ferries during a typhoon in 1954 that initiated investigations into the feasibility of building a tunnel. In the foreground is the Tappi construction site.

fied plan, linking the four islands of the Japanese archipelago, was adopted, and completed with the Seikan Tunnel and the Seto Bridges, which join the main island of Honshu with Hokkaido to the north and Shikoku to the south. The fourth island, Kyushu, was already linked to Honshu through the Kanmon Tunnel, opened in 1942. Following the loss of five ferries and 1,430 lives during a typhoon in the Tsugaru Strait between Honshu and Hokkaido, which is 15 miles wide at its narrowest point, an investigation was made into the feasibility of a tunnel.

The surveys established that the task would be a difficult one. The rocks of Japan are geologically young, created by volcanic action and full of faults and fissures. They are both unstable and porous, allowing large water flows—the very worst kind of rock to drill through. Treacherous sea conditions in the strait made surveying difficult, so less information was obtained than the engineers of Japanese National Railways had hoped for. In March 1964 the first shaft was drilled on the Hokkaido side, followed two years later by a similar inclined shaft on the Honshu side. The idea of the shafts was to provide a proper survey, develop a method of tunnelling through the rock, and ultimately to serve as entrances to the main tunnel.

The shafts proved that a tunnel could not be drilled without first making the rock less porous and unstable. This was done by the technique known as grouting. Small holes were drilled into the rock ahead of the advancing face, and fanning out in the shape of a cone. Into these holes a mixture of cement and a gelling agent was pumped under huge pressure, so that it was forced into all the small fissures in the rock, sealing them. Then the main tunnel was advanced through the same volume of rock, before drilling and grouting a fresh section ahead. Without such careful preparation, the tunnel workings would have been flooded almost as soon as they began.

Less than half of the 34 miles of tunnel actually lies under the sea, but this section inevitably proved the most difficult. To reduce seepage from the sea, the tunnel was cut more than 300 feet beneath the seabed. For every day's cutting of the tunnel, two to three days might be spent grouting in an attempt to improve the rock. A pilot tunnel was driven ahead of the main and service tunnels, to provide advance warning of difficult conditions, and core samples of rock were taken by a small-bore drill driven into the

rock in advance of the tunnel faces.

In spite of such precautions, there were at least four major floods, the worst occurring in 1976 and 1977, when flow rates of up to 80 tons of water a minute forced the miners to evacuate the tunnel in a hurry. In one of these incidents, in May 1976, more than 2 miles of the service tunnel and 1 mile of the main tunnel were flooded, delaying work for months. Eventually the service tunnel was detoured past the region of difficult rock, and additional grouting and special mining techniques used to get the main tunnel through the same region without further problems. Even today, with the tunnel completed and lined, four separate pumping systems must operate continuously to keep it dry. Without the pumps the tunnel would fill with water in 78 hours.

The nature of the rock made it impossible to use full-face boring machines of the type being used to cut through the chalk beneath the English Channel. Instead, the engineers were forced to use conventional mining methods,

breaking up the rock with explosives before clearing it away with mechanical excavators.

Because of the length of the tunnel, special facilities had to be provided for ventilation and fire prevention. Air is pumped into the tunnel through inclined shafts on either side of the strait, flowing through the pilot tunnel into the centre of the main tunnel and then outward through both outlets of the main tunnel. A steady breeze of about 2 miles an hour is enough to keep the air in the tunnel fresh, and prevent overheating from the heat generated by the trains. In the service tunnels, which run alongside the main tunnel through the sub-sea section, the air pressure is slightly higher, ensuring that air flows from the service tunnel into the main tunnel, and not the other way round. This would be vital in the event of a fire, because it would prevent smoke entering the service tunnels, which are the escape route for passengers.

If a fire did break out, the train's driver would try to take it out of the tunnel as quickly as possible, but because of the length of the tunnel

The single-bore tunnel *has twin 3 foot 6 inch gauge tracks, but it has been built to dimensions that will allow standard gauge (4 feet 8½ inches) Shinkansen trains to use it when the money is available. The delay in building the faster trains has removed the tunnel's raison d'être, since the time saving is not sufficient to make major inroads into alternative modes of transport.*

Railroad under the Sea

that might prove impossible. For this reason two emergency stations have been built underground, where passengers could get off the train and run down escape and rescue passages into the service tunnel. Smoke exhaust blowers are provided at these stations to remove it as quickly as possible, while emergency generators would ensure the tunnel remained well-lit.

Along the tunnel there are four heat-detection systems and sprinklers, designed to provide early warning of a fire and to put it out rapidly. Many of these facilities were designed after a disastrous fire in another Japanese rail tunnel in November 1972 killed 30 people and injured many more. "We think this is the safest undersea tunnel in existence" boasts Mr Shuzo Kitagawa, the Deputy Project Director.

Safe it may well be, profitable it is not. The total cost of the tunnel was $6.5 billion, against an original estimate in 1971 of $783 million. Together with financing costs and other incidentals, the total amounted to $8.3 billion. While the cost went up, the potential use went down. In the ten years from 1975, the number of passengers using the ferries declined by 50 percent. In 1986, before the tunnel opened, only 186,000 travelled by train and ferry between Tokyo and Hokkaido's main town, Sapporo, while 4.5 million—25 times as many—went by air, which takes 90 minutes. The decision not to run the bullet trains through eliminated any chance of reversing this trend, and there was even talk of abandoning the tunnel and using it as an underground reservoir for oil, or even for growing mushrooms. But that would have wounded the pride of Japanese National Railways unacceptably, so the tunnel was completed and brought into use. Debt repayments and operating losses are now put at $67 million a year for the next 30 years.

The daytime trains have made few inroads into the air traffic between Tokyo and Sapporo, but the sleepers have proved more successful, and three 12-car trains a night pass in each direction. Travellers on the route can watch illuminated displays in each coach which chart the progress of the train through the tunnel, showing distance covered, and depth below the sea; the maximum depth reached is 787 feet. Many passengers spend a good part of the journey taking pictures of these panels, and themselves. A stop is also made in the middle of the tunnel for two minutes to enable passengers to take pictures through the windows of panels on the tunnel wall.

Mechanical excavation (right) was employed in places but generally explosives were used, after which the surface was stabilized with a cement mixture called shotcrete and then lined with H-section steel supports and a layer of concrete 2 feet thick, or 3 feet in weak ground.

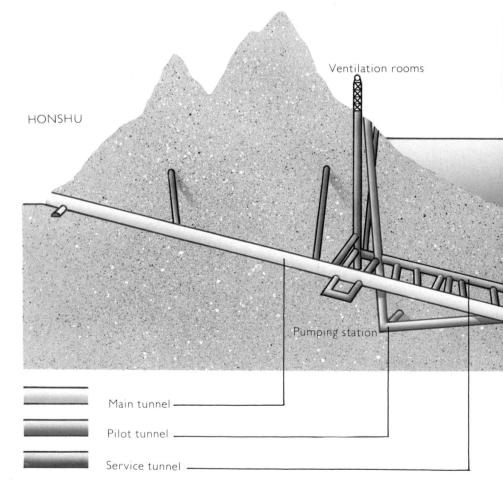

HONSHU

Ventilation rooms

Pumping station

Main tunnel

Pilot tunnel

Service tunnel

Shafts of two types connected the Tappi and Yoshioka construction sites with the tunnels: the vertical shafts were used to transport machinery, materials and shotcrete, and personnel working in the main and service tunnels; the inclined shafts conveyed workers to the pilot tunnel and was the conduit for the largest machinery, and extracted water and spoil. The inclined shafts formed the air intakes and were adapted for the forced air ventilation system, as well as providing a passage for maintenance, escape and rescue. The vertical shaft took exhaust air from the tunnel and is now a smoke exhaust shaft should fire break out in the tunnel.

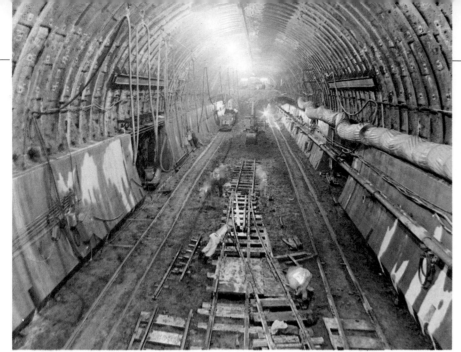

A narrow gauge railway was used in the main tunnel to bring grouting, water, concrete, grout pumps and power units to the headings and to extract spoil. A fire alarm system, radio telephone communication and loudspeakers in the tunnels were part of the safety measures.

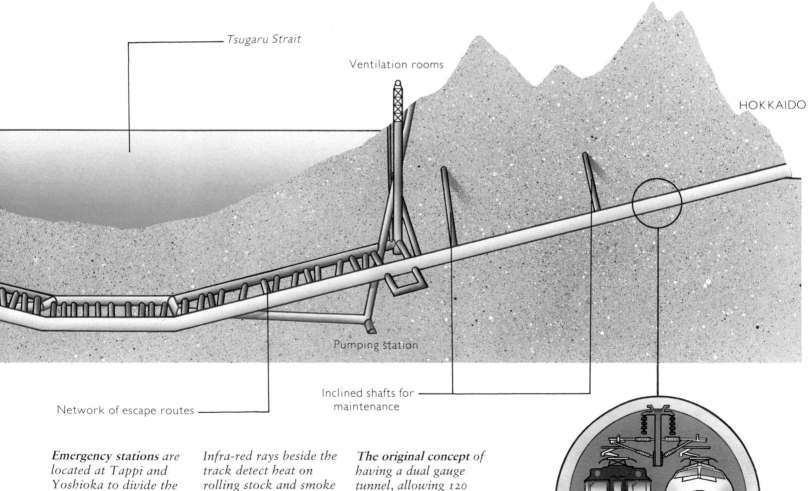

Tsugaru Strait

Ventilation rooms

HOKKAIDO

Pumping station

Inclined shafts for maintenance

Network of escape routes

Narrow gauge

Standard gauge

Emergency stations are located at Tappi and Yoshioka to divide the tunnel into manageable sections. The stations are provided with platforms for passengers to alight, with escape and rescue passages, public address system and telephones, smoke exhaust system and fire-fighting equipment.

Infra-red rays beside the track detect heat on rolling stock and smoke detectors have been installed. A control centre at Hakodate monitors conditions in the tunnels and initiates safety procedures. Extensive disaster drills are regularly carried out with emergency services.

The original concept of having a dual gauge tunnel, allowing 120 mph running of Shinkansen trains, was postponed on cost grounds. However, it is still the intention to convert the tunnel when finance allows.

Great Tunnels

The earliest tunnels were built in the tombs of Babylonian and Egyptian kings. A small tunnel is believed to have been built under the River Euphrates in the twenty-second century BC.

The mining of minerals and the walls of castles under siege kept alive the skills of tunnelling until the canal age of the eighteenth century, when the work of engineers such as James Brindley eclipsed all that had gone before. With the railways came the invention of the tunnelling shield and the use of compressed air, both to counteract the external pressure of water and to power drills.

The major mountain massifs on important routes have been bored. The future of tunnelling lies with projects such as the Channel Tunnel, which will just exceed in length the comparable Seikan Tunnel.

The Malpas Tunnel, Canal du Midi

Although comparatively short, at 528 feet, the Malpas Tunnel in south-west France is a tunnel with more "firsts" than any other: it was the first canal tunnel to be built, completed in 1681; it was also the first tunnel to be built for any form of transport; and it was the first tunnel to be excavated with the help of gunpowder, which represented a major breakthrough in technique. The Canal du Midi was the first great European canal, linking the Atlantic Ocean with the Mediterranean Sea. In its 148 miles there are 119 locks to take the canal over a summit of 620 feet above sea level.

The Rove Tunnel, Canal de Marseille au Rhône

The world's longest canal tunnel, at almost 4½ miles, was opened in 1927 to link the port of Marseilles with the Rhône at Arles. Built to take seagoing vessels, the tunnel is 72 feet wide and 37 feet high. Work began on the tunnel at the south end in 1911 and at the north end in 1914. The outbreak of World War I halted work until German prisoners of war were assigned to the tunnel. In 1916 they broke through but work on lining it was slow. Twice as much spoil was excavated from the Rove as the Simplon Tunnel, due to the size of the bore. A collapse of a section of the tunnel in 1963 has closed it to traffic.

The Channel Tunnel, Folkestone–Sangatte

The idea for a tunnel under the English Channel is almost 2 centuries old: the first proposal, in 1802, by a French mining engineer was followed by a number of schemes over the next 160 years; all were rejected by Britain for fear of jeopardizing national security. A scheme in the 1870s and '80s produced pilot tunnels from both sides before the British government put a stop to the digging. Work began again in 1973, only to cease on the grounds of economic stringency.

In January 1986 Eurotunnel was awarded the concession to build the present rail tunnel, which will comprise 2 single bores with a service tunnel between. Of the total length of 30.7 miles, 23.6 will be under the sea. The saturated chalk through which the tunnellers have to bore poses the main challenge. A seal between the cutting head of the Japanese boring machines and the cylinder behind it prevents water flooding in. The tunnel lining sections are bolted together inside the cylinder, and the cavity left behind as the cylinder moves forward is filled with compressed concrete. The tunnel will transform the prospects for rail transport in Britain and become part of the European high-speed rail network.

CHAPTER FIVE

Astronomical Constructions

Astronomers are at the edge of the greatest leap forward in understanding the Universe since the first telescopes were produced in the seventeenth century. Those primitive instruments revealed far more objects in the sky than could be seen by the naked eye, but for every new object they identified, a thousand more remained hidden. The limitations of the telescopes, and the fuzzing of the image brought about by the Earth's atmosphere, have proved frustrating obstacles to understanding.

The most obvious way around the difficulties was to build better telescopes, and site them, like those of the European Southern Observatory, high on a mountain peak where the atmosphere is thinnest. Isaac Newton showed the way, with telescopes based on mirrors rather than lenses. Since then, the mirrors have become larger and larger, capturing ever greater quantities of light so as to detect even the faintest of stars.

But to begin observations beyond the atmosphere altogether, as the Hubble Space Telescope will do, is to open new doors. It will make possible the study of individual stars that have previously been an indistinct part of a cluster. Objects infinitely remote and impossibly dim will for the first time be seen by the human eye. The findings will be combined with the results now available from radio telescopes of huge size and great sensitivity, which detect the signals emitted by exotic objects such as quasars and pulsars. Foremost among these is the Very Large Array, a dull name for a remarkable instrument constructed on a huge plateau in New Mexico.

The search for knowledge has driven scientists in many disciplines to build ever bigger and more expensive machines. Nowhere is this more likely to produce dramatic discoveries than in astronomy, which could be set for its most productive decade since the 1920s.

Astronomical Constructions
Space Telescope
Very Large Array
European Southern Observatory

Cosmic Time Machine

Fact file

The world's most powerful gatherer of information about the Universe

Coordination agency: Marshall Space Flight Center, Huntsville, USA

Built: 1977–85

Length: 43 feet

Diameter: 14 feet

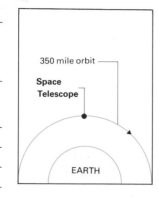

350 mile orbit

Space Telescope

EARTH

A complex satellite the size of a railroad car spent five years waiting for the opportunity to transform our picture of the Universe, its launch delayed by the Challenger disaster in 1986. The Hubble Space Telescope was to provide the clearest and deepest view of the universe astronomers had ever enjoyed. Floating above the disturbing effects of the atmosphere, the Space Telescope would be able to observe the heavens using ultraviolet and infrared rays as well as visible light, picking up objects far too distant or too faint to be seen on Earth, and so remote that light from them takes billions of years to reach us. By seeing so far, the Space Telescope would look backwards into the past, to events that took place 14 billion years ago when the Universe was young. It would be able to see objects 25 times fainter than anything visible from Earth-based telescopes, and explore the universe in ten-times greater detail than before.

Its launch on 24 April 1990 represented the beginning of the greatest opportunity for discovering new information about the Universe since Galileo directed the first simple telescope at the skies almost 400 years ago. Seldom has euphoria at a successful space launch been so abruptly cut short, for Hubble was sent into space with a serious visual defect: the mirror that focused the light had been curved with perfect precision, but in the wrong shape.

Astronomers have known for a long time that the view of the Universe from above the atmosphere would be much clearer than it is from Earth. The twinkling of the countless stars in the sky is caused by atmospheric disturbance bending the waves of light that reach us. So the first proposals for a space-based telescope are older even than space travel itself. They came in 1923 from Hermann Oberth, the German pioneer who developed many of the key concepts in space exploration, and inspired the generation that produced the first rockets.

In 1962 the US National Academy of Sciences recommended developing a large space telescope, an option supported by similar groups in 1965 and 1969. The launch of space observation satellites by NASA in 1968 and 1972 further whetted the appetite, but it took the development of the space shuttle to provide the means for launching a really large telescope into space. The European Space Agency became involved in 1975, funding was finally in place by 1977, and the telescope was ready by 1985.

The Space Telescope is 43 feet long and 14 feet in diameter, weighing just over 11 tons. It is wrapped in several layers of shiny metallic foil, which reflects most of the sunlight and prevents overheating. It is essentially similar to a large optical telescope on Earth, using mirrors rather than lenses to focus the light. The very biggest have mirrors 200 inches in diameter in order to collect light from the widest possible aperture, and hence detect the most distant of objects.

The Space Telescope's mirror is 94 inches in diameter, made of a special type of glass which expands and contracts very little with changes of temperature. It took the Perkin-Elmer Corporation 4 million person-hours of work to cast and

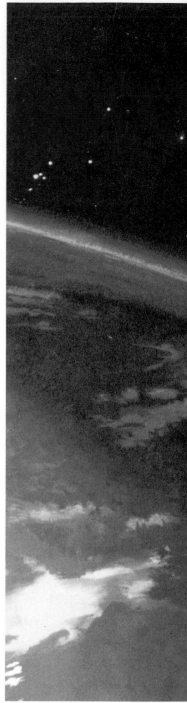

The Space Shuttle was central to the concept of the Space Telescope: Discovery placed the telescope in orbit and a Shuttle will carry astronauts to service it every 5 years.

polish it. The finish they achieved was staggering. The curvature was accurate to within two-millionths of an inch; that means that if it were scaled up to the size of the Earth, no irregularity on its surface would be greater than 12 inches. Its resolution—the ability to separate two distant objects—should have been sufficient to distinguish the headlamps of a car 2,500 miles away.

The mirror glass is covered with an aluminium reflecting surface. Mounted well inside the cylindrical body of the telescope, it would reflect light forward to a second mirror 12 inches across and 16 feet farther forward. This mirror would return the light through a 2-foot hole in the middle of the primary mirror to the focal plane where the scientific instruments are mounted.

There are five such instruments: two cameras, two spectrographs, and a photometer. The Wide Field Camera would investigate the age of the Universe and search for new planetary systems around young stars. Despite the camera's name, the width of its view is actually very limited, only 2.67 arc seconds, so that it would take a montage of 100 images to get a picture of the entire Moon. But this narrow view gives far better resolution of distant objects. The second camera, the Faint Object Camera, has an even narrower gaze, only a fortieth as great as the Wide Field Camera, but extends the telescope's range to the limits and produces the sharpest views. Many objects

The telescope's mirror pointing system is so accurate that it could fire a laser over 400 miles and hit an object the size of a coin, despite the fact that it is moving around the Earth at a speed of 17,000 mph.

Cosmic Time Machine

The telescope's covering is several layers of shining metallic foil which reflects most of the sunlight and prevents overheating. Electrical power is provided by 2 solar arrays, each wing containing 24,000 solar cells, supplemented by 6 batteries to store electricity while the satellite is hidden from the Sun by the Earth.

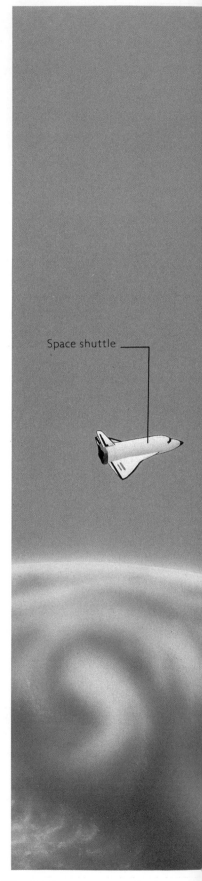

Space shuttle

barely visible from Earth would appear as blazing sources of light to this camera.

The two spectrographs would analyse the spectra of light from the objects viewed. From the various characteristic wavelengths given off by different atoms, spectrographs enable astronomers to determine precisely what elements are present in the bright objects they are looking at. The Faint Object Spectrograph would study the chemical properties of comets or compare the composition of galaxies close to the Earth with those far away. The High Resolution Spectrograph would study the chemical composition, temperature and density of interstellar gas, and the atmosphere of planets in our solar system.

The final instrument, the High Speed Photometer, would measure the brightness of the objects in space, looking for clues that black holes actually exist and providing an accurate map of the magnitude of stars.

Soon after the Hubble's launch in April 1990, however, efforts to focus it showed that something was wrong. Further tests made clear that the main mirror was seriously flawed. Shaping and polishing such a large telescope mirror to such refined tolerances requires the use of instruments, called "null correctors", which tell you when the shape is right. Perkin-Elmer used two such instruments, one relatively crude and the other much more precise. Although the cruder instrument indicated that the main mirror had been polished to the wrong shape, evidence from the more sophisticated device assured them all was well. Subsequent investigation showed that a lens in this instrument was a minute

fraction of an inch out of place. This produced a corresponding error in the shape of the mirror. It may seem small, but in optical terms it is huge.

The effect of the mistake has not, however, proved quite as disastrous as might have been expected. What has been lost is not resolution, but sensitivity; instead of being able to observe images a billion times fainter than those visible to the naked eye, the telescope can manage only those 50 million times fainter. While the images can be corrected using computer enhancement, in order to achieve this the blurred areas surrounding the images have to be thrown away. This cuts out some of the most distant objects, including planets around nearby stars and very distant quasars, but it leaves a lot that can be successfully seen.

Among the most brilliant images are those of planets in the solar system, taken with a resolution about ten times sharper than any Earth-based instrument. One such image was the first taken of the distant planet Pluto and its moon Charon in which they appeared as discs rather than as spots. Hubble has also taken a picture of what astronomers believe may be the hottest star ever seen, some 33 times hotter than the Sun's temperature of 11,000°F (6,000°C).

Already, then, Hubble has achieved worthwhile results. A rescue mission is planned in the next few years to replace the main camera with one specially designed to correct for the mirror's sharpness. Assuming that this mission is accomplished, Hubble, named after the man who first showed that the universe is expanding, may yet prove a splendid success.

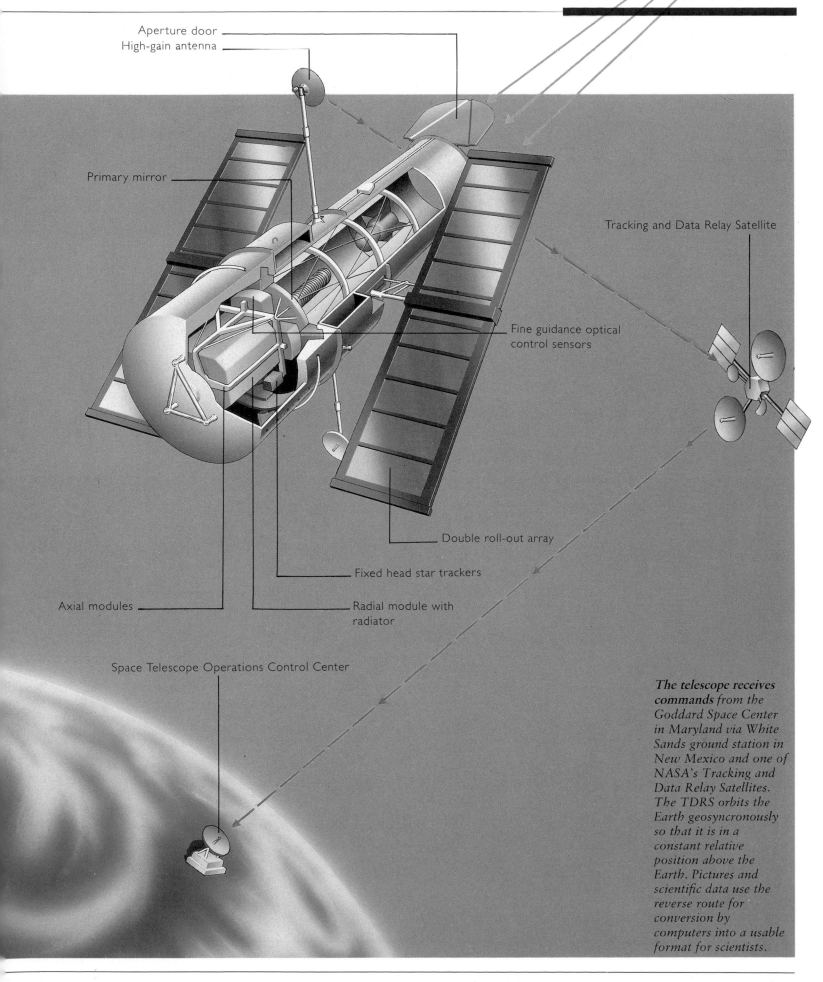

Aperture door

High-gain antenna

Primary mirror

Tracking and Data Relay Satellite

Fine guidance optical control sensors

Double roll-out array

Fixed head star trackers

Axial modules

Radial module with radiator

Space Telescope Operations Control Center

The telescope receives commands from the Goddard Space Center in Maryland via White Sands ground station in New Mexico and one of NASA's Tracking and Data Relay Satellites. The TDRS orbits the Earth geosyncronously so that it is in a constant relative position above the Earth. Pictures and scientific data use the reverse route for conversion by computers into a usable format for scientists.

The Ultimate Radio Telescope

The world's most powerful radio telescope is to be found on a high, flat plain in New Mexico. From this remote and quiet spot it scans the heavens, producing radio images of stars, galaxies and other exotic objects as sharp as the photographs from the best optical telescopes. Its detailed pictures of some of the millions of objects in the sky that emit radio waves are used to try to understand the huge forces at work: curved filaments a million light years long; objects so dense that light itself cannot escape from them; thin channels across space carrying huge quantities of energy; and the faint blush of radiation that mantles the sky—the last vanishing echo of the Big Bang which began it all 15 billion years ago.

Radio astronomy was invented in the 1930s by an engineer at Bell Telephone Laboratories, Karl Jansky, who was trying to find the source of the crackles and hisses that interfered with transatlantic radio transmissions. Using primitive apparatus, he established that the radio signals came from the heart of the Milky Way. After World War II, more sensitive instruments were built to attempt to point more accurately at radio sources in the sky, to see if they were identical to visible objects, and to resolve their fine structure. Because the signals are so faint compared with terrestrial radio waves, big dish-shaped antennae are needed to detect them, and the first, the 250-foot Jodrell Bank telescope in Cheshire, England, was completed in 1957.

The bigger the dish, the greater the sensitivity and the more accurately it can pinpoint objects in space. But there is a limit to how big a dish can be built, particularly when it has to be steered and pointed with exquisite accuracy. From quite early in the history of radio astronomy it was realized that the effect of a very large dish could be simulated by combining the signals from several smaller ones some distance apart.

The Very Large Array (VLA) in New Mexico is the ultimate expression to date of this type of telescope. One of four telescopes run by the US National Radio Astronomy Observatory, it consists of 27 dishes, arranged alongside three straight rail tracks fanning outward from a central point. Each dish is 82 feet in diameter, its parabolic surface formed from aluminium panels accurate to 20 thousands of an inch over their whole surface. The movable part of the antenna, the dish itself, weighs 100 tons, while the whole structure weighs 235 tons. Each of the 27 dishes can be pointed anywhere in the sky

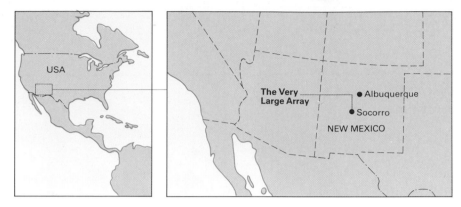

with an accuracy of 20 seconds of arc—equivalent to one 180th of the diameter of the Moon.

Two of the three tracks running outward are 13 miles long, while the third measures just under 12 miles. Each has nine dishes arranged along it. The tracks make it possible to move the dishes in and out, which achieves the same effect as the zoom lens on a camera. Four different configurations of the dishes are possible. In the A configuration, they are distributed along the full lengths of the tracks, giving the greatest resolution for observing small, intense radio sources. In the D configuration, they all cluster within 650 yards of the centre, which enables large, diffuse sources to be studied with lower resolution but higher sensitivity. Configurations B and C are intermediate settings.

To move a dish, a special transporter picks it from its pedestal, carries it to the nearby track, transports it to a different position, then sets it down on another pedestal with a precision greater than a quarter of an inch. Using a pair of transporters, it takes about two weeks to reconfigure the telescope completely, and the process is carried out on a cycle in which the VLA returns to its original configuration every 15 months.

The first design studies for the VLA were drawn up in the early 1960s, and a formal proposal from the NRAO for funds made in 1967. Approval from Congress in 1972 enabled work to begin in 1974, and the whole array was finally completed in 1981. Each dish cost $1.15 million, and the whole telescope was built for $78.6 million, very close to the estimates.

The site chosen, 7,000 feet up on the plains of San Augustin 50 miles west of Socorro, New Mexico, was ideal. Because of the height and the desert climate, there are few clouds to blur the images. Mountains around the site cut out interference from radio, TV and military bases. The terrain is flat, making it easy to move the

Fact file

The world's most powerful radio telescope

Builder: US National Radio Astronomy Observatory

Material: Aluminium

Diameter of dishes: 82 feet

Weight of dishes: 100 tons

All 27 dishes point to the same object in the sky, in a similar fashion to other multi-dish radio telescopes. The VLA represents a quantum leap from the first 2-dish telescope built by the California Institute of Technology near Bishop, California, in 1959. A 3-dish array built at Cambridge, England, in 1963 discovered in 1967 pulsars—radio sources that produce bursts of emissions every few seconds.

The Ultimate Radio Telescope

dishes around, and the site is far enough south to be able to see 85 percent of the sky.

Radio waves from all 27 dishes are amplified a million times by receivers and fed into an underground waveguide which runs along the tracks to the control room at the centre of the array. It is here that the signals from the 27 dishes are combined to create the image. Because some of the waves have travelled farther, from the outlying dishes, their signals will be delayed by a tiny fraction of a second, which is enough to destroy the image. To make the necessary correction, the signals from some of the dishes are automatically delayed before they are all combined in the correlator and passed to a computer for analysis.

The calibration computer first analyses the data for any defects, which might include stray signals from satellites or radar installations. These are removed automatically, and the cleaned-up signals combined using a mathematical technique known as a Fourier transform. The effect is to convert the signals into an image in much the same way that a lens converts light into a picture. The radio image is stored on the computer as a sequence of numbers on a grid, each number representing the strength of the signal, and each grid point a position in the sky. Transmitted to a TV screen, the numbers are displayed as a picture.

Further processing is necessary to produce a crisp image. First, there is a lot of "noise" from stray radio signals that appears like a shower of snow on the picture. This can be removed by averaging the signals over several hours of observation. Then there are distortions arising from the fact that the 27 dishes cover only a small

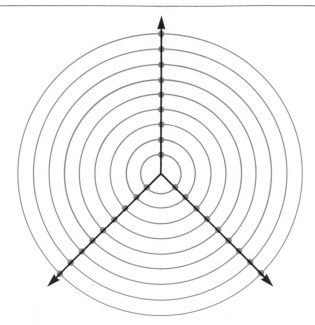

Radio waves (left) are reflected off the curved surface of the dish on to a second subreflector at the focus of the dish, and then to the radio receivers at its centre.

The 27 dishes arranged on the 3 railway lines are connected electronically to synthesize their signals, which are equivalent to those of a single radio telescope 20 miles in diameter.

Slight rotation of the subreflector (above), which is an asymmetric mirror, enables signals to be directed to one of 6 receivers tuned to different wavelengths. In the base of the dish are the azimuth and altitude driving motors and gears, which move throughout an observation to compensate for the Earth's rotation.

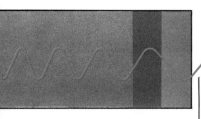

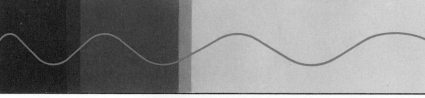

— Visible Light

Electromagnetic waves (above) range from gamma rays at the shortest wavelength end of the spectrum, at the left, to low-frequency long waves at the right, with visible light and the colour spectrum near the middle.

Cassiopieia A (right), whose ring of radio emission represents a spherical, expanding cloud of gas expelled by an explosion.

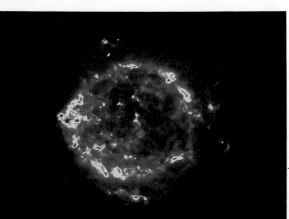

The synchronizing of signals from the 27 dishes is one of the VLA's most vital processes, for the travel time of the signals— from their source to the correlator—must not differ from each other by more than about one 1,000,000,000th of a second. The distance of many miles between dishes can cause a difference in travel time of one 10,000th of a second.

fraction of the area of the array. These can be corrected, to produce an image exactly as it would be seen by a dish the whole area of the VLA. Finally, there is the radio equivalent of the "twinkling" of stars, caused by atmospheric conditions, which can also be corrected for. The final data is stored on magnetic tape, and the images can be further enhanced by taking the tapes to supercomputers elsewhere and running them through special programs.

The VLA operates every day, 24 hours a day, except for a few holidays such as Thanksgiving and Christmas. Astronomers from the US and abroad put in requests to use the instrument, which are considered by a committee and assigned a time. The average proposal requires about eight hours of observing time, although some are completed in as little as five minutes and others need up to 100 hours. Astronomers arrive a day before their observations are scheduled, make sure all is well, and prepare a list of the sources to be observed, for how long, and at what wavelengths. The actual observations are controlled by a computer. Once they are com-

plete, the astronomers depart with their magnetic tapes back to their own laboratories to analyse, and later publish, the results.

More than 700 astronomers use the VLA every year and the images it produces are far from the fuzzy patterns of earlier radio telescopes. They show objects unimaginably far away and driven by forces so huge it is difficult to comprehend them. The radio waves from the source Cygnus A, a galaxy consisting of billions of stars, have taken 600 million years to reach us. Analysed by the VLA, they show two clouds on either side of the galaxy, caused by electrons trapped by magnetic fields. The electrons themselves are speeding away from a bright spot at the very centre of the galaxy.

More dramatic still is the radio source Cassiopeia A, a huge boiling mass of material expanding at a speed of 10 million miles an hour away from the centre of a gigantic supernova that exploded in 1680. Or, to be accurate, that is when we on Earth saw it exploding. The actual explosion took place 9,000 years earlier, for that is how long it took the signals to reach us.

Recorder of the Heavens

Fact file

The source of the world's best pictures of the sky

Builder: European Southern Observatory

Built: 1964–

Altitude: 7,800 feet

No of telescopes: 15

On a high mountaintop in the Atacama Desert of Chile, 375 miles north of Santiago, is a series of buildings as strange as anything left by the Incas or the Aztecs in Latin America. Dotted around the slopes are 15 telescopes, housed in shiny silver-coloured buildings with white domes. Here astronomers from eight European countries repair to watch the night skies far from the atmospheric pollution and all-pervading light which have made optical astronomy in Europe increasingly difficult.

Observing the skies from the surface of the Earth has certain intrinsic drawbacks. The atmosphere, even when clean, introduces blurring into the images as the light from stars passes through it. The old Royal Observatory established at Greenwich in 1675 (now a London suburb) was, by 1850, suffering from the drawbacks of its location.

Today nobody would dream of building a telescope in a city, or even close to one. Britain's best telescopes are now based on a mountain in the Canary Islands; the major observatory in the US is at Kitt Peak, in Arizona, almost 7,000 feet above sea level. And the nations belonging to ESO—Belgium, Denmark, West Germany, France, Italy, the Netherlands, Sweden and Switzerland—have chosen La Silla (The Saddle), a long ridge 7,800 feet above sea level in the empty vastness of the Atacama Desert.

Because the site is high, the air is thin and there is less of it above the telescopes for the light from stars and galaxies to pass through, so there is much less blurring. Rain and cloud are exceptionally unusual, and La Silla enjoys more than 300 clear nights every year. There is relatively little difference between day and night temperatures, a great advantage because problems can be caused by the expansion and contraction of instruments as the temperature rises and falls.

A site in the southern hemisphere is also highly desirable because so much optical astronomy has, until recent times, been conducted in the north. The south gives the best views towards the centre of our own galaxy and of the Magellanic Clouds, two companion galaxies to our own. The combination of all these features makes La Silla one of the world's finest observatories, where in the opinion of astronomers the best and sharpest pictures of the sky are taken.

Of the 15 telescopes at La Silla, all but one are optical instruments. Eight are financed by ESO, the rest by member countries. The odd one out is a radio telescope, SEST (the Swedish-ESO Submillimetre Telescope), a 48-foot dish which has been listening to very short wavelength radio signals from space since 1987. This instrument is especially well sited because such wavelengths are usually absorbed by water vapour in the European atmosphere. At La Silla it can thrive in the dry air, making observations of molecules in the space between stars in our galaxy and neighbouring ones.

The most interesting telescope at La Silla is undoubtedly the 136-inch New Technology Telescope, which came into use in March 1989. This instrument uses new techniques to produce the best images of many objects in the sky. It is the most advanced land-based telescope in use.

All large modern telescopes are based on concave mirrors made of glass. Casting and polishing such huge pieces of glass to the necessary accuracy is an art form in itself. The glass from which they are made is heated to 2,600°F (1,600°C), and then allowed to cool immensely slowly—up to six months—to avoid stresses. It can then take the best part of a year for further heat treatments, and several years to grind and polish. The mirrors produced are thick and immensely heavy, which causes distortions in the structure and even the shape of the mirror itself as its position alters. A mirror that is perfectly shaped when lying on its back will not

Recorder of the Heavens

The clarity of air around La Silla is helped by ESO's ownership of 300 square miles around the site. It was bought in 1964 to prevent any development, such as mining, that might damage the crystal clarity of the air. There are no cities to cast a glow at night or create atmospheric pollution, the two major problems for European and American observatories.

be quite so perfect when it is held at an angle.

The mirror is made from low-expansion "Zerodur" glass ceramic, and is only half the thickness of a conventional mirror of the same size—less than 10 inches thick. This halves its weight from 12 tons to only 6, reducing the distortion of the supporting structure. In order to eliminate distortion of the mirror itself, which would otherwise be unacceptably large in such a thin piece of glass, it is supported by a unique "active optics" system.

Under the mirror are 78 supports, controlled individually by computer. Light from a star is analysed, and its deviation from the ideal shape—the diffuseness of the image—generates signals which activate the supports, altering the shape of the mirror until a perfect image is obtained. In this way, the mirror always has the right shape, whatever its position. The distortions may be only a few millionths of an inch, but correcting them makes a lot of difference, producing images of stars or other objects at least three times sharper than any other ground-based telescope of the same size.

The NTT is mounted on a thin layer of oil, only a thousandth of an inch thick, which enables it to rotate about a vertical axis. The temperature of the oil is controlled to within 0.1°C to avoid the generation of heat which

The biggest of the conventional refracting telescopes at La Silla is a 140-inch instrument commissioned in 1975. It occupies the biggest dome on the highest point of the site (right). The NTT has eclipsed it for finely resolved pictures.

would disturb the atmosphere around the instrument. The building in which it is housed is, like all observatories, unheated to minimize disturbances. The pointing accuracy of the NTT is ensured by computers that take into account the minute flexing of the structure and allow for it. As a result, the NTT can be pointed in the right direction more precisely than any other telescope of the same size.

The result of all this has been to produce the best images of stars and galaxies ever taken. But the NTT by no means represents the last word in telescope technology. Ahead lie bigger and even more sophisticated instruments, with mirrors 394 inches or more across. The first of these, an

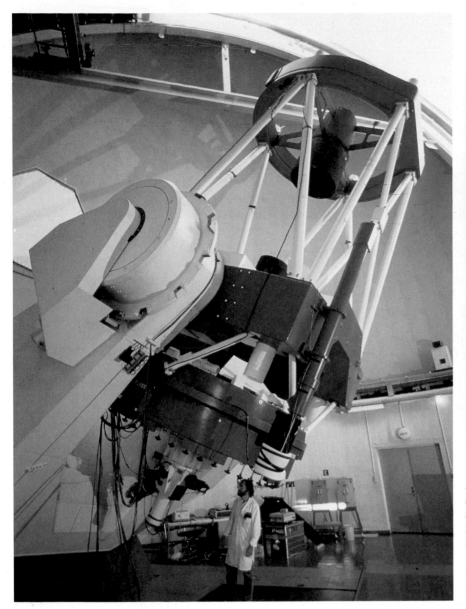

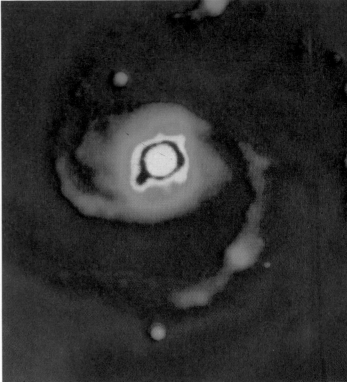

A spiral galaxy illustrates the clarity of image achievable with the sophisticated technology of the ESO. The NTT is capable of resolving, for the first time, globular clusters at a distance of 700,000 light-years, making possible the study of individual stars. In turn this allows more precise dating of clusters and the study of gas- and dust-clouds.

The immense size and weight of the larger telescopes at La Silla demand high-precision mechanics to compensate for the Earth's rotation, particularly when taking a long exposure. The NTT is equipped with computerized position encoders which achieve the greatest pointing accuracy of any ground-based telescope of comparable size.

American instrument named after its sponsor, William Keck, is due to come into operation on Mauna Kea, 13,600 feet up in Hawaii, in 1991. The Americans are also planning their own National New Technology Telescope, a 645-inch instrument planned for 1992. This should have the capacity to identify objects the size of a gold sovereign 1,000 miles away.

ESO's next step is to develop a system of "adaptive optics" designed to correct for the distortions of the atmosphere. This will be done by placing a small mirror in the telescope, and monitoring the image on it of a bright star in the field of view. Then the mirror will be automatically and rapidly deformed so as to correct any changes in the star's image caused by atmospheric disturbance. The result will be to correct also the rest of the image, producing unprecedented clarity. Tests have shown that the method works, and the next stage is to implement it in telescopes such as the NTT.

Further in the future is the next ESO project—the Very Large Telescope, or VLT, for which $232 million has already been budgeted. Once in operation by 1998, the VLT should be more powerful than all of the 20 largest telescopes currently in use. It will in fact be four telescopes, each with 320-inch mirrors, whose signals can be combined to create the same effect as a single mirror 640 inches across.

The VLT will use the same technology as the NTT, and should be sensitive enough to pick up light from objects 18 billion light years away. Work began on the first of the telescopes in 1988, although a final site for it has yet to be decided. It will be somewhere in the Atacama Desert, but not at La Silla itself. When finished, it will be possible to operate it entirely by remote control from the headquarters of ESO near Munich, without actually having to travel to Chile at all.

Gazetteer

MONOLITHIC MEMORIALS

The Americas

Crazy Horse Memorial, Custer, South Dakota, USA

Situated 17 miles from Mount Rushmore, a tribute to the Indians of North America is being carved out of the granite of Thunderhead Mountain. This colossal project, which will create the world's largest statue, was begun in 1947 by the sculptor Korczak Ziolkowski, who assisted Gutzon Borglum on Mount Rushmore. The site was chosen in 1940 by Ziolkowski and the son of the sculpture's subject, Crazy Horse, who defeated General Custer at Little Big Horn in 1876. Crazy Horse was killed by an American soldier in the following year while under a flag of truce. The sculpture depicts the chief astride a pony, and when complete will be 563 feet high and 641 feet long.

Gateway Arch, St Louis, Missouri, USA

This giant catenary arch, standing on the bank of the Mississippi River, was built in 1966 to symbolize St Louis' position as the gateway to the West. Designed by Eero Sarinen, it is a double-walled stressed-skin structure 630 feet high. The outer wall is made of ¼-inch stainless steel, the inner wall of mild steel almost ⅔ inch thick; the lower part of the gap between them is filled with concrete, the upper with cellular stiffening. In cross-section, the arch is a hollow equilateral triangle, within which lifts travel to an observation platform at the top.

San Jacinto Column, near Houston, Texas, USA

This column, at 570 feet the tallest in the world, was built in 1936–39 on the bank of the San Jacinto River to commemorate the battle that took place there in 1836 between the Texans, under Sam Houston, and Mexican troops. The concrete column, faced with creamy marble limestone, is 47 feet square at the base and tapers to 30 feet square at the observation platform. On top is a vast star, weighing nearly 197 tons.

Europe

Hadrian's Wall, Cumbria and Northumberland, England

The Romans' principal defence in Britain against invasion from the north by warlike Picts and Scots was Hadrian's Wall. Built in 122–30 at the Emperor's command, it ran between natural strongpoints from the Solway Firth, in the west, where it was made of turf, to the estuary of the Tyne in the east, where it was a grey stone structure up to 14 feet high. Along its 73 miles were forts, milecastles and signal turrets, manned by some 18,000 troops.

The wall was protected to the north by a ditch 27 feet wide and 9 feet deep, while to the south was the vallum, a 20-foot-wide, flat-bottomed ditch running between turf walls 10 feet high that served as a road. The Romans abandoned the wall in 383, when Rome itself was attacked by the Goths, but a significant part of it and 17 forts, particularly the well-preserved fort of Vercovium near Housesteads, can still be seen.

Stonehenge, Salisbury Plain, Wiltshire, England

Building of this megalithic monument began c3500 BC, before Egypt's pyramids, and continued for about 1,500 years. It was probably always the site of some form of religious ritual, but it might also have been a primitive astronomical observatory.

The final "building", whose ruins remain, consisted of a ring of sarsen stone monoliths 16 feet high and weighing up to 26 tons, linked by a continuous lintel. This ring encloses a circle of 4-ton bluestones, brought from the Welsh Preseli Mountains 200 miles away, a horseshoe of five sarsen trilithons and a horseshoe of bluestones. In the middle is the great Welsh blue-green sandstone "Altar Stone". The trilithons are made up of two standing stones and a linking lintel, fitted together with precisely shaped ball-and-socket joints.

ARCHITECTURAL ACHIEVEMENTS

The Americas

Boeing Factory, Everett, Seattle, Washington, USA

Located on the outskirts of Seattle, the Boeing Company's manufacturing facilities at Everett are the largest in the world. When it was completed in 1968, the capacity was 200 million cubic feet (70 million cubic feet more than the Vertical Assembly Building at the Kennedy Space Center). In 1980, the plant was enlarged to 291 million cubic feet to accommodate production of the 767 aircraft. Today, major parts of the assembly functions of the 747 and 767 are also housed under this one great roof.

Fallingwater, Bear Run, Pennsylvania, USA

The domestic buildings designed by the American architect Frank Lloyd Wright are amongst the most remarkable of their kind. Of these, Fallingwater is probably the best known. The house was built between 1935 and 1937 for Edgar Kaufmann, who owned Kaufmann's Department Store in Pittsburgh. Wright's first house built of reinforced concrete, Fallingwater is constructed of slabs of ochre concrete cantilevered over a waterfall with sheets of glass forming the horizontals between the planes of concrete. It reflects Wright's "organic" use of concrete, rooting his structure in the surrounding rocks by walls of rough stonework. The house has been afflicted by technical shortcomings, requiring successive heavy repairs.

Las Vegas Hilton, Nevada, USA

The largest hotel in the world, the Las Vegas Hilton occupies a 63-acre site and has 3,174 rooms and suites. There are 14 international restaurants, a casino hung with chandeliers, a 48,000-square foot ballroom and convention space with an area of 125,000 square feet. On the roof is a remarkable 10-acre recreation space, with a 350,000-gallon heated swimming pool, six tennis courts and an 18-hole putting green, as well as facilities for table tennis, badminton and shuffle board. There are 21 lifts to whisk guests up and down, and they are served in the utmost luxury by a staff of 3,600 people.

Machu Picchu, Peru

The story of the rediscovery in 1911 by Hiram Bingham of the lost Inca city, deep in the forests that cloak parts of the Andes, is one of the most romantic of archeological finds. Of all such sites, none can rival its position, surrounded by mountains and valleys on a cyclopean scale and situated at 7,975 feet above sea level. The hillsides are so precipitous that they had to be terraced, not only for the growing of food, but also to retard erosion of the soil. The terraces had a capacity to feed several hundred, and water was brought miles by aqueducts, which were still functioning when Bingham found them.

The quality of Inca masonry in the temples and houses that make up the site is as fine as that found in Cusco, where a knife blade cannot be inserted between blocks, so perfect is the join. The history of Machu Picchu is a subject of debate.

Maracana Municipal Stadium, Rio de Janeiro, Brazil

The world's biggest, this football (soccer) stadium was completed in time for the World Cup Final between Brazil and Uruguay in July 1950. It can accommodate 155,000 people seated and another 50,000 standing on the terraces. The players are isolated from the crowd by a dry moat 5 feet deep and 7 feet wide.

The Pentagon, Arlington County, Virginia, USA

The largest office building in the world, the Pentagon is the headquarters of all three branches of the armed services in the United States. Built in 1941–43, this low, five-storey block, with five sides 921 feet long, covers 34 acres, including the courtyard, and provides 3,700,000 square feet of air-conditioned floor space—sufficient for 30,000 people to work in. Built of steel and reinforced concrete with some limestone facing, it consists of five concentric rings with 10 corridors, like the spokes of a wheel, connecting them. In addition, the complex contains a huge underground shopping concourse and a heliport.

Europe

The Alhambra, Granada, Spain

Austere and formidable, the exterior of the Alhambra belies its gracious and richly ornamented interior. The conversion of the ancient fortress of Alcazába into a palace—for almost 250 years the residence and harem of Muslim rulers in Spain—began in 1238. Moorish creative genius reached its peak during the fourteenth century, when a maze of halls, columns, arcades, shady courtyards, pools and fountains was built.

With representational art forbidden by Islam, architects and artists achieved miracles of intricate abstract and geometric designs in their glazed tiles and delicate, lacelike plasterwork. The finest example of this is probably the stunning "stalactite" decorations that appear to explode in a starburst on the cupola of the Hall of the Two Sisters.

Carcassonne, Aude, France

The site of the old city, on top of a steep, isolated hill, has been occupied continuously since the fifth century BC, and towers built by the Visigoths in AD 485 can still be seen. But Carcassonne's fame rests on its medieval fortifications, the finest in Europe. Begun by the viscounts of Carcassonne in the twelfth century, they were continued after 1247 by King Louis IX of France, who constructed the outer ramparts. His son, Philip III, added further intricate defences, including the beautiful Narbonnese gate and the Tour de Trésor.

In 1355, even the redoubtable Edward, the Black Prince, found the fortress impregnable. By the end of the seventeenth century, however, the ramparts were abandoned and fell into disrepair; they were restored in the mid-nineteenth century by the great architect Viollet-le-Duc.

Castell Coch, South Glamorgan, Wales

Designed by William Burges for the 3rd Marquess of Bute and built in the late 1870s, Castell Coch bears comparison with the creations of King Ludwig II of Bavaria: both men had atavistic ideas about architecture, and produced buildings that were indulgent anachronisms. Though nominally the restoration of a castle ruinous since the sixteenth century, Castell Coch is a sham, combining the exterior appearance of a thirteenth-century Welsh castle with an interior that is one of the most exuberant products of Victorian imaginative decoration. For example, almost every surface of the vaulted Drawing Room is elaborately decorated with subjects from nature, scenes from Aesop's Fables and Greek mythology.

It is rare for an architect to be so in sympathy with a client's vision as Burges was with the Marquess of Bute; the result, here and at Cardiff Castle where the two men also collaborated, is a pair of buildings unlike any others.

Church of Notre Dame du Haut, Ronchamp, France

One of the most unorthodox church buildings ever built is the highly individual creation of Le Corbusier at Ronchamp near Belfort, erected between 1950 and 1955. Built of reinforced concrete, the church provides an interesting silhouette from all viewpoints, the roof billowing up to an acute point with an exaggerated overhang, looking like a cushion from some angles. Deeply recessed stained-glass windows of irregular shapes and size light an interior with a seeming confusion of angles and slopes.

The Colosseum, Rome, Italy

Situated near the south-east end of the Forum, the great oval Flavian amphitheatre takes its familiar name from the huge statue of Nero that stood nearby. The venue for gladiatorial fights and contests with wild animals, it was begun by Vespasian in AD 75 and inaugurated by his son Titus in AD 80. Built of concrete faced with travertine marble, at 620 feet overall and 513 wide, it is the most imposing of all remaining Roman buildings. The outer wall, 160 feet high, has four storeys, the first three arcaded with Doric, Ionic and Corinthian orders, the top one solid with Corinthian pilasters and windows. Tiers of seats, supported by concentric corridors with vaulted ceilings, could accommodate around 45,000 people. And underneath the arena, which measures 287 by 180 feet, are storerooms and dens for animals.

Gazetteer

Escorial, near Madrid, Spain

Philip II built the Escorial in 1563–84 to commemorate the Spanish victory over the French at St Quentin in 1557. The rectangular complex, measuring 675 by 525 feet, includes the large, handsome church of San Lorenzo and a mausoleum in which all Spanish sovereigns except Alfonso XIII (d1941) are buried. There are also a monastery, palace, offices, library and college, housed in five great cloisters.

The massive, sombre buildings, designed by Juan Bautista de Toledo and Juan Herrera, are made of grey granite, and are impressive rather than beautiful. The plan of the grand but austere church is that of a Greek cross, with nave and transepts of equal length, and the monumental dome is 60 feet in diameter and 320 feet high. Today the Escorial contains a magnificent collection of paintings, rare books and manuscripts.

Fonthill Abbey, Wiltshire, England

The now-vanished country house at Fonthill was one of the most fantastic houses ever built in a country not short of eccentric creations. Its creator, William Beckford, had inherited a huge fortune, derived largely from plantations in the West Indies. An admirer of the Gothic, Beckford commissioned James Wyatt to design a pile that would stand comparison with nearby Salisbury Cathedral. Eleven years of round-the-clock work by two teams, each of 500 workmen, were required to build the cruciform structure, completed in 1808.

The main part measured 312 feet by 250 feet, the Great Hall's ceiling was 80 feet high, and there were two Long Galleries, but it was the tower surmounting the crossing that astonished the few visitors admitted by the reclusive Beckford: the octagonal spire soared 276 feet into the air, but it was to prove the building's undoing. Beckford's impatience to see his house completed and a lack of scruples by the builder combined to encourage the latter to skimp on the foundations. Crucial inverted arches had been omitted, with the result that the tower fell in 1825, though not before Beckford had sold the Abbey. It was never rebuilt, and within thirty years of its construction the rest of this vast building had disappeared.

Hagia Sophia, Istanbul, Turkey

A pool of serenity in the maelstrom of modern Istanbul (formerly Constantinople), the great Byzantine church of Hagia Sophia, "Holy Wisdom", was built by Justinian in 532–37. The third church to stand on the site, the exterior is a jumble of semi-domes and buttresses, with four minarets at the corners, added later. But the interior, with an area of 9,800 square yards, and the dome, with a diameter of more than 100 feet, are magnificent.

Justinian imported red porphyry, verdantique, and yellow and white marble, and employed sculptors and mosaic artists to create the finest church in Christendom. When Constantinople fell to the Ottoman Turks in 1453, Hagia Sophia was converted to a mosque and the mosaics plastered over. Finally, in 1934, it became a museum.

Herrenchiemsee and Neuschwanstein, Bavaria, West Germany

Several of the world's most opulent and fantastic buildings were built by the eccentric, romantic King Ludwig II of Bavaria, patron of Wagner.

Herrenchiemsee, built on the largest of three islands in Bavaria's largest lake, was Ludwig's Versailles. The foundation stone was laid in 1878, and by the time of Ludwig's death in 1886, only the central block and part of one wing had been finished. But it already contained some of the most magnificent objects made for any palace: the largest porcelain candelabrum in the world, produced by Meissen; the Hall of Mirrors that eclipses that at Versailles; curtains that each weigh a hundredweight; a door with Meissen plaques in the panels.

In contrast, Neuschwanstein is a pastiche medieval castle, built on a spectacular mountain top of which over 20 feet had to be blasted away to provide a level surface. It is the castle's dramatic setting, ringed by Alpine peaks, that makes this fairytale fantasy so memorable. Work began in 1869 and the finishing touches were still being done at Ludwig's death. Besides the traditional rooms of the castle, the king's study gave access to an artificial grotto with cascade and variable lighting effects to match the monarch's mood.

Knole, Kent, England

Seen from a distance, across its 1,000-acre park, the country house of Knole resembles a medieval town. It is reputed to be the house (as opposed to palace) with the largest number of rooms—365. Eventually built around seven courtyards, the house was begun in 1456 by the Archbishop of Canterbury Thomas Bourchier, who bequeathed it to the see of Canterbury. Henry VIII coerced Archbishop Cranmer into giving it to him, and the acquisitive king enlarged it considerably, almost certainly adding the imposing west front, 340 feet long, for the enormous retinue that accompanied the monarch and visiting ministers. The Great Hall, originally intended as the room in which the household ate, measures 95 feet by 32 feet. The Cartoon Gallery is even longer, at 135 feet.

The Leaning Tower, Pisa, Italy

This round Romanesque tower, the campanile to the nearby Baptistery, was started in 1174 by Bonanno Pisano. Built entirely in white marble, with eight tiers of arched arcades, the tower is 179 feet high. It began to lean as soon as the first storey was completed, probably because the alluvial subsoil settled or the foundations were inadequate. Ingenious attempts were made to compensate for the tilt by straightening up subsequent storeys and making the pillars higher on the south side than the north. The bell chamber, finished only in 1350, was also built at an angle and the heaviest bells hung on the north, but the tower continued to lean and is currently some 17 feet out of perpendicular.

Lincoln Cathedral, England

Regarded as the finest example of Early English architecture, Lincoln Cathedral had the distinction of being the world's tallest structure between 1307, when its central spire reached 525 feet (overtaking the Pyramid of Cheops in Egypt), and 1548 when it fell in a storm. The traveller and writer William Cobbett even thought it "the finest building in the whole world". Its position atop the hill that dominates Lincoln gives it a commanding site unrivalled by any cathedral but Durham.

Building began c1075 under Bishop

Remigius and the cathedral was dedicated in 1092. Damage sustained through an earthquake in the twelfth century necessitated its rebuilding under the bishop St Hugh of Lincoln, begun c1190. Amongst the glories of the cathedral are hundreds of statues that adorn the exterior, the quality of the carving on the choir screen and in the Angel Choir, and the library designed by Christopher Wren. The spires that once crowned the two shorter, western towers were removed in the eighteenth century, despite the riotous protest of the townspeople.

Nat-West Tower, Old Broad Street, London, England

The tallest cantilevered building in the world, and the tallest office block in Britain, is the National Westminster Bank's 600-foot tower in the City of London. It has three basement levels and 49 storeys, which rest on steel and concrete supports projecting from a central tower. It was designed by Richard Seifert and completed in 1979.

The Palm House, Kew Gardens, London, England

After Queen Victoria's visit to Paxton's lily-house at Chatsworth (see p.64), it was suggested that the Royal Botanical Gardens at Kew should build a comparable structure. The two architects involved were Decimus Burton and Richard Turner: Burton had helped Paxton with the Chatsworth building, and Turner had contributed to the Palm House for the Botanic Gardens in Belfast. Work began in 1844 on the designs for what was to be the longest such building, 362 feet long, 100 feet wide in the centre and 63 feet high. Cast-iron columns supported the curved mullions of the walls and roof. A separate boiler house provided heat through pipes buried in a walk-through tunnel.

The Parthenon, Athens, Greece

The Parthenon was built as a temple to the goddess Athena in 447–438 BC. In essence, it consists of a rectangular base, 238 by 101 feet overall, with a colonnade on all four sides enclosing the two small rectangular chambers of the naos—the city's treasury and a room to house the sumptuous gold and ivory statue of Athena. The roof was low pitched, with a triangular pediment at each end. But these geometric forms are softened and enlivened by subtle variations that make the Parthenon the most perfect of ancient Greek buildings. All horizontal lines curve upward toward the centre, and the columns, which swell slightly in the middle and taper toward the top, lean inward.

The temple is built of marble blocks, precisely fitted without mortar and decorated with carvings, embellished with bronze and gold. A carved frieze ran around the top of the naos. Carved panels above the pillars and magnificent high-relief carvings on the pediments depicted the birth of Athena and the battle between Athena and Poseidon, the sea god, for Athens.

Petra, Jordan

In 1812 the Swiss traveller J.L. Burckhardt rediscovered the ancient city of Petra, "a rose-red city half as old as time", which flourished as the Nabatean capital for about 500 years from the second century BC to the early fourth century AD. What make Petra one of the world's most spectacular archeological sites are its setting, ringed by barren mountains, the fabulous carving work of the Nabateans, and the overlay of Roman buildings that was erected after their annexation of the city in AD 106. Petra is reached by a narrow gorge of $\frac{1}{2}$ mile, the Siq, that runs between almost vertical cliffs 300 feet high. This approach was impregnable, capable of being defended by a handful of soldiers.

The Nabateans were amongst the world's finest carvers of stone and the El-Khazneh, or Treasury, which is the first building seen at the end of the Siq, is the most spectacular example. Carved out of orange-pink rock, the Greek-style building was probably a temple. The Nabatean buildings that were carved into the cliff faces have been protected by the overhang and are much better preserved than the later Roman buildings. Of these, the best preserved is the amphitheatre which once held over 3,000 spectators in 33 tiers of seats. Three markets, temples, a forum, baths, gymnasia, colonnades, many shops and private houses once covered the Roman site, 2 miles long.

Pompeii, Naples, Italy

Founded in the fifth century BC, Pompeii came first under Greek influence; but by AD 79, when it was overwhelmed by the eruption of Vesuvius, it had become a town of 25,000 and a summer resort for wealthy Romans. Systematic excavation of the ruins began only in 1748, and a third of the city still remains buried.

The villas, temples, baths, civic buildings, forum and amphitheatre so far uncovered are mainly in the Roman style. They are built of brick, faced with marble or plaster, and some, notably the Casa dei Vettii, are richly decorated with frescoes. The paved streets, between high pavements, are deeply rutted by chariot wheels and frequently crossed by stepping stones for pedestrian use. The remains of buildings and people as they emerge provide graphic and moving evidence of the life of this ancient city.

Pompidou Centre, Paris, France

Designed by Richard Rogers and Renzo Piano, this huge museum and display centre, completed in 1975, is one of the most controversial of modern buildings. It has no formal façade and is constructed of gigantic steel beams and trusses painted in bright primary colours— red, blue and yellow—which are clearly visible through the glass walls, as are the external escalators and connecting galleries.

The structure consists of five floors some 360 feet long and 160 feet wide, with a public forum 1,368 square yards in extent on the ground floor. It also houses a museum of modern art with 44,800 square yards of exhibition space, research institutes for industrial creation and for music and acoustics, a library and a restaurant.

Ponte Vecchio, River Arno, Florence, Italy

Built by Taddeo Gaddi in 1345, the Ponte Vecchio was the first bridge in the West with arches smaller than a semicircle. This meant that fewer piers were needed to support it, affording a freer passage to boats and, most importantly, to flood water, for the Arno carries vast quantities of melt-water in spring.

On either side of the roadway is a two-

Gazetteer

storey gallery. The top storey acts as a corridor, linking the Uffizi Palace, which housed the offices of the ruling Medici family, with the Pitti Palace on the other side of the river. At street level there were, and still are, shops occupied by gold- and silver-smiths and jewellers.

Prague Castle, Hradčany, Prague, Czechoslovakia

Founded *c*850 as a wooden keep, the "castle" at Hradčany, the largest in the world, is, like the Kremlin in Moscow, now a complex of buildings rather than a fortress. Grouped around three courtyards, the irregular oblong of buildings covers 18 acres. A visitor penetrating the castle enters through the elaborate Matthias Gate, then passes from early twentieth-century architecture back through baroque, renaissance and Gothic to the huge medieval White and Dalibarka towers.

The most impressive buildings are the Royal Palace and the Gothic cathedral of St Vitus. Designed by Matthias of Arras in 1344, it is the third on the site; the original was founded *c*930 by Prince Wenceslas, now the country's patron saint. From at least 894, the castle has been the official seat and coronation place of Czech sovereigns; even today, the president is inaugurated in the palace in the vast, late Gothic Valdislav Hall, which is 243 feet long, 60 feet wide and 50 feet high.

The Royal Pavilion, Brighton, Sussex, England

Originally a small farmhouse, the Royal Pavilion was changed and added to over 35 years, from 1786 to 1821, to satisfy the whim of the Prince of Wales, later King George IV. Its final fantastic pinnacles and domes, owing much to Indian Islamic architecture, date from 1815. They were the work of John Nash, who for the first time in domestic architecture made much use of cast iron – other than for window frames and fireplaces – both structurally and decoratively.

Astonishing as the exterior is, the interior is even more stunning, for Nash added the huge domed banqueting hall and music room and decorated both with wild extravagance. Great dragons curl around the music room's walls and deep-red and blue ceiling, encrusted with gold; and in the exotically painted banqueting hall hangs a jewelled chandelier weighing almost a ton.

St Paul's Cathedral, Ludgate Hill, London, England

The first stone of Christopher Wren's masterpiece was laid in 1675 and the cathedral was finished in 1710. The three-aisled nave and choir are 463 feet long and 101 feet wide, and over the crossing is a shallow dome, 450 feet in diameter and 218 feet high, covered in mosaics. The dome is supported by pillars, grouped at the corners to house church offices and a staircase to the library. These pillars were originally built of stone, infilled with rubble; in the 1930s they were strengthened by the injection of liquid concrete, which perhaps helped them to withstand destruction in the bombing during World War II.

The dome consists of three shells. Above the inner one is a conical brick structure which carries the timber framework of the external lead-covered dome. It also supports the colonnaded lantern and a great golden cross that rise to 365 feet above the ground.

On the west front are two 222-foot towers, in the southern one of which hangs the 17-ton bell, Great Paul, the largest in England.

The Palace of Versailles, Versailles, France

Built on the site of a royal hunting lodge, the palace of Versailles was the triumphant product of the ambition of Louis XIV and the designs of the great architects in the classical style: Le Vau, Le Brun and Hordouin-Mansart. Begun in 1661, it was 50 years in the building. The vast palace and gardens occupy 6,000 acres.

The west, garden front, 2,197 feet long, was built largely by Le Vau in 1669, and in 1678 its open terrace was enclosed by Mansart to create the most splendid room in the palace, the Hall of Mirrors, 238 feet long. Here, 17 tall arched windows are matched by 17 dummy arches lined with mirrors set in gilded copper, and both windows and mirrors are separated by red marble pillars. A gilded stucco cornice frames the painted ceiling. The room was originally furnished with silver furniture and chandeliers, and sumptuous carpets, to reflect the Sun King's magnificence.

Windsor Castle, Berkshire, England

Begun by William the Conqueror in 1067, the royal residence of Windsor Castle is the largest inhabited castle in the world. Its plan is roughly a figure of eight, and the curtain wall extends for over ½ mile. The massive cylindrical shell keep, which dominates the town's skyline, was built by Henry I, who first used stone in the castle's construction. The keep's height has since been increased to 100 feet and the exterior wall refaced. By the end of Edward III's reign, the castle had ceased to be primarily a military stronghold and become principally a residence. Successive monarchs have altered and extended the castle, but its present appearance resembles its medieval form. Foremost of the additions is the Garter chapel of St George, begun by Edward IV.

Rest of the World

Angkor Wat, Angkor, Kampuchea

The temple of Angkor Wat, one of the largest religious complexes in the world, covers an area of nearly 1 square mile. Built of sandstone in 1113–50 under the ruler Suryavarnam II as his sepulchre, it was dedicated to the god Vishnu and represents the Hindu cosmology.

The great temple, surrounded by a moat representing the oceans, is approached across a causeway 1,000 feet long. A magnificent gateway in the outer wall— the mountains at the edge of the world— gives access to five concentric rectangular enclosures, overlooked by towers in the form of lotus buds, the tallest more than 200 feet high. The five central towers denote Mount Meru's peaks, the hub of the Universe. The courts are linked by colonnades lined with elaborate sculptures and immense decorative bas-reliefs depicting scenes from sacred Hindu legends—the temple's most remarkable feature.

Chandigarh, Punjab, India

Le Corbusier's vision for an ideal city received partial expression in the administrative capital of the Punjab, founded in 1951, for which he designed the principal buildings: the Palace of the Assembly (parliament), High Court and Secretariat.

Their massive dimensions make them appropriate symbols of government, but they have proved less than functional, not least because of the space between them—uncomfortable in the heat of the Punjab. The radical departure from any national architectural tradition was a deliberate policy of Prime Minister Nehru at the beginning of India's independence, intending the buildings to be "symbolic of the freedom of India".

Fatehpur Sikri, Uttar Pradesh, India

In 1569, the emperor Akbar built a mosque and tomb at Fatehpur Sikri to honour the hermit Salim Chisti, who had foretold the birth of his son, later the emperor Jahangir. Public buildings and palaces were the next to be erected, and the city, encircled by battlemented walls, became Akbar's capital until 1588. By 1605, due to a shortage of water, it was deserted.

Built of soft, rose-coloured sandstone, easily carved, Fatehpur Sikri is an exquisite and almost intact example of Moghul architecture. Most remarkable are the Buland Darwaza (victory gate) with its immense elephant statues; the fine façade of the Jami Masjid (great mosque); Salim's marble mausoleum with its fine traceries and enamel and mother of pearl inlays; and the palaces of Jodh Bai and Birbal.

Great Zimbabwe, Zimbabwe

The largest stone monument in Africa outside Egypt is the complex of ruins 250 miles inland from the Indian Ocean port of Sofala, known as Great Zimbabwe. The buildings of the Acropolis, or hill fortress, look down on those in the valley that lie within the Great Enclosure. This dry-stone wall, 830 feet in circumference, 16–35 feet high and at least 4 feet thick at the base, is made from blue-grey granite cut and laid like bricks. Inside are other walls forming narrow passages, three platforms, several "chambers" and a solid stone conical tower.

The builders of Great Zimbabwe and its purpose are not known, but it was probably founded around the tenth century as a centre for trade in artefacts from a flourishing Iron Age community and in black slaves for Arabia.

Hong Kong and Shanghai Banking Corporation Headquarters, Hong Kong

This masterpiece of technical innovation, designed by Norman Foster and completed in 1986, is made up of three visually distinct towers of different heights, the 47-storey central section rising to 590 feet. The entire building is suspended over an open ground-floor plaza from eight immense steel towers clad in aluminium panels. The exposed steel structure is divided into five vertical zones within which, in a method derived from bridge construction, a stack of lightweight steel and concrete decks is hung from steel suspension trusses that look like giant coathangers. These stacks were built largely from prefabricated modules made in USA, Britain and Japan.

On the south face of the building is a computer-controlled "sunscoop" of 24 mirrors, which follows the sun and reflects its rays on to the top of the 150-foot high central atrium; from here it floods down throughout the building.

Hoysaleswara Temple, Halebid, Karnataka (Mysore), India

The Hoysala dynasty, which ruled in this region for some 250 years until 1326, reached the peak of its power under Bittiga (1110–52), who took the name of Vishnuvardhana when he was converted to Hinduism. The most remarkable of the temples he erected to honour his new religion was the Hoysaleswara temple at Halebid, his capital city.

In itself, the fairly small, squat, star-shaped building is not impressive; it is the intricate sculptures with which every surface is covered that establishes the temple as the acme of Hoysala artistic achievement. Carved in soft soapstone that hardens with exposure are episodes from the lives of the princes: hunting scenes, depictions of rural life, animals, birds, and, above all, musicians and dancing girls.

There is also a huge statue of the Jain god Gommateshwara and of the bull of the Hindu god Shiva.

New Delhi, India

The city of New Delhi, on the right bank of the Jumna River, was designed by Edwin Lutyens and Herbert Baker. It was built between 1912 and 1929 to replace Calcutta as the capital and administrative centre of British India. Its broad streets are symmetrically laid out to afford wide views of fine government buildings and historical monuments, including a huge war memorial arch erected in 1921. From this arch, a broad, tree-lined avenue, the Raj Path, leads to a magnificent marble and sandstone palace. Originally the Viceroy's Palace, since Independence it has become the official residence of the Indian president.

In a prayer ground in the south of the city, Mahatma Gandhi was assassinated in 1948.

Polonnaruwa, near Sigiriya, Sri Lanka

Built in a wonderful site beside a lake, the ancient city of Polonnaruwa was once the most magnificent in Sri Lanka, formerly Ceylon. It became a royal residence as early as 368 and during the eighth century was the capital of the island. Its period of greatest importance was during the reign of the most famous Singhalese king, Parakrama Bahu I, who reigned from 1164 to 1197, and the principal ruins date from this time. The most imposing is the Jetawanarama temple, 170 feet long, whose walls reach 80 feet in height and are 12 feet thick, and the immense reclining statue of Buddha.

The Potala, Lhasa, Tibet

Its thousand windows and gleaming golden roofs visible from miles away, the imposing and powerful structure of the Potala rises high on a hill above Lhasa. For more than 300 years, until the Chinese annexation in 1951, it was the fortress-palace of the Dalai Lamas, Tibet's spiritual leaders; today it is a museum.

The whitewashed stone walls of the outer White Palace, completed in 1648, enclose the Red Palace, finished in 1694. This is the religious centre of the complex, with the monks' assembly halls, libraries of Buddhist scriptures, chapels, shrines and, most impressive, the 50-foot-high funerary pagoda of the Fifth Dalai Lama—the Potala's founder. It is made from sandalwood and covered with 4 tons of gold, studded with diamonds, rubies and sapphires.

Gazetteer

Taj Mahal, Agra, India

One of the best-known buildings in the world was an extraordinary indulgence, a personal celebration of the love felt by the seventeenth-century Moghul emperor, Shah Jahan, for his queen, Mumtaz Mahal. She died in 1631 after bearing 14 children during their 17 years of marriage. Work on the building began in the same year.

For the next 20 years, 20,000 men and women toiled to turn the drawings of an architect, whose identity remains a mystery, into the gleaming white mausoleum: skilled craftsmen were recruited from all over Asia; elephants and bullocks dragged countless blocks of marble along a 10-mile ramp of tamped earth to the construction site. The surfaces of the Taj were inlaid with precious and semi-precious stones until the troubled eighteenth century, when they were stolen. The dome is the most imposing part of the building, the finial reaching 220 feet.

The Taj was neglected after Shah Jahan's sons died, and under the Raj there was even a plan to dismantle it and sell the marble in England. Only with the revived interest in India's architectural heritage, fostered by Lord Curzon, were the mausoleum and its grounds renovated.

Schwedagon Pagoda, Rangoon, Burma

In a "nest of hundreds of smaller pagodas", on a 14-acre hilltop site dominating the city of Rangoon, is the Schwedagon Pagoda, the most magnificent Buddhist shrine in Burma.

Legend has it that the first pagoda was built here in the sixth century BC; the present stupa, dating from 1768, was raised by King Hsibyushin to replace one destroyed in an earthquake. The bell-shaped central body, which stands on a series of rectangular and octagonal terraces—the whole plated with pure gold—rises more than 300 feet in tapering sections to a gilt-iron *hti*, or "umbrella", hung with gold and silver bells. This is surmounted by a gem-encrusted vane and an orb studded with 4,000 diamonds.

FEATS OF CIVIL ENGINEERING

The Americas

Chesapeake Bay Bridge-Tunnel, Virginia, USA

The world's longest bridge-tunnel was opened to traffic in April 1964 after just 42 months' work and the expenditure of $200 million. The $17\frac{1}{2}$-mile combination of trestles, bridges and tunnels links Norfolk and the tip of Cape Charles. To keep the channel into Chesapeake Bay clear for shipping, two concrete-lined tunnels a mile long and 24 feet in diameter were taken deep beneath the main channel, joining two man-made islands each 1,500 feet long. The main part of the crossing is on $12\frac{1}{2}$ miles of precast concrete pile trestles, 31 feet wide and 25 feet above mean low water, and capable of withstanding 20-foot waves.

Golden Gate Bridge, San Francisco, USA

Although over 50 years old, this bridge is still regarded as one of the world's great civil engineering masterpieces. When Joseph Strauss completed his design for the bridge in 1930, it was for the world's longest span, at 4,200 feet, overtaken only in 1964 by the Verrazano Narrows Bridge, New York, which has a span of 4,260 feet.

More than 100,000 tons of steel, 693,000 cubic yards of concrete and 80,000 miles of cable were used in its construction. The overall length, including freeway approaches, is 7 miles. The towers are 746 feet high and there are two supporting piers, the larger of which extends 100 feet below the sea. At low tide, the roadway is 220 feet above the water.

The biggest obstacle encountered by the engineers on the Golden Gate Bridge was the construction of the foundations on account of the strong tides; deep-sea divers could work for just four periods of 20 minutes a day when the tide turned and the water was relatively slack. Several abortive attempts were made to establish a caisson within which to build the piers of the bridge, compelling the engineers to build instead a cofferdam—a watertight case

kept dry by pumping. The bridge opened in May 1937 and had cost $35 million.

Quebec Bridge, Canada

The world's longest cantilever truss span, at 1,800 feet, is situated some way up the St Lawrence from Quebec to take advantage of a narrowing of the river from its usual width of 2–3 miles to little more than $\frac{1}{4}$ mile. An earlier bridge at this point collapsed, and construction of the present bridge was begun in 1899, but was fraught with problems. Warnings of excessive deflection as work progressed were ignored until, in 1907, the bridge collapsed, killing 75 workmen. An inadequate number of rivets in one of the cantilever arms and the buckling of a web member were the cause.

The new design was for a much stronger bridge, 3,300 feet long and entailing the use of 150 percent more steel. However, disaster struck again, in 1916, when the suspended span was being lifted into place and a casting broke; the 640-foot, 5,000-ton span fell into the river, killing 13 workers. The third attempt was successful, and the opening train steamed across in December 1917. A roadway was added in 1929.

Niagara Suspension Bridge, Niagara River, USA and Canada

Amid dire predictions that it would collapse in the first high winds, the first modern suspension bridge was opened to rail and passenger traffic at Niagara in 1855. That the double-decker bridge, with a main span of 821 feet, proved safe was due to the recognition by its designer, John A. Roebling, that a suspension bridge needed to be not only strong but stable. Strength was gained from two $10\frac{1}{4}$-inch diameter cables on either side, each of which supported one of the decks, each 10 feet wide. Stability was ensured by the 64 stays and deep timber trusses between the decks. But the iron cables gradually deteriorated, and in 1897 Roebling's suspension bridge was replaced by a steel arch structure, itself replaced by the Rainbow Bridge.

Second Lake Washington Bridge, Seattle, Washington, USA

The longest floating bridge in the world—12,596 feet overall with a 7,518-foot floating section—is the Lacey V. Murrow Bridge, finished in 1963, which traverses Lake Washington on Interstate 90. The lake was too deep, at 150 feet, to bridge conventionally, but there are no currents and no ice, so a pontoon bridge was the ideal solution. Each of the 25 reinforced concrete pontoons measures 350 feet long, 60 feet wide and 14 feet to the roadway; pontoons are divided internally into watertight compartments. As well as the floating section, there are three reinforced concrete girder spans to allow small ships to pass.

Europe

Southend Pier, Essex, England

The world's largest pier was built to serve a resort that was already popular by the beginning of the nineteenth century. The first, wooden, pier was begun in 1829 and was extended from 1,800 feet to 1¼ miles in 1846. In 1887 it was almost entirely rebuilt by Arrol Bros to a design by J. Brunlees. The new pier was 6,600 feet long, and was improved and extended on several occasions, to reach almost 7,000 feet.

Piers had two principal functions: to enable visitors to walk away from the beach into healthier sea air, and to enable pleasure steamers to ply the seaside resorts without the use of rowing boats to ferry passengers ashore. Many piers incorporated a theatre or at least a café and shops. At Southend an electric narrow gauge railway linked the shore with the three-tiered pavilion structure at the seaward end where coastguard and lifeboat stations were provided.

Forth Railway Bridge, Fife, Scotland

The graceful design for a cantilever railway bridge across the Firth of Forth by John Fowler and Benjamin Baker (who designed the tube for the journey of Cleopatra's Needle to London) was the first use of steel for a major bridge in Europe. Suspicion over the use of steel after disappointing results in some Dutch railway bridges led to a Board of Trade prohibition on the metal's use for bridges until 1877. The three piers support cantilever arms of 680 feet which are joined by two suspended spans, each of 350 feet, making two main spans of 1,710 feet, which made it the world's longest span between its opening in 1889 and completion of the Quebec Bridge in 1917.

Royal Albert Bridge, Saltash, Devon, England

The last great work by the brilliant and versatile engineer Isambard Kingdom Brunel was the viaduct taking the Cornwall Railway across the Tamar estuary into Devon. It was notable in being the first major work in which compressed air was used to expel water from a caisson—a working chamber in which foundations can be dug below the surrounding water.

Brunel developed the principle behind his earlier, smaller bridge at Chepstow to produce a twin-span bridge reached by short, curving approach spans. The two central spans are a combination of arch and suspension bridge, the upper chord consisting of a huge wrought-iron oval cylinder from which two chains are suspended to form the lower chord. The spans, each of 455 feet and weighing 1,060 tons, were built on the river bank and floated into position. Brunel did not witness the opening by the Prince Consort in May 1859, being critically ill; he died four months later.

Pontcysyllte Aqueduct, Shropshire, England

Thomas Telford's aqueduct across the Dee Valley broke new ground in using for the canal trough and towpath a material new to this application—cast iron. By the time construction began in 1795, a number of cast-iron arch bridges had been built, following Abraham Darby's pioneer structure of 1779 at Ironbridge. But Telford incorporated the canal trough itself in wedge-shaped sections, which bolted together through flanges at each end, the wedges building up to form arches that rested on masonry piers. Even after building an embankment at each end, 19 spans each of 53 feet were necessary to bridge the valley, making the aqueduct 1,007 feet in length. Opened in 1805, the aqueduct still carries boats on the Ellesmere Canal.

Afsluitdijk, Zuider Zee, Netherlands

The Zuider Zee was formed in the thirteenth century when the North Sea, surging inland, captured an existing lake. Over the centuries, attempts were made to reclaim the flooded land, but large-scale reclamation only became possible through one of the world's greatest feats of civil engineering, the construction in 1927–32 of the Afsluitdijk, a sea dam 20¼ miles long and 25 feet high. Built in two parts, this split the Zuider Zee into the Ijsselmeer and the Waddenzee.

In shallow areas, two walls of boulder clay were built up and sand pumped into the space between them; the sloping dam walls were faced with brushwood bundles and stone. In two deep areas, sill dams extending 11½ feet below the average sea level were built first. The dam's width at sea level is 293 feet.

Four polders—reclaimed land—totalling 700 square miles have already been returned to agricultural and urban use, and another 155 square miles will be added with the completion of a fifth polder, the Markerwaard. The Ijsselmeer will become a freshwater lake 540 square miles in extent.

Thames Barrier, River Thames, Woolwich, London

The barrier across the Thames—1,706 feet long and 105 feet high—is the world's largest tidal river barrier. After almost 13 years of planning and building, it was opened by Queen Elizabeth II in 1984. Designed to protect vulnerable areas along the river from flooding by the North Sea, it consists of 10 movable steel gates, 9 piers and 2 abutments. Four large rising sector gates, each 200 feet wide and weighing some 1,300 tons, span the main navigational channels; two 103-foot rising sector gates provide two narrower channels; and adjacent to the abutments are four falling radial gates.

To facilitate shipping, when the rising sector gates are opened, they rotate about 90 degrees until their curved surface is housed in a shaped recess on the river bed and their flat upper surface is flush with the river bottom. The gates are operated by a hydraulically powered mechanical system.

Gazetteer

Tower Bridge, River Thames, London

Probably the best-known sight in London is the elaborate gothick Tower Bridge over the Thames. The first bridge encountered by shipping, it was designed by Horace Jones and John Wolfe Barry and built between 1886 and 1894. The bridge is made of iron, clad in Portland stone and grey granite, and consists of two counter-weighted bascules (from the French for see-saw) and two suspended spans that connect the 205-foot main towers with the shore. Each of the bascules is made up of four main 100-foot girders, with cross-bracings, and weighs around 1,000 tons. Originally they were operated hydraulically and took about 6 minutes to open; today they are opened electrically in 1½ minutes. Pedestrians can cross the bridge even when it is open by means of high-level walkways between the towers.

Rest of the World

Carthage Aqueduct, Tunisia, North Africa

The longest aqueduct of ancient times was this channel of 87½ miles, built by the Romans during the reign of Emperor Hadrian (117–138). It brought water from the inland springs of Zaghouan to huge underground cisterns built earlier by the Carthaginians at Maalaka on the outskirts of their city.

The piers supporting the channel stood some 15 feet apart and were 15 feet high by 12 feet thick. The channel itself was 3 feet wide and 6 feet high, and it has been calculated that it had a capacity of 7 million gallons a day.

"The Giant Peter", Himeji Central Park, Hyogo, Japan

The largest Ferris wheels in the world today are "The Giant Peter" and its companion wheel at Tsukuba, also in Japan, which can carry 384 people. Both wheels measure just under 279 feet in diameter—29 feet more than the original wheel designed by George Ferris, which was built at Chicago in 1893.

Kariba Dam, Zambezi River, Zambia and Zimbabwe

Downstream of the Victoria Falls, where the great Zambezi River used to thunder through the Kariba Gorge, stands the Kariba Dam. One of the world's largest dams and, at 420 feet, the fourth highest in Africa, the concrete arch structure measures 1,900 feet along the crest. The dam was built in 1955–59 and first filled in 1963. Some 50,000 people living along the banks of the Zambezi had to be resettled as Kariba Lake, the reservoir formed by the dam, grew to 175 miles long and 32 miles across at its widest, and thousands of wild animals had to be moved to safety. Kariba's hydroelectric project supplies almost all Zambia's electricity needs, and also serves a large part of Zimbabwe.

Mohammadieh Noria, Hamah, Syria

Where river banks are steep, as on the River Asi (Orontes) at Hamah, one of the most efficient ways of raising water is by means of a noria, or waterwheel. This wheel, one of several at Hamah dating from Roman times, has a diameter of 131 feet and is the largest in the world. The tall, undershot wheel is lightly built from timber in a complex design, with a chain of scoops around the rim. As the revolving scoops reach the river, they fill, and at the top discharge the water into a towering aqueduct which carries it to the fields for irrigation.

Nurek Dam, Vakhsh River, Tadjikistan, USSR

The highest dam in the world is this earth embankment dam with a clay core close to the border with Afghanistan. Started in 1962 and finished only in 1980, the dam is 984 feet high and 2,310 feet along the crest and was designed to withstand severe earthquakes, which are common in the region. Water from the dam, which has a volume of 2,048 million cubic feet, is used to generate electricity and to irrigate more than 2½ million acres of land in the Amu-Darya area.

UNDERGROUND ENGINEERING ACHIEVEMENTS

Europe

Thames Tunnel, London, England

The tunnel that links Wapping and Rotherhithe is arguably the most historic tunnel ever built: it was the first underwater tunnel and the first to be built with the use of a tunnelling shield, which became the normal method of tunnel boring. The shield's function is to protect the roof and sides of the tunnel until the lining of brickwork has been completed, and to facilitate manual or mechanical excavation. The credit for these distinctions goes to Marc Brunel and his even more remarkable son, Isambard Kingdom Brunel, who at the age of 20 was engineer in charge.

The Brunels began work in March 1825, sinking a shaft at Rotherhithe in which the tunnelling shield was installed. Work progressed more slowly than anticipated, partly due to the difficult nature of the ground, which also made working conditions in the tunnel extremely injurious to health. Two inundations flooded the workings, the second almost killing the younger Brunel and causing work to come to an end through lack of finance. A government loan enabled work to be resumed after seven years. By this time, Marc Brunel had improved the design of his tunnelling shield, and he drove the tunnel through to Wapping by 1843. It became a tourist attraction, venue for art exhibitions and markets, as well as a way for pedestrians to cross the river. Its cost and the modest returns compelled the company to sell out in 1865 to the East London Railway, which adapted it for steam trains. Today electric Underground trains still use the twin tunnels.

Metro, Moscow, USSR

Moscow has the third largest metro system in the world, at 132 miles. The first section, constructed by the cut-and-cover method, was opened in 1935. Work was carried out largely by pick and shovel under the direction of the future Soviet leader Nikita Krushchev. During World War II, the 16 miles of completed line acted as an air raid shelter, as did the London Underground tunnels. Construction continued during the war, the first deep-level tube opening in 1943. Subsequent lines have been built at a depth of 100–160 feet, which is deeper even than the London deep-level tubes.

Moscow's Metro is famous for the opulence of some of its stations and for their sense of spaciousness; some are decorated with marble, ornate plasterwork, chandeliers and murals. Despite being the busiest system in the world, with 2,500 million passenger journeys a year, it is probably also the cleanest: litter or graffiti are rarely seen.

ASTRONOMICAL CONSTRUCTIONS

Europe

William Herschel Telescope, La Palma, Canary Islands

Sited above the clouds, almost 8,000 feet up on the volcanic island of La Palma, is the world's third largest single mirror telescope, and the most powerful. Named after the eighteenth-century astronomer, the altazimuth telescope, driven by mini-computers and pointed and supported by 10,000 tons of equipment, took 12 years to build. It was completed in 1987.

The 17-ton mirror, $14\frac{1}{2}$ feet in diameter, is made of special non-expanding glass ceramic, polished to an accuracy of 10,000th of a millimetre and then covered with a film of aluminium weighing 1/57th of an ounce. The telescope, so sensitive that it could detect a candle flame 100,000 miles away, is used to collect photons—particles of light—which are deflected on to a mass of detection devices to give astronomers information about immensely distant heavenly bodies.

The most important of these intstruments is the spectrograph, which splits light into its constituent rainbow colours; from the shift of the colour band toward one or other end of the spectrum, astronomers can tell if the star is approaching the earth or moving away from it.

Bibliography

Beaver, Patrick. *A History of Tunnels* Peter Davies, 1972.

Beaver, Patrick. *The Crystal Palace* Hugh Evelyn, 1977.

Bergere, Thea and Richard. *The Story of St Peter's* Frederick Muller, 1966.

Boyd, Alastair. *The Essence of Catalonia* André Deutsch, 1988.

Briggs, Asa. *Iron Bridge to Crystal Palace* Thames and Hudson, 1979.

Coe, Michael D. *Mexico* Thames and Hudson, 1962.

Cossons, Neil and Barrie Trinder. *The Iron Bridge* Moonraker Press, 1977.

David, A. Rosalie. *The Egyptian Kingdoms* Elsevier, 1975.

Descharnes, Robert and Clovis Prevost. *Gaudi* Bracken Books, 1971.

Dmitrev-Mamonov, A.I. and A.F. Zdiarski. *Guide to the Great Siberian Railway* David & Charles Reprints, 1971.

Dorin, Patrick C. *Canadian Pacific Railway* Superior Publishing, 1974.

Fedden, Robin and John Thomson. *Crusader Castles* John Murray, 1957.

Fryer, Jonathan. *The Great Wall of China* New English Library, 1975.

Garlinski, Jozef. *Hitler's Last Weapons* Julian Friedman, 1978.

Ghosh, A. (Ed.). *Jaina Art and Architecture* Bharatiya Jnanpith, 1974.

Gladstone Bratton, F. *A History of Egyptian Archaeology* Robert Hale, 1967.

Gorringe, Henry H. *Egyptian Obelisks* C.H. Yorston, 1885.

Habachi, Labib. *The Obelisks of Egypt* Dent, 1977.

Hayden, Richard Seth and Thierry W. Despont. *Restoring the Statue of Liberty* McGraw-Hill, 1986.

Hayward, R. *Cleopatra's Needles* Moorland, 1978.

Hopkins, H.J. *A Span of Bridges* David & Charles, 1970.

Hughes, Quentin. *Military Architecture* Hugh Evelyn, 1974.

Hunter, C. Bruce. *A Guide to Ancient Mexican Ruins* University of Oklahoma Press, 1977.

Irving, David. *The Mare's Nest* William Kimber, 1964.

Joyce, Thomas A. *Mexican Archaeology* Philip Lee Warner, 1914.

Kamil, Jill. *Luxor: A Guide to Ancient Thebes* Longman, 1973.

Lawrence, T.E. *Crusader Castles* Oxford, 1988.

Longmate, Norman. *Hitler's Rockets: The Story of the V-2s* Hutchinson, 1985.

Louis, Victor and Jennifer. *The Complete Guide to the Soviet Union* Michael Joseph, 1976.

Macadam, Alta. *Blue Guide: Rome and environs* A. & C. Black, 1989.

MacFarquhar, Roderick. *The Forbidden City* Reader's Digest, 1972.

Mackay, Donald A. *The Building of Manhattan* Harper & Row, 1987.

Masson, Georgina. *The Companion Guide to Rome* Collins, 1985.

Meyer, Karl E. *Teotihuacán* Reader's Digest, 1973.

Murname, William J. *The Penguin Guide to Ancient Egypt* Allen Lane, 1983.

Rice, B. Lewis. *Epigraphia Carnatica* Mysore Government Central Press, 1889.

Romer, John. *Romer's Egypt* Michael Joseph/Rainbird, 1982.

Ruffle, John. *Heritage of the Pharaohs* Phaidon, 1977.

Sanders, Catharine, Chris Stewart and Rhonda Evans. *The Rough Guide to China* Routledge and Kegan Paul, 1987.

Sandstrom, Gosta. *The Crossing of the Alps* Hutchinson, 1972.

Sandstrom, Gosta. *The History of Tunnelling* Barrie & Rockliffe, 1963.

Sivaramamurti, C. *Panorama of Jain Art* Times of India, 1983.

Smith, Rex Alan. *The Carving of Mount Rushmore* Abbeville Press, 1985.

Speer, Albert. *Inside the Third Reich* Weidenfeld and Nicolson, 1970.

Stierlin, Henri. *Ancient Mexican Architecture* Macdonald, 1968.

Stott, Carole. *Astronomy in Action* George Philip, 1989.

Thompson, J. Eric. *Mexico before Cortez* Charles Scribner's Sons, 1933.

Tompkins, Peter. *Mysteries of the Mexican Pyramids* Thames and Hudson, 1976.

Tupper, H. *To the Great Ocean* (Trans-Siberian Railway) Secker & Warburg, 1965.

von Hagen, Victor W. *The Aztec: Man and Tribe* New American Library, 1958.

Watkin, David. *A History of Western Architecture* Barrie & Jenkins, 1986.

Yarwood, Doreen. *The Architecture of Europe* Batsford, 1974.

Young, Richard. *The Flying Bomb* Ian Allan, 1978.

Zewen, Luo, Dick Wilson, J.P. Drege and H. Delahaye. *The Great Wall* Michael Joseph, 1981.

SECTION II:
Vehicles

CHAPTER ONE

ACROSS THE OCEANS

For most of humankind's history, the immensity of the oceans created a barrier that seemed impenetrable. Small boats might skirt along a coast to fish and trade, or explore a modest ocean like the Mediterranean, but the Atlantic appeared boundless and the Pacific was unknown. At the outer edge of the great oceans lay an emptiness where no one might venture with any certainty of a safe return.

Suddenly, in medieval Europe, the constraints of geography were broken by navigators who struck out boldly across the oceans. They had ships capable of great journeys of exploration, but, more important, they had an idea of how the Earth was made that convinced them and their patrons that such voyages would be possible and worthwhile. To overcome the dangers of the open sea they had first to subdue the doubts in their own minds. In the space of a few years Columbus had discovered the New World and Magellan had circumnavigated the Earth, feats of courage and seamanship that transformed human perceptions.

Since these pioneering voyages, the oceans have been travelled by a huge variety of ships. Some have been designed for speed, like the tea clipper *Cutty Sark* and the liner *Mauretania*, while others made a virtue of their ordinariness, like the humble Liberty ships that kept the supply lines open during World War II. Men like Joshua Slocum and Francis Chichester have challenged the oceans alone, responding to an adventurous instinct. They endured hardships of a quite different kind from the crew of the nuclear submarine *Nautilus*, who sat in air-conditioned comfort as they faced the unknown dangers of the first journey beneath the Arctic ice cap.

Yet, in spite of all the changes and the development of new technologies like satellite navigation, the oceans still retain something of the dread they had for ancient man. On land nature has been largely tamed, but at sea it retains its power to terrify and to subdue. In this section we examine some of the more remarkable craft that have set to sea and follow the voyages that made them famous.

Pioneer Voyage to the New World

The three small ships that first sailed to the New World in 1492 occupy one of the most puzzling gaps in the history of exploration. Everybody knows that they were commanded by Christopher Columbus and financed by King Ferdinand and Queen Isabella of Spain. Most would agree that the small fleet—the *Santa Maria*, the *Pinta* and the *Niña*—discovered America, although these days the more particular are inclined to say they merely "encountered" it, out of respect for the aboriginal Indian peoples who predated Columbus. However we describe it, the voyage was of huge and lasting importance to world history, yet the vessels that made the journey are ill-documented and poorly understood.

"Nobody knows what *Niña*, *Pinta* and *Santa Maria* really looked like," wrote Samuel Eliot Morison in his biography of Columbus, *Admiral of the Ocean Sea*. There have been plenty of attempts to draw the ships, or even to build copies of them, but each has inevitably involved a lot of guesswork. None of the reproductions sails as well as Columbus's ships did, suggesting that they had some secret now lost which accounted for their excellent performance.

No original plans exist for the caravels, the ships that made possible the great age of discovery in the fifteenth and sixteenth centuries. Contemporary drawings lack details, and no wreck of a caravel has ever been unambiguously identified. It has been said that more is known of the ships of ancient Greece and Rome than of the caravels that extended the European imagination across the oceans.

Santa Maria was the largest ship in Columbus's fleet and therefore his flagship, but she was not his favourite vessel. She was broader in the beam than the *Pinta* or the *Niña*, suggesting that she was probably not a caravel at all, but a cargo vessel of the type known in Spain and Portugal as a *nao*. For voyages of discovery, speed is worth more than cargo capacity and Columbus wrote in his journal that *Santa Maria* was unwieldy and not well-suited to the task. He put the blame on the people of Palos, the Spanish port that had been ordered by King Ferdinand and Queen Isabella to put the ships at his disposal as recompense for certain offences they had committed against the crown.

But in fact the royal decree demanded two caravels, not three, and these were duly provided: the *Pinta*, which belonged to Christobal Quintero of Palos, and the *Niña*, which belonged to Juan Nino of the nearby town of Moguer. Officially the *Niña*'s name was the *Santa Clara*, but in those days ships usually had nicknames given by the crew, often taken from the name of the owner.

Two ships were insufficient for Columbus's purposes, so a third had to be hired by the crown to make up the fleet. None of the shipowners in Palos who owned caravels was willing to let them be hired, so Columbus had to be content with a *nao* belonging to Juan de la Cosa of Santona, near Santander. She was called *Santa Maria* but because she had originally been built in Galicia was known by the crew as *La Gallega*.

Santa Maria was only slightly larger than the other two ships, perhaps a little over 80 feet long and 28 feet in the beam. She was rated at 90 to 100 tons, which meant that she could carry that many tuns, or barrels, of wine. Since a Spanish *tonelada* of wine contained 213 gallons, it weighed almost a ton in weight. The *Niña* and the *Pinta* were shorter than the *Santa Maria*, at around 70 to 80 feet long, but they were about 3 feet narrower in the beam and, at 60 tons, had less cargo capacity.

When the ships finally sailed on 3 August 1492, it marked the culmination of a long campaign by Columbus to be allowed to undertake a voyage of discovery. He believed that by sailing far enough westward he would eventually reach the shores of Asia, a conception of geography that left the entire American continent out of account. Nobody knew it was there, and Columbus had wrongly calculated that the circumference of the Earth was about 18,750 miles, some 6,300 miles too short. This led him to claim that it would be possible to sail to the coasts of Asia if he set off westward and kept on going for long enough.

After failing to persuade the Portuguese to support his expedition, Columbus sent his brother Fernando to England to try to solicit support from King Henry VII. Nothing came of this so Fernando next tried King Charles VIII of France. Columbus himself was about to travel to France to press his suit when Queen Isabella was persuaded by a priest to take the proposition seriously. She summoned Columbus, and

FACT FILE

Columbus's flagship on his first voyage to the New World

Date: 1492/93

Duration: 7 months 12 days

Christopher Columbus (1451–1506)
Born in Genoa, Columbus went to sea as an illiterate young lad. After many years on merchant ships, he developed a conviction that the Atlantic Ocean was quite narrow and that Asia could soon be reached by sailing west. Three further voyages of exploration followed Columbus's epic voyage; they met with only limited success and he was to die at Valladolid in Spain a frustrated and embittered man.

Pioneer Voyage to the New World

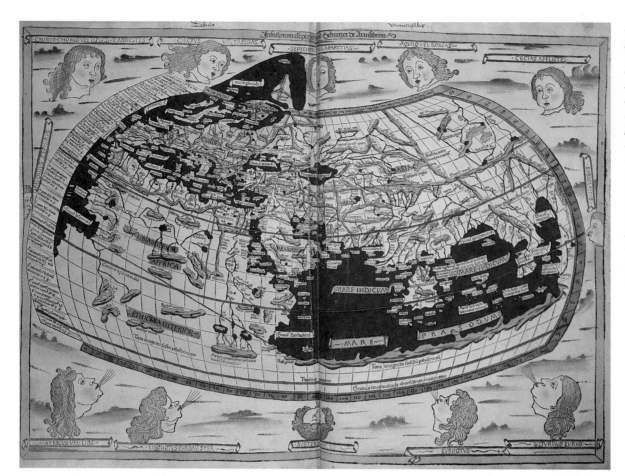

A map of the world published in 1482 at Ulm in Germany and based on Ptolemy's system of latitude and longitude. Ptolemy's work was lost with the fall of the Roman Empire, and it was only in 1400 that a manuscript copy of his Geographia, *with maps, was found in Constantinople. He gave winds both names and personalities, illustrated here in the border.*

eventually agreed to finance the expedition.

Some historians consider that Columbus's trump card was his recognition of the existence of the trade winds, which he believed would blow him all the way to the Indies if he stuck to the southerly part of the ocean, and all the way back if he took a more northerly course. Although his geography was hopelessly muddled, his instinct about the winds was right, and may have helped him convince the queen.

On 17 April he signed an agreement with Ferdinand and Isabella covering the terms under which the expedition would operate. Columbus was to be appointed admiral, and would become viceroy and governor-general of any "islands and mainlands which he may discover or acquire". He would be entitled to 10 percent of any valuable merchandise he might obtain. For their part, the king and queen would provide the ships and pay the crews four months' wages in advance. The people of Palos were ordered to provision these ships within ten days, a timetable which could never have been met. In fact, it was ten weeks before they were ready to sail.

Ninety men sailed in the three ships. On *Santa*

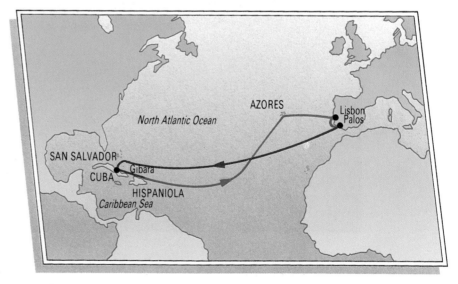

Columbus's first landfall in the Caribbean was the island called Guanahani by the natives and which he named San Salvador. He explored the islands of Cuba and Hispaniola before heading back to Spain 155 days after first setting out.

ANNIVERSARY RECONSTRUCTIONS

The reconstructions being built for the 500th anniversary celebrations include copies of all three ships, financed by the Spanish government at a cost of $4 million. These pictures illustrate the *Santa Maria* at Barcelona. A copy of *Santa Maria* is being built for the Japanese government. Geo-Arts of Bath, Maine, plans to reproduce the whole squadron, while the city of Columbus, Ohio, and the Mexican government are content with copies of *Santa Maria*. A citizen in Florida is building a copy of *Nina*.

Maria, Columbus was assisted by the captain and owner of the ship, Juan de la Cosa. The flagship also carried a pilot, a royal inspector, a surgeon, a secretary, a man who could interpret from Hebrew, Aramaic and Arabic, and about 30 artisans, including a carpenter, a caulker, a cooper and a master gunner. The *Pinta* was commanded by Martin Alonso Pinzón, while his brother Vicente Yanez Pinzón commanded the *Niña*. The owners of both ships also sailed with the fleet.

The voyage started with problems. Columbus had to put in to Lanzarote, the closest of the Canary Islands, to repair the *Pinta*'s rudder and to replace the *Niña*'s lateen (triangular) sail with square sails which would be better suited to the following winds which Columbus expected from here onward. All this took time, and it was 8 September before the fleet finally set sail again.

The fleet sailed swiftly. According to Dr Morison, during one five-day stretch it averaged 8 knots running before the favourable winds, an excellent performance. The maximum speed of the two caravels appears to have been about 11 knots, which compares quite well with the speed of any sailing ship except fast clippers or racing yachts. On 10 October, the fleet covered 59 leagues, equivalent to more than 215 miles, and the crew began to grow restless, so far had they now strayed from familiar waters. Columbus

Pioneer Voyage to the New World

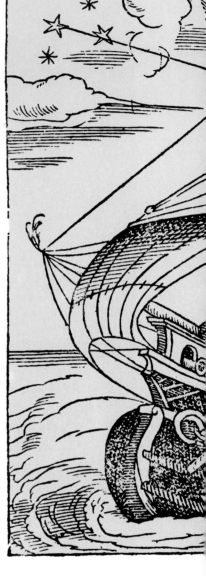

reassured them, and two days later the crew of the *Niña* found a twig floating in the water, encouraging evidence that land might be near. On 12 October, a lookout on the *Pinta* sighted land, and two hours after midnight the fleet hove to about 7 miles from the shore to await daylight.

The land Columbus had found was a small island in the Caribbean, which he named San Salvador. Subsequently he sailed to Cuba, landing at a point thought to be near Gibara, and to an island he called Hispaniola (now shared between Haiti and the Dominican Republic). He found such friendly natives there that he determined to found a settlement. But on Christmas Eve disaster struck when control of the flagship was left overnight in the hands of a boy who allowed it to drift ashore on to the reef. Realizing that the *Santa Maria* was lost, Columbus abandoned ship and transferred the crew to the *Niña*. He set up the first Spanish settlement in the New World and left some 40 settlers to establish it. On 4 January 1493, he set sail back to Spain.

Both Columbus and Pinzón, the captain of the *Pinta* who had meanwhile engaged in some freelance exploring, had collected quantities of gold from the natives they met. On the way home they met a terrible storm and Columbus feared that all his discoveries would be lost before he could report them to the Spanish crown. Finally they made landfall at the Portuguese island of Santa Maria, the easternmost of the Azores. From there they sailed home, surviving another terrible storm, in which waves swept continuously over the decks of the two small ships. They reached Lisbon, where they were welcomed by the Portuguese king, and then sailed on to Palos, arriving on 15 March 1593.

The completion of the voyage was testimony to the excellent qualities of the ships, particularly the two caravels, and to Columbus's abilities as a navigator. Yet frustratingly little is known of the details of the ships' construction: historians believe that any such details were deliberately kept secret by the Portuguese and Spanish for reasons of strategy. As a result, no drawings were allowed to be published.

Most caravels had a tall deck at the stern, raised well above the level of the main deck. This was called the tolda, and later evolved into a fully developed sterncastle, a platform from which the ship would be navigated and from which attacks on other ships could be launched. To begin with, caravels did not have a similar raised portion at the front because this would

EARLY NAVIGATION METHODS

When Columbus set sail in 1492, navigational methods were rudimentary. The Phoenicians in the first millennium BC undertook preplanned ocean voyages, reaching the Azores and the Scilly Islands by their knowledge of the stars. The Scandinavians developed navigational skills during the first millennium AD, sailing regularly to Iceland and Greenland by AD 900.

The first navigational aids were the astrolabe, magnetic compass and chart. The first two may have been in use by *c*. 1300, but it was not until the early fifteenth century that the first attempt at scale maps was made. The accuracy of early compasses was reduced by ignorance over the angle between magnetic North Pole and the true North Pole.

have got in the way of the lateen sails. But on the later square-rigged caravels, the bow was raised to form a tilda, which developed into a forecastle. It is assumed that the *Santa Maria* had both a forecastle and a sterncastle, but the details remain obscure.

Unless the wreck of a caravel is discovered, these questions are unlikely to be answered. In 1976, treasure hunters in the Turks and Caicos Islands found a wreck that appears to have been a caravel or small warship of the sixteenth century, but little was left for the nautical archaeologists to pore over. Their best hope remains that of finding what is left of two caravels beached by Columbus on his last voyage

The astrolabe (*far left*) *was a simple device used to measure the altitude of the Sun or a star. A thick graduated ring of brass is suspended by a cord to hang vertically. Pivoted at the centre of the ring is an alidade, or sighting rule, which was turned on its axis to align with the star and the altitude reading was then taken from the ring. The difficulty of using it on a pitching deck is obvious, so navigators were provided with a platform mounted on gimbals (left). This picture is taken from* Le Cosmolabe . . . *by Jacques Besson, published in 1567.*

The precise function of the vertical timbers attached to the outside of the hull remains a mystery. They may have been fenders or designed to reinforce the attachment of the shrouds to the hull. It is not known whether the caravel's stern was rounded or square or whether it had a crow's nest for lookouts.

in 1503. With timbers penetrated by worms and leaking heavily, the *Capitana* and the *Santiago de Palio* were deliberately driven ashore by Columbus in St Ann's Bay, off the northern coast of Jamaica, on 23 June 1503.

It is assumed that the two caravels were gradually covered by sand and silt and may still be in a reasonable state of preservation. In recent years a series of attempts has been made to discover what may be left of them, using increasingly sophisticated scientific instruments to probe beneath the mud. Nautical archaeologists from Texas A. & M. University are leading the search, using sonar devices to try to detect the presence of timbers. If they succeed,

the 500th anniversary of Columbus's voyage may be marked by fresh understanding of the remarkable vessels he used.

The absence of knowledge is not, however, preventing the building of a series of replicas to mark the 500th anniversary celebrations. At least ten reproductions of the various ships used by Columbus are either built or planned. It seems plain that 1992 will see more caravels sailing the seas than have been afloat since the sixteenth century, although whether any of them will bear close resemblance to the originals is open to doubt. Nevertheless, it should make for an enjoyable celebration of a crucial anniversary in European and American history.

Circumnavigating the Globe

On 6 September 1522, seventeen weary men sailed into the harbour of Sanlucar de Barrameda in southern Spain aboard a small vessel, the *Vittoria*. They were the only survivors of the greatest journey ever undertaken, 42,000 miles around the world, more than half of it through waters no Christian had ever entered. As a feat of seamanship and navigation it had no equal, yet the man responsible was not on deck as *Vittoria* crept to her berth. Ferdinand Magellan had not survived to see his voyage through, and those who did had reason to disparage his achievement and cast doubt on his leadership. As a result, Magellan has never enjoyed the fame that he undoubtedly deserves.

He had set out three years before in order to find a new route to the Spice Islands of the Far East. These were what are now known as Indonesia, a group of islands centred on the Moluccas. They produced coconuts, palm oil, hemp, various dyes, sandalwood, spices and pepper. Today it seems strange that such products could excite the greed of kings, but without pepper medieval society would have been hard-pressed to survive. In central and northern Europe there was such a shortage of winter fodder that more than three-quarters of all cattle and sheep had to be slaughtered each autumn and their carcasses cured.

For that, both salt and pepper were needed; and while salt was easily to be had, pepper had to be imported from the Indies. It was a hugely profitable trade, making middlemen rich at every stage, all the way from the point of production. Small wonder that an alternative direct route to the Indies was desperately sought, and that the Spanish crown should have agreed to finance an expedition by the Portuguese navigator Magellan to try to find it.

The potential gains of the voyage help to explain the tensions on board the five ships that set sail under Magellan's command: the *San Antonio* (120 tons), the *Trinidad* (110 tons), the *Vittoria* (90 tons), the *Concepcion* (90 tons) and the *Santiago* (75 tons). These ships were caravels, stout cargo ships about which we know pathetically little. They had three masts, square sails and a simple deck. Below deck was an open bilge and a lower deck that effectively ran like a shelf around the inside of the hull. Life on board these ships was insanitary, uncomfortable and often short.

Magellan had not won the command without inspiring jealousy, and the ships were provi-sioned in an atmosphere poisoned by political intrigue. Connections at court had won a number of people positions in the fleet which they did not merit by experience or personal qualities, while ordinary seamen were reluctant to sign on. They had not been told the object of the voyage, but knew they had to enlist for at least two years.

Magellan ordered sufficient food to be loaded aboard the ships—including 213,800 lb of biscuit, 72,000 lb of salt beef and 57,000 lb of salt pork—but much of it was pilfered. And, as we now know, the rations lacked the very thing that the crew would need to fend off the dreaded scurvy. Without vitamin C in the form of fruit or green vegetables, more sailors died from scurvy than from wind, wave or shipwreck. Magellan did not know this, or he could have saved himself and his men much grief. Instead, he ordered cheeses and enough wine to give each of his men almost a pint a day.

The fleet also carried huge quantities of spares for making repairs along the way, a shallow draught boat for exploring inshore, and an adequate armoury for fighting their way out of trouble. The cargo consisted of quantities of copper and mercury, bracelets, bells, cheap knives, mirrors, scissors and combs, fishhooks, cloth and crystals cut into the shape of jewels, enough to exchange for a full cargo of pepper for the return journey. There were 277 men at the farewell mass in the dockyard church; only 1 in 15 was to see his homeland again.

Already mutiny was in the minds of some who resented Magellan's command and resolved to murder him at the first opportunity. But he refused to rise to their taunts and provide an excuse. Setting a course southward, his intention was to cross to the mainland of South America, and then travel down the Brazilian coast until he reached the southern cape and could turn west.

He then expected to cross a narrow ocean and reach the Moluccas swiftly. There were at least two serious errors of geography here: first, the southerly extent of South America and second, the width of the Pacific Ocean. Magellan can hardly be blamed for these mistakes, however, for no man had sailed this way before.

As the fleet crossed the equator, Magellan's chance came to deal with his rebellious subordinates. The boatswain of the *Vittoria* had been caught in the act of sodomy, and Magellan ordered a trial. The three Spanish captains of the other ships attended and took the opportunity of

FACT FILE

The first ship to sail around the world

Date: 1519–22

Duration: 3 years

FERDINAN:MAGAGLIANES

Ferdinand Magellan (c.1480–1521)
Born at Villa de Sabrosa in Trasos-Montes, Magellan spent his early years as
an attendant at the Portuguese court of John II. He first went to sea on a
voyage to India in 1505, followed by visits to the Spice Islands. Falling from
favour for alleged trading with the enemy in Morocco, Magellan went to
Spain, where he won the support of Charles V for his epic journey. This
portrait hangs in the Uffizi Gallery in Florence.

Circumnavigating the Globe

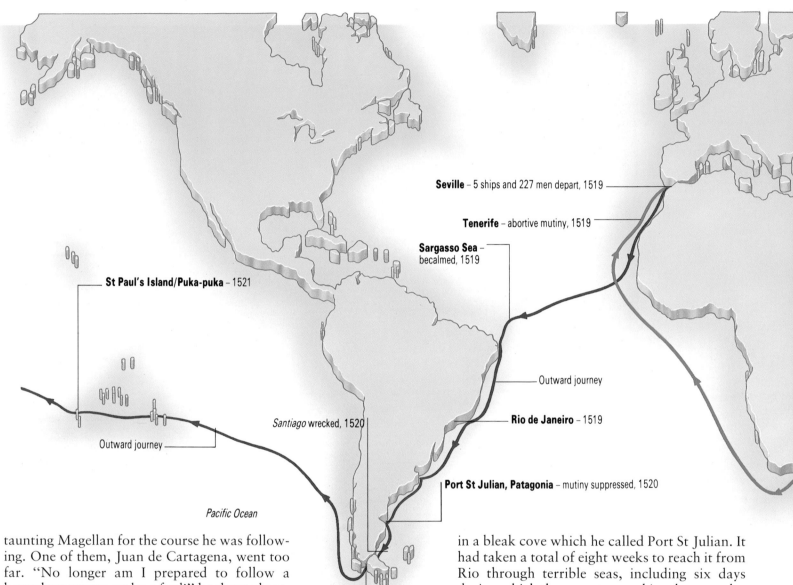

Seville – 5 ships and 227 men depart, 1519

Tenerife – abortive mutiny, 1519

Sargasso Sea – becalmed, 1519

St Paul's Island/Puka-puka – 1521

Outward journey

Outward journey

Rio de Janeiro – 1519

Santiago wrecked, 1520

Port St Julian, Patagonia – mutiny suppressed, 1520

Pacific Ocean

Tierra del Fuego – desertion of *San Antonio*, 1520

taunting Magellan for the course he was following. One of them, Juan de Cartagena, went too far. "No longer am I prepared to follow a hazardous course set by a fool!" he shouted out. Magellan accused him of mutiny, stripped him of his command and threw him in irons.

Led by the flagship *Trinidad*, the fleet ploughed south. Delayed by the doldrums in the Sargasso Sea, they finally found a wind and made the coast of Brazil early in December. After two weeks' resting in the bay of Rio de Janeiro, where to the joy of the crew the Guarani Indians willingly sold their daughters for a shiny bell or a cheap German knife, they sailed on down the coast. When the wide estuary of the River Plate was reached, they confidently sailed into it, believing that it must be the southern cape that would lead them toward the Indies. They realized to their disappointment that it was a river, and sailed on.

By the end of March, with the winter fast approaching, Magellan was forced to anchor

in a bleak cove which he called Port St Julian. It had taken a total of eight weeks to reach it from Rio through terrible seas, including six days during which the *naos*, trapped in a bay on a lee shore, had been forced to tack hopelessly to and fro to avoid being driven aground. As they struggled on, they sighted penguins, the first Europeans ever to see them, but no sight of human beings. It was a tired and disaffected crew who finally dropped anchor in the cheerless bay of St Julian.

Here the Spanish captains attempted another mutiny, which Magellan with an element of luck was able to crush. The ringleader, the released Cartagena, was banished with a priest on to the mainland of Patagonia—a miserable prospect, but Magellan would have been within his rights to execute him. Another Spaniard, Gaspar de Quesada, was beheaded, the executioner his own secretary who took on the task in exchange for a pardon. Quesada's body, together with that of another Spaniard, Captain Luis de Mendoza,

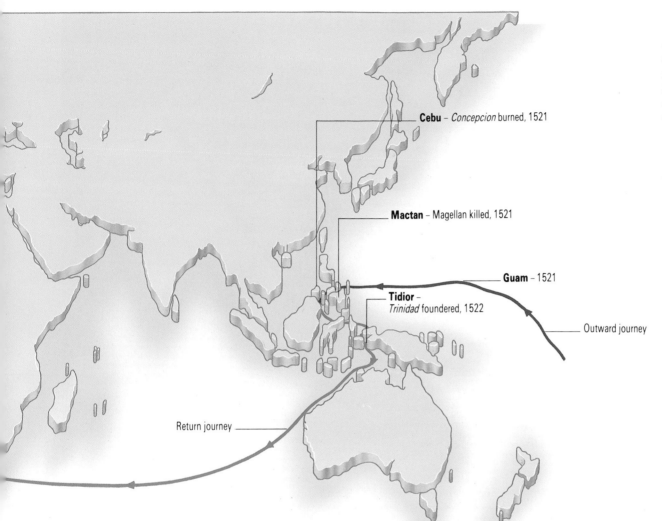

Cebu – *Concepcion* burned, 1521

Mactan – Magellan killed, 1521

Guam – 1521

Tidior –
Trinidad foundered, 1522

Outward journey

Return journey

The principal human discovery of Magellan's voyage was the race of giants standing about 7 feet 6 inches tall, found in Patagonia. They are described by Pigatta in the only chronicle of the voyage to survive. Later travellers, like Sir Francis Drake, concur in reports of the existence of the now extinct race; all that remains is the name Patagonia—land of the big feet. Magellan took two of the friendly giants aboard, but neither survived.

The trading caravels forming Magellan's fleet remain a mystery to maritime archaeologists. There are no accurate illustrations of them, but these Portuguese carracks were a development of the caravels, with high fore and stern castles.

Circumnavigating the Globe

who had been killed in the mutiny, were drawn, quartered and strung up on gibbets.

In this freezing and gruesome place the fleet spent its winter with Magellan's authority now unquestioned. Stout huts were built, the provisions shifted to them, and the ships drawn up on shore and repaired. Here Magellan discovered to his consternation that only half the provisions he had ordered had in fact been loaded. He set the crew to hunting, fishing and trapping to make good the deficiencies.

By the time Magellan was ready to sail, the *Santiago* had been lost in a storm. Just 300 miles farther south, Magellan finally found a strait which he began to explore. It was the *San Antonio* and the *Concepcion*, advancing alone, which discovered that the strait indeed led into a wide expanse of ocean which stretched as far as the eye could see toward the setting sun. Magellan was overjoyed and determined to sail on, but the *San Antonio* mysteriously disappeared. Her crew had had enough and were sailing back to Spain with defamatory accounts of Magellan's leadership in an attempt to justify their desertion.

On the large island that lay to the south, Magellan's men saw the campfires of the Indians, and named the place Tierra de los Fuegos (land of the fires). As they emerged into the ocean, which Magellan optimistically named the Pacific, he thought they would have only a few days' sailing to reach the Spice Islands. In fact, it was two miserable months before they sighted land, by which time the crew were reduced to eating ox-hides, sawdust and rats. Even rats eventually became so scarce that they had to be auctioned off to the highest bidder.

Magellan was unfortunate in the course he chose, which passed north of the Society Islands and led him into the empty reaches of the Pacific. Scurvy took its toll, and men began to die. By mid-January, a third of the crew were so ill they could hardly walk and only a handful could manage the sails or the helm. When they finally did sight an island, on 24 January 1521, it was uninhabited, and they were forced to sail on. (We now believe that this island, named St Paul's by Magellan, was Puka-puka, the most northerly of the Society group.)

Finally, after another agonizing month, they made landfall on some inhabited islands near Guam, about 1,700 miles northeast of their destination in the Moluccas. Here there was a row with the native people, many of whom were

The channel now called the Magellan Strait did not look promising as a passage to the Pacific when Magellan entered it in 1520. It seemed too narrow and overpowered by mountains to be the right channel, but it wound its way between the peaks and led into the huge expanse of the eastern Pacific. Varying in width from 2¼ to 70 miles, the strait is 365 miles long. Although not thoroughly explored until 1826–36, it was charted in the sixteenth-century Vaz Dourado map, from the collection of the Duke of Alba.

slaughtered and their food stolen to feed the starving European crew. After a rest, they went on, reaching the Philippine island of Cebu early in April.

Here at last was a known land, with a recognizable language and the unmistakable artefacts of the East. Magellan realized that after 555 days he had reached the Indies and if he continued he would complete a circumnavigation of the Earth. It was a moment of triumph he did not have long to enjoy, for instead of making immediately for the Moluccas he lingered in the Philippines and found a taste for preaching the gospel of Christ. He erected a cross on a hill and took possession for Spain of the group of islands.

Today the Philippines remain the only Christian nation in Asia. Having converted the local ruler, Magellan rashly promised to help him deal with his enemies. The Rajah replied that he did, indeed, have a dispute with the neighbouring island of Mactan, and Magellan sailed to visit the might of the Spanish armouries on these poor innocents. The result was disaster: not only did he fail to conquer the people of Mactan, but he was himself killed in the battle. Deserted by his

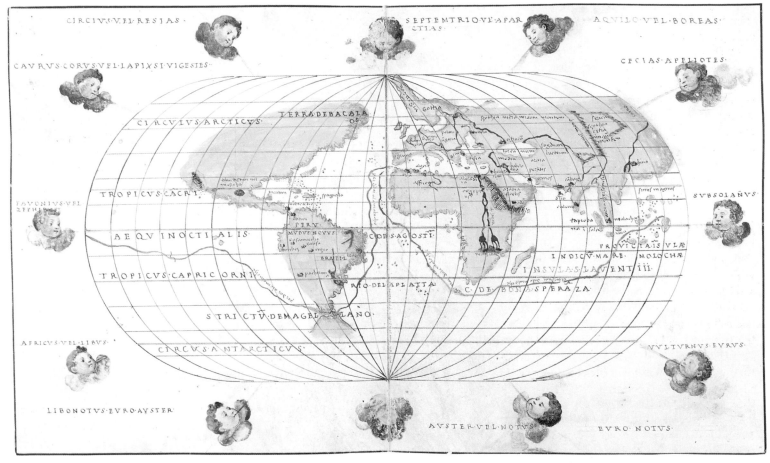

Spanish officers, Magellan was speared to death in shallow water by the enraged natives. "And so they slew our mirror, our light, our comfort and our true and only guide" wrote Antonia Pigafetta, the chronicler of the voyage, whose loyalty to Magellan was unquestionable.

What followed was muddle and chaos. The Rajah owed no loyalty to those who had betrayed Magellan, and took the first opportunity to slaughter as many as he could. The rest escaped and roamed the seas as pirates, stealing cargoes from any ship they met. Early in November 1521, the *Trinidad* and the *Vittoria* reached the Spice Islands, *Concepcion* having been burned—together with most of Magellan's papers—because she was unseaworthy.

In January 1522, *Vittoria* set sail alone, for by this time *Trinidad* too was unfit for sea. As *Vittoria* struggled home, men died of hunger, disease and scurvy. The 17 men who finally staggered ashore were all that was left of the 277 who had sailed. Among them was the captain, Juan Sebastian del Cano, to whom went the honour of being the first circumnavigator of the Earth. But the real honour was Magellan's.

The discoveries of men like Vasco da Gama and Columbus *gave a great impetus to chartmaking in Spain and Portugal. Few charts that predate 1500 still exist, but many fine sixteenth-century charts survive, including this 1554 map by the Genoese Battista Agnesi showing Magellan's route (above). The tradition of placing representations of winds around a map goes back to Ptolemy's maps. Evidence survives that globes were used in navigation during the sixteenth century. On the right is a facsimile of the globe made by Georg Hartmann (1489–1564), a German maker of navigational instruments.*

Convoy of Floating Prisons

t five o'clock on the morning of Sunday 13 May 1787, a fleet of 11 ships weighed anchor at the Mother Bank outside Portsmouth. It was barely dawn as the ships dropped out of sight of land, on a spring morning which offered little comfort to 759 wretches huddled below, chained and in pitch darkness. Never before had so large a fleet attempted so ambitious a voyage.

Their destination was Botany Bay on the southeastern coast of Australia, discovered 17 years before by Captain James Cook and now designated a penal colony for those unfortunates who had offended against the law of England. It was a destination as remote to the eighteenth-century imagination as the Moon is to ours, an oubliette for the petty criminals who now lay below decks. Ahead was a journey of eight months to a continent occupied by strange, wild men and even stranger creatures.

The First Fleet was led by the frigate *Sirius*, the flagship of the expedition's commodore, Captain Arthur Phillip. It was accompanied by another armed ship, *Supply*, and three store ships, *Golden Grove*, *Fishburn* and *Borrowdale*, which carried sufficient food and stores to last two years. The convicts were carried in six ships—*Scarborough*, *Lady Penrhyn*, *Friendship*, *Charlotte*, *Prince of Wales* and *Alexander*— each accompanied by a detachment of marines. Below, the convicts cowered in the darkness, for they had no portholes, and candles or lamps were not permitted for fear of fire. The air was fetid with the stink of vomit and worse; the stench from the bilges rose and overpowered them. Many must have felt they would have preferred a public execution at Tyburn.

Transportation of criminals was nothing new in English law. Banishment had first been ordered as a punishment for rogues and vagrants in the reign of Queen Elizabeth I and transportation to the American colonies had begun in the seventeenth century. But the American War of Independence had closed off that option, leaving Britain with a growing number of criminals and no clear idea what to do with them. To the educated and cultured minority in the eighteenth century, the cities seemed every bit as threatening as do parts of New York to smart Manhattanites today. With no police force, a rising population, the easy availability of gin, and the

moral authority of the Church in decline, there was a justified fear of crime. The penalties for breaches of the law were extraordinarily harsh.

Among those aboard the First Fleet (as Australians call it) was a 70-year-old woman, Elizabeth Beckford, sentenced to seven years' transportation for stealing 12 lb of Gloucester cheese. A West Indian man, Thomas Chaddick, was aboard for the crime of entering somebody's kitchen garden and picking 12 cucumbers. A nine-year-old chimney sweep, John Hudson, the youngest on board, was being transported for seven years for stealing some clothes and a pistol. The oldest convict was 82-year-old Dorothy Handland, who had got seven years for perjury.

The transports that carried the convicts were not purpose-built. They were ordinary sailing ships of the day, in reasonable condition. The oldest, *Scarborough*, had been launched in 1781. They ranged in size from the *Alexander*, at 452 tons, to the *Friendship*, at 278 tons. Even the *Alexander* was only 114 feet long and 31 feet in beam, and it had to carry 213 male convicts, together with 2 lieutenants and 35 marines, not counting officers and crew.

The convicts had been put aboard the ships several months before they sailed, causing Phillip considerable anxiety. "It will be very difficult to prevent the most fatal sickness among men so closely confined," he warned the Admiralty. Sure enough, in March typhus broke out and 11 of the prisoners on board *Alexander* died. The convicts were taken off the ship, which was scrubbed with creosote and quicklime to purify it. Another five convicts died, but the outbreak was brought under control and even served a useful purpose, for it enabled Phillip to insist on proper food which was being denied him by a dishonest contractor.

The man entrusted with command of the First Fleet was a solid, reliable sort. Arthur Phillip was half-German, the son of a language teacher from Frankfurt who emigrated to London and married an English girl. Phillip's career in the Royal Navy had not been especially distinguished, and his own marriage had failed. Twice he had retired from the Navy to his farm at Lyndhurst in the New Forest, but had been drawn back by the sea. For several years during the 1770s he had served in the Portuguese Navy, once delivering 400 convicts from Portugal to Brazil without

FACT FILE

The long journey by ordinary British merchantmen taking the first convicts to Australia

Scarborough

Built: 1782

Overall length: 111 feet 6 inches

Width: 30 feet 2 inches

Height between decks: 4 feet 5 inches

The founding of Australia by Captain Arthur Phillip, RN, is depicted in this painting by Algernon Talmage, RA (1781–1839), which hangs in the Royal Commonwealth Society, London. Convicts were chained at the neck and hands (left) for the walk from prison to barges at Blackfriars, which took them to transports down the River Thames.

Convoy of Floating Prisons

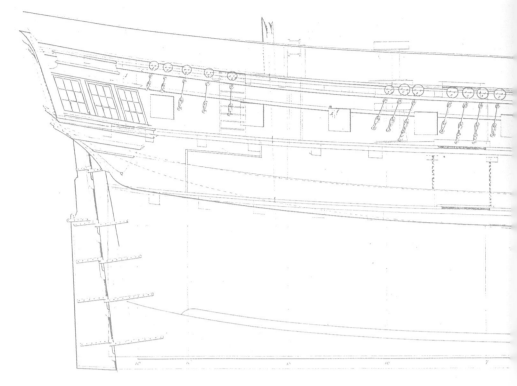

losing a single man, a remarkable achievement.

By 1782 he was at last master of a ship of the line, the 64-gun *Europe*, but in 1784 he retired again on half pay to his farm. In 1786 he must have been surprised to be entrusted with a long and difficult voyage in command of unwilling convicts, to a land where he would be responsible for setting up a penal colony in the wilderness. But he turned out to be an excellent choice, an honest man who would not be fobbed off with half measures and who supervised every detail of the preparations. More than once he wrote furiously to the Admiralty about the conditions of the prisoners and the inadequate provisioning of the fleet.

As far as he could, Phillip insisted on a decent diet for both crew and convicts. The bane of long sea voyages was scurvy, caused by vitamin C deficiency and first conquered by Captain Cook who, during his voyages between 1768 and 1771, issued sauerkraut, a liquor made of malt, and a meat broth reduced until it became a kind of cake. The juice of citrus fruits would have been more effective, but Cook was unaware of that, even though it had been discovered nearly 20 years earlier by Dr James Lind.

For short journeys to the Americas, scurvy was less of a problem, but Phillip realized that if his fleet lacked the right provisions on their long voyage, many would die. "The garrison and the convicts are sent to the extremity of the globe as they would be sent to America—a six-week's passage," he complained.

Once at sea, things went more smoothly. The official history of the voyage records one attempt at mutiny aboard *Scarborough*, detected and frustrated by the officers. The leaders were brought to the *Sirius* and punished, presumably by flogging. The fleet reached Tenerife on 3 June, where one prisoner escaped but was quickly recaptured. The next port of call was Rio de Janeiro, far south enough to pick up the westerlies across the South Atlantic for the Cape of Good Hope. As they slipped south and the weather became hotter, conditions aboard deteriorated.

Rats, cockroaches, lice, bedbugs and fleas proliferated, crawling up from the bilges and tormenting convicts and crew alike. In the doldrums, water was rationed to three pints a day, but then the wind freshened and the fleet reached Rio on 4 August. A month was spent provisioning before Phillip set sail for Cape Town, where another month was spent buying plants, seeds and livestock for the new colony.

HMS Sirius *began her existence as an East India Company merchantship named* Berwick *in 1780. Within a year,* Berwick *was gutted by fire and bought by the Royal Navy. She was put into dry dock and rebuilt as a storeship (above) in 1782, to carry anything from water casks to powder and shot. In October 1786 she was renamed* Sirius *and classified as sixth rate— a ship of no fewer than 26 guns and no more than 28. Apparently a slow sailor,* Sirius *was 110 feet long, 32 feet wide and weighed 540 tons. Although Captain Phillip travelled on her,* Sirius *was under the command of Captain John Hunter. She was wrecked off Norfolk Island in the South Pacific in 1790.*

Out of Cape Town, the weather turned dark and gloomy, with the occasional violent storm. On 19 January 1788 Botany Bay was sighted, and the next morning they were anchored. Of roughly 1,000 people aboard the 11 ships, 48 had died—40 convicts, 5 convicts' children, one marine, the wife of another, and the child of a third. This may sound terrible, but in the circumstances of the time it was a remarkable achievement, one of the greatest feats in the annals of navigation. Later transports, under less efficient leadership, did far worse. The Second Fleet, which sailed between July 1789 and January 1790, lost 267 prisoners out of roughly 1,200 at sea, and at least another 90 after landing. On the *Scarborough*, which completed the first voyage without losing a life, 73 out of 253 died.

Captain Phillip quickly found that Botany Bay was unsuitable for a penal colony. It had a shallow harbour, a shortage of fresh water, and a bare and open soil. Leaving the convicts ashore, he sailed north to investigate another harbour noted favourably by Cook from a glimpse as he sailed past its narrow entrance. It had everything that Botany Bay lacked: deep anchorages, "where a thousand sail of the line may ride with the most perfect security", good landings, fresh water and eucalyptus trees. It was, Phillip told Lord Sydney of the Admiralty, "the finest harbour in the world". He named it Sydney Cove. Today it is better known just as Sydney, one of the world's greatest cities.

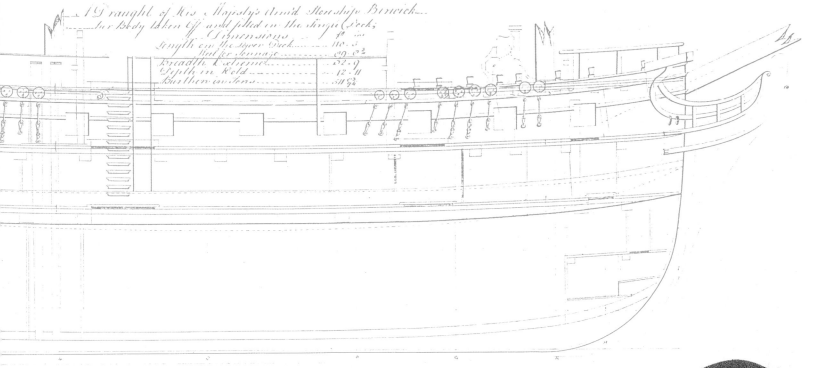

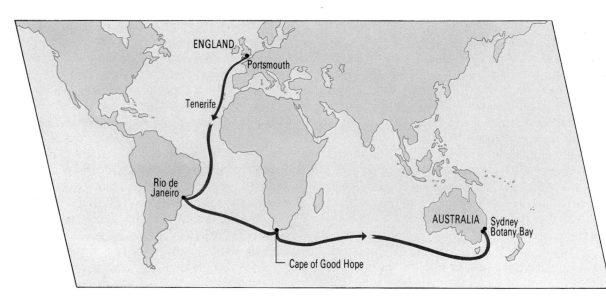

Captain Arthur Phillip *(1738–1814) was born in London and trained at Greenwich before joining the navy in 1755. After serving with Admiral Byng in the Mediterranean, he was at the taking of Havana in 1762. He became the first governor of New South Wales, guiding the colony for four years until ill-health forced him to return to England. He was made a vice admiral in 1810.*

Captain Phillip's concern with diet *on the eight-month voyage was reflected in the time spent provisioning. The fleet stocked up in Rio, and in Cape Town, the Friendship's female convicts were transferred to other ships and it was filled with 500 animals— bulls, cows, sheep, pigs and poultry.*

For the bicentennial celebrations *of the founding of Australia in 1988, the voyage of the First Fleet was re-enacted by reconstructions of vessels that either took part in the voyage themselves or were thought to resemble ships associated with the early history of the country. These included HMS Bounty (right).*

Alone Around the World

Joshua Slocum was born in Nova Scotia in 1844. His family included several seafarers, but his father was a farmer. He left home at the age of 12 when his father beat him for making a model ship when he should have been grading potatoes. He signed on as a sailor and by the age of 26 had command of a barque. In the course of a full life, he acquired enormous knowledge, not only learning the skills of sailing and navigation, but boat-building too. Surprisingly few photographs have survived of Spray *to help artists depict the boat's epic journey (opposite).*

FACT FILE

First boat to carry a lone sailor around the world

Built: 1892–94

Length: 36 feet 9 inches

Width: 14 feet 2 inches

Weight: 9 tons net

At the age of 51, Captain Joshua Slocum set out to sail around the world, alone. No man, he asserted, had done it before, which seemed reason enough to try. Slocum was a tough sea captain from the age of sail, adaptable and not easily cast down by circumstance. He had little formal learning, but he could write with a wry, simple-hearted charm; his *Sailing Alone around the World* remains one of the great classics of the sea. The only thing he could not do was swim.

The boat in which Slocum was to undertake his journey was an ancient sloop called *Spray*. She was a virtual wreck when Slocum found her, but in 13 months he had rebuilt the sloop as strong as he could make her.

When finished *Spray* "sat on the water like a swan," Slocum wrote, and sailed so securely that he found he could set course, lash the tiller and go below to sleep in the certain knowledge that she would not wander.

He spent a season fishing in *Spray*, but by this time had resolved to sail her around the world, serving as captain, mate and crew. On 24 April 1895 he left Boston, and after fitting out in Gloucester, Massachusetts, he set sail on 7 May. He called at a few ports up the coast and at one of them bought an old tin clock with a broken face and no minute hand for the sum of $1. This was the timepiece he used to navigate during the entire voyage.

Spray made good time, covering 1,200 miles in the first eight days, her sails drawing steadily all night as Slocum dozed in between going aloft from time to time to make sure all was well. He passed several ships, shouting messages to them as he went; one Spanish captain, who was 23 days out from Philadelphia, sent him a bottle of wine across, slung by the neck. The loneliness, once conquered, never returned.

Slocum stopped briefly in the Azores, then sailed for Gibraltar. Here the Royal Navy made a great fuss of him, giving him a berth alongside several great battleships. The governor came to visit and signed his name in Slocum's log. Vegetables and milk were supplied by the Admiralty, and a tug was provided to tow *Spray* out of harbour when Slocum sailed. He left Gibraltar westward, crossing the Atlantic once more, bound for Brazil. Once in the swing of the trades, the sailing was easy and Slocum spent his time reading and writing, or making small repairs to rigging and sails. Flying fish that landed on the deck provided most of his meals, together with biscuits and potatoes.

He made landfall at Pernambuco, then sailed on to Rio. Leaving Rio for Cape Horn, Slocum encountered a northerly current which made it necessary to hug the shore, but in doing so he ran aground. With great difficulty he managed to lay out the anchor to hold the sloop firm, carrying anchor and cable in his little dory which was swamped by the weight and the waves breaking over it. "I grasped her gunwale and held on as she turned bottom up, for I suddenly remembered I could not swim," Slocum wrote. After repeated efforts he managed to right the boat and clamber aboard, and with one of the oars which he had recovered he was able to paddle to the shore to rest.

Soon *Spray*, high and dry on the beach, was surrounded by curious and acquisitive locals, but Slocum bought them off with a few biscuits, and with the help of two other men was able to refloat his ship on the next high tide. She had been damaged, but not mortally, and was easily put right at Montevideo, where the local agents of the Royal Mail Steamship Co. docked and repaired her for nothing, as well as giving Slocum £20. He was happy to have it, for he had set off with very little money and was dependent during his voyage on gifts or what he could earn. Ahead lay the greatest challenge of the whole trip, Cape Horn.

Slocum planned to squeeze through the Magellan Strait rather than sailing around the very tip of Cape Horn. He was warned that foul weather was not the only danger he might face. The Fuegians who inhabited those remote regions were neither friendly nor law-abiding, and Slocum was advised to wait for a gunboat to accompany him, or at least to carry a crew to help fight off attacks. He could find nobody.

As Slocum sailed between the remote islands of the Magellan Strait, he soon met the Fuegians. When the weather permitted, they came out in canoes to beg and threaten. Slocum, anxious not to show them he was alone, rigged an old piece of bowsprit forward as a lookout, dressing it as a seaman and attaching a line to it so that he could create the impression it was alive. Several times he was forced to fire over the heads of boarding

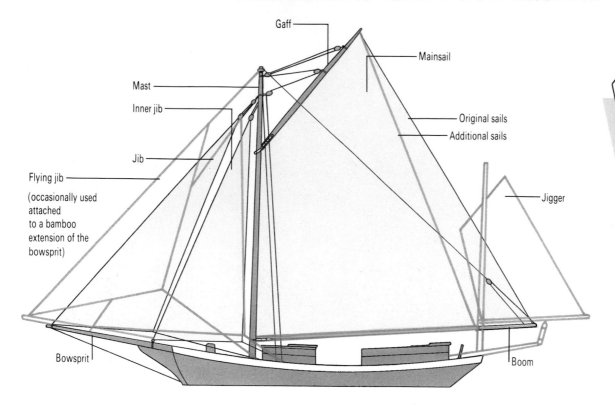

Gaff

Mainsail

Mast

Inner jib

Original sails
Additional sails

Jib

Flying jib

(occasionally used
attached
to a bamboo
extension of the
bowsprit)

Jigger

Bowsprit

Boom

THE REBUILDING OF SPRAY

Slocum found *Spray* propped up in a field at Fairhaven, Massachusetts. To rebuild her, he used local timber which he steamed, bent and caulked himself. The planks were of Georgia pine 1½ inches thick, the keel was a stout oak, the deck 1½-inch pine pinned to beams 6 inches square. He created a cooking galley and a cabin 10 feet by 12. Between

cabin and galley was a midship hold sufficient to store water and salt beef for many months.

Her rig began as a sloop but was altered to a yawl during the journey. For a ship's boat, Slocum found an old dory and cut it in half, boarding up the end where it was cut. It also served as a tub to wash clothes in and as a bath.

parties, and when he finally escaped from the strait he was caught by a tremendous storm.

Stripped of her sails, *Spray* bore south under bare poles, two long ropes paid out astern to steady the ship and stop her broaching. Under these conditions, Slocum cooked an Irish stew, for his taste for proper food seldom deserted him. As he was swept south around Cape Horn he began to make plans to head for Port Stanley in the Falkland Islands, so hopeless was it to contemplate beating north. But suddenly he saw land and made for it. It was Cockburn Channel, leading him back into the strait from which he had so recently escaped.

He broke away from the treacherous waters of the Horn on 13 April 1896, next making landfall at Juan Fernandez, the island where Alexander Selkirk, prototype for Robinson Crusoe, lived alone for almost five years. Slocum visited Selkirk's cave and a local woman made him a new flying jib in exchange for some of his tallow.

Then he was away across the Pacific to Samoa, where he met the widow of Robert Louis

Stevenson and passed some idyllic days. Reluctantly he left, and "crowded on sail for lovely Australia", a nation which he knew well.

Slocum lingered in Australia for nine months, visiting Sydney and Melbourne and cruising around Tasmania. The Australians showed an enormous interest in his voyage, and he gave many public lectures, as well as charging people sixpence to visit *Spray*. Eventually he left, sailing north of Australia to the Keeling Cocos Islands, Rodriguez and then Mauritius.

In South Africa Slocum had a memorable encounter with Paul Kruger, the president of the Transvaal. Kruger believed the world was flat, and retorted sharply when told that Slocum was sailing around the world that it could not be.

Finally all there remained of the great journey was yet another crossing of the Atlantic, for the third time. Slocum reached his native shore by way of the Caribbean, then up the eastern seaboard of the US to drop anchor in Boston on 27 June 1898, "after a cruise of more than 46,000 miles round the world, during an absence of

After crossing the Atlantic, Slocum had intended to travel through the Mediterranean and down the Suez Canal, but the danger of attack by pirates along the North African coast changed his mind. Slocum's accurate navigation was remarkable because he measured his longitude by calculating with a sextant the distance between stars. He was then able to work out the time at the Greenwich meridian using tabular data first produced in the late 1750s. Comparing that with local time enabled him to calculate his longitude.

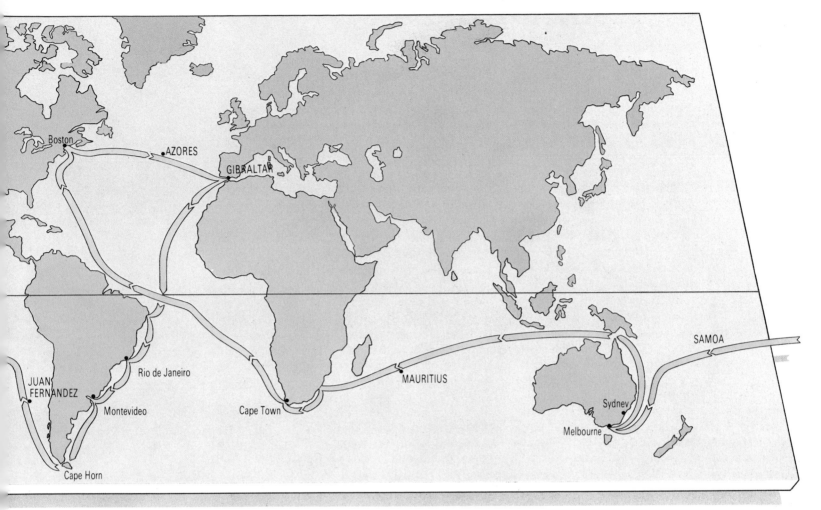

Slocum read avidly *during his voyage. He had been warned that the Fuegians of southern Patagonia would probably try to board his boat. To deter such interruptions to his sleep or reading, Slocum used a bag of carpet tacks that an Austrian sea captain had given* him *en route. He spread them over the deck while he anchored near the Cockburn Channel; he was woken about midnight by howls that were "like a pack of hounds . . . They jumped pell-mell, some into their canoes and some into the sea."*

three years and two months." He was well and weighed a pound more than when he had sailed. As for *Spray*, "she was still as sound as a nut, and as tight as the best ship afloat. She did not leak a drop—not one drop!" A few days later Slocum took her right home, tying her up at Fairhaven, Massachusetts, to the same cedar pile driven into the bank to hold her when she had been launched. "I could bring her no nearer home," he noted.

Slocum's appetite for sailing never diminished. Almost every winter he sailed *Spray* down to Grand Cayman in the West Indies, and in November 1909, at the age of 65, he set out once more, outward bound from Bristol, Rhode Island, for the River Orinoco. He was never seen again. Most likely *Spray* was run down in the night by a steamer while Slocum was below. For years afterward there were rumours that Slocum had been seen on some South American river or another, for he appeared indestructible. But he was finally declared legally dead. His book, and his reputation, remain imperishable.

The Wooden Fortress Against the Ice

Seldom has a ship been given a more appropriate name than the SS *Discovery*, which carried Captain Robert Scott on his first voyage to Antarctica in 1901. *Discovery* was a robust ship, built in Dundee, Scotland, strong enough to spend two winters locked in the Antarctic ice and emerge undamaged. Later, after spending many years as an ordinary trading ship, *Discovery* was re-equipped and sent on a pioneering scientific cruise in the southern oceans, establishing many of the basic data upon which the science of oceanography is founded.

Scott's voyage of 1901 was the most ambitious scientific expedition that had ever sailed from England. The questions he sought to answer were fundamental ones: how large was Antarctica, how deep the ocean surrounding it, how impenetrable the ice cap that surmounted it? His crew were to make meteorological observations every two hours and a painstaking magnetic survey of the regions south of the 40th parallel. They were to explore the greatest unknown landmass in the world, striking farther south than anyone had gone before.

The expedition was sponsored by the Royal Society and the Royal Geographical Society, funded to the extent of £45,000 by the government, and supported by the Admiralty. To carry this expedition the first ship ever built in Britain for scientific exploration was commissioned.

Immense care went into deciding what form *Discovery* should take. Should she follow the saucerlike lines of *Fram*, the Norwegian polar ship, which survived pack ice by riding upward under its pressure? Or should she be based on the shape of the old whalers, tough, seaworthy craft whose record spoke for itself? The expedition's sponsors opted for the latter, specifying a ship 172 feet long by 33 feet broad, and made of wood, for no other material could provide the combination of elasticity and strength needed to survive the pack ice. By October 1899, when the lengthy specification was issued, few shipyards in Britain still had the skills to build in wood, and only one firm with sufficient experience responded. So it was in Stevens' Yard, on the River Tay, that the keel was laid in March 1900.

The ship was built spectacularly strong, with huge beams and a double thickness of hull. The bow was even tougher, made of huge pieces of oak fitted together and fastened by strengthening bolts. At the bow a layer of steel was laid on top of the timber, to produce greater strength when *Discovery* crashed into the ice, riding upward on it before crashing down under her own weight to break it.

Discovery was undoubtedly strong, but she was not a graceful sailor. She was slow and rolled horribly and, despite the many-layered hull, she leaked mysteriously and persistently. The only time the leaks stopped was when she was trapped in the pack ice. For the rest of the time, the pumps were at work, since even the most careful examination in dry dock in New Zealand failed to find the source of the leak.

After sailing to New Zealand and unsuccessfully seeking to stem the leak, *Discovery* set off south on Christmas Eve 1901. There were 44 men on board, mostly very young. Scott himself was only 33, and the average age was 25. The ship passed without too much trouble through the belt of sea ice that lies around Antarctica, and reached land. On 21 January they passed Mount Erebus and were in sight of the great ice sheet which extends outward from the land for 500 miles. Then Scott retraced his steps and, having found a sheltered anchorage in McMurdo Sound, decided to spend the winter there.

It was an unwise decision, for it was to be two winters before the ice shifted enough to allow *Discovery* to escape. Soon the winter set in, and the expedition was left alone in an isolation now impossible to imagine. There was no radio, nor any hope of messages reaching them until the following summer. It was dark, for in the winter the Sun never rose above the horizon.

The following summer was spent in observations and expeditions, Scott making an epic but mismanaged journey inland. He had too few dogs, and those he did have were grossly overloaded, so could hardly pull the sledges. The group of three who set off—Scott, Ernest Shackleton and the expedition's surgeon, Dr Edward Wilson—were provided with wholly inadequate amounts of food, of the wrong sort, and tents which could not easily survive the kinds of winds that are common in Antarctica.

They had just $7\frac{1}{2}$ ounces of pemmican, a cake of dried meat, to eat a day; today it is known that at least a pound a day is necessary to keep going in such conditions. The men worked heroically, none more so than Scott, but emerged exhausted

Discovery *was trapped by ice,* near Observation Hill (above), *for two winters. The crew (left) did not have to endure the privations of some marooned expeditions. Breakfast consisted of porridge, bread and marmalade, the main meal of seal or tinned meat and a fruit tart. On the mess deck, "shove ha'penny" was the favourite entertainment, while the wardroom held debates on issues such as women's rights and enjoyed lantern slide talks.*

The Wooden Fortress Against the Ice

and near to death. There was evidence here of the same kind of blind heroism that was later to lead Scott to disaster on his final bid to reach the Pole in 1910–12.

As summer arrived, so did a relief ship, the *Morning*, bringing mail and fresh supplies, to find *Discovery* still firmly anchored by the ice and with little chance of escaping. The expedition settled down for another winter. When summer finally came around again, fruitless efforts were made to escape by cutting through the ice with saws. The ice was 7 feet thick and froze up again almost as soon as it had been cut.

That summer not one relief ship but two had arrived, *Morning* and *Terra Nova*, sent by the Admiralty which had panicked unnecessarily. They brought orders that if *Discovery* could not be freed by the end of February, Captain Scott was to abandon ship and return home in the relief ships. This proved unnecessary because a swell arrived to break up the pack ice and quite suddenly *Discovery* was free. What followed, however, was even more alarming and might have broken a weaker ship into fragments.

Leaving her harbour, *Discovery* almost immediately ran ashore. The wind got up and the heavy sea pounded the ship on the shore, breaking off the false keel. She was aground for eight hours, grinding relentlessly to and fro, but by good fortune drifted off again and set sail for New Zealand. Next her pumps failed, and the leak, grown worse after two years in the ice, threatened to sink her. At last steam was raised in an auxiliary engine on deck and the pumps were made to work. *Discovery* was saved. There remained only a broken rudder to replace and she was able to make New Zealand.

When the expedition returned in triumph to London, having achieved much, *Discovery* was soon forgotten. She was sold to the Hudson's Bay Company in 1905 and for six years sailed to and fro carrying supplies from West India Dock, London, to Hudson Bay. From 1912 to 1914 she lay idle in dock until World War I provided new opportunities. She sailed to Russia, and then worked briefly for the French Ministry of Commerce. In August 1916, she sailed to rescue members of Ernest Shackleton's expedition, stranded after their ship was crushed by ice, but arrived after Shackleton had contrived his own escape in an open boat. *Discovery* went back to routine trading until in 1923 she was bought by the Crown Agents for the Colonies to undertake scientific research in the South Seas.

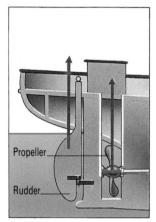 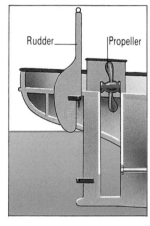

The frame of Discovery *(above) was of English oak 11 inches thick, covered by planking 4 inches thick. Outside that were two layers of planking, one 6 inches thick and the other 5. The frames were placed close together so that for much of her length* Discovery's *hull was a full 26 inches thick. Three tiers of beams ran from side to side, 11 inches square and in the lower levels no more than 3 feet apart.*

The rudder was protected by an overhanging stern, since the rudder and propeller were always the weakest points of an Antarctic ship. In case of damage, the propeller and rudder could be detached and raised through the upper deck for repair (left).

She spent two years carrying out a variety of work, including studies of the population of whales, until in 1925 she was commissioned again to visit the Antarctic as part of a joint British-Australian-New Zealand scientific expedition. On two expeditions *Discovery* surveyed another 1,500 miles of Antarctic coastline to add to the 1,000 miles surveyed under Scott.

She passed after this into the hands of the government of the Falkland Islands, and then, in 1937, to the Boy Scouts. Moored along the Embankment she was a familiar sight to Londoners for 50 years, until finally she was taken back to Dundee for restoration and to become part of a museum in the town where she was built. Few ships have been responsible for more distant or more dangerous voyages, or can claim to have located more territory than *Discovery*. Few have been more soundly built or have survived more perils.

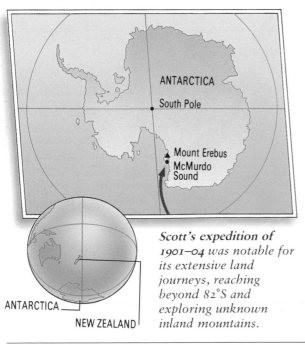

Scott's expedition of 1901–04 was notable for its extensive land journeys, reaching beyond 82°S and exploring unknown inland mountains.

Discovery's accommodation *had been well planned for her crew to come through two icebound winters (above) in good spirits. Individual cabins for officers were provided off a wardroom 30 feet by 20, but as a result of their position over the freezing coal bunkers they were rather cold. The crew's quarters were larger and warmer. Discovery's propensity to roll (left), even in modest seas, contributed to the loss of sheep from the decks on the way south.*

263

Exploring the Antarctic

The search for a great south land, or Terra Australis Incognita, preoccupied explorers of the sixteenth and seventeenth centuries. Credit for confirming its existence goes to Captain James Cook who undertook three voyages between 1772 and 1779. A series of modest discoveries preceded the "heroic" age of Antarctic exploration, which produced some of the most remarkable stories of human courage and endurance: Scott, Oates, Shackleton and Amundsen have become household names.

Since World War II, scientific discovery has replaced geographical discovery and the area has been uniquely protected from commercial exploitation and pollution by the Antarctic Treaty. Pressure from some countries to allow the mining of minerals places the world's last unspoiled wilderness in jeopardy.

The Terra Nova *(above) was the three-masted barque which took Captain Robert Scott (left) on his fatal Antarctic expedition of 1910–13. Scott and four companions perished on the return journey from the South Pole to base camp. They had reached the pole only to find that the Norwegian Amundsen had beaten them to it. Built in 1884 and weighing 749 tons, the* Terra Nova *had been the "biggest whaling ship afloat".*

The **Endurance** *(left), a* **Norwegian sealer** *of 350 tons, carried Sir Ernest Shackleton's Imperial Trans-Antarctic Expedition of 1914–16 to the Weddell Sea. In January 1915 the ship was trapped by ice floes off the Caird Coast. After nine months of tremendous pressure, beams began breaking and Shackleton gave orders to abandon ship. When they left the ship the next day, decks had buckled, masts had snapped and spears of ice had penetrated the bulkheads. In mid-November the party watched her sink. The 800-mile journey by Shackleton and 5 others in a 22-foot boat to South Georgia to organize the rescue of the expedition has been called the most remarkable boat voyage in history.*

The **first mechanical vehicle** *to be used on Antarctica was the Arrol-Johnson motor car (below), taken by Shackleton on his British Antarctic Expedition of 1907–09. Driven by a 15-hp air-cooled engine, the car was fitted with special steel-ribbed tyres. It proved of little use on soft snow, however.*

265

The Longest Journey into Battle

FACT FILE

The arduous voyage of the Russian Baltic fleet to a disastrous defeat by the Japanese at Tsushima

Date: October 1904–May 1905

Distance: 18,670 miles

Duration: 222 days

Admiral Heihachiro Togo (top) was trained in England and commanded the Japanese fleet at Tsushima. The Russian leader was Admiral Sinovi Petrovich Rozhestvensky (above).

Few more hopeless journeys have ever been undertaken than the voyage of the Russian Baltic fleet during the winter and spring of 1904/05. A poorly equipped and badly led navy set out on mission impossible: to sail 18,000 miles around the world, without benefit of friendly ports or coaling stations, in order to engage a Japanese fleet which had already proved its effectiveness. In the heat of war, many ill-considered decisions are made, but seldom one as fateful as that of Tsar Nicholas II to send 45 ships and 10,000 sailors to disaster.

The war between Russia and Japan, two nations which both had imperial designs on Manchuria and Korea, had gone badly for the Russians. On 5 February 1904 the Japanese commander-in-chief, Admiral Heihachiro Togo, launched an attack on the Russian Pacific fleet as it lay at anchor at Port Arthur, the most northerly ice-free port in the Pacific. Serious damage was done, but it was not mortal; the Russian fleet in the East still outnumbered the Japanese and for the next year engaged in a series of skirmishes as the war raged on land and the Japanese closed in on Port Arthur. An attempt by the Russians to break out and link up with their cruiser squadron at Vladivostok failed, and in desperation the tsar readied the Baltic fleet to steam around the world to relieve the blockade.

A curious selection of vessels old and new was assembled under the command of Admiral Sinovi Petrovich Rozhestvensky. His flagship was the *Suvorov*, a modern battleship designed for a displacement of 13,500 tons and a speed of 18 knots. But so much additional weight had been added, much of it in unnecessary fittings in the officers' quarters, that she weighed 15,000 tons, was top heavy and could reach only 16 knots at the most.

Some of the other battleships were worse: the *Alexander III* was good for only 15 knots, while the brand-new *Borodino* had had no time for trials to sort out her troublesome engines, which overheated at any speed greater than 12 knots. The *Orel*, another battleship, was plagued with troubles from the start: a fire, a near-sinking, and then the discovery that her propeller shaft had been coated with emery and brass filings in an attempt to sabotage her. The *Svetlana* was a modern ship capable of 20 knots, but was only a lightly armed cruiser.

The rest of the major warships were a poor lot in the opinion of Captain Vladimir Semenov, who had served in the Pacific fleet but had made his way back to Russia and was now aboard the *Suvorov*. Some were a joke. The cruiser *Dmitri Donskoi* was so old she had originally been rigged for sail as well as steam, while the *Almaz* was the commander-in-chief's yacht to which some armour and a few light guns had been added. The fleet could move only at the speed of its slowest member, which was 11 knots.

The sailors included a smattering of criminals who had been called up in order to get them out of the way. Small wonder that there was an air of alarm verging on panic in the fleet when it finally left Russian waters on 16 October 1904.

Men and officers were prey to a series of absurd rumours, of which the least probable but most widely believed was that the North Sea was full of Japanese torpedo boats. Nobody tried to explain how such tiny boats could have made their way around the world without detection, although the Russians suspected British conniv-ance. The fact that Britain, though neutral, had supported Japan's side in the war deepened Russian doubts about British motives.

On 18 October the fleet fired on an innocent Danish trawler, and two days later on the Dogger Bank opened fire again on a fishing fleet out of Hull, believing it to be the fabled Japanese torpedo boats. One trawler, the *Crane*, was sunk and five more hit; two sailors were killed and six injured. In the pandemonium the Russians began firing at themselves; the cruisers *Aurora* and *Dmitri Donskoi* were hit and the chaplain of the *Aurora* was killed.

Thomas Carr, senior skipper of the Gamecock fleet of fishing vessels, kept a very stiff upper lip. In his report to the fleet's owners, he wrote laconically: "I don't know whether they mistook us for Japanese, or whether they were practising on us to get their hand in. There must be a mistake somewhere: they ought to have known that we were only innocent fishermen." He signed the letter Thomas Carr, "Admiral".

On the *Suvorov*, the fleet's engineer-in-chief, Eugene Politovsky, wrote in a letter to his wife: "Imagine the feelings of the people in these ships! They were, no doubt, fishermen. Now there will be a universal scandal." He was right. The British government mobilized the Home fleet

***A popular classic woodblock** by Hampo, issued by the Japanese in 1905.*

The Longest Journey into Battle

and called the Channel fleet, then at Gibraltar, to a state of alert. By the night of 26 October the Royal Navy had 28 battleships either at sea or ready to go to sea, and for a while the prospect of war seemed quite possible.

Rozhestvensky, shadowed by four British cruisers, made his way through the Channel and south to Vigo Bay, in Spain. His explanation of the incident was unconvincing, but the Russian government offered reparations and agreed to cooperate in an inquiry. They detached a few officers from the squadron to give evidence. One of them, a Captain Klado, was no great loss to Rozhestvensky, for he was a troublemaker who spent as much time writing critical articles for the newspapers as serving as a naval officer. On his return to St Petersburg, Klado immediately began arguing that the fleet needed further reinforcements, with the result that some even older ships were sent to support Rozhestvensky.

His squadron had meanwhile split in two, the smaller vessels being sent through the Mediterranean and the Suez Canal, while the battleships with deeper draught took the long route around the Cape of Good Hope. Their greatest problem was coal. Before setting off they had been loaded to the gunwales with the stuff, *Suvarov* carrying more than 2,200 tons although she had bunkers for only half as much. There was coal everywhere, Semenov remembered, "not only up to the neck but over the ears". Coal was stored in bags on deck, in the lifeboats, in the heads, even in the food lockers.

Even so, it was nothing like enough, and with most of the world's coaling stations controlled by the British, the Russians had devised an extraordinary scheme to keep their ships steaming. A deal had been struck with the German Hamburg-Amerika Line to provide 62 colliers along the route, carrying 340,000 tons of coal to be transferred in neutral ports if possible but failing that outside the 3-mile territorial limit.

Loading the coal at sea was a horrible job, especially in the tropics. At Dakar in Senegal, where temperatures inside the bunkers reached 115°F, a young lieutenant, son of the Russian ambassador in Paris, dropped dead of heatstroke. Coal dust was everywhere, in the cabins, in the cupboards, in everybody's clothes. Rozhestvensky's temper, never calm, was by this time close to boiling point. His main interest seemed to be to keep the fleet in perfect lines, exploding with rage when any of the ships deviated. After a volley of oaths, the order would

Damage to a Hull trawler from the incident at Dogger Bank. The sense of paranoia that led to Russian ships firing on British trawlers was fuelled by fanciful reports sent by Hekkelman, the head of the Russian intelligence agency. Based in Copenhagen, he had a hundred observers and nine boats to gather information, and sent warnings of Japanese torpedo boats. The incident produced demands from the British press and some members of Parliament for retribution, but an offer of compensation was accepted.

come: "Signal that idiot a reprimand!"

The fleet at last arrived at Madagascar to hear the news that Port Arthur had fallen to the Japanese, with the complete elimination of the Russian Pacific fleet. Rozhestvensky also heard the equally unwelcome news that reinforcements he had not sought and did not want were on their way. Overcome by exhaustion and despair—or perhaps even suffering a stroke—he retired to his cabin for several days, emerging pale and dragging one of his feet as he walked. He now had to sail the rest of the way to Vladivostok while the whole of the Japanese fleet lay in home waters waiting for him.

For weeks after its departure from Madagascar the fleet simply disappeared. Without radio communication, nobody knew where it was as it struck out across the Indian Ocean, making regular rendezvous with the colliers. This was the first time that a modern battle fleet had ever made such a long journey across open sea, relying on no friendly port for assistance. On 8 April it was sighted off Singapore, steaming at a steady 8 knots, all the ships trailing great masses of vegetation just below the water line.

By 12 April they were at Cam Ranh Bay in

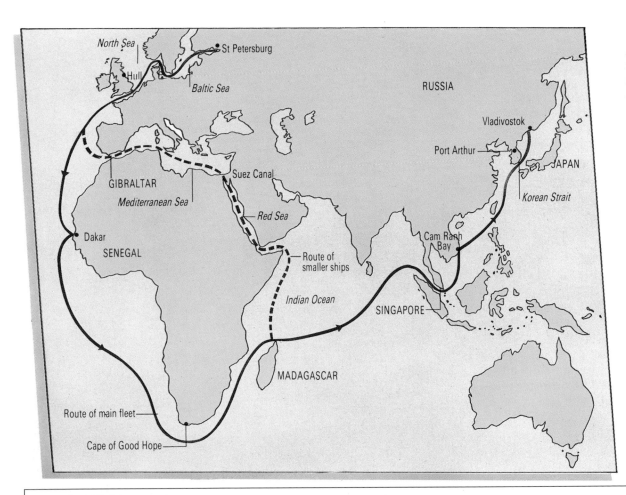

The route after the **Dogger Bank debacle** *took in Vigo, where the* Daily Mail *correspondent Edgar Wallace elicited good copy from drunken Russian seamen. The smaller ships left to sail through the Suez Canal; the bigger ships sailed to Dakar and then around the Cape of Good Hope to Madagascar, stopping in isolated bays in French, German and Portuguese colonies to coal on the way. During two months of gunnery practice off the island few targets were hit, but one shell hit a Russian cruiser, and in manoeuvres two battleships had a gentle side-on collision.*

COALING AT SEA

The most difficult part of taking 40-odd ships halfway around the world was the provision of coal for the voracious steam boilers. Most battleships had 20 boilers, one had 24. The desire of the German government to curry favour with Russia enabled Rozhestvensky's fleet to rely on German colliers. Agreement was reached with the Hamburg-Amerika Line to provide 340,000 tons of coal.

Rozhestvensky's fear of running short of coal led to frequent coaling at points between Denmark and Korea, and a stipulation that all ships should carry 50 percent more than their bunker capacity. The exertion of coaling in the tropics, and the dirt created by having coal stored in every possible place, did nothing for the crew's health or morale.

Generally, coaling was done using wicker baskets or sacks that the men carried on their backs or their shoulders—a long and laborious method. The delay to ships through the time taken to replenish a ship's bunkers encouraged the Royal Navy to begin in 1912 a programme to build British ships with oil-firing.

The Longest Journey into Battle

French Indochina (now Vietnam) where they halted for a full month to let the reinforcements catch them up. Given their deficiencies, the second squadron had made good time and reached Cam Ranh Bay on 8 May. But they added little punch; there was an elderly battleship, *Nikolai I*, an old cruiser and three coastal defence ships, together with seven auxiliary vessels. Rozhestvensky now had 45 fighting ships and numerous auxiliaries, some of which he sent to Shanghai but others he was obliged to keep with the fleet. Since they could make only 9 knots and had to be protected in a convoy, the whole fleet was slow and unwieldy.

Finally, though, it was ready for battle. The sensible course was to try to reach Vladivostok without encountering the Japanese, for then Rozhestvensky could rest, refit and prepare the fleet for battle without the encumbrance of the supply ships. But his best chance of doing so would be to go up the east coast of Japan, a longer route which would mean coaling off the coast. Up the Korean Strait was a shorter route, but it made direct contact with the Japanese more likely. For reasons we do not know— pride, fatalism or a desire for battle—he chose the Korean Strait. Admiral Togo guessed correctly that is what he would do and lay in wait.

On 27 May, on a moonlit morning, the Japanese sighted the Russian fleet. By 7 a.m. Japanese cruisers were shadowing it as it sailed northeast at 8 knots in misty weather and a heavily rolling sea. By 1.40 p.m. both battle fleets were in sight of one another, and the biggest naval battle since Trafalgar began. They were proceeding on parallel courses, in opposite directions, when Togo gave the order to turn about. He wanted to put his best ships in the right position to cause the maximum damage for the longest time, but he ran the risk that as his ships turned and masked each other's guns they would be vulnerable to the Russians.

The manoeuvre came off, and soon the Russian battleships were under withering fire. The Japanese concentrated on the *Suvarov* and the *Oslyabya*, the flagship of the second-in-command, Rear-Admiral Felkerzam. In fact, as Rozhestvensky knew but the rest of his fleet did not, Felkerzam already lay dead in his cabin. Ill since leaving Madagascar, he had died on the night of 23 May but the commander-in-chief had kept the fact secret for fear of spreading despondency.

Oslyabya, burning from end to end, turned

over and sank. The *Suvarov* was hit repeatedly, shells felling all but one funnel and one mast, and injuring many on the bridge, including Rozhestvensky. When *Suvarov*'s steering gear was disabled, the stricken ship left the line. By 3 p.m., the Russians were in disarray as the Japanese pounded them continuously. By the end of the day, *Suvarov*, *Borodino* and *Alexander III* had joined *Oslyabya* on the bottom and the rest of the fleet was scattered. Only one cruiser and two destroyers reached Vladivostok intact.

In all, on this and succeeding days, the Russians lost 34 warships and 4,830 lives, against 3 Japanese torpedo boats and 110 lives. There can hardly ever have been such a one-sided battle, or such a final and numbing defeat. After its epic journey around the world, the Russian Baltic fleet had stumbled naively to destruction.

The lesson was not wasted on other naval strategists. The Japanese victory had come from speed, better gunnery and superior leadership. The future of naval combat lay with swift ships, carrying big guns, as the British Admiralty had realized. The keel of a new class of battleship, HMS *Dreadnought*, had already been laid.

The cruiser Dmitri Donskoi *was the older of the two armoured cruisers in Rozhestvensky's fleet, built in 1883 with a full ship rig. She was damaged during the battle of Tsushima on 27 May 1905, and was scuttled the following morning off the island of Matsushima.*

The battleship Orel (left) was built in a yard on Galeray Island, St Petersburg, and launched in 1902. She was 397 feet long, and fully laden, she displaced 15,275 tons. Crewed by 29 officers and 796 men, the Orel was, like other Russian ships, painted black except for the canary yellow funnels, which helped the Japanese gunners. The upper deck of the Orel after the battle (below) indicated the severity of the damage sustained. The ship was amongst the remnants of the fleet which Rear-Admiral Nebogatoff surrendered the day after the battle.

The Aleksander II class battleship Imperator Nikolai I, flagship of Rear-Admiral Nebogatoff who commanded the reinforcements sent to catch up with Rozhestvensky. Launched in 1889, the Nikolai I was old and slow, but still the best of the "old flatirons and galoshes" as Captain Vladimir Semenov called them in his account of Tsushima. Nikolai I was surrendered to the Japanese.

The Indian summer of the clippers *witnessed some memorable races between clippers and steamships. This painting by David Cobb commemorates the occasion in 1888 when* Cutty Sark *overtook the P&O's crack new mailboat* Britannia *on the final run up the coast of Australia from Gabo Island to Sydney. Unloading the tea at East India Docks (right) was done as quickly as possible: the first of the new crop commanded the highest prices.*

Survivor of the Great Tea Race

The clippers that carried valuable cargoes of tea back from the Chinese ports in the middle years of the nineteenth century were some of the fastest sailing vessels ever built. The best of them could handle the shifting winds of the South China Sea as readily as the roaring forties or a brisk blow in the English Channel. Built for speed, they also possessed endurance and the power to fly before the fiercest storms, outpacing the mountains of green water that threatened to overwhelm them from astern. They were quite small ships, of 800 tons or so, with limited cargo capacity but able to navigate the poorly charted rivers and waters along the Chinese coast. The most famous of them, now preserved at Greenwich in London, was the *Cutty Sark*.

The tea clippers were racers, their job to be first back to London with the new crop of tea from the ports of China. Large bets were placed on these races by indulgent owners who treated their ships like thoroughbred racehorses. To be first back was both a commercial advantage and a source of pride. Ordinary trading ships would reduce sail and "snug down" each night, but for the clippers the rule was to cram on more sail in the hurry to be home. With favourable weather, they could complete the voyage from Shanghai in 90 days or less, and great prestige attached to the first ship home. On its maiden voyage to Australia in 1869 the great *Thermopylae* made Melbourne in 61 days, port to port.

In 1872 *Thermopylae* and *Cutty Sark* had a famous race home from China. They loaded together at Shanghai and sailed the same day, 18 June, but the first few days of fog and a dead calm produced little progress. At last, on 23 June, the wind picked up. By 26 June, both ships were off Hong Kong and in sight of each other. In light winds, *Thermopylae* showed at her best, but *Cutty Sark* regained at night much of what she had lost during the day. By 1 July, the ships had lost sight of each other. Through the South China Sea *Cutty Sark* met quirky weather, violent squalls, which carried away four sails, being followed by calms.

On 15 July, *Thermopylae* was again sighted in the Java Sea, and the two clippers beat through the strait between Java and Sumatra only a few miles apart. Captain George Moodie of *Cutty Sark* was well pleased to have held *Thermopylae*

over this tricky section of the voyage, for ahead lay the trades where he was confident *Cutty Sark*'s power would tell. He was right: with three consecutive daily runs of 340, 327 and 320 miles, *Cutty Sark* romped ahead, and the two clippers were never in sight of each other for the rest of the voyage.

In the middle of August, when *Cutty Sark* lay 400 miles ahead in the Indian Ocean, a tremendous storm struck her. The wind howled from the west, blowing a strong gale with heavy squalls. At 6.30 a.m. on the morning of 15 August, in the storm's last gasp, a heavy sea under the stern of the ship tore the rudder from its eyebolts, leaving *Cutty Sark* without a means of steering. The brother of the ship's owner, Robert Willis, recommended making for a South African port, but Moodie would have none of it and set about fitting a jury rudder at sea.

As luck would have it, two stowaways were aboard *Cutty Sark*, a carpenter and a blacksmith. They were set to work, together with the rest of the ship's company, to create a jury rudder out of a spare spar 70 feet long which the clipper carried in case of breakages. A forge was set up on deck for the blacksmith to make bolts and bars from the ship's stanchions. More than once the whole fire was swept away, and the smith himself was washed half overboard. Fixing the rudder in place was another awkward task, completed by 21 August when to everyone's delight it was found that it worked well. By this time, it is reckoned, *Thermopylae* was some 500 miles ahead, having caught and overtaken *Cutty Sark* while she lay stationary.

Ahead lay heavy weather, through which *Cutty Sark* had to be nursed, for her makeshift rudder could not be risked. She ran into a head gale which kept her down to only 465 miles in eight days, and the eyebolts holding the rudder came away. Once more the rudder was hauled on deck, repaired and refitted.

Finally, the last lap of the voyage from the Azores to the Channel was accomplished against strong gales, and *Cutty Sark* passed Dungeness in Kent on 17 October. *Thermopylae* had finished a week ahead, but *Cutty Sark*'s performance in making the Channel from the Cape with a jury rudder in 54 days was considered a marvellous achievement. *Thermopylae* had taken 115 days, *Cutty Sark* 122. The fastest

FACT FILE

The most famous of the celebrated tea clippers

Date built: 1869

Length: 212 feet 6 inches

Width: 36 feet

Registered gross weight: 963 tons

Sail area: 32,000 square feet

Survivor of the Great Tea Race

passage that year was by *Normancourt*, which left Macao on 14 September and made it home for Christmas after a passage of 96 days.

The clippers owed their inspiration to the eighteenth-century Yankee schooners, ships that had the ability to skim over the surface of the water. By the 1850s these had developed into fast passenger vessels, weighing more than 2,000 tons and carrying a huge area of sail. The tea clippers were smaller but with a similar racing profile: a sharp pointed bow, three masts raked astern and a set of sails that looked too powerful for what were really quite small vessels. To design such a ship successfully called for the nicest of judgement, for it had to be tough as well as fast.

Cutty Sark was commissioned by the ship-owner Captain John Willis, determined to produce a clipper to beat *Thermopylae*. Willis picked a young designer, Hercules Linton, who had recently started building ships on the Clyde at Dumbarton near Glasgow with a partner named Scott. The ship was built in 1869, a time when wooden construction had not yet given way entirely to iron. *Cutty Sark* used both, in what was known as composite construction.

Although designed for the tea trade, *Cutty Sark* carried every sort of cargo during her long career. Before loading the tea she would be cleaned out and fumigated, then lined with

Cutty Sark in dry dock at Greenwich (above). Her composite construction produced a tremendously rigid ship. The keel, frames and other main structural parts were of iron, with the outer skin in wood. The lower part of the masts was also of iron, and the deck of teak. Below, her cabins were panelled in teak and bird's-eye maple, and the captain was provided with a four-poster bed instead of the usual bunk. The cabin doors had yellow cut-glass handles, and the saloon a fireplace to keep the crew warm. She seldom leaked, and her pumps had little use. Even when 25 years old, she arrived in Hull with a cargo of wool after a voyage from Australia on which her pumps were not used.

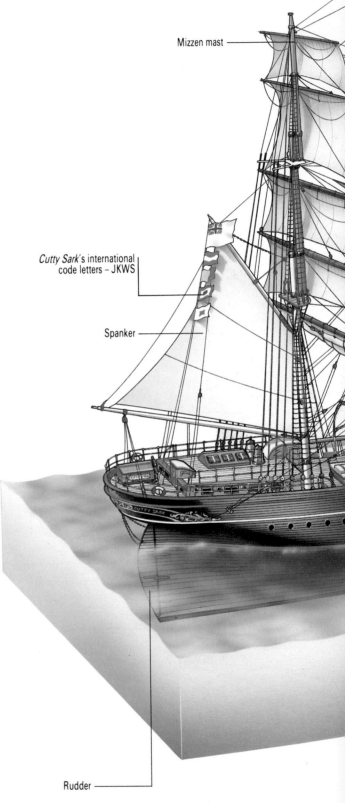

Mizzen mast

Cutty Sark's international code letters – JKWS

Spanker

Rudder

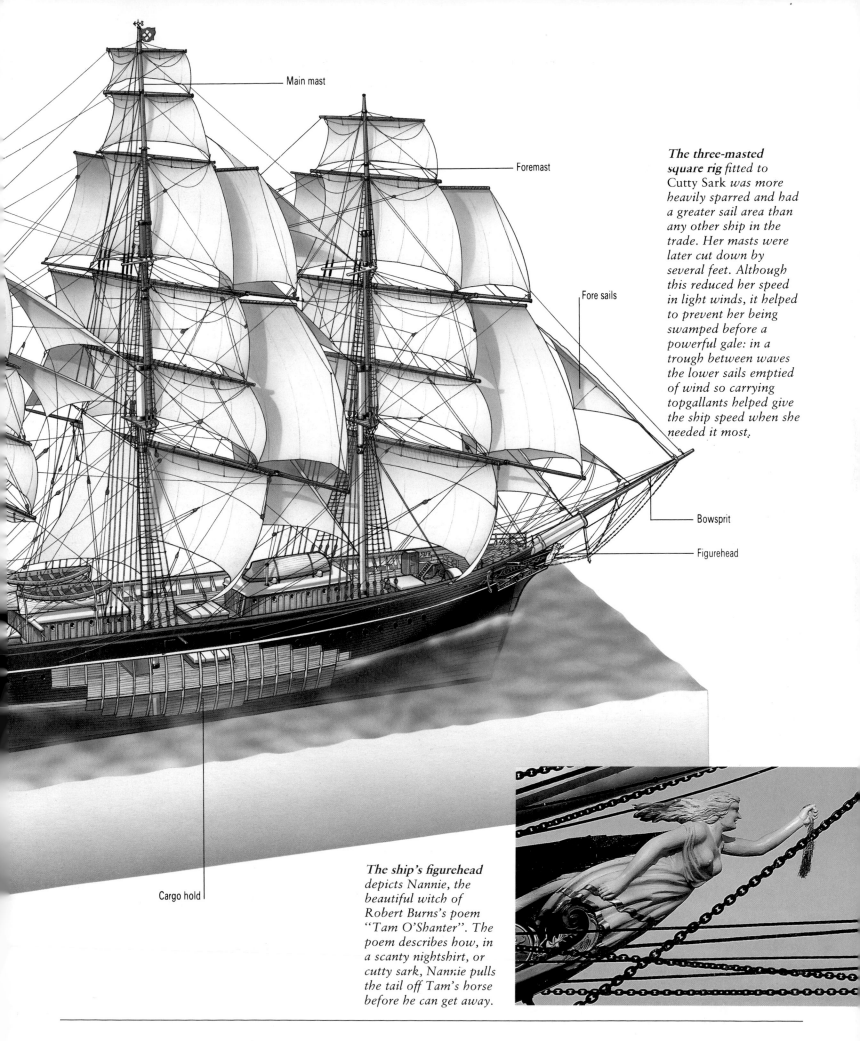

Main mast

Foremast

Fore sails

The three-masted square rig fitted to Cutty Sark *was more heavily sparred and had a greater sail area than any other ship in the trade. Her masts were later cut down by several feet. Although this reduced her speed in light winds, it helped to prevent her being swamped before a powerful gale: in a trough between waves the lower sails emptied of wind so carrying topgallants helped give the ship speed when she needed it most.*

Bowsprit

Figurehead

Cargo hold

The ship's figurehead depicts Nannie, the beautiful witch of Robert Burns's poem "Tam O'Shanter". The poem describes how, in a scanty nightshirt, or cutty sark, Nannie pulls the tail off Tam's horse before he can get away.

Survivor of the Great Tea Race

bamboo matting before the chests of tea were brought aboard and stowed. There was considerable skill in filling her awkwardly shaped holds, and in guessing how much ballast, in the form of washed stones, should be loaded below the cargo. Too much and the ship was down to her gunwales before the cargo was half-loaded; too little and she would spend the voyage home rolling on to her beam ends.

On the outward voyages *Cutty Sark*, like other clippers, would carry general cargoes to Australia, then load up with coal for Shanghai, before returning with the tea. It was a pattern that did not last very long; the Suez Canal had opened the tea trade to steamers, and by the end of the 1870s the clippers were forced to earn their livings elsewhere. Several turned to the Australian wool trade. *Cutty Sark* could cram as many as 4,500 bales of wool, worth almost £100,000, into her holds.

In 1885 *Cutty Sark* made a memorable passage from Australia, reaching Ushant in the mouth of the English Channel in 67 days and beating the rest of the fleet, including *Thermopylae*, by more than a week. But by 1895 the slow rise of the steamship had finally made sail uneconomical, and John Willis sold his most famous ship to a Portuguese company, Ferreira, which gave her its own name. Now she traded between Lisbon, Rio and the Portuguese colonies in Africa, with regular visits to New Orleans. In 1905 she turned up in Cardiff, with images of saints stuck up around her decks, then disappeared again.

In 1914 she appeared in the River Mersey at Liverpool with a cargo of whalebone and oil, and was visited by hundreds of sightseers. She loaded up with coal and bricks and sailed again for Africa just as World War I was breaking out. In 1916 she was dismasted in a storm off South Africa, narrowly escaping complete destruction. Her owners could not afford to replace the masts as they had originally been, so she was re-rigged as a brigantine until she was finally put up for sale in 1920.

Her new owner, also Portuguese, had some repairs carried out, and sailed for London, where the old ship was once more the centre of attention. As she left, a gale blew up and *Cutty Sark* was forced to take refuge in Falmouth, where an old seafarer, Captain Dowman, saw her and bought her for £3,750. So finally *Cutty Sark*'s career of more than 50 years came to an end, and she eventually went into retirement in dry dock at Greenwich.

TALL SHIPS

The graceful clippers and full-rigged, three-masted ships were gradually superseded during the last two decades of the nineteenth century by the four-masted barque. Until the mid-nineteenth century, barques had been relatively small sailing ships, but gradually larger vessels were built, particularly for the grain and nitrate trade between South American ports and Europe. Some were as heavy as 5,000 tons. Technological advances helped to make possible the increase: the replacement of rope by wire enabled much larger sails to be set; winches and capstans took over the control of yards and sails from block and tackle.

World War I took a heavy toll of sailing ships, which were mostly broken up rather than lost to naval action. Within a few years of the war most had gone from the main ports of the world. Some sail training ships remained and many decaying vessels could be found in far corners of the world, like the Falkland Islands. The rescue of a few is testimony to the affection felt for the age of sail.

The **Falls of Clyde** *(below) was built at Glasgow by Russell & Company in 1878. With a wrought-iron hull, she was 1,748 tons net and 266 feet long. She sailed to ports in India, Australia, the Far East and the United States before being sold to the Matson Line in 1898. It used her on a San Francisco to Hawaii service until 1921. Her sailing days over, she was taken to Alaska for use as a fuel store. She was subsequently rescued and eventually found a home at Honolulu in Hawaii.*

The Mersey was one of the last ships built for Captain James Nourse who specialized in trade to India and remained loyal to sail while rivals were changing to steamships. Built by Charles Connell of Glasgow and launched in 1894, Mersey was 270 feet long and weighed 1,713 tons. She was designed as a general purpose cargo vessel, and it is thought that Nourse used her as a coolie ship, taking indentured labour from Mauritius to the West Indies and returning with a cargo of sugar. By 1908 Mersey was used as a training ship by White Star Lines; although cadets would serve on steamships, it was policy to train them in the principles of navigation on sailing vessels. In 1911 she became part of the Transatlantic Motor Ship Co. of Christiana (now Oslo), Norway, and was given the name of the company. She changed hands several times in Norway before returning to Britain in 1923 to be broken up.

Racing Elegance

No more beautiful racing yachts have ever been built than the magnificent J-class which competed for the America's Cup in 1930, 1934 and 1937. Sleek, fast and carrying tall Bermudan rigs, the big yachts were racing machines *par excellence*, designed and built for nothing else. They needed wealthy enthusiasts to commission and sail them, for no expense could be spared if they were to prove competitive. For the first time, high technology became an integral part of yacht racing. The J-class yachts were also the closest Britain has ever come to lifting the America's Cup, in a thrilling series of races in 1934.

Earlier contests for the cup had been between yachts that often differed markedly in size and sail plan, with time handicaps being given in an attempt to ensure they competed on level terms. Some of these yachts were even bigger than the J-class; *Reliance*, the American defender of the cup in 1903, carried 16,159 square feet of sail, ten times that of a modern 40-foot yacht. She was the biggest yacht ever to sail in the America's Cup and easily defeated the challenger, *Shamrock III*.

One difficulty faced by any challenger from Britain was that it had to be solid enough to cross the Atlantic. In 1929 it was agreed that in future both defender and challenger should be built to the same minimum standards established by Lloyd's, and should sail against each other on equal terms, with no handicaps. The yachts were to conform to the New York Yacht Club's J-class, which permitted a waterline length of between 75 and 87 feet. The rules also specified the Bermuda rig, with its tall, narrow sails which drove the yachts more efficiently than the old gaff rigs.

For the 1930 series Sir Thomas Lipton, a millionaire and perennial challenger for the cup, went to Britain's top yacht designer, Charles Nicholson. The result was *Shamrock V*, a graceful but fairly conventional design with steel frames and deck beams and a hollow spruce mast. In spite of the 1929 Wall Street crash, no fewer than four defenders were built—*Enterprise*, *Yankee*, *Weetamoe* and *Whirlwind*. Their differences were not very obvious to the naked eye, their sail area being identical within 1 percent. Although *Enterprise* was the shortest, at 80 feet, she won the trials.

The truth was that *Enterprise* represented a leap forward in yacht design, stripped of all normal fittings and using a light, strong duralumin mast, 12-sided and held together with 80,000 rivets. It was stepped in a watertight steel tube filled with a dense liquid which gave it more flexibility. This incredible mast weighed 4,000 lb, 50 percent less than the conventional hollow wooden mast, and was so delicate that it had its own crew member, a "mast nurse", to look after it. It cost as much as the whole of *Shamrock V*.

The boom was equally extraordinary. It was triangular, with a broad flat top wide enough for two men to stand abreast, giving it its name, the Park Avenue boom. All along its length were transverse tracks into which the slides attached to the foot of the mainsail were fixed. This enabled the curve at the foot of the mainsail to be trimmed to the optimum for wind conditions.

John Nicholson, son of *Shamrock V*'s designer, admits that he felt rather despondent when he heard of these innovations after arriving in the US. His premonitions proved only too accurate. *Enterprise*, chosen to defend the cup after a close-fought series of eliminators, easily beat *Shamrock V* in four straight races at Newport, Rhode Island. As well as a considerable technological edge, *Enterprise* was brilliantly helmed by Harold S. Vanderbilt, who

The Rhode Island course (right) has been used for the America's Cup races in most years since 1852. However, San Diego has hosted the race and in 1986/87 it was held in waters off Fremantle, Western Australia. The America's Cup was originally presented in 1851 by the Royal Yacht Squadron at Cowes, the premier yacht club of Britain, to the winner of a race around the Isle of Wight. It was won by a 170-ton schooner America, *entered on behalf of the New York Yacht Club against 15 British yachts.*

FACT FILE

The most graceful racing design for the America's Cup

Endeavour I

Built: 1933

Length (at waterline): 83 feet 4 inches

Weight: 143 tons displacement

Sail area: 7,560 square feet

Endeavour I was considered the best J-class yacht of her day, though she failed in the challenge against the American defender Rainbow *in 1934.*

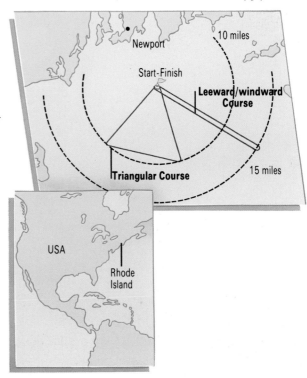

Racing Elegance

Sir Thomas Sopwith (b.1888) made three challenges for the America's Cup; he is pictured (left) at the helm of the boat in which he made the challenge, Shamrock V. Sir Thomas was president of the Hawker Siddeley group that made its name building aircraft, many of which he designed. Besides owning three J-class yachts for his challenges, he later built a 1,620-ton motor yacht, Philante, which became the royal yacht of King Haakon of Norway, who renamed her Norge.

Harold Stirling Vanderbilt (1884–1970), businessman, author and yachtsman, successfully defended the America's Cup on three occasions. He helped William Vanderbilt establish the Vanderbilt Marine Museum on Long Island. His defender for 1930 was Enterprise, a J-class bare of all but essential fittings (right).

organized his crew into a flawlessly efficient unit.

For the next challenge, in 1934, Nicholson responded by building for Sir Thomas Sopwith a much more technically sophisticated boat, *Endeavour*. By this time, the rules had changed to ban masts weighing less than 5,500 lb, which eliminated the possibility of another defence by *Enterprise*. The depression was at its gloomiest, but Vanderbilt put together a syndicate of yachtsmen to build a defender, *Rainbow*, designed by Starling Burgess.

Using as much equipment as possible from *Enterprise*, *Rainbow* was built for $400,000, a rock-bottom price, and sailed off against *Yankee*, one of those eliminated in the 1930 trials. To begin with, *Yankee* showed *Rainbow* a clean pair of heels, beating her ten times in succession in preliminary races. Vanderbilt then added 5 tons of ballast to *Rainbow* and his yacht began to improve. In the trials proper, *Rainbow* narrowly won and was chosen to defend the cup.

Endeavour was a worthy challenger, probably faster than *Rainbow*. She was 83 feet 4 inches long at the waterline and was made of steel throughout, except for her decks, joinery and rudder. Her mast was of welded steel, her boom of hollow spruce and constructed so that by the use of struts and tension wires it could be bent to give the sail the right aerodynamic profile. However, during trials in the English Channel the boom broke, and a hastily made Park Avenue boom replaced it.

Just before *Endeavour* was due to leave England, Sopwith's professional crew went on strike. Disdaining to negotiate, he sacked them all and put together a crew of amateur sailors from the Royal Corinthian Yacht Club; they had virtually no time to train together and many had never sailed J-class yachts before. This was a fateful error which almost certainly cost Sopwith the cup, for in every respect except the crew, *Endeavour* was a match for *Rainbow*.

The first race was called off for lack of wind with *Rainbow* well ahead, but when it was repeated two days later *Endeavour* won handily by 2 minutes 27 seconds. The second race also resulted in victory for the challenger, by 51 seconds. The third race was a different matter. After two legs of the triangular course, *Endeavour* was 6½ minutes ahead and the defender apparently beaten.

Vanderbilt handed over the wheel to Sherman Hoyt, a clever tactician who knew that Sopwith would always attempt to cover an opponent and

steal his wind, however far ahead he might be. Hoyt therefore set a course well wide of the finishing line and tempted Sopwith to cover him. When *Endeavour* came about in failing winds she lost headway and was forced to tack again. Coming up behind with better winds *Rainbow* was through, forcing Sopwith to go about again. *Rainbow* passed the finishing line 3½ minutes ahead having made up 10 minutes on a single leg. Instead of being 3-0 down, Vanderbilt was losing only 2-1, with another four races to go.

The fourth race was marred by one of those rows without which no America's Cup series would be complete. When Vanderbilt refused to yield to a legitimate Sopwith manoeuvre as the two boats closed on each other, Sopwith issued a protest. But because he did not raise the protest flag until he neared the finishing line more than a minute behind, the committee refused to hear it. The decision caused fury. The result, however, was to put the two yachts level, 2-2. The fifth race went to *Rainbow*, though not without a

Shamrock V was designed by Charles Nicholson for Sir Thomas Lipton. It was to be Sir Thomas's fifth and last challenger. He was in his eightieth year, and felt confident of victory. Shamrock crossed the Atlantic with her designer, her manager and sailing master on board, while Sir Thomas made the passage in his luxurious steam yacht Erin. The race was an easy victory for the defender, Enterprise. Shamrock was bought by Thomas Sopwith after Lipton's death in 1934.

Racing Elegance

slice of luck. After a spinnaker split, Vanderbilt gybed in order to pull it in, and a man went overboard. He fortunately held on to a sheet and was quickly hauled aboard, and a race that was nearly lost was won by *Rainbow*.

The final race was desperately close. The two yachts were never far apart around the course, but *Rainbow* finally won by a bare 55 seconds, and the cup was retained. Never was Britain to come closer to winning, for the 1937 series was lopsided, the brilliant defender *Ranger* proving the fastest J-type ever built and easily defeating Sopwith's *Endeavour II*. Both defender and challenger were at the limit of the class, 87 feet along the waterline, and were equipped with bunks, panelling and other accommodation which the racers of 1930 had lacked. This was the result of a change of rules, which since 1934 had insisted the yachts be fully equipped.

Ranger was designed by Starling Burgess and Olin Stephens and was perfectly designed for the conditions of Newport. With a bulbous stem and

flattened stern she was not beautiful, but her speed was unquestionable. She easily defeated rival defenders and then won the actual races by a straight 4-0 victory. In the final race she covered the 10-mile leg dead to windward in 1 hour 14 minutes, an average speed of 8.01 knots, which still stands as the highest authenticated speed ever made good to windward by a sailing ship. *Endeavour II* finished 4 minutes behind.

This was virtually the last time the great J-class yachts raced. They were expensive to build and to race, for in anything over a stiff breeze there was always a serious danger of a mast being lost. Sailing in English regattas in 1935, both *Endeavour* and *Yankee* lost their masts, and *Ranger*'s expensive duralumin mast was swept overboard near Cape Cod.

The unsuitability of the J-class for ordinary sailing may help explain why so few have survived into modern times. *Ranger* was broken up for scrap during World War II, the same fate that befell many of these great yachts.

ENDEAVOUR RESTORED

World War II put a temporary stop to the America's Cup, but the real tragedy of the war for the sailing fraternity was the loss of several J-class yachts for scrap. The huge cost of restoring the few survivors has deterred all but a few. *Endeavour* has been rebuilt by Elizabeth Meyer, and *Shamrock* was restored by Camper & Nicholson at Gosport in Hampshire during the 1970s. *Shamrock* was renovated again, at the Museum of Yachting in Newport, Rhode Island, also under Elizabeth Meyer. *Velsheda* has been restored and is now based at Southampton.

The restoration of Endeavour *ranks as one of the most thorough and expensive rescues of a yacht. Work began in Calshot (top right) before the boat was* *sold to the American Elizabeth Meyer, who completed her rebuilding, first at Calshot and then in Holland (left and above).*

Queen of the Atlantic

"If ever there was a ship which possessed the thing called soul, the *Mauretania* did," declared Franklin D. Roosevelt in August 1936, as the old liner was being broken up in Rosyth. The most famous ship ever to sail the Atlantic, she deserved in his view a more fitting end. "Why couldn't the British have remembered the *Mauretania*'s faithfulness—taken her out to sea and sunk her whole—given her a Viking's funeral, this ship with a fighting heart?"

Sentiment, however, comes pretty low on the shipowner's order of priorities, and by 1935 *Mauretania* had reached the end of her natural life. From her maiden voyage in November 1907 to her final trip in September 1934, she had been the flower of the North Atlantic, holder for 18 years of the Blue Riband for the fastest crossing and capable even in her final years of an astonishing turn of speed.

At her launch she was the biggest ship afloat, just a few feet larger than her sister ship the *Lusitania*, torpedoed by a German U-boat off the coast of Ireland in May 1915. With her four funnels and crisp lines, *Mauretania* looked more like a huge yacht than an ocean liner: "a ship which was a ship and not a damned freight-house" as Roosevelt put it.

Mauretania was the product of a battle for supremacy in the Atlantic trade, and British worries that they were losing control of their merchant fleet to J.P. Morgan's International Mercantile Marine Company. In 1897 the *Kaiser Wilhelm der Grosse*, owned by Norddeutscher Lloyd, had captured the Blue Riband, and its successor in holding this important speed record was another German ship, the Hamburg-Amerika Line's *Deutschland*. The Cunard Steamship Company recognized that these fast German ships were winning the majority of the traffic at a time when immigration from Europe to the US provided a buoyant market. The takeover of White Star Lines by IMM in 1902 alarmed the Admiralty, for it appeared that Britain's Merchant Navy was falling into the hands of foreigners and would soon be unavailable for military service in time of war.

To meet these twin challenges, Cunard and the British government did a deal to build two high-speed express liners. In return for a loan, an operating subsidy and a guarantee of mail contracts, Cunard undertook to design the ships to suit the Admiralty, staff them with British officers and a crew at least three-quarters British, and make them available for war service at prescribed rates. The results of this contract were two of the finest ships ever seen.

Much of the success of the *Mauretania* and the *Lusitania* arose from the choice of motive power—steam turbines rather than the reciprocating engines which drove the German ships. Steam turbines were then in their infancy, but Cunard convinced itself of the virtues of the turbine by comparing two identical ships, the *Caronia* and the *Carmania*, the first having reciprocating engines, the second turbines. *Carmania* was quicker and used less fuel. For the same amount of coal, she could produce an extra knot. She was also smoother and the engine room could be much smaller, leaving more room for passengers. The huge weight of reciprocating engines in the stern could be avoided, giving better weight distribution. The case for the turbine was proved.

The contract for building *Mauretania* went to Swan Hunter and Wigham Richardson at Wallsend on the River Tyne. Many changes were made as the design proceeded, but it was finally fixed on a ship 790 feet long and 88 feet broad which was to have a gross weight of 31,938 tons.

The *Mauretania* was launched on 20 September 1906, just 25 months after her keel was laid. The Dowager Duchess of Roxburgh named her, in the Cunard custom, after one of the ancient Roman provinces: in this case, a barren stretch of Sahara desert then called Spanish West Africa but now an independent nation, once more rejoicing in its original name. A ton of soft soap, $14\frac{1}{2}$ tons of tallow and 113 gallons of train oil did their work, and *Mauretania* slid slowly into the Tyne.

Mauretania was then fitted out in considerable splendour. The country-house architect Harold Peto designed the interior in an eclectic Edwardian style. Huge amounts of timber were used: French walnut veneer in the staircases, mahogany in the lounge, maple in the drawing room, weathered oak in the triple-decked dining room. The carving was spectacular: 300 craftsmen were brought from Palestine to the Tyne to spend two years creating high-relief mouldings, columns, capitals and bulkhead walls.

The first-class dining room was entirely

FACT FILE

The largest and one of the most sumptuous ships afloat in the 1920s

Date built: 1905–07

Length: 790 feet

Power output: 78,000 horsepower

Maximum speed: 29.7 knots

Registered gross weight: 31,938 tons

covered in straw-coloured oak, carved in a sixteenth-century style attributed to François I of France. The first-class lounge, or music room, 79 feet 6 inches long by 55 feet wide, was decorated in late eighteenth-century French style, with Aubusson tapestries and 16 lilac-coloured fleur-de-pêche marble pilasters. There was a high glass dome and crystal chandeliers, which appeared to hang free but were in fact locked in position so they did not swing when the Atlantic turned unfriendly. Cunard insisted on old-fashioned, bolted-down chairs, a nineteenth-century notion soon replaced by heavy but moveable furniture.

On 17 September 1907, *Mauretania* slipped out of the Tyne on some preliminary trials. Carrier pigeons took the results back daily to the builders. Her speed was fine, but there was a

Mauretania *leaving the* **Tyne** *for preliminary trials by T. Henry. The vibration that soon became apparent was caused by alternating stresses in the propellers that reacted with the hull in an unpredictable way. The vibration was reduced by fitting one-piece cast propellers. A silver match case embossed with the date 1907 (left) was given to first-class passengers. The brooches were for sale on board the ship.*

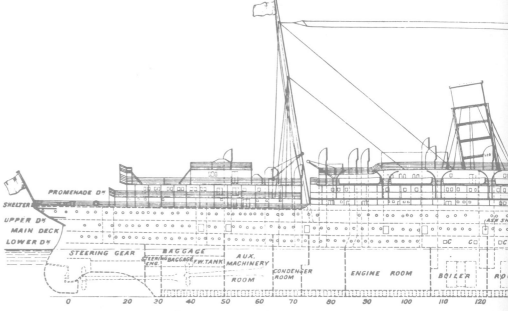

distressing vibration, just what they had hoped to avoid.

On her official trials, *Mauretania* satisfied the Admiralty by steaming 1,216 miles in two days at an average of 26.04 knots, and running the measured mile at 26.75 knots. Her first transatlantic crossing, in November 1907, was made into the teeth of a 50 mph gale, so no records were set. But on the return journey, despite a delay for fog, *Mauretania* got home in 4 days, 22 hours and 29 minutes, an average of 23.69 knots, and captured the Blue Riband from her sister ship *Lusitania*.

She held it until the maiden voyage of Norddeutscher Lloyd's *Bremen* in July 1929. Even then, *Mauretania* was not finished. Returning from New York in August 1929, she averaged 27.22 knots, completing the crossing in 4 days, 17 hours and 50 minutes. Between Eddystone Light and Cherbourg, 106 miles, she averaged 29.7 knots, an astonishing achievement for a ship 22 years old and designed for 25 knots. On 26 September 1934, the day after the *Queen Mary* was launched, she left New York for the last time. She was sold for scrap, her fittings removed and auctioned, her steel recycled into weapons for the war that was approaching. One man got a bargain, paying $20 a letter for the brass bow letters of her name.

Mauretania made a total of 318 return trips across the Atlantic during her career, as well as 54 cruises in the Mediterranean and Caribbean, particularly popular with Americans in the days of prohibition. Painted white, she looked, said a crew member, "like a bloomin' wedding cake", but no amount of white paint could conceal the fact that she was not really designed for cruising. With no air conditioning, few private bathrooms and no swimming pools, cruising in southern seas was a sweaty business. But still *Mauretania* maintained her record of speed and exceptional reliability. On one of her runs to Havana from New York in the early 1930s, she managed to beat the previous record by 13 hours and 28 minutes.

Few ships are as well remembered as *Mauretania*, for she symbolized a whole era in travel. Although more graceful in recollection than in reality—the majority of her passengers travelled third class—it is not mere nostalgia that has given her an affectionate place in the history of ships. Swift, elegant, reliable and safe, she served Cunard magnificently and for a generation made them kings of the North Atlantic.

The quadruple screws, *each 17 feet in diameter, were driven by six Parsons turbines—four for going ahead and two for going astern. Steam was raised by 25 boilers in four boiler rooms which required a complement of 250 stokers to feed them 1,000 tons of coal a day. They were converted to oil after World War I.*

The plates were fixed to the framework by rivets, *of which four million were used, ranging in size from ¼ inch to 8 inches. The weight of rivets alone was 1,013 tons. The steel plates that formed the hull were more than an inch thick.*

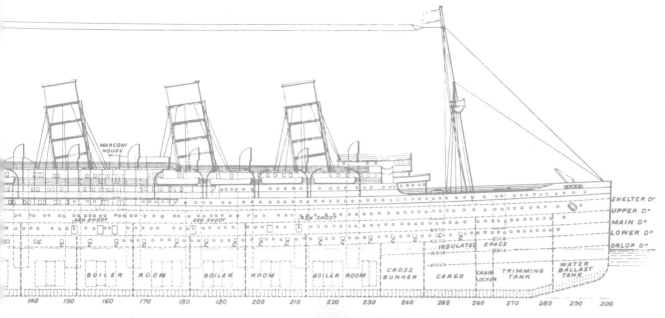

MARCONI
HOUSE

ASH SHOOT   ASH SHOOT   ASH SHOOT   SHELTER Dᴷ

UPPER Dᴷ

MAIN Dᴷ

INSULATED SPACE   LOWER Dᴷ

ORLOP Dᴷ

BOILER ROOM   BOILER ROOM   BOILER ROOM   CROSS BUNKER   CARGO   CHAIN LOCKER   TRIMMING TANK   WATER BALLAST TANK

140   150   160   170   180   190   200   210   220   230   240   250   260   270   280   290   300

Mauretania *carried 2,145 passengers in greater safety than most ships. Her bottom was double plated and divided into separate cells like a warship. Some 175 compartments with watertight doors through the bulkheads, many of which could be closed from the bridge, made the ship less liable to sink.*

Golden Years of Transatlantic Luxury

The development of transatlantic steamship services began in 1838 with the 700-ton *Sirius*. Two years later the Liverpool-based Cunard Line won the British government contract to carry mail across the Atlantic; steamship sailings began between Liverpool and Boston.

The facilities of the early transatlantic ships were fairly basic, but they became gradually more opulent. Cunard's supremacy was eclipsed during the 1890s but construction of the *Lusitania* and *Mauretania*, launched in 1907, restored Cunard's fortunes. After World War I, the *Ile de France* set higher standards of luxury. Soon most new transatlantic liners were equipped with such facilities as swimming pools, squash courts, theatre, concert hall and vast apartments—the first-class dining room of the *Normandie* was 300 feet long.

Construction of grand liners continued during the 1930s and after World War II. The number of passengers grew to 1.2 million in 1958, but the start of jet airliner services in that year heralded the end of transatlantic liners.

Dancing on the promenade deck of the Aquitania *in 1922. With* Mauretania *and* Berengaria, Aquitania *was one of the "Big Three" of the Cunard fleet in the 1920s. Regarded as having the most sober character of the three, she drew passengers "of social consequence, people of title . . .". She lived to become the last four-funnelled liner, being withdrawn in 1939.*

The lounge on the **Duchess of Bedford,** *a Canadian Pacific Railway liner built by John Brown in Glasgow. Launched in 1928, she spent most of her life on the route between Liverpool and Montreal. She was renamed* Empress of India *and then* Empress of France *before being broken up in 1960.*

Competition between shipping lines extended to food, with tempting dishes listed in ornate menus (above). The quantities of food and drink required for a transatlantic voyage were prodigious: 425 lb smoked salmon, 1,150 lb beef fillet, 70,250 eggs, 2,400 bottles of champagne, 48,000 bottles of mineral water and 15,000 cigars. To be one of the seven guests to dine at the captain's table was the ultimate recognition of a person's status: the fifteen guests invited to pre-prandial cocktails changed each evening, but the composition of the captain's table was the same throughout the voyage.

The Pompeian Bath on the P & O liner Viceroy of India, *built by Stevens of Glasgow and launched in 1928. She sailed on the London to Bombay route until World War II, during which she was torpedoed off Algiers.*

Wartime Heroes Built by the Mile

*As efficiency in yards
grew, Liberty ships were
built increasingly
quickly. The SS Pierre
Dupont was launched at
Portland, Oregon, on 31
August 1942 (opposite).
The only preserved
Liberty ship, launched
in June 1943, may be
seen near Fisherman's
Wharf, San Francisco
(below). Jeremiah
O'Brien has
occasionally been
steamed up and taken
out to sea laden with
fare-paying passengers.*

During World War II—or so the story goes—a lady was invited to the California shipyard of Henry Kaiser to launch a ship. Arriving at the launching platform, she found the bottle of champagne ready, but no sign of a ship. Had she come to the wrong yard, or on the wrong day? "No, ma'am," came the reply. "You just start swinging the champagne and the ship will be along soon enough!"

At the time, this must have appeared a pardonable exaggeration, for US shipyards were performing miracles of ship production never achieved before or since. In the month of September 1942 three new ships were delivered every day, a total of 93 in a single month. One of these ships had been launched just ten days after its keel was laid, and completed in another five days. Over the year as a whole, 8 million tons of shipping were launched in US yards in a desperate effort to keep up with the appalling losses inflicted by the Axis powers.

Mass production had been made possible by the adoption in January 1941 of a standard design of cargo ship. The Liberty ships, as they were called, were accepted with some reluctance by the US Maritime Commission, for they appeared ugly, sluggish and out of date, and their basic design was British. In practice they became the commonest ships afloat, and instead of the five-year life they had been given, many were still providing good service in the 1970s as

tramp steamers flying many different flags. Others were converted into troopships, oil tankers, army tank transports, a hospital ship and even a mobile nuclear power station.

In 1937, the US Maritime Commission had begun a peacetime programme of equipping its merchant navy with modern high-speed tankers and cargo vessels, at a rate of 50 ships a year. These were excellent ships, with turbine engines that gave them speeds of up to 17 knots. In November 1940, the Commission produced its first all-welded ship and showed that this method of production could save 600 tons of steel. The intention was to re-equip with up-to-date ships a merchant navy that had stagnated since World War I; there had therefore been little enthusiasm for a visit in September of a delegation from Britain intent on ordering 60 ships, to be built in American yards.

The design the group brought with them was unambitious, based on a ship called *Dorington Court* which had been designed and built by the Sunderland shipyard of J.L. Thompson & Sons in 1939. Using modest engines of 2,500 hp, the *Dorington Court* could carry 10,000 tons of cargo at 11 knots; slow but economical. Admiral Emory Land, Chairman of the US Maritime Commission, found little to praise in these "simple, slow" ships, suspected that Britain was going to lose the war anyway, and felt the Commission should dissociate itself from the whole idea by allowing the British to purchase the ships outright. The British agreed, but found there were insufficient slipways available in the US to build them; new yards would have to be laid out and new techniques, such as welding, used if the contracts were to be fulfilled.

By January 1941, it was clear that the American shipbuilding programme had been overtaken by events. The tonnage being sunk by German U-boats underlined the need for lots of cheap ships, which could be "built by the mile and chopped off by the yard". There was no time to create a new design, and Admiral Land was forced to accept that the British might, after all, have been right.

The plans of the 60 Ocean-class ships already ordered by Britain were modified and adopted for the new programme, announced by President Franklin Roosevelt in February. The president seemed no more impressed with the design than

Wartime Heroes Built by the Mile

The Oregon Ship Building Corporation at Portland built 322 Liberty ships on 13 slipways designed specially for their construction. Of the 18 yards building Liberty ships, the Oregon Corporation produced the highest number of ships per slipway, and launched one vessel ten days after keel laying. This record was exceeded by the No. 2 yard at Richmond, California, which established an unbeaten figure, assembly taking just over four days and outfitting another three.

Land, calling the ships "dreadful-looking objects". But Land, having reluctantly embraced the idea of mass-producing tramp steamers, realized that they needed a better image if the programme was to succeed. In a brilliant stroke he named the ships a "Liberty fleet", and soon they were known as Liberty ships.

The ships which the American yards set to building were not quite the same as the British original. Oil was used instead of coal to fire the boilers. The shape of the hull was simplified to reduce the number of plates which had to be shaped by heating and pressing, eliminating many double curves at bow and stern. The superstructure was reorganized so that all crew accommodation was midships, considered safer for Atlantic convoys and also cutting the expense of piping, heating and outfitting.

Steel decks were specified instead of wooden ones, and items such as radio direction finders, fire detection equipment, emergency generators and life-raft radios were omitted. The ships were not fitted with gyro compasses and many went to

sea with inadequate anchor chains. As steel ran short, the original specification of 300 fathoms of chain was reduced to 240 and later to 210. The only improvements on the British original were the provision of searchlights, domestic refrigerators and running water in the cabins, which doubtless reflected the different expectations of American merchant seamen.

Nine shipyards were established early in 1941 to make the ships. Many of them were completely new yards manned by workers with no experience of shipbuilding, but this did not matter much. Liberty ship production was an assembly process in which the component parts of the ship, produced in factories in 32 states, were welded together as rapidly as possible. Engines and boilers were interchangeable, while whole bow and stern sections were prefabricated ready for dropping into place.

The names of the ships were taken from famous Americans. The first, named *Patrick Henry* in honour of the American patriot who cried "Give me liberty or give me death!", was

Prefabrication of components was vital to achieve the rate of ship production required. The yards were assembly points for some 30,000 parts, all produced off site. Many of the yards had none of the usual shipyard machine tools and equipment. Here a deckhouse section is swung over a slipway in 1943.

Moored Liberty ships lined up at Withington, North Carolina, one of eight sites where ships were mothballed after World War II. Some vessels re-entered service during the Korean and Vietnam wars, but as their condition deteriorated and they became technically obsolete, they were sold for scrap en bloc.

Women worked on construction in increasing numbers as the war progressed. After June 1944, shipbuilding had an "urgency" rating for workers and many more women were taken on. By September 1944, 31 percent of the work force at the Oregon Corporation were women. Riveting was a hard and noisy job. Although some yards welded all joints, the older yards used rivets in the frames, seams and deckhouses. Later, after a series of Liberty ships had broken in half, strengthening sections were riveted in.

launched on 27 September 1941, ten weeks before the attack on Pearl Harbor brought the US into the war. It was the first of 2,710 ships which stretched the *Dictionary of American Biography* to its limits.

Some 200 Liberty ships, almost 7½ percent of production, were supplied to Britain under the lend-lease provisions and were all given names beginning with Sam—*Samadang, Samaritan, Samgara.* Americans believe the Sam prefix indicates the beneficence of Uncle Sam, but the real explanation is more mundane. Sam, it turns out, stands for "Superstructure Aft of Midships" in British Ministry of War Transport jargon.

In 1947, when the British economy was at full stretch and the ships were desperately needed, the US demanded them back. Eventually, about 100 of them were bought by British shipping companies, for £135,000 each.

Many of the Liberty ships were lost to enemy action during the war, no fewer than 50 going down on their maiden voyages. Seven took part in the ill-fated convoy PQ17 from Iceland to

north Russia in June 1942, and four were sunk. Armed with their single 4-inch gun, a few took part in heroic naval actions. The *Stephen Hopkins* gained fame for sinking the much better-armed German raider *Steir* after a battle which left them both immobilized and sinking.

The many Liberty ships that emerged intact in 1945 did not all enjoy a quiet retirement. The *Benjamin R. Curtis,* renamed the *Grandcamp,* caught fire when loading ammonium nitrate fertilizer in Texas City on 16 April 1947. When firemen were unable to put the blaze out, the ship was towed into the stream but exploded before she could reach a place of safety. The blast set off a series of other explosions which destroyed most of the dockyard, a chemical plant and many other buildings. Fires burned fiercely for several days, setting light to another ship which also exploded, destroying a second Liberty ship, *Wilson B. Keene,* which was moored alongside, and forcing the evacuation of the town. Over 500 people died, and the *Grandcamp* vanished without trace, such was the force of the blast.

Record-Breaking Hydroplane

time Campbell was in no position to stop. The expense of building K7 had virtually ruined him, and he now had to try to cash in on his fame. When he was invited to Lake Mead in Nevada for a regatta he saw the chance of making some money, and accepted. There on 16 November 1955 he broke his own record, putting up the speed to 216.2 mph. He was now into a rhythm, inching up the record, with each attempt calculated to generate publicity and income.

Billy Butlin, founder of the holiday camps, offered a £5,000 prize for every new water speed record gained by a British pilot in a British boat—an open invitation to Campbell to continue annual runs, gaining the record each time but not by too much. In September 1956, at Lake Coniston, he put it up to 225 mph; the following November, also at Coniston, to 239.07. Both times Butlin was as good as his word, handing over cheques for £5,000. In 1958 Campbell reached 248 mph, in a boat originally designed for a maximum speed of 250 mph. On several occasions he had exceeded the design speed, producing a worrying tendency for the bows to lift. But Campbell was undeterred and in 1959 he increased the record to 260.35 mph. Now his ambition was to reach 300 mph.

Before that, however, he had set a new land speed record in July 1964 at a dry lake, Lake Eyre in Australia, reaching 403.1 mph to beat John Cobb's record. He became determined to do the double—the land and water speed record in the same year. With just eight hours to spare on 31 December 1964 he achieved a new record of 276 mph on Lake Dumbleyung in Western Australia. It was his finest moment. From that day, things began to go wrong.

By this time people had begun to tire of Campbell's record attempts. A sensible man would have retired K7, now ten years old and 30 mph beyond her design speed, and gone into some other business. He had nothing left to prove. But by now money was short, Campbell had no business left to return to, and record-breaking was all he understood. To reach 300 mph he acquired a new engine, a Bristol-Siddeley Orpheus with another 1,000 lb of thrust.

Bluebird arrived at Coniston in November 1966. The new engine's power was too much for the old air intake, sucking in pieces of metal and destroying the engine. A new one was fitted and the intakes modified. Still *Bluebird* refused to fly, ploughing into the water and putting out the engine just as it had at the beginning of its long

career. Villa fitted extra ballast to the aft, and finally Campbell was able to make a full-speed trial. Although he reached 250 mph, the boat kept tramping, and 300 mph seemed impossibly elusive. As Christmas came, the press and the timekeepers announced they were going home. Campbell sent his own team home and then, on Christmas Day, went out alone and ran the boat at over 280 mph in perfect conditions.

On 4 January 1967 conditions were finally right for a record attempt. The team assembled in the early morning while it was still dark and launched the boat. On his first run Campbell covered the kilometre at 297 mph. Villa, listening on the radio circuit, heard the figure announced and was then astonished when Campbell said "Stand by. Am making my return run". He had not waited to refuel, or for the wash from his first run to settle down.

As *Bluebird* came back down the course again at full speed, Campbell hit the swell, which was worse than usual because he had used a water-brake to slow him at the end of the first run. *Bluebird*'s bows lifted and she became airborne. She turned over, hit the water nose first and started somersaulting, flinging off parts of her structure at every contact with the water. When the spray subsided, the broken hull of *Bluebird* lay on its side in the water. Nearby floated Campbell's helmet, a mangled life jacket, a teddy bear mascot. But of Campbell himself there was no sign. Skin divers later located the wreck, lying in 50 feet of murky water, but Campbell's body was never found. His attempt to live up to his father's reputation had finally cost him his life.

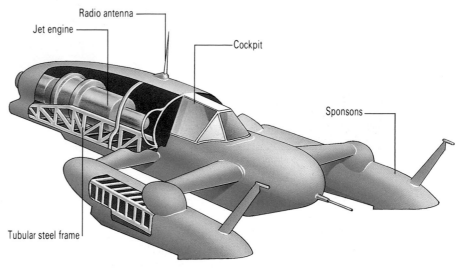

Radio antenna
Jet engine
Cockpit
Sponsons
Tubular steel frame

K7 (above) was designed by Ken and Lew Norris and built of high-tensile aluminium alloy by a bus builders, Salmesbury Engineering Ltd, in England. To increase his chances of winning the world speed record on water, Campbell decided K7 had to be powered by a jet engine, unlike its predecessor, K4, which was a prop-rider. Campbell had to mortgage his house and sell his engineering business to pay for K7. The boat was unveiled by Lady Wakefield and tested on Ullswater in the Lake District. It took some months to cure the tendency for K7's bows to nose into the water like a submarine.

Bluebird on Lake Coniston in September 1958 during the attempt to reach 250 mph. Foul weather wasted many days but Campbell set a new record of 248 mph after having to cram three runs into one hour: rules stipulated that the two-way run had to be done within one hour and K7 had reached only 188 mph on the first.

The final moment on Coniston, 4 January 1967. At 320 mph, Campbell reported over the intercom that the bows were tramping: "Passing close to Peal Island and we're tramping like mad ... full power ... tramping like hell here ... I can't see much and the water's very bad indeed ... I can't get over the top ... I'm getting a lot of bloody row in here ... I can't see anything ... I've got the bows up ... I've gone ... Oh."

Veteran Circumnavigator

FACT FILE

The fastest solo circumnavigation

Built: 1965/66

Length: 54 feet

Weight: 11½ tons

Sail area: 2,403 square feet

Francis Chichester was not a happy man when he sailed from Plymouth on 27 August 1966. His aim was to sail alone around the world with only a single stop, in Sydney, but instead of leaving on his great adventure with a light heart he was ill, depressed and far from confident about the sailing qualities of his 54-foot ketch, *Gipsy Moth IV*. The book he later wrote about the voyage begins with a sustained grumble. Unlike his predecessor Joshua Slocum, for whom sailing alone around the world was a long and enjoyable holiday, Chichester set out like a monk doing penance.

Chichester was not new to adventure. In 1929 he had learned to fly, bought an aircraft, and flown it single-handed to Australia. Other epic journeys were made, but in 1953 Chichester gave flying up in favour of sailing. When the first single-handed transatlantic race was organized in 1960 he entered, and won; he also completed the transatlantic races in 1964 and 1966. He began to believe that it might be possible to realize his dream of circling the globe alone, but in a boat, not an aircraft.

The more Chichester thought about the

Francis Chichester (1901–72) aboard Gipsy Moth IV *near Tower Bridge, London, before setting off on his circumnavigation. His intention was to follow much the same course as the tea clippers over the 14,000 miles to Sydney, which he hoped to reach in a similar time, about 100 days. Sydney was to be the only stop, to save time. After his voyage around the world, Chichester made a triumphant return to England (opposite). In 1971, he crossed the Atlantic alone in* Gipsy Moth IV, *but died the following year after becoming ill on a race.*

project, the more possible it seemed. He was not interested in simply completing the trip, as Slocum had—he wanted to do it faster than any other small boat had managed.

Chichester's ambition was to reach Sydney in 100 days, then sail on and complete the circumnavigation in another 100 days. To achieve that would need a boat that was both fast and manageable. For long periods it would have to sail itself, using self-steering gear, and the key to success would be Chichester's ability to select the right course and rig to make good progress while he was asleep. The sails must not be too big or unwieldy to be handled by a single man—particularly one who was just a few weeks short of his sixty-fifth birthday when he set off.

Yet Chichester allowed his judgement over the design of the yacht to be overruled. He had wanted a boat 48 feet long, but the designer John Illingworth asserted that *Gipsy Moth IV* would be so easy to handle that she could be longer, and thus faster. When launched, *Gipsy Moth IV* turned out to be so tender that she would lay almost on her beam ends in a modest blow. This, says Chichester, "put ice into my blood", for how would a yacht that could be blown flat in the Solent behave when she met the gales of the huge Southern Ocean?

To try to stabilize her she was put into dry dock, her keel removed, and more lead added. This increased her weight, of course, so that Chichester finished off with a boat both bigger and much heavier than he had originally wanted. Moreover, she still heeled to 35 degrees which could prove dangerous in big seas.

All this sapped Chichester's confidence, and things were made worse by an injury he suffered when he slipped on the saloon skylight and hurt his hip. He set off from Tower Pier in the Thames on 12 August, and sailed around to Plymouth with his wife Sheila and son Giles on board. The voyage proper began when he crossed the Royal Ocean Racing Club's start line off Plymouth Hoe as the gun fired at 11 a.m. on 27 August.

For the first couple of days he was seasick and found the sailing hard. The self-steering gear did not seem to work well and would not hold the boat on course if all sails were set. But in the first four days he sailed 556 miles, which cheered him up. He passed Madeira and in the warmer waters began to enjoy himself. Every time a serious

Veteran Circumnavigator

squall hit the boat, however, things went wrong. The self-steering would not hold the course and *Gipsy Moth IV* would tear off at great speed, but in the wrong direction. Under these circumstances it was very difficult to lower sails and regain control while trying to steer the boat.

Despite the problems, he was making good time. By his 32nd day out, he reckoned he lay only 40 or so miles behind the position of *Cutty Sark* at the same point on one of her voyages. By the middle of October, *Gipsy Moth* had rounded the Cape of Good Hope and was halfway to Australia. Ahead lay 7,000 miles of running down the winds along the clipper way, one of the greatest sails in the world. By this time Chichester had had a spell of calms and was well behind *Cutty Sark*'s timetable, but he felt more cheerful.

The roaring forties, however, proved tough sailing. When the wind really blew and Chichester attempted to flee before it under bare poles, he found *Gipsy Moth* would do nothing but lie broadside on to wind and waves. Only by hoisting a storm jib could she be persuaded to sail. Chichester was dumbfounded. All his earlier yachts had steered easily downwind under bare poles. Broaching to under a heavy sea was the fate that clipper captains feared most, for if the sails went into the sea they were likely to founder. *Gipsy Moth*'s chances were better than that, but it was still impossibly uncomfortable, and Chichester was making slow progress.

On 15 November, with 2,750 miles to go to Sydney, disaster struck. The self-steering gear broke, two steel plates 6 inches wide and $\frac{1}{8}$ inch thick sheering clean through. Chichester thought his dream was over and decided to put into Fremantle, which was much closer than Sydney. Without the self-steering, he would be lucky to be able to sail for more than ten hours a day, and the rest of the journey to Sydney would take three months.

But during the day he started experimenting with the sails, creating a jury rig which would hold *Gipsy Moth* nearly on course, as long as the wind was astern. To his delight, it worked, and he decided to head for Sydney after all. The hope of reaching it in 100 days was gone, but he would still make good time.

Ahead, however, lay a tough sail through the Bass Strait and north to Sydney Harbour. The weather was rough, the currents unfavourable and *Gipsy Moth* continued to sail badly. Chichester noted bitterly in his log "I fear *Gipsy Moth IV* is about as unbalanced and unstable a

The rounding of Cape Horn (above) presented nothing to compare with the seas Gipsy Moth IV *encountered during a storm on the first night out of Sydney. Chichester later estimated, from marks made by objects flung about the cabin, that the masts went between 45 and 60 degrees below the horizontal. It was pitch dark, and he had the feeling of the boat being on top of him as things rained down from every locker.*

boat that there could be". Finally he sailed into Sydney at 4.30 p.m. on 12 December after 107 days 5½ hours.

In Sydney Chichester took advice from a number of yachtsmen on how to improve the sailing qualities of *Gipsy Moth IV* before he left on 29 January 1967. Almost immediately he hit trouble. The next night, *Gipsy Moth* was hit by a freak sea, and virtually turned turtle. Slowly she righted herself without going completely over. The result of the upset was an appalling mess, the loss of several sails, winches and other gear, and a bilge almost full of water. But Chichester was still alive, and *Gipsy Moth* still afloat.

The rounding of Cape Horn was the part of the voyage that had most frightened Chichester before he set off. As he expected, he found fearsome seas and winds gusting to 60 knots, but no disaster befell. By 26 March he was around the Horn and halfway home, heading up through

Outward journey
Homeward journey

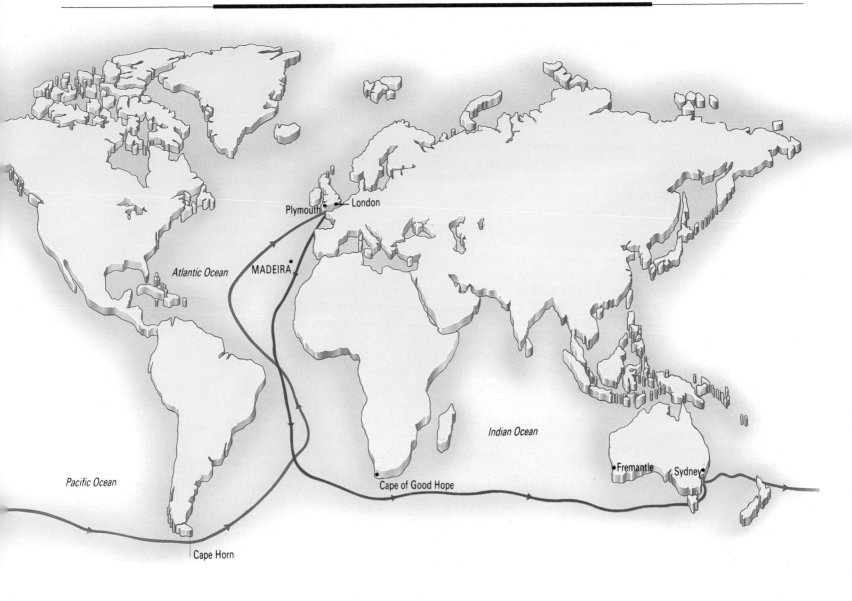

Plymouth • — London

Atlantic Ocean

MADEIRA •

Pacific Ocean

Indian Ocean

• Fremantle   Sydney •

Cape of Good Hope

Cape Horn

the South Atlantic Ocean with 8,000 miles to go.

Much of the way was easy, pleasant sailing, and even *Gipsy Moth* seemed to be enjoying herself at last. He reached Plymouth on 28 May, a passage of 15,517 miles in 119 days, at an average speed of 130 miles per day. He had completed the fastest ever circumnavigation of the world in a small boat, 9 months and 1 day, of which the sailing time was 226 days. He had also broken records for the longest passage and for a week's run by a single-hander.

After arriving in Plymouth, Chichester paid the price for the way he had driven himself, collapsing with a duodenal ulcer. This delayed his triumphal return to London until the beginning of July. He arrived at Greenwich on 7 July and was knighted by the Queen in the Grand Quadrangle of the Royal Naval College. Nearby, his yacht is preserved close to *Cutty Sark* whose great runs so inspired him.

As Chichester stepped ashore in Sydney, *he was faced by a press conference of over 100 journalists, quite a change from three months of his own company. The changes made to Gipsy Moth IV in Sydney proved beneficial. The yacht's handling improved, reducing her tendency to broach in a following sea, which had caused Chichester such concern while crossing the Indian Ocean.*

The Longest Journey under the Sea

The Arctic ice cap floats on top of a deep and unexplored ocean. Unlike the Antarctic, no land lies beneath the wilderness of broken ice, but until the development of the nuclear submarine the ocean remained as inaccessible as any place on Earth. Sir John Ross, the explorer, described the Arctic sea ice as "a floating rock in the stream, a promontory or island when aground, not less solid than if it were a land of granite". He exaggerated, but not by much; in reality the Arctic ice has the strength of rather poorly made concrete. But it is certainly tough enough to ensure that no surface ship will ever be able to plough its way through to the pole.

The idea of getting there under the ice, however, had been taken seriously by several explorers. The Australian Sir Hubert Wilkins had led an expedition to the edge of the ice in an old American submarine in 1931. In the 1950s, submarines had crept beneath the ice for a distance of several miles before retreating. In principle, there seemed no reason to suppose that the right vessel could not sail clean under the polar ice cap and emerge unharmed on the other side. Nobody really knew how far down the ice penetrated at the shallow edges of the ocean, so there was a risk that a submarine might find itself trapped between the ice above and the ocean floor below, isolated, out of contact and beyond rescue. The only way to find out was to try.

Ordinary submarines were really unfit for the journey. When submerged they depend on electric power, but the batteries that store it have only a limited life before the submarine must surface and recharge by running its diesel engines. Optimists like Wilkins believed there would be sufficient polynias—open stretches of water in among the ice—for him to surface at regular intervals to run his engines. Even if he were right, finding them would require luck.

The development of the nuclear submarine transformed the position. Here at last was a vessel which could realize Jules Verne's dream of 20,000 leagues under the sea. A nuclear submarine equipped with a system for reconstituting the air its crew breathes can stay down for months on end. Unlike a diesel submarine which constantly dives and surfaces, the nuclear submarine finds its natural habitat in the deeps.

This revolution in submarine technology was brought about largely by one man, the remark-able Admiral Hyman Rickover of the US Navy. In 1946 Rickover, then a captain, had studied nuclear physics and became convinced that a nuclear reactor could be squeezed down small enough to power a submarine. Many people laughed at him, for the first nuclear piles were just that—enormous piles of uranium and graphite as big as a couple of city blocks. Rickover refused to be daunted.

For three years he fought a bureaucratic guerrilla campaign to have his idea taken seriously. His master stroke was to get himself appointed head of the Nuclear Power Division in the Navy's Bureau of Ships and simultaneously chief of the Atomic Energy Commission's Naval Reactors Branch. He could now send memos to himself, approve his own ideas, and move ahead at startling speed. By January 1954 the first nuclear submarine, called *Nautilus* in honour of Jules Verne, was ready for launch. The following January she sailed for the first time.

Nautilus was a triumphant vindication of Rickover's ideas. Her performance was staggering. She could cruise under water at more than 20 knots, was highly manoeuvrable, could go very deep and was reckoned to be 50 times as difficult for anti-submarine forces to catch as a diesel submarine. By the time she first needed refuelling, two years after her shakedown cruise, she had travelled 69,138 miles.

If any vessel had the capacities to cruise below the Arctic ice cap, *Nautilus* did. A number of

FACT FILE

The submarine that first sailed under the Arctic ice cap

Built: 1953/54

Length: 320 feet

Diameter: 28 feet

Maximum speed: 20 knots

Commander William Anderson (middle below) with Lt Commander Frank Adams (left) and Lt William Lalor, Jr., aboard Nautilus *after their successful voyage. Looking at the edge of the ice cap, the submarine's crew breathe their last fresh air before diving under it (right).*

The Longest Journey under the Sea

influential people, including Senator Henry Jackson of the State of Washington, had been pressing for the attempt to be made, and the US Navy agreed, although some admirals opposed risking their only nuclear submarine in such a hazardous operation. In great secrecy the captain of *Nautilus*, Commander William R. Anderson, prepared for the trip. No announcement was to be made in advance, in case *Nautilus* failed. Elaborate cover stories were prepared, suggesting that *Nautilus* was bound for Panama, and the crew packed their tropical gear. In fact the destination was to be Portland, in England, via the North Pole.

The first attempt to penetrate the ice failed. *Nautilus* approached the ice cap by navigating through the Bering Strait that divides Alaska from Siberia, reaching the shallow Chukchi Sea. To reach the deep Arctic Basin it was necessary to find a way through this sea without meeting any ice that came too close to the bottom to allow *Nautilus* through. They saw the edge of the ice and plunged beneath it, navigating in a shallow region with the seabed 40 feet below and the deepest ice 50 feet above them.

Suddenly the instruments showed a huge chunk of ice ahead, a mile wide and more than 60 feet thick. Beyond lay an even more formidable barrier, which swooped down and down toward the seabed. *Nautilus* crept forward, its officers certain that any moment they would hear the grinding sound that meant they were trapped between the ice ceiling and the seabed. They cleared the massive block of ice with a bare 5 feet to spare, and Anderson knew the mission had failed; to go on risking his ship in those waters would be foolhardy. He gave the order to turn south, and abandoned the attempt on the pole. *Nautilus* sailed for Pearl Harbor, its crew sworn to secrecy, for Anderson still hoped to make a second attempt later in the year.

They set off again on 23 July and returned to the Bering Sea in six days—an average speed of 19.6 knots, all of it spent deep under water where submarines cruise better, free from storms. This time, he found the ice had retreated, but it was still necessary to thread his way through the Chukchi Sea. Despite steaming to and fro, they failed to find a passage, and Anderson decided to turn his attention eastward to the Barrow Sea, where a deep valley ought to provide a gateway to the western Arctic Basin.

They found it and submerged with relief in an area that looked safe. The water was deep, the

ice far above, and Anderson increased speed to 18 knots and set course for the pole, 1,094 miles away. Beyond that another 800 miles would bring them to the Greenland-Spitzbergen edge of the pack ice.

From here on, the expedition was almost an anticlimax. *Nautilus* found places where the seabed rose almost vertically toward the ice, but there was always ample space to slip through. At the pole itself, reached on 3 August 1958 at 11.15 p.m., the sea was measured as 13,410 feet deep. *Nautilus* emerged from the ice within a few miles of where it expected, a tribute to good navigation under difficult conditions. The transit had taken 96 hours to cover 1,830 miles. Since then, operations by nuclear submarines beneath the ice have become almost commonplace.

A routine check of the torpedo tubes as the ship glides beneath the Arctic ice. The only technical problem was a leak in a water condenser, cured by a liquid made to plug leaking car radiators. Conditions aboard Nautilus *were quite luxurious, with a juke-box, ice cream and cola machines in the mess— which converted to a 50-seat cinema—a library with 600 books and a darkroom.*

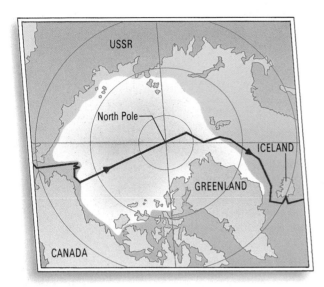

The route pioneered by Nautilus *might be of great benefit to commercial shipping if nuclear cargo-carrying submarines are ever built—or so Captain Anderson considered. It would cut 4,900 miles and 13 days off the route from Japan to Europe, a new submerged North-West passage.*

SIR HUBERT WILKINS

The first attempt to explore the Arctic by submarine was made by Sir Hubert Wilkins, an Australian adventurer. Sir Hubert, who spent most of his life in the US, persuaded the American government in 1931 to back his efforts to reach the pole in a submarine. For a fee of $1 a year for five years, the US Shipping Board let Wilkins have a 1918-built "O" class submarine, which he renamed *Nautilus*.

Wilkins expected to find open water every 25 miles or so, giving him a fair margin of safety with his 125-mile submerged range. If he was trapped beneath the ice, he planned to bring into use hollow ice-cutting drills mounted on top of the submarine.

From the beginning things went wrong: one of *Nautilus*'s two engines broke down in mid-Atlantic, through incompetence or deliberate sabotage. *Nautilus* was towed to Devonport dockyard in

Plymouth for repairs, which took three weeks. By the time she reached the polar ice it was too late in the year for an attempt on the pole.

Inside *Nautilus* conditions were horrible. It was cramped and so cold that ice formed on the walls. When they finally submerged, the grinding and tearing noises made by the hull scraping along the ice so terrified them that they promptly surfaced. In fact there was little damage, but even the toughest found these ghastly noises hard to bear, and after a few days Wilkins admitted defeat.

He limped into Bergen and was granted permission to scuttle her off Norway. The trip had been a disaster, but Wilkins remained convinced that a submarine would succeed where he had failed. He lived just long enough to see his prediction come true, dying on 30 November 1958.

Nautilus **enters Portland harbour** *in England to a rousing welcome on 12 August 1958, just nine days after reaching the North Pole. To release news of the success to the world as quickly as possible, it had been arranged that a helicopter would rendezvous with the submarine off Reykjavik, Iceland, and fly Captain Anderson to Iceland from where a plane would take him to Washington to report to President Eisenhower. A press conference was held, after which Captain Anderson was flown to England to rejoin* Nautilus *off Portland. The submarine would then enter the Royal Navy's submarine base. When the submarine returned to the United States, New York honoured the crew with a ticker-tape parade.*

Blue Riband-Winning Catamaran

In June 1990 the world's biggest catamaran, the *Hoverspeed Great Britain*, broke a record that had stood for 38 years. It covered the 2,800 miles between the Ambrose light-vessel, New York, and Bishop Rock off the Isles of Scilly in 3 days, 7 hours and 54 minutes. In doing so it broke the record set by the liner SS *United States* on her maiden voyage in July 1952, and won the Blue Riband for the fastest Atlantic crossing.

It was a victory that nearly caused a battle in court, for the US Merchant Marine Museum was reluctant to give up the Hales Trophy, awarded to the holder of the Blue Riband, to what it saw as a mere channel ferry. "Even if they come here and claim it, we're not going to give it to them," said Frank Braynard, curator of the museum. "The trophy was intended for great liners, not for toy boats, and this is a toy boat." On the other side of the Atlantic the captain of the *Great Britain*, John Lloyd, was equally certain that he and his crew had won the trophy fair and square. As it berthed in Falmouth, *Great Britain* flew a 30-foot blue ribbon. "The trophy is ours. No ifs and buts, it belongs to us," he said. "A trophy that collects dust is not a trophy; it is a souvenir and it is cheapened by not being competed for."

The catamaran had already come a long way before it began its record-breaking Atlantic run. Built in Hobart, Tasmania, by International Catamarans, it had sailed across the Pacific, through the Panama Canal and up the coast of the United States to Somerset, Massachusetts, where it entered a dock for some strengthening work to be done on the superstructure, to cure a problem of vibration. The Atlantic crossing was merely the final leg of a journey to Britain to begin work as a ferry capable of carrying 450 passengers and 80 cars between Portsmouth and Cherbourg, or on other Channel routes.

The catamaran, or SeaCat, was seen as a successor to the large hovercraft, which have been used as car ferries since the early 1970s, and as a pre-emptive strike against the Channel Tunnel, expected to come into operation in 1993. By halving the crossing time of a regular ferry, Hoverspeed hoped to attract and hold passengers in what is likely to be a tough battle in one of the world's busiest waterways.

The SeaCat is capable of a top speed of 42 knots, giving it a comfortable theoretical margin over the *United States*, which averaged 35.6 knots on its record trip in 1952. But Captain Lloyd did not attempt to drive the catamaran flat out. To begin with, indeed, it seemed that he was going too slowly to stand much chance of a record. "We started off doing 35 knots," he says. "At first, when we realized how slowly we were going, it was tempting to throw open the throttles but I knew if we simply sat tight the boat would pick up speed itself as it consumed the 217 tonnes of fuel on board. By the time we reached the UK, we were doing 38 knots, keeping the engines at maximum continuous rpm."

There were just 10 tons of fuel left when the boat reached Falmouth, having averaged 36.65 knots for the crossing, just over a knot faster than the *United States*.

Captain Lloyd had not lingered in New York waiting for good weather, but had set out as soon as the boat was ready. In fact, he was lucky. "We saw nothing that I would call big seas," he says, nor did they meet ice or much fog. Conditions for an Atlantic crossing were about as good as they could have hoped for.

As they approached the Scillies and the end of the course, Lloyd and the SeaCat crew held a meeting to discuss what to do if, at that late stage, something went wrong. Reluctant to break out the champagne until the moment the Bishop Rock was astern, Lloyd admits: "We could have celebrated the night before our arrival, but I knew that if we did the engines would play up. So that night we planned what to do if one of the four failed. Could we make it on three engines?" Fortunately for them, the situation never arose and the catamaran passed the finish line and reached Portsmouth with all four engines running strongly.

The SeaCat has more in common with the great ocean liners than meets the eye. They used the well-established principle of a long, narrow hull to get maximum speed through the water, and so does a catamaran. The difference is that a catamaran has two narrow hulls, with the accommodation arranged as decking linking the two together. The catamaran form has been in use for thousands of years in the Pacific and Indian oceans, and its name derives from a word in the Tamil language of southern India, *kattumaram*, which means trees tied together. Sailing catamarans have proved that they are the fastest in many classes of racing, combining light weight

FACT FILE

The world's largest catamaran

Date launched:
January 1990

Overall length: 242 feet 10 inches

Power output: 20,000 horsepower of thrust

Maximum speed: 42 knots

with the ability to carry a lot of sail without capsizing. When they do capsize, however, they are much harder to right than a conventional hull, which has made some long-distance sailors wary of them.

A conventional ocean liner cuts straight through the waves with its narrow hull. There is little buoyancy at the bow, so a liner does not pitch, tending instead to plough through the waves. While this produces an easy motion, it means that seas can sweep right over the deck in rough conditions. The SeaCat's twin hulls are also designed to pierce the waves, but because

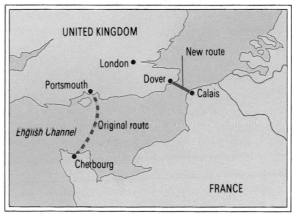

Hoverspeed Great Britain *beneath the New York skyline. The catamaran spent longer in the United States than anticipated, in dry dock at Somerset, Massachusetts, while the superstructure was strengthened to eliminate vibration.*

Blue Riband-Winning Catamaran

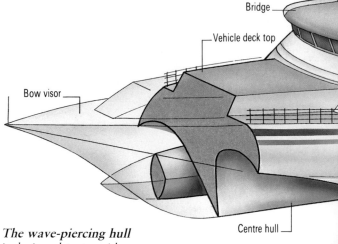

The wave-piercing hull is designed to provide a balance between high speed and passenger comfort. It took six years to refine the concept.

the passenger accommodation is carried high above them it stays dry.

The craft is very short in comparison to its breadth—242 feet 10 inches long by 84 feet 7 inches across—which means that the hulls must pierce the waves if pitching is to be controlled. On some early Channel runs, Hoverspeed did indeed find that the motion was unpleasant enough to cause seasickness, and shifted some ballast forward to try to correct the problem.

The hulls are linked by a bridging structure which is shaped on the underside like a third hull. In normal conditions this is lifted clear of the water, but in extreme weather it provides a third source of buoyancy. The shape of the underside is designed to reduce the shock impact of waves. The hulls and superstructure are made of welded aluminium, with access to the vehicle deck through the stern. The passenger saloon, 65 feet 7 inches wide, is fitted with airline-type seats, the centre section raised by 3 feet so that all passengers can see through the side windows. There is a separate lounge bar at the stern and an observation deck. The passenger area is mounted flexibly to reduce vibration.

Manoeuvring is facilitated by two water jets on each side, fitted with steering and reversing controls. The other two water jets are powered up when outside the harbour to bring the catamaran up to its maximum speed.

The *Great Britain* was not the first ship to break the record held by the *United States*. In 1986 Richard Branson crossed in three days and eight hours in his powerboat *Virgin Atlantic*

The welded aluminium hulls are joined by an arched bridge structure which incorporates a central third hull form. Above them is a vehicle deck, surmounted by a superstructure which contains air-conditioned passenger space. This is supported on anti-vibration mountings.

Challenger, but his claim to the record was disallowed by the Hales Trophy trustees because his boat was not built for commercial service. Nothing daunted, Branson commissioned his own trophy, a sculpture of Bishop Rock lighthouse, and when his own powerboat record was beaten in 1989 by an American, Tom Gentry, he handed over the sculpture.

The considerations that prevented Branson and Gentry from claiming the Hales Trophy did not apply to *Great Britain*. Although the catamaran was not on a scheduled run, and did not carry passengers, the British-based trustees of the trophy decided that it did in fact meet the

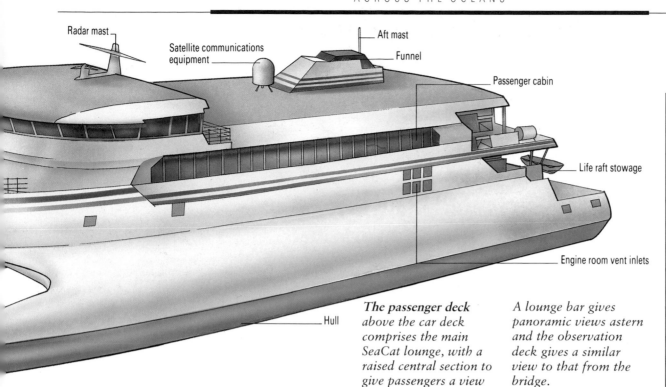

Radar mast

Satellite communications equipment

Aft mast

Funnel

Passenger cabin

Life raft stowage

Engine room vent inlets

Hull

The passenger deck *above the car deck comprises the main SeaCat lounge, with a raised central section to give passengers a view of the sea on both sides.*

A lounge bar gives panoramic views astern and the observation deck gives a similar view to that from the bridge.

The SeaCat's power *is provided by four 16-cylinder Ruston diesel engines mounted in the wide hulls. Manufactured by GEC at Newton-le-Willows on Merseyside, the engines each produce 5,000 hp at 750 rpm. Medium-speed diesels have never before been fitted in a high-speed craft; it eliminates the need for gearboxes, since the engines are coupled directly to the largest water jets ever made.*

Until Harold Keates Hales first presented, in 1935, the trophy named after him, there had been no formal recognition of the vessel that held the record for the fastest crossing of the Atlantic. However, a notional trophy was the Blue Riband (or Ribbon) of the Atlantic. The first ship to hold it was one of the original Cunard wooden paddle steamers, the *Arcadia*, built in 1840. Fierce competition has since led to the Riband being held by all the great transatlantic lines. Hales himself was a self-made engineer with a passion for speed.

requirements. Commander Michael Ranken, secretary to the trustees, said: "We are a legally constituted trust and have the power to say who has won. The Hoverspeed vessel is eligible because it was built for commercial service. I wish there was a little less nostalgia about."

In fact, the trust deed of the trophy, originally commissioned by Harold Hales, MP for Hanley, Staffordshire, in England, to encourage "the craft of speed" in marine engineering, made no mention of a restriction to ocean liners. It was to be awarded to that ship which made the crossing at the highest average speed, without undue risk to the ship or her passengers or crew. The

trustees had no hesitation in awarding the trophy to Hoverspeed and the *Great Britain*, and the New York museum, faced with the prospect of going to court under English law, had no choice but to accept the verdict.

The Hales Trophy, a 4-foot-high silver and gilt sculpture showing scenes of Atlantic vessels from the fifteenth to the twentieth centuries supported by the god of the sea Neptune and his wife Amphitrite, was finally surrendered. In a ceremony in the pool of London in November 1990, it was presented to James Sterling of Hoverspeed by Lord Callaghan, Britain's prime minister from 1976 to 1979.

309

CHAPTER TWO

OVERLAND BY ROAD

ne of the greatest but least remarked upon differences between our lives and those of the wealthier citizens of the eighteenth century is in the ease of transport. The middle classes then lived in houses no worse designed and often rather better built than our own, read good books and listened to music still enjoyed today. Until they set foot out of doors they lived a recognizably civilized life. When they embarked on journeys, however, they descended into an agony of discomfort and delay which had no respect for rank.

The Habsburg emperor Charles VI visited England in 1703 and set out from London to visit Petworth in Sussex, a distance of only 50 miles. The journey took three days, the imperial coach overturned a dozen times, and only by hiring labourers to walk alongside and help push him through the mud did Charles VI finally reach his destination.

It was the invention of the railway, the bicycle and, finally, the car that annihilated distance. Where once even the nobleman's coach could hope for no more than 4 mph, the lone cyclist by the end of the nineteenth century could bowl along at 10 mph, roads permitting. In 1884 the American cyclist Thomas Stevens cycled all the way around the world, a remarkable achievement for, as he himself was the first to admit, most of the journey was made over roads hardly improved since the Middle Ages.

Early in this century an even more dramatic improvement was brought about by the automobile, which proved in the Peking to Paris car race of 1907 that no part of the world was beyond its reach. Again, much of the success of the winning Itala was the result of a recognition by its owner, Prince Borghese, that the race would be won not on the roads but across mountains, along railway tracks and through rivers. The same applied more than 60 years later to the expedition that crossed the Darien Gap in Central America, a wilderness of forest and bog that had defeated many earlier attempts.

The car has become, of course, more than just a means of transport. It is an object of beauty and a sporting machine as well. In this section we explore a few episodes in man's love affair with the car which, in spite of pollution and congestion, shows no sign of diminishing.

Wheeling Around the World

Thomas Stevens, journalist, traveller and evangelist for the bicycle, set out in 1884 to ride alone around the world. His journey was not so much a ride as a pioneering essay in the sport now known as cyclo-cross, for Stevens carried his bicycle almost as often as he rode it. It was an 1883-model Columbia Expert, and singularly ill-suited to the task. It weighed at least twice as much as a modern machine, and riding it even on sound roads was hazardous. Downhill, it was easy to tip straight over the front wheel head first on to the road. Such accidents were known in cyclists' slang as headers, taking a purler, or coming a cropper, expressions which survive long after the bicycles have disappeared.

Despite these drawbacks, it was the penny-farthing (known as an "ordinary" to distinguish it from the new-fangled geared bicycles with their diamond-shaped frames which were soon to displace it) that created the first great boom in cycling in the 1870s.

The ordinary appealed particularly to smart young men who wanted to cut a dash. By 1883 the Cyclists' Touring Club of Britain had more than 10,000 members, and the first long-distance records had been established between Land's End and John o'Groats. Nobody, however, had yet crossed the United States, let alone ridden around the world, when Stevens set off from San Francisco in California on 22 April 1884.

Stevens carried pathetically little: no coat, or tent or sleeping bag, and nothing to eat or drink. He had a sheet of oiled cambric which could be worn as a poncho or draped over the bicycle as a kind of tent. In a small case he carried medicines, matches, a map, a notebook, a pen and ink, and his League of American Wheelmen badge. His bicycle had solid tyres, so he needed no puncture outfit, but he did carry a .38 Smith & Wesson revolver and ammunition as an insurance against some of the wilder folk he expected to meet. He was 29 years old.

What sort of man was he? Born in England, he had moved to the US as a child. To judge by the huge, two-volume account he later published of his exploits, he was tough and resourceful but not very sophisticated. As Stevens innocently blunders his way through Turkey, Persia, Afghanistan and China, the reader anticipates the difficulties long before they occur to the traveller.

His first challenge was the Sierras, the snow-covered mountains of California, which he covered on foot, walking along the railroad track and carrying his bicycle. Next came the wild country of Nevada, where only sagebrush flourished in the sandy desert. In the town of Carlin, he demonstrated the bicycle to people who had never seen one by riding it around the pool table in the hotel bar. In the Humboldt Mountains he came upon a mountain lion, and fired his revolver at it twice without doing it any harm at all.

He set his daily target at 40 miles, a considerable distance when two-thirds of a typical day involved walking. Through the Great Plains he passed the homesteads that were beginning to spring up in country hitherto occupied by buffalo and cattle, and found a few ridable roads, although it was a lucky day on which he did not suffer at least one header. By 4 August he had reached Boston, and he spent the winter of 1884/85 in New York, where he wrote some articles for *Outing* magazine. Next spring he set off once more, as their special correspondent, on his ride around the world.

First stop was Liverpool, where he disembarked from the SS *City of Chicago*. Riding to London he was astonished by the smoothness of

FACT FILE

The first journey around the world on two wheels

Model: Columbia Expert

Diameter of front wheel: 50 inches

Date of journey: 1884–86

Distance wheeled: about 13,500 miles

The penny-farthing was invented in 1870 by James Starley of Coventry, England. The pedals were attached to the front wheels, and each turn of the pedal took the rider forward 13 feet. The seat was set back too far to exert maximum force, yet the handlebars were too close for comfort.

Thomas Stevens, as depicted in his two-volume account of his epic
journey, Around the World on a Bicycle.

The mountain paths through the Sierra Nevadas were so treacherous that after a few slides Stevens chose to walk through railroad tunnels. There was barely room for a man and bicycle to cower at the side as the trains rumbled through, their black smoke making the darkness more intense.

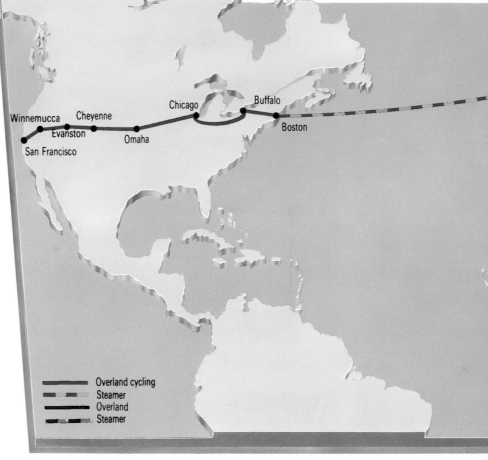

Overland cycling
Steamer
Overland
Steamer

the roads, and pleased that he did not have to dismount for horses, the English variety having long since got used to swells whooping by on their strange machines. When he reached Newhaven for the crossing to France, he realized that it was the first 300 miles of road he had ever covered without coming a cropper.

Through France, Germany, Austria and Hungary Stevens made good time. In Belgrade, the capital of Serbia, the last contacts with organized cycling died out. Close to the Bulgarian frontier a team of horses and a light wagon challenged Stevens to a race. The road was flat and Stevens went full speed, but the wagon kept up and they finally drew up together at the frontier post, the horses' sides white with sweat.

Stevens's greatest difficulty in Turkey and Kurdistan was to escape from the mobs of people anxious, indeed insistent, that he should show them how to ride. In narrow, crowded streets riding a penny-farthing was not easy, but he was given little choice. The Smith & Wesson came in handy when he was stopped by two would-be highwaymen, but in general Stevens found Turkish hospitality overwhelming.

In Persia, Stevens was summoned by the Shah to ride with him from Tehran to the summer palace at Doshan Tepe. Stevens was told to

The route Stevens took had to be altered radically on only two occasions. His arrest in Afghanistan compelled him to return to Constantinople to take a steamer to India. But it was in China that he encountered the most serious problems. He spent the first night in a Chinese village inn, amidst opium smokers and mosquitoes. The next night was worse. Pursued by hostile villagers, Stevens fled to an island in a river to escape them, then scrambled on to the next village. So it went on, the mutual incomprehension made worse by the lack of any means of communication. He was finally ordered to abandon his route through the country.

sprint, then to ride over rough stones, and finally to keep his balance when going as slowly as possible, in order to show what the first bicycle ever to appear in Persia could do. He spent the winter of 1885/86 in Tehran, sharing bachelor quarters with a group of staff from the telegraph office, and in March set off again, heading through Turkestan and southern Siberia.

He was arrested in Afghanistan and sent back to Herat, on the grounds that continuing would be too dangerous and that it would be impossible to guarantee his safety. Returning to Constantinople (present-day Istanbul), he took a series of ships to Karachi. From there he went by rail to Lahore, reasoning that it was as close as he could get to Furrah, in Afghanistan, where his journey had been so rudely interrupted.

In India Stevens found a magnificent road for cycling, "an unbroken highway of marvellous perfection from Peshawar to Calcutta," broad, level and smooth, and shaded on either side by trees. The only trouble was the appalling heat. A day or two's experience of the midday sun soon showed him that the Indian climate was not to be trifled with, and he even overcame his antipathy to alcohol when offered a "peg"—a big brandy and soda—by some servants of the Raj. Thus fortified, he reached Calcutta and took a boat to

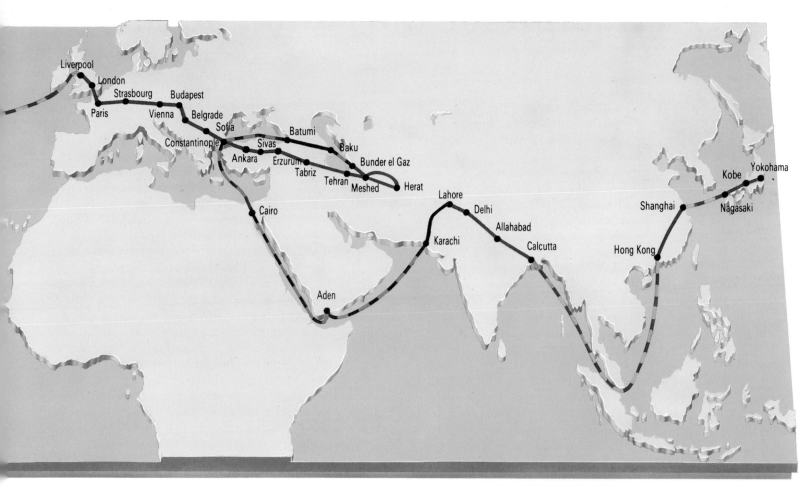

Hong Kong. Ahead lay the final stretch through China and Japan before crossing the Pacific back to his starting point in San Francisco.

Stevens's progress through China was less a bicycle ride than a series of arguments with bewildered officialdom. In Kingan-foo, a mob attacked Stevens who almost resorted to the Smith & Wesson before escaping in some peril into the Manchu quarter of the town, where the chief magistrate rescued him. At this point, it became clear even to Stevens that cycling across China was not really a practicable proposition, and at the insistence of the authorities he made the rest of the journey to Shanghai by riverboat, before catching a ferry to Nagasaki.

Japan proved a much more straightforward proposition. While life at a Chinese village inn had nearly unhinged his reason, the equivalent in Japan seemed close to paradise. Even the roads were good, so Stevens completed his journey to the port of Yokohama in high spirits.

There, on 17 December 1886, his journey by bicycle ended, and it remained only to cross the Pacific aboard the *City of Peking* for San Francisco. It had been an extraordinary journey and his fame was secured; others may bicycle around the world but nobody can take from Stevens the distinction of doing it first.

The return to Herat in *the heat was exhausting for Stevens, in low spirits at not being able to reach India overland. One of his escorts kindly exchanged his horse for Stevens's bicycle for part of the journey, but soon fell off and broke two of the spokes. The bicycle was repaired in Herat.*

Stevens warmed to Japan and its people. "The Japs are a wonderful race," he wrote. "They seem to be the happiest people going, always smiling and good-natured, always polite and gentle, always bowing and scraping." He was impressed by the awareness of Western dishes, when he was served beef and onions.*

A Triumph for the Automobile

FACT FILE

The first transcontinental car race

Date: June–August 1907

Distance: 9,200 miles

Duration: 61 days

Winner: Prince Scipione Borghese/Itala

Prince Borghese undertook a reconnaissance of the first stretch of the race, the Nankow Mountains outside Peking. He was convinced the cars could get through, but only by dragging them up on ropes hauled by porters and animals, then lowering them down the other side.

On the morning of 31 January 1907, the Paris newspaper *Le Matin* issued what it called a stupendous challenge: "Is there anyone who will undertake to travel this summer from Paris to Peking by automobile?"

This was a bold suggestion. Cars were still in their infancy and for most of the distance there would be no roads to drive them on. Within a few days it was clear, nonetheless, that plenty of people were prepared to take the idea seriously. One of the first to respond was the Marquis de Dion, president of the de Dion-Bouton motor company and founder of the Automobile Club of France. In a letter delivered to *Le Matin* the same day, he declared: "The roads are abominable and often exist only as lines on a map. However, it is my belief that if a motor car can get through, the de Dion-Bouton will get through . . . I take up this challenge here and now, provided that I have one other car against me as competitor and travelling companion."

De Dion soon had his wish. In the first flush of enthusiasm there were at least a dozen entries, but these began to shrink as the difficulties became plain. *Le Matin*, meanwhile, changed its mind and decided the race should begin in Peking and end in Paris, rather than the other way around. Finally, five cars turned up in the Chinese capital on 10 June 1907 for the start.

Two came from de Dion-Bouton—standard lightweight 10-hp voiturettes, driven not by the company's founder but by professional drivers. There was a Dutch Spyker, a curious three-wheeled Contal, and an impressive 40-hp Itala, entered by Prince Scipione Borghese, an Italian diplomat and explorer who took the whole enterprise with great seriousness.

The cars they were driving were typical of the Edwardian era. The Itala was the biggest, a four-cylinder racer ordered by Borghese direct from the factory with minimal modifications. It had four speeds, right-hand drive, a conical clutch, magneto ignition, leaf springs, and could do about 8 miles to the gallon in favourable conditions. It was fast, able to reach 50 mph and heavy. The de Dion-Boutons, by contrast, were almost dainty, light 10-hp machines which their manufacturer believed would perform better on rough roads than the heavier Itala. The Spyker lay somewhere between the two extremes, with a 15- to 20-hp four-cylinder engine, extra low gears and larger than normal wheels to increase ground clearance.

All the participants agreed that they would travel in convoy through China and Mongolia, as far as Irkutsk in Siberia, offering each other assistance if needed, although this agreement seems to have been only reluctantly entered into by Borghese. Meanwhile, the Spyker's driver, Charles Godard, extracted enough money from a Dutch diplomat to pay for the petrol, which was being left at staging points along the way.

The five cars drove off in a line, led by one of the de Dion-Boutons and followed by a detachment of army officers on horses. All traffic on the northern side of the city had been banned as the cars accelerated through the Gate of Virtue Triumphant, leaving the cavalry behind. It was splendid, but short-lived, for two cars immediately took a wrong turning and were lost before they had even left the city. Borghese impatiently went on while the rest gathered themselves and followed. It began to rain.

The next day the first of the great passes over the mountains was tackled. Ropes were tied to the cars and porters urged into reluctant effort as they strained to drag the vehicles up muddy tracks between the rocks close to the Great Wall. Sometimes picks had to be used to clear away boulders, and coming down was even more

"Pékin-Matin."

LE PRINCE BORGHÈSE
premier du raid PEKIN-MATIN
sur sa voiture 24 HP ITALA
60 jours de voyage dont 44 de marche effective

A Triumph for the Automobile

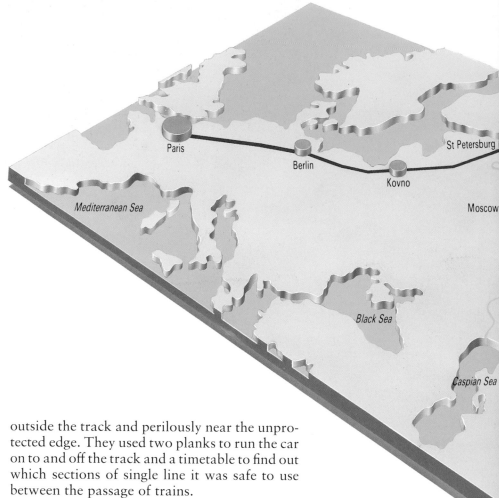

alarming, every man deployed to hold the cars back as the drivers stood on the brakes. Finally, seven days after leaving Peking the caravan reached the Mongolian border. They had covered 200 miles and had 9,000 to go.

Now at last they could drive, for the ground was flat even if it was not a road. Ahead lay a dash across the Gobi Desert, skirting around the whitened skeletons of oxen and camels which had tried, and failed, to make the same crossing. The three-wheeled Contal had been left behind, out of petrol, and its crew almost died before they were picked up by nomads and returned to Peking, claiming they had been betrayed.

To be fair, Godard had left some petrol behind for the Contal, a chivalrous gesture for it left him with too little to get across the Gobi himself. He believed that the de Dion-Bouton drivers, seeing his plight, would spare him enough of their fuel to get to the next staging-post at Udde. They did give him some, but not enough, and the Spyker coughed to a halt. The de Dions promised to send some fuel from Udde by camel while Godard and his companion, a French journalist named Jean du Taillis, waited. They had a long and agonizing wait, without food and water, before fuel arrived and they could escape. They, too, were lucky to survive.

The Italians, always anxious to press on, were the first to reach the Mongolian capital of Urga (now Ulan Bator). Meanwhile Godard and du Taillis in the Spyker drove nonstop from Udde to Urga, covering 385 miles in 24 hours, an astonishing performance for two men who a couple of days before were dying in the broiling heat of the Gobi.

Finally the great River Iro was reached. As the river was too deep to ford under the car's own power, the magneto was removed to avoid damage, the Itala hitched to yet more oxen, and dragged across, the water gurgling over the floor of the car and threatening to sweep it away. The magneto was refitted and the Itala was off, heading for Kia Khta and Russian soil. Here they believed that they had reached proper roads at last, for they had now reached the line of the Trans-Siberian Railway.

Unfortunately, the coming of the railway had led to a neglect of the roads. Vital bridges across rivers were down, and fording the rushing Siberian waters was impossible. There was only one option—to take the car on to the railway line and drive on the sleepers across the bridges, one wheel between the tracks and the other

outside the track and perilously near the unprotected edge. They used two planks to run the car on to and off the track and a timetable to find out which sections of single line it was safe to use between the passage of trains.

Behind Borghese came the two de Dions and the Spyker, enduring much the same difficulties. Instead of driving along the track, they put their cars in freight wagons and arrived in Irkutsk on the evening of 3 July, hard on the heels of the Italians who had left that very morning. By this time, Godard's car was very sick. The magneto was playing up and the rear axle had lost its oil after being holed by a stone. He plugged the hole

Prince Borghese's Itala had few modifications: strengthened frame, stronger springs and wheels, and the largest possible tyres, made by Pirelli of Milan.

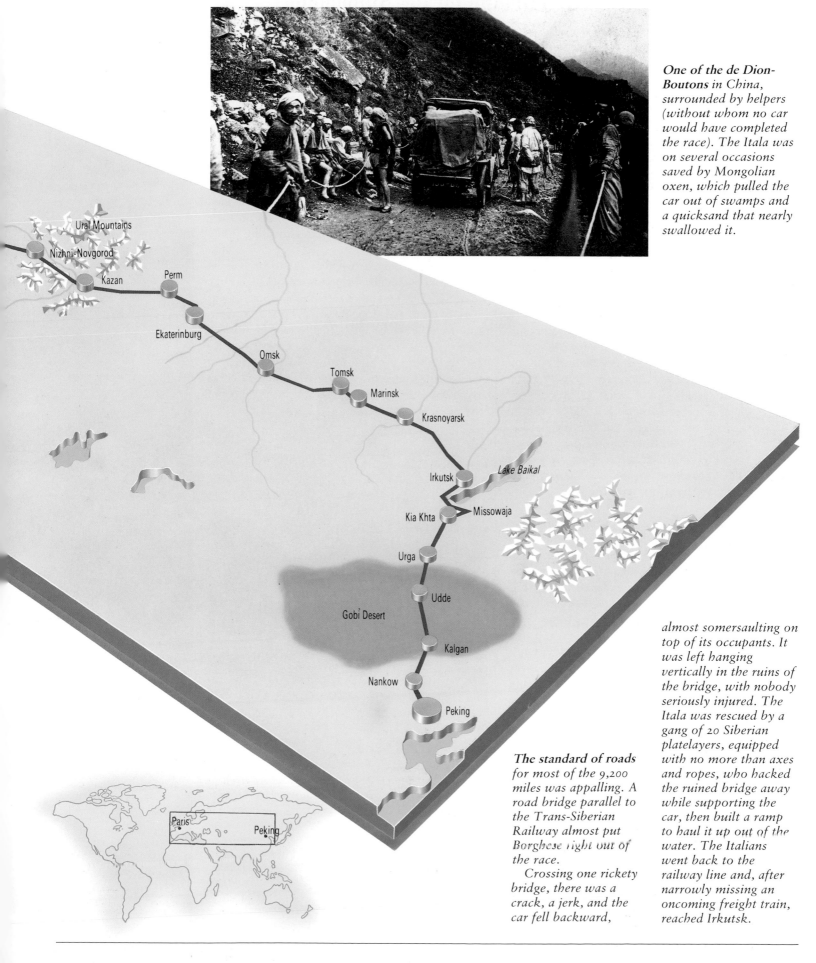

One of the de Dion-Boutons in China, surrounded by helpers (without whom no car would have completed the race). The Itala was on several occasions saved by Mongolian oxen, which pulled the car out of swamps and a quicksand that nearly swallowed it.

The standard of roads for most of the 9,200 miles was appalling. A road bridge parallel to the Trans-Siberian Railway almost put Borghese right out of the race.

Crossing one rickety bridge, there was a crack, a jerk, and the car fell backward, almost somersaulting on top of its occupants. It was left hanging vertically in the ruins of the bridge, with nobody seriously injured. The Itala was rescued by a gang of 20 Siberian platelayers, equipped with no more than axes and ropes, who hacked the ruined bridge away while supporting the car, then built a ramp to haul it up out of the water. The Italians went back to the railway line and, after narrowly missing an oncoming freight train, reached Irkutsk.

A Triumph for the Automobile

with a piece of bacon and refilled the axle with oil, but even a man with his innocence of motor mechanics knew this would not be enough. He cabled to the manufacturer of the car in Amsterdam for spares while the de Dions went on.

Help took some time coming, the spares being held up in Moscow for ten days by bureaucrats, but when Godard got going again he performed a miracle of driving. In 14 days he covered around 3,500 miles, a distance that had taken Borghese three weeks and the de Dions nearly five. Day after day he drove until his hands were raw. But even as he was doing it, a court in Paris was sentencing him to 18 months imprisonment for obtaining money under false pretences from the Dutch consular officials in Peking.

The Italians, marshalled by the superefficient Borghese, were now forging on toward Moscow. After a carriage-maker in Perm had rebuilt a collapsed wheel, they entered Moscow in triumph, the roads lined with Cossacks on horseback at 100-yard intervals to greet them. They stayed for three days of celebration before leaving on 31 July. Ahead lay only 2,500 miles of metalled road to the finish in Paris, covered with no difficulty. Borghese arrived in Paris to the sound of a brass band playing the march from Verdi's *Aida*.

Behind, the de Dions and the Spyker had become embroiled in political manoeuvres. While *Le Matin* had been obliged to accept that an Italian car had won the race, it could not face the fact that the two French cars still running might yet be beaten by the Dutch. In fact the three, reconciled after their privations, had agreed to finish in convoy. This was not good enough for *Le Matin*, which arranged to have Godard arrested in Germany on the false pretences charge. Du Taillis was disgusted at this and made sure that the Spyker and its driver got the recognition they deserved for a remarkable performance, for unlike the others the car ran the whole way virtually without a service.

The race had proved that the motor car could, indeed, go anywhere and that, all other things being equal, a large and powerful car will perform better than a small and light one. It was a triumph for the automobile, but it did little for the successful manufacturers. Itala, de Dion-Bouton and Spyker have long since joined the list of makes that have gone under in the tough competition of the motor industry. The memory of the great Peking to Paris race remains to make them immortal.

THE CHALLENGE OF 1908

Even at the time, the New York–Paris car race, sponsored by French and US newspapers, was regarded as a farce. The race began in the middle of winter. The seven contestants—a Protos from Germany; a Sizaire-Naudin, Werner, Motobloc and de Dion from France; a Zust from Italy; and a Thomas Flyer from the United States—struggled through the worst blizzards for 10 years on their way to San Francisco, sometimes covering just 7 miles a day.

Cars were shipped to either Japan or Russia, where the incompetent organizers changed the route and rules for the umpteenth time. Siberia was a sea of mud, and stops for repairs were frequent. Although the Protos had been disqualified by being railed to Seattle for repairs, it re-entered the race and was ahead for most of the way. Its entry into Paris was ignored; the popping of champagne corks awaited the arrival of the Thomas at the offices of the newspaper *Le Matin*.

The 60-hp Thomas Flyer (above) *was built in Buffalo, N.Y. Captained by Montague Roberts and later George Schuster, the car returned to drive up Broadway. The victors were congratulated by President Roosevelt.*

The departure from Broadway (right) *on Lincoln's birthday, 12 February, was watched by 250,000 people. Bands played the four national anthems and the cars set off on the 21,000-mile, 170-day race.*

Race to the Channel

In January 1930, a journalist named Dudley Noble carried off a very neat publicity stunt for the Rover car company, beating the famous Blue Train from the south of France to Calais. Soon the same feat had been achieved in a Vauxhall, and advertisements were placed in the British motoring magazines to celebrate the fact. The French authorities were not very amused, and nor was Woolf Barnato, chairman of the Bentley company and a well-known racing driver who won the Le Mans 24-hour race three years running in Bentley sports cars.

Barnato regarded beating the Blue Train as hardly worth bothering about. The train went from Cannes to Paris via Marseilles, which took it well out of its way, and then spent more than three hours wending its way across Paris from the Gare d'Orléans to the Gare du Nord. In a late-night argument with friends in Cannes, Barnato wagered he could do a lot better than either the Rover or the Vauxhall. His bet, he said later, was laughed off as a joke, for he asserted that not only could he reach the Channel before the train, but could actually cross it and be in England before the train pulled into Calais. "All right," he said, "we'll have no bet but I say I shall do it, just to prove my contention that beating the Blue Train deserves little merit."

The car Barnato planned to drive was a Bentley Speed Six saloon with very dashing coachwork by Gurney, Nutting & Co. of Chelsea, London. The car was based on the chassis of the famous Bentley Speed Six, normally an open car with a bonnet which went on for ever and coachwork in the familiar British racing green. The Speed Six is the classic Bentley, introduced in 1929 and winning at Le Mans for the next two years at the hands of Barnato. It also won the six-hour race at Brooklands in 1929 and the Double-Twelve and the 500 in 1930.

The car Barnato drove against the Blue Train was mechanically identical but had closed coachwork. He is said to have sketched the design on the back of the proverbial envelope for the coach-builders to copy. It was an early example of "fastback" styling, with the bluff Bentley radiator and bonnet followed by a sleek, low roof sweeping down at the rear.

Gurney, Nutting told Barnato that with a roof that tumbled so steeply they could not build a full four-seater, but were able to find room in the back for a seat set sideways between two cocktail cabinets. It was a pioneer GT car, with all the dash of a sporting Bentley and the comfort of a saloon. It weighed some 2½ tons, did 10 miles to the gallon and was capable of comfortably more than 100 mph. The rear window was a mere 2 inches high, which must have made rear vision tricky, but Barnato does not appear to have been the sort of driver who spent much time looking backward. W.O. Bentley regarded him highly: "The best driver we ever had, and I consider the best British driver of his day . . . the only driver who never made a mistake."

He opted to take with him a friend, Dale Bourne, a well-known amateur golfer who could take over the driving if Barnato became too tired. They sat in the Carlton Bar in Cannes until they heard that the train had left, at 5.54 in the evening of 13 March 1930. They finished their drinks in no particular hurry, and left.

The trip had required a certain degree of planning, because Barnato had to be sure of finding supplies of petrol in the middle of the night, by no means as easy then as it would be now. He topped up first at Aix-en-Provence, after a mere 100 miles, providing enough petrol to reach Lyons, where he had arranged for a garage to stay open after midnight. The next fuel stop was at Auxerre, where a petrol tanker had been paid to wait on the bypass to fill the Bentley. Arriving in Auxerre a little behind schedule at 4.20 a.m., Barnato took a while to locate the tanker which had driven into town rather than staying on the bypass.

By this time it was raining hard, which slowed him down so much that he reached Paris three-quarters of an hour late. Soon after leaving Paris he had a burst tyre and, as he had brought only one spare with him, he slowed down a little to make sure of preserving it to the finish. He pulled into the quayside at Boulogne at 10.30 a.m., allowing an hour for breakfast and for his papers to be processed before catching the 11.30 ferry. Quickly through the customs on the other side, Barnato and Bourne were soon touring gently up to London. They had proved their point, for they were in England long before the Blue Train reached Calais and saw no reason to hurry.

"On getting to London," Barnato later wrote, "I noticed the clock at Victoria on the Vauxhall Bridge Road signified the time as 3.20 p.m. I said

FACT FILE

The Speed Six Bentley that beat the Blue Train from Cannes to the English Channel

Built: 1925

Engine capacity: 6.5 litres

Power output: 160 horsepower

Maximum speed: 100 mph

LE NOUVEAU TRAIN BLEU VERS LA COTE D'AZUR

to Dale: 'Do you know, we've got to London before the train has got to Calais?' So to confirm this we clocked into Bourne's club, the Conservative in St James's Street. Then I thought we ought to register our arrival with the Royal Automobile Club. The news of our successful run had apparently already preceded us, for the hall porter was waiting with the time clock message stamping machine to 'mark our cards'."

Over the rough French roads of the day Barnato had driven between Cannes and Boulogne at an average of just over 45 mph. He might have been quicker but in case his elaborate arrangements for refuelling failed, he had filled the boot with spare cans of petrol, as a result of which he had so much weight in the tail that he could not do more than about 80 mph without

The oil painting by Terence Cuneo (b.1907) that illustrates a fictitious moment in the race between the Paris, Lyons and Mediterranean Railway 4-8-2 and Woolf Barnato's Bentley. "Le Train Bleu" (left) was even more luxurious than the Orient Express. It attracted the most fashionable clientele and was celebrated in paintings and by the eponymous ballet score by Milhaud.

Race to the Channel

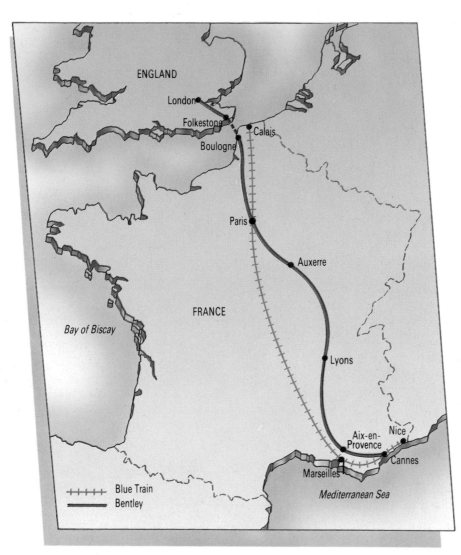

British passengers were conveyed from London to Calais by the Club Train, operated by Georges Nagelmackers's La Compagnie Internationale, which also ran the Blue Train and the Orient Express. In Paris the Calais portion was united with coaches from Berlin, St Petersburg, Warsaw and Vienna, allowing time for shopping before dinner in the train's Pergola Restaurant. From Marseilles the train swung east to run along the Riviera through Antibes to Nice. The train helped create the Côte d'Azur.

the springs bottoming. The average speed, very high by the standards of the day, only went to show, Barnato said, what a high average can be maintained over a long distance by not stopping for refreshments. He drove the whole way except for two hours near Paris, where his eyes needed a rest from the strain of driving in fog and rain.

The French motoring authorities were incensed when they heard of the exploit, accusing Bentley of advertising an unofficial trial. In fact, no advertisements were placed, although the story was reported in the motoring press. The French Society of Motor Manufacturers banned Bentley from the 1930 Paris Salon and attempted to impose a fine of £160 on the Bentley company for racing on the roads of France without their permission. The fine was never paid.

Barnato did not hold on to the car for long, for later in 1930 it was advertised for sale in *Autocar* as a "Special Streamline Coupé" indistinguish-

able from new, an exceptional bargain at £345. Subsequently the car was owned by Lord Brougham and Vaux, and by racing driver Charles Mortimer before being sold in 1941 to Reg Potter, who stored it for many years in a garage in the Midlands.

Finally, in 1968, the car enthusiast Hugh Harben persuaded Potter to sell it. By this time it was looking sorry for itself but a complete rebuild restored it to more or less original condition. Harben made a few changes which today's restorers would frown at, fitting a sun roof and deepening the letterbox shaped rear window. But by the time he had finished, the car was once more in magnificent condition.

The Speed Six remains one of the most interesting cars from Bentley's great years. The irony is that it is remembered for a feat carried out by Barnato simply to demonstrate how insignificant it was to beat the Blue Train home from the south of France.

Hugh Harben bought the Bentley in 1968, by which time it was in a poor state of repair. With a good deal of work he restored the car almost to its original condition (left). It is now deep green below the waist line whereas before it was plain black. When Barnato sold the car in 1930, the advertisement (below) referred to him as "a world-famous racing motorist".

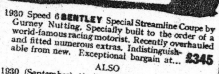

BENTLEY BARGAINS

1930 Speed 6 **BENTLEY** Special Streamline Coupe by Gurney Nutting. Specially built to the order of a world-famous racing motorist. Recently overhauled and fitted numerous extras. Indistinguishable from new. Exceptional bargain at... **£345**

ALSO

1930 (September) 4½ litre **BENTLEY** Vanden Plas tourer. New tyres. D.W.S. Jacks. As new £265 throughout **£265**

AND

1929 4½ litre **BENTLEY** Sun Saloon. Recent overhaul cost £100. Receipts available... **£215**

Many other secondhand bargains in all makes.

FRANCE, RADFORD & Co., Ltd.
48, ALFRED PLACE, South Kensington Station, S.W.7. Kensington 6642 3.

The Speed Six had a fixed-head long-stroke engine of six cylinders and 6.5 litres, capable of producing 160 hp at 3,500 rpm. The single overhead camshaft was driven by three coupling rods from the crankshaft and operated 24 small-diameter valves through rockers. The chassis was simple, with semi-elliptical springs front and rear. Later Bentley Continentals were to have a somewhat similar shaped roof, sweeping down to the rear. Woolf Barnato is seen here proudly standing next to his new car.

Across the Darien Gap

A narrow isthmus, coiling and twisting like a length of rope, joins together the two great landmasses of North and South America. At its thinnest, the neck of land provides the point at which the Caribbean is joined to the Pacific by the Panama Canal. To the south, straddling the border between Panama and Colombia, lies an area of swamp, jungle and mountain which is so impenetrable that no road or railway has ever been cut through it. For 200 miles the jungles of the Darien Gap prevent all movement and cut off South America from Central and North America as tightly as a cork seals a bottle. It is the only break in a highway that otherwise runs from the Arctic Circle to Tierra del Fuego.

In the early 1970s a group from the US, Panama and Colombia tried to prove that this gap could be bridged. They inspired an expedition which set out to be the first to drive all the way from north to south, taking specially prepared vehicles through the swamps and jungles of the Darien Gap, acting as pathfinders for the engineers who would one day build the road. A team of British servicemen and civilians, led by Major John Blashford-Snell of the Royal Engineers, set out to show that the gap could be crossed using a new model of vehicle, the Range-Rover, made by the Rover company.

Major Blashford-Snell and his party would not be the first people ever to cross the gap. That had been done on foot, and even in vehicles, but never in a single campaign. Previous crossings had been interrupted and resumed the following season, or had been abandoned altogether. The full journey, from Alaska to Tierra del Fuego, was 18,000 miles long. All but 250 miles of it was pretty straightforward motoring, although an accident in Canada raised doubts about the wisdom of using a new vehicle on such a demanding journey; it took 12 days for the parts to be sent from England to repair it. But much greater difficulties lay ahead.

Blashford-Snell had insisted that an advance reconnoitre should be done to assess the difficulties. A young Irish explorer, Brendan O'Brien, walked the course on foot, returning exhausted, covered in insect bites, and obviously ill. Once discharged from the Hospital for Tropical Diseases, O'Brien reported that the job might be possible but he wanted no part of it.

Only slightly daunted, the major assembled a large party, including 25 Royal Engineers, a Beaver aircraft and helicopters to provide airdrops during the crossing, 28 pack ponies, together with scientists, veterinarians and additional support from the armed forces of Panama and Colombia. It began to assume the proportions of a wartime task force: 59 men and 5 women linking up with 40 Panamanian and 30 Colombian servicemen in early January 1972.

Despite careful planning, the first few days of real jungle exposed the weaknesses of the equipment. As a form of mechanical packhorse the expedition had taken some "Hillbillies"—small vehicles like tracked wheelbarrows that in English conditions could carry a 500 lb load, steered by a man holding on to two handles at the back. In the swamps of Darien, the tracks were quickly clogged with mud which set solid in the heat. Unless the tracks were cleared out every 200 yards, progress was impossible. Eventually the Hillbillies had to be abandoned.

More serious were the problems with the Range-Rovers. Designed as a luxury road car with cross-country capability, the Range-Rover was not really up to the job of crunching through the jungle on non-existent tracks, and hauling itself and its considerable loads up steep hills. Within 25 miles both front and rear differentials on one vehicle had blown up, tossing gear teeth through the axle casings as they exploded. When the other vehicle tried to tow the wrecked one out, its differential also failed. It was an embarrassing way to discover a weakness in the vehicles, the more so when it took a month for spares to reach the jungle and they promptly failed again.

By this time Blashford-Snell was growing anxious. He knew that they had only 100 days to make the crossing if the weather were not to turn against them. Time was passing and very little progress had been made. Close to desperation, he bought a secondhand Land-Rover from a dealer in Panama. It had been in an accident and had a dented roof, but this was unimportant.

Fortunately the Land-Rover performed superbly, running for 70 days in four-wheel drive, and for almost the entire time in first gear. On impossible slopes—and some were nearly vertical—the winch was used to haul the vehicle up. The only problem was that at a certain point

FACT FILE

The most gruelling test of man and machine

Date: 1971/72

Distance: 17,000 miles

Duration: 190 days

the slope would become so steep that petrol stopped reaching the carburettor and the oil warning light came on. The drivers gritted their teeth and pressed on.

If the vehicles were finding the trip a bit of a strain, the same could be said for the participants. It was an endless slog, days of hard work and poor rations interrupted by nights of discomfort amid the ghastly noises of the jungle. Saws whining, axes swinging, the advance party hacked their way forward, creating a path wide enough for the Range-Rovers to drag themselves through. Dozens of bridges were built to cross streams and ravines. Every night Blashford-Snell made contact by radio with his far-flung party,

calling base camp to fly in spares and rations. Tempers frayed as the jungle took its toll. Several members of the party had to be flown out, unfit to continue the nightmare journey.

In front was a team of Gurkhas, tough men from the mountains of Nepal who have served with distinction in the British Army for generations. Behind them were the engineers with the Land-Rover, chain saws, axes, aluminium bridging ladders and tools. Then came a long caravan of men, women and horses, with the Range-Rovers bringing up the rear. The scientific party had scooted off to carry out their work.

Drama turned into tragedy. Captain Jeremy Groves, acting as reconnaissance officer for the

The two Range-Rovers were heavily overloaded at the beginning, contributing to the strain on the differentials. These were broken by the flywheel effect of the special tyres with which the vehicles were fitted to cross swamps. Five differentials failed and had to be replaced by Rover engineers flown out from Britain.

The Pan-American Highway stretches from the Arctic Circle to Tierra del Fuego apart from a 200-mile break where the jungles and swamps of the Darien Gap have prevented the construction of a road or railway.

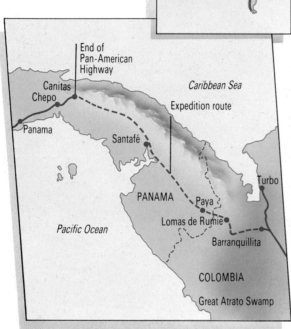

main party, was being taken by boat with an officer and five Colombian marines to a gunboat which would carry them to the Atrato River. In rough water, their boat went down. Groves was carrying a briefcase full of vital documents and cash, and like the others was dressed in full kit, with boots, a revolver and a machete. Grabbing the briefcase he made for the shore, which he reached exhausted and nearly spent. Struggling to a nearby Shell depot to call for help, he found the Colombian officer, the only other survivor. When bodies of the drowned marines were washed ashore, they had been hideously disfigured by crabs.

By this time, the party was divided and discontented. Several were unhappy with Blashford-Snell's leadership, while those responsible for the Range-Rovers were worried that an expedition intended to provide good publicity would merely emphasize the vehicle's failings. Those unused to the Army command structure found it difficult to respond to Blashford-Snell's

orders when they thought them to be wrong.

But in reality it was too late to quibble. They would have to sink or swim with the leader they had; and it would have needed a man of superhuman qualities and saintly patience to keep this heterogeneous party happy. Blashford-Snell remained openly confident, not wishing others in the party to become aware of his doubts. Wearing a white pith helmet which made him look like a nineteenth-century British colonialist, he became the lightning conductor for the expedition's woes.

Two of the worst sections of the journey lay across Pucuru Heights and the Atrato Swamp. In both cases rafts were used to transport the vehicles around impossible obstacles and, using the edges of rivers as carriageways, the Range-Rovers drove through torrents of water pulling rafts behind them. On more than one occasion the vehicles slipped into the river, but by changing the oil three times, drying plugs and points, and flushing the cylinders out with petrol, the engines

Thousands of trees had to be felled in the Darien Gap by power saws to clear a path for the Range-Rovers. In Major Blashford-Snell's words, "Our prison, for that is what it was, was illuminated by a dull green light, which at times gave an almost translucent appearance to this eerie world. Great trees rose up like pillars reaching for the sun . . . day and night, the jungle resounded to the drip, drip, drip of the condensed humidity and the occasional crash of some giant tree at the end of its life."

were once again coaxed back into action.

Crossing the swamp, Blashford-Snell remembers, was really hideous. The rafts were used but could not move because the surface was covered with a dense mat of logs and water hyacinth. Machetes were useless against this tangle, and the answer was found in lengths of detonating cord, flung out ahead of the rafts and exploded to cut up the beds of weed. Using this method, the expedition could advance in 20-yard stages.

By this time, Blashford-Snell admits, common sense had ceased to exist. "Many had gone down with disease and mental stress. We were all suffering from trench foot, and one man went mad when he saw a Land-Rover being winched up a cliff, he was so sure it was going to crash down and kill somebody. We had got through nine back axles on the Range-Rovers, and a relief party of Colombian soldiers had been ambushed by guerrillas and killed."

All in all, things had not gone too well, but at last the end was in sight. On 24 April the expedition crossed the bridge into Barranquillita with flags flying. The inspector-general of the province met them, declared a public holiday, and the exhausted soldiers made straight for a well-earned beer in the local bars. It had taken them 99 days. By 26 April they were in Bogotá, and from here it was a simple enough drive to Tierra del Fuego, which they reached in the depths of winter, cabling to Blashford-Snell, now back in London: "Mission Accomplished".

The expedition had cost the princely sum of £19,000, not counting the contributions in kind, including rafts and vehicles. It had nearly been, in Blashford-Snell's words, "the biggest failure of all time". But in spite of the problems and the rows, in spite of the fragile vehicles, the snakes, the hornets and the horrors of the jungle and the swamp, they had got through. As far as creating a road across the gap, the expedition was a failure, for no road has yet been built. But it certainly has its place as an astonishing footnote in the annals of humankind's conquest of nature.

The Atrato Swamp would have been impassable without the Avon Rubber company raft, the only one of its kind in the world, which could carry a car. The 40-odd miles of swamp was a green morass of water covered with weed that was sometimes so thick that explosives or chain saws had to be used to clear a channel for the raft. Surveyors lowered a drum of concrete into the swamp; at 1,000 feet it had still not reached the bottom. Mosquitoes, snakes and alligators all added to the trials of crossing the swamp.

Mercedes and Moss: a winning combination

FACT FILE

The fastest time ever set in the Mille Miglia

Mercedes-Benz 300 SLR

Date built: 1954

Engine capacity: 3,000 cc

Power output: 290 horsepower

Maximum speed: 170 mph

1955 Mille Miglia

Distance: 998 miles

Duration: 10 hours, 7 minutes and 48 seconds

Average speed: 98.5 mph

Stirling Moss was born in 1929, the son of a racing driver who had competed in the Indianapolis 500. By the age of 14, Stirling Moss was already an accomplished racing driver, and he joined the Mercedes-Benz racing team in 1954 at the age of 24. He retired in 1961 after 16 Formula 1 wins. Few victories gave him as much satisfaction as the Mille Miglia (opposite).

Motor racing is a modern sport, but has quickly acquired its own legends. Among the most romantic is a race in Italy that was run 24 times between 1927 and 1957: the Mille Miglia. It consisted of a single lap 1,000 miles long, always beginning and ending at Brescia, although the route and distance varied slightly from year to year. On ordinary roads, the fastest cars of the day—and some of the slower ones—took part in an event that combined festival and competition. Hundreds of thousands lined the route, which wound over mountain passes and cut through historic cities such as Florence, Rome and Siena.

The drivers and co-drivers had to be ready and willing to change a wheel or carry out emergency repairs themselves, for their support crews were usually far away. When Juan Fangio came second in 1953, he did so in an Alfa Romeo which was steering on only one front wheel, the other track rod having broken. In 1947 Tazio Nuvolari, in a Ferrari, first lost a mudguard, then his bonnet. Finally, his seat broke loose from the chassis so he threw it away, grabbed a sack of oranges and sat on that instead.

The race went over roads that were rough and unprepared: blind corners, level crossings, manhole covers and other hazards made it exciting and also very dangerous. The only safety precautions, laughably inadequate, were straw bales lining the route in towns and villages.

The cars left from Brescia at one-minute intervals, with the fastest leaving last, which provided plenty of action along the way as the faster cars caught up and overtook the slower ones. All sorts of cars were entered, some of them hardly suitable for racing; in the later years there was even a class for bubble cars. But the real interest was focused on the fast machinery starting last, mostly Alfa Romeos before the war and Ferraris afterward.

Few foreign teams were prepared to make the trek to Italy to take part in so chancy an event, and non-Italian winners were therefore rare. The race was never won outright by a British or a French car, and only three times by German ones. The most celebrated of these wins came in 1955, when a young Englishman, Stirling Moss, drove a Mercedes-Benz to victory. The fame of Moss's win was ensured by an account of the race written by his passenger, Denis Jenkinson,

and published in *Motor Sport*. It instantly became a classic of sports writing, later inspiring a television play, *Mille Miglia*, by Athol Fugard.

Jenkinson and Moss had worked out that the only way a non-Italian could hope to win the race was by applying science. It was impossible to expect a driver to know every corner, brow, curve and level crossing on the course; even the top Italian drivers who had regularly competed in the race knew only a few sections perfectly. The answer lay in creating pace-notes, details of the course written down on paper from which Jenkinson could read as the race progressed. These are now commonplace in rallies, but were then a novel idea.

Moss and Jenkinson made several trips around the course (writing off one car and breaking the engine on another) and eventually acquired 17 pages of notes, which concentrated on places where they might damage the car, such as railway crossings, sudden dips in the road, bad surfaces and tramlines. The difficult corners were classified into three categories: "saucy ones", "dodgy ones" and "very dangerous ones", and where the road went over a brow Jenkinson made careful note as to whether it turned sharply or went straight on.

This meant that if Moss trusted him, he would be able to take blind brows at full speed, knowing that the road went straight on. A system of hand signals was arranged to convey the information, for it was impossible to converse in the car once under way. Jenkinson wrote down his pace-notes on a strip of paper 17 feet long, carried on rollers in a box with a window on the top; a handle turned the rollers.

A new Mercedes-Benz sports racing car, the 300 SLR, was the car that Moss and Jenkinson were to drive. There was a huge entry for the race that year—521 starters, who began leaving at 9 p.m. on the evening of 1 May. The turn of Moss and Jenkinson did not come until 7.22 a.m. the following morning when the silver 300 SLR, number 722, was finally flagged off. Ahead were Fangio, Karl Kling and Hans Herrmann in similar cars; behind were the Italians Eugenio Castellotti, Umberto Maglioli and Piero Taruffi in Ferraris. Denis Jenkinson takes up the story:

"We had the sun shining full in our eyes, which made navigating difficult, but I had written the notes over and over again, and gone

Mercedes and Moss: a winning combination

over the route in my imagination so many times that I almost knew it by heart, and one of the first signals was to take a gentle S-bend through a village at full throttle in fourth gear, and as Moss did this, being quite unable to see the road for more than 100 yards ahead, I settled down to the job, confident that our scientific method of beating the Italians' ability at open-road racing was going to work.

"Barely 10 miles after the start we saw a red speck in front of us and had soon nipped by on a left-hand curve. It was 720, Pinzero, number 721 being a non-starter. By my right hand was a small grab rail and a horn button; the steering was on the left of the cockpit, by the way, and this button not only blew the horn, but also flashed the lights, so that while I played a fanfare on this Moss placed the car for overtaking other competitors. My direction indications I was giving with my left hand, so what with turning the map roller and feeding Moss with sucking sweets there was never a dull moment.

"On some of these long straights our navigation system was paying handsomely, for we could keep at 170 mph over blind brows, even when overtaking slower cars, Moss sure in the knowledge that all he had to do was to concentrate on keeping the car on the road and travelling as fast as possible. This in itself was more than enough, but he was sitting back in his usual relaxed position, making no apparent effort, until some corners were reached when the speed at which he controlled slides, winding the wheel from right to left and back again, showed that his superb reflexes and judgement were on top of their form.

"Cruising at maximum speed, we seemed to spend most of the time between Verona and Vicenza passing Austin-Healeys that could not have been doing much more than 115 mph, and, with flashing lights, horn blowing and a wave of the hand, we went by as though they were touring. Approaching Padova Moss pointed behind and I looked round to see another Ferrari gaining on us rapidly, and with a grimace of disgust at one another we realized it was Castellotti. The Mercedes-Benz was giving all it had, and Moss was driving hard but taking no risks, letting the car slide just so far on the corners and no more. Entering the main street of Padova at 150 mph we braked for the right-angle bend at the end, and suddenly I realized that Moss was beginning to work furiously on the steering wheel, for we were arriving at the corner

The Italians' love of the motor car made the authorities more indulgent toward the idea of races over public roads than those in most countries. *Ordinary traffic was banned from the roads, but the only safety measure was a line of straw bales in towns. A fatal accident in the 1957 Mille Miglia convinced people that racing cars and crowds should be separated.*

much too fast and it seemed doubtful if we could stop in time.

"I sat fascinated, watching Moss working away to keep control, and I was so intrigued to follow his every action and live every inch of the way with him, that I completely forgot to be scared. With the wheels almost on locking point he kept the car straight to the last possible fraction of a second, making no attempt to get round the corner, for that would have meant a complete spin and then anything could happen. Just when it seemed we must go head-on into the straw bales Moss got the speed low enough to risk letting go the brakes and try taking the corner, and as the front of the car slid over the dry road we went bump! into the bales with our left-hand front corner, bounced off into the middle of the road and, as the car was then pointing in the right direction, Moss selected bottom gear and opened out again.

"All this time Castellotti was right behind us, and as we bounced off the bales he nipped by us, grinning over his shoulder. As we set off after him, I gave Moss a little handclap of appreciation for showing me just how a really great driver acts in a difficult situation.

"More full-throttle running saw us keeping the Ferrari in sight, and then as we approached a small town we saw Castellotti nip past another Ferrari and we realized that we were going to have to follow through the streets, until there was room to pass. It was number 714, Carini, so soon, and this encouraged Moss to run straight round the outside of the Ferrari, on a right-hand curve, confident from my signals that the road would not suddenly turn left.

"Approaching the Ravenna control I took the route-card board from its holder, held it up for Moss to see, to indicate that we had to stop here to receive the official stamp, and then as we braked towards the 'CONTROLLO' banner across the road, and the black and white chequered line on the road itself, amid waving flags and numerous officials, I held my right arm well out of the car to indicate to them which side we wanted the official with the rubber stamp to be. Just beyond the control were a row of pits and there was 723, Castellotti's Ferrari, having some tyre changes, which was not surprising in view of the way he had been driving.

"With a scream of 'Castellotti!' Moss accelerated hard round the next corner and we twisted our way through the streets of Ravenna, nearly collecting an archway in the process, and then out on the fast winding road to Forli. Our time to Ravenna had been well above the old record but Castellotti had got there before us and we had no idea how Taruffi and the others behind us were doing.

"Now Moss continued the pace with renewed vigour and we went through Forli, waving to the garage that salvaged the SLR we crashed in practice, down the fast winding road to Rimini, with another wave to the Alfa Romeo service station that looked after the SLR that broke its engine. I couldn't help thinking that we had certainly left our mark round the course during practice. Ever since leaving the start we had had the rising sun shining in our eyes and now, with the continual effects of sideways 'G' on my body, my poor stomach was beginning to suffer and, together with the heat from the gearbox by my left buttock, the engine fumes, and the nauseating brake-lining smells from the inboard-mounted brakes, it cried 'enough' and what little breakfast I had eaten went overboard, together with my spectacles, for I made the fatal mistake of turning my head sideways at 150 mph with my goggles lowered. Fortunately, I had a spare pair,

and there was no time to worry about a protesting stomach for we were approaching Pesaro, where there was a sharp right-hand corner.

"We were beginning to pass earlier numbers very frequently now, among them some 2-litre Maseratis being driven terribly slowly, a couple of TR2 Triumphs running in convoy, and various saloons, with still numerous signs of the telling pace, a wrecked Giulietta on the right, a 1,100 cc Fiat on the left, a Ferrari coupé almost battered beyond recognition and a Renault that had been rolled up into a ball.

"Through the dusty, dirty Adriatic villages we went and all the time I gave Moss the invaluable hand signals that were taking from him the mental strain of trying to remember the route, though he still will not admit to how much mental strain he suffered convincing himself that I was not making any mistakes in my 170 mph navigation. On one straight, lined with trees, we had marked down a hump in the road as being 'flat-out' only if the road was dry. It was, so I gave the appropriate signal and with 7,500 rpm in fifth gear we took off, for we had made an

Crowds were particularly dense at the start and finish of the race. Jenkinson described the start of the race at Brescia: "As the flag fell we were off with a surge of acceleration and up to peak revs in first, second and third gears, weaving our way through vast crowds lining the sides of the road. Had we not been along this same road three times already in an SLR amid the hurly-burly of morning traffic, I should have been thoroughly frightened, but now, with the roads clear ahead of us, I thought Moss could get down to some uninterrupted motoring."

Mercedes and Moss: a winning combination

error in our estimation of the severity of the hump. For a measurable amount of time the vibromassage that you get sitting in a 300SLR at that speed suddenly ceased, and there was time enough for us to look at each other with raised eyebrows before we landed again. Even had we been in the air for only one second we should have travelled some 200 feet through the air, and I estimated the 'duration of flight' at something more than one second. The road was dead straight and the Mercedes-Benz had a perfect four-point landing and I thankfully praised the driver that he didn't move the steering wheel a fraction of an inch, for that would have been our end."

By the control in Rome, Moss and Jenkinson were told they were in the lead by almost two minutes, leading Taruffi, Herrmann, Kling and Fangio. Their average speed to Pescara had been 118 mph, to Rome 107. Very soon after Rome they saw Kling's Mercedes off the road among the trees, badly wrecked, but it had no effect on Moss. On the next pass a brake grabbed, locked the wheels and the car spun. "There was just time to think what a desolated part of Italy in which to crash, when I realized we had almost stopped in our own length and were sliding gently into the ditch to land with a crunch that dented the tail. 'This is all right,' I thought, 'we can probably push it out of this one' and I was about to start getting out when Moss selected bottom gear and we drove out—lucky indeed!

"The approaches to Florence were almost back-breaking as we bounced and leaped over badly maintained roads and across the tram-lines, and my heart went out to the driver of an orange Porsche who was hugging the crown of the steeply cambered road. He must have been shaken as we shot past with the left-hand wheels right down in the gutter. Down a steep hill in second gear we went, into third at peak revs, and I thought 'It's a brave man who can unleash nearly 300 bhp down a hill this steep and then change into a higher gear.' At speeds of up to 120–130 mph we went through the streets of Florence, over the great river bridge, broadside across a square, across more tramlines and into the control point.

"Up into the mountains we screamed, occasionally passing other cars, such as 1900 Alfa Romeos, 1100 Fiats and some small sports cars. Little did we know that we had the race in our pocket, for Taruffi had retired by this time with a broken oil pump and Fangio was stopped in

Jenkinson (centre) and Moss (right) at the end of the race talking to Daimler-Benz engineer Rudolf Uhlenhaut. It was usual to end a race with face blackened from fumes, road dust and dust from the linings of comparatively primitive brakes. Jenkinson recalled Stirling Moss's comment on their victory: "I'm so happy that we've proved a Britisher can win the Mille Miglia, and that the legend 'he who leads at Rome never leads at Brescia' is untrue—also, I feel we have made up for the two cars we wrote off in practice."

Florence repairing an injection pipe, but though we had overtaken him on the road we had not seen him as the car had been hidden by mechanics and officials.

"At the top of the Futa Pass there were enormous crowds all waving excitedly and on numerous occasions Moss nearly lost the car completely as we hit patches of melted tar, coated with oil and rubber from all the competitors in front of us, and for nearly a mile he had to ease off, the road was so tricky.

"On we went, up and over the Raticosa Pass, plunging down the other side in a series of slides that to me felt completely uncontrolled but to Moss were obviously intentional. Amid great crowds of people we saw an enormous fat man in the road, leaping up and down in delight; it was the happy body-builder of the Maserati racing department, a good friend of Stirling's, and we waved back to him.

"Down off the mountain we raced, into the broiling heat of the afternoon, into Bologna at close on 150 mph and down to the control point. We were away so quickly that I didn't get the vital news sheet from our depot. Now we had no

idea of where we lay in the race, or what had happened to our rivals, but we knew we had crossed the mountains in 1 hour 1 min, and were so far ahead of Paolo Marzotto's record that it seemed impossible. Looking up I suddenly realized we were overtaking an aeroplane, and then I knew I was living in the realm of fantasy, and when we caught and passed a second one my brain began to boggle at the sustained speed. Going into Piacenza we passed a 2cv Citroen bowling along merrily, having left Brescia the night before, and then we saw a 2-litre Maserati ahead which shook us up perceptibly, for we thought we had passed them all long ago. It was number 621, Francesco Giardini, and appreciating how fast he must have driven to reach this point before us, we gave him a salutary wave as we roared past.

"The final miles into Brescia were sheer joy, the engine was singing round on full power and after we passed our final direction indication I put my roller-map away and thought 'if it blows to pieces now, we can carry it the rest of the way'. The last corner into the finishing area was taken in a long slide with the power and noise full on

and we crossed the finishing line at well over 100 mph, still not knowing that we had made motor racing history, but happy and contented at having completed the whole race and done our best.

"From the finishing line we drove round to the official garage, where the car had to be parked, and Stirling asked 'Do you think we've won?' to which I replied 'We must wait for Taruffi to arrive, and we don't know when Fangio got in'. At the garage it was finally impressed upon us that Taruffi was out, Fangio was behind us and we had won. We clasped each other in delirious joy, and would have wept, but we were too overcome and still finding it hard to believe we had won."

Their final time for the 998-mile course had been 10 hours, 7 minutes, 48 seconds, an average of 98.5 mph. Fangio, driving alone, was half an hour behind, and then came Maglioli in his Ferrari and Giardini in his Maserati. Moss and Jenkinson had created a record that was never to be beaten, for an accident at the 1957 race, and the realization that fast cars and crowds do not mix, brought the Mille Miglia to an end.

The restored Mercedes 300 SLR which Moss drove to victory, now in the Mercedes-Benz Museum in Stuttgart. The car has a 2,982 cc, 300 hp version of the straight eight-cylinder engine that had proved so successful in Formula 1 racing in 1954, fitted into a space-frame chassis made from small-diameter tubes welded together to make a strong structure. Suspension was by double wishbones and longitudinal torsion bars at the front, and swing axles, also with torsion bars, at the rear. There were large drum brakes, mounted inboard, and a five-speed gearbox set behind the final drive.

Supremacy at Le Mans

When Jaguar first won the Le Mans 24-hour race in 1951, the winning XK120C had never been in a race before. There was no sponsorship, no racing budget, no car transporters—the winning car drove to and from the track—and racing success was incidental to the main business of making cars. Only the Jaguar team leaders (first Stirling Moss and later Mike Hawthorn) were full-time racing drivers. Between 1951 and 1957, in those days of innocence, Jaguar's competition department won a string of successes, including five wins at Le Mans and victories at the other great circuits.

By the early 1980s, however, these triumphs were becoming a distant memory. Jaguar had been absorbed into the British Motor Corporation and allowed to languish. The quality of the cars was poor and it seemed that Jaguar was doomed to join other British motoring names like Riley and MG in the graveyard. Three things saved the company: privatization, John Egan (who arrived as chief executive in 1980 at the nadir of Jaguar's fortunes) and Tom Walkinshaw, a Scottish racing driver and developer of racing cars who believed that Jaguar's XJ-S might win races with him at the wheel.

The new regulations for international touring cars introduced in 1982 provided the opportunity, with a new class for cars that were based on their road-going counterparts, with only small modifications to engines, transmission and braking systems. Walkinshaw persuaded Egan that the XJ-S could be competitive in this new class, but was told that he would have to organize the entire programme from his own headquarters at Kidlington, near Oxford.

With sponsorship from the French oil company Motul, Walkinshaw entered the XJ-S for the 1982 season and did well. The following year he had a close battle with the BMW 635CSi, losing the championship on the very last race. But in 1984 there were no mistakes: the XJ-S won seven of the first nine races, making Walkinshaw champion driver. He also won the Francorchamps 24-hour race, the touring car equivalent of Le Mans. At last it was possible to imagine Jaguar repeating its great wins of the 1950s at the apogee of sports-car racing, Le Mans.

That, however, would never be possible with the XJ-S, for in the intervening years Le Mans had changed dramatically. No longer was it possible to imagine driving a car to the track under its own power, or winning with a slightly modified road car. Today Le Mans is a competition for out-and-out racing cars designed and built in the same way as their Grand Prix cousins. They may bear the names of the great marques—Porsche, Mercedes, Ferrari or Jaguar—but they bear little relation to the showroom products that these companies sell.

In fact, by the time that Walkinshaw began to develop a Le Mans Jaguar, a similar car was running in United States events, developed by a company called Group 44. Its XJR-5, using the Jaguar V-12 engine and driven by Bob Tullius, enjoyed some success in North American events, and it appeared as a Jaguar at Le Mans in both 1984 and 1985. Walkinshaw also entered an XJ-S in those races—though in a different class—so there was the curious sight of two Jaguar teams, neither of them under the full control of the company and hailing from different continents, running in the same races.

Tullius finished 13th at Le Mans in 1985, but by then Jaguar had decided that his car, designed for American regulations, could not be a winner in Europe. They backed Walkinshaw and his company, Tom Walkinshaw Racing (TWR), who in turn hired Tony Southgate, a well-known and successful designer of racing cars, to produce a new car, named the XJR-6.

The car that Southgate produced was based on the same V-12 engine used by Tullius, the engine that powers Jaguar XJ-12 saloon cars and was originally designed by Walter Hassan and Harry Mundy in the late 1960s. At 7 litres capacity, the normally aspirated V-12 with a single overhead camshaft on each bank of cylinders produced 700 bhp at 7,000 rpm. Its drawback was its weight, and to make up for that Southgate used lightweight components to try to get close to the weight limit for the class of 1,874 lb. He used the Du Pont plastic Kevlar, reinforced with carbon fibre, to produce a strong mid-engined car, with the engine itself acting as a load-bearer carrying the rear suspension.

Although a 48-valve engine had been tried initially in one of Tullius's Group 44 cars, Walkinshaw and Southgate chose the 24-valve unit for the XJR-6. The car was completed in the summer of 1985 and made its first appearance in Mosport, Canada, in August. It immediately

A Jaguar at dawn in the 1989 Le Mans, which proved an interruption to Jaguar's wins, when a Mercedes took the chequered flag. The previous year three of the five Jaguars completed the race (left), with the car of Jan Lammers, Johnny Dumfries and Andy Wallace winning the race—the first Jaguar victory since 1957. Lammers drove 176 of the 394 laps.

Supremacy at Le Mans

The Le Mans 24 hours can be lost in the pits, even if the pit stop is only for refuelling. In the 1988 race, the battle between the Porsche driven by Stuck, Bell and Ludwig and the leading Jaguar hinged on fuel, since drivers have a fuel allocation and incur penalties for exceeding it. Jaguar's success has been partly due to their superior fuel consumption: Lammers had $4\frac{1}{2}$ gallons left, Stuck less than half a gallon.

showed speed, sweeping past two Porsches, but suffered a wheel bearing failure, probably as a result of the exceptional downforce achieved by Southgate's design.

The first win for the XJR-6 came in the 1986 season, when Eddie Cheever and Derek Warwick drove the car to victory in the Silverstone 1,000 kilometres (621 miles). There was also a win at the Nurburgring, but none of the three cars entered at Le Mans was still running at the finish. A defiant mechanic from the TWR team spray-painted "We'll be back" on the deserted timing box by the pits before the disconsolate team left for home.

Over the winter of 1986/87, TWR made a number of improvements to the car, which began the 1987 season under the designation XJR-8. Several times during 1986, races had been lost due to engines cutting out as a result of fuel starvation, so for 1987 the three fuel tanks were reduced to one, with a better arrangement for picking up the last drops of fuel.

The 1987 season was a triumph, with Jaguar winning the World Sports Car Championship, which they had never contrived to do in their great days in the 1950s. They won eight of the ten races to finish well ahead of five different Porsche teams, but still the ultimate prize eluded them. At Le Mans, three Jaguars started, and one completed the course in fifth place.

For 1988 yet more changes were made to the car, which by now had become the XJR-9. Five Jaguars were entered for the race, but in practice the Porsche 962Cs proved quickest, taking the first three places on the grid with the first Jaguar occupying fourth place. For the first five hours

In motor racing tyre technology is tested to its limits, and sometimes beyond with tragic consequences. At the 1955 Le Mans a burst tyre caused a Mercedes to crash; the driver and 85 spectators were killed. An explosive tyre failure on a Sauber-Mercedes during practice before the 1988 race led to the team's two cars being withdrawn when no satisfactory explanation for the burst could be established.

the race was led by a works Porsche, but the number two Jaguar, driven by Jan Lammers, Johnny Dumfries and Andy Wallace, was never far behind.

The leading Porsche's engine blew up just before half time, and the race developed into a battle between the Lammers Jaguar and a works Porsche driven by Hans Stuck, Derek Bell and Klaus Ludwig. These three Porsche drivers had between them ten Le Mans wins, and Bell was going for his sixth win, and a hat trick.

Klaus Ludwig was unlucky enough to run out of fuel some two and a half hours into the race, losing a couple of laps as he limped back into the pits with the engine popping and banging, and some help from the starter motor. Refilled, the car went perfectly again and began to gain on the Jaguar, which had taken the lead. Though Hans

The winning XJR-9 in the 1988 race. After Ludwig's Porsche had lost time refuelling, he had to turn up the turbo boost to try and catch the Jaguar, running the risk of exceeding his fuel allocation. His only hope lay in a prolonged downpour of rain, which would slow all the cars and enable the Porsche to use less fuel. There was a localized half-hour of rain, but this only delayed the Porsche when it went into a major slide.

Andy Wallace, Johnny Dumfries and Jan Lammers (left to right) celebrate their famous 1988 win. It was a brilliant combination, although some were surprised at the choice of 27-year-old Andy Wallace who had never driven at Le Mans. He proved the wisdom of his selection. During practice he climbed his way up to being the 15th fastest driver.

Stuck drove as hard as he could, Lammers and his co-drivers were always ahead.

At the finish the Jaguar had just 2 minutes and 36 seconds in hand after covering 394 laps, or more than 3,000 miles, in the 24 hours. It was one of the closest finishes seen at Le Mans for many years, and the first time Porsche had been beaten in the race for six years. Porsches came second and third, with another Jaguar fourth, and Porsches occupying the next seven positions. Sir John Egan said: "Le Mans is part of Jaguar's heritage. I felt we had to win again in the 1980s to prove ourselves."

Nor was it to be Jaguar's last win in the race, for in 1990 they scored a one-two, after also coming first and second in the toughest endurance race in the United States, the Daytona 24 Hours. Nobody could now doubt that Jaguar was back.

The Fastest Set of Wheels

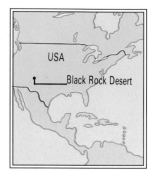

FACT FILE

Holder of the world
land speed record

Date built: 1979/80

Length: 27 feet

Power output:
Approx. 34,000
horsepower

Maximum speed:
650 mph

*Richard Noble
developed an ambition
to break speed records
when still a child,
inspired by the exploits
of John Cobb and
Malcolm and Donald
Campbell.*

The appeal that appeared in several motoring magazines in September 1977 was brief and to the point. "Wanted—650 mph car designer" it said. The man who had placed it was Richard Noble, a young businessman with not much experience of fast driving but an ambition to gain the world land speed record. Among those who read the story was John Ackroyd, an engineer who thought he could do the job. It was to take them more than six years to prove they were right.

The car they built was a jet engine with wheels. The days when the land speed record could be won with a conventionally propelled car, using an engine driving wheels through a gearbox and transmission, disappeared in the 1960s. The record for this type of car is still held by Donald Campbell's *Bluebird*, at 429.3 mph. Much faster speeds require either a jet engine or a rocket, but the choice between the two is by no means straightforward.

A rocket car does not need an air intake, so it can be slimmer, proportioned like a pencil. By contrast, a jet car must be much broader to accommodate its air intake, increasing drag and reducing acceleration. In practice, designers of record-breaking cars usually make do with what is readily available and, in the case of Richard Noble's car, *Thrust 2*, that was a Rolls-Royce Avon engine from a Lightning fighter that had come to the end of its life with the RAF.

*The size and shape of
Thrust 2 were dictated
by the engine, which
ran down the centre of
the car. The cockpit had
to be placed on one
side, balanced by an
empty cockpit on the
other. The frontal view
was dominated by the
huge inlet for the jet
engine, allowing a
limited but adequate
view forward for the
driver.*

By the time Noble appealed for help to design a record-breaking car, he had already built a jet-powered car of his own, *Thrust 1*. This was a simple machine, based on racing-car practice and a Rolls-Royce Derwent engine that he had bought from a dismantler for £200. Its chassis he found lying disused in a factory.

Thrust 1 gave Noble some brisk rides before he turned it over at about 140 mph during a run at RAF Fairford in Gloucestershire. It bounced and rolled over three times, but Noble stepped out unhurt. To go any faster, he realized, the project would need to be professionally organized and backed. He started with just £175.

The first thing he needed was another engine. Oddly enough, engines are one of the easiest things for designers of record-breaking cars to find because there are always jet fighters being scrapped and their old engines, despite being in excellent condition, are worth little. Soon Noble acquired an Avon engine from the RAF for £500, and it formed the basis around which the car was designed. The engine was 25 feet long, weighed 3,700 lb, and in its final form produced 16,800 lb of thrust, using full reheat. That is equivalent to nearly 34,000 hp, or approximately the same as 40 Formula 1 Grand Prix cars.

It was during tests on a one-tenth scale model in the British Aerospace wind tunnel that Noble and Ackroyd realized that *Thrust 2*, initially intended merely as a stepping stone toward a record car, might itself be capable of breaking the record. By 1980 the car was making its first tentative runs at RAF Leconfield and at RAF Greenham Common. The car proved a handful, but its performance was impressive. *Thrust 2* accelerated to 100 mph in two and a half seconds, then up to 200 mph in a further three seconds. In order to stop in time, Noble had to release braking parachutes even before he reached the end of the measured mile, so that they would fill with air just in time to stop him before he ran off the end of the runway.

At Greenham Common he set six new British land speed records, including the flying mile at 248.87 mph, without using reheat. Any higher speed would have sent him off the airfield and wrecked the car. These records were achieved without the full bodywork, the car running down the runway like a jet-propelled bedstead.

By 1981 the bodywork was complete and it

The Fastest Set of Wheels

The chassis was designed by Ackroyd on the space-frame principle, a series of struts and beams welded together to form a rigid box over which the body panels could be mounted. The space-frame was made by Tube Investments, using the same tubing that is used to make racing bicycles. GKN agreed to make the chassis at the company's expense. The steering was by rack and pinion, Ackroyd finding a heavy-duty system normally used in Leyland buses perfectly suitable.

The state of the track in the desert was the crucial factor in the final attack on the record in 1983. Ackroyd's solid wheels were designed to rise and plane over the surface, rather than plough through it. If it had been too crumbly, the drag would have been enough to wreck the attempt. Solid wheels had several advantages: they could be smaller and lighter, were cheaper, impervious to punctures and blow-outs and did not need a large stock of spares.

was time for a real record attempt. To find a sufficient stretch of flat ground, record breakers have for decades made for the dried beds of America's great salt lakes, usually to Bonneville in Utah. For the record attempt, the conventional wheels with tyres which Noble had used in Britain had been replaced by solid aluminium wheels 30 inches in diameter. This was possible because the surface of the salt flats is not rigid but has some degree of give, making it possible to use a solid wheel.

Nobody had tried this before, so it was a step in the dark; but in reality there was little choice, as no tyre company could be found willing to develop tyres for the speeds envisaged.

Thrust 2 did just enough at Bonneville in 1981 to keep the project alive. A problem of low-speed stability and the tendency of the wheels to cut ruts in the salt limited speeds, but Noble managed a two-way average of 418.118 mph over the flying kilometre. It was a long way short of the 622 mph world record, held by Gary Gabelich, but it was progress. Unfortunately, just as these runs were achieved, the rain began and the salt was soon flooded and unsuitable for record breaking. The team came home.

In June 1982, Noble came close to wrecking the car, when he failed to deploy the parachutes soon enough in a test run at Greenham Common. Realizing he was not going to stop in time, he put the car into a high speed swerve at 180 mph and slammed on the brakes. It skidded for 4,000 feet across the grass in a series of bounces, throwing dirt into the intake engine, before it finally stopped. A single error had done £22,000 worth of damage, but fortunately the engine had survived unscathed.

The car was rebuilt ready for a second attempt at the record, but it was late in the year before it was ready, and once again the weather intervened. Bonneville was flooded and in desperation the team sought an alternative site. They found Black Rock Desert in New Mexico, and put in some encouraging runs, reaching an average of over 590 mph for the measured mile. But Noble was still 30 mph short of the world record. There seemed to be insufficient power, the track was crumbly and several team members had to get home. The 1982 attempt was abandoned.

Noble knew that he had just one more chance; the sponsors who had financed the record attempt had been patient, but they could not wait for ever. During the winter of 1982/83, Rolls-Royce adjusted the Avon engine to produce more power, while Ackroyd altered the underside of the car, trying to smooth out the airflow. In September 1983, they were back at Black Rock ready for what everybody recognized would be their last attempt on the record.

The car performed well, but a series of

Tie-down tests at Reno airport in Nevada to check minor but vital modifications were made prior to the successful runs in September 1983. The tests in England had relied on the brakes to hold the car on full thrust from the engine until the reheat flame lit. The procedure in the desert was to measure speed over a flying kilometre or mile, in which Thrust 2 would take progressively longer run-ins to build up speed in steps. The car was always driven flat out for maximum acceleration. This used up 10 gallons of kerosene per mile. The smaller amount of fuel required by a jet engine compared with an even thirstier rocket was a major factor in the choice of engine. The amount of fuel required by a rocket weighs a car down at the start and makes it dangerously lively by the end of the run, at maximum speed.

niggling problems prevented Noble from beating the record. The engine refused to produce full power or the reheat failed to come on. They were close, but not quite there. They tried finding different tracks across the salt, even changing the 6-inch wide wheels for 4-inch ones, but that made things worse rather than better.

Finally, on 4 October, Noble managed a run in one direction of 624 mph, fractionally over the record, and turned for the return run. To gain a record, the speed is averaged over two runs in different directions and must exceed the previous record by 1 percent so the second run would need to be faster if Gabelich's 622.407 mph was to be beaten. On the return run, *Thrust 2* did everything that was expected of it, achieving 642.971 mph and peaking at a speed of just over 650 mph, its design speed. The two-way average was 633.468 mph—a new world record.

Across Africa on an Air Cushion

Late in 1969 one of the most unusual expeditions ever launched set out across the African continent. Its objective was to complete a journey of 5,000 miles through ten countries in less than three months, using a hovercraft to travel along the great highways of Africa, its rivers. It was one of the largest expeditions ever mounted in Africa, and the first time an air-cushioned vehicle had ever travelled on its own power south of the Sahara. The regions through which it went were among the most unexplored and undeveloped in the world, with some of the highest concentrations of disease. The purpose was to study the geography and wildlife, and to investigate how effective the hovercraft would be as a means of transport in a region with few roads.

The leader of the expedition was David Smithers, a journalist, publisher and explorer who knew Africa well and had, in 1968, led an expedition by hovercraft from Manaus on the Amazon through the Orinoco in Venezuela and finally into the Caribbean. The success of that expedition had convinced Smithers and his backers, the International Publishing Corporation and the Royal Geographical Society, that the hovercraft could accomplish things beyond any other form of transport.

The hovercraft had been invented in Britain in the early 1950s by an electronics engineer, Christopher Cockerell. His first experiments involved an old vacuum cleaner and a coffee tin, but he moved quickly to the first working model, a flying saucerlike craft that drew air in with a fan, and blew it out in the form of an annular ring around the periphery of the craft. He tried it over water, and it worked. With official support, patents were taken out and a full-scale hovercraft was built by Saunders-Roe. This was SR.N1, launched in May 1959, which demonstrated the feasibility of the principle. Later that summer it crossed the English Channel. It proved as effective over land as over water, making it the first truly amphibious vehicle.

By the time Smithers came to organize his expeditions, a much bigger and more practical hovercraft was available. The SR.N6, or Winchester class, was designed as a passenger ferry, able to carry 38 people at maximum speeds of 52 knots. The actual hovercraft, No. 018, was already four years old and had been used as a ferry and for charter work. To complete the journey it would have to travel through sea, swamp, sand, bush, rice fields, reeds, rapids and lakes, carrying at least 2 tons more than it was designed for. A total of 30 scientists, technicians, writers, cameramen and crew took part in the expedition, although not all of them were present all the time.

The journey began at Dakar in Senegal with a short sea voyage up the coast to St Louis, then on to the Senegal River. Shell had provided fuel dumps at 250-mile intervals along the route, mostly in fair-sized towns, and for the first section of the journey to Timbuktu in Mali, most nights were spent in comfortable lodgings.

On the very first day, after leaving the town of Richard Toll in Senegal, the hovercraft proved its value. They had decided to explore some swamps impassable to normal vehicles and travelled all day through empty country with not a soul in sight, disturbing enormous flocks of flamingos and pelicans, until the swamps dwindled and disappeared. Soon they were lost. Whichever way they turned, the water petered out and they could find no landmarks. Finally the pilot, Peter Ayles, opted to take to the bush. Ploughing majestically through grass taller than a man's height, the SR.N6 finally found its way back to the swamp and then to open water.

This side trip cost more fuel than planned, so an unscheduled stop had to be made at Kaedi, on the Mauritanian side of the Senegal River. At this small village the expedition was able to purchase 77 gallons of cooking kerosene—three months' supply for the village—and carry it back to the hovercraft in a selection of tin cans and other vessels. The Gnome engine ran happily enough on this fuel, producing a cloud of black smoke.

At Kayes in Mali, the first of the planned portages was carried out. One object of the expedition was to find out how quickly the hovercraft could be dismantled, loaded on to railway wagons, and then reassembled. The first problem at Kayes was getting the hovercraft out of the river and up 200 feet of steep bank on to the railway car. Ayles unloaded everything from the vehicle, took it back across the river, gave it full throttle and made a run for the bank.

"Everyone waited for the dull, rending crunch that would end our safari," Smithers wrote later. "Instead, completely obscured by clouds of

FACT FILE

The longest hovercraft journey

Built: 1968

Length: 48 feet 5 inches

Width: 23 feet

Power output: 900 horsepower

Weight: 10 tons

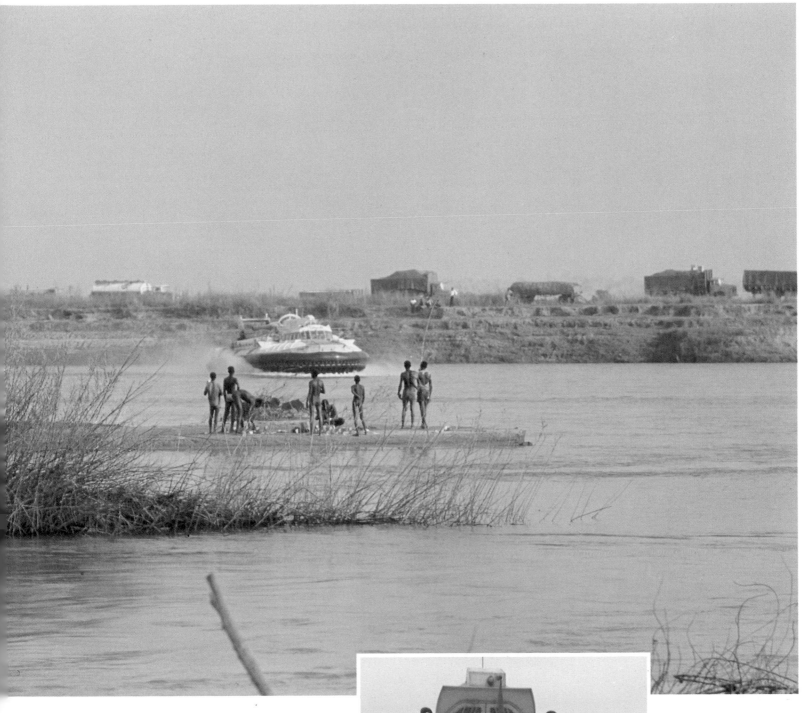

spray and dust, the giant craft roared up the bank and settled gently on its skirts as though it were an everyday affair." Next the engineers had to disassemble the craft, a job that took six men virtually the whole day in broiling heat. Finally it was in pieces small enough to attach to the railway flat-car with twists of rusty wire, all that the local agent for the railway could provide.

At Bamako the railway reached the Niger River and the hovercraft was reassembled. Here the expedition struck north toward the Sahara along the Niger, a river so broad that at times it seemed like a sea, until they reached Timbuktu, the golden city where the sand and water meet. Between there and Gao the hovercraft startled

*The SR.N6 crosses the **Benue River** at Garoua in Cameroon. The captain of Garoua's only ferry was mesmerized by the hovercraft and crashed his boat, which sank. Traffic built up (above) and included the lorries ordered to take SR.N6 overland to the Logone River at Yagoua. David Smithers (left) in Kinshasa.*

Across Africa on an Air Cushion

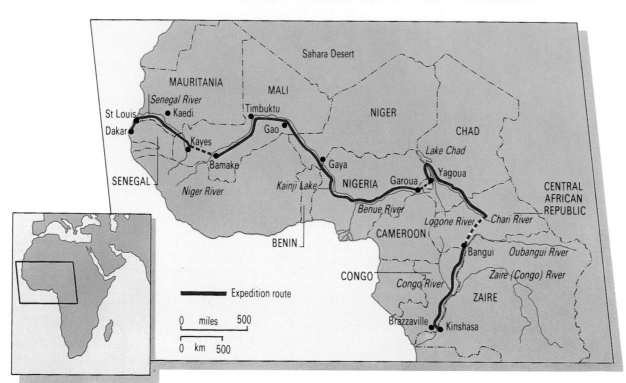

The route followed
rivers wherever
possible; the sections
overland caused
problems, but SR.N6
exerted so little pressure
on hover that it could
cross fields of crops
without damaging
them. For most of the
journey, the expedition
was overwhelmed by
kindness; they were
given messhui—a sheep
roasted on spits—on 12
successive nights.
President Bokasa of the
Central African
Republic and President
Mobutu of Zaire were
given a demonstration
of SR.N6.

*The hovercraft drawn
up on the north bank of
the Niger River, west of
Timbuktu, during a
stop for scientists to
make observations. The
team was made up of
scientists of many
disciplines—hydrology,
parasitology,
entomology, zoology
and anthropology.*

herds of hippo in the river, scattering them in panic. Although several submerged, fortunately none surfaced again directly beneath the hovercraft's skirts, and they all got clean away.

At the border between Mali and Niger lay the Labezanga rapids, hitherto uncrossed and with a fearful reputation. People asked with incredulity: "Are you really going to cross them?" to which the members of the expedition gave the answer "Yes, of course," as confidently as they could. In the event, it was all a bit of an anticlimax. There were one or two eddies and swirls, and a drop of a few feet, but in the hovercraft it was scarcely noticeable.

Near Gaya, a low bridge which did not appear on the maps blocked the river. To get around it the hovercraft had to cross rice paddies and sorghum fields, while Smithers and co-pilot Don Paterson held ropes to steady it. Finally, after edging under power cables, crossing a road and sliding down a bank, the hovercraft was back in the river the other side of the bridge. At Kainji Lake in Nigeria, a worse problem arose. Here there were supposed to be locks to drop vessels 100 feet from the top of a dam, but rats had eaten the cable insulation and the lock gates would not open. A 2-mile trail through the bush, followed by a descent into the river aided by some bulldozers manned by Canadian engineers, bypassed that obstacle.

After exploring Lake Chad, which involved a portage over the mountains by lorry, the expedition set off south again. Another portage was needed, again by lorry, to get from the Chari River to Bangui on the headwaters of the Congo. By now the two British Hovercraft Corporation engineers, assisted by the pilot and co-pilot and other obliging members of the expedition, were getting quite skilful at taking the SR.N6 apart and putting it together again.

Passing through the Congo, the expedition crossed the equator and celebrated with champagne. But soon disaster struck. Travelling along a channel between Congo-Brazzaville and an island the propeller hit an overhanging tree and one blade was broken. They began to drift as the engineers took a hacksaw to the other blades to

A bridge built over the Niger River by the French at Gaya on the border of Niger and Benin was built so low that few craft could pass under it. The plan was to use a gentle slope on the Benin bank of the river, but the prospect of war between the two countries made that impossible. A steep bank on the Niger side had to be negotiated instead, and a crop of 12-foot-high sorghum then had to be crossed before the river was rejoined.

re-balance the propeller. Going ashore things got awkward, for Congo-Kinshasa (Zaire) was in a state of near-war with Congo-Brazzaville.

Sensing danger, Smithers managed to get the expedition back on board and set off, although it was by now quite dark. By 11 p. m. they reached the confluence of the Congo and the Oubangui rivers and anchored, but then it became clear that the hovercraft had taken on a lot of water. They had to start the engines again and find somewhere safer to moor. Eventually, at 4. 30 a. m., they found a reed bed and hovered on to it, before collapsing exhausted.

From here to Kinshasa was relatively easy going, although the river was clogged with water hyacinth which would have prevented any other form of transport moving. The expedition entered Kinshasa accompanied by a flotilla of powerboats, sirens hooting, crowds cheering, flags waving. A Congolese guard of honour scattered in alarm as the hovercraft mounted the concrete slipway of the Lever plantation in a cloud of spray. The journey was over. It had taken 83 days, and provided the scientists aboard with unique opportunities for studying specimens. It had also demonstrated clearly how the hovercraft could go to places beyond the ken of any other vehicle. It had completed the last 300 miles with half a propeller, and throughout the expedition experienced no mechanical failures except for one ignition plug.

David Smithers hoped the success of the expedition would lead to hovercraft like the

SR.N6 being used in many ways in developing countries. The British government of the day was, however, reluctant to help and the African governments were too poor and too disorganized to help themselves. "The hovercraft could have done so many things," he says now, "it could have been a ferry, a bus service, an ambulance, or a flying doctor for many areas that desperately needed it." Even the successful SR.N6 that completed the trip did not survive long. The Ministry of Defence took it to the Ivory Coast for a demonstration, and wrecked it. Christopher Cockerell's invention had proved itself, but nobody seemed to care.

Transport over mountain watersheds on three occasions required the dismantling of the hovercraft, enabling it to be loaded on to railway wagons or lorries. Convicted murderers were loaned by the local prison governor to help the loading at Yagoua, Cameroon.

CHAPTER THREE

OVERLAND BY RAIL

T he Duke of Wellington had no doubt that railways were a mixed blessing. They would, he said, "enable the lower orders to go uselessly wandering about the country". How right he was. The nineteenth century has often been depicted as an age when the working class was oppressed. It is true that factory labour was no picnic, but the same steam engines that made it possible also provided a means of escape. No longer need people be tied to the same hearth from birth to burial.

The duke was present at the opening of the first great railway, between Liverpool and Manchester. Its success, much greater than expected, led to a tremendous and uncontrolled boom in railway building. Lines were constructed everywhere and thousands of locomotives built to pull the trains. Many of them were memorable machines. *Rocket*, still the most famous of engines, pulled the carriages in 1829 to open the Liverpool to Manchester line. The "American" 4-4-0 type of engine, the most numerous ever built, helped develop the United States and played a major part in the Civil War. The underground railway civilized London—for a while—and then spread to a host of other cities. The Orient Express brought luxury and style to continental travel.

In the twentieth century the railways have faced stiffer competition, from cars and aircraft. In the 1930s this competition was met by designing fast and comfortable trains which attempted to establish a new image. The American and Canadian expresses and, in Britain, the trains pulled by the likes of *Mallard*, the fastest-ever steam locomotive, kept up for a while a pride and confidence in the future of railways.

A new round of the battle began with the Japanese Shinkansen and the French high-speed train, the TGV. At a time when many countries have come to accept the need to contain pollution from cars, the TGV is an example of what can be done with modern technology to provide faster journey times between city centres than cars or aircraft can match. If the TGV really represents the future of the train, the revolution begun by *Rocket* more than 160 years ago still has some way to go.

Trial by Steam

Seldom has the human imagination been so rapidly enlarged as in the month of October 1829, when the directors of the Liverpool & Manchester Railway held a public contest to determine what form of locomotion was best suited to their new line. People to whom 8 mph in a stagecoach had been a dizzying experience were overnight introduced to speeds three times as great.

The event responsible for this change was the Rainhill Trials, a spectacle that combined the excitements of science fiction with those of the race track. The six competitors were given their own colours and listed on a race card, grandstands were erected for the public to view the events, a prize was offered to the winner, and there were even allegations of "nobbling" from the unsuccessful.

Few had ever seen a locomotive before, or had any conception of the technical merits of the contestants. At the time, steam engines were regarded as plodding heavyweights, barely capable of outpacing a man. The astonishment of the crowd when the locomotive *Novelty* sped by at 28 mph was captured by the correspondent of the *Liverpool Mercury*: "It actually made one giddy to look at it," he wrote, "and filled thousands with lively fears for the safety of the individuals who were on it, and who seemed not to run along the earth, but to fly, as it were, on the 'wings of the wind'. It is a most sublime sight; a sight, indeed, which the individuals who beheld it will not soon forget."

Novelty, built in just seven weeks by the London engineers John Braithwaite and John Ericsson and named after a theatre, was the popular favourite. Lightly built and swift, it seemed to the eyes of the time the most beautiful of all the entries. Much less strongly favoured was the ultimate winner, George and Robert Stephenson's *Rocket*, the only entry which met all the demands of the trials successfully and was still running soundly at the end.

Two of the entries now sound like a joke. *Cyclopede*, entered by Thomas Brandreth of Liverpool, was powered by two horses walking on an endless platform like the tracks of a tank, running around gear wheels on the vehicle's axles which transmitted the drive. *Cyclopede* could manage 6 mph with its horses at full stretch, too slow to meet the requirements of the

trials, so it was not taken seriously by the judges. An even less likely competitor was the *Manumotive*, a manually propelled vehicle entered by a Mr Winans, which put in a brief appearance but stood no chance of meeting the requirements of covering 70 miles at a minimum of 10 mph and pulling a load three times the engine's weight.

The triumphant *Rocket* was largely the work of Robert Stephenson, son of the engineer who had laid out the Liverpool to Manchester line, George Stephenson. Between them, the Stephensons had both genius and long experience, for George had built his first locomotive at Killingworth colliery in Northumberland in 1814. It demonstrated that the weight of the engine could provide sufficient adhesion between iron wheels and iron rails to pull substantial loads, as long as the gradients of the track were not excessive. Later, in 1825, Stephenson had provided locomotives for the world's first railway to operate a scheduled passenger service, between Stockton and Darlington. The first of these, *Locomotion*, weighed 8 tons and could pull a train weighing 50 tons at 5 mph along a level track.

The Liverpool & Manchester Railway was aiming at much greater speeds, and as the line neared completion the directors seem finally to have asked themselves how they could be achieved. Would locomotives suffice, or should the trains be pulled by cables operated by stationary steam engines located at 21 points along the line? The trials were an opportunity for the locomotive engineers to show that they could do the job. The prize was £500, over and above the cost of purchasing the winner, for "a Locomotive Engine which shall be a decided improvement on any hitherto constructed," as Henry Booth wrote in an advertisement in the *Liverpool Mercury* calling for entries.

It was fortunate that Booth himself was not among the judges, or the cries of malpractice from the defeated would have been louder. It was Booth who seems to have been responsible for one of the novelties in the design of *Rocket*— the multi-tube boiler which enabled it to maintain steam pressure so well. This provided a large heating surface of 134 square feet, enabling *Rocket* to raise steam in around 40 minutes and to maintain it even when running at full power. Neither *Novelty* nor Timothy Hackworth's *Sans Pareil*, its main rivals, had such an efficient

FACT FILE

Prototype for the world's first class of successful passenger locomotive

Date built: 1829

Weight: 4 tons 3 cwt

Driving wheel diameter: 4 feet 8½ inches

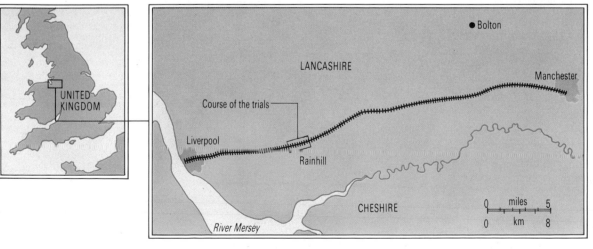

Rocket *passes a grandstand* at the Rainhill Trials, followed by Hackworth's Sans Pareil and Braithwaite's and Ericsson's Novelty. Begun on 6 October 1829, the trials were watched by 10,000 to 15,000 people who lined the 1½ miles of track along which the competition was held.

Trial by Steam

boiler. George Stephenson, a dour, ungenerous man, never gave Booth credit for suggesting this boiler design, which had been invented in France by Marc Seguin.

The Stephensons were able to run their engine at Killingworth before the trials, to sort out any small problems. It was then dismantled, taken by road to Carlisle and then by barge to Bowness on the Solway Firth, and finally by steamer to Liverpool, where it arrived on 18 September.

The rules stipulated that the engines were to be fuelled and watered and attached to trains three times their own weight. They were then to make a trip of 32½ miles by going to and fro along the track ten times, the distance chosen because it was equivalent to that between Manchester and Liverpool. The engines could then be refuelled before repeating the same task, the whole 65 miles—or 70 if the starting and stopping distances are included—to be completed at an average of more than 10 mph. On Thursday 8 October, *Rocket* duly completed this test, averaging 16 mph, and at one point reaching 29 mph. Despite several attempts and some good performances, neither *Novelty* nor *Sans Pareil* was able to match it. Both engines broke down more than once, and neither managed to complete the course.

There could be no doubt who had won the trials, and George and Robert Stephenson were immediately given orders for more locomotives. The first of these, *Meteor*, *Comet*, *Dart* and *Arrow*, were to be delivered within three months. During 1830 a series of excursions was run along the line to reassure the public that it was indeed possible to travel at 30 mph without giddiness or disturbances of vision while watching the scenery go by. The line was formally opened on 15 September, when eight locomotives, including *Rocket*, were made ready to carry 772 people from Liverpool to Manchester.

The first train, pulled by the locomotive *Northumbrian* and with George Stephenson driving, carried the prime minister, the Duke of Wellington, and members of his government. The high spirits of the morning were to be overshadowed by a tragedy: William Huskisson, MP for a Liverpool constituency, fell in front of *Rocket* which ran over his left leg. By early evening he was dead. As Frances Kemble, a young girl travelling on one of the trains, wrote: "The contrast between our departure from Liverpool and our arrival at Manchester was one of the most striking things I ever witnessed."

Rocket's driving wheels were 4 feet 8½ inches in diameter to help the locomotive attain the speeds looked for by the judges. These large wheels were driven directly through cranks by two cylinders inclined at an angle of about 35 degrees and mounted high on the boiler. This caused an awkward swaying action at speed, compelling the driver to hold on to anything at hand to stay on his feet. The position of the cylinders was later altered. Exhaust steam from the cylinders was blown through the funnel which was as tall as possible to create a good draught through the firebox.

Chimney

Chimney support

Piston

Boiler

Connecting rod

Driving wheel

Rocket's cylinders were 8 inches in diameter, and the piston had a stroke of 17 inches. Their location high up beside the firebox was unusual; it was not long before nearly all locomotives had their cylinders mounted at the front close to the smokebox. But it was the boiler that gave the engine its revolutionary significance. The heating surface of the water was increased by replacing the usual 2 to 3 large tubes by 25 smaller copper tubes, which can be seen behind the wheel.

The Stephenson family by an anonymous artist, with George Stephenson (1781–1848) showing the miner's safety lamp he invented to his son Robert (1803–59). The mine to the rear may be Killingworth where George Stephenson completed his first engine Blucher in 1814. Father and son had equally illustrious careers, primarily as builders of railways, although a locomotive building company, Robert Stephenson & Co., achieved renown.

Cylinder

Control levers

Firebox

Footplate

Water barrel

Civil War Combatant

FACT FILE

The locomotive used in the Chattanooga railroad expedition

Built: 1855

Driving wheel diameter: 5 feet

Weight: 22½ tons

James J. Andrews was from Kentucky, though born in the "panhandle" of western Virginia, and had worked as a "spy and secret agent" for the Union before the expedition. He was described by a high-ranking officer as "true as steel, and very smart". The locomotive chase between General *and* Texas *was to inspire many artists' impressions (opposite).*

The American Civil War was the first great conflict in which the railways played an important part. On both sides, many of the locomotives used were 4-4-0-type engines, among the most successful wheel configurations ever built. Easily the most famous was the *General*, completed by Rogers Locomotive Works in Paterson, New Jersey, in December 1855. In 1862, *General* was involved in one of the most spectacular incidents of the war, when it was taken over by a group of Union soldiers in an operation behind Confederate lines which led to a hectic chase along the track.

The object of the raid was to disrupt Confederate communications, particularly along the 135 miles of track linking Atlanta to Chattanooga. A plan was devised to destroy bridges on the track by stealing a train, driving it along the track and setting light to the wooden trestle bridges. Unable to pursue the raiders because of the damaged bridges, the Confederates would also be prevented from reinforcing their lines.

It was an ingenious plan, made possible by the ease with which agents could be infiltrated behind enemy lines. Twenty-two men under Captain James Andrews were detached from the Union army and, dressed in civilian clothes, they slipped through the lines at night.

They split into several groups, arranging to meet at the town of Marietta. Among their number were several who had experience as train drivers. They slept the night at Marietta, arranging to catch the first northbound train in the morning, due in at daybreak. They bought tickets separately, so as not to arouse suspicion, and got on to the crowded train when it drew in. The plan was to seize the train when it reached Big Shanty, 8 miles from Marietta, where it stopped to allow the passengers to get off for breakfast, a normal practice in those days.

The train was full, and the line guarded along its length by armed men. Could it be seized by a mere 20 men (two had overslept and missed the train) and make its escape before anybody noticed? As one of the party, William Pittenger, wrote later with pardonable exaggeration: "The annals of history record few enterprises more bold and novel than that witnessed by the rising sun of Saturday morning, 12 April 1862."

When the train stopped, the driver, fireman, guard and most of the passengers got off. The raiders moved smoothly into action. All but three cars were uncoupled, four of the men got aboard *General*, and the rest of the party, who had been keeping guard, jumped into an open boxcar. At the order, the steam valve was opened and they were off. As the people on the platform gasped and leaped for their muskets, *General* clattered off into the distance.

It had all gone very smoothly, but soon there was a setback. *General*'s driver, knowing that the train was about to stop for breakfast, had allowed the fire to run down, and the raiders quickly ran out of steam. They stopped, threw more wood into the firebox and in three minutes they were away again. It was unfortunate that the track was a single one, for it meant that the raiders would have to adhere to the timetable to pass trains coming the other way in loops.

In addition, they would have to cut the telegraph wire, which ran along the track, to prevent signals being passed ahead of them. There was no telegraph at Big Shanty, but they did not know how quickly their pursuers might reach one, so they stopped again to cut the wire. At the same time, others tried to wrench up the line behind their train, although it was difficult because they did not have the right tools.

At the first station reached, Cass, *General* took on wood and water. The man who supplied them was told by Andrews that the train was a special, carrying ammunition, and that the regular train was coming on behind. So persuasive was his manner that he was believed. The first major station, at Kingston, was 32 miles from Big Shanty and was reached in two hours.

Here the raiders were given the unwelcome instruction to wait for the local freight, which was coming the other way and running behind time. When it came it carried a red flag, indicating that another was behind it—and when that finally arrived it, too, gave notice that yet another train must come through before *General* could advance. For more than an hour the raiders were forced to sit silent in their train.

Meanwhile the dispossessed driver of *General*, Captain William Fuller, had not been inactive. First he had run after it on foot with two other railway employees because he had the idea that the train had probably been seized by escaped convicts who would drive it only a mile or so before abandoning it. A few miles out of

Civil War Combatant

Big Shanty he saw the broken telegraph line and realized the matter was more serious.

But at that moment he also saw a party of workmen with a hand car, which he immediately mobilized for the chase. In a hand car, he reasoned, he might easily manage 7 to 8 mph, half the speed of the train, and stand some chance of catching it at Kingston. They set off as fast as they could, and almost immediately came off the track where it had been damaged, landing in a ditch. They were uninjured, put the car back on the track and continued the pursuit.

Fuller knew he had just one chance. The only locomotive on the track this side of Kingston belonged to an iron furnace, located up a private track 5 miles long. If it happened to be near the main line, he would take it over and use it to pursue *General*. As they approached the branch line, the exhausted pursuers, who by now had covered 19 miles, saw to their joy that the engine, *Yonah*, was on the main track, aimed for Kingston and already steamed up. Fuller and his men leaped aboard and set off in pursuit. They reach Kingston just 20 minutes after *General* had finally managed to leave, and here Fuller transferred to one of the waiting freight trains.

The crew of *General* continued to put obstacles in the way of their pursuers, throwing out rail ties and tearing up track, and eventually Fuller was forced to stop by a long break in the line. Once again he continued the pursuit on foot, and within a mile met a freight train coming toward him. This was a train that had been held up to allow *General* past. Fuller explained the situation and quickly resumed the pursuit in the freight train, whose locomotive was another 4-4-0, *Texas*. His luck was holding, while Andrews's was running out. Fuller left behind the freight cars at the next station and went off full tilt in *Texas*.

By now he was hard on the heels of *General*, whose crew could hardly believe it when they heard a train whistle behind them. Frantically they threw more ties on to the track, hoping to reach a bridge and set it on fire before Fuller could catch them. Both trains were flat out, doing 60 mph or more, and *General* attempted to slow its pursuers by detaching cars and allowing them to roll back. Each time Fuller slowed down in time, coupled on to the car, and continued.

The 15 miles to the town of Ringgold were covered in the quickest time Captain Fuller ever managed in 22 years as a driver. Soon he was within half a mile of the raiders, who in

Near Big Shanty, *where the raiders took over the train, was a Confederate training camp. Captain Fuller, in charge of the train until it was seized, at first thought that it had been taken by deserters who had been reported as absconding from the nearby camp.*

desperation set their only remaining freight car on fire, with the idea of releasing it on the next bridge. Fuller and his men quietly came up to it and pushed it off the bridge. By now *General* was almost out of fuel. Everything combustible aboard the train had been crammed into the fire, and there was nothing left to burn.

Reluctantly, Andrews and his party were forced to abandon the train and take to the woods. As they did so, they put the train into reverse, hoping to ram the pursuers—but they left the brake on the tender, and *General* did not

The Western & Atlantic Railroad 4-4-0 Texas *was the best engine that Captain Fuller commandeered for the chase. Built by Danforth, Cook & Co. of Schenectady, New York, in 1856, it is now preserved in the Cyclorama Building at Grant Park in Atlanta, Georgia.*

General *was built in 1855 by the Rogers Locomotive Works in Paterson, New Jersey, for the Western & Atlantic Railroad. Later in the Civil War,* General *was the last W & A engine to leave Atlanta when it was evacuated by Hood's army.*

Survivors of the Union raiders in front of the memorial statue at Chattanooga cemetery. Front from left to right: John Porter, William Knight, Jacob Parrot, ?, Daniel Dorsey; rear: William Bensinger, ?. Of the 22 men, 8 were executed, including Andrews, 8 escaped and the remaining 6 were later paroled. General *itself is preserved at Union station, Chattanooga.*

have enough steam left to move. The raiders, who were unarmed, were pursued by Confederate forces and within a few days all had been rounded up.

There was a military trial, and eight of the party, including Andrews, were sentenced to death and executed. The rest were imprisoned, but eight contrived to escape in October 1862 from prison in Atlanta, Georgia. The remaining six were paroled the following year. The survivors erected a monument to their fallen comrades in the National Cemetery at Chattanooga; on the top is placed a small model of *General*.

Both *General* and *Texas* (or what is purported to be them) still survive. *General* is kept in the Union station at Chattanooga, and occasionally run, though not on wood. Oil is used, and the fuel tank is concealed under a huge pile of fake wood. *Texas* is kept in Grant Park at Atlanta. Many other examples of this remarkable American locomotive also survive in museums across the United States, but none is as famous as these two, which played their part in one of the strangest stories of any war.

Locomotives under London

FACT FILE

The pioneer
underground steam
railway

Date opened:
January 1863

Length: 3¾ miles

Traction: Steam

By the mid-nineteenth century, London's streets had become almost impassable. While transport outside the capital was being transformed by the railways, within the city there was congestion and squalor. A man could travel swiftly from Windsor or Oxford to a London terminus, but it then took him as long again to reach his office in the City.

Transfers between the great stations established by the rival railway companies were inconvenient, dirty and slow. The roads were clogged, the pavements filthy, public transport by horse-drawn omnibus was unreliable, and the cabmen were notorious for insolence and extortion. One physician declared with a straight face that a woman he knew had suffered a miscarriage "by incautiously venturing over the broken and rugged country that lies between Cavendish and Portman squares". The immemorial cry went up: "Something must be done!" But what?

Sir Charles Pearson, solicitor to the City of London, had few doubts. The railways, he declared, must be allowed to bring their lines right into the centre of the city, rather than decanting passengers at what was then the perimeter. He wanted a grand terminus at Farringdon Street, linked to all the railway lines to the north, northeast and northwest. This plan was never realized, but by the early 1850s two different schemes had been hatched: for a City Terminus Railway linking King's Cross to Farringdon Street and a North Metropolitan Railway running from King's Cross to Edgware Road, near Paddington.

In 1854 the two rival schemes were merged, and the House of Commons approved a railway to run underground over the whole route. It would link Paddington in the west to King's Cross and then go on to terminate at Farringdon Street in the City. It would be the world's first underground railway.

It was another six years before ground was broken. The railway companies were of several minds, the City was recalcitrant, private investors doubtful, and the Crimean War an inconvenient distraction. Finally, and largely thanks to the enthusiasm of the indomitable Pearson, work began at the end of January 1860.

The work of digging was done by teams of navvies who worked all night by the light of blazing flares. The line they created was covered by an elliptical brick arch, with a span of 28 feet 6 inches, over vertical walls three bricks thick and rising 11 feet. The load-bearing roof was made of cast-iron girders between 1 foot 6 inches and 2 feet 6 inches deep, spaced 6 to 8 feet apart. Where possible, the line was left open to the sky, for it was clear that ventilation was going to be a major difficulty.

In promoting the railway, the engineers had cheerily dismissed the problems of providing clean motive power as easily solved. Locomotives could be built that would emit no noxious smoke or steam, they declared, although no such design then existed. Early in 1860 Robert Stephenson was given a contract to build a smokeless locomotive and by October 1861 had produced a machine that seemed to fit the bill. The engine had a small firebox and a large mass of firebricks stowed away in a chamber in the boiler barrel.

The principle was to run at full blast in open sections of the track, generating enough heat to bring the bricks to white heat, so that they would supply enough steam to keep the trains moving in the closed sections. To reduce emissions still further, steam was condensed through a cold water tank under the boiler. The principle sounded fine, but the reality was rather different.

When tested in 1861 over a stretch of the Great Western's line near Paddington, the "Ghost", as it was known, performed poorly. It took three hours to raise steam, and once in motion steam pressure fell quickly before it came to an ignominious stop. The Ghost was quickly abandoned, and an agreement was reached that the service would open using locomotives of the GWR fitted with condensing devices to reduce the steam somewhat. With the death of the Ghost went the hope that the railway could be the pure, clean and comfortable experience its promoters had promised.

On 2 April 1862 the tunnels were virtually complete when the Fleet River took a hand. Along the retaining wall of the terminus at Farringdon it ran in a poorly built sewer pipe, 10 feet in diameter. This suddenly burst, filling the tunnel with sewage 10 feet deep as far back as King's Cross. The opening of the railway had to be postponed until January 1863, when a huge celebration was planned.

Seven hundred people were invited to travel

Baker Street station (above and left) was illuminated by daylight as well as gas lighting. This was made possible by the shallow depth of the railway, built throughout by the "cut and cover" method of construction. An open trench was cut, restraining walls were built on each side and the works roofed over. To avoid houses, the route followed roads almost entirely. The railway was built to accommodate the 7-foot gauge of the Great Western trains, as well as the 4 feet 8½ inches used by every other railway company in London. Three rails were laid for each line, with both types of train sharing the rail nearest the platform.

Locomotives under London

from Paddington to Farringdon Street where a banquet was laid out for them. The prime minister, Lord Palmerston, was expected, but declined to come on grounds of age, explaining in addition that he wished to remain above ground for as long as possible.

The next day the public had their first chance of sampling the railway and took it in their thousands. From 8 a.m. every station on the line was crowded with people, so many that for long periods they had to be turned away. The trains, built to the generous GWR proportions, were admired. They had carpeted floors, well-upholstered seats, panelling on the walls, and were lit by gas lamps fed from rubber bags contained in cylinders or boxes on the roof. There were three classes, but nobody was allowed to stand; the rule book, indeed, expressly forbade it on pain of being forcibly removed from the train.

Passengers generally seem to have found the ventilation acceptable, but the same cannot be said of the company's employees, who were forced to spend much longer underground. On the first day two men working at Gower Street station were overcome by the fumes and had to be taken to University College Hospital to recover. The success of the line meant that by the end of January trains ran every four minutes during the day, beyond the capacity of the ventilation system. On 7 March, when Princess Alexandra of Denmark arrived in London for her marriage to the Prince of Wales, 60,000 used the Metropolitan Railway in a single day as they rushed to see her. By April, more than two million people had been carried.

The company tried to minimize the effects of the sulphurous fumes in the tunnels, even persuading doctors to claim that they were therapeutic for those suffering from respiratory complaints. Guards, policemen and porters working for the railway petitioned the directors to be allowed to grow beards in the belief that the fumes might thereby be filtered, and their request, after discussion at a GWR board meeting, was granted. Eventually large fans were put into the tunnels to try to keep the air clear.

Soon after opening, the Metropolitan Railway fell out with the GWR, which was running as many of its own trains down the lines as it could, cutting the profits available for the company that actually owned the line. As the GWR had provided the rolling stock, it believed it had a stranglehold over the line and threatened to withdraw its trains. The Metropolitan quickly

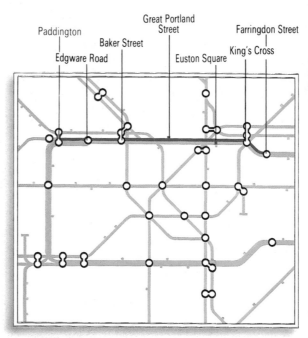

A trial run over the railway was organized on 24 May 1862 for dignatories, seen here at Edgware Road (below). The engineer of the Metropolitan Railway, John Fowler, is in the nearest wagon, wearing a pale-coloured suit and hat; on his right is the chancellor of the exchequer William Gladstone. The western end of the line was almost complete by the time this train was run. These dignatories were witnessing the creation of the first part of the London Underground system (above), which is still being enlarged.

Excavation at King's Cross, with the Great Northern Railway terminus beyond the workmen's hut. Engineers had many problems to overcome: keeping the cuttings buttressed to avoid damage to buildings above; underpinning walls; diverting sewers; and maintaining road traffic before the line was roofed over. East of King's Cross, along the old valley of the Fleet River, the railway cleared slum housing— an incidental benefit of much urban railway construction.

An "A" class 4-4-0 tank engine, one of the 24 original locomotives ordered from Beyer, Peacock of Manchester at a cost of £2,280 each. The engines were based on a design already supplied to the Tudela & Bilbao Railway in Spain, and were painted dark green. They had condensing apparatus to reduce steam in the tunnels and save water.

appealed to the other railway companies, who provided standard gauge trains, and ordered locomotives of its own from Beyer, Peacock & Co. of Manchester.

Unsatisfactory as steam power was bound to be, the underground's passengers had to put up with it until 1889, when electrification finally dispelled the dirt and smell. By then the Metropolitan had expanded into the District Line, a closely linked but technically independent company. Inevitably they fell out, arguing over the rights to different portions where the two lines overlapped, and the District acquired its own engines. Despite the disputes above ground and the smoke below, the public took to the new railways with enthusiasm, for they offered cheap, swift travel across the capital, something that no other form of transport has provided, before or since.

The Most Luxurious Train

Georges Nagelmackers was born in 1845 at Liège in Belgium. His father was involved with railway finance, and his family well placed to exploit royal connections to further his ventures. He died in 1905 at his chateau in Ville-preux-les-Clayes.

FACT FILE

Date: 1883–1977

Distance: 1,896 miles

Duration: 81 hours 40 minutes (1883)

It was an odd group that gathered at the Gare de l'Est in Paris on 4 October 1883. Among them were diplomats, journalists, bankers, a Belgian cabinet minister, a Romanian general, a distinguished French doctor, a writer from Alsace and a Dutchman named Jansson who appeared to be none of these things, but did not care to say what he was. Each man carried a revolver. They were greeted by flunkeys in eighteenth-century costume.

The party of 40 was the responsibility of a young Belgian, Georges Nagelmackers, founder of the Compagnie Internationale des Wagons-Lits et Grands Express Européens. The occasion was the inauguration of a new service which Nagelmackers had been trying to establish for more than a dozen years, and the VIPs he invited along were among the first to experience the joys of the freebie, travelling first class at somebody else's expense in the hope that they would bring lustre and publicity to the enterprise.

In that respect, the journey was a triumph, producing long articles in *The Times* and *Le Figaro*, as well as interviews and even books: just the kind of international reception Nagelmackers was seeking. The Orient Express was launched with a splash, a champagne-and-caviare experience at a time when most international train journeys were brutish and long.

Georges Nagelmackers's idea was to run a luxury train owned by him over tracks belonging to others, crossing frontiers without fuss while its passengers were cosseted by servants and insulated from the horrors of customs officials and the risks of brigandage. The inspiration had come to him in the 1860s, when as a 21-year-old fleeing from a disappointment in love—he was spurned by an older woman—he went to the United States.

There he experienced the mixed blessings of long-distance railway travel, rejoicing in the fact that a single train could take him right across the nation, but appalled by the crowding and discomfort involved. In those days trains had no toilets, and meals were taken in a hurry during brief stops. The food was usually awful and the train conductors were apt to blow the whistle for departure before you had had time to eat it. One British traveller, J.W. Boddam-Whetham, travelled in a Pullman sleeping car and reported that the horrors of the experience were indelibly impressed on his mind. The heat was intolerable, and the bunks so close together that it was not unusual to wake up with a stranger's feet resting on one's face.

Nagelmackers did, however, identify one overwhelming advantage in the cars operated by George Pullman—through running. Instead of having to change trains at a junction between different railroads, passengers could stay in the same cars while they were transferred to a different train. Although obvious in retrospect, this was not the usual practice at the time. Travellers between New York and Chicago had to make five changes of railroad, unless they chose to travel Pullman.

As Nagelmackers knew, the situation in Europe was even worse, with national borders adding to the confusion. He conceived the idea of a European network of trains, comfortable and well run, which passengers could make their home during the long journeys across the Continent. All that was needed was to persuade the railways of the benefits of the idea. They would collect the normal fares from anybody using the special cars, while Nagelmackers would cover his own costs and make a profit from the supplements he would charge.

For one reason or another this brilliant idea took a while to catch on. The Franco-Prussian War of 1870 put paid to the plan for a train between Paris and Berlin. And although Nagelmackers did well for a while running trains full of British empire-builders through Europe to Brindisi, where they boarded P & O ships for India, Ceylon and Australia, it was hardly what he had had in mind. That came to an end anyway when P & O cast in their lot with the French, who had built the first tunnel under the Alps and refused to let Nagelmackers use it.

His company faced bankruptcy, from which it was saved only by the timely intervention of an American, Colonel William d'Alton Mann. Frustrated by the Pullman company in his ambitions to set up a service of what he called "boudoir cars" in the US, Colonel Mann brought one to Europe. Nagelmackers was impressed, but had no money left, and Mann offered to go into business with him.

Mann was a rogue and a confidence trickster, whose source of money was never very clear, but he did Nagelmackers several good turns. He

*The **steamer journey** from Varna was obviated by the opening of
the last section of line to Constantinople in 1889, as advertised by
the Wagons-Lits Company.*

The Most Luxurious Train

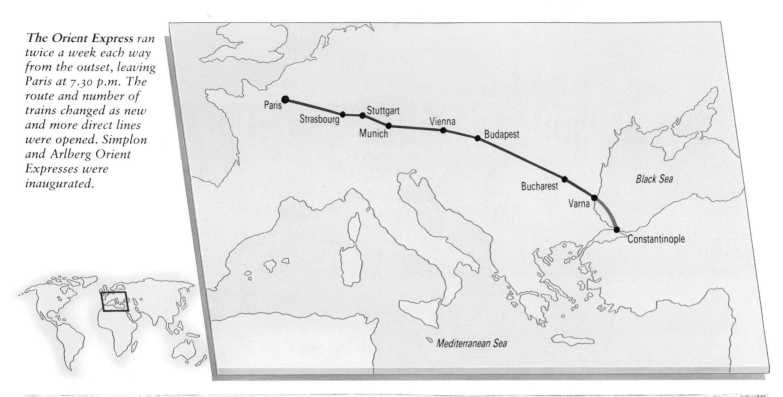

The Orient Express ran twice a week each way from the outset, leaving Paris at 7.30 p.m. The route and number of trains changed as new and more direct lines were opened. Simplon and Arlberg Orient Expresses were inaugurated.

The first restaurant car of the Orient Express had a ceiling covered in embossed Cordoba leather, walls lined with Gobelins tapestries, and velvet curtains. The five-course dinner was cooked by a chef from Burgundy, "not merely of the first order but a man of genius", as one satisfied traveller put it.

saved the company from ruin and saw off, by the clever use of black propaganda, an attempt by Pullman to establish himself in Europe. The open Pullman cars, he told the European railway companies, were an invitation to debauchery. Respectable women would be importuned in their beds by strangers, while unmarried couples would use the cars for their liaisons.

Mann was persuasive, and his boudoir cars gained business while Pullman languished. But just as success was beckoning, Mann got bored. Nagelmackers, seeing his opportunity, raised fresh capital and paid off Mann, who returned to the US with $5 million in his pocket. Pullman tried to do a deal with Nagelmackers, and was

shown the door. The stage was finally set for the Orient Express.

To begin with, Nagelmackers had done no more than attach individual cars to existing trains, but the Orient Express was designed to be an entire train in itself. As his 40 guests clambered aboard in Paris in October 1883, they entered a world entirely under the control of Nagelmackers and his company. The compartments, called coupés, were like miniature sitting rooms, with two red plush armchairs, Turkish carpets on the floor and silk wall coverings. At night, a comfortable double bed folded downward out of the walls. Between each coupé was a bathroom, and in a coach at the rear of the train

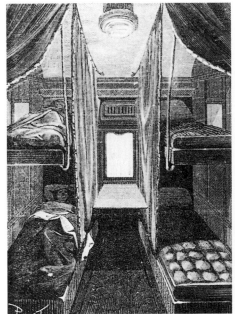

A compartment prepared for sleeping (far left) could quickly be converted into use for passengers by day (left). The beds were originally covered with silk sheets, wool blankets and counterpanes filled with the lightest of eiderdown. The early toilet cabinets (middle) had porcelain basins set in Italian marble with vials of toilet water and lotions beside them.

The dining car was panelled in mahogany and teak inlaid with rosewood and decorated with carved scrolls, cornices and scallops. Diners could place small articles in the racks supported by gilded brackets that ran the length of the car on both sides. Gold-framed etchings by leading nineteenth century artists hung on panels between the windows, and huge gas chandeliers gave a soft glow to the proceedings—the gas mantle had yet to be invented, and the naked flames had to be kept low to minimize the risk of fire. During the inaugural journey, a gipsy band came aboard at Tsigany in Hungary to give a concert of waltzes and czardas in a dining car temporarily cleared of furniture. As they struck up "La Marseillaise", the chef emerged from the kitchen, red-faced and eyes ablaze to lead the singing.

The Most Luxurious Train

King Boris III of Bulgaria (on the right) could not be restrained from driving locomotives of the Orient Express, especially inside his own country. On one occasion he stoked the fire too energetically and it blew back into the cab, setting the fireman's clothing ablaze. As the fireman leaped from the footplate to his death, King Boris urged the train on, alighting at Sofia to solicit the congratulations of the passengers for having arrived on time in spite of the accident.

ROMANCE AND INTRIGUE

Often exaggerated stories of skulduggery or illicit liaisons on the Orient Express have provided fertile ground for novelists and film-makers. *Stamboul Train* by Graham Greene was published in 1932, followed two years later by Agatha Christie's *Murder on the Orient Express*. In Ian Fleming's *From Russia, with Love*, the fight between 007 and a Soviet agent takes place aboard the train, and the plot of Eric Ambler's *The Mask of Dimitrios* is interwoven with its route. Alfred Hitchcock set *The Lady Vanishes* (1938) aboard the Orient Express.

Murder on the Orient Express was made into a film in 1974, starring Anthony Perkins, Vanessa Redgrave, Sean Connery, Ingrid Bergman, Albert Finney as Inspector Poirot, Rachel Roberts, Wendy Hiller, Michael York, Jacqueline Bisset and Lauren Bacall.

were shower cubicles. There was a smoking room, a ladies' boudoir and a library.

The destination of the train was Constantinople (now Istanbul), the Sublime Porte, capital of the Ottoman Empire and the point where Europe becomes Asia. To Victorians this was an exotic and dangerous place, for their concept of European civilization stretched no farther east than the borders of Hungary. Since rails had yet to be laid all the way to Constantinople, the journey was a complicated one, but it started easily enough.

From Paris the train crossed into Germany, through Strasbourg (then, of course, German), Stuttgart, Munich, Vienna and Budapest. At Augsburg, in Germany, there was a setback, for it was found that the dining car had an overheating axle box. Fortunately Nagelmackers had a spare ready at Munich, although it was an older type—a six-wheeler rather than a bogie car—and it ran so poorly that it became almost impossible to pour wine without spilling it.

In Bucharest, the journey took on a surreal quality. King Charles of Romania invited the entire party to visit him at his new summer palace at Sinaia, four hours away up a branch line in the mountains. Decanted at the station, they made their way to a hotel where a buffet had been prepared. Summoned into the presence of the king, they then had to walk up a mile and a half of muddy, unsurfaced road in pouring rain before arriving in a filthy condition.

Next the travellers entered Bulgaria, by crossing the Danube. No bridge existed yet, so they were forced to leave the train, cross by boat, and get aboard another train, operated by Austrian Oriental Railways, on the other side. It was five years before Nagelmackers's dream of a continuous track all the way became reality. Bulgaria was an eye-opener, a rather barren and melancholy country whose people seemed steeped in despair and hopelessness.

At Votova station, they were told that a fortnight before a gang of brigands had attacked the station, garotted the stationmaster, carried off his daughter and were about to set light to the place when they were disturbed and ran off, leaving their victims grateful to be still alive. The passengers on the Orient Express tightened their grip on their revolvers. Finally they arrived at Varna on the Black Sea, where a steamship was waiting to take them to Constantinople.

The return journey was relatively uneventful, enlivened when the train was joined in Vienna by fare-paying passengers, among them some elegant young women. The corridors of the train, wrote *The Times* correspondent de Blowitz, became like the pavement of the Rue de la Paix as the beautiful young ladies emerged from their compartments impeccably turned out to promenade under the scrutiny of the male passengers.

So the first journey of the Orient Express ended with precisely the impression that Nagelmackers had hoped to convey: glamour, comfort, elegance and a hint of intrigue and excitement. Who could resist it? Soon the train began to appear in novels, just as it later did in films. Extraordinary stories, not all of them untrue, began to gather around it. At least two government agents, one of them an American military attaché, either fell, jumped or were thrown to their deaths from the train.

King Boris III of Bulgaria, a train fanatic, could not be dissuaded from taking the controls when the Orient Express passed through his country. Wearing white overalls made for him in Paris, King Boris would spend long hours on the footplate, itching to get his hands on the controls. Firm instructions were given to drivers that he should not be permitted to do so, for his love of speed greatly exceeded his comprehension of the signalling system.

The Orient Express was never transport for the masses. Its fares were astonishingly expensive: £58 per person, or £160 for a couple with a servant. At that time, £160 would pay the annual rent for a substantial house in London, or keep a working-class family fed, clothed and supplied for a whole year. The people who could afford to travel on Nagelmackers's train were the truly rich, a class which did not long survive the nineteenth century. The arrival of high taxes on income and inheritance, World War I, and the depression of the 1930s transformed Nagelmackers's luxury train into a pale imitation.

After Nagelmackers died in 1905, his successor, Lord Dalziell, combined the Compagnie Internationale with Thomas Cook and Sons Ltd and the English Pullman Company, and catered for the beginnings of mass tourism. Rather than carrying a few extremely rich people, trains were filled with larger numbers, at lower fares and in less comfort. Thus was the Orient Express democratized, and its standards reduced; by the 1970s the train did not even boast a restaurant car for large parts of the journey.

Then, in the 1980s, a saviour emerged in the form of James Sherwood, an entrepreneur who

THE RESTORATION WORK

Restoration of the carriages for the Venice-Simplon Orient Express was undertaken in the 1980s by workshops in Belgium, Germany and England. The Pullman car *Audrey* (above) was once part of the Brighton Belle that ran to London Victoria. In all cars, marquetry panelling was restored or replaced, woodwork french polished, marble wash basins fitted, the electrics entirely rewired, new light shades made, based on a design by René Lalique, and new carpets woven in Yorkshire. No expense was spared to create a train that would measure up to the high standards of the original Orient Express.

had made his fortune running Sea Containers Ltd. Conspicuous consumption, long regarded as rather vulgar, was back in fashion as paper fortunes were made on the stock markets. Sherwood acquired and restored a series of carriages to create two trains, one to carry passengers from London to Folkestone, the other from Boulogne to Vienna, under the name Venice-Simplon Orient Express. Most of the sleeping cars are 50 years old, but magnificently restored, and the journey to Venice takes 30 hours. A second train, run by a Swiss entrepreneur, Albert Glatt, under the name Nostalgic Istanbul Orient Express, runs occasional trips from Paris to Istanbul and Bucharest, also using old rolling stock.

Goliaths of the Mountains

The great age of the luxury trains in the United States began in the days of the Depression and finally petered out during the late 1950s. In Canada, where the lines are longer and the scenery even more dramatic, the romance of the transcontinental journey survived, albeit unprofitably, until quite recent times. There has never been a better way to see the US or Canada than by train, a fact that railway managements exploited successfully until the greater speed of the airlines and the hurry even of modern tourism defeated them.

In the second half of the nineteenth century, both Canada and the US were united by railways that ran from shore to shining shore. In Canada it was possible to cover virtually the entire journey over the rails of a single company, which was never the case in the US. There, the railroads were regional rather than national, although by European standards they still covered huge territories. By 1900, more than 90 percent of the rail lines that would ever be built in North America were already in place. The pioneer era, when merely to cross the country by train was a kind of miracle, was replaced by the need to market the trains as an enjoyable experience.

Never was this more urgent than in the 1930s. In 1933, at the height of the Depression, trains in the US averaged only 43 passengers per run. The answer lay in new trains, with glamorous names and better standards of service. These great trains were powered both by steam and diesel, for it was a period in which the two prime movers were contesting supremacy.

The Pennsylvania Railroad used steam on the Broadway Limited—4-6-2 Pacifics of conservative design but great reliability. On some sections of the line, these K4 Pacifics could maintain average speeds in the region of 75 mph, making them among the quickest steam trains in the world. Often, in the great level stretches west, two K4s were coupled together to provide the motive power, their economical running making such prodigal use of locomotives feasible. Over the Allegheny Mountains, three K4s were needed to take the Broadway Limited up the 1 in 58 incline of Horseshoe Curve.

The rival Twentieth Century Limited also used steam, a fabled series of engines with a 4-6-4 layout known as the Hudsons. By 1938 the schedule for the New York to Chicago trip was down to 16 hours, giving an end-to-end speed of 59.9 mph, including seven stops totalling 26 minutes. In the fashion of the 1930s, some of the locomotives of both the Broadway Limited and the Twentieth Century Limited were given streamlined shapes, from the designers Raymond Loewy and Henry Dreyfus.

Any passenger reaching Chicago under the power of steam could continue by diesel, on one of the most glamorous trains of all, the City of San Francisco. In 1937, the Southern Pacific, the Union Pacific and the Milwaukee Road, over whose lines the train ran, bought from General Motors the world's most powerful diesel locomotives. The City of San Francisco exemplified the elegance of Art Deco, gleaming silver without and leather and chrome within. The power units, the longest locomotives that had ever been built, contained six 900-hp, 12-cylinder diesels, capable of pulling a 600-ton train at speeds of up to 110 mph. She made the trip in 39 hours; the cheapest ticket cost just $5, while the most expensive, at $22, provided a suite that slept four and had its own sofa and bathroom. Three meals a day cost an extra 90 cents.

On 12 August 1939 the City of San Francisco came off the rails near Harney in Utah, after a saboteur had damaged the track; 24 people died. The train went on running through the war, and in 1952 was trapped for five days by a blizzard in the Sierras. By careful husbandry, the crew fed 230 people with two meals a day, though by the time rescue came dinner was a frugal affair: spaghetti without sauce, a frankfurter, and half a cup of coffee per passenger.

Canadian railways, too, were noted for their spectacular trains. For many years the rival lines, Canadian Pacific and Canadian National, ran their cross-country trains in competition. It was possible to travel west by Canadian Pacific, covering 2,881 miles in 87 hours 10 minutes, and return by Canadian National, which had 2,930 miles to cover but much easier grades, so that its overall time was hardly different. That way, the traveller saw more scenery and had a taste of the different operating methods of the two railroads.

In the late 1920s Canadian Pacific introduced locomotives of its own design which were quickly recognized as outstanding. The 2-10-4 Selkirks were unusual among ten-coupled locomotives in being used for express passenger

FACT FILE

The heaviest engines ever built for the Canadian Pacific Railway

Selkirk 2-10-4

Date built: 1938–49

Number built: 36

Length: 97 feet 10⅝ inches

Driving wheel diameter: 5 feet 3 inches

CANADIAN PACIFIC

CANADIAN PACIFIC STEAMERS
CONNECT DIRECTLY WITH
CANADIAN PACIFIC EXPRESS
TRAINS TO EVERY PART OF
CANADA

Agent:

service. Normally engines with ten driving wheels are ideal for freight trains because of their exceptional traction, but are limited in speed because a locomotive can only be so long if it is to get around curves, and that means that if ten driving wheels are used, they must be small. This in turn usually limits top speeds.

For most of the CPR's 2,881 miles from Montreal to Vancouver the going was easy, but there were two awkward sections—the northern shore of Lake Superior and the 262 miles over the mountains between Calgary and Revelstoke. To haul the CPR's flagship train—the Dominion, weighing 1,300 tons—up inclines as steep as 1 in

A parlour car of the 1930s reflects the attention paid to the comfort of passengers before the airlines began to erode the railways' supremacy. Rivalry was between railway companies rather than modes of transport. The advertising art of the 1930s (right) now commands high prices among collectors.

369

Goliaths of the Mountains

45 required prodigious pulling power. Speeds on those sections were slow, no more than about 10 mph uphill and 25 to 30 mph down, because in addition to the slope the sharp curvature of the track had to be taken into account. To get the long 2-10-4s around these curves it was necessary to widen the track from 4 feet 8½ inches by 1¼ inches and to provide the leading axle with nearly an inch of free play. On the flat, the big Selkirks could reach 65 mph.

In 1953, when American railways were beginning to sense the competition, Canadian Pacific resolved to modernize its two transnational services, the Canadian and the Dominion. It ordered from the American coachbuilding company Budd of Philadelphia a total of 173 new stainless-steel cars, to be pulled by diesel locomotives. Each train had dome cars, with windows in the roof to look up at the spectacular scenery, and the new timetable cut 16 hours off the journey between Montreal and Vancouver, although eastbound the reduction was a more modest 10½ hours. The Canadian, the faster of the two services by half a day, quickly became one of the most famous trains in the world.

Canadian National retaliated by improving its own timetables, and buying from US railroads any luxury streamliner cars that were no longer wanted. The bold effort certainly increased traffic, but not enough to justify the expenditure, and by 1978 Canada's two railways operated a joint service over at least part of the track. Finally, in 1990 it was announced that the Canadian, a national institution since its introduction almost 40 years before, would stop running on a regular timetable.

In a declaration of faith in the future of rail, however, VIA Rail (the company that now operates all CN and CPR intercity trains) has refurbished the famous stainless-steel cars that caused such a sensation when they were introduced in 1955. At a cost of $200 million, air-conditioning, showers, interior design and the domes themselves have been restored and improved. The cars have been completely refitted from top to bottom, making them better than new, according to VIA officials. In the early 1990s, as all the cars are completed, new services are to be introduced. The first, in the spring of 1991, is the Western Transcontinental, between Vancouver and Toronto via Edmonton. VIA believes that the trains will uphold Canada's reputation for providing some of the most sensational railway journeys in the world.

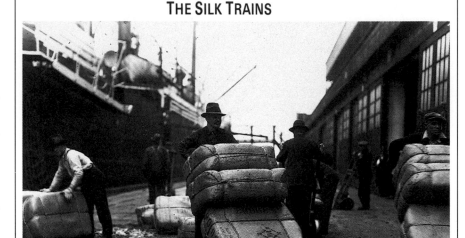

THE SILK TRAINS

Unloading the silk at Vancouver began before the first passengers disembarked, so crucial was every minute in the race to transport it to New York—not only is silk perishable, but the shorter the transit time, the lower the cost of insurance. Longshoremen unloaded the bales in cargo slings or by conveyor, once achieving the unloading of 7,000 bales in three hours. The silk was wrapped in burlap and tied up in a bale weighing about 130 lb and measuring 3 feet by 2 feet by 1 foot. A 30-ton boxcar, lined with protective paper, could be loaded in 15 minutes. The value of the silk on the first CN special train was $2 million, at a rate of $9 per 100 lb.

The most precious cargo ever carried by the Canadian railways, to judge by the efforts made to run the trains to time on a fast schedule, was not passengers but silk. For almost 50 years the trains carrying the silk from Pacific ports to New York had the freedom of the tracks. Ordinary trains were shunted into sidings and elaborate security precautions introduced to protect the valuable cargo.

The silk trains were the result of a determined marketing drive by the president of Canadian National, Sir Henry Thornton. Silk is perishable, so any time that could be saved on its journey to the Silk Exchange in New York was worthwhile. Thornton, determined to wrestle the business away from Canadian Pacific, organized CN's first silk special on 1 July 1925. It was to be handled like a relay race; every 150 miles or so train crews and engines were to be changed and running gear lubricated.

Seldom have freight trains run faster than the silk specials. A typical time for the journey to New York was a fraction over four days. For speed, the locomotives were those normally used for passenger trains, and over some sections they reached 90 mph. Between 1925 and about 1936, competition for the business was intense, with CN, CPR and the Great Northern competing neck and neck. The best year was 1929, when the railroads shared revenues from half a million bales of silk, valued at $325 million. The largest silk train that ever ran was in October 1927. That consisted of 21 cars containing 7,200 bales worth $7 million—the product, somebody estimated, of two billion silkworms.

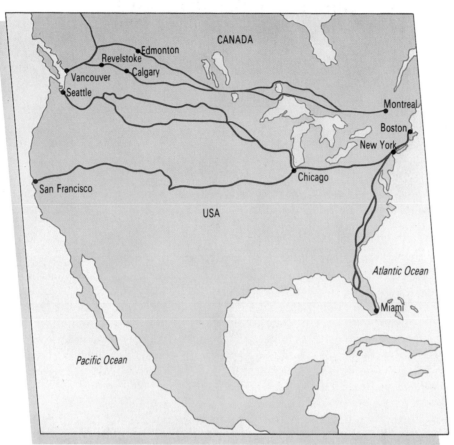

The new, named trains brought glamour and profitability to travel by long-distance expresses. Among the best known were the Twentieth Century Limited and its rival, the Broadway Limited, which both ran between New York and Chicago; the Empire Builder (Chicago to Seattle); the Canadian Pacific's Canadian (Montreal to Vancouver); the Orange Blossom Special (Boston to Miami); and the two rival trains that ran between Chicago and San Francisco, the City of San Francisco and the San Francisco Zephyr.

An eastbound Canadian Pacific train climbs the steep grade out of Field, British Columbia. The train has emerged from one of the two spiral tunnels designed to ease the gradient, and the lower portal can be seen beneath the first coach. The leading locomotive is a 2-10-4 Selkirk. The final example of the class, No. 5935, was the last steam locomotive to be built for the Canadian Pacific Railway, in 1949.

The Ultimate in Steam Power

The biggest, heaviest, most powerful steam locomotives ever built served the mountainous Wyoming division of the Union Pacific Railroad for 20 years from 1941. "Big Boy", as the class of locomotive was universally known, was a prodigy of steam power, able to pull trains weighing up to 4,200 tons up the 60-mile climb of the Wasatch Mountains unaided.

Before the arrival of Big Boy, this stretch of line had tested a long series of powerful engines. At first, helper engines were needed to shove the freight trains up the hill, but later the line acquired more powerful locomotives, with the idea of a single locomotive doing the job unassisted. No sooner were the new locomotives in service than the trains got bigger. Finally, in the early part of 1940, Union Pacific's Research and Mechanical Standards Department was ordered to design and construct an even more powerful engine. The result was Big Boy, by most reckoning the largest locomotive ever built and the one that combined the greatest pulling ability with an impressive turn of speed.

The order was for an engine able to pull 3,600 tons over the Wasatch unassisted. In just a year the first Big Boy was built and ready, a tribute to the excellence of American locomotive engineering. To do the job, Union Pacific estimated, an engine capable of 135,000 lb of tractive effort would be required. To transmit this amount of force to the rails would need sixteen 68-inch wheels in two sets of eight, and the engine's weight of more than 530 tons dictated at least four wheels for the lead and trailing trucks. Thus the 4-8-8-4 configuration was settled on.

To get around the curves along this awkward stretch of line, the engine had to be articulated—joined in the middle by a hinge, with one set of eight driving wheels each side of it. Clearly the boiler itself could not be hinged, so the bulk of its weight was borne by the rear set of driving wheels and on corners it slid across the front set on a support, hanging out by as much as 2 feet on a 10 degree curve.

The idea was not new, having originally been proposed by the French engineer Anatole Mallet in 1884. In Europe Mallet's principle was used mainly for narrow gauge railways, but in the US big Mallet articulateds were used for freight duties. Their speed was usually limited to 30 to 40 mph by vibration of the front frame, since at higher speeds great damage would be done to track and to wheels.

Improvements in the 1920s and '30s solved the vibration problem and better steam connections enabled high-pressure steam to be supplied to both sets of driving wheels—in the earlier engines only the rear set was fed with high-pressure steam, while the forward set operated at low pressure. In 1936, Union Pacific ordered forty 4-6-6-4 "Challenger" locomotives, which performed very well and provided the confidence to go ahead with the even bigger Big Boys.

The American Locomotive Company, of Schenectady, New York, was given the job of building the engines, sharing the design job with Union Pacific. Legend has it that the type got its name when a foreman at Alco chalked the name Big Boy on the smokebox of one of the early engines. Union Pacific had the idea of calling the type Wasatch, but publicity in the newspapers ensured that Big Boy was the name that stuck.

Everything about the engines was huge. The firebox was 20 feet long and 8 feet broad, plenty big enough for a family to sit down and have dinner. To toss the coal into its vast interior would have been beyond even the brawniest fireman, so a mechanical stoker was fitted which, with skilful operation, could be encouraged to throw the coal into the farthest reaches of the firebox. The tender could carry 28 tons of coal and 24,000 gallons of water, ample to get the big trains over the toughest sections of the track.

The main frames were huge castings, supplied by the General Steel Castings Company of Granite City, Illinois. The articulated joint between the leading unit and the main frame was designed so that it could transmit a load of several tons from the rear unit to the front one, thereby evening out the load carried by the driving wheels. In the Challengers, the joint had both horizontal and vertical hinges, so that the engine could adjust to humps and hollows in the track as well as curves. In the design of Big Boy the horizontal hinge was left out and the vertical hinge was designed to shift weight to the front wheels, helping to prevent slipping. To cope with humps and hollows, the wheels were mounted on individually sprung axles so that the suspension could accommodate uneven ground.

The cabs on the Big Boys were among the biggest on any steam locomotive, with room for

FACT FILE

The world's largest and most powerful steam locomotive

Date: 1941–44

Length: 132 feet 10 inches

Power output: 135,375 lb tractive effort

Diameter of driving wheel: 5 feet 8 inches

Weight: 539 tons 12 cwt

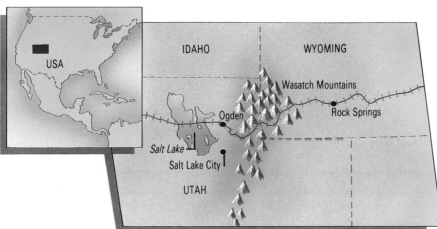

No. 4019 attacks the second part of the climb up the Wasatch Mountains after a stop for coal, sand and water. The engine was withdrawn from service in January 1962 after running 1,043,352 miles. The weight of the locomotives compelled Union Pacific to re-lay much of the route with 130 lb/ft steel rail.

The Ultimate in Steam Power

four people on seats and for a couple more standing. Even in the coldest winters the cabs were hot, but they rode very smoothly. For a huge locomotive, Big Boy ran well, able to reach speeds of up to 80 mph on straight and level stretches without rolling. But it really showed its mettle on the slow grind over the continental divide in the centre of the United States for which it had been designed.

Here the locomotives would pull steadily at about 15 mph, generating their maximum pulling power on the stretch between Cheyenne, Wyoming and Ogden, Utah, where on the notorious Sherman Hill a slope of 1 in 65 ran up to Sherman Summit at 8,013 feet. Leaving Ogden going east was a solid 60 miles of uphill grades, most of it around 1 in 88 as the rails climbed from 4,300 feet to 7,230 feet. Although designed to carry 3,600 tons over this section, the Big Boys showed that they could manage more and were regularly harnessed to 4,200-ton trains.

The huge publicity the Big Boys had enjoyed during their rapid construction ensured great interest in the first run, which took place in September 1941. A dormitory car was fitted behind engine No. 4013 for the run, to carry officials, test men and photographers. Behind that came a line of 100 fruit cars, all empty. With two long, moaning shrieks from its whistle and a black smudge of smoke from the short stack, 4013 started smoothly from Summit, in Omaha, attached to its first train.

Across Nebraska the stations were lined with people who had heard about the new engine. By late evening the train was in Sidney, Nebraska, and in the early hours of the morning it left Cheyenne for Sherman Hill, where an early fall of snow had dusted the lines. Between Tipton and Bitter Creek, Wyoming, it reached a speed of 72 mph and rode so smoothly it felt no more than 55. The following day saw an eastward run over the long climb the Big Boys had been designed to conquer, this time pulling a 3,500-ton train.

Again the line was crowded with spectators as the full power of the engine was unleashed. The smell of steam mixed with that of hot lubrication oil, and the sound of the thunderous exhaust combined with the clatter of cinders thrown out of the huge firebox landing on the cab roof as 4013 climbed the hill out of Echo, the toughest section. When the run was over, the weight of the train was recalculated and it was realized that 4013 had carried 3,800 tons, 200 more than the rated capacity.

The Big Boys proved highly successful engines, easy to run and reliable. With trains of regular weight and in normal conditions it was almost impossible to cause the wheels to slip, remarkable for articulated locomotives. Occasionally they were used on passenger trains, although their stock in trade was the less glamorous but profitable freight. They are recorded as producing 6,290 horsepower at 40 mph, consuming 100,000 lb of water and 44,000 lb of coal an hour in the process.

As time went by, experience allowed greater and greater loads, and the gradients were also trimmed by deviations, so that Big Boys could lift 6,000-ton trains up Sherman Hill by the end of their working lives in the early 1960s. The last were retired in 1962; six are preserved and can be seen at various locations in the US, from California to New Hampshire. None, alas, is still in working order.

The controls at the back of the firebox with the steam-operated butterfly firebox doors in the centre. The vertical lever on the right was the regulator, which determined the amount of steam being fed into the cylinders. The mechanical stoker fed coal into the firebox by a screw conveyor that passed underneath the cab footplate. The length of the firebox made it difficult to feed satisfactorily.

The boiler of the first Big Boy, No. 4000, is lowered on to its frames at the American Locomotive Company's works in Schenectady, New York. The plates used in the boiler barrel were $1\frac{3}{8}$ inches thick and the boiler pressure was a high 300 lb/sq in.

No. 4002 all set to go. The Big Boys were liked by both the crews and management. Union Pacific president Arthur Stoddard regarded them as "more than tools of an era—they were a symbol of the finest in transportation. Everyone on the line was proud of their performance and talked about it."

Streamlined Greyhound of the Rails

FACT FILE

The world's fastest steam locomotive

Date built: 1938

Length: 71 feet

Maximum speed: 125 mph

Gauge: 4 feet 8½ inches

Driving wheel diameter: 6 feet

Weight: 166 tons

One Sunday in July 1938 the steam engine *Mallard* set a speed record that has never been equalled. Down Stoke Bank, south of Grantham in Lincolnshire, it pulled seven coaches weighing 240 tons at a speed of 125 mph—some say 126. It was the high watermark of steam, and one of the last records set in an era of intense competition on land, sea and in the air that came to an end with World War II. After the war steam lingered on British tracks for 23 more years, but the glory had gone.

The driver of *Mallard* on the morning of 3 July 1938 was Joe Duddington, who drove with his cloth cap turned back to front in traditional style. Her designer was the chief mechanical engineer of the London & North Eastern Railway, Sir Nigel Gresley, who had produced the first of a long line of 4-6-2 Pacific locomotives in 1922 and had steadily improved them ever since.

In 1935, the LNER introduced the Silver Jubilee service between London and Newcastle, promising to complete the journey in four hours at an average speed of 67.08 mph. It was competition with road and air travel, as well as the traditional rivalry with the London, Midland & Scottish Railway which ran over the west coast route to Glasgow, that inspired the LNER to introduce its new train. But there were also continental influences at work in Gresley's mind.

In 1934, he had visited Germany and had been impressed by the "Fliegende Hamburger", an express service between Berlin and Hamburg. This Flying Hamburger, as we are unfortunately obliged to render it in English, was a lightweight diesel train of only three coaches which covered the 178-mile journey at an average speed of 77.4 mph. Impressed by the smoothness of the train at 100 mph, Gresley asked its designers to calculate how quickly a similar train would cover the London–Newcastle run. They quoted him four and a quarter hours for a three-coach train carrying 140 passengers.

Gresley and his board thought the train too cramped by British standards, and worked out that a modified A4 Pacific class locomotive might well achieve the same times with a train of much greater weight, capacity and comfort. To secure a sufficient margin of power, Gresley determined on a few modifications to cylinders and boiler and on streamlining to reduce wind resistance.

Gresley's streamlined A4 Pacifics were quickly put into service and the Silver Jubilee trains proved a huge success, attracting 100 percent loadings almost every day. The cost of the locomotives and the seven-coach trains was recovered from fare supplements alone within three years. *Mallard*, the 28th of the class to appear, emerged from the workshop in March 1938 at a cost of £8,500 and was given the number 4468.

At the time, the speed record for steam trains was claimed by the German railways for one of their own streamlined engines, No. 05.002, which reached 124.5 mph on 11 May 1936. On 27 August the same year, a Silver Jubilee train on a regular run south, pulled by No. 2512 *Silver Fox*, reached 113 mph, a record which still stands as the fastest ever reached by a steam engine on a normal service. Considerable damage was done to the engine during this run, including a broken big end on the middle of the three cylinders.

Fast running of the Silver Jubilee services depended on testing and improvement of the brakes, and it was during one of these tests that Gresley decided to go for the record. He selected *Mallard* and chose a quiet Sunday morning for the attempt, an out-and-out record run. Driver Joe Duddington was accompanied on the footplate by fireman Tommy Brae and locomotive inspector Sid Jenkins. Behind *Mallard* were a dynamometer car to measure the speed, an

Gresley's inspiration for the streamlining came from the racing-car designer Ettore Bugatti who had produced a streamlined railcar for Italian railways. Gresley claimed streamlining was vital to achieve the desired performance; some ascribed it to a concern with image. The side panels over the wheels impeded access for maintenance and were later removed. No. 4468 Mallard leaves the National Railway Museum at York (opposite) to work a train.

Streamlined Greyhound of the Rails

antique vehicle originally built in 1906, and seven coaches.

"I'd taken expresses along at, well—60, 70 or 80 mph," Duddington later told the BBC, "but this day we were going out to see just what we could do. I accelerated up the bank to Stoke summit and passed Stoke [signal] box at 85. Once over the top I gave *Mallard* her head and she just jumped to it like a live thing. After three miles the speedometer in my cab showed 107 mph, then 108, 109, 110—getting near Silver Jubilee's record of 113, I thought—I wonder if I can get past that—well, we'll try, and before I knew it the needle was at 116 and we'd got the record. They told me afterwards there was a deal of excitement in the dynamometer car and when the recorder showed 122 mph for a mile and a half it was at fever heat.

"Go on, old girl, I thought, we can do better than this. So I nursed her and shot through Little Bytham at 123 and in the next one and a quarter miles the needle crept up further—123½—124—125 and then for a quarter of a mile, while they tell me the folks in the car held their breaths—126 miles per hour. That was the fastest a steam locomotive had ever been driven in the world—and good enough for me, though I believe if I'd tried her a bit more we could have got even 130."

Back in the dynamometer car was a representative of the Westinghouse Brake and Signal Company, P.T.W. Remnant, who had managed to squeeze himself aboard for the record run even though no brake tests were planned. His account coincides pretty closely with that of Duddington. They began with a slight disadvantage, he said, because (as ever) the line was subject to Sunday maintenance and there was a speed restriction outside Grantham station. There were wry smiles as the speed fell back to 18 mph. But *Mallard* accelerated powerfully up the bank to Stoke summit, passing it at 75 mph according to the dynamometer record.

As the train was running at over 100 mph, Remnant walked back through the length of it. "There was a good deal of movement at the front; the middle gave one a floating impression, and the ride at the back was pretty rough. The guard looked as though he had had enough. Some of the more inventive newspapers the next day carried tales of the engineers 'having tea without a drop being spilt'. In fact, I believe there was a little broken crockery."

As the train approached a bend in the track at Essendine, with 123 mph recorded on the

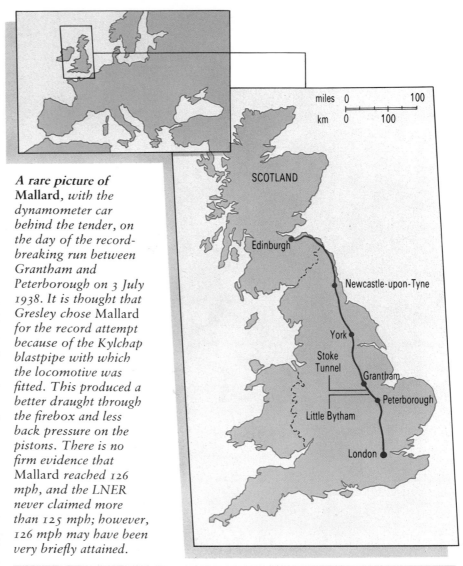

A rare picture of **Mallard**, *with the dynamometer car behind the tender, on the day of the record-breaking run between Grantham and Peterborough on 3 July 1938. It is thought that Gresley chose* Mallard *for the record attempt because of the Kylchap blastpipe with which the locomotive was fitted. This produced a better draught through the firebox and less back pressure on the pistons. There is no firm evidence that* Mallard *reached 126 mph, and the LNER never claimed more than 125 mph; however, 126 mph may have been very briefly attained.*

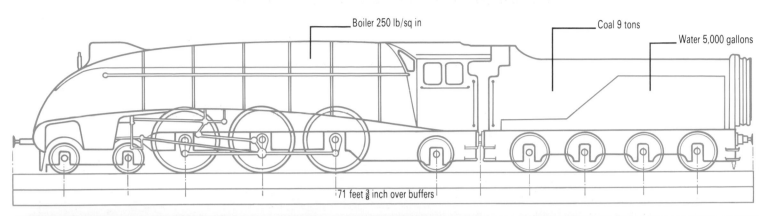

Boiler 250 lb/sq in

Coal 9 tons

Water 5,000 gallons

71 feet ⅜ inch over buffers

speedometer in the cab, the order was given to ease up. There were handshakes and smiles as people stuck their heads out of the window, to be greeted with a powerful smell. This was the "stink bomb", a device built into the centre big end bearing of A4 Pacifics to provide warning of the bearing overheating. In Peterborough station the fitters soon had the fairing off the driving wheels, to reveal that the big end bearing had indeed failed. The return to London was made behind an older and less glamorous engine.

After *Mallard*'s record run, Gresley made preparations for a further attempt to raise the record to 130 mph, but the war intervened. The smart trains of the 1930s made way for over-loaded troop carriers groaning out of King's Cross, and standards of maintenance suffered. The lines were soon no longer fit for record attempts, and the spirited competition between the old railway companies gave way to the uniformity of the nationalized British Railways.

In the 1950s things began to improve, and *Mallard* and her sister A4s ended their careers in the early 1960s in a blaze of glory. In May 1960, the failure of a diesel engine obliged *Mallard* to run the service to and from Newcastle every day for a week—a total of 3,750 miles. Renumbered by British Railways as 60022, *Mallard* ran its last scheduled trip on 25 April 1963, and retired to the Museum of British Transport at Clapham.

This was not quite the end. After the closure of Clapham in 1975, and the move of exhibits to the National Railway Museum in York, it was suggested that *Mallard* be restored to working order. By 1985 it was in steam once more. Since then it has been regularly seen pulling excursion trains, a remarkable survivor still as powerful and impressive as the day it was built.

Mallard at York station with a special train. The slight dip immediately behind the chimney was an accident. Gresley had intended to make the top of the boiler flat. A plasticine model was made in this shape for wind tunnel tests, but by accident somebody's finger made a small indentation behind the chimney. When this was tested, it was found that the smoke lifted away from the chimney more effectively, giving the driver better visibility, so this shape was used.

The Quest for Speed

From the time of the world's first steam-operated railways in Britain, speed has been a major factor in giving railways a commercial advantage over rival forms of transport. Even in the age of the aeroplane, railways in Europe are striving for ever higher speeds to extend the distance over which they can beat the airlines on city centre to city centre timings.

The TGV is only one of a number of high-speed trains that are being built to link the cities of Europe by a high-speed network. Proposals for similar schemes on the east coast of North America are under consideration. The need to counter the growing pollution caused by road transport has given an added sense of urgency to the development of fast, cleaner rail services.

During the 125 years that the steam locomotive was the dominant form of power on the railways, speeds built up steadily: 100 mph was reached in 1904, and the record was steadily increased during the 1930s to reach 125 mph. It took over 110 years of development to reach this speed by steam; it took just 36 years to raise the speed record for an electric train from 150 mph in 1954 to 319 mph in 1990. The record for diesel traction is 144.9 mph, set by a British high-speed train in 1986.

London Midland & Scottish Railway 4-6-2 No. 6222 Queen Mary *climbing to Shap summit in Westmorland with the Coronation Scot. Five streamlined Pacifics were built for this special service between London and Glasgow. They were a development of the "Princess Royal" Pacifics and intended for continuous high-speed running.*

A rare example of streamlining outside Europe or North America were the Japanese-built SL7 Pacifics, built in 1934 and used on the Asia Express of the South Manchuria Railway. This one is preserved at Shenyang, China.

The last streamlined steam locomotives *operating in commercial service are the WP Pacifics of Indian Railways. No. 7200, the first of a class of 750 locomotives, was built by Baldwin Locomotive Works in Philadelphia in 1947.*

Great Western Railway *4-4-0 No. 3440 City of Truro is reputed to have been the first engine to reach 100 mph, down Wellington bank in Somerset in May 1904. Now preserved, she is seen here at Haxby, Yorkshire.*

Train for the 21st Century

When the French high-speed train set off from the Gare de Montparnasse on 18 May 1990, the officials responsible were pretty sure it would prove an interesting trip. They were confident enough, anyway, to invite 150 journalists to watch and to carry aboard the Minister of Transport, Michel Delebarre. They departed ten minutes late because a roe deer had somehow vaulted the protective fences and found its way on to the track, but it was efficiently removed after being anaesthetized with a dart. French Railways (SNCF) was making a public attempt to beat its own speed record, set just two days before at 317 mph.

The train was France's latest candidate for the title of the world's fastest train. The Japanese bullet trains—pioneers of high-speed railways—have been left behind. The French "Train à Grande Vitesse", or TGV, has set new standards for fast rail travel, operating since 1981 between Paris and Lyons at speeds of 168 mph—37 mph more than the Japanese bullet trains. On 26 February 1981, the TGV set a record of 236 mph and won the title of the world's fastest train.

The pride of SNCF was dented, therefore, when on 1 May 1988 the West German prototype of its new InterCity Express set a new record of 252 mph on the Fulda–Würzburg line. But SNCF had another trick up its sleeve—a new line linking Paris to the Atlantic coast, and an improved TGV to run on it. On 6 December 1989, the TGV Atlantique (TGV A) reached 300 mph, recapturing the Blue Riband of the tracks. On 9 May 1990, it went even faster, reaching 317 mph on a stretch of line near Tours, before edging it up a fraction, to 319 mph, on 16 May. This is more than twice as fast as the fastest-ever diesel train (145 mph by a British Rail HST between York and Darlington on 9 November 1986) and half the speed of the fastest Airbus, the real competition for high-speed railways.

The TGV is an excellent example of how an old and apparently mature technology can be given a new lease of life. When research began in 1969 into trains capable of more than 150 mph, many assumed that such speeds would be possible only if the familiar steel wheels on steel tracks were replaced by the concept of magnetic levitation—trains hovering a few inches above the track on a cushion of magnetism. But the levitation experiments were not very successful. According to François Lacôte, SNCF's chief engineer in charge of TGV programmes, "It was the failure of our experiments with magnetic levitation that needled us into developing the TGV at the outset. Twenty years later, we still feel we have the right formula."

That formula consists of light, streamlined, high-powered electric trains running on a purpose-built track. Only passengers are carried, leaving the track clear of slow-moving goods trains, which can use the older tracks. The high power means that gradients steeper than those on conventional railways can be tolerated, with slopes of up to 1 in 30, which reduces the distance the lines must cover. Here speed itself is an advantage because the kinetic energy stored in a train travelling more than 150 mph carries it up hills on momentum alone.

The lines have no level crossings—no tunnels, even, on the original TGV line to Lyons—and there are no height restrictions under bridges. Modified signalling equipment, sophisticated design of bogies and carriages, and a special two-stage pantograph to collect the current from an overhead wire at 25,000 volts complete the package. No breakthroughs and no radical new technologies were needed to create a railway faster than anything that had gone before.

The driver of the train on the morning of 18 May was Michel Massinon, aged 45, a man whose childhood dream was to join SNCF and drive trains. During the run on 9 May he had been the first driver ever to exceed 310 mph. With him in the cab on both occasions was Daniel Vigneau, the engineer who had organized the record-breaking runs. Behind them were two ordinary TGV coaches and three buffet coaches converted into electronic laboratories and staffed by 40 technicians. The entire train weighed 258 tons. The record run began at Dangeau, 71 miles from Paris, where the railway divides, one line heading to Le Mans and the other to Tours.

By mile 76 the speed was up to 186 mph, and 248 mph was passed 7½ miles later. 260...267... 280...290...307, the speed crept upward as Massinon crammed on full power. The train swooped into the new station at Vendôme at 307 mph. If it had wings it would long since have taken off, but instead it had been given a special skirt to create down force and keep it on the

FACT FILE

The world's fastest train

TGV Atlantique

Date built: 1985/86

Length: 781 feet

Power output: 12,000 horsepower

Maximum speed: 320 mph

Gauge: 4 feet 8½ inches

Weight: 472 tons

track. Screens in the technicians' coaches showed that the wheels were indeed lifting a fraction from the rails, but fortunately not all were doing so at the same time.

In the cab the driver had his eyes firmly on the track—"never look sideways" is his technique for driving at very high speed. The motors were at full power, alarms designed to sound in case of danger were silent and the camera installed on the roof showed that the pantograph was remaining in perfect contact with the catenary wires carrying the current.

At mile 101 the speed crept past 310 mph. The final downward stretch of line beckoned, where the record would be won or lost. At mile 103.6, everybody held their breath. In a cloud of dust the train shot by the watchers at the track-side at

320 mph, a new record. "We were flat out, using all the power," said M. Vigneau later. M. Massinon said: "I was so busy that I didn't have time to think of the record. I had to stick to all the parameters we had set in advance, the speed at certain points, and to remember that some of the curves had speed limits . . . Our idea was to reach the maximum speed at a very precise point because after that the slope is less helpful. As soon as I passed that section, I put on the brakes. This was everybody's success, everybody in SNCF."

To set up the record attempt, SNCF engineers had adjusted a few details on the train and the track, for they knew that they were approaching the absolute limit of the TGV's performance. The slope was gently downhill, and the driving

The Train à Grande Vitesse Atlantique is a development of the earlier orange, grey and white sets for the first high-speed line to Lyons. The number of trailer cars was increased from eight to ten, the interiors were redesigned with extra facilities, more powerful and compact motors enabled the number to be reduced from twelve to eight and more powerful disc brakes were fitted.

Train for the 21st Century

TGV A trains serve 25 million people in towns from Brest in the north to Hendaye close to the border with Spain in the south. Provision has been made to extend the dedicated TGV line around Le Mans for trains to Brittany via Rennes.

wheels of the train had been increased in size by 1 inch to 3 feet 6 inches, marginally increasing the gearing. The catenary cable was under more tension than usual—3.3 tons instead of 2.8—to diminish the curve of the wire and reduce the danger of the pantograph losing contact with it, and with only five coaches instead of ten, the power to weight ratio was doubled. The wind was favourable, blowing at 11–14 mph.

After the record run, there was only one word of disappointment from an SNCF official. He had been hoping to beat the 321 mph achieved by an unmanned Japanese vehicle using magnetic levitation. There is, however, little comparison between a proper train, albeit one prepared for a record attempt, and a pre-prototype Japanese vehicle. The SNCF therefore felt quite justified in claiming that the TGV possessed a greater potential than other forms of ground transport.

The record represented the culmination of a long process of development. When the TGV studies began, it was assumed that traction would be provided by gas turbines, but the energy crisis of the early 1970s changed the plans. France invested heavily in nuclear power stations, using indigenous sources of uranium, so it was logical to electrify the TGV.

As speed rises, so does wind resistance. The smooth shape of the train and the design of the bogies are therefore particularly important. The TGV has fewer bogies than a conventional train, each being shared by neighbouring coaches. As well as reducing wind resistance, this "articulated" system makes it possible to arrange the seating in between the bogies, so that no passenger actually sits over the wheels.

At very high speeds, the shock when the train runs into a tunnel or passes another going the other way can be considerable, enough even in extreme cases to dent the bodywork of the train, and certainly to make passengers' ears pop. Unlike the line to Lyons, the TGV A line does have tunnels, some of them with speed limits. Railways in west Germany have solved this problem with pressurized trains, like aircraft, which work well but are heavier and more costly to build and run. SNCF believes an adequate and much cheaper answer can be found in careful aerodynamic design and hermetic door seals.

Because trains run to the centre of cities, they can compete on journey times with aircraft even if their average speed is lower. Paris–Lyons takes just two hours by TGV, a time which cannot be matched by airlines. In addition, the train uses

The ten trailer cars have seats for 116 in three first-class cars and 485 in six second-class cars; the tenth car provides a bar and buffet. New facilities include a nursery with bottle warmers and changing table, three telephones, a kiosk for groups of up to 17 people, and tables with greater privacy for meetings. Fares are the same as those on other express trains.

far less energy—the equivalent of 3½ pints of oil per passenger per 60 miles covered on the original TGV, now cut to just over 2½ pints by the TGV A. That compares with the 12 pints used by an Airbus on the same basis. Every TGV saves France 100,000 tons of oil a year.

With the success of the TGV, the future now looks bright for high-speed railways. New lines are to be built from Paris to the Channel Tunnel and to Brussels, and another line to Strasbourg is under discussion. The line to Lyons could be extended to the Mediterranean coast. A total of 13 new lines have been proposed by SNCF, some of which would require government subsidy. France, a large and still relatively underpopulated country, is ideal for railway building, with empty rural areas through which the noisy TGV

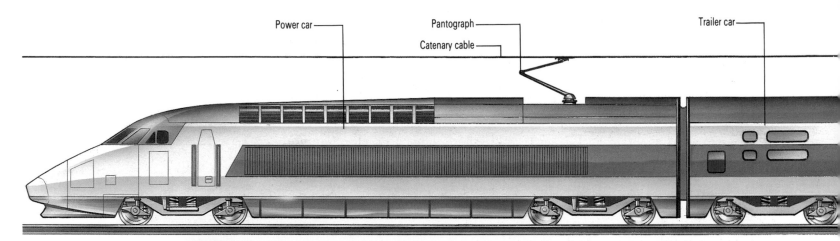

Power car — Pantograph — Trailer car —

Catenary cable —

The traction units, or power cars, of the TGV A trains – one at each end of the train – produce a total of 12,000 hp from their eight self-controlled synchronous motors, which are also used for braking. The steel disc brakes can bring a TGV A train running at 186 mph to a stop in 2 miles. This provides a margin of safety to run a train every 5 minutes. Experiments now being carried out with carbon fibre disc brakes, similar to those used on the European Airbus, may reduce the distance needed for stopping, which would permit closer spacing of trains.

lines can be routed with a minimum of protest. Some French towns have even campaigned vociferously to be included on a new TGV line. In much more crowded Britain, fear of noise and disruption tends to be greater than the enthusiasm for faster, cheaper and cleaner travel.

SNCF has so far failed to persuade its German opposite number, the Deutsche Bundesbahn (German Federal Railway), to collaborate on the TGV, so the French and German systems are in rivalry for the new lines proposed to link western Europe together. Although the Germans began before the French, it will be 1991 before the InterCity Express trains come into operation, linking Hamburg to Munich on two routes via Würzburg and via Frankfurt and Stuttgart. Like the TGV, the ICE has two power units, with 12

coaches between them. The goal of the programme is to develop a train capable of travelling twice as fast as a car, and half as fast as an aeroplane—an objective achieved in the experimental run in May 1988 which reached 252 mph.

There is much at stake in the contest between the two systems, and there is the prospect of competition from the Italians, the Japanese and perhaps the Canadians. The European Commission is working on plans for a Europe-wide express rail system, using 11,800 miles of existing, updated and new lines. This could involve the building of between 400 and 500 trains in the next ten years, a market worth up to £4 billion. Small wonder that a battle is going on to establish the prestige that comes from running the world's fastest trains.

The risk of drivers missing signals at normal operating speeds of up to 186 mph necessitated provision of a display on the control panel in the train's cab. If the driver fails to respond to a signal advising a reduction in speed, the brakes are automatically applied. The TGV A routes are controlled from a signal centre in Paris which is in radio contact with all trains.

CHAPTER FOUR

THROUGH THE AIR

Everybody has heard of Icarus and his doomed attempt to escape from Crete which ended when the Sun melted the wax holding his wings. Fewer may know of a Chinese legend about the emperor Shun, who lived from 2258 to 2208 BC. He understood the laws of aerodynamics and put them into practice when a granary that he was building burst into flames while he was on the top floor. "He donned the work clothes of a bird and, flying, made his escape," the story goes.

Fantasies about flying are clearly common to all cultures, but it was not until the eighteenth century that they became reality. It must have been extraordinary to be present when men first defied gravity in a lighter-than-air machine. Only in this century have we finally learned to fly—not by donning the work clothes of a bird but in machines that carry us faster, higher, and in greater comfort than any bird has flown.

It was the Montgolfier brothers who discovered the remarkable properties of hot air and another set of brothers, Wilbur and Orville Wright, who first flew a powered aircraft. Sensational as it seemed, the Montgolfiers' invention proved a dead end until revived for fun in the 1960s, although the gas balloon which first flew only a few days later had much greater promise before the crashes of R101 and the *Hindenburg* destroyed confidence in airships.

The Wrights' invention, by contrast, transformed travel and warfare within half a century. The demonstration by Alcock and Brown, and later by Lindbergh, that aircraft could fly the Atlantic opened the way to international air travel, which from small and hair-raising beginnings has become a huge industry. Faster, higher, bigger; the history of our conquest of the air has been marked by superlatives, some of which are chronicled here. At the end, we come full circle, to a hot-air balloon carried by the winds across the Atlantic and the Pacific oceans, using exactly the same principles that the Montgolfiers demonstrated more than 200 years ago.

Up and Away

FACT FILE

The first successful
hot-air balloons

First Montgolfière

Date built: 1783

Width: 35 feet

Volume: 28,000
cubic feet

Third Montgolfière
(in modified form)

Date built: 1783

Height: 75 feet

Width: 46 feet

Volume: 60,000
cubic feet

The age of flight began on 4 June 1783 in the Place des Cordeliers in Annonay, a French market town not far from Lyons. As the people of the town began gathering there late in the morning, two brothers, Joseph and Etienne Montgolfier, directed four workmen who were assembling a wooden platform. Two masts held with ropes were erected on each side of the platform, each with a pulley at the top. Over the pulley ran two ropes, attached at one end to an eye on a large piece of fabric which lay in a heap on the platform. By pulling the ropes, the fabric was raised so that it hung between the poles. It was made of sackcloth lined with three thin layers of paper, and at the base it had an open mouth about 8 feet square.

When all was complete, the brothers waited for the members of the local Diocesan Assembly, who were holding their annual meeting in Annonay. The Montgolfiers were keen to ensure that what happened next was seen by officials who could vouch for it. A brazier filled with burning shreds of wood and dry straw was placed under the mouth, and as the hot air filled the fabric it rose, straining on the ropes. Etienne gave the order to let go, and the balloon soared straight up to 3,000 feet, carried a mile and a half by wind, until it settled again to earth, landing on a stone wall. The brazier tipped over, set light to the fabric, and the whole affair was destroyed.

No person had been carried on this first flight of a hot-air balloon, but the principle had been clearly demonstrated. The next day the Montgolfiers petitioned the members of the assembly to record their approval of the experiment, thus making clear who had been the first to conquer the air. To this day, a hot-air balloon is called in French a Montgolfière.

The two brothers who had devised this extraordinary spectacle were the sons of Pierre Montgolfier, a paper-maker. It was Joseph, the dreamer, who was without doubt the progenitor of the hot-air balloon. There are many stories about how he devised the idea. One says that he watched a girl blowing soap bubbles, and saw them rise; another, that one day he was drying his wife's petticoat over a fire, and saw it fill with hot air and billow upward.

Joseph was well aware of the recent advances in chemistry, including the discovery by Henry Cavendish in 1766 of "inflammable air"—

hydrogen. He knew, too, that hydrogen was a very light gas and had considered the idea of filling a balloon with it in order to fly. He dismissed this possibility because of the expense of acquiring the gas, but others did not, and while he and Etienne were experimenting with their hot-air balloons, other pioneers in France were trying to make the hydrogen balloon a reality. The bid to be the first men to fly was a race between the proponents of the hot-air balloon and those of the hydrogen balloon.

After the successful demonstration in Annonay, Etienne went to Paris to publicize the balloon and carry out further demonstrations. While he was there, the first test of a hydrogen balloon was carried out in the Champ de Mars by the French physicist J.A.C. Charles, who had contrived to generate sufficient hydrogen to fill a rubberized bag 12 feet in diameter. The "Charlière" worked well, rapidly ascending to 1,500 feet and disappearing over the Seine. It came down about 12 miles north of Paris near Ecouen, where terrified peasants attacked it with pitchforks. Etienne now had a serious rival.

He had meanwhile constructed a second Montgolfière, 70 feet tall and 40 feet in diameter, which he intended to demonstrate to the royal family at Versailles. It was made in the wallpaper factory of a friend, Jean-Baptiste Reveillon, who added some colourful touches in the form of brilliant strips of wallpaper. Unfortunately the first attempt to demonstrate it coincided with a rainstorm, and the balloon soon collapsed, looking hopelessly bedraggled. It did just enough, however, to encourage Etienne to proceed, but this time he resolved to make a balloon which would be resistant to fire, wind and water. To ensure that the Versailles demonstration was really impressive, he decided to jump one step ahead of the Charlière by sending animals aloft.

Etienne and his friends built the balloon in just four days and nights. Made of taffeta coated with varnish, it was smaller than the one destroyed by the rain, but had a lifting force of almost 700 lb, quite sufficient for the sheep, duck and rooster which had finally been chosen as crew. The demonstration, on 19 September 1783, was a triumph. The balloon lifted off and, despite losing some hot air when it was tilted by the wind, continued on its way for eight minutes before landing gently with its animals still alive.

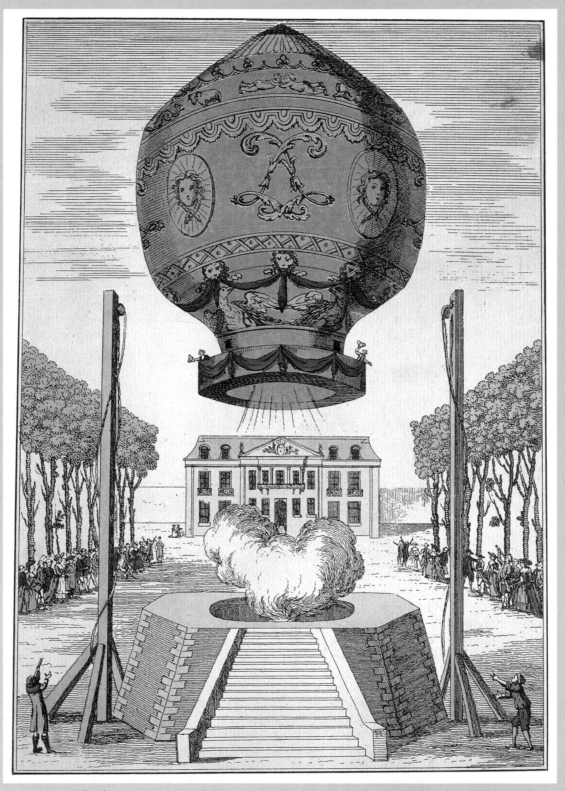

The first manned free flight, on 21 November 1783. Etienne Montgolfier had
hoped that the event would be kept secret, but it proved impossible and a large
crowd gathered at the Château de la Muette on the western outskirts of Paris.
It was the home of the two-year-old dauphin and his elder sister; Benjamin
Franklin was a near neighbour and an engraving was made of the first flight as
seen from his terrace.

Up and Away

The third Montgolfière was built in four frantic days and nights. The urgency was caused by the imminent date for the royal demonstration at Versailles on 19 September 1783 and by the destruction by rain of the second balloon. A large platform was built with a circular opening 15 feet in diameter which contained an iron stove. The king watched the flight with his field glasses and sent people to check on the condition of the animals when the balloon came down just over 2 miles away.

King Louis XVI and his court were impressed.

Next, Etienne determined to try a manned flight. He modified the Versailles balloon, increasing its capacity by 50 percent. The burner was suspended below the balloon, within reach of the passengers who could toss fresh fuel into it with a pitchfork, but far enough away so as not to set the fabric alight.

The public demonstration set for 21 November was preceded by several tethered experiments, in at least one of which Etienne himself may have gone aloft. This demonstration is generally taken to be the first manned flight, and indeed it was the first in which the tethering ropes were disconnected. The crew consisted of a young scientist, Jean-François Pilâtre de Rozier, and a nobleman, François Laurent, the Marquis d'Arlandes. Both had been keen to take their chances in Etienne's balloon.

This time the launching place was the garden of the Château de la Muette, on the western outskirts of Paris, where the infant dauphin lived under the care of the Duchesse de Polignac. The first attempt at a tethered test failed when wind tilted the balloon and brought it ignominiously to the ground. Repairs took an hour and a half, by which time the wind had abated. It took eight minutes to reflate the balloon, and at 1.54 p.m. it was off.

As he looked down, d'Arlandes was struck most by the silence of those on the ground. They seemed immobilized and, thinking they needed reassurance, he waved a handkerchief. De Rozier soon complained that d'Arlandes was not doing enough to keep the fire burning, so they both fed it with fresh straw. The wind was carrying them along the Seine, so they stoked the fire again, and d'Arlandes gave it a poke with his pitchfork. As it blazed up, he felt himself lifted as if by the armpits. "Now we're really climbing," he shouted, but at that moment there was a popping noise high in the rigging.

Looking upward, d'Arlandes saw that part of the fabric was smouldering, creating small holes.

Machine Aërostatique de 126 p.ds de haut sur 100 p.ds de large.

Elevée dans les Champs appellés les Brotteaux, hors de la Ville de Lion, le 19. Janvier 1784, par M. Montgolfier, en vertu d'une Souscription de 12.ᵉ par personne. Le 16. Janvier, ne prévoyant pas l'effet de l'humidité que le balon avoit essuyé par les mauvais tems, on mit le feu, alors l'humide raréfié et reduit en vapeurs corroda les toiles et mit le feu a la calotte, il fut éteint en une minute. l'ecole du 16. fit prendre des mesures plus réflechies. Le 19. on fit secher les toiles, et on mit 2 heures a gonfler le balon ou l'on n'avoit employé cy devant que 27 minutes. Dans l'Etat de perfection ou l'on crut qu'il etoit: M. Montgolfier, M. Pilatre de Rosier, M. le Prince Charles de Ligne, M. le C.ᵗᵉ de la Porte, M. le C.ᵗᵉ de Dampierre, M. le C.ᵗᵉ de Laurencin, et M. Fontaine de Lion, entrerent dans la galerie. Ces 7 Titans pesoit avec le lest 16000, ce fardeau immense s'éleva a la hauteur de 3000 pieds en 13 minutes a la satisfaction de plus de 100000 Spectateurs qui exprimerent leur enthousiasme par mille crys de joye. En forçant le feu pour s'élever plus rapidement il se fit une ouverture verticale de 4 pieds ½ qui fut le terme du Voyage, qui ne dura que 15 minutes, et les Voyageurs descendirent dans une prairie près de Lion, sans aucun accident.

The Montgolfier brothers—Joseph (1740–1810) (top) and Etienne (1745–99)—were opposites in temperament. Joseph was ingenious, interested in science but impractical in everyday life. His brother was businesslike and had trained as an architect, but was recalled to his father's paper mill when the eldest brother died. Joseph was later created a Chevalier de la legion d'honneur.

Le Flesselles, the fifth Montgolfière, was designed by Joseph for Jacques de Flesselles. It took off from Lyons, after rivals for a place in the balloon drew pistols to enforce their claim, on 19 January 1784, watched by 100,000 spectators. The fabric tore, causing a harsh landing.

They were right over Paris, so they could not put down. Fortunately d'Arlandes put out the flames with a sponge attached to his pitchfork.

Once past the Port Royal, open ground appeared and d'Arlandes was all for putting down, but de Rozier warned that they were approaching two windmills. De Rozier threw on another bale as the balloon went between the mills. It cleared a pond and landed with the windmills a hundred yards on either side. They had been in the air 25 minutes and had travelled 5 miles. Most of their fuel remained unburned.

Etienne had launched his balloon just in time. Only ten days later Professor Charles and Marie-Noël Robert took off in their Charlière for a flight of more than 25 miles, lasting two hours. When they landed Robert alighted and Charles went on for a second solo flight, rising to 10,000 feet and making a series of observations of temperature and pressure. After 35 minutes he opened the valves and settled slowly down again, landing gently near La Tour de Laye. In less than two weeks, not one but two flying machines had been successfully demonstrated.

The Monoplane that Hit the Headlines

The moment when Charles Lindbergh finally came down to earth after his epic flight alone across the Atlantic was when he met King George V at Buckingham Palace. The king, who insisted on seeing Lindbergh alone, leaned forward and said: "Now tell me, Captain Lindbergh, there is one thing I long to know. How did you pee?" It was, said Lindbergh, a question that put him at his ease. He explained that he had carried an aluminium container for the purpose, and had dropped it when he was safely over France and no longer needed it. "I was not going to be caught with the thing on me at Le Bourget," he explained. In some remote hedgerow it may rest to this day, for aluminium

does not corrode. The rest of Lindbergh's aircraft, *Spirit of St Louis*, is in the Smithsonian Institution in Washington, the only survivor of the planes that raced to be the first to fly from New York to Paris nonstop.

It was Lindbergh who won that race, and his the name that is remembered. Nobody now recalls his rivals, who came so close to denying him the prize. Some have even forgotten that the Atlantic had been flown before, by Captain John Alcock and Lieutenant Arthur Whitten-Brown, in a Vickers Vimy bomber in 1919. The two-man team departed from Newfoundland, and ended nose-first in an Irish bog. It is the glamour of the lone aviator, who set off from a proper

FACT FILE

The first solo flight across the Atlantic

Date built: 1927

Wingspan: 46 feet

Length: 27 feet 8 inches

Power output: 237 horsepower

Maximum speed: 129 mph

airfield and landed at another, that has lasted.

Lindbergh began his career as a barn-storming pilot in the early 1920s, touring the farm lands of the Midwest. The technique was to raise interest by flying low over a town, showing off a few stunts, then to sell tickets at $5 a ride. Lindbergh grew skilful at standing on the wings, even when the pilot threw the plane into a loop. But it was a precarious life, and in 1924 he enlisted in the US Army as a flying cadet. A year later he got his wings, went on the reserve list, and found a job as a pilot flying mail from St Louis to Chicago.

Within a year he had twice had to parachute from aircraft that had run out of fuel in poor weather. The day after the first of these mishaps,

he took a day off and went to the cinema. On a newsreel he saw a report of a huge new aircraft designed by Igor Sikorsky to carry a crew of four across the Atlantic to Europe. Flown by a French pilot called René Fonck, the Sikorsky was aiming to win a $25,000 prize for the first crossing from New York to Paris or the shores of France, or vice versa. The prize had been put up in 1919 by a Frenchman, Raymond Orteig, who ran two hotels in New York.

Lindbergh immediately began to take an interest in the race. He found Fonck's plans poorly conceived. Why take four men to fly a single plane? Why carry two radio sets, when one would do? Why decorate the interior of the plane

The crowd waiting to welcome Lindbergh at Croydon Aerodrome near London was so great that police lines broke and people ran on to the runway just as he was about to land, compelling him to take off again. Lindbergh had flown from Paris to Brussels and come on to England on 29 May. King George V awarded Lindbergh the Air Force Cross.

The Monoplane that Hit the Headlines

with red leather, and even provide a bed? To an aviator of Lindbergh's experience, raised in simple planes that cut out every frill, this seemed wasteful. It would be better to strip the machine to its limits, carry a single man, and use the extra space for fuel. His doubts proved justified when Fonck set out for Paris on 20 September 1926, failed to get airborne, and crashed into a gully at the end of the runway killing two members of the crew. It was at this point that Lindbergh realized he could do better.

He determined to fly the Atlantic alone, in a single-engined plane. He had some trouble explaining the wisdom of this idea to potential backers, but he was a persuasive young man and had soon raised $15,000 from St Louis businessmen, sufficient to buy the aircraft he needed. Fokkers refused to sell him one, and the Wright-Bellanca company, who made a suitable monoplane, would only let him have one if they were permitted to choose the crew. Guessing they would not choose him, Lindbergh turned them down. The only company that was prepared to help was the Ryan Aircraft Company of San Diego, California.

By luck, Lindbergh had stumbled on the best men in America to make his dream come true. While the rivals in the race suffered crashes, the Ryan company worked flat out on Lindbergh's

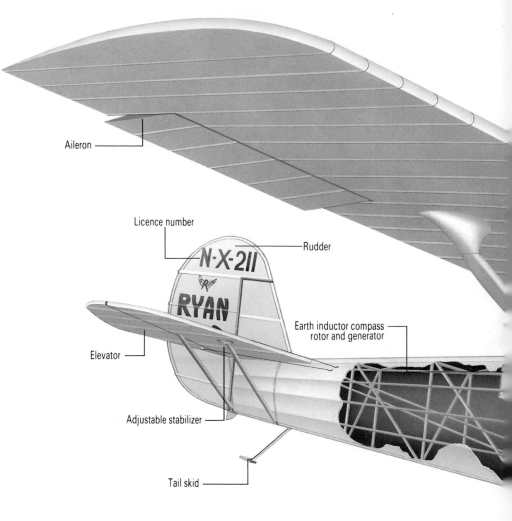

Aileron

Licence number

Rudder

Elevator

Earth inductor compass rotor and generator

Adjustable stabilizer

Tail skid

Lindbergh was impressed by the people at the Ryan Aircraft Company in San Diego, although their premises were in a dilapidated building on a waterfront reeking of dead fish. Hours of overtime were needed to construct the new design in less than two months. On the test flights the plane exhibited good reserves of power. These would stand her in good stead when laden with fuel for the Atlantic crossing; some rivals had crashed on takeoff due to lack of power. The Wright "Whirlwind" J-5C engine produced 220 hp at sea level, turning over at 1,800 rpm.

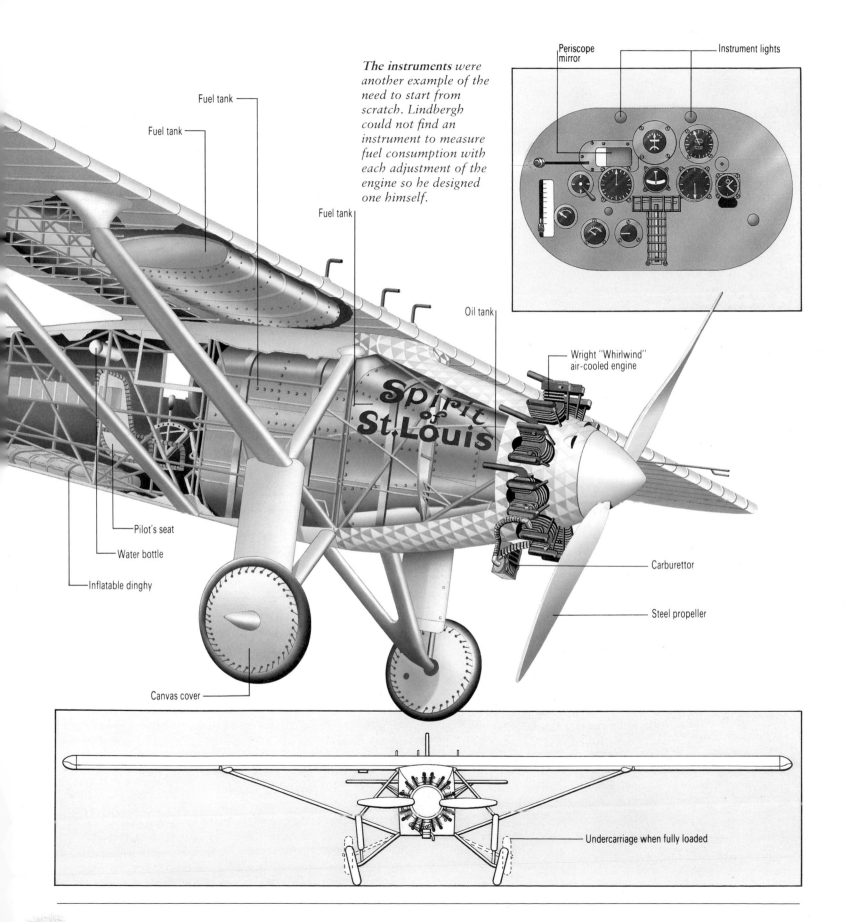

Fuel tank

Fuel tank

Fuel tank

The instruments were another example of the need to start from scratch. Lindbergh could not find an instrument to measure fuel consumption with each adjustment of the engine so he designed one himself.

Periscope mirror

Instrument lights

Oil tank

Wright "Whirlwind" air-cooled engine

Pilot's seat

Water bottle

Inflatable dinghy

Carburettor

Steel propeller

Canvas cover

Undercarriage when fully loaded

The Monoplane that Hit the Headlines

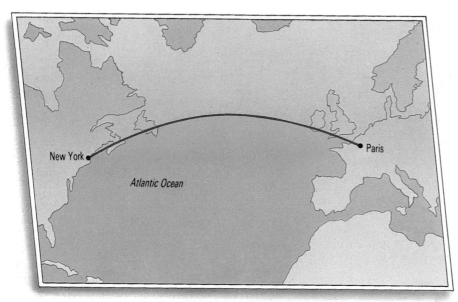

Lindbergh rightly considered lightness a key to success. As a result, safety and personal equipment were kept to a minimum. He did not even take a parachute. The list comprised an air raft with pump and repair kit, a canteen of water (8 pints), an Armbrust cup that condenses moisture from the breath, a knife, ball of cord, ball of string, large needle, flashlight, four red flares from a railroad sealed in rubber tubes, match safe and matches, a hacksaw blade, five cans of army emergency rations and five ham sandwiches. During the flight, he drank most of the water but ate little of the food, thinking that it increased his desire to sleep.

plane, the *Spirit of St Louis*. The chief designer was Donald Hall, and the monoplane he created had some novel features.

In most aircraft of that era, the pilot sat behind the engine but in front of the fuel tank, a position Lindbergh considered very dangerous. He decided to put the tank in front of him, which meant that he had no view forward, except by leaning out of a side window. Lindbergh explained that this was no serious disadvantage, since during takeoff the pilot could not see forward anyway, because of the engine high in the nose ahead of him. During normal flight he would not need to look ahead, because he would not be in any normal air lanes; for landing, he could see out sufficiently to get down safely. He wanted no night-flying equipment, and no parachute, in order to save a few pounds in weight. (He did take a rubber dinghy, in case of ditching in the sea.)

In order to speed up the building process, he agreed to let Hall use tail components from an existing Ryan model, although they would diminish the stability of the aircraft. It would not matter, Lindbergh argued, on an aircraft that was designed to be flown by an experienced pilot who would spend all of his time with his eyes on the compass and trying to steer a course above the waves.

Lindbergh decided to fly a great circle route, the shortest distance between two points on the Earth's surface. He drew the route on maritime charts of the Atlantic, and flew along it as best he could judge, setting his course by compass and making allowance for the wind by watching the spray from the waves below. It was a rough and

ready method but, as he explained, it would be accurate enough to ensure that he reached the European coast, and that was what mattered. He could still win the prize as long as he landed in France, and the design of the aircraft gave it a theoretical range of 4,100 miles—500 miles more than his great circle route. That ought to be enough to ensure a landfall even if his calculations were out.

The *Spirit of St Louis* made its maiden flight on 28 April 1927, just over two months after the order had been placed with the Ryan company. By 8 May Lindbergh was ready to fly to New York, when news came that two French airmen had set off from Paris on their bid to cross the Atlantic the other way. It looked as if all Lindbergh's efforts would be in vain. But Charles Nungesser and François Coli came down somewhere in the Atlantic in their Levasseur biplane, *L'Oiseau Blanc*, and were never seen again. Hope of finding them alive had not receded before Lindbergh took off for France, and he received requests to search for them in the area where it was thought they may have come down.

Once in New York, Lindbergh became obsessed by weather reports. As an experienced mail pilot, he knew he dared not try to make the trip in unfavourable weather, but also that he could trust the forecasters to give him advance warning of when the weather would improve. On the evening of 19 May, the good news came. Just after daybreak the next morning, weighed down with a full fuel load, the *Spirit of St Louis* was ready to go. It had never taken off fully laden, and the weather in New York was miserable, whatever the forecasters had said. In rain and over a muddy runway, Lindbergh opened the throttle and began to gain speed. He felt the tail go up, but then come down again. The plane splashed through a puddle, skimmed the next one, and was up. He cleared a set of telephone lines at the edge of the field by a bare 20 feet, and was gone.

Although he had laughed at the suggestion of carrying a periscope to see out, he nevertheless took one. For much of the journey he flew low over the sea, at an altitude where the greatest danger was colliding with the masts of ships. Peering through his periscope, which he lowered from the left side of the fuselage, he looked out for landmarks. But for most of the time, his eyes were on his chart, which lay on his lap, and a compass by which he steered. To conserve fuel, he cruised at a speed of 100 mph, which would

Landing at Le Bourget (above) was made difficult by the lack of feeling induced by exhaustion. Thousands of people greeted Lindbergh and the plane was damaged by the pressure of the crowd and by those wanting a souvenir. Two companies of soldiers and countless police could not restrain the crowd. It was 4.15 a.m. before Lindbergh got to bed—63 hours since he had last awoken. Dressed in full flying kit, Lindbergh (left middle) poses before leaving for home.

give him 50 hours of flying on what ought to be a 36-hour flight.

Eleven hours saw him over Nova Scotia, and heading across the Atlantic. There followed a long night of fighting off sleep and trying to keep on course. In the morning, he saw some trawlers, and seeking directions flew low above them. They ignored him, so rather than waste fuel, he flew on. An hour later, he saw land, and recognized it from his charts as the southern coast of Ireland. People waved to him from the ground.

He was next seen over Cornwall and then over the French coast at Cherbourg. By 9.52 p.m. he saw the Eiffel Tower and began to look for Le Bourget airport. The first time he missed it, but he turned round and tried again, landing to a huge welcome from an ecstatic crowd that had been warned of his arrival. He had flown from New York to Paris in 33 hours 30 minutes. He was the most famous man in the world.

Flying Farther and Faster

The great distinction of being the first to fly in a heavier-than-air machine was achieved by Orville Wright, at Kitty Hawk, North Carolina, on 17 December 1903. Between 1896 and 1902, Orville and Wilbur Wright learned enough about aerodynamics from experiments with gliders to begin work on a powered aeroplane. They built their own four-cylinder engine which drove two propellers by chain drives. Scepticism about the chances of success was reflected in the fact that just five people turned out to witness the first flight of 12 seconds.

Since that momentous day, aviators and aeroplane companies have worked to break new ground, either in terms of endurance and average speed over a long haul, or by raising through steady increments the speed of the world's fastest aircraft. Records in the first category were being established throughout the 1920s and '30s; after World War II, the target was the sound barrier and then Mach 2 and 3.

Amelia Earhart (above), born in Kansas, was the first woman to fly the Atlantic as a passenger, in 1928. Four years later, she became the first woman to fly alone across the Atlantic, in a monoplane. The flight took 13½ hours. In 1937, she set off around the world in a twin-engined Lockheed Electra, but went missing over the Pacific.

Amy Johnson, born in Hull, England, flew solo to Australia in 19½ days in 1930, just three days short of the record. Her epic flights to Japan via Siberia in 1931 and to Cape Town in 1932 set new records. She is seen here (right) just before setting off for Cape Town. On a flying mission in 1941 she disappeared over the Thames Estuary.

The Wright brothers were refused recognition or financial help for their aviation experiments in the United States, so in 1908 Wilbur Wright went to France to try to obtain support there. This time large crowds watched the flights in their *Flyer* biplane. A vast improvement on earlier models, in which the pilot lay prone on the lower wing beside the engine, in this *Flyer* both pilot and engine were upright. Wilbur flew from Hunardières-Le Mans (above) and achieved a flight of 2 hours 19 minutes, winning the Michelin Cup and securing many orders for the Wright biplane. He returned in triumph to the US and the brothers turned over their bicycle factory to the manufacture of aeroplanes. After Wilbur died in 1912, Orville sold his interest and went into research.

The Schneider Trophy was first presented in 1913 by Jacques Schneider for success in a speed competition between seaplanes of any nation. The award stimulated aircraft development and had a major effect on World War II, since the competition led to the development of the Spitfire fighter that helped the RAF win the Battle of Britain. The Supermarine S.6 (above) was powered by a Rolls-Royce R type engine of 1,950 hp, which was a precursor of the Merlin engine fitted to the Spitfire. The S.6 won the 1929 race and set a world speed record with a speed of 357.7 mph.

The Lockheed SR-71 Blackbird (left) was put into service with the United States Air Force in the early 1960s and was the fastest military plane in the world. Able to cruise at Mach 3 (1,865 mph) and reach an altitude of 15 miles, most of the SR-71's airframe was built of titanium and coated with a heat-radiating black paint that could also absorb radar waves. Used as a spy plane, the SR-71's cameras could focus on a golf ball from a height of 14 miles. The plane's operating costs were so great they were taken out of service in 1990.

The Doomed Airship

Rigid airships represent one of the most fascinating dead ends in transport history. During the 1920s many saw them as the aerial equivalents of the great liners, gliding silent through the night sky as their passengers slept. They offered space, comfort and—by the standards of the time—speed. Britain, France, the US and Germany all built airships in the conviction that they represented the future. It took seven disasters and the loss of 266 lives between 1921 and 1937 to show them how wrong they had been. Of these accidents none was more profoundly shocking than the loss of the R101 in October 1930.

The R101 and its sister ship, R100, were Britain's attempt to catch up with the German lead in rigid airship design, which had begun in 1900 with Count Ferdinand Zeppelin's LZ-1. A rigid airship was more than just a bag full of gas or hot air with a basket hung below. It had a metal or wooden framework covered in fabric, with passenger accommodation inside the envelope. The lightweight hydrogen gas was contained in bags made of goldbeaters' skin, inside the cover and harnessed to the structure.

Also attached to the structure were engines, with propellers, capable of driving the airship at speeds of up to 70 mph. The rigid airship seemed particularly safe, because it did not depend on forward motion—and hence on unreliable engines—to keep it aloft, as aircraft did. It floated on the air like a liner on the ocean, the very image of soundness and security. This was a terrible illusion.

In Britain, the airship's greatest champion was Lord Thomson, a successful soldier who in 1924 became secretary of state for air in the first Labour government. He had no doubt that one day the British Empire would be linked together by airships and he quickly launched a programme to build two of them. No ideologue, he arranged for R100 to be built by private industry, while R101 was entrusted to the Royal Airship Works at Cardington in Bedfordshire.

Both had the same specification: a gas capacity of 5 million cubic feet, sufficient in theory to carry 100 passengers with 8 tons of mail and cargo for 3,135 nautical miles at a speed of 55 knots. Five million cubic feet of hydrogen gives a theoretical gross lift of 151.8 tons, from which must be subtracted the weight of the airship, engines, fuel and ballast to calculate the payload.

Unfortunately, but perhaps inevitably, the weight of both airships turned out to be considerably greater than their designers anticipated. Consequently, when R101 was completed in June 1929, its disposable lift was only 46.8 tons, instead of the 63.3 tons intended. By the time fuel, ballast, crew and food were loaded, that left just 9.3 tons available for passengers, mail and cargo, instead of the 24.2 tons intended.

In spite of these problems, R101 was an impressive sight as it was walked out of the huge shed at Cardington by 400 men holding on to ropes. It was the biggest airship ever built—732 feet long, 140 feet high, and with an outer cover that was almost 5 acres in area. R101 was by quite a margin the biggest vessel in the world.

The lack of lifting capacity was, however, a serious embarrassment. One problem with airships was the need to carry a large amount of deadweight in the form of ballast, for there was no way of replenishing the gas in mid-flight. If leaks in the gas bags or an increase in temperature caused the craft to sink, the only way of correcting the situation was by dumping water ballast overboard. An airship flying without adequate amounts of ballast was dangerous and hard to control, so arrangements were made to collect rainwater falling on the cover in flight to replenish the ballast tanks.

It is clear that in spite of its apparent security, the airship operated in a very narrow safety envelope. Apart from the risk of fire there was the danger of the fragile gas bags puncturing, of loss of lift because of changes in temperature, or of damage from severe weather. Violent storms could carry airships upward like the leaves in autumn, as R100 found on a visit to Canada in 1930 which nearly ended in disaster. Navigation instruments were primitive in the extreme.

With the benefit of hindsight, it is hard to share Lord Thomson's conviction that airships had a future. Yet his ambition was to inaugurate a regular service to India, via Ismailia in Egypt. The trip by R100 to Canada, although hair-raising to the participants, had ended in apparent success. Now it was necessary to fly R101 to India with the secretary of state for air aboard. Lord Thomson wished this pioneering journey to take place while the Imperial Conference of 1930 was meeting in London, so that he could

return in triumph and address the delegates. Many have subsequently blamed the disaster on Thomson's impatience, although that was only one element in the tragedy.

To prepare for the journey, R101 had been modified in an attempt to increase lift. An extra bay had been added to its length, and the network of wires that held the gas bags in place had been let out to increase capacity. This meant that the bags were now rubbing against the actual structure of the airship, which they were not supposed to touch. A huge number of holes were made in the bags, which needed patching. To prevent the same thing happening again, sharp edges on the structure were covered in soft wadding to protect the bags. Frederick McWade, the airworthiness inspector at Cardington, reported that he was unhappy with this solution and could not grant R101 a permit to fly; his objections were overruled and were not brought to the attention of Lord Thomson.

All was made ready for the departure to India. In addition to Lord Thomson, the passenger list featured all the leading airship designers from Cardington, including the director of airship development, Wing-Commander R.B.B. Colmore. It now seems rash in the extreme to fill an experimental flight with so many top brass, but there was complete optimism, bordering on complacency, that all would go well.

R101 beside the docking tower at the Royal Airship Works. Excessive weight was a key factor in R101's loss: it weighed 113.4 tons instead of the intended 90 tons. Lord Thomson was not warned about the need to restrict luggage and brought an Axminster carpet weighing almost half a ton as well as 254 lb of trunks and champagne.

The Doomed Airship

The Beardmore Tornado diesel engines which powered R101 were a major reason for the miscalculation of the airship's weight. Although diesel engines are reliable and economic to run, they are heavy in relation to other engines. However, the higher flash point of diesel fuel compared with petrol was a safety factor.

The lounge of R101 was 60 feet long by 32 feet wide and was on the upper accommodation deck, along with a dining room for 50 people and the cabins. On the lower floor were a smoking room, electric kitchens, crew's quarters and further cabins. The total floor area available to passengers and crew was 7,780 square feet, the size of a large country house.

Lord Thomson's timetable, already delayed by the alterations to R101, made a departure early in October vital if he were to return in time to address the conference. It was the first time R101 had left the British Isles, and ahead lay two long legs, from Cardington across France and down the Mediterranean to Ismailia, and then by way of Baghdad and the Gulf to Karachi. The first, some 2,235 nautical miles, was scheduled to take 48 hours, the second, 2,135 nautical miles, another 46 hours.

Departure was set for the evening of 4 October 1930, and the luggage was loaded. By the time all was ready and the secretary of state was on board, delay became impossible even though the weather forecasts for France were bad and becoming worse. R101 set off into the teeth of the fiercest gale it had ever experienced, though such was the cheerful spirit of those on board that it did not fail to make its customary tour of Bedford after leaving the tower. Flying barely 600 feet above the houses, it weighed 160 tons—the greatest load ever lifted by any aircraft at that time. After its farewell circuit the airship set off toward London.

As it flew over London, people came out into the streets to watch. Looking up they could see faces silhouetted in the large windows of the passenger cabin. As it crossed the Kent countryside just south of Hawkhurst, R101 sent a radio message to the Met Office asking for further weather forecasts. It passed over Bodiam Castle and crossed the coast 4 miles east of Hastings.

As R101 crossed the Channel, calcium flares were dropped from the control car into the sea, igniting to produce a brilliant light. By watching

the flares, R101's navigators could estimate their drift. By mid-Channel the wind was up to 44 mph, with fierce gusts, and R101 flew at no more than 800 feet. The passengers had eaten and were now smoking in the special room set aside for that purpose. Across the Channel R101 made only 24.8 knots into a rising headwind.

By midnight it was west of Abbeville and flying at 1,500 feet to clear high ground; but in gaining height it had spilled gas, at the same time as adding more than 5 tons of weight as a result of rain absorbed by the cover and collected in the ballast tanks. At this point, R101 was almost certainly flying about 4 tons heavy, sustained in the air by the aerodynamic effect of its motion.

Over the wooded country between the Somme and the Bresle R101 flew on, with just the crew on watch awake. By now the wind was blowing

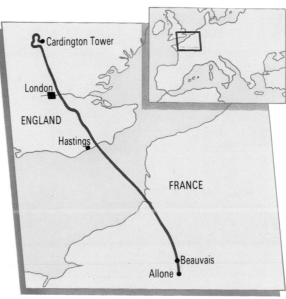

The fire that devastated R101 was started when the calcium flares used to aid navigation ignited in the wet undergrowth. The fire started just below the passenger accommodation and quickly spread to the gas bags. R101 was a mass of twisted metal in minutes. Amongst the passengers were Air Vice-Marshall Sir Sefton Brancker, director of civil aviation, and the best of the design engineers, Squadron Leader Michael Rope.

403

The Doomed Airship

at 50 mph, but all five engines were running well. The speed over France was down to 23.6 knots as R101 battled against the wind, constantly blown eastward off its course to Orly airfield.

By 2 a.m., the change of watch, R101 had almost reached the Beauvais Ridge at a ground speed of no more than 20 mph. Seven minutes later the ship suddenly dipped, pointing toward the ground before righting herself. She then dived again and nosed quietly into the ground. Within seconds R101 was in flames. In less than two minutes it had gone, consumed by a terrible fire that killed 46 of the 54 on board, including the secretary of state for air and all the leading British airship specialists.

What had happened? The most scrupulous analysis of the accident, carried out by Sir Peter Masefield for his book *To Ride the Storm*, has revealed the most likely course of events. He believes that in battling against the storm R101 had almost certainly damaged its outer cover, a known weakness in the design. Much of it had been replaced when it had been found to be rotten, but a critical section near the front had been retained. There had been no full-speed trial after the repairs and before the flight, so the cover had never been fully tested. R101 had flown into the worst storm of its life, and had ploughed on at full speed, in order to meet the secretary of state's timetable.

There had just been a change of watch, and the new coxswain had not had time to get used to the handling of the ship in the difficult conditions when it hit a region of turbulence. The chances are that the cover was damaged, and the fact reported to the men on the wheel, who reacted by throttling back the engines in order to spare the cover further damage. But R101 was flying heavy and needed speed to maintain height. As it slowed, it lost dynamic lift, went into a dive and brushed gently into the ground at hardly more than 10 to 15 mph.

The destruction of R101 spelled the end for British airships. R100 never left the shed at Cardington again, and plans for R102 and R103 were abandoned. The Germans continued their work until 1937, when the *Hindenburg* burst into flames at its mast in New Jersey. After that, all the high hopes that had inspired a generation of designers lay in ruins. The first vehicle to meet R101's specification—to carry 100 passengers more than 3,000 miles—was a heavier-than-air machine, the Bristol Britannia series 300 turbo-prop airliner, in 1956.

LEVIATHANS OF THE SKIES

Within 18 months of the Montgolfiers' flights, a hydrogen-filled balloon had crossed the English Channel and seemed to point the way forward. The military used them in the American Civil War (1861–65), and the first powered dirigible was built in Germany in 1872. Their potential was developed most notably by Count von Zeppelin. His 420-foot-long LZ 1 flew for $1\frac{1}{4}$ hours in 1900. Competition between Britain, France, Germany and the United States to develop the airship was intense, despite serious accidents and losses. The loss of the *Hindenburg* ended enthusiasm for the airship.

LZ 129, the Hindenburg, *under construction at Friedrichshaven. Completed in March 1936, the* Hindenburg *was the largest airship ever built, with a length of 813 feet and a capacity of 7 million cubic feet. She exploded in May 1937 while docking at Lakehurst, New Jersey.*

Professor Salomon Andrée and two companions attempted to reach the North Pole by balloon in 1897, setting off from Spitsbergen, Norway, aboard the specially built Eagle. With a capacity of 170,000 cubic feet, the Eagle was fitted with sails which were intended to direct it. The three were not seen again until their frozen bodies were discovered 33 years later. A diary found on Andrée revealed that the balloon had been abandoned three days after departure because it continually struck the ice. Then began a 200-mile trek across the frozen wastes.

The Graf Zeppelin *was the first commercial airship to cross the Atlantic, on 11 October 1928, flying from Friedrichshaven to Lakehurst in New Jersey. The next year, the* Graf Zeppelin *accomplished the first around-the-world airship flight with* passengers and mail. Thereafter it operated a regular service between Germany and Rio de Janeiro. With accommodation for 20 passengers, the Graf Zeppelin *was 772 feet long and had a capacity of 3.7 million cubic feet. It was broken up for scrap in March 1940.*

Opening up the East

No experience in flying is quite the equal of taking off and landing on water. While an airliner must operate from a busy airport, with its crowds, queues and tiresome delays, a flying boat can make use of any stretch of water. It can pick up its passengers from a beach or a harbour, taxi out between the yachts and speedboats, gain speed to the heady scent of hot oil and the spatter of salt spray against the windows, and translate itself into another element. This is flying with the magic put back in. Unfortunately, there are only a few flying boat services left, mostly in holiday areas like the US Virgin Islands, so few people have a chance to enjoy a wonderful experience. There was a time, however, when flying boats were thought to hold the future to aviation.

In the 1930s, before war brought down the curtain, it was possible to fly all the way to the Far East in a flying boat, making stops in dozens of exotic places and taking two weeks over the journey. The airline, Imperial Airways, stopped at places that are hardly places at all: Rutbah Wells and Sharjah, Gwadar in Baluchistan, Kanpur, Akyab, and the islands of Lombok, Sumba and Timor.

The journey was accomplished in aircraft that were laughably slow, though by the last years of the 1930s the route was served by a magnificent flying boat, the Short S-23, better known as the Empire class. Until recently, it was possible to meet old colonial officers whose eyes would grow misty at the mention of *Canopus*, or *Coriolanus*, or *Caledonia*, or *Corsair*—four of the Empire class boats, built by Short Brothers beside the River Medway at Rochester in Kent.

It was in 1928 that Imperial Airways first planned its long-distance routes to destinations in the Empire. For services to India and Africa, Short Brothers provided the S-8 Calcutta, an all-metal biplane flying boat with three engines. The Calcutta carried a crew of 4 and 15 passengers, and could cruise at 80 mph.

A couple of years later Short produced the Kent, also a biplane, which was used by Imperial on the Mediterranean stretch of the run to India. The Kent had four engines, the first ever passenger aircraft so equipped, and could cruise at 105 mph. Only three Kents were ever built. Each had space for 16 passengers in a roomy saloon with comfortable armchairs.

In 1935, Imperial Airways' ambitions began to widen, as they contemplated passenger services throughout the Empire, and across the Atlantic. Imperial issued to British companies a request for an aircraft, and Short Brothers once more came to their aid.

They produced a design for a large flying boat, able to carry 24 passengers, with a single high wing. It was bigger, faster and more powerful than any plane built in Britain, and Shorts suggested it might be sensible first to build a prototype to see how well it flew. Imperial responded by saying there was no time for that, and ordered 28 of the new boats off the drawing table. So was born one of the most handsome aircraft that ever flew, the Short S-23 "C" Class Empire flying boat.

The prototype, *Canopus* (named after an ancient Egyptian city), was launched at Rochester on 4 July 1936. Its four 920-hp Bristol Pegasus engines gave it a top speed of 200 mph and a cruising speed of 165 mph. It weighed 18 tons, but the design of its deep hull enabled it to "unstick" from the Medway in only 17 seconds on its maiden flight. The major advantage of the Empire type was its 700 mile range.

Canopus went into service on the Mediterranean run in October, and on 12 December *Centaurus* left with the first of the air mail bags to Egypt, and *Caledonia* departed on an experimental flight to India. The boats were rolling out of the Rochester plant at the rate of two a month. By June 1937, a total of 14 had been delivered and the first proving flight to Singapore had been undertaken. By February 1938, enough Empires were available to start a regular service to Singapore.

Travelling east by flying boat was not without its awkward moments. During 1938 one boat collided with an Italian submarine; *Ceres* was forced down on to Lake Dingari in Tonk, India, and became solidly bogged down in mud. In 1939, *Centurion* was written off by a gust of wind while landing on the Hooghly at Calcutta, and *Connemara* was burned at Southampton. In August *Challenger* crashed in Africa.

Even one of these accidents today would cause a tremendous furore, but airline passengers of the 1930s were a phlegmatic lot. It was a great adventure and, like all adventures, involved an element of risk. To those used to small, draughty

FACT FILE

The world's longest flying boat service, operated by Short S-23 "C" class Empire flying boats

Built: 1935/36

Wingspan: 114 feet

Length: 88 feet

Power output: 4 × 920 horsepower

Maximum speed: 200 mph

The first of the Empire flying boats, Canopus, *takes off from the River Medway with Rochester Castle, Kent, in the background (above). She left Rochester on the first route-proving flight, to Rome and Alexandria, in October 1936, returning on the first scheduled flight. Imperial Airways promoted the exotic nature of many of the places on the Empire route (left).*

Opening up the East

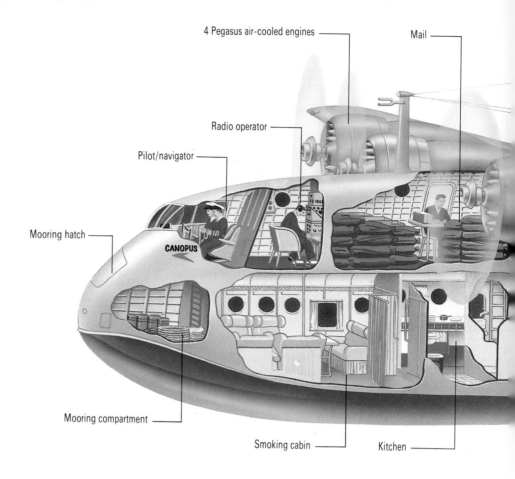

4 Pegasus air-cooled engines

Mail

Radio operator

Pilot/navigator

Mooring hatch

CANOPUS

Mooring compartment

Smoking cabin

Kitchen

and uncomfortable aircraft, the Empires were a revelation. One anonymous passenger, who wrote for *Imperial Airways Gazette* an account of his flight aboard *Calypso* to Singapore in March 1938, arrived at Southampton with a cabin wardrobe-trunk, a set of golf clubs, a suitcase, a heavy dispatch case and a typewriter. *Calypso* on this trip carried 3 tons of mail, 2 tons of cargo, and a few passengers, a couple of them young men going on their first contract to the newly opened oil fields in Bahrain.

From Southampton *Calypso* flew at 11,500 feet toward Marseilles. At this height it was chilly, so the steward gave out blankets and came round with cups of hot Bovril. Lunch consisted of soup, hot or cold meat and vegetables, sweet, cheese and dessert. At Marseilles the landing was made at Lake Marignane, a few miles from the city, after a flight of almost five hours. Here passengers spent their first night, before taking off again at 6.45 the next morning for Italy, landing this time on Lake Bracciano, 30 miles north of Rome. After refuelling, *Calypso* flew on to Brindisi, for more fuel and oil. Here the passengers were taken off in launches for customs examination before reboarding and flying on to Athens, landing in Phaleron Bay.

After a second overnight stop in Athens, *Calypso* took off again at 8.30 a.m., and landed for fuel in Mirabella, a landlocked bay on the northeast coast of Crete. Here Imperial Airways had moored the motor yacht *Imperia*, a floating depot and wireless station where the passengers took tea. After another 400-mile hop, *Calypso* landed on the harbour at Alexandria and taxied to her mooring between local craft.

After takeoff at six the following morning, *Calypso* flew over Port Said and Haifa, before landing on the Sea of Galilee near Tiberias. The passengers watched in amazement as the altimeters went down below sea level, for the Sea of Galilee lies 700 feet below the Mediterranean. After refuelling, it was off over the desert to Lake Habbaniyeh in Iraq, for more fuel to take *Calypso* as far as Basra. Over the marshlands between the Tigris and Euphrates rivers the local Marsh Arabs were known sometimes to take pot shots at passing flying boats, at least once with fatal results. That night was spent at Shatt-el-Arab, where *Calypso* met *Clio*, homeward bound, and *Calpurnia*, which had brought the King of Iraq to open a new airport and hotel.

An early start the following day called for the use of flares in the waterway to mark the takeoff

path. Stops were made in Bahrain, Dubai, Gwadar and Karachi, where *Calypso* landed among the shipping in the harbour. The run to Calcutta the next day involved stops at the sacred Lake Raj Samand in Udaipur, and the reservoir at Gwalior—reputed to be the hottest place in India. A final stop at Allahabad, then to Calcutta, where a porpoise jumped out of the water a few yards ahead of the flying boat as it landed on the Hooghly. From Calcutta the route took *Calypso* on to Akyab on the northern end of the Bay of Bengal, then over southern Burma to Rangoon, and on to Bangkok. One more day, and a single stop at Penang, finally brought the flying boat to Singapore.

Few air routes have ever been so romantic, and although the journey may seem endless to those familiar to modern jets, it was fast compared to the only alternative, steamers. But hardly had the Empire service become fully established than it was brought to an end by the war, and never resumed. Those unique craft, half boat, half plane, had only a brief and brilliant flowering before being replaced by something altogether more mundane.

The interior layout provided two decks forward of the wing spar. The upper flight deck had stations for captain and first officer at side-by-side dual controls, storage for mail bags and a purser's desk. There were also places for a radio operator and flight engineer on longer hauls. On the lower deck, the mooring compartment in the bow contained anchors; aft was a smoking lounge with seats for seven passengers, two toilets, the steward's galley and a midship cabin with seats that converted into bunks for three passengers.

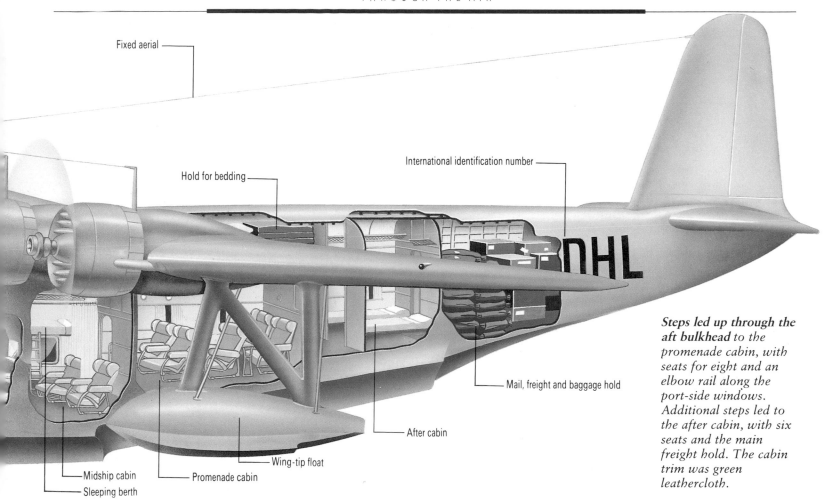

Fixed aerial

Hold for bedding

International identification number

Midship cabin

Sleeping berth

Promenade cabin

Wing-tip float

After cabin

Mail, freight and baggage hold

Steps led up through the aft bulkhead to the promenade cabin, with seats for eight and an elbow rail along the port-side windows. Additional steps led to the after cabin, with six seats and the main freight hold. The cabin trim was green leathercloth.

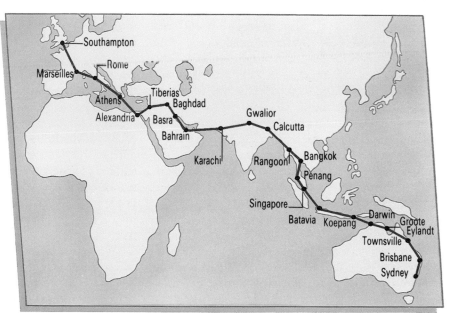

An air service from Britain to Australia began in late 1934, but until the introduction of flying boats in 1937/38, Imperial Airways planes operated the leg to Singapore and Hong Kong only. The regular flying boat service to Karachi began in 1937, and from July 1938 it went on to Darwin in Northern Territory. The thrice-weekly service, run by Imperial Airways and Qantas Empire Airways, was subject to repeated delays. Connections on to Sydney were provided by conventional aircraft. After World War II, the service resumed with Sunderlands and Sandringhams.

Rescue from the Skies

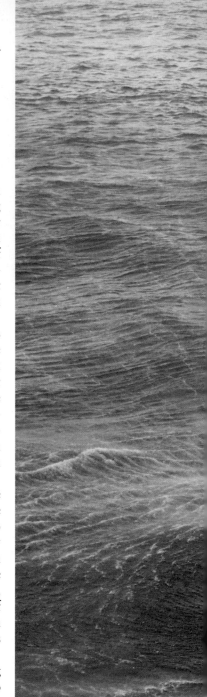

From the waters of northern Norway to the Bay of Biscay, Europe's western seaboard is patrolled by helicopters which have achieved a series of near-miraculous rescue operations. Men, women and children have been snatched from ships, oil rigs, life rafts, mountain tops and vertiginous crannies high in cliffs. No two rescues are quite the same; all they have in common is the immense relief of the victims as they see the familiar profile of the Westland Sea King coming into sight and their anxiety as they wait to be hauled aboard.

The Sea King, with its long range, big cabin, legendary reliability, and instruments which enable it to locate a tiny life raft 250 miles from base in the dead of night and thick fog, has become the champion at search and rescue missions. Hundreds of people owe their lives to the remarkable helicopter which first flew as the Sikorsky S61 in 1959.

One of the most dramatic rescues of all happened when the 1979 Fastnet race was devastated by a freak storm. A highlight of the yacht-racing calendar, the Fastnet that year had 300 entries. Winds gusting to force 11 scattered the fleet, and one of the biggest peacetime rescue operations ever undertaken was launched.

The waves ran at 40 to 60 feet and virtually every yacht in the race suffered some degree of distress, from extreme discomfort to mortal danger. Six Sea Kings, flying for three days through salt spray which filled the air up to 1,000 feet, rescued 73 people. Another 17 yachtsmen died. The Sea Kings' engines swallowed so much salt that they had to be washed out during refuelling stops on the ground.

During the 1985 Fastnet race, a Sea King made another dramatic rescue when the pop singer Simon Le Bon and members of his crew were trapped in the overturned hull of his yacht *Drum*. Le Bon, lead singer with the group Duran Duran, was asleep when a force 8 gale ripped the keel off his boat and overturned it. Trapped in the hull with five crew members, Le Bon was rescued by Petty Officer Larry Slater, a Royal Navy frogman dropped from a Sea King, who swam through the hatch into the hull and pulled them out one by one.

The Sea King was originally designed by Sikorsky helicopters in the United States as a platform from which to seek and destroy enemy submarines and ships. It made its first flight in 1959, and in 1966 was the subject of a licensing agreement between Sikorsky and Britain's major helicopter manufacturer, Westland. Since then Westland has sold 320 Sea Kings out of a total of 1,400 of the type manufactured. American production of the model has now stopped, but Westland continues to make it at its factory in Yeovil, Somerset.

From the beginning Westland made Sea Kings specifically tailored for the search and rescue role, omitting the sonar equipment used to track submarines and extending the cabin 5 feet farther aft, in order to find room for more survivors. By the mid-1970s Westland was producing the Sea King HAR Mk3, with twin Rolls-Royce Gnome engines, a two-tank fuel system and comprehensive equipment for the search and rescue function.

It is a combination of features that makes the Sea King such an effective life-saver. One of the most important is size: it is small enough to operate from ships at sea, yet big enough to carry 20 survivors and 4 crew. In extreme cases, even more people have been carried. It has huge doors, necessary for the winching operations, and two engines which provide a degree of reassurance when operating over water. It can operate on one, if necessary, as long as the load is not too great.

At a cruising speed of 115 mph, the Sea King can operate for nearly six hours, but it is also extremely effective at low-speed hover just above the sea. There is provision for automatic transition from forward flight to hover, and height hold which will maintain the aircraft at any height between 0 and 140 feet, within a couple of feet. The pilot can set the controls so that the Sea King automatically slows down over a distance of half a mile before settling at a preset hover height over the sea. When departing, the pilot can select autotransmission up, which will fly the aircraft to a preset height and a speed of 103 mph before he has to take over manual control.

The stories of rescues performed by Sea Kings are extraordinary. Often divers must be sent down to help crewmen on sinking ships escape, putting themselves into appalling danger. In 1989, the 18,000-ton Pakistani-registered *Murree*, bound for Egypt from London with building materials, foundered 25 miles off Start Point in

FACT FILE

The definitive search and rescue helicopter

Date built: 1959–

Length: 57 feet 2 inches

Diameter of rotor blades: 62 feet

Range: 870 miles

A German Sea King lifts a survivor from a life raft *(above)*. The West German navy ordered enough Sea King airframes to equip a complete search and rescue squadron. Sea Kings were used during the Falklands War in 1982, most memorably to rescue survivors from the blazing landing ship Sir Galahad *(left)*, at Bluff Cove. Eventually the ship was towed out to sea and sunk as a war grave.

Rescue from the Skies

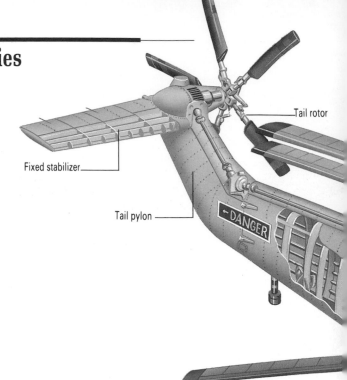

Tail rotor

Fixed stabilizer

Tail pylon

←DANGER

IGOR SIKORSKY

The specification of the most modern Sea Kings (right) maintains the helicopter's reputation as a world leader in air-sea rescue. Its tactical air navigation system (TANS) computes, from a variety of input data, wind velocity, track, groundspeed and present position. It also calculates bearing and distance to a selected point, as well as the time needed to reach it.

The hundreds of people rescued by helicopters owe their lives ultimately to Igor Sikorsky, the first man to establish the configuration of the modern helicopter. A pioneer aviator in pre-revolutionary Russia, Sikorsky designed a series of aircraft, culminating in the remarkable Grand, the world's first four-engined aircraft, which he first flew in 1913. In 1918, he departed for the United States, and during the 1920s and '30s he designed a series of aircraft and flying boats.

In 1939, he turned again to a dream—creating an aircraft that would take off and land vertically. His earliest attempts failed for lack of power; but by 1936 the first flights had been made in helicopters with two rotors, and Sikorsky determined to solve the problems of creating a stable aircraft using one main rotor for lift.

His first experiments with the VS-300 involved sitting amidst a box framework with a large rotor above and secondary rotors at the tail to provide stability. Improvements led, by 1942, to the XR-4 variant of the VS-300, with the main rotor providing lift and forward motion, and a single tail rotor to prevent the aircraft whirling around. Manufactured during the war as the R-4, Sikorsky's helicopter made the first aerial rescue under combat conditions in Burma in April 1944.

Sikorsky always believed the helicopter's role would include rescue missions and he experimented using a winch attached to a US Navy version of the R-4. The first air-sea rescue, by a US Army Sikorsky R-5, took place on 29 November 1945 off Long Island Sound.

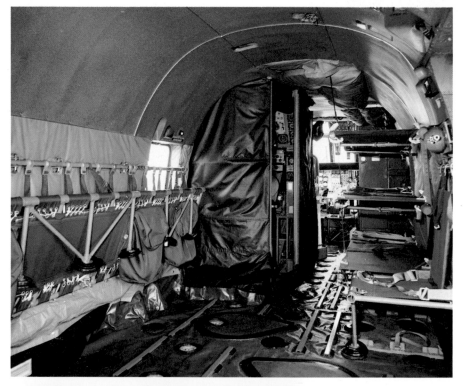

The cabin of a German Sea King (above and left), showing the enlarged space in the search and rescue versions, created by moving the after bulkhead. The cabin is 24 feet 11 inches by 6 feet 6 inches, providing seats for 20 survivors and 4 crew, although as many as 27 people have been carried in extremis.

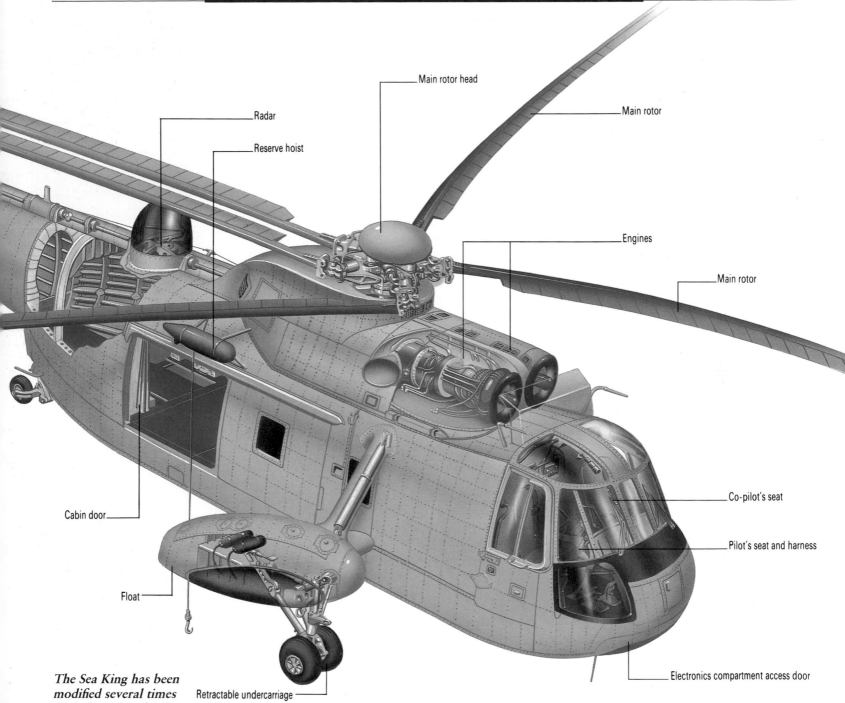

Main rotor head

Radar

Main rotor

Reserve hoist

Engines

Main rotor

Co-pilot's seat

Pilot's seat and harness

Cabin door

Float

Electronics compartment access door

Retractable undercarriage

The Sea King has been modified several times since the original US navy version was first made. The Sea King built by Westland today (above) is very different from the American standard. Besides its search and rescue role, the Sea King has been adapted for anti-submarine warfare, for anti-surface vessel combat and for logistic support and troop transport. There are over 1,400 Sea Kings in service worldwide.

Devon. The bows of the ship were already awash when the first Sea King landed diver Steve Wright on board. He helped to winch 30 crew from the ship to safety, but by then the *Murree* was sinking fast. His colleague Dave Wallace was sent down to help. They managed to get the last ten crew off on to the second Sea King just seconds before the ship gave a huge lurch and began to turn over.

"There was an almighty bang," said Wallace later, "and we could see the boys in the aircraft signalling us to jump. We were slipping down the deck and I got my foot caught in a rope. As soon

as I got free I jumped and Steve went over the rail at much the same time. I knew it was a long fall, and I went very deep into the water. It felt like an age before I came up again, and when I did I could see the ship's stern towering above us. We both thought we were going to be sucked under so we swam like hell to get away, and then the winchman came down and we got hooked on and taken back up again. It could not have been closer. It was last second stuff and very frightening, there's no doubt about that." Together the two Sea Kings had rescued the entire 40-strong crew of the *Murree* in 100-mph winds.

Aerial Fire-Fighters

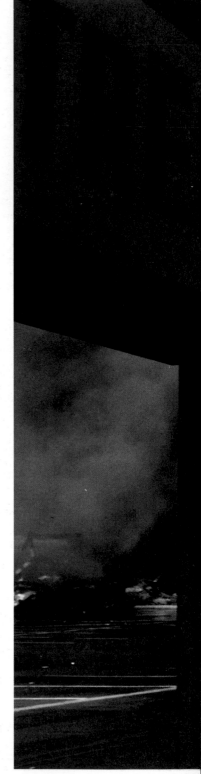

The days of barnstorming are long over for most pilots, who today must abide by increasingly restrictive regulations. Some airline captains, bored by long flights when all the work is done by autopilots, complain that they are beginning to lose their edge. It is not a complaint ever heard from the crews of the Canadair CL-215, perhaps the last fliers outside the air forces of the world who have the chance to fly a big aircraft to the limit of their ability. The CL-215 is an amphibious plane designed for one specific purpose: dousing fires, especially forest fires, with 6 tons of water at a time, then skimming across a lake to pick up another load. It requires hair-trigger judgement, great skill and a lot of confidence. It is never boring.

Canada is a land of forests and lakes. In the fire season between April and October, lightning strikes and human carelessness often set the forests ablaze. There is plenty of water in the lakes to fight the fires, but getting it to where it is needed was an impossible task before the development of fire-fighting aircraft—first the Canso and later the much bigger CL-215. For 20 years the CL-215s have been proving their value, not only in Canada but also in France, Spain, Yugoslavia and other countries. There is no other aircraft like it, and flying it is an experience that would soon shake a jaded airline pilot out of the rut.

In many ways, the CL-215 is an anachronism. Years after the jet and the turboprop have taken over, the CL-215 still uses piston engines, 18-cylinder Pratt & Whitney Double Wasps originally chosen for their rapid acceleration and good low-speed performance. Some of the aircraft have now been converted to turbo-prop operation but most of them still have the thunderous 2,100 hp radials.

The CL-215 is a flying boat, a type of aircraft that is now a rarity in the skies. Most important of all, despite its size, it still needs to be flown like a fighter, swooping down on lakes at a steep angle, taking off again fully laden at the very limits of its capability, then flying at treetop height through smoke and ashes to release its water in a one-second burst whose accuracy depends entirely on the judgement of the crew.

The CL-215 emerged from a market research programme by Canadair in the early 1960s. Careful study of how forest fires start and spread showed that substantial amounts of water needed to be delivered in a very short time to have much chance of putting them out. The biggest aircraft that could be operated at reasonable cost turned out to have a payload of 1,200 gallons of water. To be able to lift water from any convenient lake it would need to be an amphibious flying boat. The first aircraft, bearing the registration letters CF-FEU-X, made its maiden flight in October 1967.

To reduce production costs, the CL-215 is a simple slab-sided box, made of aluminium alloy. The water is carried in the lower part of the hull, and picked up by two probes which descend and dip into the water, their openings facing forward. The movement of the aircraft, at speeds of 92 mph, is sufficient to fill the tanks in 10 seconds. The probes are lowered as the aircraft descends toward the water, and non-return valves prevent the water escaping. As soon as the tanks are full the pilot selects full power and takes off again.

Once in the air, a small amount of fire retardant is added to the water, to improve its ability to douse flames. The retardant also creates a foam effect which acts as a target for other aircraft following behind. In a big fire, a team of CL-215s working together make a series of runs. A single load would never be sufficient to douse a fire, but might delay its spread for 15 minutes or so. As long as the aircraft is capable of returning with another load within 8 to 10 minutes, it stands every chance of bringing the fire under control or at least of stopping its spread. A team of aircraft working together, if there is a suitable lake nearby, can deliver a full load every few minutes.

The skill of the pilots is tested at every stage of the operation. Very often, they will be landing on lakes they have never seen before, and there is no way to judge from the air whether the water is deep enough—the CL-215 needs 4 feet 6 inches of water—or whether there are sunken obstacles that will foul the probes.

Once a lake has been selected, the pilot approaches with the probes down. As soon as the probes are in the water, power is increased to compensate for drag and increasing weight. Once the tanks are full, in about 10 to 12 seconds, full power is selected and the CL-215 takes off at just under 92 mph. Often, if the

FACT FILE

The piston-engined planes that water-bomb fires

Date built: 1972–

Wingspan: 93 feet 10 inches

Length: 65 feet

aircraft is carrying a full load of fuel as well, these takeoffs may be made in an overweight condition, so the pilot keeps his finger on the water release button. In an emergency, if it looks as if he is not going to manage to clear the trees at the water's edge, he can release the cargo in a second.

Bombing the fires also requires great skill. The heat can be stifling as the CL-215s come in over the forests at heights of between 100 and 150 feet.

If they flew any higher, their water would be dissipated before it could have any real effect on the flames. The final approach is usually made through choking smoke and always in severe turbulence caused by the hot air rising from the fire. Strong wind shears may be experienced from violent low-level winds.

To help to reduce side slip, the turboprop-fitted CL-215, designated CL-215T, has large endplates at the wing tips. The engine's greater

A CL-215 drops 6 tons of water on a fire. Although the capacity of the CL-215T is the same, the greater power, speed and quick start mean a 119 percent increase in the number of tons of water delivered in the first hour of a mission.

415

Aerial Fire-Fighters

power helps the rate of climb and acceleration, and the pilot no longer has to endure the heat of fires as air-conditioning is now fitted.

The aircraft fly over the fires at 115 to 126 mph, and can opt either to drop their entire load in a single burst, or to open the two bomb doors successively to produce a narrower but longer spread. As the water drops away, the aircraft surges upward, but there is no danger of losing control because the tanks are placed close to the centre of gravity. Judgement of when to release the water is simply a matter of experience, although care must be taken to avoid any fire-fighters on the ground, who could easily be killed by 6 tons of water falling on them.

One of the greatest dangers is colliding with "cheekos"—tall, dead trees that blend into the background and cannot be seen until the very last moment. Fortunately, the CL-215 is an extremely strong aircraft. Once, a pilot heard a clatter as he flew over a fire, but sustained little damage. He was astonished when a forester brought him a sample of the tree which he had felled, a massive branch that would have brought most other aircraft down.

One of the most dramatic operations undertaken by the CL-215 was the fight against a fire close to the town of Val d'Or in Quebec in 1972. To control this fire took four CL-215s and two Canso aircraft, working together. During the battle one pilot spotted a small but very violent fire in a nearby wood just a few hundred yards from a railway junction and a propane and petrol storage plant.

The fire was "crowning"—sweeping through the very tops of the trees—always an indication of great heat intensity. At virtually the same moment a second fire broke out 1½ miles to the east. Careful control was needed to coordinate the attack on two fires less than 2 miles apart, but soon the aircraft were dropping their loads of water at one-minute intervals. Every few circuits an aircraft would detour and drop its water from a greater height on to the roofs of houses, to protect them from flying embers. The fire was eventually stopped just 20 feet from the propane storage tanks.

In the space of two hours, the six aircraft had made 65 drops, totalling just under 300 tons of water. The single operation saved the propane plant, worth £160,000, and other property, the total value of which was equal to half the cost of operating Quebec's fleet of fire-fighting aircraft for a whole season.

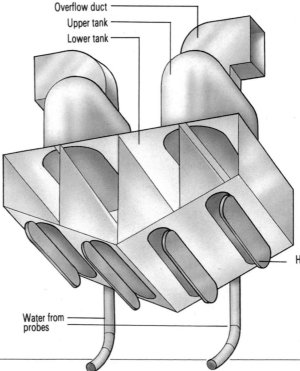

Overflow duct
Upper tank
Lower tank
Hydraulic door system
Water from probes

The water is released through doors that form the bottom of the two tanks located on each side of the aircraft's centreline. These doors are normally unlatched by an electrically controlled hydraulic system, but there is also a manual release system for emergencies. As speed is of the essence, the tanks can be filled in about 10 seconds.

The water tanks are empty in less than a second, once the release button has been pressed (above), causing a pronounced upward pitch. A similar but opposite reaction is felt landing on the water at high speed (left) when a severe nose-low pitch can cause inexperienced pilots to lose control. The record for the number of pick-ups and drops in a day is held by a Yugoslavian CL-215, at 225.

Juggernaut of the Air

FACT FILE

The world's largest aircraft

Built: 1985–88

Wingspan: 290 feet

Length: 276 feet

Power output: 311,700 lb of thrust

Cargo load: 250 tons

The principal difference between the An-124 and An-225 lies in the twin fins at each end of the tailplane of the An-225, the larger aircraft (opposite). This is designed to make it easier to carry loads mounted on top of the fuselage. The droop of the wings can be seen clearly as the An-225 comes in to land (below).

The biggest aircraft in regular service in the world's airlines is the Boeing 747 jumbo jet, able to carry more than 400 passengers over distances of 8,400 miles. Only one American aircraft, the Lockheed C-5 cargo aircraft, is bigger, although its engines are less powerful. The Soviet Union, however, has now produced not one but two aircraft that dwarf even the C-5. When the second of these, the gigantic Antonov An-225, arrived at the 1989 Paris air show with the Soviet space shuttle *Buran* (Snowstorm) riding on its back, there were gasps of amazement. The An-225, or Mriya (Dream), had rewritten almost all the superlatives of the aviation industry.

It was a product of the Antonov design bureau in Kiev, led by chief designer Pyotr Balabuyev. To the already gigantic An-124, which first flew in 1982, the Antonov team had added a longer body, bigger wings, more engines and more wheels. At the back, looking down on the football field of the cargo hold, is an area where 70 passengers can be seated. The An-225 is the first aircraft able to take off with a gross weight of more than a million pounds; fully laden it leaves the ground weighing 1,320,750 lb, or 600 tons. It can lift a cargo load of 250 tons, against the C-5 Galaxy's 132 tons.

The An-225 was designed for a specific purpose: carrying the Soviet space shuttle, its huge rocket launcher, or other heavy pieces of

equipment for the oil, gas or electricity generating industries to wherever they are needed in the Soviet Union. Confidence that this could be done had been gained after experience with the An-124, which itself was a huge aircraft. In the mid-1980s, the An-124 took all the world records for maximum weight lifted and long-distance endurance. On 6/7 May 1987, an An-124 covered 12,521 miles without refuelling, around a circuit that took it from Moscow to Astrakhan, Tashkent, Lake Baikal, Petropavlovsk, Chukot Peninsula, Murmansk, Zhdanov and back to Moscow, arriving with some fuel left.

The An-124 is powered by four Lotarev D-18T turbofans, each producing 51,950 lb of thrust. Its wingspan is 240 feet, while its hold is 118 feet long, 21 feet across and 14 feet 5 inches high. It lands on ten wheels. All these figures are, however, easily exceeded by the An-225, which is an An-124 stretched in every direction. Instead of four engines, it has six; its wingspan is increased to 290 feet by adding an extra section that carries the two additional engines, and the length of the cargo hold is increased to over 141 feet. The total length of the aircraft is nearly 276 feet and when it is parked on the runway a double-decker bus can drive under its wings.

Design of the An-225 began in 1985, and it made its first flight on 21 December 1988. On 22 March 1989 it set a total of 106 world and class records in a single day, taking off at a gross weight of 1,120,370 lb and flying 1,250 miles at a speed of 505 mph and at heights of up to 40,000 feet. According to deputy aviation minister Vladimir Ivanov, who spoke during a visit of the An-225 to the 1990 Farnborough air show, the huge aircraft does not need a special runway.

The total cost of the An-225 programme has been £150 million, but it is not clear how many will be built. In September 1990 a second was almost complete, and six crews had been trained to fly the aircraft. Pyotr Balabuyev said "There will be others, but not very many. And so far as we can see, this is about as big as we can get."

The principal purpose of the An-225 is to fly the shuttle orbiter *Buran* from the factory where it is built to the Baikonour Cosmodrome for launch. *Buran* is believed to weigh 70 tons, too heavy for the modified M-4 bomber which had been used for similar tasks before.

In November 1988, the *Buran* orbiter was

Juggernaut of the Air

The carrying capacity of the An-225 was put to use in the 1990/91 Gulf crisis, carrying Bangladeshi refugees to safety (above). The cargo hold is 141 feet long and loading is facilitated by the fact that the entire nose section swings upward. The aircraft can be made to "kneel" by retracting the nosewheel and settling on to two extendable feet to give the floor an upward slope. The 16 landing wheels (right) are independently sprung to help the aircraft tolerate makeshift runways.

disaster of 1986. Leaving the children in the US for medical treatment, the An-225 flew back to Kiev with 200 tons of medical supplies on board for other Chernobyl victims.

If the Soviet shuttle has hit problems, the An-225 may find that its primary purpose no longer exists, but there are likely to be plenty of other things it can do. Many large machines or structures, such as turbogenerators, boilers or oil industry equipment, are difficult to transport by road or rail. Often they have to be transported in pieces and reassembled on site. The An-225 makes it possible to carry loads never before carried by air, not only in the USSR but in other countries too. In the post–Cold War climate, the Soviet authorities could well create a successful business shifting heavy loads.

The An-225 might also come to the rescue of a British development for launching satellites. Hotol is a space plane which uses a revolutionary engine able to convert from a jet to a rocket high in the atmosphere. As originally conceived, Hotol (standing for horizontal takeoff and landing craft) would take off from a normal runway using its engines as air-burning jets. When it reached the upper limits of the atmosphere, it would start burning rocket fuels in the same engines, making the transition from aircraft to space plane. The difficulty is that the British government has declined to contribute to the £6 billion cost of developing Hotol.

Late in 1990, British Aerospace and the Soviet authorities began discussing whether it would be possible to launch Hotol from the An-225. It would be carried to the aircraft's ceiling and then released, burning rocket fuel to put it into orbit. If this proved feasible, BAC engineers believed it would be possible to reduce the cost of developing Hotol to £2.5 billion, largely because they could eliminate the air-breathing engine. This might then cut the cost of launching satellites to as little as $8 million a shot, against the $70 million a launch of the US shuttle. Hotol would go into space, and then re-enter the atmosphere and land at an ordinary airport like the shuttle.

BAC believes there would be an enormous market for such a system, and if the feasibility studies work out, intends to approach European governments and the European Space Agency for support. Projects like the American space station desperately need a cheap, re-usable launch system if they are ever to work. Perhaps the An-225, the world's biggest aircraft, could help provide it.

launched from Baikonour for the first time, making two unmanned orbits of the Earth before coming in to land under automatic control. Since then there have been no further flights, suggesting problems in the development of *Buran*. As a result, the An-225 has been underemployed, although it has been used to carry bulky engineering equipment to remote sites in Siberia, and during the Gulf crisis it was used to rescue a large number of refugees displaced by the Iraqi invasion of Kuwait.

In March 1991, an An-225 went to the US, carrying two children suffering from radiation injuries as a result of the Chernobyl nuclear

An An-225 performing the task for which it was primarily designed: carrying the space shuttle Buran. *Although the estimated 70-ton weight of* Buran *would be within the capacity of the An-124 with its 125-ton payload, it may be that parts of the huge Energia booster used to put the shuttle into orbit are too heavy for the An-124. Energia was first tested in May 1987 and is one of the biggest rocket boosters ever made, able to put 100 tons into orbit around Earth.*

Captain Charles "Chuck" Yeager (right) was a classic test pilot—cool, laconic and determined. On the nose of the P-51 he had flown in Europe at the end of World War II, he had written the name "Glamorous Glennis", after his wife. He had the same legend inscribed on the X-1 (above).

Edwards Air Force Base in California is famous as the landing site used for the space shuttles. When the X-1s used it, the air force base was named Muroc.

Beyond Mach 1

Toward the end of World War II, the air forces of Britain and the United States began experimenting with speeds close to the speed of sound. In 1943, a Mk IX Spitfire, one of the fastest fighters of the day, was used for a series of tests during which it dived from 40,000 feet at speeds which approached Mach 0.9—90 percent of the speed of sound.

The flights produced some curious results because the Spitfire did not really have a structure strong enough for speeds like these. The front edge of the tailplane had a tendency to bend upward, which meant that the elevator was enveloped in the slipstream and ceased to work normally. In fact, under these circumstances it was found that the controls reversed, so that any attempt by the pilot to pull out of the dive merely pitched the aircraft's nose even farther down. In 1946, Geoffrey de Havilland, the son of the founder of the company, was killed when his de Havilland 108 failed to emerge from such a dive.

The strange changes that seemed to set in close to the speed of sound led to the belief that it might be a barrier. One possible origin of this phrase was a remark by Dr W. F. Hilton of Armstrong-Whitworth, who suggested that as aircraft neared the speed of sound, drag would suddenly increase "like a barrier against the future". De Havilland's death lent credibility to the prediction, and the myth of the sound barrier was born.

Why it was ever believed is a mystery, for rifle bullets had long been travelling faster than the speed of sound without coming to grief. The wind tunnels available in the late 1940s could not reproduce supersonic conditions, so it was left to the test pilots to find out for themselves. Physical theory, first enunciated by Ernst Mach in the nineteenth century, indicated that there would be a change in the behaviour of the air at these speeds because the aircraft would overtake its own pressure wave. At normal speeds, these pressure waves spread away ahead of the aircraft; at transonic speeds, the aircraft would catch up with its own waves, compressing the air and causing instability.

In 1944, a research programme was launched in the US to investigate the question. The Army Air Force and the National Advisory Committee on Aeronautics (NACA) agreed to design a rocket-propelled aircraft, and a contract was signed with the Bell Aircraft Company of Buffalo, New York, on 16 March 1945. The design was largely a matter of fumbling about in the dark, but the team sensibly set out by basing the shape of the aircraft on an object that was known to fly straight at supersonic speeds, the .50 calibre bullet.

The result was a short, rather fat fuselage, straight wings and a very clean profile. The absence of propellers or a jet engine intake simplified the design, which was ready by the middle of October. The aircraft was called the Bell XS-1, X standing for experimental and S for supersonic. The S, however, was quickly dropped and it became known as the Bell X-1.

The first flight was made on 25 January 1946, with Bell test pilot Jack Woolams at the controls; the aircraft was taken aloft by a B-29 bomber, which was to be normal practice. On these first flights the rockets were not used, but the X-1 was simply glided down to land to test its flight characteristics. Woolams's report was enthusiastic. He had reached a speed of 275 mph and found the X-1 rock steady and easy to fly. After another nine test flights the decision was made to move the whole operation to Muroc Air Force Base in the Mojave Desert of California, a huge dry lake bed ideal for flying because of its vast flat area and the fact that the weather is perfect 350 days a year.

The first powered flights were made at Muroc by another Bell test pilot, Chalmers "Slick" Goodlin, who took the X-1 up to Mach 0.8, the figure guaranteed by Bell in their original contract. When this had been achieved, the first two X-1s were handed over to the Air Force. The first Air Force test took place with Captain Charles E. "Chuck" Yeager at the controls. According to Tom Wolfe, who chronicled the birth of the US manned space programme in his book *The Right Stuff*, Yeager celebrated this first flight by executing a barrel roll with a full load of rocket fuel, then pointed the aircraft vertically upward and accelerated to Mach 0.85—but this incident is not mentioned in more restrained histories.

Gradually the test flights got faster and faster as Yeager edged toward Mach 1. He experienced the buffeting that had become familiar but was convinced that the closer he came to Mach 1 the smoother it would become. He appears to have been quite genuinely unimpressed by the fears of

FACT FILE

The first manned aircraft to break the sound barrier

Built: 1945/46

Wingspan: 28 feet

Length: 31 feet

Power output: 6,000 lb of thrust

Maximum speed: 957 mph (Mach 1.45)

Beyond Mach 1

Yeager broke his own record on several occasions. On 26 March 1948, he reached 957 mph (Mach 1.45), the fastest ever reached by the X-1. In subsequent X-craft he reached yet more prodigious speeds, taking the X-1A to Mach 2.44 (1,650 mph) on 12 December 1953. In principle, it was possible for the X-1 to take off from the ground normally, but to make optimum use of the fuel, it was usually carried to high altitude underneath a B-29 bomber (above), before it was released and the rocket engines were ignited.

the engineers that the speed of sound would prove an impenetrable barrier. By his eighth flight Yeager had pushed X-1 to Mach 0.997, the very verge of the sound barrier. The attempt to break through it was set for 14 October 1947.

Two days before takeoff, Yeager took his wife Glennis out to a bar called Pancho's for a drink. About 11 p.m. , he decided it was a good time to take a ride on a couple of the horses that were kept at the bar by its owner, a woman called Pancho Barnes. Galloping back toward the bar, Yeager failed to see that a gate had been closed, ran straight into it and fell off, breaking two ribs. The next day, in some pain, Yeager realized that if he told the Air Force about his injury he would be taken off the flight, so instead he went to see a doctor in nearby Rosamond, who taped up his ribs and told him to keep his right arm still for a fortnight. The next day, at dawn, Glennis drove him over to Muroc for the flight.

By this time, Yeager was in considerable difficulty. His side hurt badly and he could

hardly move his arm. The major problem that faced him was how he was going to close the hatchlike door of the X-1 after he had climbed down into it from the B-29, for that involved pushing a handle forward with his right hand. He confided in the flight engineer, Jack Ridley, who solved the problem by cutting about 9 inches off a broom handle, which Yeager could use as a lever to close the handle with his left hand. Neither Ridley nor Yeager told anybody else of the problem.

At 7,000 feet Yeager climbed down the ladder from the B-29's bomb bay and into the tiny cockpit of the X-1. Ridley slotted the door, which had no hinges, into place, and with the broom handle Yeager managed to close the latch. Then the B-29 climbed to 29,000 feet, went into a shallow dive and then pulled up, releasing the X-1 like a bomb being thrown forward. Yeager ignited the rockets and was immediately thrown backward so hard that he could hardly get his hands to the controls. He shot upward to

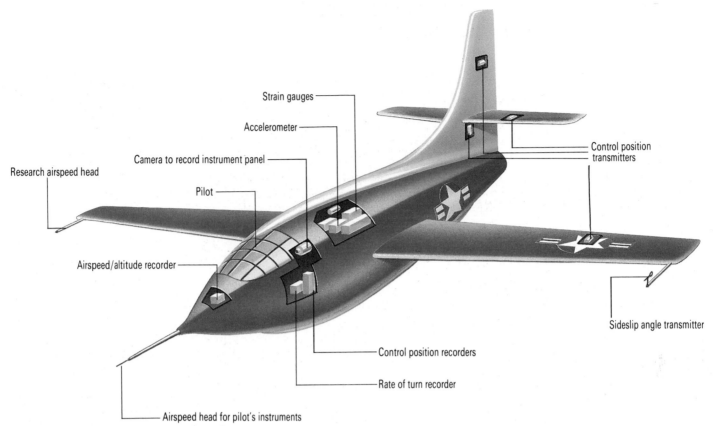

Research airspeed head

Camera to record instrument panel

Strain gauges

Accelerometer

Control position transmitters

Pilot

Airspeed/altitude recorder

Airspeed head for pilot's instruments

Control position recorders

Rate of turn recorder

Sideslip angle transmitter

The X-1 that broke the sound barrier can be seen at the National Air and Space Museum in Washington (above). It was one of only three built. The second is on display at Edwards Air Force Base, the third was destroyed by fire.

The X-1 was simple and very strong, made of aluminium and designed to withstand stresses 18 times those of gravity. It was 31 feet long and weighed just over 12,000 lb. Most of the fuselage was filled with two large stainless-steel fuel tanks, one of which contained liquid oxygen, the other ethyl alcohol. The fuel was fed to a single four-chamber rocket motor; each chamber fired separately and was capable of 1,500 lb of thrust.

40,000 feet and then nosed the X-1 over for the record attempt. At Mach 0.87 he reported a mild buffet, but by Mach 0.96 he was telling Ridley that his elevators were working well again.

Seconds later, without any evidence that anything dramatic had happened, the needle jumped to Mach 1.06. "Say, Ridley, make another note, will you," Yeager said. "There's something wrong with this machometer . . . it's gone kind of screwy on me." This was Yeager's way of conveying that he had exceeded Mach 1 without allowing outsiders who happened to be tuned to the right frequency to understand. As he did so, those on the ground heard a boom sound across the desert floor—the first sonic boom ever from a manned aircraft. When Yeager landed, the instruments were checked and confirmed that he had indeed gone supersonic.

This was the achievement that everybody interested in flight had been waiting for, but for some unexplained reason the Air Force put a total blackout on the news. Nobody was to be told that an American, in an American aircraft, had broken the sound barrier. It was two months later before the news appeared, as a leak in the magazine *Aviation Week*. The Air Force was furious and even contemplated legal action, but such a step would have been pointless.

In a very short time, the X-1 had shown all the fears about the sound barrier to be imaginary. Its example has since been followed by hundreds of different aircraft.

The Big Bird

Few aircraft have survived a more difficult gestation than Concorde, the world's first commercial airliner to fly scheduled services faster than sound. Assailed by economists, noise campaigners, cost cutters and fainthearts, and built in an unlikely collaboration between two countries traditionally suspicious of each other, Concorde emerged to discomfit its critics. Not only was it strikingly beautiful, but it worked, solving almost all the awkward problems of supersonic passenger travel. Only the bottom line let it down, for it was never built in sufficient numbers to recoup its huge development costs. To that extent, at least, its critics were right: but if every human endeavour were to be judged solely by profit and loss, it would be a dull world.

When aircraft first approached the speed of sound, it was seen as a barrier, a region of instability where the normal rules of aerodynamics no longer applied. Experience with the Bell X-1 in the US and the Fairey Delta 2 in Britain showed, however, that supersonic flight could be achieved by aircraft of the right configuration. The shape chosen for the Fairey Delta 2, which achieved a world air speed record for a jet aircraft of 1,132 mph in March 1956, was a sharply swept delta wing, and no tailplane.

At transonic speeds, several designs with tails had suffered problems as the airflow over the wings caused buffeting at the tail surfaces. Fairey decided, therefore, to dispense with the tail altogether, a bold move because it cast doubt on how controllable the aircraft would be.

The gamble succeeded, but another question then presented itself. The slender delta wing form worked well at supersonic speeds, but could it produce sufficient lift at low speeds during takeoff and landing? A small experimental aircraft, the Handley-Page 115, was built and showed that such a wing could indeed provide low-speed lift, without needing complex flaps or slots. However, the higher drag of such wings could only be overcome by carrying more fuel. Were it not for the greater efficiency of jet engines at supersonic speeds, long-distance supersonic transports (SSTs) would be impossible.

By 1961, it was apparent to aircraft designers in both Britain and France that a supersonic transport aircraft could be built. The French favoured a range of 2,000 miles, while the British insisted that an aircraft that could not cross the Atlantic would be worthless. A deal to build

FACT FILE

The first supersonic airliner

Built: 1965–67

Wingspan: 83 feet 10 inches

Length: 202 feet 4 inches

Power output: 38,050 lb of thrust

Maximum speed: Mach 2.04

A mock-up of the flight deck (left), showing the ram's-horn-shaped control columns and the flight engineer's panel on the right. Concorde has a greater thrust to weight ratio than subsonic aircraft so the feeling of acceleration on takeoff (right) is more pronounced. Fuel has to be moved from one tank to another or "burned off" prior to takeoff to make sure that the centre of gravity is positioned at a specific point. This is particularly important for stability, since Concorde does not have a tailplane. Fuel is redistributed throughout the flight.

The Big Bird

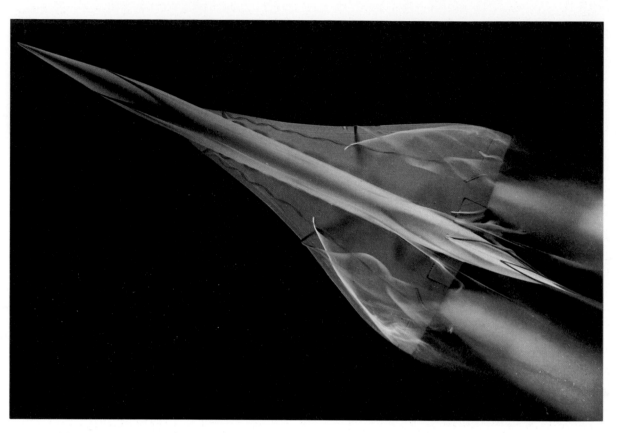

The intricate patterns of airflow over the wings and fuselage of a model of Concorde are revealed by a hydrodynamic tunnel test. The penalty of the slender delta wing necessary for supersonic speeds is its greater drag. The ratio between the lift produced by such a wing and the drag it generates is much less advantageous than conventional wings. To overcome this might have involved carrying so much fuel that there would have been no room for passengers. However, jet engines become more efficient at supersonic speeds because more air is crammed into them.

both versions was signed between Britain and France in November 1962, providing for equal distribution of costs and revenues. There was no provision in the treaty for either partner to withdraw. The medium-range version was later dropped, as the British view was adopted.

The designers of Concorde had little room for manoeuvre. When they began, the only people to have flown as fast or as high as Concorde were military pilots wearing pressure suits and provided with oxygen supplies—yet they were planning to carry more than 100 passengers, on regular services, in air-conditioned comfort.

At 60,000 feet, Concorde's cruising altitude, the air pressure is only one-tenth that at ground level, which meant that Concorde's fuselage had to be very strong to withstand the pressure differential. If it were made too strong, however, it would be too heavy. The payload on a long-haul trip was already small, only 5 percent of the all-up weight, compared with 10 percent for subsonic jets, and 20 percent for today's jumbo jets. A small error in engine performance, lift, drag or any other variable could have eliminated it altogether, which would mean that Concorde could cross the Atlantic only if it were not carrying any passengers.

The actual development of Concorde took

place against a background hum of political discord, dismay about the rising costs, and public apathy. The Labour government elected in Britain in 1964 attempted to cancel the project, but found that their Conservative predecessors had provided no get-out clause, for fear that the unreliable French would let them down. In fact, it was the British who proved the more faint-hearted. Reluctantly the teams at British Aerospace and Sud Aviation were allowed to continue their work, as the costs mounted.

On the other side of the Atlantic, attempts to develop a more ambitious SST, bigger and faster than Concorde, were running into the sand. Boeing had been chosen for the job and had submitted a swing-wing design which would have been the longest aircraft ever built, capable of carrying 300 passengers at Mach 2.7 at heights of up to 70,000 feet. Boeing, however, had bitten off more than they could chew. In 1969, they abandoned the swinging wings and went for a delta shape like Concorde's. Speed would still have been Mach 2.7, necessitating a titanium fuselage. In 1971 the project was cancelled.

While officials on both sides of the Atlantic chewed their pencils, Concorde took shape. On 2 March 1969, the first Concorde to fly, 001, lifted off from Toulouse in the hands of test pilot

The Concorde production line at Filton, Bristol, was in the hangars originally built for the manufacture of the Bristol Brabazon. The 16 production Concordes were completed between 1973 and 1979. Further production was made prohibitively expensive by the disposal of the French jigs at Toulouse by December 1977 and those from Filton, after a period of storage, in October 1981.

Mach 2 is the limit that will allow aluminium alloys to be used in aircraft construction. Beyond Mach 2, the flow of air over the fuselage causes excessive heating, requiring the use of more expensive high-temperature materials like titanium or stainless steel. This is part of the complex balancing of options that went into the design of Concorde. From the point of view of the engines, an ideal maximum speed would have been Mach 3, because their efficiency goes on increasing up to that speed. In the case of Concorde, a speed of Mach 2.04 was chosen because that reduced the temperature of the fuselage from 313°F to 261°F, easing problems with the handling of fuel and oil.

The Big Bird

BAC chief test pilot of Concorde, Brian Trubshaw (left) with Roy Radford, another BAC test pilot, aboard the British prototype 002. Concorde was tested for six years before entering commercial service. While the test pilots were putting the pre-production Concordes through their paces, structural tests on a specimen were carried out by the Royal Aircraft Establishment at Toulouse and at Farnborough where a supersonic "flight" was simulated. The airframe was covered in ducts linked to a hot air supply to replicate the heating and cooling of a flight. A specimen was also placed in a thermal duct with full fuel tanks and the cabin pressurized to reproduce the correct load.

André Turcat. Thirty-five minutes later he landed and declared: "The big bird flies". It would have been a serious disappointment if it had not. One month later the first British-assembled Concorde prototype, 002, took off from Filton with BAC's chief test pilot, Brian Trubshaw, at the controls. It had taken more than six years to get Concorde into the air, but it was to be another six before it carried paying passengers for the first time.

Concorde was not, however, the only SST in the air. The Soviet Union produced the TU 144, an aircraft similar in conformation to Concorde and which flew two months earlier. The TU 244 was designed to carry 121 passengers at Mach 2.35 over 4,000 miles, an impressive specification on paper. In reality it was never achieved.

In 1973, the modified TU 244 crashed at the Paris air show, which did little to inspire confidence. Nevertheless, it beat Concorde into service, flying mail and freight between Moscow and Alma-Ata for the first time in December 1975. The chances are that the TU 244 never achieved its design specification, and may have needed to use full afterburners during supersonic cruise, making it totally uneconomic. By 1985, if not sooner, it was out of service. "Concordeski", as it had been christened in the West, was an expensive failure.

No supersonic aircraft had ever been certified for passenger use, so the Concorde test pro-

gramme was exhaustive. Every conceivable mode of failure was explored, from stalls to multiple engine failures. Fatigue testing of a complete fuselage began. On 1 October 1969, 001 achieved Mach 1 for the first time and on 4 November 1970, it reached Mach 2. In 1973, the second pre-production aircraft, 002, broke the Washington–Paris record, setting a time of 3 hours 33 minutes.

By October 1973, 001 had been retired to the French Air Museum at Le Bourget, and in December that year the first production Concorde, 201, flew for the first time. By September 1974, a total of 3,000 hours of flight testing had been completed. During 1975 the first certificates of airworthiness were issued on both sides of the Channel. Finally, in January 1976, both British Airways and Air France were ready to make their maiden flights.

At 11.40 a.m. on 21 January the British Airways Concorde took off from Heathrow for Bahrain. At the same moment, the Air France aircraft took off for Rio de Janeiro via Dakar. Neither was a viable route, but the potentially profitable American destinations were still closed by environmental arguments. Those on board the British Concorde were greatly cheered by the tremendous reception they had from the emir of Bahrain, who gave them a banquet.

While destinations all over the world were sniffily turning their faces against Concorde, Bahrain welcomed it with open arms. Perhaps, after all, it might yet convince others that it was not the threat they believed it to be. Eventually, the US authorities allowed a Concorde service to Washington and New York, although by the time they did, the damage was done; both Pan American and TWA had cancelled their options to buy the aircraft.

A typical flight on the Atlantic route begins for the crew two hours before takeoff, as they go through the flight plan at Heathrow. Knowledge of the winds and temperatures along the proposed flight path is important for calculating the amount of fuel required—typically around 90 tons for a passenger load of 100.

Takeoff, at around 250 mph, is fairly quickly followed by turning off of the afterburners to reduce noise around the airport. At the same moment the rate of climb is reduced to compensate for the diminished thrust. Some 7 miles from Heathrow power is increased and the nose, which is lowered to improve visibility during taxi and takeoff, is raised into its flight position.

Between 6,000 and 32,000 feet Concorde climbs at 400 knots, increasing its Mach number toward 0.93 as the air gets thinner. As the speed rises, the centre of lift of Concorde's wing moves toward the rear and, to keep the aircraft balanced, the centre of gravity must also be moved backward by about 2 feet, accomplished by pumping fuel backward.

As Concorde crosses the coast, it changes gear. The reheaters are lit, first on the inboard and then on the outboard engines. With a perceptible nudge Concorde accelerates and soon exceeds Mach 1. At Mach 1.3 the complex engine inlets begin to rearrange themselves to achieve the best compression of the airflow entering the engines. At Mach 1.7 the afterburners are switched off, for now the increased speed has begun to improve the efficiency of the engines. Mach 2 is reached at about 50,000 feet, 40 minutes after takeoff.

At cruising height, 58,000 to 60,000 feet, the sky above is black, like space, and the temperature of the air is −58°F. But friction heats up the fuselage of the aircraft to more than 212°F, and it expands by 8 inches. Between the bulkhead and the engineer's panel, a gap opens up wide enough for the engineer to put his fingers in.

Two hours out of London, Newfoundland can be seen. Deceleration begins over the ocean before New York is reached, to ensure that Concorde is subsonic at least 35 miles out to sea.

As the aircraft slows, its angle of attack must be increased to maintain lift, which means that the nose must be drooped, first by 5 degrees and on final approach by 12.5, to preserve visibility forward. As speed falls below 253 mph, drag actually increases, a feature unique to Concorde which necessitates a modest increase in power to accommodate it.

Landing is made at 188 mph, which thanks to the paradoxical nature of the drag on Concorde, requires more power than 219 mph. At this speed, Concorde's fuel consumption is ten times greater than at supersonic cruise, for her engines are not optimized for dawdling. In case of delays at New York, an extra 15 tons of fuel are carried, sufficient for 50 minutes in a stacking pattern. As Concorde lands, the tyres produce a brief flurry of smoke which flows outward and around the wing tips, evidence of the vortex lift which enables the delta wings to function at low speeds.

Since those first flights, Concorde has carried millions of passengers to many different destinations, some on scheduled services and some on special charter flights. Speeds and heights that once were the realm of the test pilot have become almost routine, although such is the expense of Concorde flights that they still have a special aura. More than 30 years after it was conceived, Concorde is still the most sensational shape in the air, looking as advanced today as it did when it was first rolled out.

The choice of the four Bristol-Siddeley Olympus turbo jet engines mounted under the wings was crucial: to operate efficiently at all speeds would require very complex inlet arrangements and afterburner nozzles, all under computer control. The Olympus appeared to be the only suitable engine. That this engine existed at all was in defiance of British government policy, for it had decreed that all jet engine development should be concentrated in one company, Rolls-Royce. Against official wishes, the Bristol Aeroplane Company had persisted with the remarkable Olympus, capable of producing over 38,000 lb of thrust with full reheat. This pre-production Concorde has its nose in the flight position.

Ballooning in the Jet Stream

When Richard Branson, entrepreneur and founder of the Virgin group of companies, and balloonist Per Lindstrand came down in the frozen wastes of the North West Territories of Canada on 17 January 1991, they had achieved a unique double—crossing first the Atlantic and then the Pacific oceans in hot-air balloons. Strangely, the feat received little recognition, for the first allied bombing raids in the Gulf war had just been launched.

The challenge of crossing both the great oceans of the world by hot-air balloon had long been considered impossible. Both had been crossed by helium-filled balloons—the Atlantic in 1978, by the American team of Ben Abruzzo, Maxie Anderson and Larry Newman, flying *Double Eagle II*, and the Pacific in 1981, by a four-man crew led by Rocky Aoki of Japan.

To make such a crossing in unpowered balloons, it is necessary to fly at above 20,000 feet to take advantage of the jet stream winds, which blow at up to 200 mph. Nobody had ever flown a hot-air balloon in such winds, and many thought it impossible. To survive so high also requires a pressurized capsule, previously considered too heavy for a hot-air balloon. Thirdly, theory said that no hot-air balloon could carry sufficient propane gas to cross the 3,000 miles of the Atlantic, never mind the more than 6,000 of the Pacific. The task of solving these problems was given to the British firm of Thunder & Colt, of Oswestry, Shropshire, the largest manufacturer of leisure balloons in the world.

Richard Branson and Per Lindstrand were captain and chief pilot. Branson has become a household name for exploits such as the attempt to win the Blue Riband with the Atlantic Challenger. Lindstrand worked on high-altitude aircraft in the Swedish air force before founding Colt Balloons. The company Thunder & Colt designed both the Atlantic balloon and the Pacific one (opposite).

Per Lindstrand, an expert balloonist, believed that the answer to the fuel problem lay in using the heat of the Sun to keep the balloon hot, thereby reducing fuel requirements. The final design for the *Virgin Atlantic Flyer* was a vast envelope of laminated fabric, capable of holding more than 2 million cubic feet of hot air, standing 172 feet high and 166 feet broad.

The *Atlantic Flyer* was launched from Sugarloaf, Maine, early in the morning of 2 July 1987. Immediately there was a crisis as one of the propane tanks fell off as the balloon lifted. In addition, the balloon carried up with it one of the sandbags that had been used to hold it down, and when they reached 9,000 feet Branson climbed out of the capsule and cut the rope holding it with a penknife. The ascent of the balloon was so swift that none of the helicopters trying to take pictures could stay with it as it rose at 1,200 feet a minute. Branson and Lindstrand left the coast at around 25,000 feet, travelling at over 100 mph.

About 200 miles off Gander in Newfoundland they met an intense low-pressure front that buffeted them for three hours. On the instructions of their meteorologist, Bob Rice, they resisted the temptation to come down to calmer air below the storm, sticking firmly to their cruising altitude of 27,000 feet. It was snowing, dark, and the balloon kept shaking but eventually they came through into clear air, as Rice had predicted.

Just before dawn on 3 July they passed the midpoint of the Atlantic. By 2.33 p.m. they crossed the coast of Donegal, just 29 hours and 23 minutes after taking off. Now only the problem of landing remained, and that was to prove the stickiest part of the trip.

Because they had travelled so fast, Branson and Lindstrand still had three full fuel cells on the capsule. Not wanting to land with the fuel aboard, Lindstrand brought them down over Limavady, in Northern Ireland, aiming to come close to the ground and release the tanks at a safe height. But he overdid it and crashed heavily on to the ground, breaking off the tanks. Having lost 2½ tons, the balloon took off like a rocket again before Branson and Lindstrand had time to jettison the canopy.

They were now aloft again, without their spare fuel tanks, and wondering where to come down. Reasoning that the landfall in Limavady

Ballooning in the Jet Stream

had established ground contact and thus completed the crossing, Lindstrand decided to ditch in the Irish Sea as close as he could to the coast of England. As they touched the water, they fired the explosive bolts to separate the capsule from the canopy, but they failed to work—the battery was flat. Now the huge canopy was towing the capsule along like a speedboat.

They both climbed on top of the capsule and prepared to jump. Lindstrand went, but Branson hesitated. Five seconds later the balloon was up to 100 feet, Lindstrand in the water and Branson clinging on. The situation was now desperate. None of the chase helicopters had seen Lindstrand bale out, so were unaware that he was in the water; and Branson was soaring up with the burners at full tilt, turned on to try to provide a soft landing. He turned them off and came down through cloud, seeing to his intense relief a Royal Navy frigate, the HMS *Argonaut*, just below.

This time there was no mistake; Branson bailed out a few seconds before the capsule hit the sea. He was rescued by a Royal Navy helicopter, and provided instructions on where to find Lindstrand. Happily he too was fished out of the sea alive. Both men were cold, shocked and shaking. The entire flight, to "landing" in Limavady, had taken 31 hours 41 minutes.

Having beaten the Atlantic, it was inevitable that Branson and Lindstrand would attempt the Pacific. An even bigger balloon with a capacity of 2.6 million cubic feet was designed for this purpose, standing as high as the Statue of Liberty. The takeoff point this time was Miyakonojo, nearly 600 miles southwest of Tokyo, chosen because it lies under the course of the jet stream and is safely out of Tokyo airport.

After a smooth takeoff at 3 a.m. on 15 January, all went well until after seven hours of flight the first fuel tank was empty, the balloon cruising easily at 30,000 feet. They decided to dump the empty fuel tank but, to their horror, when Branson pulled the switch on the tank release panel, the balloon tilted and soared upward to 36,000 feet. Not only had the empty tank gone, but it had taken with it two full ones.

This might have spelled disaster, but a quick calculation showed that they still had perhaps 35 hours' worth of fuel left, enough to reach the coast of North America. Landfall was made at Juneau, Alaska, at 2.30 a.m., but it was impossible to land at night so the balloon swept on, crossing the Rockies before dawn enabled a descent to be attempted.

The eight propane burners needed to produce the initial lift were arranged in banks of two. All eight Thunder & Colt B3 units were used during takeoff. During the flight, only one bank was used at any one time. The mouth of the envelope, where the burners fed the hot air in, was protected by black fire-resistant fabric.

The frozen tundra of the North West Territories was ideal for landing because of its flat, wide-open spaces. Unfortunately there was a blizzard blowing, with winds of 35 knots. The cloud ceiling was only 1,000 feet but when the balloon finally emerged their ground speed was more than 30 mph, which made a landing on a frozen lake the preferred option. They hit the ice, jettisoned the canopy immediately, and slid to a stop. The temperature was −20°F and the nearest road was 153 miles away. It was four hours before a helicopter picked them up.

Having conquered both Atlantic and Pacific, all that remains is a flight right around the world. Knowing Branson's appetite for adventures, many expect him to try that one day.

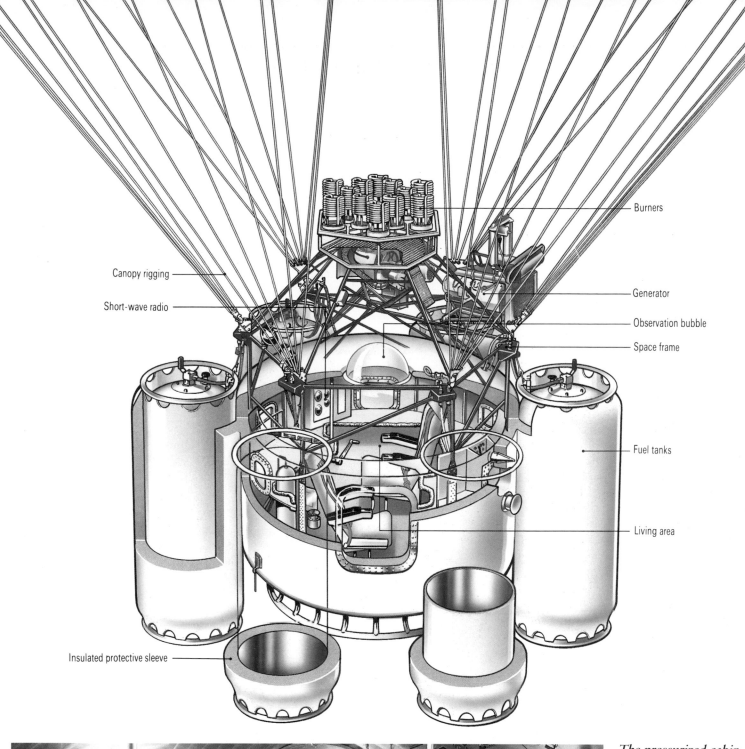

Burners

Canopy rigging

Short-wave radio

Generator

Observation bubble

Space frame

Fuel tanks

Living area

Insulated protective sleeve

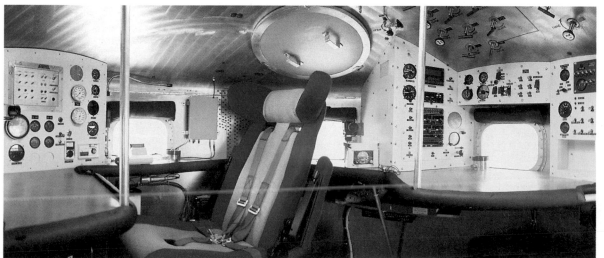

The pressurized cabin of Virgin Atlantic Flyer *was made of aluminium rolled into a cylinder almost 8 feet in diameter and 8 feet high. Aluminium domes were fitted at each end, the upper one having a window so that an eye could be kept on the burners. Ports in the side provided views of the surroundings from the airline-style seats.*

CHAPTER FIVE

INTO SPACE

I n 1961, humankind for the first time left its own environment. After thousands of years of gazing at the stars, we now have the technology to explore them. So far we have done no more than dip a toe into the immensity of space; but if past history is any guide these first steps will lead eventually to expeditions that will leave our own solar system, just as the medieval mariners first set sail across the oceans.

The history of space travel may be short, but it is full of incident. To begin with, few believed in it except for the pioneers of rocketry in Russia, Germany and the United States. As late as the 1950s a British Astronomer Royal declared that space travel was "bunk", but by the dawn of the 1960s Yuri Gagarin had proved him wrong, riding into space in a small and primitive Vostok spacecraft and returning alive after a single orbit.

Soviet successes stimulated a response from the United States, shocked that they should have been overtaken. This response was the Apollo programme, the brilliantly successful attempt to put a man on the Moon. In later Apollo missions, the astronauts were provided with their own vehicles to make the process of exploration easier.

After the success of the Moon landings, space travel has entered a quieter phase. The American and Soviet space shuttles, originally intended to make the orbiting of satellites easy and cheap, have failed to do so. The US programme was set back by the *Challenger* disaster and a series of more minor technical problems, while the Soviet programme remains a mystery—a single unmanned launch in 1988 being followed by a long silence. The Russians have, however, developed the ability to remain in space for very long periods in the Mir space station, building up the experience which will be necessary for establishing colonies in space or on the Moon.

In the following pages we look at a few highlights in the history of space travel. If, as most people expect, the future involves manned missions to the planets, their success will depend on the data gathered in the few years since the world was stunned to hear that a man had gone into space for the first time.

Gagarin's Momentous Orbit

The night before he was launched into space, Yuri Gagarin slept soundly. We know this because under his bed, close to the launch pad at Baikonour Cosmodrome, officials of the Soviet space programme had fitted special sensors. They wanted to be sure that the first man in space was thoroughly rested before he took his chances strapped into a cramped capsule on top of the Soviet Union's SS-6 intercontinental ballistic missile.

The space programme that culminated in Gagarin's flight on 12 April 1961 had its origins in pre-revolutionary Russia. Konstantin Tsiolkowski, born near Moscow in 1857, was a brilliant engineer who believed that the only form of propulsion possible in space would be the rocket. In 1903 he wrote an article that first suggested the use of liquid fuels in rockets and anticipated the need for a multistage rocket, with each stage dropping away as its fuel was exhausted. Tsiolkowski was a theoretician—he did not put any of these ideas into practice—but his judgement proved to be uncannily accurate.

After the revolution in 1917, Soviet interest in space travel was stimulated by a society called the Group for the Study of Jet Propulsion. In 1932, the Moscow and Leningrad branches were amalgamated by the government to form the State Reaction Scientific Research Institute, with Sergei Korolyev at its head. It was a brilliant appointment, for Korolyev was later responsible for all the Soviet Union's early success in space exploration. Without him it is likely that the first man in space would have been an American.

World War II, and the success of Germany's V-2 missiles, showed that orbital flight was not beyond imagination. In their attacks against London and Antwerp, the V-2s reached heights of 50 miles, taking them to the very edge of the Earth's atmosphere. Encouraged by this, and armed with information obtained from captured German specialists, Joseph Stalin ordered a serious study of ballistic missiles soon after the war. The Soviet Union started producing its own V-2s from German plans, using them to carry dogs in high-altitude biological research flights. By 1953, Korolyev had designed a multistage missile as powerful as 20 V-2s. Known in the West as the SS-6, it was the first intercontinental ballistic missile, able in theory to reach America from its launch sites in the USSR.

Nikita Khrushchev, who had succeeded Stalin, gave approval for the SS-6 programme, and the first successful launch was on 3 August 1957, four months before the first US ICBM, *Atlas*. Korolyev had always wanted to use his launcher to put up a satellite, and Khrushchev now saw the opportunity to steal a march on the Americans. Korolyev was told to put a satellite into orbit as quickly as he could.

In just six weeks an SS-6 launcher was united with a simple satellite consisting of a globe 22 inches in diameter, with four aerials and a radio transmitter. The whole satellite, called *Sputnik*, weighed 184 lb and was launched successfully on 4 October 1957. As it circled the Earth, its beeping sound provided powerful evidence of the Soviet lead in space flight, causing something of a panic in the US. The national gloom deepened when on 6 December the US Vanguard rocket, attempting to put a tiny $3\frac{1}{2}$-lb satellite into orbit, rose a few feet from its pad and crashed.

By then, the Soviet Union had launched its second Sputnik, a much more significant satellite, for it weighed half a ton and carried a live creature, a dog called Laika, together with the systems needed to keep the creature alive in the vacuum of space. Now the Soviet intentions were clear. It had the ability to lift very large payloads into orbit, and it was interested in testing how living systems would fare in space. Poor Laika was not, however, provided with any means of coming down again, so she died of asphyxiation when her air supply ran out, and was cremated when *Sputnik 2* re-entered the Earth's atmosphere after three months in orbit.

The Soviet Union and the United States now began a race to be first to send a man into space. The Russians had the advantage of a powerful rocket, but the Americans, after their slow start, were focusing their resources on the problem. It took the Russians two years to design their first manned spacecraft, *Vostok* ("East"), and it set a pattern that has been followed ever since. Designed for automatic operation, *Vostok* could be launched manned or unmanned. This made it possible to carry out a series of unmanned tests without risk to life before the first cosmonaut took his chances.

The spacecraft itself required more work because, unlike the Sputniks, it had to be designed to re-enter the atmosphere safely and

FACT FILE

The first journey by a person in space

Date: 12 April 1961

Distance: Single orbit of Earth, about 25,000 miles

Duration: 1 hour 48 minutes

make a soft landing on the ground. That meant it needed retrorockets to slow it down, a heat shield to resist the blistering temperatures on re-entry, and some sort of parachute—although it was always the intention that the cosmonauts should eject and come down independently. The spacecraft was ready for testing early in 1960.

Things did not go as smoothly as Korolyev would have liked: in testing the ejection system, a pilot was killed; the first orbital tests of the system, on 15 May 1960, in which a dummy took the place of the cosmonaut, failed. The launch was successful and the spacecraft entered a stable orbit, but when the order was given to fire the re-entry rockets, the spacecraft was facing in

The launch of Vostok 1 *(above) was celebrated with commemorative posters (right). The spacecraft was propelled by an SS-6 rocket with an extra stage; this was powered by a single rocket engine, burning alcohol and liquid oxygen. The SS-6's core was made up of thick-walled, heavy steel tanks to contain its fuel—liquid oxygen and kerosene.*

Gagarin's Momentous Orbit

The planners of the orbit of Vostok 1 *appear to be working with very basic equipment in comparison with the sophistication of contemporary ground controls. But they performed their work well:* Vostok 1 *landed only 6 miles from the calculated point. The most crucial decision was the point at which the re-entry burn was made; the wrong angle or position would almost certainly have led to the loss of the spacecraft. Some test flights had failed due to such an error.*

the wrong direction because a sensor had failed. Instead of re-entering it went into a useless orbit from which it eventually re-entered and burned up in October. In July, a launch failed when the rocket refused to ignite on the pad.

Further failures preceded two completely successful tests in March 1961, when officials at last decided the spacecraft was proven enough to carry a man. The risks were emphasized when on 23 March a cosmonaut was killed in a fire while testing the spacecraft on the ground.

In view of the chequered history of the test programme, Gagarin's flight had been reduced from the planned 6 to 18 orbits to a single orbit. Gagarin went aboard at about 7.30 a.m. on the morning of 12 April and while the countdown proceeded, music was played to him through his headphones—a practice which continued for Soviet manned launches for many years. Whether this helped relax Gagarin is not clear, for during the launch his pulse rate rose to 158.

The engines fired at 9.07 a.m. and with a roar *Vostok* was launched into space.

Throughout the short flight all systems worked well, and Gagarin's main job was to observe them. The engineers in charge do not seem to have had much confidence in the ability of cosmonauts to control their spacecraft and preferred to rely on the automatic systems. *Vostok* did possess a manual system for orienting itself for retrofire, but there was no need to use it; the retrorockets fired as the spacecraft came around the world over Africa, and the capsule separated successfully.

At a height of 22,750 feet the capsule hatch was blown off and Gagarin was ejected, landing by parachute. The capsule also landed by parachute but it was feared that the shock of impact might be too violent. The two came down southwest of Engels in the Saratov region, where a titanium monument, 130 feet high, now marks the spot. Many subsequent reports

Control of Vostok 1 was firmly in the hands of ground control (left), since Soviet doctors feared that a cosmonaut might become mentally disturbed in flight. The descent module (above) was known as Charik, or "little ball", and measured only 7 feet 6 inches across.

Major Yuri Gagarin (below left) with Nikita Khrushchev at Vnukovo airport on his return to Moscow on 14 April 1961. Tragically, Gagarin did not live long to enjoy his fame: he died on a routine training flight in a Mig-15 trainer on 27 March 1968.

suggested that Gagarin had landed inside the capsule, but they were not true.

The Russians deliberately obscured the issue because the rules of aerospace records demand that the pilot be in charge of the vehicle, or at least in it, throughout the voyage. If they had admitted that Gagarin had bailed out at 22,000 feet the flight might not have been acknowledged as a first by the Fédération Aéronautique Inter-nationale. The FAI did ask a lot of questions, but eventually admitted the flight as a first; it would have been pedantic to do otherwise. In fact, all the Vostok cosmonauts ejected as Gagarin did, so the legally minded could argue that the first manned flight, takeoff to landing, was made by American John Glenn in February 1962.

That is not, of course, the way the world saw it. The handsome, cheerful Gagarin became a celebrity overnight. For the first time man had set foot outside his own planet, an event as historic as the voyages of Magellan and Columbus.

Man on the Moon

FACT FILE

The first Moon
landing

Date: July 1969

Distance: 952,702
miles

Duration: 195 hours

The Apollo 11
*command and services
modules* (opposite)
*photographed from the
lunar module in orbit
around the Moon. On
the surface below them
is the Sea of Fertility.
Six hours after landing
on the Moon, Neil
Armstrong was the first
human being to set foot
on an extraterrestrial
surface (below).*

The night of Monday 21 July 1969 was unique in human history. While four billion or so people slept on Earth, two of their kind were spending the night on the Moon, the first creatures ever to set foot there. It was the culmination of an ambitious programme launched eight years earlier by President John F. Kennedy and carried out with exemplary efficiency by the US National Aeronautics and Space Administration (NASA). By the success of the Apollo programme, as it was called, the US was able to vault ahead of the early lead in space exploration established by the Soviet Union.

The mission to the Moon was born of pride and frustration. America's leaders could not believe that they had been left behind by their Soviet rivals, and Kennedy resolved to find a dramatic way of catching up. In his address to Congress on 25 May 1961, Kennedy declared: "I believe that this nation should commit itself to achieving the goal, before the decade is out, of landing a man on the Moon and returning him safely to Earth."

Many questioned whether it was wise to declare both an objective and a timetable before it was certain that the job could be done. At the time of the president's speech, the US had yet to achieve even a full Earth orbital flight.

NASA had, however, already been working on a proposal for a three-man spacecraft able to go into orbit around the Earth or the Moon. That would be launched by the *Saturn 1* rocket, with its 665 tons of thrust. Actually landing on the Moon would require a much bigger launcher, with five times the power, larger than anything so far developed anywhere. It would also need a spacecraft capable of navigating across space, landing on the Moon, taking off again, and making it back to the Earth. Nobody had yet worked out quite how to do this, but proposals were soon being discussed.

The best, it was decided, involved making the assault on the Moon in a series of steps. First a spacecraft would be put into Earth orbit. Once there, it would fire rockets to take it out of Earth orbit and toward the Moon. When it reached the Moon it would not land directly, but again go into orbit. If all went well up to that point, a special landing craft would separate from the lunar orbiter, descend to the surface and land. When the mission was complete, part of it—the ascent module—would take off again, rendezvous with the orbiter which was still circling the Moon, and transfer the crew. The orbiter would then escape from Moon orbit and return to Earth, re-entering the atmosphere and landing in the sea.

To make it work, however, NASA would have to learn a lot of new tricks. One was finding, tracking and locking on to another spacecraft in space. Another was to design controllable rocket engines for the lunar lander so that the pilot could use them as delicately as a helicopter's rotors to land on the Moon. Yet a third was to devise an absolutely reliable rocket to get the lander off the Moon again, for if that failed the crew would be stuck there with no hope of rescue. And before a landing could be risked, more would have to be learned about the surface of the Moon itself.

NASA set about answering those questions in a systematic way. The problems of rendezvous and docking were solved during the Gemini missions, while work on the huge *Saturn 5* went on in parallel. Unmanned missions were sent to land on the Moon, sending back pictures and data more detailed than any that could be obtained from Earth. It was clear that the Moon's surface was firm, if not exactly flat. There were thousands of craters, but it looked as if there were sufficient flat places to land safely. Precisely where the astronauts landed would be left to their judgement.

When complete, *Saturn 5* was a prodigious piece of engineering. The noise it made—190 decibels—is the loudest sound that man has ever produced. Firing it was the equivalent to setting off an explosive under a naval destroyer balanced upright and blowing it 30 miles into the air, without breaking a single thing on board. *Saturn 5* was tested for the first time in November 1967, with an unmanned spacecraft, and worked perfectly.

The success had come at a good moment, for earlier in 1967 the programme had suffered a terrible blow, when a fire aboard an Apollo spacecraft being checked out on the ground killed three astronauts. They were breathing pure oxygen, and a spark set plastic in the spacecraft alight. The fire revealed many design failings, which were corrected, but it delayed the first manned launch for 18 months.

Man on the Moon

That mission, *Apollo 7*, was launched into Earth orbit in October 1968. It worked well, paving the way for the first trip around the Moon in *Apollo 8*, launched in December 1968. Frank Borman, James Lovell and William Anders spent 20 hours circling the Moon, taking photographs, including Borman's famous shot of the Earth rising above the lunar horizon.

Apollo 9 was an Earth orbit mission in which the astronauts practised removing the lunar module from the third-stage rocket casing in which it was stored during launch, docking with it, and test-firing its engines. *Apollo 10*, in May 1969, was a full dress rehearsal for the actual landing, except that the astronauts stopped short 10 miles from the lunar surface before returning and docking with the lunar orbiter. So finally, with just six months to go before the deadline set by President Kennedy, all was ready.

Three astronauts had been selected for the crucial *Apollo 11* mission: Neil Armstrong, Edward (Buzz) Aldrin and Michael Collins. Launch from Cape Canaveral on 16 July went perfectly and the voyage to the Moon was routine. On 19 July they reached the Moon, fired the service module rockets and went into lunar orbit. On Sunday 20 July, while Collins stayed in the command module (codenamed *Columbia*), Armstrong and Aldrin got into the lunar module (*Eagle*) and separated on the 13th orbit.

While *Eagle* was around the far side of the Moon, Armstrong fired the descent engine and started toward the surface. As he approached he saw that they were heading for an area strewn with boulders, so took over manual control. At 9.17 p.m., as the descent engine came close to running out of fuel (it had only 2 percent left), the module made contact with the surface. The 500 million people watching television on Earth heard Armstrong say: "Contact light. OK, engine stop . . . Houston, Tranquillity Base here, the *Eagle* has landed."

At this point of maximum excitement, Armstrong and Aldrin were supposed to sleep for four hours, a plan now recognized as absurd. Instead, the two men had a meal, and then prepared to take the first walk on the Moon. It took them nearly six hours to eat, set up the spacecraft for a quick getaway if that should be needed, and put on their bulky spacesuits. Finally, Armstrong moved with deliberation down the stairs, put his foot on the ground, and uttered a sentence carefully composed and committed to memory in advance: "One small

Aldrin descends the ladder from Eagle *to join Armstrong on the Moon. They set up a TV camera, placed a US flag on a pole, gathered rock samples, took a call from President Nixon, and set up various experiments. These included a laser reflector that enabled scientists to measure the distance of the Moon from Earth to within 6 inches. Finally, and controversially, they left their rubbish on the Moon before re-entering the lunar module.*

step for man. One giant leap for mankind."

Aldrin soon joined Armstrong on the Moon for 2½ hours before they got back into the lunar module to sleep. After 22 hours on the Moon, they fired the engine to put them back into lunar orbit, aboard *Eagle*'s ascent stage. It simply had to work, and it did. There was a wobble as *Eagle* docked, but all was well. Armstrong and Aldrin then joined Collins in the command module, jettisoning the ascent module, and fired their propulsion rockets behind the Moon to bring them out of orbit and back on course to Earth.

They arrived home to a splashdown on 24 July at 17.50 BST, just 30 seconds later than had been predicted at the start of the 195-hour mission. In eight days, they had travelled almost a million miles and set foot on a planet no living thing had ever visited before. A mission designed with the precision of a clock had run like clockwork.

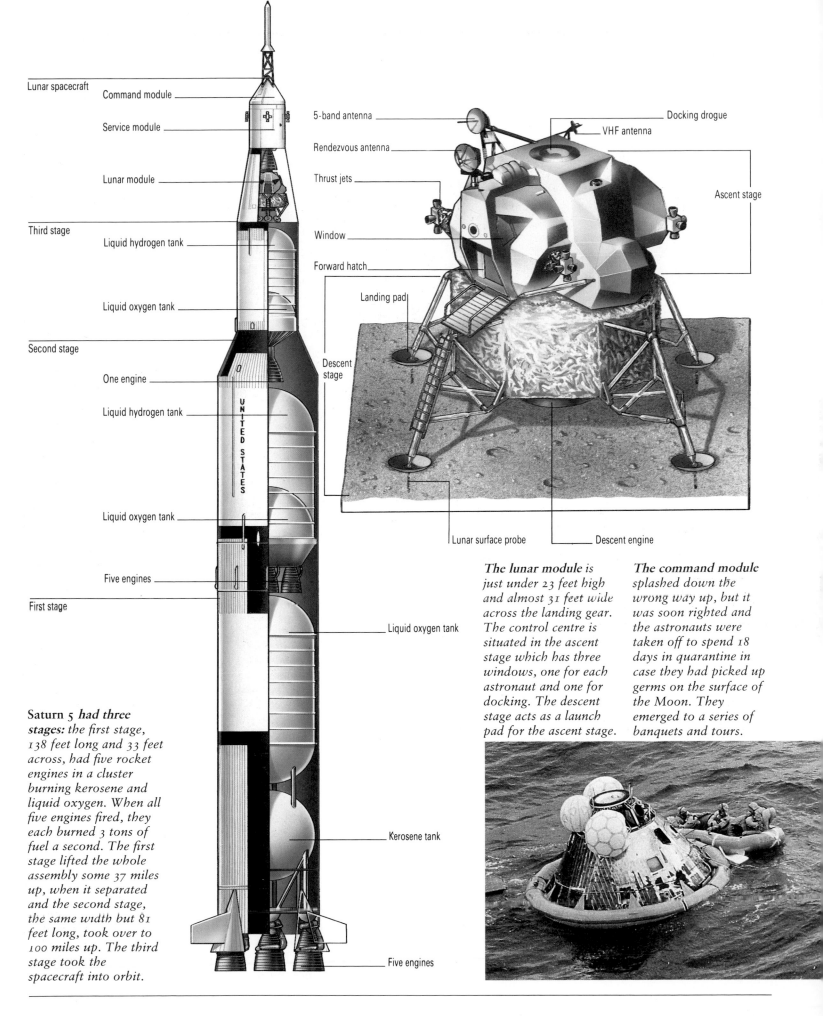

Lunar spacecraft

Command module

Service module

Lunar module

Third stage

Liquid hydrogen tank

Liquid oxygen tank

Second stage

One engine

Liquid hydrogen tank

Liquid oxygen tank

Five engines

First stage

Liquid oxygen tank

Kerosene tank

Five engines

5-band antenna

Rendezvous antenna

Thrust jets

Window

Forward hatch

Landing pad

Descent stage

Docking drogue

VHF antenna

Ascent stage

Lunar surface probe

Descent engine

Saturn 5 *had three stages:* *the first stage, 138 feet long and 33 feet across, had five rocket engines in a cluster burning kerosene and liquid oxygen. When all five engines fired, they each burned 3 tons of fuel a second. The first stage lifted the whole assembly some 37 miles up, when it separated and the second stage, the same width but 81 feet long, took over to 100 miles up. The third stage took the spacecraft into orbit.*

The lunar module is just under 23 feet high and almost 31 feet wide across the landing gear. The control centre is situated in the ascent stage which has three windows, one for each astronaut and one for docking. The descent stage acts as a launch pad for the ascent stage.

The command module splashed down the wrong way up, but it was soon righted and the astronauts were taken off to spend 18 days in quarantine in case they had picked up germs on the surface of the Moon. They emerged to a series of banquets and tours.

Lunar Explorer

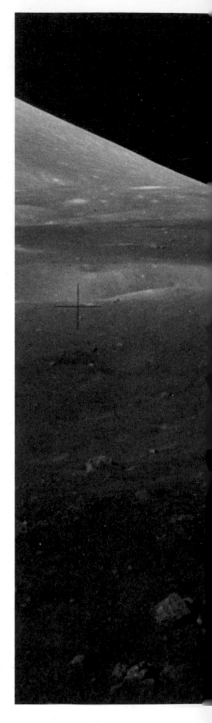

Three vehicles that are never likely to be given a parking ticket have been sitting stationary and unattended for the past 20 years. It could be half a century or longer before anybody sees them again, although each cost millions of dollars to make and has no more than delivery mileage on the clock. The lunar rovers carried to the surface of the Moon by the last three Apollo missions in the early 1970s are among the oddest wheeled vehicles ever built. Their existence is evidence, if any were needed, that Americans cannot imagine life, anywhere, without the automobile. To ensure that the Moon had been truly claimed for humankind, it had to be driven over as well as trodden on.

More seriously, the rovers enabled the astronauts on the *Apollo 15, 16* and *17* missions to travel more widely and with much less risk than they could have done on foot.

Designing a vehicle to be carried to the Moon presented special difficulties. The payload of the Apollo spacecraft was limited, so the rovers had to be made extremely light, and the cargo space was small so that they had to be able to fold up like a portable bicycle. In the one-sixth gravity experienced on the lunar surface, supporting the weight of the astronauts was less demanding than it would have been on Earth, but this meant that the rovers could not be test-driven before they reached their destination. If an Earth-

FACT FILE

The first wheeled vehicle used extraterrestrially

Built: 1969/70

Length: 10 feet 2 inches

Maximum speed: 10 mph

Range: 57 miles

weight astronaut had sat in the rover it would have collapsed. Special normal-gravity models had to be made to teach the astronauts how to drive them.

The job of designing and building the lunar rovers was awarded to the Boeing aircraft company. The purpose of the vehicles was to transport the astronauts around the lunar surface while using far less energy, and so consuming less oxygen and cooling water. In this way it would be possible to double the time the astronauts could remain on the surface. They could travel much farther from their landing point, and also do more useful work.

The need for the rovers had been realized from the start, but was brought home during *Apollo 14* when Alan Shepard and Edgar Mitchell had to tow some scientific equipment a mile across the Moon's surface, climbing almost 400 feet to the rim of Cone Crater. After two hours and ten minutes they were still not there, and visibly tiring. Shepard's heart rate rose to 150, and Mitchell's to 128 before they turned back short of their destination. Getting about on the Moon was clearly an exhausting job in the cumbersome space suits.

The lunar rover, designed and built by Boeing in only 17 months, was a light-alloy vehicle which weighed only 460 lb but was capable of carrying 1,080 lb, more than twice its own

The **Apollo 15** *mission in July 1971 (above left) was the first to use the rover, travelling 2½ miles from the lunar module* Falcon. *During the Apollo 17 mission in December 1972, the rover went on two drives. The second lasted for an hour and took Dr Jack Schmitt and Eugene Cernan 4 miles from the module (above).*

Lunar Explorer

weight. This payload consisted of two astronauts plus equipment, reckoned at 400 lb each, together with another 280 lb of tools, equipment, television and communications gear and lunar samples. By comparison, the average family car can carry only half its own weight.

Power was provided by a quarter-hp electric motor in each wheel, fed from two independent 36-volt battery systems. If either of these broke down, the other was capable of getting the vehicle back to base. Both front and rear wheels could be steered, using a T-shaped hand controller in the middle of the console between the two astronauts. Pushing the controller forward made the rover move forward, while moving it sideways steered to right or left. Pulling it backward applied the brakes. The rover's maximum speed was 10 mph, and its batteries gave it an operational lifetime of 78 hours. In practice, however, its range on the Moon was limited to a radius of 6 miles from base, so that if it broke down the astronauts would be able to walk back.

The rover was designed to be able to climb hills of up to 20 degrees, and to clamber over obstacles and small crevasses. The astronauts found that the ride on the lunar surface was so bumpy that in one-sixth gravity they would have been thrown out of the vehicle if they had not used the seat belts provided. The rovers were also fitted with a sophisticated navigation system, set before they drove off, which used the Sun-angle as a bearing to tell them the precise distance and direction back to the lunar module at any time.

Unpacking the rover after landing on the Moon was designed to be simple. It was fitted into a pie-shaped quadrant of the descent stage of the lunar module during flight, and unfolded itself after the astronauts had pulled on two nylon operating tapes in turn before removing a series of release pins. The rover was fitted with a radio for continuous communication with mission control and a TV camera which could be turned on when it was stationary.

The first time the rover was used was during the *Apollo 15* mission, launched in July 1971. David Scott and James Irwin landed in a basin near Hadley Rille on 30 July. They had some problems deploying the rover, and on their first outing could not make the front wheels steer. It functioned satisfactorily with rear steering only, however, so they drove 2½ miles to the edge of Hadley Rille and turned on the TV cameras for the first time. Scott then collected some geologi-

cal samples, using a drill to produce cores of moon rock 3 feet long which were found to contain 57 separate layers of soil, dating back 2,400 million years.

They made two further trips out of the lunar module, covering a total of more than 17 miles. During the final outing they collected 170 lb of rock samples, including one piece of rock 4,150 million years old. Finally they left the rover with the TV camera running as they took off from the Moon, providing a dramatic two seconds as the screen briefly showed the red and green flame as the ascent stage rocket fired.

Apollo 16, in April 1972, also made good use of the lunar rover. At the end of the first trip out of the lunar module, which had landed at Cayley

Commander Eugene Cernan preparing to board the lunar rover during the Apollo 17 mission. In the background is the south massif of the Taurus Mountains, which reach 6,986 feet. Mission control was anxious that Cernan and Schmitt had driven as far as 4 miles from the module, since it would have taken 2¾ hours to walk back.

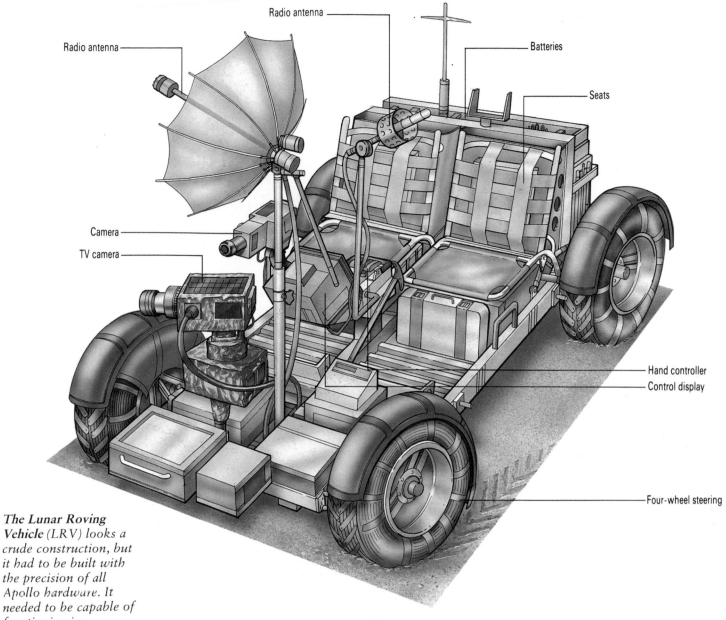

Radio antenna

Radio antenna

Batteries

Seats

Camera

TV camera

Hand controller

Control display

Four-wheel steering

The Lunar Roving Vehicle (LRV) looks a crude construction, but it had to be built with the precision of all Apollo hardware. It needed to be capable of functioning in temperatures of up to 250°F, and in a vacuum which meant that air cooling could not be employed. The rover has enabled astronauts to visit and send back pictures of parts of the Moon that could not have been reached on foot. Unfortunately, it was impossible to send back pictures from the vehicle while it was on the move as the antenna can be unfurled for transmission only when it is stationary.

Plains, John Young drove the rover around and around in tight circles as fast as he could to test wheel grip. Later a rear mudguard fell off the rover, exposing the astronauts to a constant cloud of dust. Exactly the same happened during the *Apollo 17* mission, in December 1972, after Eugene Cernan, the mission commander, had accidentally knocked off a rear mudguard. So much dust was being scattered over them and their equipment that the astronauts were advised to make a temporary mudguard by taping together four lunar maps and clipping them to the vehicle.

Cernan and his colleague, geologist Dr Harrison (Jack) Schmitt, used the rover to make the longest trips yet across the lunar surface. During

their three trips they covered a total of 22 miles, loading up the rover with a massive 250 lb of moon rock. During the final trip the rover was taken up mountain sides so steep that its wheels, made of wire mesh, were dented, fortunately without affecting its performance.

Apollo 17 was the last mission to the Moon, and humans have not set foot on it since. The three rovers left behind are unlikely to be much use to any future explorer—their batteries will be flat, and they were not designed to withstand the bitterly cold temperatures of the Moon indefinitely. As things stand, there are no further plans for exploring the Moon, so it may be a long time before anybody sets eyes on the three vehicles which proved so useful.

The Retrievable Spacecraft

In the history of space exploration sketched out by NASA, the space shuttle was supposed to occupy the same role as the Douglas DC-3 does in aviation: a cheap, utterly reliable workhorse that would transform space flight into a mundane affair. Reality has been crueller. While it has flown well and carried out many space "firsts", including the rescue of a broken-down satellite for repair, the shuttle has failed to make space travel either cheap or safe. Its launches cost just as much as conventional rockets, and nobody who saw it either live or on television can forget the *Challenger* disaster of 28 January 1986, when a shuttle blew up with its crew of seven just after launch from Cape Canaveral.

Designed as a space plane that could take off from and land in ordinary airfields, the space shuttle has been the victim of too many compromises, most of them forced on it by tight budgets. Nor has the copy of the shuttle produced by the Soviet Union performed any better: *Buran* ("Snowstorm"), uncannily similar in appearance to the shuttle, made one unmanned flight in 1988 but then disappeared from sight. The manned flight promised for 1989 was postponed, apparently indefinitely.

Conventional rockets, used only once, will never be an inexpensive form of travel. So when NASA started work on the shuttle in 1972, it made sense to envisage a re-usable spacecraft that could make many flights. Original plans suggested that by 1991 the shuttle fleet would have completed 725 flights, at a rate of 60 a year, each one costing as little as $20 million. All these figures now look absurdly optimistic.

The designers of the shuttle had to produce a vehicle that could function in two quite different environments. In orbit, it is a spaceship, controlled by small rocket motors. In the atmosphere it is a 200-ton glider, which can be controlled aerodynamically and brought in to land, in theory at least, on any runway long enough to accommodate it. Because it has no engines for use in the atmosphere, it has only one chance to land, using gravity to generate enough speed to fly. Its small wings produce little lift, so the shuttle lands fast, at more than 200 mph. So far, thanks to the skill of the pilots, landing has proved no problem.

Liftoff, however, is another matter. In an ideal world, the shuttle would take off like a regular aircraft, using jet engines that would convert themselves high in the atmosphere into rockets to propel it into space. Such "space planes" have been designed, but none has yet been built. The shuttle, by contrast, blasts off like a conventional rocket, with all the same complexities.

Its main engines use liquid hydrogen and oxygen fuel, which are difficult to handle and need a huge external fuel tank. On their own, the main engines provide insufficient lift, so they are supplemented by two solid-fuel boosters strapped on to the tank and discarded before the shuttle goes into orbit. The empty boosters parachute into the sea for recovery and re-use, but the big external tank is discarded after a single launch. Many of these design features were introduced to save development costs, but they added to operational costs, thereby undermining the rationale of the shuttle.

Two of the most difficult features to get right were the main rocket engines and the insulation of the shuttle orbiter to prevent it burning up during re-entry. The shuttle has three main engines, each with enough thrust to power two

FACT FILE

The world's only operational spacecraft to land like a plane

Columbia (OV-101)	
Date built:	1974–76
Wing span:	78 feet
Length:	122 feet

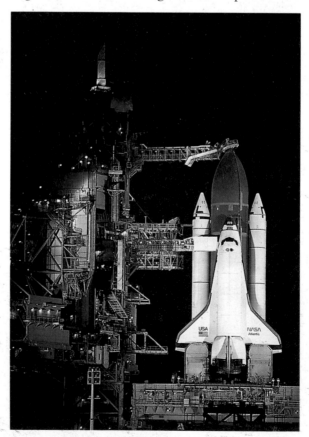

The shuttle project was given the green light by President Nixon on 5 January 1972. In July a $2,600-million contract was awarded to North American Rockwell Corporation as the principal contractor, and by May 1973 the design was almost complete. Work began in June the following year on the first shuttle, which was to be used for gliding tests. Two launch pads are available at Cape Canaveral where Atlantis is prepared for takeoff (left). Discovery was launched (right) on 13 March 1969 to deploy the final Tracking and Data Relay Satellite to complete the TDRS network.

The Retrievable Spacecraft

and a half jumbo jets. The engines work by mixing and igniting liquid oxygen and liquid hydrogen, which are stored in the external tank. The two liquids, at extremely low temperatures, have to be pumped at huge pressures into the combustion chamber where they react, creating pressures 220 times that of the atmosphere.

It was hardly surprising that developing these engines caused a lot of headaches. In tests between March 1977 and November 1979 there was a run of 14 failures, but eventually the engines were made to work. They have not failed in use, even if servicing them between missions has proved more difficult than hoped.

A second major difficulty was with the ceramic tiles that are used to insulate the shuttle against the temperature of re-entry. Earlier spacecraft had used ablative heat shields which protected their occupants by gradually burning off as they re-entered. For a re-usable spacecraft something more permanent was needed, so it was decided to cover the surfaces of the shuttle with silica-based tiles about the size of the tiles on a bathroom wall. These materials are such astonishingly good insulators that it would be quite possible to touch one side of a tile with your finger while the other side was red-hot.

To cover the surface of the orbiter requires 31,000 tiles, each of which has to be stuck on individually, with a small gap between them to allow for expansion and contraction. Sticking these tiles on proved a long and tiresome job, for it was found to the horror of the engineers that they could easily be pulled off. Curing the problem on the first shuttle, *Columbia*, took more than a year from September 1979 and involved a work force of 1,400 people.

The solid fuel boosters, by contrast, seemed to offer few problems, although it was eventually the failure of one of them that caused the *Challenger* disaster. Solid boosters had never before been used for manned missions. Although they are reliable, they have the drawback that once ignited they cannot be turned off again, nor can the power they deliver be controlled as a liquid rocket's can. Without them, however, the shuttle would not get far off the pad; the two boosters provide 5.8 million lb of thrust, against the 1.4 million lb of the main engines.

Eventually, some years after the scheduled date, the first shuttle was ready for launch. A final test of the engines was carried out on the pad at Cape Canaveral on 20 February 1981, running them for 20 seconds to make sure they

The solid fuel boosters (left) are placed either side of the tank; each is 150 feet long and 12 feet in diameter and is filled with 1.1 million lb of propellants that burn within two minutes. The propellant consists of aluminium powder, aluminium perchlorate, a small amount of iron oxide catalyst and a binding agent that sets the mixture to the consistency of hard rubber. The shuttle's three main engines (above) have the greatest thrust-to-weight ratio of any engine ever developed, and they are designed to burn for $7\frac{1}{2}$ hours, or for 55 missions.

were really working. They were, and launch was set for 10 April. The commander was John Young, a veteran of two trips to the Moon, who was 50 and wore spectacles, the first astronaut ever to do so in space. His pilot was Robert Crippen, who had never been in space before.

The first attempt to launch *Columbia* failed when a tiny computer malfunction was detected 16 minutes before liftoff. It took five hours to sort out the fault, which meant that the external tank had to be emptied, so the launch was put off until Sunday 12 April, 20 years to the day since Yuri Gagarin made the first manned space flight. This time the count went smoothly. A few seconds before liftoff the main engines were ignited, and their performance was instantly scrutinized by a mass of instruments and analysed by computers. If there had been anything wrong, it would have been possible even in those few seconds to abort the launch before the solid boosters ignited. All was well, the boosters were lit and with a tremendous roar and a huge cloud of white exhaust *Columbia* leaped from the pad at just after 7 a.m. local time.

After 2 minutes and 12 seconds the boosters burned out and were jettisoned to splash down in the Atlantic 5 minutes later for recovery. By now *Columbia* was 31 miles up and travelling at 2,900 mph. The main engines ran for a further 6 minutes, cutting out 8 minutes and 34 seconds after launch, when *Columbia* was travelling at 17,502 mph and had reached a low Earth orbit. The final orbit was achieved by firing the orbital manoeuvring system engines four times, putting *Columbia* into a stable 170 by 172 mile orbit.

As soon as Crippen opened the payload bay doors it was apparent that *Columbia* had lost some tiles during launch. They were, however, in areas where the temperature was not expected to get dangerously high. From the cabin it was, of course, impossible to see the critical underside of the orbiter, and there was concern that tiles might have fallen off from there too, imperilling the return to Earth.

After two days in orbit, the astronauts

The shuttle's pilots sit in front of large windows and control the orbiter like an aircraft, with columns and foot pedals, while in Earth's atmosphere. In space the craft's attitude is controlled by 44 small rocket thrusters around the nose and rear.

THE FATED MISSION

Shuttle mission 51L had been dogged by frustrating minor technical hitches which delayed the eventual takeoff, on 28 January 1986. The seven astronauts boarded the *Challenger*; the main engines were fired at 11.38 a.m. local time, and the computers verified that all was well with them and the boosters were ignited. Once the level of thrust constantly exceeded the weight of the assembly, the explosive restraining bolts were detonated and the shuttle left the launch pad. In the 74th second of the mission, at an altitude of 10 miles, flames appeared around the base of the tank. It exploded and engulfed *Challenger* in flames. The steel casing of the right booster had ruptured, playing flames on to the tank. The disaster shocked the world, and set back the US space programme by years.

The Retrievable Spacecraft

The Remote Manipulator System (above and right) is the key to manoeuvring satellites out of and into the shuttle's payload bay. The 50-foot-long jointed robot arm, built by the Canadians, is stowed along the payload bay. Electrically operated from one of the flight deck windows that overlooks the payload bay, the arm has flexible joints and a rotating wrist. Manoeuvring the large satellites that shuttles have carried and placing them in a precise orbit is a highly skilled operation. A close-up TV camera on the "forearm" assists the operator.

prepared to return. First, Young rotated *Columbia* so that it was going backward, then fired the manoeuvring engines to slow it down by 200 mph and bring it back into the fringes of the atmosphere. After another orbit *Columbia* began to dig into the atmosphere with its nose angled up by 40 degrees and the thermal tiles glowing red. Radio contact with Earth was lost for 16 minutes when the temperature rose high enough to ionize the air around *Columbia*, obliterating radio signals, but this had been expected and caused no anxiety.

When *Columbia* emerged from radio silence it was 35.6 miles above the Earth and travelling at ten times the speed of sound. It was landing not at Canaveral but on the wide-open expanses of Edwards Air Force Base high in the Mojave Desert of California. To lose speed *Columbia* went through a series of S-curves, lining up for final approach to the runway. With no power available, Young had to get it right; the shuttle cannot go around again if it misjudges its approach. There was no mistake. The wheels came down seconds before *Columbia* hit the runway at 215 mph in a copybook landing.

The cargo bay of shuttles (left) was designed with satellites in mind. Placing satellites in orbit or repairing them for communications companies can be lucrative work. This often requires a space walk by astronauts wearing suits (above) that provide water, heat, oxygen, radio contact and waste disposal for up to seven hours. The bay is 60 feet long and 15 feet wide, big enough for four satellites. Once in orbit, the two pairs of payload bay doors swing open to expose heat exchangers for the shuttle's electrical systems.

Satellites are sent into their geostationary orbit at a height of 22,000 miles by rocket motors, since the shuttle cannot climb above 690 miles.

Most often, an electric turntable spins the satellite like a top before a spring is released to send it on its way. The rocket motors are fired once it is a safe distance from the shuttle.

Life in Space

From the first unfortunate animals sent into space to the more recent tests on humans, much of the United States and Soviet space programmes has been directed at understanding more about the effects of weightlessness. This is vital if a space station is to be built. The Soviets lead the field in long-term exposure to weightlessness: Valery Ryumin has spent a cumulative total of 361 days in orbit, while Anatoly Berezovoy was on board the space station *Salyut 7* for 211 days in all. Predictably, psychological pressures have proved more taxing than the physical problems, although a constant diet of largely dehydrated food also becomes a trial.

A major incentive behind this work is the prospect of harvesting both energy and minerals in space. A giant solar collector and satellite could convert the Sun's energy into electricity which would be transmitted to Earth as microwaves. A collector built on a flimsy scale to take advantage of weightlessness would have to be built in space, working from a space port.

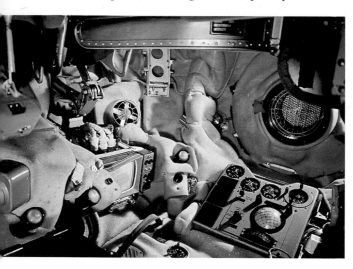

The cabin of Voskhod 1, the first three-man rocket, which took Soviet cosmonauts Vladimir Komarov, Konstantin Feoktistov and Dr Boris Yegorov on 16 orbits on 12/13 October 1964. It was the first time a medical man had flown in space and the first time light sports suits rather than space suits were worn.

Space shuttle astronauts (right above) queue up to select their space food in the galley on the orbiter Columbia on flight 611, launched on 12 January 1986. Daniel Brandenstein, commander of the space shuttle Columbia on its STS-32 mission of 19/20 January 1990, celebrated his 47th birthday in space with an inflatable cake (right).

The 51-D shuttle mission aboard Discovery *broke new ground in the United States space programme when Jeffrey Hoffman (left) and David Griggs (right) carried out the first unplanned space walk. It was supposed to be a routine mission, launched on 13 April 1985, to place two comsats, communication satellites, in orbit. On the first day, the $65 million Anik C1 comsat was successfully ejected, but when an attempt was made to release the $85 million Syncom 4-3 comsat, there was no sign of life.*

It was decided that the fault probably lay with an arming lever on the side of the comsat, so Hoffman and Griggs donned space suits to try to fix it. A makeshift device was used to try to trip the lever. Although the method worked, nothing happened and later examination of photographs indicated that the lever was already fully extended, so the problem with the comsat was internal.

On 27 August 1985 Discovery was launched to try to repair the satellite and save the huge investment. The mission was a complete success. Its commander, Joe Engle, commented: "It was one of the most fantastic things I've ever been involved with. Five months ago we had no idea we'd be doing this . . ."

ACROSS THE OCEANS

Gokstad and Oseberg Viking Longships *c.* ninth century Norway

Two Viking longships uncovered by archaeologists in Norway have been rebuilt and put on display in the Viking Ship Museum in Oslo. Both ships were well preserved by the blue clay in which they were buried. The Gokstad ship was discovered in a burial mound at Sandefjord in 1881, while the Oseberg ship was found in a mound near Tönsberg.

Respectively 76 feet and 70 feet long and each with a beam of 17 feet, the longships would have been used for raiding, often far from the Norse homelands. Despite having neither keel nor deck, longships made remarkable journeys, reaching Iceland, Greenland and the Mediterranean. During the winter, longships were generally hauled ashore until the spring.

Built almost entirely of oak, the Gokstad longship was designed to undertake longer journeys. Her hull was clinker-built with 16 planks contoured to form an identical bow and stern.

Henry Grâce à Dieu 1514 England

When launched at Erith in Kent in June 1514, *Henry Grâce à Dieu* was the largest warship in the world. Built on the orders of Henry VIII, *Great Harry*, as she was better known, had four pole masts, three of which had two circular tops—platforms from which soldiers could fire muskets on to the enemy below.

In common with many ships of her day, *Great Harry* had a large forecastle and sterncastle. She is thought to have weighed 1,000 tons and had a complement of 700 men. Although armed with 21 heavy bronze guns and 231 lighter weapons, *Great Harry* took no part in an engagement, since she was destroyed by an accidental fire at Woolwich, London, in 1553.

HMS *Victory* 1765 Britain

Nelson's flagship at the Battle of Trafalgar in 1805 is one of the best-known warships from the days of sail. *Victory*'s elm keel was laid down in 1759 at Chatham, but it was six years and 2,000 oak trees later before she was launched. Weighing 2,162 tons and mounting 100 guns, *Victory* was one of only five first-rates in the Royal Navy which then comprised 300 ships.

Her first action came in 1778 against the French, and thereafter *Victory* was the flagship of a succession of admirals in campaigns against France. By the end of the eighteenth century, *Victory* was old, but a shortage of good timber prevented her replacement and she was extensively refitted between 1800 and 1803. After the victory at Trafalgar and the death of Nelson in the battle, she was rebuilt and became the flagship of the commander-in-chief at Portsmouth, where the ship is now open to the public.

Charlotte Dundas 1801 Scotland
Clermont c. 1805 US

These two vessels may be said to have inaugurated the age of steam afloat. *Charlotte Dundas* was the creation of William Symington who built for the governor of the Forth & Clyde Canal, Lord Dundas, a steamboat that could reliably haul two other craft on the canal.

The canal's proprietors thought the wash would erode the canal's banks so *Charlotte Dundas* was laid up; her remains were photographed in 1856 just before they were broken up. A model based on the remains indicates that the boat had a paddlewheel inset into the hull toward the stern, driven by a crank powered by a single double-acting cyclinder.

Robert Fulton studied Symington's boat before building the world's first commercially successful steamboat, *Clermont*, which plied the Hudson River between Albany and New York from 1807. The single vertical-cylinder engine, built by Boulton & Watt of Birmingham, England, drove a pair of 15-foot paddlewheels mounted on each side of the hull.

SS *Great Eastern* 1858 Britain

The third and last steamship built to the designs of the remarkable engineer Isambard Kingdom Brunel was one of the most extraordinary vessels ever built. The *Great Eastern* was more than twice as long and three times as heavy as any other ship afloat, and the enormous difficulties that were encountered during her construction and launch served to undermine the health of her creator.

The ship was intended to carry 4,000 passengers and 6,000 tons of cargo to India or Australia without recoaling. With a gross tonnage of 18,914 tons and a length of 680 feet, the *Great Eastern* had a pair of paddlewheels and a propeller, driven by different engines, as well as sails. She was the first ship to have a cellular, double-skin hull. Her career was a failure. She was too large to be viable and spent more time as an exhibit in United States ports than carrying passengers across the oceans; her one triumph was the laying of the first transatlantic telegraph cable, in 1866. The ship was broken up in the River Mersey in 1889.

Gloire 1859 France
HMS *Warrior* 1860 Britain

It is a matter for debate whether the French *Gloire* or the English *Warrior* was the first true battleship, taking the term to mean a capital ship of a navy built of iron or steel. *Gloire* was a frigate with a displacement of 5,600 tons, clad in armour plate almost $4\frac{3}{4}$ inches thick. However, beneath the iron was a ship of oak.

HMS *Warrior* had three skins to her hull: an inner 1 inch of wrought iron sandwiched 18 inches of teak between the outer skin of 4 inches of wrought iron. Her iron construction and watertight bulkheads returned naval supremacy to the Royal Navy; Napoleon III called the ship "the black snake amongst the rabbits".

USS *Monitor* 1862 US

John Ericsson's shallow-draught ironclad gave its name to a whole class of naval vessels, although his ship for the Union navy was only a limited success. Born in Sweden, Ericsson had emigrated to the United States after a period in England, during which he had entered a locomotive in the Rainhill Trials of 1829, won by the Stephensons' *Rocket*.

When the Union learned that the Confederate navy was converting a wooden ship, *Merrimak*, into an ironclad, plans were made for a response. Ericsson's design was accepted, and *Monitor* was launched in 1862. Two guns were mounted in a revolving turret which was to revolutionize naval design. The encounter with *Virginia*, as *Merrimak* was renamed, was indecisive, and *Monitor* foundered off Cape Hatteras on the last day of 1862.

Milestones

Turbinia 1894 Britain
Built by Brown & Hood at Wallsend-on-Tyne in 1894 to a design by Charles Parsons, *Turbinia* was the world's first turbine vessel. Although *Turbinia* was only an experimental 100-foot launch, her influence was immense. It was at Queen Victoria's Diamond Jubilee Review at Spithead in 1897 that *Turbinia* made her mark, achieving 34 knots and outstripping the vessels that attempted to intercept her. It encouraged Cunard to adopt turbines for the *Lusitania* and *Mauretania* and the Royal Navy to order two turbine submarines, *Viper* and *Cobra*.

Turbinia is preserved at Exhibition Park, Newcastle-upon-Tyne.

HMS *Dreadnought* 1906 Britain
Like the USS *Monitor*, HMS *Dreadnought* gave her name to a whole line of battleships. The first "all big gun" battleship, *Dreadnought* was launched at Portsmouth in February 1906 after being under construction for just eight months. Rather than carry a range of guns, she carried ten 12-inch guns, which enabled her to outgun anything else afloat. Her steam turbines also gave her a speed that would eclipse any other battleship in the world, her top speed being 21½ knots. Her superiority prompted the start of the "Dreadnought race" with Germany and Japan. During World War I there was only one engagement between Dreadnoughts, an inconclusive affair at Jutland in 1916. The Dreadnought formula of high speed, heavy protection and big guns continued until after World War II.

USS *North Carolina* 1940 US
Launched before the United States entered World War II following Pearl Harbor, USS *North Carolina* represents the final stage in the development of the battleship. By the time her keel was laid in 1937, it was evident that the principal threat to capital ships came from aircraft. Her antiaircraft armament was increased with each refit, and by the end of World War II, she had 96 AA guns, supplemented by twenty 5-inch guns; these could fire shells with proximity fuses, fitted with miniature radios that detected the presence of an aircraft within effective range and exploded to shower the plane with shrapnel fragments.

But *North Carolina*'s prime purpose was as a mobile gun platform; she had nine 16-inch guns which were never fired against another battleship, but were used to bombard land and lesser sea targets throughout the war. Her 121,000-hp engines could propel her loaded displacement weight of 44,800 tons at a maximum speed of 25 knots. She was a lucky ship, losing only 6 men in her company of 2,000 during 300,000 miles of war at sea.

North Carolina is preserved at Wilmington, North Carolina.

OVERLAND BY ROAD

Bicycle 1860s US, France and Britain
Extraordinary as it may seem, none of the sophisticated civilizations of the ancient world appear to have had any concept of the bicycle. The first evidence that anyone had considered this means of transport appears in the sketches of a student of Leonardo da Vinci, but as it is included among caricatures and pornographic drawings, it is unlikely that even then—the late fifteenth century—the idea was being taken seriously.

In 1817 Baron Karl von Drais produced the hobby-horse—a body set on two wheels with a handlebar for steering. Although it had no pedals and was powered by the rider pushing his feet along the ground, it attained such speeds that a hobby-horse is reported to have beaten a coach and four in a race from London to Brighton. The bicycle with pedals emerged more or less simultaneously in the US, France and Britain in the 1860s, inspired by the work of Pierre Michaux of Paris who is credited with the first "velocipede".

Two inventions of the 1880s increased the bicycle's practicality and popularity. The Rover Safety Bicycle, designed by John Kemp Starley, was the first to feature a chain-driven rear wheel. This meant that speed was no longer dependent on the size of the wheel, an engineering achievement which led to the fall from favour of the unstable penny-farthing. The second invention was that of the pneumatic tyre by John Boyd Dunlop—what had until then been popularly known as the "boneshaker" now became a reasonably comfortable means of transport.

Model T Ford 1908 US
Although Karl Benz is credited with the production of the world's first practical automobile with an internal combustion engine, the massive growth in the popularity of the motor car must be attributed to Henry Ford (1863–1947). The Ford Motor Company was founded in 1903 and by 1915 was the largest automobile producer in the world, with over 500,000 Model Ts on the road. Ford pioneered mass production: parts or subassemblies were delivered to the production line with precision timing, so that by 1913 a complete chassis for the Model T could be produced in 93 minutes.

The Model T Ford was the first ever popular car. At its launch in 1908, Ford said, "I will build a motor car for the great multitude"—and he did. Before this time, cars had been the preserve of the rich. The Model T cost $500 in 1913 and $290 by the time it was withdrawn from production in 1927. Ford produced 15.5 million Model Ts—and changed people's lives as radically as any other modern development.

Harley-Davidson c.1910 US
In the early days, motorcycles were not as popular in the US as in Britain and Europe. This may be because the motor car was much cheaper and more readily available in the US; or because the distances a traveller was likely to cover in Europe were small enough to make the comparative discomfort of a motorcycle more tolerable. In any event, it is surprising that what became known as "the motorcycle magnificent" should have developed in a Milwaukee basement around the turn of the century.

The first Harley-Davidson product was a 3-hp, single-cylinder vehicle. Before World War I their motorcycles were widely used by policemen, telephone companies and postal services. During World War I they consolidated their reputation for power, reliability and speed—one model averaged an incredible 89 mph over a 100-mile test.

Expansion in the 1920s added the characteristic bomb-shaped tank, hooded mudguards and wide wheels to the already familiar low saddle position. And throughout this century, with the rise and fall of British, European and Japanese manufacturers, the Harley-Davidson has remained the ultimate "bikers' bike".

Milestones

Bugatti c.1920 France

It is difficult to define a "classic car"—it must simply have something about it that makes it unforgettable. Anything from the unpretentious Austin Seven to the incomparable Rolls-Royce can be included in a list of classics.

Bugattis deserve a place in such a list because they can be likened to thoroughbred racehorses—beautifully designed, impeccably produced and a joy to handle. The Bugatti company, which flourished and produced beautiful cars throughout the 1920s, was founded in France by an Italian, Ettore Bugatti, son of a furniture designer and brother of a sculptor.

Bugattis were nothing if not stylish. As early as 1919, Ettore was criticized for producing a very fast car with poor brakes. "I build my cars to go, not to stop," he is said to have replied.

Volkswagen Beetle 1937 Germany

The Volkswagen company was founded in Wolfsburg in 1937 by the German government. Its brief, as its name suggests, was to mass produce an inexpensive "people's car". The man brought in to design the car was Ferdinand Porsche, whose name is usually associated with sportier vehicles.

The VW factory was destroyed during World War II, along with most of Wolfsburg, but as German industry was rebuilt after the war, automobile manufacture concentrated largely on the people's car. By the mid-1950s, Volkswagen produced over 50 percent of the motor vehicles in West Germany.

Although it was soon one of the most popular cars in Europe, the Volkswagen was not at first a great success in the US. One of the reasons was certainly its Nazi connections, but the American public had not yet recognized the disadvantages of their larger, "gas-guzzling" cars. A brilliant advertising campaign run in 1959 changed all this: it not only emphasized the appeal of the small car, it gave the Volkswagen its popular name—the Beetle. In the early 1960s the Beetle was the most successful imported car in the US.

For 40 years Volkswagen traded on the success of its original model, hardly refining it at all. But by the early 1970s other small car manufacturers were producing more advanced and more attractive rivals.

Volkswagen was forced out of its complacency and began to produce other, sportier models like the Golf/Rabbit. But the Beetle, like the Morris Minor and the Citroën 2CV, retains its place in the hearts of lovers of unpretentious cars.

Mini 1959 Britain

The Suez Crisis of 1956 caused the first international oil shortage of the automobile era and led directly to a demand for smaller, more economical cars. The greatest of these was the Mini, created by the British Motor Corporation's chief designer, Alex Issigonis, who had already shown his genius with the development of the much-loved Morris Minor.

Issigonis's masterstroke lay in giving the Mini a transverse engine—simply turning the Morris Minor's engine through 90 degrees, so that it could be mounted on top of the transmission. The bonnet which covered it was shorter than anything ever seen on a saloon car. But although the Mini itself was tiny, 85 percent of its volume was passenger space: it was remarkably uncramped for such a compact car.

The Mini was cheap, reliable, safe and easy to park—but somehow it was more than that. It rapidly became a British national institution and a symbol of the 1960s, often seen painted with Union Jacks or psychedelic, flower power patterns. Indeed, it attained such cult status that a facsimile edition was launched to celebrate its thirtieth birthday in 1989.

E-Type Jaguar 1961 Britain

The E-Type Jaguar was the attainable sports car of the 1960s. The fact that it had an enormous potential market in the US (in the years before the imposition of a speed limit that curtailed the pleasures of sports-car driving) meant that the manufacturers could keep the price to a realistic level. Owning an E-type need not be a fantasy or a privilege reserved for pop stars—without losing any of its glamour, the E-type became a car the man in the street could just about afford.

The charisma of the E-type lay in its glorious, streamlined shape, but it also boasted a mighty 3.8-litre engine and was the first Jaguar with independent rear suspension, an innovation which made it sturdy, reliable and a joy to handle.

Formula 1 Racing Cars—the Cosworth Engine 1967 Britain

Racing cars are divided into "formulas" or categories defining the size and power of the car—and the most powerful and theoretically the most exciting are classed as Formula 1. In the early 1960s, motor racing was still based on 1500 cc unsupercharged engines, which meant that many sporting models of private cars were faster and more challenging than anything on the Grand Prix circuit. The sport was losing its thrill for drivers and spectators alike.

In 1966, the definition of a Formula 1 car was increased to 3000 cc and motor racing was revolutionized by the invention of the Ford-Cosworth DFV engine. A compact and supremely efficient four-overhead-camshaft unit, the 405-hp Cosworth swiftly became the standard engine for Formula 1 cars and dominated the Grand Prix circuit. The engine had been produced specifically for Lotus, although they had exclusive use of it for only one year, and a Lotus 49 with a Cosworth engine, driven by Jim Clark, won the Dutch Grand Prix in 1967 on its first outing—itself a remarkable achievement.

Clark and his Lotus teammate, Graham Hill, won four more Grand Prix in the course of the year. The engine was subsequently adopted by almost all other major manufacturers and by the time the 3000 cc unsupercharged engine was banned in 1985, cars powered by the Ford-Cosworth DFV had won 155 Grand Prix.

Sunraycer—the Solar Car 1987 US

Sunraycer was produced by General Motors as their entry for the 1987 World Solar Challenge—a 2,000-mile race across Australia intended to encourage the development of solar power for automobiles. Not only did it win, it beat the second placed car by 20 hours.

In some ways, Sunraycer is one of the most successful cars ever produced. Its coefficient of drag—the means by which a car's aerodynamic efficiency is tested—is comparable to that of an aeroplane wing. Its body is exceptionally sleek, with only two small fins to improve stability in cross winds interrupting its smooth lines. It is made largely of lightweight aluminium and powered by solar cells covering all the body except the nose.

However, the cost of production was over $1 million, and it remains to be seen whether it will ever be practical to manufacture such a vehicle on a commercial scale. Drawbacks yet to be overcome include the fact that Sunraycer seats only one person, that it has no headlights, and that it is impossible to put the top in place from the driving seat.

OVERLAND BY RAIL

Lafayette 4-2-0 1837 US
In 1837 William Norris of Philadelphia delivered the first of eight locomotives to the Baltimore & Ohio Railroad. They incorporated several important developments from the Stephensons' *Rocket* of 1829. It had a leading bogie underneath the smokebox, which both improved weight distribution and helped to guide the locomotive smoothly through curves. The cylinders were placed beside the smokebox outside the frames, with the valves placed in a chest on top of the cylinders. The axle of the driving wheels was located in front of the firebox rather than behind, which served to increase the weight placed upon them and so improved adhesion.

The locomotives, the first of which was named *Lafayette*, were a great improvement on the B & O's vertical-boilered locomotives which were all the company owned before the Norris 4-2-0s. Their success led to export orders for railways in Austria, Germany and even Britain, which was at the time the leading producer of railway locomotives.

Merddin Emrys 0-4-4-0 1879 Wales
The Festiniog Railway double Fairlies represent a major development in the history of the steam locomotive. Built to take slate from the quarries of North Wales to the harbour at Porthmadog for shipment, the railway was built to a gauge of 1 foot 11½ inches. Its steep gradients and lack of power in the railway's early engines caused congestion. In 1864, Robert Fairlie, a consulting engineer in London, patented a double bogie locomotive, and received an order from the FR; the first locomotive, *Little Wonder*, was built in 1869. Two more Fairlies followed, and in the third, *Merddin Emrys*, the Fairlie reached its final form. The locomotives immediately proved their worth by hauling twice the load of the railway's previous engines.

A Fairlie double boiler is built as a single unit, with continuous space for water and steam, although there are two fireboxes with separate firedoors. The engine has two sets of wheels, cylinders and valve gear. By the time of Fairlie's death in 1885, 52 railways worldwide were using locomotives based on his patent. Three double Fairlies are still at work on the Festiniog Railway, now a tourist railway.

Jones Goods 4-6-0 1894 Scotland
The remote Highland Railway of Scotland was responsible for introducing the 4-6-0 locomotive to the British Isles. Designed by the railway's brilliant locomotive superintendent, David Jones, the Jones Goods were influenced by some 4-6-0s built in Glasgow for service in India. The 4-6-0 was to become one of the most successful of wheel arrangements for express locomotives, found all over the world, so it is surprising that it took 34 years from the construction of a 4-6-0 in Britain, built for an overseas railway, until an engine of this type was ordered by a British company.

The Jones Goods performed sterling work over the long and steep gradients of the Highland Railway north of Perth, hauling passenger trains as well as goods. With driving wheels of 5 feet 3 inches diameter, they were well suited to hill climbing. Few locomotives have required such little modification to their basic design over a 40-year life. Most were withdrawn from service during the 1930s, but one survives in the Museum of Transport, Glasgow.

Class P8 4-6-0 1906 Prussia
Few 4-6-0s were built in such numbers or found their way on to the railways of so many countries as the P8 class 4-6-0s, first built in 1906 for the Royal Prussian Union Railway (KPEV). They were intended for express passenger work on hilly routes, having driving wheels of 5 feet 9 inches diameter. However, it was found that they were better suited to secondary passenger and mixed traffic use, although they continued to work some expresses. Fitted with superheaters, long-travel piston valves and Walschaert's valve gear, the P8s proved exceptionally efficient locomotives.

By 1918, 2,350 had been built for KPEV. Because many P8s were handed over as part of war reparations after both world wars, or remained in formerly occupied countries where they had been used by the Germans, P8s could be seen on passenger trains in Belgium, Czechoslovakia, Greece, Yugoslavia, Poland, Romania and the USSR. The last was withdrawn from service in West Germany in 1975, although at least eight have been preserved.

K4 Class 4-6-2 1914 US
The 425 K4 Pacifics built between 1914 and 1927 handled all the express trains of the Pennsylvania Railroad until after World War II. A development of the earlier Pacific classes which the railway had operated since 1907, the K4s had driving wheels of 6 feet 8 inches diameter and proved remarkably economical. During the 1930s most of the class were fitted with a mechanical stoker to relieve the fireman of the arduous task of feeding the 70-square-foot grate. The famous designer Raymond Loewy devised a streamlined casing for one engine which regularly operated the Broadway Limited that ran between New York and Chicago. Over the steepest part of the route, on which the gradient was sometimes 1 in 58 (1.72 percent), three K4s were sometimes needed to haul the train.

Two K4s survive, one at Horseshoe Curve, near Altoona, Pennsylvania, where most of the class were built, and one at Strasburg, Pennsylvania.

Castle Class 4-6-0 1923 Britain
The first Castle class 4-6-0, No. 4073 *Caerphilly Castle*, was the most powerful locomotive in Britain when it was built at the Great Western Railway's workshops in Swindon. This power was achieved with an economy that was the envy of the other three main line railway companies in Britain, since the Castles used just 2.83 lb of coal per drawbar-horsepower-hour, when other locomotive engineers thought that they were doing well to produce a figure of around 4 lb.

The four cylinders and inside valve gear made access for maintenance difficult but helped to produce a wonderfully balanced locomotive. The driving wheel diameter of 6 feet 8½ inches helped the Castles to run at high speed, and for some years No. 5006

Tregenna Castle held the world record for an average start-to-stop speed of 81.7 mph over the 77¼ miles between Swindon and London Paddington.

Caerphilly Castle is preserved in London's Science Museum, No. 4079 *Pendennis Castle* operates on a private railway in Australia, and several are able to work special trains over main line and preserved railways in Britain.

Pioneer Zephyr 1934 US

The first self-propelled diesel train built by General Motors was put into service after four years' development work, on 26 May 1934. The three-car train ran between Denver and Chicago on the Chicago, Burlington & Quincy Railroad, cutting the usual journey time of 27 hours 45 minutes to just over 13 hours, an increase in average speed from 37 mph to 78 mph. General Motors presented this as a triumph of the diesel engine, when in fact it was a new approach to train operation. The lightweight, stainless-steel train had a limited carrying capacity, and other railroads soon showed that similar improvements in speed could be effected with steam.

Nonetheless, the concept caught on, although self-propulsion soon gave way to locomotive-hauled trains. The Pioneer Zephyr can be seen at Chicago's Museum of Science & Industry.

Class 05 4-6-4 1935 Germany

Although only three locomotives of this class were built for the German State Railway, they had a major impact when new. They were intended to be the steam engineers' answer to the German high-speed diesel railcars that had reached 100 mph in 1931. The limited capacity of the railcars made them unsuitable for many routes, and they were expensive to build. The Class 05 was a streamlined, three-cylinder locomotive with unusually large driving wheels, of 7 feet 6½ inches diameter, and exceptionally high boiler pressure at 284 lb/sq in. The streamlined casing went almost down to the rails and was painted red. The intended high speeds made good brakes vital, so a pair of blocks was fitted to all wheels, including bogie wheels, except those on the leading axle which had a single block.

Expectations were fulfilled when the Class 05 achieved an authenticated world speed record of 124.5 mph on 11 May 1936. This was eclipsed two years later by the London & North Eastern Railway's *Mallard* in Britain. After being stored during World War II, they were rebuilt with new boilers and without their streamlined casing. One has been preserved, at the German National Railway Museum in Nurnberg, in its original condition.

Class 59 4-8-2 +2-8-4 1955 Kenya

For 25 years the metre-gauge Class 59 Garratts held the distinction of being the largest and most powerful steam locomotives in the world, once the "Big Boys" on the Union Pacific in the US had been withdrawn. The Class 59s were the last of a line of Garratt classes built for the Kenya & Uganda Railway, later East African Railways, and were designed to haul freight trains over the 350 miles between Mombasa and Nairobi. The line has a ruling gradient of 1 in 65 (1.5 percent) and the earlier Garratts could not cope with the demands of traffic. The 59 class had driving wheels of 4 feet 6 inches diameter and produced a tractive effort of 83,350 lb, twice that of the most powerful passenger locomotive operated in Britain.

The Garratt was conceived by an English engineer, Herbert Garratt, who interested locomotive builders Beyer, Peacock of Manchester in an articulated locomotive with high-pressure cylinders at each end of two sets of wheels. Between them is the boiler unit, and water tanks over the two sets of motion help to provide weight for adhesion. The first Garratt was built for Tasmania in 1907, but it was in Africa that the type had the greatest impact, especially in South Africa.

No. 18000 A1A-A1A 1950 Britain
No. 18100 A1A-A1A 1950 Britain

At the end of World War II, the increasing use of diesel traction in the United States and the work done on aircraft gas turbines during the war encouraged British railway companies to look to these forms of motive power as possible successors to steam. The simplicity of gas turbines over diesels appealed to the Great Western Railway, which ordered two such locomotives, one from Brown Boveri in Switzerland and one from Metropolitan Vickers in England.

The Swiss gas turbine, No. 18000, was delivered in 1950, by which time the GWR had been nationalized to become part of British Railways. The unit produced 2,500 hp to drive a generator that supplied current to four traction motors, driving the outer axles of each six-wheeled bogie.

The Metro-Vick locomotive, No. 18100, was delivered a year later and produced 3,500 hp, enabling it to start trains on the Devon banks that were twice as heavy as those the Swiss engine could get under way. However, the principal flaw of the gas turbine was its inefficiency when not working at full load. When other regions of BR gained experience of diesel-electrics, interest in the gas turbine waned and both were withdrawn from regular service by the end of 1960.

Shinkansen 1964 Japan

Shinkansen means "new line", and the significance of the celebrated Shinkansen trains lies more in their method of operation than in technical development. The Japanese had the courage to fund a totally new railway, accepting two prerequisites for the successful attainment of average speeds of 100 mph: a wider gauge than the standard 3 feet 6 inches of Japanese National Railways; and the need for a line dedicated to frequent high-speed trains to guarantee a reliable service.

Their investment was amply rewarded by a 300 percent increase in traffic between 1966 and 1973 over the new 4-foot-8½-inch gauge line between Tokyo and Osaka. The line had been opened for a year of moderate speed running in 1964, leading to the introduction of services running at up to 130 mph the following year. Each 16-car train has 15,872 hp at its disposal, produced by sixty-four 248-hp motors, one to each axle to ensure high acceleration. New generations of Shinkansens have been produced since the original 480 cars.

Class DD40 AX "Centennial" 1969 US

To take their mammoth freight trains over the Sherman Hills of Wyoming, Union Pacific had to use six or seven diesels on a single train to replace the steam "Big Boy" 4-8-8-4s. The answer to this unsatisfactory arrangement was the "Centennial" diesel-electric, built by General Motors to produce 6,600 hp from two 16-cylinder engines driving two four-axle bogies. It was the most powerful and the largest prime mover unit in the world, with a length of 98 feet 5 inches.

The class name was chosen to commemorate the centenary of the Union Pacific Railroad, the central section of the first transcontinental railroad, which opened in 1869. The use of two engines in a single unit saved a set of electrical control gear, but the modular nature of modern control gear, in which faults can be easily diagnosed and repaired, has diminished the value of this saving.

In common with most railroad companies, Union Pacific has reverted to buying off-the-shelf locomotives since they are more cost effective, but the "Centennials" remain the ultimate development of the most common form of traction on the railways of the world.

ETR 401 Pendolino 1976 Italy

This was the first successful train to have a tilting mechanism that would allow a 9-degree angle. Previously, the first commercial tilting train, the Class 381 on Japanese National Railways, had been limited to 5 degrees. The advantage of a tilting train is that it obviates the need to build a new railway line to achieve significantly higher line speeds, which is the method chosen by SNCF with the TGV.

The tilt mechanism of the Pendolino is made up of accelerometers and gyroscopes, and has been used to good effect on the sharp curves of the line between Rome and Ancona that runs through the Apennines. A new generation of Pendolino trains, the ETR 450, has extended their use, and other countries, such as Sweden, are using comparable technology in the ceaseless quest for higher speeds to capture traffic from road and air transport.

THROUGH THE AIR

Sopwith Camel 1917 Britain

During the early part of World War I, the Royal Flying Corps, forerunner of the RAF, had depended largely on the tiny Sopwith Pup. By 1916, it was apparent that German aircraft technology was outstripping the British, and that a replacement for the Pup was needed.

The Sopwith Camel was therefore introduced in 1917. With its propeller, engine, fuel tank, armament and cockpit all crammed into a comparatively small space at the front of the aircraft, the Camel had extraordinary manoeuvrability, but this feature also had its disadvantages. Although the plane could be turned very tightly, it was difficult to control under those circumstances and was liable to spin rapidly without warning.

Nevertheless, the Camel became the most successful fighter of its age. Between July 1917 and November 1918, Camels destroyed 1,294 enemy aircraft, more than any other in the entire course of the war, and played a particularly significant role in the Battle of Cambrai in March 1918.

Hawker Hurricane 1935 Britain

Developed by Hawker and first flown as a prototype in 1935, the Hurricane was the RAF's first eight-gun monoplane fighter. Like the Spitfire, it had machine-guns mounted on the wings (previous fighter planes had had a smaller number of guns mounted in the fuselage). Although inferior in performance to the Spitfire, it made up in sturdiness and the solidity of its gun platform what it lacked in manoeuvrability. In their first year in combat, Hurricanes shot down some 1,500 Luftwaffe aircraft, almost half the total for all British fighter aircraft over that period.

Douglas DC-3 1936 US

The 21-seater DC-3 flew its first scheduled service for American Airlines in 1936. Its cheapness and reliability made it popular both as a passenger aircraft and for military transport in the US and Great Britain during World War II; by 1945, 10,000 DC-3s had been built. After the war the US Air Force sold many of its aircraft to air forces from Argentina to Yugoslavia; over 2,000 DC-3s are still being used in a military capacity outside the US. Later models could accommodate 36 passengers, but the plane's range never exceeded 1,510 miles and its normal cruising speed was a mere 170 mph—the modern DC-10 has a range and speed more than three times greater. Nevertheless, small airlines throughout the world continue to rely on the DC-3 and it remains the most widely used air transport in history.

De Havilland Comet 1952 Britain

In May 1952, the first commercial jet-propelled aircraft, a BOAC Comet, made its maiden flight from London to Johannesburg. It had five scheduled stops along the way, and the journey took a little under 24 hours, but the effect on long-distance travel was as dynamic as that of Concorde 25 years later. The other end of the world was suddenly accessible.

The de Havilland Comet had been developed in Britain during World War II, with an eye to commercial transport in peacetime. In the United States, military jet aircraft were already in use, but commercial manufacturers had not yet exploited the possibilities. In fact, the Comet was so far ahead of its rivals that none of the other aircraft companies had any clear idea of how to compete.

Jet-propulsion was only a part of the breakthrough in technology that this plane represented—its structure and aerodynamics were also far in advance of anything that had been built so far, and the pressure attained in the cabin was double that of any previous airliner, allowing a cruising height of 40,000 feet.

By 1954, Comet 2 could fly nonstop from London to Khartoum, a distance of 3,064 miles in six and a half hours. And, perhaps most significantly of all, passengers had discovered that the new airliner could cope with bad weather much better than its predecessors.

Vickers Viscount 1953 Britain

The first aircraft designed for turboprop propulsion, the Vickers Viscount almost single-handedly prevented an American monopoly of the world civil aviation market for twenty years after World War II. The chief designer at Vickers in the late 1940s, George Edwards, was not only responsible for the Viscount—he became one of the most prominent figures in the British aircraft industry and was involved in the development of both the VC10 and Concorde.

The Viscount's strength lay in its Rolls-Royce Dart engines. The Dart was a well-established and reliable, if basic, piece of technology. A chief executive of Rolls-Royce in the 1960s described it as "agricultural machinery"; on the other hand, he had to admit, nobody had ever junked a plane with a Dart engine.

The results of the Viscount's first test flight were spectacularly good, but just at that moment British European Airways, potentially the plane's principal customer, announced the purchase of 20 rival aircraft. Edwards's faith in his design was justified within two years, however, when BEA also ordered 20 Viscounts. Air France, Aer Lingus, the Australian airline TAA and TCA (now Air Canada) all bought the aircraft in its early years.

BEA flew the first scheduled Viscount service from Heathrow to Nicosia in 1953 and the aircraft continued in production until 1964. Even today there is a thriving secondhand market for Viscounts, with ex-airline models often being bought by corporate customers.

Boeing 707 1958 US

The development of the Boeing 707 entailed one of the greatest commercial risks in modern aviation history. The British-built de Havilland Comet had shown the world the advantages of jet travel and American companies had to compete. Boeing, known more for their fighters than their commercial aircraft, were aware of the need for in-flight refuelling in air force jets and were already working on the concept of a "jet tanker". It seemed to them that a civil version of the same craft could be their answer to the Comet. It would be powered by a lighter variation of the fuel-efficient Pratt & Whitney engines Boeing had used in their hugely successful B-52 bombers.

Unable to sell this idea up front to commercial airlines or to the US Air Force, or to draw on government funding, Boeing took the decision to develop a prototype using $15 million of their own money. This was in 1952. It was an enormous sum of money. No one could have predicted that the same basic craft would still be in production 30 years later.

By 1954, the $15 million budget had long since been exceeded, but the USAF had ordered enough tankers to subsidize the development of the civil aircraft. The following year, Douglas—a far greater force than Boeing in commercial aircraft manufacture—announced the launch of their DC-8, in direct competition with the proposed 707. Pan Am bought both aircraft, while United opted exclusively for the DC-8. Expensive modifications to both craft followed as Boeing and Douglas tried to keep one jump ahead of each other.

Pan Am flew the first scheduled 707 flight from New York to Paris in 1958, and the battle between 707 and DC-8 continued throughout the 1960s. Douglas finally abandoned production of the DC-8 in 1972, but the Boeing continued to sell—admittedly in smaller numbers and largely in its military form—well into the 1980s.

Airbus 1972 France, Germany, Netherlands and Spain

The wide-bodied, twin-engined airbus produced by Airbus Industrie is the financial and technical brainchild of French, German, Dutch and Spanish expertise. It was Europe's first significant contribution for many years to what had been very much an American-dominated market—but it was a very significant contribution indeed.

European manufacturers wanted to develop a short-to-medium-haul aircraft that would seat 250 to 300 people, be economical to run and minimize congestion at Europe's overcrowded airports. The aircraft they produced was ordered not only by European airlines but by one major American carrier and, increasingly, by airlines around the world, particularly in the Far East. Within ten years of its launch, Airbus had pushed Boeing into second place in the wide-bodied market, and celebrated a million hours of accident-free flying.

TU-160 1988 USSR

Since the late 1980s, with the end of the Cold War, Westerners have become more aware of the advanced state of Russian aeronautical technology, which reaches its peak in the TU-160, the largest and one of the fastest strategic bombers in the world. It is appreciably faster than its equivalent in the US Air Force, the B-1B Lancer, and can cruise at almost twice the speed of sound. The TU-160 has broken innumerable records in tests of speed and performance, most notably flying a 620-mile course at a speed of 1,068 mph carrying a load of 66,137 lb.

INTO SPACE

Sputnik 1 1957 USSR

The first artificial satellite was launched into space by the Soviet Union on 4 October 1957. Called Sputnik—the Russian for traveller—the satellite was little more than a small sphere fitted with three radio antennae, which it used to broadcast a simple "bleep" to Earth as it made its orbit. The purpose of Sputnik was to advertise Soviet success in building an intercontinental ballistic missile, and at that it was a brilliant success. American opinion was shocked at this evidence of Soviet superiority, and at once began the expansion of its own space programme.

Apollo 13 1970 US

The flight of Apollo 13, the third manned mission to the Moon, was an epic journey saved from catastrophe by a series of brilliant extemporizations. Launched on 11 April 1970, Apollo 13 was well on its way to the Moon with its crew of three (Jim Lovell, John Swigert and Fred Haise) when an oxygen tank exploded. Without oxygen their fuel cells could produce no power, and they were forced to take to the lunar module, the space age's first lifeboat. They coasted around the Moon, correcting their course with the lunar module's engines, and returned to Earth in a cold, powerless vehicle with too little water to drink. Finally they managed a safe splashdown in the Pacific, weak and dehydrated. They had made it, but only just.

Apollo-Soyuz 1975 (US–USSR)

The first and so far only joint project between the Soviet and American space project was the Apollo-Soyuz test project, the "handshake in space". An American Apollo spacecraft, launched on 15 July 1975, made a rendezvous and docked with a Soviet Soyuz spacecraft launched the same day. The two crews moved between the two spacecraft, shook hands, shared meals and toasted each other with soup. The joint project, a result of the period of detente between the superpowers, was meant to signal a new era of cooperation in space—but the Cold War quickly resumed after the Soviet invasion of Afghanistan in 1979 and the experiment was not repeated.

Bibliography

Ackroyd, John. *Just for the record: Thrust 2* CHW Roles & Associates, 1984

Anderson, William R., with Blair Jr., Clay. *Nautilus 90 North* Hodder & Stoughton, 1959

Andrews, Allen. *The Mad Motorists* Harrap, 1964

Barzini, Luigi. *Peking to Paris* Alcove Press, 1972

Bernacchi, L.C. *Saga of the Discovery* Blackie, 1938

Bobrick, Benson. *Labyrinths of Iron* Newsweek Books, 1982

Booth, Henry. *An Account of the Liverpool and Manchester Railway* reprinted Fran Cass & Co., 1969

Botany Bay, the voyage of Governor Phillip printed for John Stockdale, London, 1789

Braddon, Russell. *The Hundred Days of Darien* Collins, 1974

British Trans-Americas Expedition Report (no date)

Brooks, Clive. *Atlantic Queens* Haynes, 1989

Burton, Anthony. *The Rainhill Story* BBC, 1980

Campbell, Gina and Meech, Michael. *Bluebirds* Sidgwick & Jackson, 1988

Carey, John (ed.). *The Faber Book of Reportage* Faber, 1987

Carlson, Robert E. *The Liverpool & Manchester Railway Project, 1821–31* David & Charles, 1969

Carrick, Robert W. *The Pictorial History of the America's Cup Races* W.H. Allen, 1965

Chichester, Francis. *Gipsy Moth Circles the World* Hodder & Stoughton, 1967

Cochrane, Dorothy, Hardesty, Von, and Lee, Russell. *The Aviation Careers of Igor Sikorsky* University of Washington Press for NASA, 1989

Cookridge, E.H. *The Orient Express* Allen Lane, 1979

Dorin, Patrick C. *Canadian Pacific Railway* Superior Publishing Co., 1974

Douglas, Hugh. *The Underground Story* Robert Hale, 1963

Duke, Neville, and Lanchbery, Edward. *Sound Barrier* Cassell, 1954

Freeman Allen, Geoffrey. *Luxury Trains of the World* Bison, 1979

Freeman Allen, Geoffrey. *Railways Past, Present and Future* Orbis, 1982

Gillespie, Charles Coulston. *The Montgolfier Brothers and the invention of aviation* Princeton University Press, 1983

The Great Age of Exploration Reader's Digest, 1971

Grierson, John. *Sir Hubert Wilkins, Pilgrim of Exploration* Robert Hale, 1960

Gunston, Bill. *Flights of Fantasy* Hamlyn, 1990

Heine, William C. *Historic Ships of the World* David & Charles, 1977

Higham, Robin. *Britain's Imperial Air Routes 1918 to 1939* G.T. Foulis, 1960

Hogg, Garry. *The Hovercraft Story* Abelard-Schuman, 1970

Hollingsworth, Brian. *North American Locomotives* Salamander, 1984

Honeywell, Eleanor. *The Challenge of Antarctica* Anthony Nelson, 1984

Howarth, D. *The Dreadnoughts* Time-Life Books, 1980

Hughes, Robert. *The Fatal Shore* Collins Harvill, 1987

Huntley, John. *Railways in the Cinema* Ian Allan, 1969

John, Anthony and Dear, Ian. *The Early Challenges of the America's Cup* Columbus, 1986

Kemp, Peter (ed.). *The Oxford Companion to Ships & The Sea* Oxford University Press, 1976

Kratville, William. *Big Boy* Kratville Publications, Omaha

Lacey, Robert. *The Queens of the North Atlantic* Sidgwick & Jackson, 1973

Landstrom, Bjorn. *Columbus* Allen & Unwin, 1967

Landstrom, Bjorn. *The Ship* Allen & Unwin, 1961

Lawrence, Mike. *The Mille Miglia* Batsford, 1988

Leggett, Robert C. *Railways of Canada* David & Charles, 1973

Lindbergh, Charles. *The Spirit of St Louis* Scribner's, 1953

Lubbock, Basil. *The Log of the Cutty Sark* Brown, Son and Ferguson, 1928

Ludovic (ed.). *A Book of Air Journeys* Collins, 1982

MacGregor, David. *Clipper Ships* Argus, 1979

MacKay, Donald. *The Asian Dream* Douglas & McIntyre, 1986

Masefield, Sir Peter. *To Ride the Storm* William Kimber, 1982

Mauretania, facsimile reprint of articles from *Engineering*, Patrick Stephens, 1987

Miller, Jay. *The X-Planes* Orion, 1988

Mondey, David (ed.). *The International Encyclopedia of Aviation* Octopus, 1977

Mosley, Leonard. *Lindbergh* Hodder & Stoughton, 1976

Newkirk, Dennis. *Almanac of Soviet Manned Space Flight* Gulf Publishing, 1990

Nicholson, John. *Great Years in Yachting* Nautical Publishing Co., 1970

Orlebar, Christopher. *The Concorde Story* Temple Press, 1986

Osman, Tony. *Space History* Michael Joseph, 1983

Page, Martin. *The Lost Pleasures of the Great Trains* Weidenfeld & Nicolson, 1975

Pittenger, William. *Capturing a Locomotive* J.B. Lippincott, 1882

Politovsky, Eugene. *From Libau to Tsushima* John Murray, 1906

Rails Across Canada VIA Rail, 1986

Rutherford, Michael. *Mallard, the record breaker* Newburn House, 1988

Sawyer, L.A. and Mitchell, W.H. *The Liberty Ships* David & Charles, 1970

Simpson, C.R.H. *The Rainhill Locomotive Trials* Rainhill Trials Celebration Committee, 1979

Slocum, Captain Joshua. *Sailing Alone around the World* Rupert Hart-Davis, 1948

Specifications for the "Discovery" Royal Geographical Society, 1899

Stevens, Thomas. *Around the World on a Bicycle* Sampson Low, Marston, Searle, and Rivington, 1887; Century, 1988

Talbot, Frederick A. *The Railway Conquest of the World* William Heinemann, 1911

Tremayne, David. *The Fastest Man on Earth* 633 Club, 1986

Turnill, Reginald. *Spaceflight Directory* Frederick Warne, 1978

Villa, Leo and Desmond, Kevin. *The World Water Speed Record* Batsford, 1976

Walder, David. *The Short Victorious War* Hutchinson, 1973

White, William J. *Airships for the Future* Sterling, 1978

Wilson, Andrew. *Space Shuttle Story* Hamlyn, 1986

Wolfe, Tom. *The Right Stuff* Jonathan Cape, 1980

Yenne, Bill. *All Aboard! The Golden Age of American Rail Travel* Dorset Press, 1984

Index

Acknowledgments

Conversion Tables

1 inch = 2.54 cm
1 foot = 0.3048 metre
1 yard = 0.9144 metre
1 mile = 1.6093 km

1 square foot = 0.092 square metre
1 square yard = 0.8361 square metre

1 pint = 0.568 litre
1 gallon = 4.546 litres

1 lb = 0.4536 kg
1 cwt = 50.8 kg
20 cwt = 1 ton
1 ton = 1.016 tonnes

$C = \frac{5}{9} \times (F - 32)$
$F = \frac{9}{5} \times C + 32$

1 hp = 746 watts = 0.746 kilowatt

1 knot = 1.15 mph = 1.852 km/h
Mach 1 (at sea level) = 760 mph = 1,222 km/h

Picture Credits

l = left; *r* = right; *c* = centre; *t* = top; *b* = bottom

13 Ancient Art and Architecture Collection; **14, 15** The Illustrated London News; **17** The Photo Source; **18** Topham Picture Source; **19***l*, *tr* and *cr* Marc Riboud/The John Hillelson Agency; **19***br* Bruce Coleman Inc; **20–23** Alex Webb/Magnum; **24** Robert Harding Picture Library; **25** Richard Laird/Susan Griggs Agency; **26** UPI/Bettmann; **27** The Image Bank; **28** UPI/Bettmann; **29** The Image Bank; **30, 31** UPI/Bettmann; **33** Mark Wadlow/USSR Photo Library; **34** V.Shustov/Novosti; **35***tl* and *r* Tass; **35***b* USSR Photo Library; **38** Ancient Art and Architecture Collection; **39, 40** Robert Harding Picture Library; **41** John P. Stevens/Ancient Art and Architecture Collection; **42–3** David Hiser/Photographers Aspen; **44** Loren McIntyre; **45***l* Werner Forman Archive; **45***r* Hutchison Library; **46***tl* Robert Harding Picture Library; **46***tr* Ancient Art and Architecture Collection; **46***b* Tony Morrison/South American Pictures; **47***t* E. Streichan/The Photo Source; **47***b* Tony Morrrison/South American Pictures; **49** Ancient Art and Architecture Collection; **50** Robert Harding Picture Library; **51** Topham Picture Source; **52, 53** The Image Bank; **54***t* Tony Stone Associates; **54***b* Stephanie Colasanti; **55** Robert Harding Picture Library; **56***t* The Image Bank; **56***b* Mischa Scorer/Hutchison Library; **57** Scala; **58–9** Marc Riboud/The John Hillelson Agency; **60** George Gerster/The John Hillelson Agency; **62, 63** Stephanie Colasanti; **65** Guildhall Library/Bridgeman Art Library; **66, 67** Ann Ronan Picture Library; **68***tl* Mary Evans Picture Library; **68***tr* The Mansell Collection; **69***tl* Sefton Photo Library; **69***tr* Mary Evans Picture Library; **69***b* Architectural Association; **70** Robert Harding Picture Library; **71** Ancient Art and Architecture Collection; **72** Topham Picture Source; **73, 74***tr* Robert Harding Picture Library; **74***b* The Image Bank; **75** Robert Harding Picture Library; **76** Stephanie Colasanti; **77** Robert Harding Picture Library; **78***c* Ann Ronan Picture Library; **78***bl* and *r* Hulton-Deutsch Collection; **78–9** Ann Ronan Picture Library; **79***r* Mary Evans Picture Library; **79***bl, c* and *r*, **80***tl* Hulton-Deutsch Collection; **80***tr* and *b*, **81** Roger-Viollet; **84** The Image Bank; **85** Angelo Hornak; **86, 87** UPI/Bettmann; **88** The Illustrated London News; **89** UPI/Bettmann; **90–1** Alan Smith/Tony Stone Associates; **92***t* Bruce Coleman Inc; **92***b* Rene Burri/Magnum; **93***t* Bruce Coleman Inc; **93***b* Art Seitz/Gamma Liaison/Frank Spooner Pictures; **95** Bavaria/Lauter; **96** Bavaria/Hans Schmied; **97***t* Bavaria/Martzik; **97***c* Susan Griggs Agency; **97***b* Bavaria/Holl; **98, 99** The Image Bank; **102** Popperfoto; **103***l* The Image Bank; **103***r* Robert Harding Picture Library; **105***t* Bruce Coleman Inc; **105***b* Mike Powell/All-Sport; **106***t* Andrea Pistolesi/The Image Bank; **106***b* The Image Bank; **109** Canadian National Tower; **110***t* Panda Associates Photography; **110***b* Canapress Photo Service; **112***l* Robert Harding Picture Library; **112***r* The Image Bank; **113***l* Orion; **113***r* Northern Picture Library; **114** S. Tucci/Gamma/Frank Spooner Pictures; **115** Mike Yamashita/Colorific!; **116***tl* and *r* Gamma/Frank Spooner Pictures; **116***b* Mike Yamashita/Colorific!; **117** Gamma/Frank Spooner Pictures; **118** Sophie Elbaz/Gamma/Frank Spooner Pictures; **119***t* Associated Press; **119***b* Associated Press/Topham Picture Source; **120***l* Gamma/Frank Spooner Pictures; **123, 124, 125** Peter Menzel/Colorific!; **128** Marc Riboud/The John Hillelson Agency; **129** Georg Gerster/The John Hillelson Agency; **130** Sally and Richard Greenhill; **132, 133***t*

Bayes/Aspect Picture Library, **391** *tr* and *br* H. Roger-Viollet; **392** Hulton-Deutsch Collection, **392–97** Popperfoto; **398** *t* and *b* Hulton-Deutsch Collection, **398** *bl* Popperfoto; **399** *t* National Motor Museum, **399** *b* Chris Allen Aviation Library; **400–402** *t* Quadrant Picture Library, **402** *b* Topham Picture Library; **403** Popperfoto; **404–5** *t* Luftschifbau Zeppelin/MARS, **405** *b* Popperfoto; **407** Shorts Brothers/MARS, **407** *(inset)*–**409** British Airways Archive; **410–11** Westland Helicopters Ltd, **411** Press Association; **412** *t* United Technologies Corporation Archive, **412** *c* and *b* Westland Helicopters Ltd; **414–17** Canadair; **418** Aviation Picture Library; **419** Quadrant Picture Library; **420** *t* SIPA/Rex Features, **420** *b* M. Roberts/The Research House; **421** Aviation Picture Library; **422** *t* USAF/The Research House, **422** *b* Quadrant Picture Library, **422–23** USAF/The Research House, **423** Quadrant Picture Library; **424** Smithsonian Institution; **425** Smithsonian Institution/Aviation Picture Library; **426** Bristol Museum/Aviation Picture Library, **426–27** Steve Krongand/The Image Bank; **428** British Aerospace/MARS; **429** Aviation Picture Library; **430** British Aircraft Corporation; **431** Quadrant Picture Library; **432–33** Boccon-Gibod/SIPA/Rex Features; **434–35** Thunder & Colt; **438–39** Novosti/Science Photo Library; **440–41** *l* TASS; **441** *tr* Novosti/Science Photo Library, **441** *br* V. Haende-Rothe/TASS; **442–45** NASA/Science Photo Library; **446** NASA/The Research House, **446–47** Salaber/Liaison/Frank Spooner Pictures; **448** NASA/Science Photo Library; **450** Luis Castañeda/The Image Bank; **451** Roger/Ressmeyer, Starlight/Science Photo Library; **452–56** NASA/Science Photo Library, **456** *l* Novosti/Science Photo Library; **457** NASA Science Photo Library.

Artwork Credits

Craig Austin: 27 *r*.
Trevor Hill: 50–1, 66–7, 130–1, 162–3, 168–9, 179, 248–49, 278, 300–301, 314–15, 318–19, 340, 358, 364, 403, 408–9, 412–13.
Andrew Popkiewicz: 31.
Simon Roulstone: 15, 27 *c* and *cb*, 41, 45, 55, 61, 73, 93, 100–1, 106–7, 111, 125, 204–5, 208–9, 220, 242, 255, 258–59, 274–75, 324, 328, 346, 351, 371, 378–79, 384–85, 435, 445.
Paul Selvey: 108, 130 *tl*, 136–7, 170, 172–3, 191, 216–17, 262–63, 296, 305, 307, 356, 360, 388, 396, 425
Ian Howatson: 373, 422, 394–95.
Mick Saunders: 269, 308–9, 332, 337, 416, 449.
All maps in Section I by Technical Art Services Ltd.

The author and publisher would like to express their gratitude to the following for their kind assistance in the production of this book:

Airship and Balloon Company, Telford; Col. J. Blashford-Snell; British Airways Archives, Heathrow; HoverSpeed, London; London Library; Peter Mills, SNCF, London; Rear-Admiral R.O. Morris; Mystic Seaport Museum, Connecticut; National Maritime Museum, London; Graham Slatter, R.G. Todd and David Topliss; National Motor Museum Library, Beaulieu; Nautilus Memorial, Groton, Connecticut; Charles Noble; Science Museum, London; Short Brothers PLC, Belfast; David Smithers; Smithsonian Institution, Washington; SNCF, Paris; Thunder & Colt, Oswestry; Virgin Atlantic Airways, Crawley; Westland Helicopters, Yeovil.

The publishers gratefully acknowledge the permission granted by HarperCollins for the use of material from *Columbus* by Bjorn Landstrom. They are also grateful to *Motor Sport* for permission to quote from an account of the Mille Miglia by Denis Jenkinson.